D0601747

The World of Fashion Merchandising

Mary G. Wolfe
St. Michaels, Maryland

Publisher
The Goodheart-Willcox Company, Inc.
Tinley Park, Illinois

Library of Congress Catalog Card Number 2001040872
ISBN-13: 978-1-56637-891-8
ISBN-10: 1-56637-891-5

5 6 7 8 9 10 03 07 06

Library of Congress Cataloging-in-Publication Data
Wolfe, Mary Gorgen, 1941-
The world of fashion merchandising / by Mary G. Wolfe.
p. cm.
Previous edition copyright 1998.
Includes index.
ISBN 1-56637-891-5
1. Fashion merchandising. I. Title.
HD9940.A2W65 2002
687'.068'8—dc21 2001040872

Introduction

The World of Fashion Merchandising brings to life the business aspects of the fashion world. It presents the basics of market economics, textiles, design, and promotion. It gives an in-depth view of the entire textile/apparel/retail soft goods chain. It also offers a comprehensive study of retail fundamentals and strategies for retail success.

The World of Fashion Merchandising has hundreds of color photographs and other illustrations to add interest and a deeper understanding of its content. It contains an extensive glossary that defines fashion and apparel terms used by industry professionals. The book

- describes the latest concepts of manufacturing, mass customization, and niche specialization;
- stresses marketing as the basis for successful fashion merchandising activities that satisfy the changing consumer market;
- explains new computer technologies, such as robotic manufacturing, automatic replenishment of floor-ready merchandise, and Internet retailing;
- discusses fashion industry globalization, business consolidation, and environmental issues;
- gives details about the many career opportunities related to fashion and how to prepare for them, including entrepreneurship.

The World of Fashion Merchandising is presented in an easy-to-understand format. It uses simple, direct language. Each chapter begins with learning objectives and ends with review materials to make learning more meaningful and enjoyable. This book provides knowledge that will help you enter a career in the wonderful world of fashion!

About the Author

Mary Wolfe has worked in all segments of the fashion industry, from textiles research to retail sales. She designed for a national sportswear firm before opening her own apparel business. She gained recognition as the personal fashion designer for the wife of a U.S. Vice President. As a consultant to several garment manufacturers, she has assisted with collection designs and pattern specifications.

Mary received the Outstanding Faculty Member Award for her teaching of fashion-related courses at the University of Delaware. She has been a New Jersey Woman of the Year and has been listed in *Outstanding Young Women of America* and *National Dean's List.* Mary is also the author of *Fashion!* and a book on pattern making. She received her bachelor's degree in Textiles and Clothing from Iowa State University and her master's degree in General Business (M.B.A.) from West Chester University of Pennsylvania.

Table of Contents

Part 1 Basic Fashion and Business Concepts

Part 2 Textile/Apparel Building Blocks

Part 3 Designing and Producing Apparel

GGT · Niebuhr
R·H·MACY & Co
MACY'S

Part 5 Strategies for Retail Success

Dior
Christian Dior

Boscov's

Part 1

Basic Fashion and Business Concepts

CHAPTER 1

The Meaning of Clothing and Fashion

After studying this chapter, you will be able to

- explain the basic reasons people wear clothes.
- state why people make various clothing choices.
- describe fashion in terms of art and science, and private and public awareness.
- summarize economic and political influences on fashion.
- define basic fashion terms.

The Reasons for Wearing Clothing	
Physical need:	protection
Psychological needs:	adornment identification
Social needs:	modesty status

1-1 Clothing has always satisfied one or more of the human physical, psychological, and social needs shown here.

Throughout history, clothing has had great meaning. Clothing has reflected and continues to reflect the handicraft skills, artistic imagination, and cultural rituals of people. Clothing also has and continues to be an indicator of advances in technology. However, the reasons people wear clothes have been the same throughout time. Additionally, the meaning of many fashion terms has remained constant.

Reasons for Wearing Clothing

In ancient times, clothing of simple design was made from items found in nature, such as animal skins or plants. Today, there are many different styles of clothing made of various fabrics, trimmings, and other materials. From the beginning, clothing has satisfied basic human physical, psychological, and social needs, as summarized in 1-1.

Physical Need

Clothing provides for the physical need of *protection,* or physical safeguards. Garments help prevent harm to the body resulting from weather, environmental dangers, occupational hazards, and enemies.

As protection from weather, clothing provides comfort, 1-2. Coats, gloves, and long underwear protect people from cold temperatures. Windbreakers and water-repellent jackets provide protection from wind and rain. Wide-brimmed hats and light, airy fabrics offer protection from the sun and heat.

As protection from environmental dangers, shoes protect feet from soil, hard and sharp objects, and hot and cold surfaces. Astronauts wear suits that provide life-sustaining atmospheric conditions. Medical workers wear sterile gloves and face masks to reduce the transfer of germs. Cyclists wear helmets to protect their heads in case of accidents, 1-3.

As protection from occupation hazards, special garments protect workers from contamination, chemicals, radiation, and fires. As technology has developed, special "occupational clothing" has evolved. Hard hats and safety goggles are required at many job sites. Athletes often wear protective helmets, gloves, and pads for protection. The special shoes worn by basketball players are designed to protect them from slipping. Blue jeans and cowboy boots, that are now fashionable, were first worn by ranchers for occupational protection.

Saxony Sportswear Company

1-2 Sweaters, wool vests, long pants, and leather jackets all provide warmth by preventing body heat from escaping into the air.

AKZO NOBEL Twaron®

1-3 Helmets, such as this one, are reinforced with tough fibers that cannot be torn or punctured if they collide with hard objects.

AKZO NOBEL Twaron®

1-4 This flexible, bulletproof vest is worn by law enforcement officers under their regular uniforms to protect them from being shot in the chest or back.

Finally, protection from enemies was provided long ago by body shields and suits of armor. Today, soldiers use helmets to protect their heads, and camouflage fabric helps soldiers hide in outdoor environments. Police officers wear bulletproof vests to protect their bodies from gunfire, 1-4. Also, reflective vests and jackets make runners and cyclists more visible to motorists.

Psychological Needs

The psychological reasons for wearing clothing are adornment and identification. They affect a person's mental attitude or morale in a positive way.

Adornment

Adornment, or attractive decoration, has been found in all civilizations throughout history. It enhances a person's self-concept, providing a psychological feeling of well-being through beauty, 1-5. *Beauty* is a quality that gives pleasure to the senses and a positive emotional reaction. It also can attract the opposite sex and create envy in rivals. Most psychologists believe that adornment is essential to human life.

Being adorned with clothing gives people a positive psychological feeling. It allows them artistic expression, showing their creativity. This can attract favorable attention and contribute to feelings of self-esteem. Wearing clothing that is artistically designed, or combining garments in artistic ways, makes us more attractive. Further adornment can occur with jewelry and makeup. Large sums of money are spent each year on products to adorn our bodies and improve our personal appearance.

Culture often determines the type of adornment people use. ***Culture*** is a society's set of social norms or values. The way one culture views beauty may be different from how others view it. Some cultural groups paint their bodies or wear rings through their nose, lips, or ears. Folk costumes illustrate the different fabric textures and patterns that cultures consider to be beautiful, 1-6. The desirability of certain decorations is determined by the standards and traditions of each society.

Peoples' ideas about beauty and adornment change over time as fashions change. Also, various people have different thoughts about beauty and adornment because of personal experiences. For instance, a professional athlete and an opera singer would probably have different adornment preferences.

Jeanswear Communications/Ruff Hewn

1-5 Adornment does not have to include shiny gowns or sparkling jewelry. This tasteful outfit, well coordinated with a belt and jacket, adorns this woman perfectly for her to feel fashionable and confident in her activities.

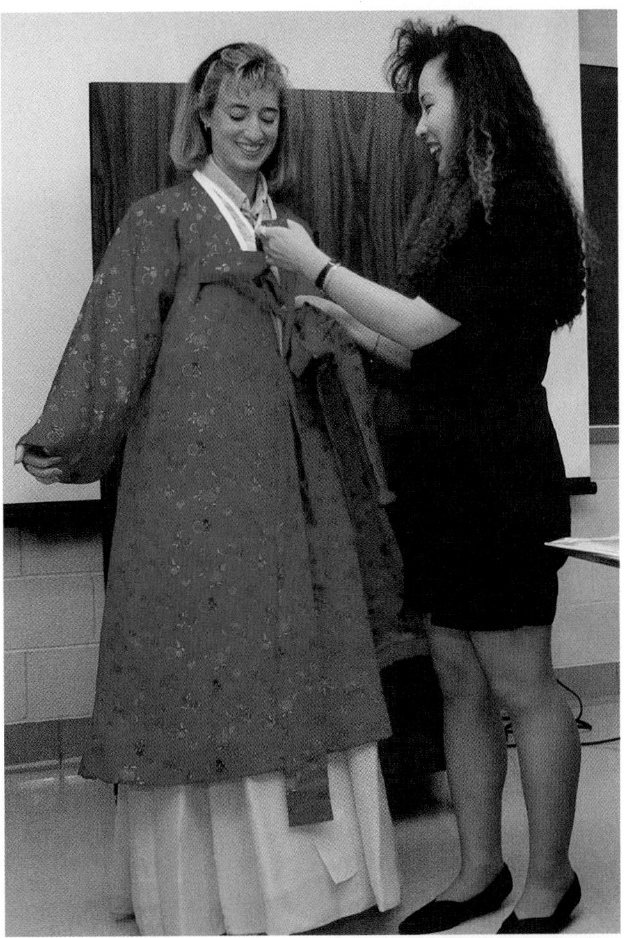

Ball State University-Indiana

1-6 This Korean gown is of a colorful brocade over a longer silk dress, beautifully constructed in a traditional Korean design.

Identification

Identification is the process of establishing or describing who someone is or what he or she does. Clothing identifies people in these ways. By dressing like others in a group, clothing satisfies the psychological need to belong. For instance, people belonging to certain professions, social groups, associations, or countries often dress alike. It indicates what "role" people play or what skills they have.

Uniforms are one way of identifying roles. Uniforms are articles of clothing that are alike and specific to everyone within a certain group of people. As symbols of group identity, uniforms provide a sense of belonging, such as for members of a sports team. Uniforms can show positions of authority, such as for police or military officers. They can also decrease racial, religious, and other barriers, since all people in a particular group appear to be alike.

Identification can also be achieved with emblems, colors, badges, patches, special jewelry, and ceremonial garments. Class rings identify the wearers with others in the group, giving a psychological feeling of unity. Caps and gowns identify graduating seniors. Wedding dresses identify brides, 1-7.

David's Bridal

1-7 A long white gown, and a veil on the head would most likely be worn by a bride on her wedding day.

The regular clothing of many people can be considered a type of "psychological uniform," because everyone dresses almost alike. Most students wear the same general kinds of pants, shirts, sweaters, and shoes to school. Male and female lawyers might wear dark suits to work. People of similar ages and interests often gain confidence and acceptance by dressing alike. They feel comfortable and secure by following informal "rules of dress" that are set by silent understanding.

Some businesses and schools have ***dress codes*** that are written or unwritten rules of appropriate attire. Although uniforms may or may not be worn, clothing must fall within a certain range of options, 1-8. Besides achieving group identity, clothes within the dress code help group members maintain a certain discipline of behavior. This might come from the symbolic meaning of the clothing or the way the clothes look or feel. For instance, a business suit helps a person conduct herself or himself in a businesslike way.

Social Needs

The social reasons for wearing clothing are modesty and status. People are socially accepted, and sometimes admired, because of their attire.

The Fashion Association/Lands' End

1-8 Most professional males wear a tailored suit, a white or light-colored shirt, and a necktie to work. It is a clearly understood dress code at many offices.

Modesty

Modesty is the covering of the body according to the code of decency of a particular society. It dictates the proper way to cover the body to eliminate embarrassment or shame. Our standards of decency are molded by our culture and social system. Each society has its own accepted standards of modesty.

The standards of our society about modesty have changed through the years. In the 1800s, it was immodest for American women to let their ankles show. The body was almost completely covered, even for swimming and tennis. In the late 1900s, however, miniskirts and bikini swimsuits became acceptable.

Status

A person's ***status*** is his or her position or rank in comparison to others. "Good" or "high" status is usually associated with recognition, prestige, and social acceptance. Clothing is sometimes used to gain a higher rank in society, along with social acceptance and peer approval. Some people seek higher status with expensive fur coats, jewelry, or garments with designer labels. Others show what they have achieved by wearing service stripes or medals on a military uniform or a school letter on an athletic jacket. All of these items raise the status of the wearer.

Combined Needs

Today, people wear clothes because of a combination of physical, psychological, and social needs. Several human needs are fulfilled to different degrees at the same time.

People receive pleasure from their apparel, and project their creativity while fulfilling their basic needs for wearing clothing. Clothing carries a highly visible message about who a person is or is not, 1-9. It can also indicate who that person would like to be.

JCPenney

1-9 Analyze this fashion in relation to protection, adornment, identification, modesty, and status.

Why People Select Certain Clothes

Besides physical, psychological, and social needs, additional factors influence clothing choices. People's values and attitudes affect clothing selections, as well as their tendencies toward conformity or individuality. Personality traits also influence clothing choices.

Values and Attitudes

Values are the ideas, beliefs, and material items that are important to an individual. They are the underlying motivations for a person's actions. They form the basis for a person's decisions, lifestyle, and personal code of ethics. ***Attitudes*** are a person's feelings or reactions to people, things, or ideas. They are formed from values. Values and attitudes have a major influence on apparel selections.

Values and attitudes are learned and passed from one generation to another. Family members, friends, and the community are important in forming them, as well as ethnic and cultural traditions. These traditions include customs, language, and social views of people's heritage or nationality. Traditional cultural fashion influences are indicated in 1-10. In the United States, where different ethnic groups co-exist, the way people dress is one means of providing a social bond within each group.

Economic and social conditions affect people's values and attitudes toward the selection of clothing. Also, how people spend their money shows their personal values. Some splurge on many clothes and accessories. Others have few clothes, preferring to spend their money on recreational activities, or to use their money for a car or other large purchase.

Some people select comfortable clothing because they value their own comfort, 1-11. Others choose bargains because they value economy. Some people prefer the latest look in clothes, or expensive items, because they want to be noticed and to gain prestige.

The Fashion Association/Pronto Uomo, Div. of Mondo Inc.

1-11 This soft knit shirt and easy-fitting slacks show that the person wearing them values comfort in his fashion.

Fashion Institute of Technology; John Senzer, Photographer

1-10 Traditional values and attitudes are perpetuated in the beauty of fashions from various cultures.

Advertising can influence people's values and attitudes. Ads try to create a stronger desire for particular products. They play to consumer desires for economy, status, easy care, adventure, and comfort.

Since needs and values change over time, age influences clothing selections, too. Young children need comfortable, sturdy clothing. School-age children also often want to fit in with their friends. The clothes in 1-12 are examples of clothes that appeal to teens. Young adults may need economy, but probably also want sex appeal. Prestige and status may be desired during middle age, and comfort is important, again, to the elderly.

Fashion professionals who make or sell clothing items try to identify the values and attitudes of their customers. Then they can produce and stock the items that will be preferred, and ultimately bought, by specific groups of consumers.

Jeanswear Communications/Bugle Boy

1-12 Teens like to dress in similar fashions to their friends.

Conformity Versus Individuality

Pressure from other people has a great influence on how people dress. ***Conformity*** means obeying or agreeing with some given standard or authority. Early in life, children learn from parents and teachers about what they are expected to wear. Peer group pressure is also a major force that contributes to conformity. By conforming to a dress code, a safe feeling of belonging is achieved through approval. However, too much conformity can mean a loss of personal individuality.

Individuality is self-expression. It is the quality that distinguishes one person from another, or makes each person unique. When people choose clothing styles and colors that are different from those of their friends, they are communicating their individuality, 1-13. They are rejecting peer pressure and conformity.

Most people balance the influences of conformity and individuality in their clothing. They want to express themselves as individuals but also want to be part of a group. Their clothing choices depend on their moods, different settings and situations, and age and maturity. Preteens may value conformity. During the late teens, they may prefer to express their individuality. In adulthood people worry less about either extreme. They settle into their own comfortable patterns of dressing that make them feel good.

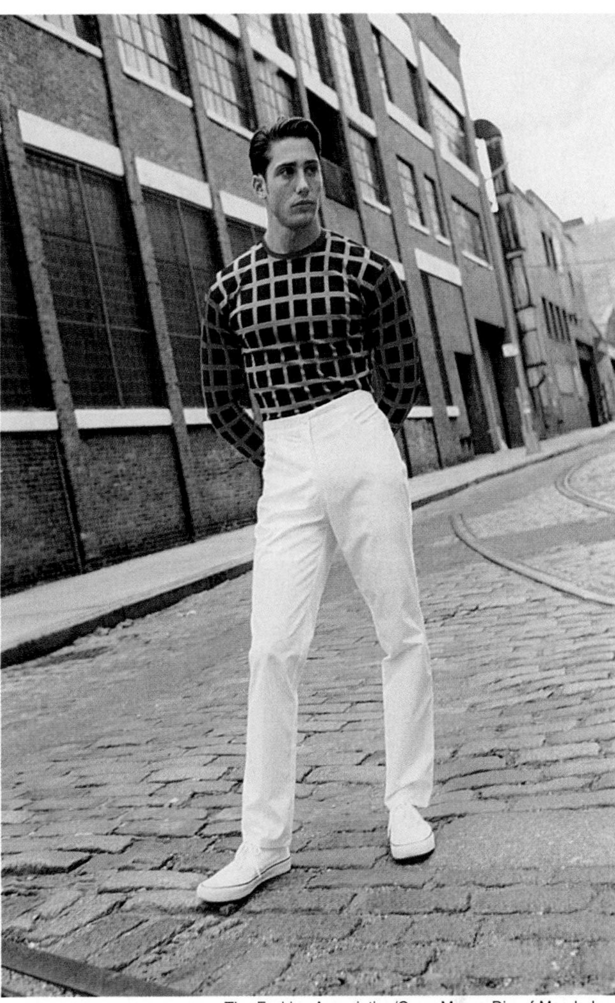

The Fashion Association/Gene Meyer, Div. of Mondo Inc.

1-13 By dressing in a colorful, fashion-forward outfit, this man is showing his own creativity as an individual.

Personality Traits

Personality can be defined as the total characteristics that distinguish an individual, especially his or her behavioral and emotional tendencies. Personality traits are often indicated by the way people dress. For instance, studies have shown that people who like lots of decoration in their apparel tend to be very sociable. People who prefer comfortable clothes tend to have self-control, and to be confident, outgoing, and secure, 1-14. Those who prefer economy, rather than spending lots of money on their wardrobes, are usually responsible, alert, efficient, and precise.

Needs Versus Wants

Needs and wants are other factors that influence people's clothing choices.

A ***need*** is something a person must have for existence or survival. It is necessary for his or her basic

Liz Claiborne

1-14 This woman is indicating her secure self-confidence with the comfortable ensemble she is wearing.

Liz Claiborne

1-15 The garments this woman is wearing allow her to do exercises properly, but she could also exercise in regular shorts and a T-shirt.

protection, modesty, comfort, or livelihood. For instance, a person who lives in a cold climate *needs* a heavy coat to stay warm. If he or she has a suitable coat that is out of style, he or she doesn't really *need* a new one. The old one can keep him or her warm. However, he or she probably *wants* a new one!

A ***want*** is a person's desire for something that gives him or her satisfaction. The item would be wonderful to have, but the person can get along without it.

Many people find it hard to distinguish between needs and wants. When someone craves something, obtaining that item seems to be a need in that person's mind rather than a want. Also, there are varying degrees of need. The most basic needs give people protection from the environment. Others are determined by personal values, culture, lifestyle, resources, peer group, and standard of living. A college graduate who is beginning a new career may need a business suit for the job, even though he or she could live without it. Or, a certain uniform may be needed to participate in a sport because the player would not be able to function in that activity without it. Do you think the outfit in 1-15 is a need or a want for the person wearing it?

As you can see, the way people dress is a combination of many factors in their lives. To be successful in the fashion business, it is important to understand the reasons why consumers make specific decisions about the apparel they buy and wear. Fashion marketers try to satisfy consumer needs and wants, and entice consumers into buying what they sell.

Ongoing Fashion Perspectives

Some subtleties of fashion have always existed, but are not often discussed. They include the fact that fashion is considered to be both an art and a science. Another fact is that fashion is both highly personal and very public. Also, fashion is influenced by economic, political, and other events.

Fashion as Art and Science

Fashion is both an art and a science at the same time. As an art, fashion encompasses ongoing creativity in its products. Unlike many other businesses where conformity is always the norm, fashion thrives on innovative, forward-thinking ideas. The most successful fashion designers and marketers use color, texture, line, and other aspects of design to the best

Hong Kong Trade Development Council

1-16 The designer of this gown, Flora Cheong Leen, has used design skills to create an artistic evening fashion.

Monsanto Fibers

1-17 Science has allowed the fibers in these socks to have the best possible characteristics for their use.

advantage, 1-16. They offer products that creatively complement current trends.

Fashion is also a science. Most textile fibers are made through a combination of chemistry and technology. New fibers might be created that absorb or repel moisture. The socks in 1-17 have been engineered to be absorbent, soft, and stretchy. In the past, when technology enabled heavy plastics to take clear dyes, brightly colored rain boots were all the rage! With current technology enabling extremely fine fibers to be made, tightly woven lightweight fabrics are made into water-resistant sports apparel, 1-18.

New apparel manufacturing and modern retailing methods are also based on technological advancement. New commercial sewing equipment might enable a certain type of sleeve to be produced efficiently, resulting in a new fashionable style that incorporates that sleeve design. Scientific technology continues to revolutionize the way apparel items are designed, mass-produced, distributed, and sold.

DuPont Supplex® Nylon

1-18 This snowboarding suit, made of lightweight and breathable fabric, is soft, durable, and wind- and water-resistant. Technology also enables it to be washable and to resist fading.

Private and Public Fashion Viewpoints

On a private level, we have seen that fashion satisfies physical, psychological, and social needs. Personal clothing choices are affected by many individual responses, including how people view themselves. Many private factors would contribute to the outfit being worn by the person in 1-19. Then her apparel choices would also reflect her personal image outwardly to the public, since all others can see how she is dressed.

The textile/apparel industry also keeps new fashions secretive and private as they are being designed. However, as soon as they are produced, they become very public. Fashion is constantly in the public spotlight through the press and other media. Promotion to the public creates rapidly rising expectations among consumers. Consumers excitedly anticipate seeing, hearing about, and wearing the new fashions.

Fashion is also public because shifts in the economy and the makeup of the population affect fashion. The art and science, and private and public aspects of fashion always blend together, although few people realize the impact of these relationships.

Economic, Political, and Other Influences on Fashion

Fashion reflects economic conditions, political issues, current events, and popular entertainment. It is "a mirror of our times." It indicates the way we think and live at a given point in time.

Historic clothing has revealed many details about the lifestyles of people from various past cultures. Current fashions will reveal much about our lifestyles to future generations. Some experts say that if a fashion magazine or catalog were left from today for people to

JCPenney

1-19 Although people privately choose what fashions they want to buy or wear, and how they want to combine articles of clothing, their choices become very public when the outfits are worn.

read centuries from now, it would tell more than volumes of books written by philosophers, novelists, or scholars!

Historic clothing shows that economic and political factors have always had a great influence on fashion. Centuries ago, people dressed according to what was allowed for their "social class." For instance, members of royalty in some countries were the only ones permitted to wear silks, pearls, embroidery, and the color purple because these items were rare and expensive. Thus, these items also became status symbols.

Economic and political factors still affect fashion. People's moods are reflected in the way they dress. For instance, in an era of hard times, clothing usually gives a serious, conservative image. People tend to lose interest in their appearance. In better times, when people's spirits are high, they dress in styles that are more fun and provocative. Styles are brighter and more adventurous, since people are more willing to try new, different fashions. This supports the theory that if the standards of dress change quickly, the basic social structure of the society has probably changed.

The Fashion Association/Hanes

1-20 During years the Olympics are held, fashions available to consumers often reflect a supportive influence.

Liz Claiborne

1-21 This outfit is comprised of slacks, a sweater, and a shirt. All are separate garments, even though they are put together into one coordinated ensemble.

Popular entertainment causes fashions to imitate a character of a movie, an actor, or a rock star. As movies, concerts, and other modes of entertainment are publicized, consumers want to identify with them. Patriotism shows in fashions to support and emulate athletes during the years of Olympic events, 1-20. Consumers feel good when their fashions imitate the look of people who are recognized or idolized.

Fashion professionals should be aware of all of these relationships of apparel to society. With this knowledge, fashion trends can be predicted and understood. Greater business success should result.

Fashion Terminology

A ***garment*** is an article of wearing apparel, such as a dress, suit, coat, evening gown, or sweater. Three separate garments are shown in 1-21. Examples of *garment parts* are the sleeves, cuffs, collar, waistband, and other components that make up each complete garment.

Accessories are the articles added to complete or enhance apparel outfits. Examples of accessories are belts, hats, jewelry, shoes, gloves, and scarves. Notice the accessories added to the outfit in 1-22.

A ***style*** is identified by distinct features that create an overall appearance. Styles exist in architecture, furniture, painting, music, and most other forms of expression. In apparel, each style is a particular design, shape, or type of garment, with unique characteristics that make it different from others. Examples of styles are A-line skirts, Bermuda shorts, safari jackets, and crewneck sweaters, 1-23.

"Style" is also used to describe a condition. Certain trendsetters and fashion leaders are said to have style or to be stylish. This means that they have a nice, distinctive manner setting them apart from others. This term is often used in fashion shows, to describe how attractive an outfit is.

Fashion is the display of the currently popular style of objects or activities. In apparel, a fashion is the prevailing type of clothing that is favored by a large segment of the public at any given time. It is the clothing that the majority of people are purchasing and using at a particular time. A style does not become a fashion until it gains popular acceptance. It remains a fashion only as long as it is accepted.

JCPenney

1-22 This suit is nicely accessorized with shoes, handbag, scarf, and sunglasses.

Monsanto Fibers

1-23 Two distinct sweater styles are shown here. They are a crewneck sweater on the man and a turtleneck sweater on the woman.

A style may come and go in fashion acceptance, but always remains as that style. The styles that are fashionable this year may seem very unfashionable in a few years. What is in fashion constantly changes, creating an ongoing process.

High fashion items are the very latest or newest fashions. They are usually innovative, expensive, and of fine quality, 1-24. They are designed for, and accepted by, the limited number of people who are the first to adopt fashion changes. They sometimes seem too extreme and unusual for the general public. Later, high fashion ideas may be modified and copied to appeal to the majority of consumers. They are then mass-produced and widely sold at lower prices to become mass fashion.

Mass fashion, or volume fashion, accounts for the majority of sales in the fashion business. These styles

Hong Kong Trade Development Council

1-24 This elegant gown, designed by Barney Cheng, includes unusual design ideas, exquisite materials, and quality construction.

are sometimes said to be "homogenized" because they are produced in such large quantities and accepted by such a mass of people that they all seem to be alike, even though they are produced and sold by many different companies.

A ***design*** is a particular, or unique, version of a style. A style can be put together in many new designs by using different fabrics, colors, trims, and combinations of ideas. A jumpsuit, for instance, always has pants attached to a top, but it might have long or short sleeves, different types of collars, and different pockets and trim. Each version is a different design of the jumpsuit style. To move fashion forward, different variations of garment parts are combined in creative ways into new garment designs, 1-25.

The terms "style" and "design" are often used interchangeably in the fashion industry. However, they have different meanings if they are to be used correctly.

Avant-garde clothes are the most daring and wild designs. They are too unconventional and startling to be considered fashions of the times. Most features of these garments disappear completely after a few years. Avant-garde clothes are used to draw attention to the wearer. They are often worn by rock groups on stage. Sometimes teenagers wear versions of avant-garde clothing or hairstyles to show their individuality.

A ***fad*** is a temporary, passing fashion. In clothing, it is an unusual garment, accessory, or look that has great appeal to many people for a short period of time. It has a sudden burst of popularity and is imitated by many to flood the market. Soon after it reaches its height of popularity, its extreme design causes its acceptance to wane and it dies out quickly.

Fads provide a feeling of adventure for the wearers, as well as a sense of belonging to a group. They are often popular only with a specific group of consumers, such as high school or college students. A fad accompanied by a display of emotion or crowd excitement can become a *craze* or a mania. Stores have a hard time keeping such items in stock because people are so eager to buy them. Eventually, most fads fade

JCPenney

1-25 The length of the sleeves and hem, contrasting trim, matching tops, print of the skirt, and other aspects make the design of this outfit unique.

away. However, if a faddish item is well-designed and meets a clothing need, it may become a style.

A ***classic*** style or design is one that continues to be popular over an extended period of time, even though fashions change. It is almost always acceptable, however minor changes may give it a more updated look. The suit in 1-26 is a classic style. Classics were originally sought-after fashion items, but their general appeal has kept them popular. They are considered to be fashion basics by retailers. Consumers make "investment purchases" of classics because these garments can be worn year after year.

Classic garments are characterized by simple, stylish lines that prevent them from being easily dated. They are quite practical, and universally appealing. Some examples of classic garments are button-down shirts, blazers, shirtwaist dresses, and loafer shoes. These styles have been acceptable for many decades, but reappear periodically as fashions. Blue jeans are now also considered to be classics, 1-27.

A ***ford*** is a style or design that is produced at the same time by many different manufacturers at many different prices. The same basic look sells in large quantities at all price levels. It is also called a *best-seller* or a *runner.*

Hart Schaffner & Marx/Hartmarx Corporation

1-26 Men's classic dark suits never go out of acceptance even though fashion updating may slightly change the width of the lapels or fullness of the trousers.

Wrangler Hero

1-27 Blue jeans started as sturdy work pants long ago and are now universally worn as stylish classics.

A ***fashion look*** refers to a total accessorized outfit. One person's fashion look at a particular time might be well-coordinated with a dress, hose, shoes, jewelry, and purse. Another person's fashion look might be a ripped pair of jeans, oversized shirt with tails hanging to the knees, colorful print vest, and sandals. Different fashion looks are often identified with a celebrity or certain groups of people, or result from the influences of cultural or world events. Apparel and home furnishing lines, such as Laura Ashley and Ralph Lauren, have developed distinctive fashion looks, 1-28. Some fashion looks are more widely adopted by consumers than other fashion looks.

Taste, in fashion, refers to the prevailing opinion of what is attractive and appropriate for a given person and occasion. *Good taste,* therefore, means sensitivity not only to what is artistically pleasing, but also to what is appropriate for a certain situation and a specific individual. Clean blue jeans and a cowboy shirt may be an attractive outfit, but if it is worn to the opera it may not

Laura Ashley / JUSCO Co., Ltd.

1-28 The Laura Ashley look is known for tasteful English prints and accessories, resulting in an overall "genteel appearance."

be considered in good taste! Tight pants or bikini swimsuits might be fashionable, but if they are worn by people who don't have slender bodies, they may be in poor taste. Garments that are no longer in fashion are also not in good taste, even if they are well designed. On the other hand, some less artistic designs that have high acceptance are considered to be in good taste. Good taste is often considered to be a well-designed outfit with fashion acceptance worn by someone on whom it looks appropriate.

Summary

People throughout history have worn clothing to satisfy basic needs. Physically, clothing offers protection to the human body. Psychological needs are satisfied by the adornment and identification gained from clothing. Clothing also satisfies the social needs of modesty and status. Most fashion experts believe that a combination of these needs are fulfilled in varying degrees at the same time through people's clothing.

A person's values and attitudes, learned from the family and experiences, play an important part in clothing selection. Conformity is weighed against a desire for individuality. Personality traits, and wants versus needs also have an influence upon a person's clothing choices.

Other ongoing relationships between apparel and society should also be kept in mind. Fashion is both an art and a science, involving both creative thinking and the use of technology. Fashion is both highly personal and very public. Additionally, fashion reflects the economic conditions, current events, political issues, and popular entertainment of a society at a given time.

For success in the fashion business, it is essential to know and understand clothing terms. Fashion professionals should be able to distinguish between styles, fashions, fads, and classics. Other important concepts include accessories, designs, and taste.

To Know

adornment
culture
dress code
modesty
status
values
attitudes
conformity
individuality
need
want
garment
accessories
style
fashion
high fashion
mass fashion
design
avant-garde
fad
classic
ford
fashion look
taste

To Review

1. Clothing provides protection to the human body from four main categories. Name these and give one example of each.
2. How does adornment fulfill psychological needs?
3. How does identification fulfill psychological needs?
4. Why are dress codes often used by schools and businesses?
5. What molds a society's standards of decency toward how people cover their bodies?
6. Give three examples of clothing items or features that give people higher status in our society.
7. Explain how a person's values and attitudes affect the selection of certain clothes.
8. Explain how conformity versus individuality affects the selection of certain clothes.
9. Explain how personality traits affect the selection of certain clothes.
10. Give an example of a clothing need versus a clothing want.
11. In what ways is fashion an art? In what ways is fashion a science?
12. Explain the statement, "for individuals, fashion is both highly personal and very public."
13. Explain why clothing tends to look "perkier" during prosperous times.
14. Why are some styles said to be "homogenized"?
15. Describe a current fashion.
16. Explain why avant-garde clothes are not considered to be fashions of the times.
17. Give three examples of classic garments.
18. What does "good taste" in fashion mean?

To Do

1. Visit the library and research at least three examples of how animal skins or plants were used as simple clothing in ancient times. Sketch your examples, or photocopy them from reference books. Tell how each example satisfied the wearer's physical, psychological, and/or social needs.
2. Cut at least two pictures from magazines, catalogs, or newspapers to illustrate protective clothing. Mount them on paper and explain why such clothing is necessary. Also try to describe the technological advances that have made the clothing possible.
3. Find at least two pictures of people wearing uniforms and mount them on paper. Write down your impressions of what each uniform communicates to others.
4. Ask two or more older people about the clothing they wore when they were your age. Did their clothes reflect traditions of their cultures? Did they follow different codes of modesty? Did garments provide the physical protection needed for their jobs? What forms of decorative adornment were popular? Write a short report about what you learned.
5. Research why fashion is "a mirror of our times." Present an oral report to the class that explains the expression. Show as many examples as possible to make the meaning clear.

CHAPTER 2

Fashion Movement

After studying this chapter, you will be able to

- explain the role of fashion leaders and followers in fashion movement.
- state the theories of fashion movement.
- describe the stages and time spans of fashion cycles.
- analyze the main principles of fashion movement.
- compare factors that speed up or slow down fashion movement.
- relate the importance of fashion change.

The fashion business is in a constant state of change. Because new designs are continually being created, and consumers steadily replace their old clothes with new ones, fashion is one of the greatest forces affecting the economy. An understanding of the constant movement of fashion is essential for success in the fashion business.

Understanding Fashion Movement

Consumer desire for new fashions causes garment silhouettes and details to constantly change, as indicated in 2-1. Different fashions constantly come in and go out of popularity. This ongoing change in what is considered to be fashionable is called ***fashion movement***. It causes consumers to discard the old fashions and purchase new ones. If fashions did not change, fashion businesses would not survive.

Everyone, from the original designer to the final consumer, benefits from and encourages the movement of fashion. People become bored with the old and enjoy change and variety. Fashion changes occur because people's views about politics, religion, leisure, and success change. New technology constantly produces new and better fibers, fabrics, and finishes. Advertising and promotion encourage consumers to want new items. All of these also encourage abandoning old fashion ideas.

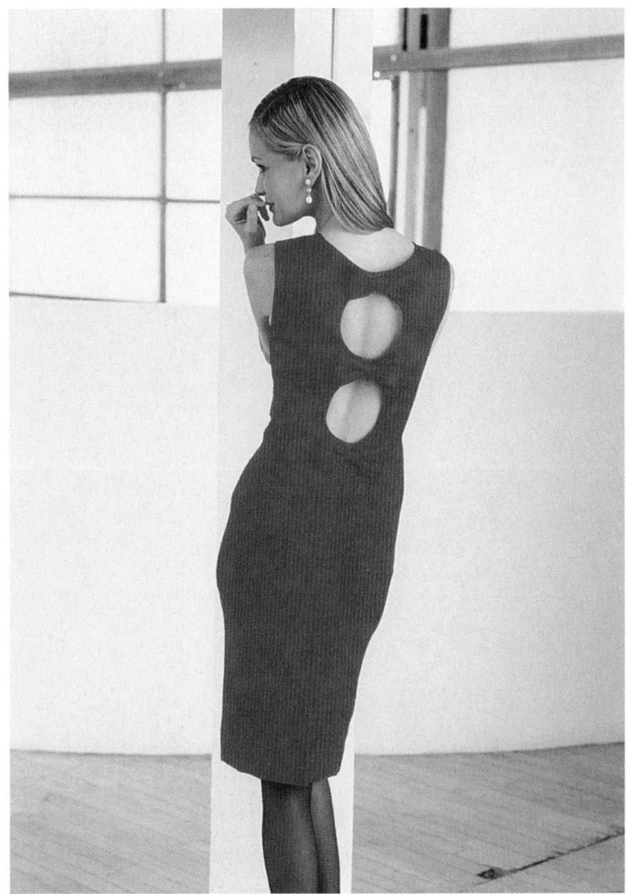

Liz Claiborne

2-1 Sometimes straight skirts to the knee, bright colors, and open design details are fashionable. At other times, different features are favored.

Fashion movement involves the ***obsolescence factor.*** This is the rejection of used items in favor of newer ones, even though the old items may retain their utility value. Most fashion items do not wear out; they just look outdated because new fashion ideas have become popular. This enables the fashion industry to prosper, which, in turn, helps the economy remain strong.

A ***fashion trend*** is the direction in which fashion is moving. It is something new that is gaining popularity and wide acceptance in the marketplace. Fashion movement involves many trends that coexist at any given time. For instance, skirts may be getting longer at the same time as sleeves are getting wider and shoes are getting "clunkier."

Fashion Leaders and Followers

In fashion movement, high fashion is first worn by the ***fashion leaders*** of the time. These are the few "fashion forward" men, women, and young people with enough confidence and credibility to start or accept new fashions. They are trendsetters. They are not afraid to wear something before everyone else does. In fact, they like to be noticed. Because of their jobs, social status, or fame, they are often in the public view. They have lots of exposure in the media, which then influences the dress of others.

In past centuries, trendsetting fashion leaders were often royalty. Today, they tend to be public celebrities, such as television, movie, and rock stars, sports heroes, and political figures. Many are in upper social classes. Others are members of specific subcultures, or simply people who are especially responsive to change.

Every community has fashion leaders. They may not create fashion, but they are the ones who first discover and display new styles within their social groups. Then, because they are the focus of much attention, others try to imitate them. While fashion leaders are wearing the new styles, other people are watching them, and forming opinions about how the new fashions would look on them. The eyes and minds of the others are becoming used to the new colors, shapes, and proportions, 2-2. They are adjusting to the new ideas.

Soon, adaptations of the fashions are worn by people in many social groups. These ***fashion followers*** wear fashion looks only when they become firmly accepted. Fashion followers wear styles after the looks receive greater publicity and promotion, and become

Fashion Institute of Technology/John Senzer, Photographer

2-2 Fashion leaders are the first to wear new color combinations, skirt lengths, and accessories.

more available in retail stores. This causes the fashions to become well-established. The fashions reach mass acceptance with the majority of the general public. Eventually the styles are worn by ***fashion laggers***, who are the last to adopt them.

The majority of people follow, rather than lead, in fashion for many reasons. Some may feel generally insecure, or be uncertain about their own tastes. They may lack interest in fashion and find it easier to conform to standards set by others. They may admire others and imitate those who they envy. Some people may dress in a certain way out of habit or custom. Also, most people do not have the time or money needed to be fashion leaders.

Although fashion leaders provide excitement for the industry, fashion followers make mass production in factories and mass distribution through retail stores economical, 2-3. The large number of fashion followers enable the fashion industry to achieve success. Also, by the time fashion followers wear a style, fashion leaders have already moved on to other styles. This keeps fashion moving.

2-3 After fashion followers accept ideas, garment designs are mass-produced and widely distributed for sale in retail stores almost everywhere.

Theories of Fashion Movement

Fashion looks may be introduced by several means. Fashion professionals need to understand how the ideas spread and are adapted to the tastes, lifestyles, and budgets of different consumer groups. Three theories explain how a fashion might travel to mass acceptance. These are illustrated in 2-4. Each theory identifies different fashion leaders who are first to wear a style, after which it spreads to fashion followers and the general public.

The Trickle-Down Theory

The ***trickle-down theory*** is the world's oldest and most accepted theory of fashion movement. The trickle-down theory assumes the existence of a social hierarchy, and suggests that fashion trends start at the top of a "social ladder" and gradually progress downward through lower levels. Fashions are accepted by people of lower socioeconomic income levels only after they have been worn by people of upper socioeconomic income levels. Fashions are eventually rejected by higher levels when they spread down to the next lower level. This implies that upper classes use fashion to symbolize their superior position. When each lower level tries to look fashionably equal, the levels above it move on to new fashions to reassert their superior position. Lower levels seek identification with those above them, and higher levels try to disassociate themselves from those below them.

The Trickle-Up Theory

The ***trickle-up theory*** suggests that fashion acceptance begins among the young or lower income groups

Trickle Theories

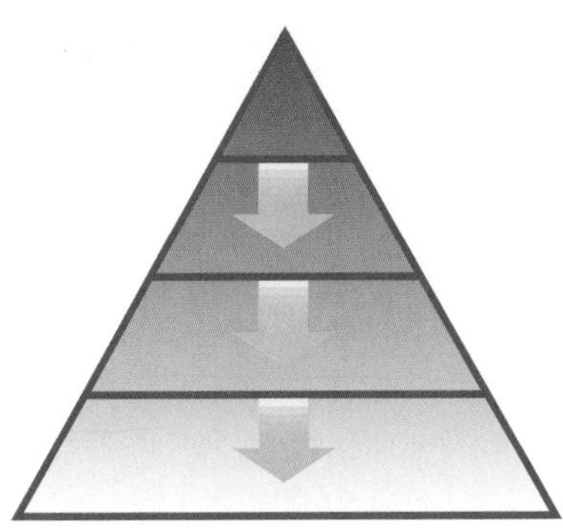

Trickle-down theory

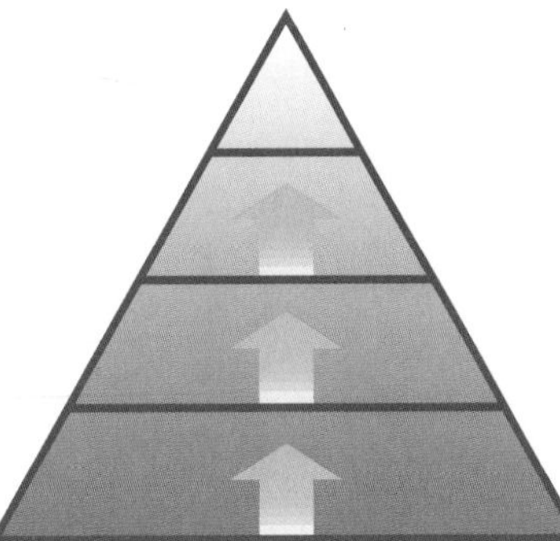

Trickle-up theory

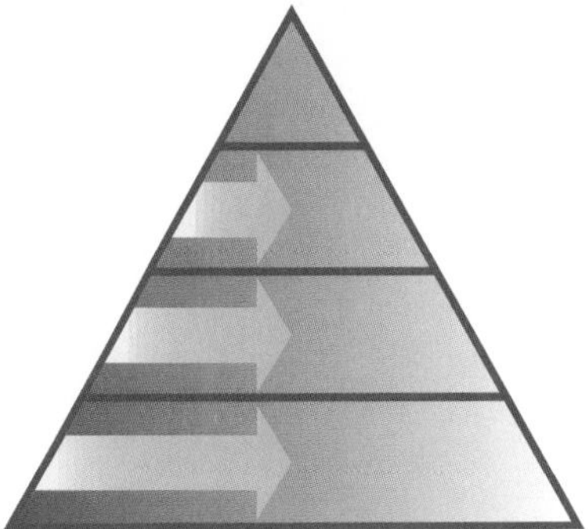

Trickle-across theory

2-4 These triangles indicate a small number of wealthy people in the top class and larger numbers of people in the social classes below that. With the colored areas showing where the fashion leaders are for each of the trickle theories, notice the arrows that show the flow to the fashion followers.

and moves upward to older or higher income groups. It is the opposite of the trickle-down theory. For instance, around 1990, less affluent teenagers were wearing ripped jeans and layers of old clothing, 2-5. Soon, that look spread into older age groups and higher income groups, and top designers produced lines of high-priced "grunge" fashions. Designers often look for trends among avant-garde youth. Similarly, fashion trends are sometimes inspired by minority groups.

The Trickle-Across Theory

The ***trickle-across theory*** claims that fashion moves horizontally through groups at similar social levels. It suggests that each group has its own fashion leaders. With today's fast-paced communications and production methods, new styles at various price levels are exposed to the fashion leaders of all social groups at about the same time. Once the fashions are well accepted by a group's fashion leaders, the styles spread through the group's population. This implies that fashion acceptance starts at the same time within several social classes. Members of each social group look at the leaders of their own group for fashion trends rather than to unknown leaders at higher or lower levels. For instance, designer fashions are copied quickly for mass production, providing similar styles at most price ranges. However, they don't become popular until the fashion leaders of each group have accepted them.

McCall Pattern Co.

2-5 "Grunge" fashions started on the streets with young people wearing old, used garments bought from thrift stores. Eventually, new garments were intentionally "distressed" with tears and holes to imitate that look.

The Fashion Cycle

Fashion change follows a definite pattern. The ***fashion cycle*** involves the ongoing rise, peak, and fall in popularity of specific styles. Each style that comes into fashion rotates through the fashion cycle. Special features of fashion goods, such as colors, textures, and fabrics also go through fashion cycles. In fact, fashion cycles exist for most products, including cars, home appliances, and sports equipment. Each popular concept eventually loses popularity because people are impressed with a newer idea.

Understanding the fashion cycle is important in fashion merchandising. A regular round of different styles is fashionable over time. As older fashions are loosing popularity, different, new fashions are emerging. When existing fashions are dying, there are seemingly more desirable ones available to replace them.

Stages of the Cycle

Each fashion moves with the same series of events:

- The new style is introduced.
- It increases in popularity.
- It is worn by many people.
- It decreases in popularity.
- Finally, it is discarded for a newer style.

Thus, the stages of the fashion cycle are introduction, rise, peak, decline, and obsolescence. These stages can be illustrated on a bell-shaped curve, 2-6. This is called the ***merchandise acceptance curve***.

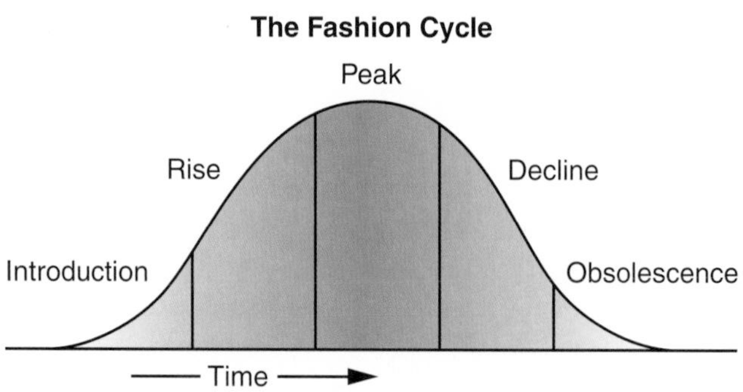

2-6 The fashion cycle, known also as the merchandise acceptance curve, has five main identifiable stages.

The Introduction

The first stage of the fashion cycle is the ***introduction***. New styles, colors, or textures are introduced. At this beginning stage, new "looks" seem unusual and are only accepted by a small number of fashion leaders. They are produced in small quantities. Retail fashion buyers purchase only limited numbers of them to test their acceptance or rejection by the store's customers. Fashion businesses try to stimulate interest in new styles being introduced, as indicated in 2-7. Promotional activities include advertising and fashion shows. Consumers either give a new fashion enough acceptance to get it started, or they immediately reject it.

The Rise

The second stage of the fashion cycle is the rise. During this time, consumer interest grows and the fashion becomes accepted by more people. Manufacturers copy or adapt the main features of the style in less expensive materials and in lower quality construction than the original styles. Mass production brings down the price of the fashion, which creates even more sales. As more consumers buy and use the fashion, it begins to gain wide-spread acceptance. Retail fashion buyers order these items in quantity so they have the maximum amount in stock. Promotional efforts try to heighten consumer desire for the merchandise and motivate consumers to buy and wear the items.

The Peak

The third stage of the fashion cycle is the ***peak***, during which fashions are at their height of popularity. This stage is also called the ***culmination stage*** or plateau. During the culmination stage, the fashion is in great demand by almost everyone. It is mass-produced in many variations. It is available at almost all retail stores and within the price range of most consumers. It may have a short or long stay in this stage, varying from a quick fad to a long-lived classic. Interest in it might be extended by updating or adding new details of design, color, or texture to the original look. During this stage, each retailer tries to persuade the public that its version of the item is best.

The Decline

The fourth stage of the fashion cycle is ***decline***. Following a fashion's highest level of acceptance, it reaches ***saturation***, in which the market has been supplied with the most it will absorb of that fashion. The fashion is overused and starts to seem dull and boring, with decreased consumer demand as it loses popularity. Many people still wear the fashion, 2-8, but they will no longer buy it at the regular price. Manufacturers stop making it. Retailers mark down the price to sell those that remain in stock and to make room for newer fashions. Stores advertise the price reduction and eventually have a major clearance or closeout to completely

Peclers c/o ESP/Ellen Sideri Partnership Inc.

2-7 Fashion services are available to offer innovative design advice and recognize future trends for introduction to manufacturers, retailers, and consumers.

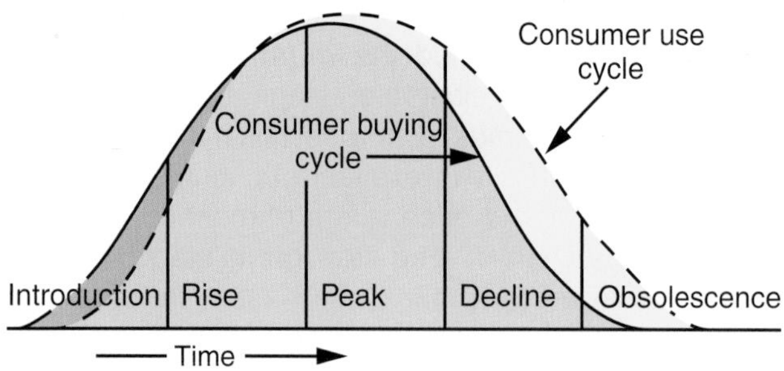

2-8 Consumers continue to use items after they would no longer buy them.

get rid of those that remain. A fashion's decline is almost always faster than its rise.

Obsolescence

The end of the fashion cycle is the *obsolescence stage*. At this time, the style is totally undesirable. Stores cannot "unload" it at any price to consumers. It is no longer worn and is rejected by almost everyone. The style fades from use completely.

The Overall Fashion Cycle

As fashions come and go, they seem to be extreme and daring when first introduced, smart and stylish when they are popular, and dowdy and out-of-date after their peak. Chart 2-9, based on one developed by James Laver, illustrates the feelings toward styles as they pass into and out of fashion. The years listed are approximate. The chart expands and contracts depending on the length of the overall fashion cycle.

Outdated styles look strange to us today because they are no longer in fashion. However, each style is considered to be attractive when it is popularly worn. It is only after many decades that old fashions become delightful again.

The Swing of Fashion Popularity
10 years before its time—vulgar and indecent
5 years before its time—bold and shameless
1 year before its time—flashy and daring
When it is in fashion—elegant and smart
1 year after its time—tacky and dowdy
5 years after its time—hideous
10 years after its time—outrageous
20 years after its time—funny
50 years after its time—odd
100 years after its time—charming
150 years after its time—gorgeous

2-9 This illustrates feelings toward fashions as they move through the years. The time taken by a fashion to complete this swing varies, but the course is always a cyclical one.

Length of Fashion Cycles

The fashion cycle has no specific standard length. The speed of movement through the cycle varies with each fashion, possibly taking from several months to several years. The time that each style spends in any of the phases of the cycle depends on the degree to which it is gaining or losing public acceptance. Thus, the line of the bell-shaped acceptance curve is a bit different for each fashion, as indicated in 2-10. Also, several fashion cycles overlap all the time.

Long-run fashions take a long time to complete the cycle. They may have slow initial acceptance, a longer time in popular demand, and/or a slow period of decline. Classics are an example of long-run fashions since they stay in general fashion acceptance for an extended period of time, 2-10.

Short-run fashions are popular for a brief period of time, usually for only one selling season. They are often easy for manufacturers to copy, and inexpensive for consumers to buy. Fads are examples of short-run fashions, since they quickly become popular and saturate the market. Then people tire of them very fast and their life cycle ends abruptly. See 2-10.

Teenagers' fashions change the fastest and have the most minor trends. Women's, men's, and children's

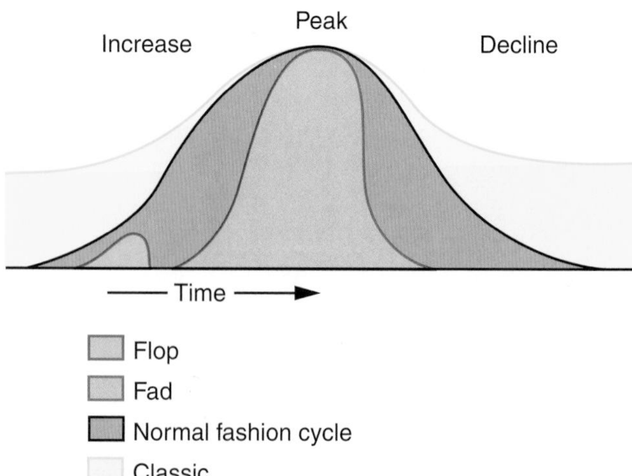

2-10 Although all fashions have a curve that goes up and down, different acceptance levels can be easily recognized if the curve is drawn for them.

apparel and accessories have varying life cycles. Those with more details tend to go out of fashion faster than simple styles. Home decorating and car styles have slower fashion cycles than apparel. Architecture and basic music styles have even slower cycles.

In past centuries, fashion cycles moved slowly. However, in the 1900s, fashion movement became faster. New fashions are always ready to push old ones out of the way. Current fashion trends seem to recur in about the span of a generation. For instance, in the 1980s, many styles reappeared from the 1950s and 1960s. In the 1990s, styles recurred from the 1970s.

Specific fashion cycles have not been as distinct recently as in past centuries. For instance, all skirt lengths are currently acceptable, from micro-mini to ankle lengths. Look at the photos in 2-11 through 2-18 to see some of the fashion looks of the 1900s. Since the mid-1980s, natural fibers and casual comfort have been widely accepted.

Breaks in cycles also occur periodically. These can be caused by radical social/political change, a natural

2-11 At the beginning of the 1900s, fashions had Edwardian elegance.

2-12 In the 1910s, fashions were influenced by early movie stars.

2-13 The carefree, jazzy, "flapper" era occurred during the 1920s.

2-14 Fashions of the 1930s were clingy, draped, and long.

2-15 In the 1940s, there was a padded shoulder look and influence of World War II.

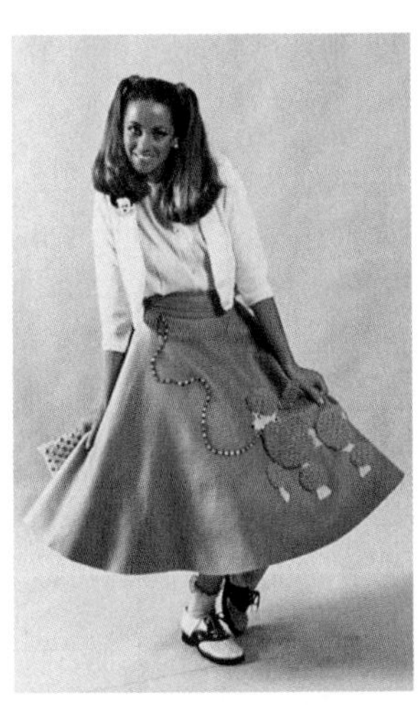

2-16 The fashion look of the 1950s included poodle skirts, stiff (crinoline) slips, and bobby socks with sneakers or saddle shoes.

2-17 The fashions of the 1960s included miniskirts, boxy jackets, and coordinated outfits influenced by First Lady, Jacqueline Kennedy.

Photos courtesy of McCall Pattern Co.

2-18 In the 1970s, men wore leisure suits and bold neckties, while women wore pantsuits. Pants for everyone were flared at the bottom, and most fabrics were of synthetic fibers.

disaster, or even an unexpected change in the weather. For instance, one drastic change occurred at the end of World War II when women quickly switched from stiff, dull clothes to soft, feminine ones.

Principles of Fashion Movement

Five basic principles of fashion movement have existed for centuries. They are fundamental to identifying and predicting fashion trends. However, applying these principles today is more challenging because of the fast pace of fashion movement. Fashions change but these principles do not. These five basic principles are:

- Consumer acceptance or rejection establishes fashions.
- Price does not determine fashion acceptance.
- Sales promotion does not determine fashion.
- Fashion movement is evolutionary, not revolutionary.
- Fashion extremes cause reversals or abrupt changes.

The Role of Consumer Acceptance or Rejection in Establishing Fashions

Consumers determine what will be in fashion. Designers and manufacturers cannot dictate what consumers should wear. For success, designers and manufacturers need support and acceptance from their customers. Consumers accept some styles and reject others. Consumers "vote for" fashions by purchasing them and "vote against" them by not purchasing them. Although designers, manufacturers, and retailers can encourage or discourage the acceptance of new fashions, consumers ultimately determine fashion acceptance.

Fashion Acceptance and Price

Although a new style may first be offered at a high price, it can quickly become available at various prices. Successful ideas that originate at any price level are soon copied in similar looking, mass-produced, ready-to-wear garments that are within the budget of most consumers. What consumers pay for an item of apparel does not indicate whether it is fashionable or not.

Sales Promotion and Fashion

Promotional activities, such as advertising and window displays, cannot sell merchandise that consumers do not want to buy. If a fashion idea is unpopular, no amount of promotional activity can be effective in creating consumer interest in buying it. Although promotional efforts by fashion businesses do help to generate more sales of already accepted fashions, they do not dictate what styles will initially be accepted by consumers. Once a fashion trend is established, however, promotion does help it to gain strength. Also, promotion cannot renew the life of a fading fashion.

Fashion Movement: Evolutionary, Not Revolutionary

People do not like drastic changes away from accepted, comfortable ideas. Thus, fashions usually evolve gradually from one style to another rather than changing quickly. Fashion change evolves through gradual movements from one season or year to the next. Shoulder widths narrow or widen gradually, not suddenly. Skirt lengths rise and fall an inch at a time, season after season. They generally do not go from mid-calf to very short lengths, or vice versa, suddenly. However, the evolutionary process through the fashion cycle is faster today than it has been previously.

Fashion Extremes—Reversals or Abrupt Changes

When fashions reach an extreme in styling, a new and different look will begin. For example, when shoulders look extremely wide and large with big shoulder pads, fashions generally move away from emphasizing the shoulder area. When garments are extremely tight, they start to move toward a roomier fit. When they reach an oversized look, they start to become tighter again. Men's neckties move from skinny string ties to very, very wide. Skirt length, from very short to very long, is a perfect example of how a fashion trend can go only so far in one direction and must eventually change.

Factors that Speed or Slow Fashion Movement

The normal flow of a fashion cycle can be affected by any number of outside influences. Those who make and sell fashion items should be aware of how certain conditions influence consumer acceptance of such merchandise. Some factors promote fast fashion movement while others cause fashion change to be slowed. Being observant of these influences helps manufacturers and retailers forecast how fast fashion trends will move through the merchandise acceptance curve. The factors are summarized in 2-19.

Factors that Speed Up Fashion Movement

Fashion movement is accelerated when demand for the products increases. This faster consumer acceptance is caused by certain factors. The following factors

Fashion Movement

Factors that Accelerate Fashion Movement	Factors that Decelerate Fashion Movement
Modern communications and mass media Good economic conditions Increased competition Technological advances Social and physical mobility More leisure time Higher levels of education Changing roles of women Seasonal changes	Bad economic conditions Cultural customs Religion Laws or other government regulations Disruptive world events

2-19 Some factors are known to speed up fashion movement while others tend to slow down the movement of various fashions through their acceptance curves.

not only speed up fashion change, but also influence the direction that fashion takes:

- modern communications and mass media
- good economic conditions
- increased competition
- technological advances
- social and physical mobility
- more leisure time available
- higher levels of education
- changing roles of women
- seasonal changes

Modern Communications and Mass Media

Modern communications and mass media spread fashion news around the world almost instantly. Centuries ago, people spread ideas only as they started to trade with other cultures. Now worldwide communication, trade, and travel lead to greater fashion exposure. They permit many fashion looks to be popular everywhere. Movies, television, magazines, and other media show the latest fashion trends to stimulate consumer buying and speed up fashion movement. Even slight fashion changes receive faster and wider publicity than ever before.

Good Economic Conditions

Good economic conditions cause changes in investment patterns and consumer attitudes. An upturn in the economy helps U.S. money have more value in relation to the currency of other countries. In strong economic times, more resources are available to create new fashions, and consumers have more money to spend on newer items. In turn, they buy new garments. Since, in most cases, fashion is a luxury, the ability to spend money enables people to replace obsolete items.

Increased Competition

Increased competition among the many manufacturers and retailers that sell fashion offers consumers a constantly changing assortment of goods. It encourages a wider variety of products that is better suited to the desires of the market. Competition also causes the products to be of better quality and keeps prices lower. Today's lower-priced, mass-produced garments are easier to discard than the fewer, higher-priced garments of the past. People now have several basic styles in their closets at a time, supplemented with some trendy items that change quickly.

Technological Advances

Technological advances encourage a wider variety of new and better products. There are new fibers and finishes, as well as new manufacturing and distribution methods. Shopping is also more convenient for consumers. Products can be available faster, manufactured quickly at all price levels. Their appearance and performance can be better. Rapid technological developments and mass production allow retailers to continually have new fashions to attract customers.

Social and Physical Mobility

Social and physical mobility means moving up the social ladder and/or moving from one location in a state or the country to another. These changes often create an increased interest in fashion and expose people to new fashion influences. More expensive or different items might be desired. Psychologically, people need different apparel. New types of garments might be needed for a different climate or different lifestyle activities.

More Leisure Time Available

More leisure time is available for some people, with paid holidays and vacations. Also, there are many more retirees today. This allows for many different lifestyles. It encourages some people to travel, participate in sports, enjoy social activities, and relax at home. This creates a need for a greater variety of clothing. The result is that people have larger wardrobes, and some have more time to shop and to buy clothing.

Higher Levels of Education

Higher levels of education also accelerate fashion movement. Consumers who have more education usually have increased earning power. They can make more retail purchases, as well as larger, more expensive ones. They often have more confidence about trying new fashions.

Changing Roles of Women

The changing roles of women have caused them to alter and expand their wardrobes. The new status of women in the past few decades has exposed them to many experiences and ideas that have changed their wardrobes. With more women in the workforce, more career clothing is needed. Women are more likely to participate in sports and to exercise, so active sportswear and exercise clothing have increased in demand, 2-20. These new buying habits contribute to faster fashion change.

Seasonal Changes

Seasonal change from spring to summer to fall to winter causes fashion change, even in fairly steady climates. Consumers desire lightweight fabrics and pastel colors in spring and summer, 2-21. They desire heavier apparel in the fall and winter, 2-22. This increases fashion demand and speeds the movement of styles through the fashion cycle.

Factors that Slow Down Fashion Movement

Fashion movement slows when consumers resist buying and wearing new styles and continue to wear clothes they already have. There is less spending for new fashion products. This lower demand for new products reduces the speed of fashion change. This is usually caused by one or more of the following factors:

- bad economic conditions
- cultural customs
- religion
- laws or other government regulations
- disruptive world events

Bad Economic Conditions

Bad economic conditions slow fashion change because consumers have less money to spend. If there is high unemployment, there is slower consumer acceptance of fashion and fewer new trends. People often try to create a new fashion look with less expensive accessories, such as belts or scarves, rather than buying new garments.

Cultural Customs

Cultural customs often include types of apparel that have been established over a long period of time and are still in existence today. Some cultures and ethnic

Monsanto Fibers

2-20 Today, women not only have careerwear and casual attire in their wardrobes, but also apparel and accessories for specific activities such as biking, jogging, or skating.

McCall Pattern Co.

2-21 Seasonal changes increase fashion movement because the pastel cotton, sleeveless, and scooped neck dress shown here can only be worn during part of the year in most geographic locations.

The Fashion Association/Newport Harbor

2-22 Different apparel is worn in cooler weather than in warmer weather, which causes consumers to buy more fashions as the seasons change.

groups prefer to wear traditional forms of dress that are passed down from one generation to another. This slows fashion movement since the new fashion trends sold in retail stores are not desired by these groups of people.

Religion

Religion also has a slowing effect on fashion change. Some religious groups feel that certain fashions lead to temptation and corruption. Although most religious groups have less influence on the dress of their members today, subtle pressures may cause their followers to avoid some modern fashion trends.

Laws or Other Government Regulations

Laws or other government regulations may slow fashion movement. In history, sumptuary laws allowed lavish clothes to be worn only by members of nobility. The apparel fabrics, colors, decorations, and expenditures of the "common people" were regulated. Today, the use of certain furs and skins of endangered species might be outlawed. Also, imported goods might be regulated by tariffs or quotas that prevent certain items from entering the country and being available to consumers.

Disruptive World Events

Disruptive world events, such as droughts or wars, cause shortages. During wartime, there may be restrictions on certain materials or amounts of fabrics that can be used for apparel. Instead, the fabrics may be needed for parachutes or military uniforms. This slows fashion movement because the scarcity prevents designers and manufacturers from making new fashions. This, in turn, prevents retailers and consumers from obtaining new fashions. Communications and trade may also be limited, further slowing fashion movement. When this happens, people might switch their fashion interest to small accessories or a different hair style to satisfy their desire for something new.

The Importance of Fashion Change

Because fashion is a product of change, understanding consumer motives and predicting fashion movement is important at all levels of the industry. Fashion manufacturers and retailers must forecast the direction in which fashion is moving and predict what styles will be accepted by the majority of consumers. It is both exciting and challenging to interpret fashion movements and to estimate their speed and outcome.

Not only does fashion thrive on change, but the business of fashion is itself changing. It operates in a much different way today than it has in even the recent past. It moves faster and reaches more people. It is more sophisticated. It is also more businesslike.

Fashion does much to stimulate our economy. Many manufacturers and retailers exist because of consumer desire to keep current with fashion trends. Consumers purchase goods to fulfill their wants and needs. Manufacturers and retailers realize that fashion meets consumers' basic desires for change.

For those who understand all aspects of fashion movement, there is a definite pattern that can be used to predict and analyze current and future fashions. Fashion cycle stages can be charted and predicted. Being able to predict fashion movement is vital to success in both the buying and the selling of fashion products.

Summary

Fashion movement is a result of different fashions continually going in and out of popularity. Fashion leaders discover and wear new styles, which are later copied and gain mass acceptance by fashion followers.

Theories of fashion movement suggest that fashion trends start with some age, income, or social groups. Then they move to other groups for greater popularity. They might move down, up, or across socio-economic levels of society.

The fashion cycle shows the predictable ongoing introduction, rise, peak, decline, and obsolescence of fashion elements. This is shown with a bell-shaped curve for each fashion trend. The curve should guide the production, promotion, and sales strategy for fashion businesses. It's length differs for each style.

Five basic principles of fashion movement help to identify and predict fashion trends. There are also factors that speed or slow fashion movement. Predicting fashion change is important for all fashion businesses. Business of the fashion industry is also changing. Knowledge of these changes is essential for success in the fashion world.

To Know

fashion movement
obsolescence factor
fashion trend
fashion leaders
fashion followers
fashion laggers
trickle-down theory
trickle-up theory
trickle-across theory
fashion cycle
merchandise acceptance curve
culmination stage
saturation
long-run fashions
short-run fashions

To Review

1. Why is fashion one of the greatest economic forces in everyday life?
2. Who encourages fashion movement?
3. If most fashion items do not wear out, why do consumers buy new clothes?
4. How many fashion trends can exist at the same time?
5. Who were most often the trendsetting fashion leaders in past centuries?
6. Why are most people fashion followers instead of fashion leaders?
7. List the three theories of how fashion might travel to mass acceptance.
8. Tell how a style goes through the five stages of the fashion cycle.
9. What determines the length of time that each style spends in any phase of the cycle?
10. Give a general example of a long-run fashion and a short-run fashion.
11. How often do current fashion trends seem to recur?
12. List three factors that could cause breaks in fashion cycles.
13. How do consumers show their acceptance or rejection of fashions?
14. What part does promotion play in the success of already accepted fashions?
15. Why do fashions usually evolve gradually from one style to another rather than change quickly?
16. List four factors that speed up fashion movement.
17. List four factors that slow down fashion movement.
18. How is the business of fashion different today, compared to the past?

To Do

1. Pick an apparel style that has been popular in the past few years. In an oral report, describe each stage of its fashion cycle (how and by whom it was introduced, how it was promoted in each stage, when it reached its peak, etc.). Show a drawing of the style's merchandise acceptance curve, showing how you think its fashion cycle has looked. Mark where you think it is in the cycle right now.
2. Study fashions from a specific year in the distant past. In a written paper, describe how the fashions looked. Then relate the styles of that time to the chart in 2-9. Explain if your feelings toward those particular past fashions agree with the chart for the corresponding number of years since they were in fashion.
3. In a written or oral report, name one of today's fashion leaders. Using newspapers, magazines, and other media, determine what trends he or she started, promoted, or strongly influenced. How popular did the trends become with fashion followers? Why? Include pictures to support the main points of your report.
4. In a small group, pick a fashion that is near the end of its fashion cycle. Analyze which trickle theory it followed as it gained popularity. Try to specifically identify where it started and how it passed to its peak. Draw a large triangle and chart your findings for a bulletin board display. Include labels and/or a short description to clarify your thoughts.
5. Describe the meaning of social and physical mobility. Then write a short story about a person or family that experiences social and/or physical mobility. Explain the apparel changes needed in your story.

CHAPTER 3

Basic Economic Concepts

After studying this chapter, you will be able to

- identify economic products as either goods or services.
- describe the role of profit, competition, and supply and demand in the free-market system.
- distinguish between the main competitive market structures.
- list the basic forms of business organizations.
- describe the concept of business cycles.
- explain the concepts of marketing and merchandising.

Fashion is big business. It is a complex, multibillion dollar industry with millions of employees. Fashion-related businesses are crucial to the U.S. economy through the materials and services they buy, produce, and sell, and the wages and taxes they pay. ***Manufacturers*** are companies that make goods. ***Retailers*** are companies that sell merchandise in small quantities to consumers. ***Consumers*** are people who buy and use the finished products, such as apparel.

The fashion industry includes all the businesses connected with designing, manufacturing, distributing, promoting, and selling textile and apparel products. The products are either goods that are manufactured, or services performed. ***Goods*** are physically made by manufacturers. The manufacturers use raw materials, production equipment, and factory workers to make the finished goods, such as garments and accessories, 3-1. Retailers perform ***services*** by buying the finished items in large quantities and selling them individually to consumers. They connect goods with users of those goods. They may also sponsor fashion shows or color

Micromattique™ by DuPont

3-1 The blouse, vest, slacks, and shoes shown here are goods that were made by manufacturers. For instance, the polyester microfiber material of the slacks was produced by machines and people at DuPont, after which the slacks were sewn by factory workers with production equipment for Casablanca.

3-2 The product of retail stores is a service because they do not manufacture goods. Instead, they buy finished goods in bulk and offer a choice of single items to consumers in a certain setting.

or wardrobe consulting. Retailers provide stores in which shoppers can choose and buy goods that were made elsewhere by manufacturing companies, 3-2. The stores have lights, displays, merchandise, and sales employees, to help them provide their services.

Fashion products, or the goods and services of the fashion industry, are constantly changing. This is done to meet the market needs of consumers.

The Free-Market System

In the U.S., products are bought and sold in a market economy. Individuals, not governments, make the key economic decisions. The economy operates as a ***free-market system***, where people freely choose how to spend their money. Their choices determine which products are offered in the market and the prices of these products. This market system has little or no government intervention, in contrast to communist command systems that have heavy government control.

In a free-market system, if you have goods or services to sell, you can charge any price you want and sell to anyone willing to pay that price. Conversely, consumers are free to buy whatever they want and can afford from whomever they choose, 3-3. The economy's businesses are responsible for fulfilling the needs of the marketplace.

Profit Motivation

The foundation of the free-market business system is profit. ***Profit*** is money left over after expenses and taxes have been deducted from the company's sales of goods or services. In other words, it is the difference between the costs to make and sell goods or services and what people are willing to pay for those goods or

JUSCO Co., Ltd./AEON Group

3-3 A free-market system allows consumers to make their own choices about where they will shop and what they will buy.

services. For example, if it costs you $25 to make or offer a garment for sale, and you sell it for $35, your profit is $10.

Profits determine whether a business succeeds and can continue to operate, or fails and must close. Also, a business with high profits is considered to be more successful than a business with low profits, even though both may continue to operate. Profit is the reward for the work of putting a desirable product into useful form and selling it to those who want to buy it.

The Significance of Competition

In a free-market system, many companies may be selling the same or a similar product. Because potential customers are free to buy where they please, the companies selling the similar products must compete for sales to those customers. ***Competition*** in our economy is rivalry between two or more businesses to gain as much of the total market sales, or customer acceptance, as possible. This is indicated in 3-4.

Since companies are essentially "fighting" against each other for business, the more competitors there are in an industry, the lower the prices will be. Companies must have low pricing to encourage consumers to buy their version of the product. This is good for consumers since they may be able to pay less for products. However, when there is more competition, the profits per item sold are lower for the businesses involved. It is easier for a business to make money if there is less competition for the type of goods or services they offer for sale.

Similarly, competition encourages higher quality goods and better service from businesses. Companies that offer quality goods that will last longer or perform better than others on the market will probably sell more than their competition if offered at a fair price.

3-4 Manufacturers of fashion goods compete with each other, and stores compete with other stores, for the limited number of consumer dollars that are spent on apparel. Stores in malls compete with others in the same mall and also in other locations.

Companies that provide better service, such as accepting credit or providing fast delivery of the products, will be chosen by more customers than their competitors who offer poor service.

Competition also encourages industries to provide a large variety of types of goods and services. If a company can be innovative and differentiate its products from its competitors, it can gain a certain additional number of customers. This desire to offer a different "twist" to products constantly creates new opportunities for businesses.

The result of these factors is that companies are always trying to stay ahead of their competitors with better price, quality, or innovation. Competition helps the economy move forward with better technology and new fashions.

The Supply and Demand Relationship

Price levels respond to the forces of supply and demand. In economic terms, ***supply*** refers to the quantities of a good or service that producers are willing and able to provide at a particular time at various prices. ***Demand*** refers to the amounts of a good or service that consumers are willing and able to buy at that time at various prices.

The supply and demand relationship affects prices because people will pay more for something that is in short supply. If there are only a few of a particular item available, consumers feel lucky to find the item at any price and are willing to pay a high price for it. Thus, the companies that make and sell that limited item can charge a higher price for it and make more profit. However, because of the higher profit opportunity, more companies then start to supply that product, it becomes more widely available, and the price goes down.

When a product is widely available, the sellers have to settle for lower prices and less profit-per-item. With high supply, consumers can find that type of product in many places and will buy it where the price is the lowest, 3-5. With competition among the many suppliers, resulting in less profit for the product, it is less attractive for businesses to sell it. Thus, some companies stop supplying that product and move on to other products that have less supply, more demand, and higher profit potential.

Demand has a big effect, too. If there is high demand for a product, people will pay a higher price for it than if demand is low. When demand goes down, the price of an item goes down because not very many people want it.

As you can see, the forces of supply and demand combine with the profit motive in a free-market system to regulate what is produced and in what amounts. The amount of goods that can be manufactured and offered for sale is limited. Also, the number of a company's

3-5 If there is an abundance of similar fashions at many stores, those at lower prices are the ones that sell.

potential customers, and those customers' dollars, are limited. The quantity of specific goods and services supplied and the quantity demanded are continuously interacting. The balance between them at any given moment is reflected by current prices on the open market. In theory, consumers get what they want and producers earn a profit by keeping up with public demand.

Impacts on Society

The free-market system uses a minimum amount of resources to achieve a maximum standard of living for consumers. This is a "win-win" situation for society because both suppliers and users benefit.

All ***resources***, or industrial materials and manufacturing capabilities, are scarce. Resources include such things as raw materials, money, equipment, and workers. Some material resources for fashion goods are shown in 3-6. Resources are used as sparingly as possible by businesses to keep prices as low as possible. This, in turn, enables a company's products to sell at competitive prices. By keeping expenses low, the level of a company's profits is as high as possible. This uses resources to the best advantage.

A ***standard of living*** indicates the way people live, based on the kinds and quality of goods and services they can afford. There are certain levels of necessities and luxuries enjoyed (or aspired to) by people at various levels of comfort and status. In the free-market system, many different products are offered at many different price levels. This provides the most selection of goods and services to the largest number of people. It enables all people to satisfy their needs and wants in the best possible ways.

Competitive Market Structures

Because competition is good for the economy, the government has passed laws that prevent any single enterprise from becoming too powerful. In theory, the ideal market structure is ***pure competition***, in which no single company in an industry is large or powerful enough to influence or control prices. If a company

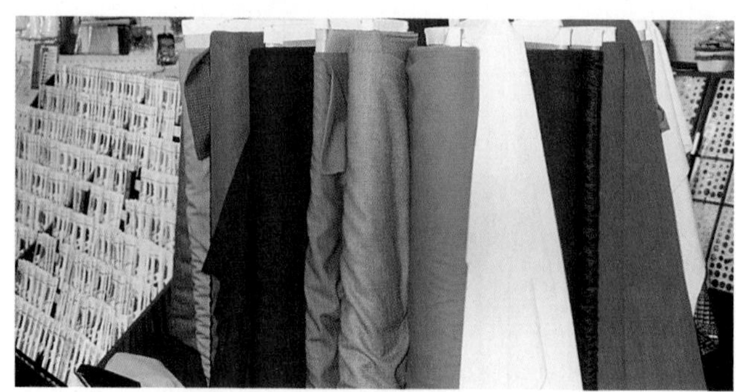

Fabrications

3-6 Raw materials to produce fashion goods include fabrics, zippers, thread, buttons, and interlinings.

becomes that powerful, it distorts the workings of the free-market system.

With such "perfect competition," there are so many buyers and sellers that no single buyer or seller can control the price of a product or the number of units sold. All the products in a purely competitive industry are very similar to each other, and the profit-per-item is low. Companies are free to enter the industry, or exit from it, without any pressure or restraints. Also, each company's existence in or out of the market does not have much effect on the market.

An example of an apparel product with pure competition is T-shirts. They are produced in abundance by many companies, are all of a similar style (even though they may have different designs on them), and are sold in many shops to almost everyone at very similar prices, 3-7. If a new company starts to make or sell T-shirts, or an existing company drops out, the overall market is not affected. Also, if one or two consumers decide to buy or not buy a T-shirt, it doesn't really affect the overall market.

Pure competition does not exist in very many industries. Some markets operate as ***oligopolies***, with only a few large rival firms offering the products. These firms dominate the market for that product and usually react to one another's actions. However, laws prohibit oligopolists from artificially setting prices by agreeing among themselves. Also, the government has the power to prevent mergers of firms that would reduce competition or lead to less competitive conditions in an industry. In the market structure of oligopoly, it is hard for new firms to enter the industry or for established firms to leave the industry.

An example of an oligopoly in apparel is blue jeans, in which there are only a few large manufacturers. Wrangler is a main supplier of jeans for the entire marketplace, 3-8. Others are Lee, Levi, and Gap. They react to the actions of one another. A non-apparel industry illustrating the structure of oligopoly is automobiles. The few car manufacturers are large corporations that dominate the industry and react to one another.

Monopolies have a market structure opposite to pure competition. A monopoly is a market in which there are no direct competitors. Only one company offers a given good or service for sale. This company has total control over products and prices, and it keeps other companies from competing.

Monopolies undermine the principle of competition. True monopolies are prohibited in the U.S. There are no textile/apparel monopolies. The government only allows some utilities (electric, water, cable TV, etc.) to operate as monopolies if they need to control all the lines in a system in order to operate. However, such legal monopolies are closely regulated so they don't charge extremely high prices, and many are now being dissolved. After all, since a monopolistic company is the only one operating in a market, the company could

3-7 Similarly styled and constructed T-shirts are sold in so many stores that a situation of pure competition exists.

Wrangler Hero

3-8 With only a few producers of popular blue jeans, each large jeans manufacturing company stays constantly aware of the design, fit, pricing, or other changes of their competition.

theoretically charge any price, and consumers would have to pay that price for its products.

Monopolies also usually have lower costs per item for their products because of economies of scale. *Economies of scale* are cost reductions resulting from large-scale mass production. If a company has no competition and produces large volumes of a product, it can be very efficient at making its products with specialized machinery and bulk orders of supplies.

There are degrees between the three main competitive structures. All industries fall between the two extremes of pure competition and monopoly, as shown on the continuum in 3-9. A *continuum* is a sliding scale from one extreme to another, with infinite possible responses falling along different points.

Basic Forms of Business Organizations

Within the free-market system, there are certain basic forms of business organizations, or types of company ownership. Each form of business organization has a characteristic structure, legal status, and size to which it is best suited. Each also has key advantages and disadvantages, and offers a distinctive working environment with its own risks and rewards. The three most common types of business organizations are sole proprietorships, partnerships, and corporations.

Sole Proprietorships

Sole proprietorships are owned by just one person, although they may have many employees. Sole proprietorships are the most common type of business in the U.S., especially in the service sector. They have the advantage of being the easiest to start or to dissolve. Most often a sole proprietership is inexpensive to form. The owner is the boss. There is an advantage of secrecy since only the owner knows what is going on in the business. The owner has freedom, independence, and flexibility in running the business. Because of this, the proprietor can make prompt decisions and take action at opportune moments. Often there is also high prestige for a person who has his or her own company and a great sense of accomplishment when that company is successful.

Sole proprietorships are subject to very few government regulations. They also have tax advantages, since the owner is taxed only at the personal rate on income earned, rather than at a corporate rate.

There are also disadvantages to sole proprietorships. Small businesses usually have limited financial resources to get started. The owner may not have much personal money to start the business and banks may be reluctant to loan money toward an unknown success or failure. If a bank does grant a loan, it may impose high interest rates on the money borrowed. This, in turn, causes many sole proprietorships to have limited profit

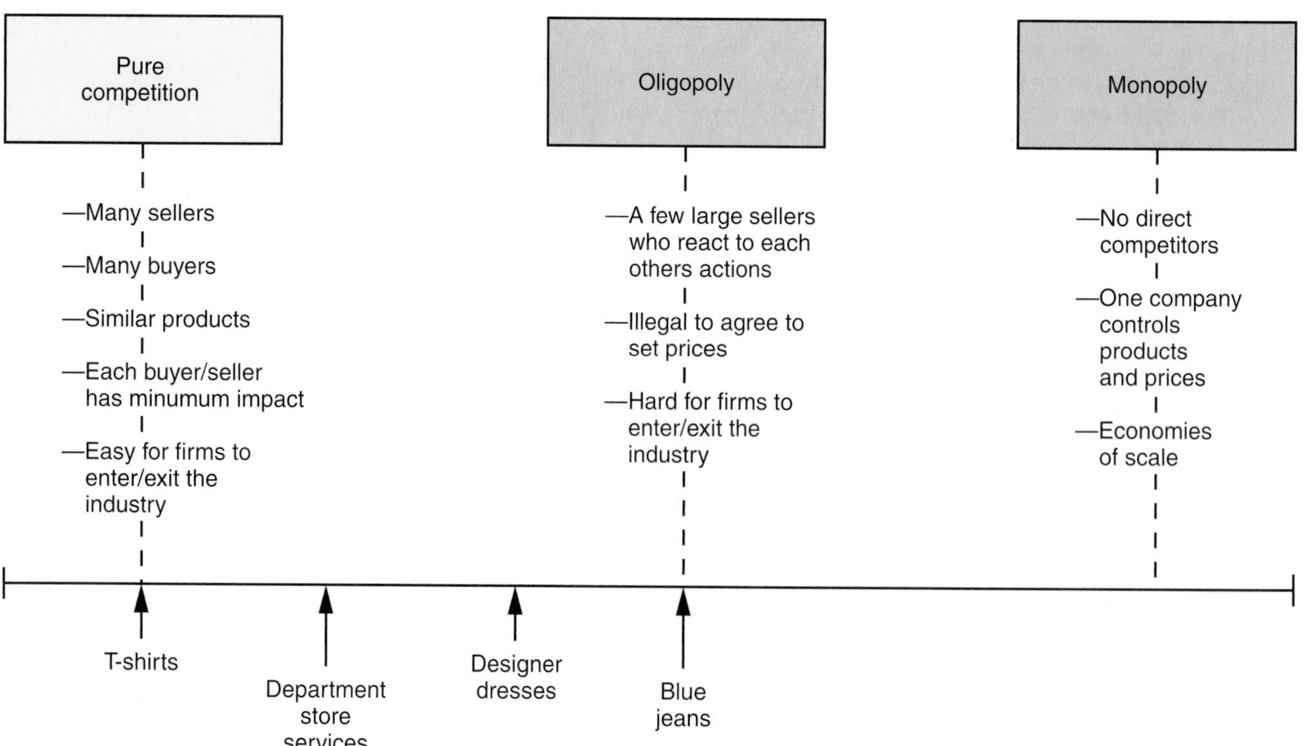

3-9 Fashion products fall mainly near the competitive end of this continuum that stretches between the extremes of pure competition and monopoly.

and growth potential. The income for the owner may be lower than what employees of large companies earn, even though more time may be spent doing the job. The prosperity of the business depends largely on the talents and managerial skills of one person.

A major risk of sole proprietorships is unlimited personal *liability*, or responsibility for the debts and obligations of the business. Since there is no legal separation between the company and its owner, any damages or debts of the business can be attached to the owner. There can be financial ruin for the owner if the business fails and has lots of debts that must be paid.

A final disadvantage of sole proprietorships is that the life of the business is limited to the life or interest of the owner. If the owner dies or retires, the business usually ceases to exist. Generally, owners who want their businesses to grow and continue, either form a partnership or corporation. If the business has been a success, an owner might sell to, or merge with, a larger business to get money from the business when he or she retires.

Small fashion shops are often sole proprietorships, 3-10. The owners have the satisfaction of independently working for themselves. However, they also have the pressure for all the decisions. They control all the profit received by the business, but are also liable for all of the debts.

Partnerships

Partnerships are unincorporated businesses co-owned and operated by two or more persons. They are fairly easy to form, although an explicit agreement should be legally drafted so each partner understands the expected obligations and rewards. Partnerships are usually inexpensive to form. Also, like sole proprietorships, they have tax advantages since profits are taxed at personal income rates rather than at corporate rates.

In general, partnerships have higher profit potential than sole proprietorships because two or more individuals are pooling their talents and taking responsibility for the business. The partners may each have different knowledge and skills that can provide combined high value. Partnerships also have higher credit ratings, enabling them to obtain financial resources for the business somewhat easier than sole proprietorships. Also, the prestige of ownership is shared, but is still very high for the partners. In addition, partnerships have longer life spans since new partners can replace retiring ones.

Partnerships can have several disadvantages. One disadvantage of partnerships is the unlimited liability of the partners, although that is shared in partnerships, rather than being all on one person's shoulders. If the business has financial problems, all the partners may suffer financially by paying the debts out of their own pockets. Another disadvantage is the potential for conflict between the partners. No two people see things exactly the same way, and inner fighting in a business can be very destructive. A final disadvantage is management confusion with more than one person having a say in the daily operations of the business. If a serious stalemate occurs in decision making, the only solution might be to dissolve the partnership. This, or the death of a partner, can create lack of continuity in the business.

Corporations

Corporations are separate legal entities. They are chartered enterprises with most of the legal rights of people. They have the right to conduct business, to own and sell property, to borrow money, to enter into contracts, and to sue or be sued. Each corporation is empowered by the state to carry on a specific line of business. Corporations tend to be larger-scale operations and provide the biggest share of total financial receipts among forms of business organizations.

Corporations are owned by *shareholders*, also called *stockholders*. The shareholders have the advantage of

3-10 Many small fashion shops in towns across North America are owned by just one person. The sole proprietor has all of the responsibility for everything that occurs with the business.

limited liability, and can only lose the amount of the investment they have put into the corporation.

Since the owners (shareholders) and management (people running the operations) of a corporation are usually separate, the owners can vote to change the management if they don't do a good job. Also, specialized managers can be employed for jobs that they are particularly good at doing.

Corporations can raise money by selling shares in "capital markets," such as stock exchanges. Because corporations can divide their ownership into shares of small denominations, their financial expansion and growth can continue as long as investors are willing to purchase additional shares of stock. The shares of stock may also be sold to or inherited by others, which gives an unlimited life span to corporations and can eventually change a company's entire ownership. No other form of business can match the success of the corporation in bringing together money, resources, and talent.

Disadvantages of the corporate form of business include the fact that corporations are complex and expensive to form and to dissolve. Costs of incorporation include charter fees, legal fees, public stock offering expenses, and printing and mailing costs for all the required documents to investors. After incorporating, legal restrictions can limit the corporation to engage in only those activities that are stated or implied in the original charter.

There is also a lack of privacy of a corporation's business information. There must be public disclosure of its operations and finances to the government and to stockholders. This puts pressure on corporate managers to achieve short-term success so the reports look good and so the stockholders receive expected dividends. The information is also then available for competitors to see.

Corporations often claim that they are taxed too heavily. Also, after corporations have paid their taxes, any profits distributed as dividends to shareholders are taxed again as personal income of the investors.

Note the advantages and disadvantages of the forms of business organizations in 3-11.

Forms of Business Ownership

Sole Proprietorship	
Advantages	**Disadvantages**
—Easy to form and dissolve —Inexpensive to form —Secrecy of operations —Freedom and independence in running business —Prestige and feeling of accomplishment for owner —Subject to few government regulations —Taxed at personal income rate —Control all profit	—Hard to obtain financial resources —Hard to make big profits —Reliance on owner for all managerial skills —Unlimited personal liability for business debts —Life of business limited to life or interest of owner
Partnership	
Advantages	**Disadvantages**
—Fairly easy to form —Fairly inexpensive to form —Taxed at personal income rate —Higher profit potential —Prestige for partners —Responsibilities/risks shared by two or more —Can continue despite changes in ownership	—Financial resources may be somewhat limited —Unlimited liability of partners for business debts —Possible conflict between partners —Lack of clear-cut management responsibilities —Problems of continuing if partner existence changes
Corporation	
Advantages	**Disadvantages**
—Unlimited life span —Easy to transfer ownership (buy/sell shares) —Limited liability for owners (shareholders) —Can raise money in capital markets —Specialized management and work skills	—Complex and expensive to form and dissolve —Public disclosure of business information —Heavy taxation —Legal restrictions —Alienation of some employees

3-11 Each of the three main forms of business ownership has specific advantages and disadvantages that distinguish it from the other forms.

Types of Corporations

In the U.S. economy, the corporation is extremely important. Of all the forms of business ownership, it is by far the most significant in terms of money, size, and power. There are several types of corporations.

Public corporations offer their stock to the general public, usually on national exchanges. They are often large businesses, with hundreds or thousands of shareholders. This is a good way to raise money for their operations. A portion of their profits are usually paid to stockholders in the form of dividends.

On the other hand, the stock of *private corporations* is not available to the general public. Most shares are owned by the executives of the corporation. This gives them complete control over their operations and protection from being taken over by outsiders. Private corporations finance any expansions out of the firm's own earnings or by borrowing from some other source.

Some small corporations are *S corporations*. They have no more than 35 shareholders and may be taxed like sole proprietorships or partnerships, rather than at corporate income tax rates.

Some corporations are not for profit. Such *nonprofit corporations* exist to provide a social service rather than to make a profit.

Business Cycles

An economy never stays exactly the same size. It grows and shrinks in up- and down-swings. These are *expansions* and *recessions*, during which national income, employment, and production all either rise (increase) or fall (decrease).

Business cycles are fluctuations in the level of economic activity over periods of several years. Although the fluctuations are natural and sometimes predictable, recessions often cause hardships for both businesses and individuals. Recessions result in a drop in *consumer confidence*, or feeling of certainty by consumers to spend their money. This causes lower retail sales, which signals factories to produce less. Companies must then lay off workers, who in turn buy even less.

Since they are less necessary, fashion products are affected more strongly than other products by recessions and expansions. In recessions, when times are tough, most people can put off buying a new outfit, but they need to continue to buy food and pay for housing and transportation. Thus, the market for fashion products "dries up" faster than such things as food and heating fuel. There is, then, a faster and deeper recession for fashion goods than for other more necessary items.

On the other hand, when the economy grows and consumers have some extra money to spend, the pent-up need and desire for apparel items quickly improves the business climate for apparel manufacturers and retailers. The market for fashion merchandise often grows faster than the general economy, 3-12. Since consumer confidence levels show results before business cycle indicators, they are used as predictors of what the economy will do in the future.

It has been shown that during recessions, consumers mainly buy small apparel items, such as inexpensive accessories that will give a new look to their old garments. During more prosperous economic times, consumers buy more costly apparel items such as dresses, coats, and suits.

The Concept of Marketing

Marketing is the total process of finding or creating a profitable market for specific goods or services. The process includes identifying customers, determining those customer's wants and needs, and providing satisfying products at acceptable prices to those customers. It also incorporates distribution and promotional activities. The marketing concept has an overall goal of satisfying customer desires while making a profit for the seller. It involves a seller and a buyer, both of whom should obtain satisfaction from the transaction.

If a manufacturing company or retailer is to be successful, the firm must have products that consumers perceive as desirable. These products must also be presented to potential customers in ways that make the customers want to buy them. To do this, the company must be marketing-oriented at all levels of the business by planning all of its operations around satisfying customer wants and needs.

In the past, manufacturers and retailers had a product-oriented approach to business rather than a marketing approach. They focused on designing and manufacturing merchandise that was easy and economical to produce, without checking the preferences of consumers. Then they would spend considerable time and money trying to convince consumers to buy the goods. This approach often resulted in low profits.

Today's marketing-oriented approach focuses on determining customer desires before goods are

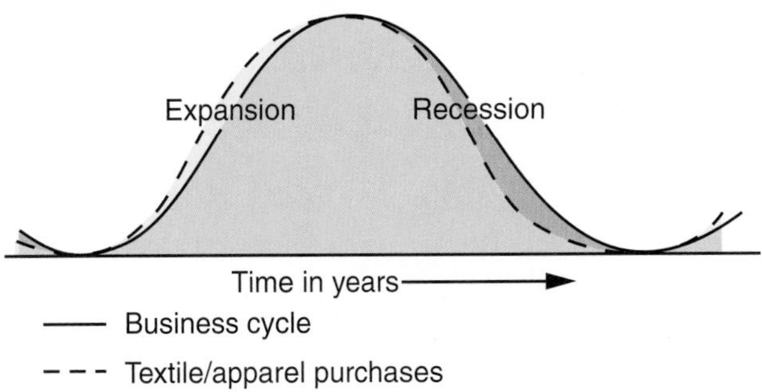

3-12 Spending for fashion merchandise is more accentuated than general spending in the economy during each business cycle.

manufactured. Companies plan their entire business around satisfying their customers. Thus, *fashion marketing*, or the making and selling of apparel and accessories that are desirable to customers, has proven to be a much better strategy.

For a successful marketing-oriented approach, the company must first define its ***target market***. This is the specific segment of a total market that a company wants as customers, and toward whom it directs its marketing efforts. Choice of a target market is usually based on some common characteristics of the market segment, such as educational level, income, or lifestyle. Then the company identifies the needs and wants of its target market. Finally, products that will meet those needs and wants are developed or selected, 3-13. The concept of target marketing is explained more specifically and fully in later chapters of this text.

Companies decide how to satisfy their target customers by creating a marketing mix that differentiates them from their competitors. A ***marketing mix*** is a blend of features that satisfies a chosen market. Its four major elements, known as "the four Ps," include:

- product
- price
- place
- promotion

Product

The first marketing task is to determine the right products. Marketing people must decide what goods or services are in demand, and then guide the process of bringing those products into existence. The needs and wants of customers must be translated into desirable products of the business, 3-14. When planning for this, both the tangible attributes of the products, such as color, fabric, and trimmings, as well as intangible attributes, such as brand name, packaging, and warranty must be considered.

Social trends often provide a clue to the types of products that consumers will want. For instance, the rapid increase in the number of working women has inspired clothing manufacturers to produce more women's business attire. The interest in physical fitness has been a boon to exercise wear.

Price

Supply and demand have a great effect on the product pricing decisions of a company. Depending on market conditions, low prices can sometimes maximize profits. The special pricing, shown in 3-15, is trying to stimulate the number of sales transacted. With low pricing, there is less profit per item, but if large amounts of items are sold, the total profit may be high. In other situations, the desirability of products may depend on a high-quality image at a high price. In that case, fewer of each item are sold but a higher profit is taken on each one. Marketing evaluates these variables.

3-13 The target market of this shop is active tennis players who like to have comfortable, up-to-date fashions on the court as well as good equipment to use.

Klopman Fabrics/Burlington Industries

3-14 Fashion marketing involves many important decisions about fabric, garment design, quality of construction, and other characteristics to satisfy customer desires.

3-15 By offering products at reduced prices, more demand is created which, in turn, causes more goods to be sold. A large consideration of marketing is the price level at which products are offered.

The overall profit potential of a product in the market is what is important to businesses, rather than the profit-per item. This is shown on the *marketing triangle*, which relates price to quantity, or the amount expected to be sold, 3-16. The low price at the bottom of the triangle indicates that a large quantity will probably be sold. A high price at the top of the triangle indicates that a small quantity will probably be sold. If the market demand quantity matches the price placement of the product on the marketing triangle, the highest total profit potential results.

Place

Place, in the marketing mix, is how and where products are offered to customers. It represents ***distribution,*** or the best ways to get the products into the hands of potential customers. Decisions must be made about the type of selling and delivery to use.

A materials supplier might sell directly to garment manufacturers at trade shows, 3-17. An apparel manufacturer might have salespeople who sell to department stores, discount chains, or other types of retailers. On the other hand, apparel producers might sell directly

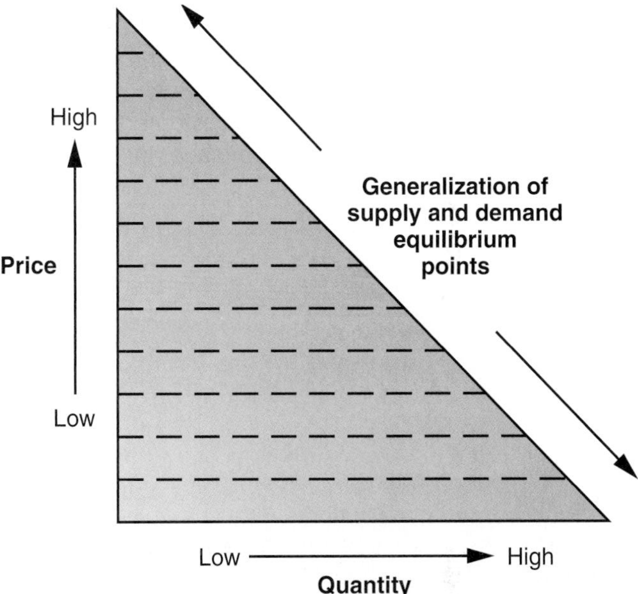

3-16 The marketing triangle shows that products with lower prices will sell in larger quantities than products with higher prices. Some products, such as designer gowns, are intentionally marketed at high prices, with only a few meant to be sold.

Bobbin, a Miller Freeman Inc. Company

3-17 A good place to sell leather, fabrics, or apparel lines might be at a trade show. However, it would not be a good place to sell single items to consumers, since it is strictly a trade event.

to consumers through their own mail-order catalogs or outlet stores. Some manufacturers use multiple distribution systems, by combining several distribution methods. They might sell to retailers as well as operating their own outlets, 3-18.

Transportation must also be considered, such as moving the goods by train, plane, or truck, 3-19. Companies try to use the most efficient methods to get goods to the right locations.

Promotion

Promotion is any nonpersonal activity that furthers the sales of goods or services to a large audience, rather than one-on-one. It encourages public acceptance of companies and their products through advertising and other promotional tools. Businesses must decide how to inform their target customers about the company's products, prices, and places of availability.

3-18 Besides selling their lines in quantity to retail stores, apparel producers often have outlet stores to sell some of their goods directly to consumers.

3-19 After manufacturers have delivered large shipments of goods to companies who sell them, they must be further distributed to individual stores in many different locations.

Promotional campaigns spread information to the marketplace and often determine the success of a marketing effort. Specific types of promotion will be studied later in this textbook.

The Concept of Merchandising

Merchandising is a major segment of marketing. ***Merchandising*** is the process through which products are obtained (designed, developed, or bought for resale) and promoted to the point of sale. This is done in response to the market demands indicated through marketing efforts. Merchandising tries to match the products of a company to existing markets to make a profit.

Marketing identifies the company's target market and determines that market's wants and needs. Manufacturing provides the products for that market. Merchandising involves varying degrees of *planning, buying*, and *selling*. Ideally, it creates the right *merchandise blend* with

- The right products
- The right quantity
- The right place
- The right time
- The right price
- The right appeal

To achieve high business profits, merchandising functions must offer the optimum merchandise blend. When goods are planned, bought, and sold correctly according to market requirements, a profit results.

Merchandising is done to some extent by all companies that deal with fashion goods. This includes textile producers, apparel manufacturers, and retailers. However, retailing concentrates almost entirely on the merchandising functions of planning, buying, and selling, 3-20. Retailing is concerned with all of the activities necessary to provide a store's customers with the goods they want to buy, when and where they want them, and at prices the customers can afford and are willing to pay. Thus, people often refer to apparel retailing as the "fashion merchandising" field. It also includes store layout, merchandise display, promotional events, and other activities that attract consumers and encourage them to buy the goods.

Successful merchandising efforts of both manufacturers and retailers, that enable profits to be made, require careful coordination of many activities. Merchandisers must consider the costs of goods as well as all other costs of receiving, handling, promoting, and selling the goods. Textile/apparel merchandising also has additional special challenges because of constantly changing fashion whims of consumers. Both manufacturers and retailers must adapt their products to ever changing consumer demand.

Successful retailing requires good marketing supported by doing effective merchandising. Marketing

JUSCO Co., Ltd./AEON Group

3-20 To stock this store with fashionable goods that please customers, merchandising employees have planned what is needed, bought the goods in quantity, and will sell them to consumers.

identifies the company's customers and determines their wants and needs. Merchandising provides the right merchandise blend. Together they result in the highest possible profits for both manufacturers and retailers, which is the main goal of both marketing and merchandising.

Summary

Economic products are sold as either goods or services in the free-market system of the U.S. Profit motivates businesses to achieve success and to continue operating. Competition helps to regulate prices, increase the quality of goods and services, and provide a larger variety of products. The supply and demand relationship also affects market prices and business profits. Conditions in the market determine what products and quantities are produced and optimize scarce resources, resulting in a maximum standard of living for consumers.

The most common competitive market structures are pure competition, oligopoly, and monopoly. At one end of a continuum is pure competition, with many sellers, buyers, companies, and products. At the other extreme is monopoly, with one company controlling the products and prices of a market segment. Fashion businesses fall between the two extremes, mainly near the competitive end.

The basic forms of business organizations have different advantages and disadvantages. A sole proprietorship is owned by one person, and is inexpensive and easy to start or to dissolve. Although there are tax and profit advantages to sole proprietorships, there are also financial and personal disadvantages. Partnerships are co-owned by two or more persons who pool their talents, resources, and liability. Corporations are separate legal entities owned by shareholders who may be separate from the management running the corporation. The many advantages and different types of corporations make this form the most significant in terms of money, size, and power in the U.S.

Business cycles are made up of expansions and recessions in the level of economic activity over a period of several years. Fashion products are affected more strongly than other products by the cycle. During recessions, consumers tend to buy small apparel items or accessories, while in prosperous times, they buy more important apparel garments.

The marketing approach of doing business is to satisfy the wants and needs of a company's target market while making a profit. Marketing-oriented companies offer a marketing mix of the right product, price, place, and promotion.

Merchandising is a major segment of marketing, involving planning, buying, and selling to offer the right merchandise blend. Although merchandising is important for manufacturers, apparel retailing concentrates almost exclusively on these functions and is referred to as "fashion merchandising." Fashion merchandising also has the challenge of constantly changing fashion whims of consumers.

To Know

manufacturers
retailers
consumers
goods
services
free-market system
profit
competition
supply
demand
resources
standard of living
pure competition
oligopolies
monopolies
sole proprietorships
partnerships
corporations
business cycles
marketing
target market
marketing mix
distribution
promotion
merchandising

To Review

1. In relation to textile and apparel products, give at least three examples each of goods and services.
2. Explain how a free-market system operates.
3. If it costs a manufacturing company a total of $8 apiece to produce shirts, and the company sells the shirts to a retailer for $10 apiece, what is the manufacturer's profit on each shirt?
4. If the retailer in question #3 has $5 of additional overhead costs (electricity, salespeople, etc.) per shirt sold, and sells each of the shirts for $18, what is the retailer's profit on each shirt?
5. How does competition affect the price of products?
6. How does competition affect the quality of goods and services offered by businesses?
7. Describe how the supply and demand relationship of a free-market system affects the price of products.
8. What does a standard of living indicate?
9. Why is pure competition the "ideal" structure for a free-market economy?
10. Why are monopolies unsuitable for a free-market economic system?
11. Explain why sole proprietorships account for more than two-thirds of all enterprises.
12. Explain why corporations account for about three-quarters of the total profits earned by American business.
13. Name one example of a business in your community for each of the following: sole proprietorship, partnership, and corporation.
14. What is the difference between a public corporation and a private corporation?
15. Describe S corporations and nonprofit corporations.
16. Explain how the market for fashion products is affected by economic expansions and recessions.
17. What is the difference between a marketing-oriented approach and a product-oriented approach to business?
18. Name and briefly describe the four Ps of marketing.
19. What are the three main functions of merchandising?
20. Describe the relationship merchandising has to marketing.

To Do

1. Visit a manufacturing company or a retailer. Observe how the company operates in relation to some of the concepts you learned in this chapter. Relate the company's activities to at least three of the following: profit motivation, competition, supply and demand, use of resources, form of business organization, products, prices, distribution, or promotion. Explain your observations to the class and answer any questions from other students.
2. Find three advertisements in the newspaper for similar products offered by different retailers. Examples might be a type of sweater, jacket, or jeans. In a written report, explain what the ads illustrate about the significance of competition.
3. Research and write a report on one of the three market structures described in this chapter (pure competition, oligopoly, or monopoly).
4. Draw a marketing triangle, with price and quantity labels shown, to use as a bulletin board display. Along the diagonal edge of the triangle, write in eight examples of fashion items and their prices in the proper locations. Put a title at the top of your display, and add a brief description at the bottom.
5. In a group of three students, divide the subjects of a textile firm, apparel manufacturer, or retailer (with each student taking one). Since merchandising involves planning, buying, and selling, describe to the class what each of you thinks the process would be for your firm. Specifically, what would the company plan, buy, and sell? Ask for additional input from the class.

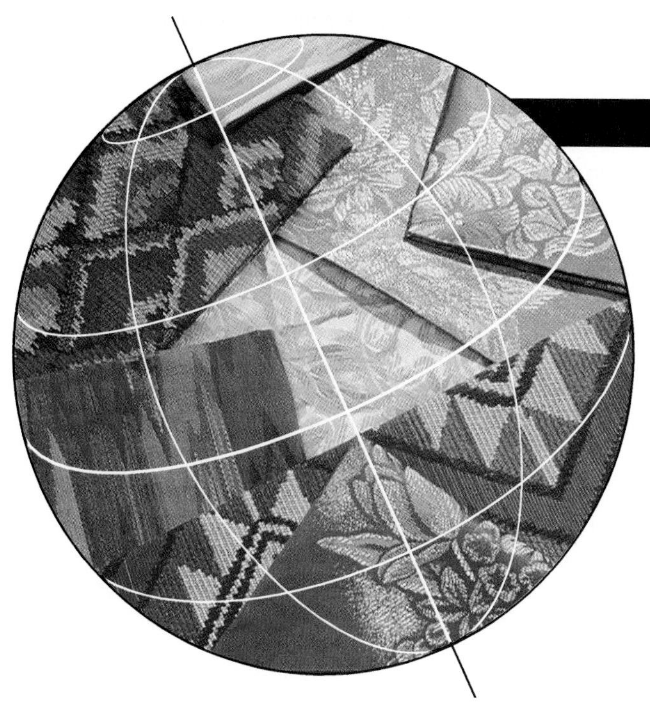

CHAPTER 4

Substance of the Fashion Industry

After studying this chapter, you will be able to

- describe the two ways of viewing the fashion industry's channel of distribution.
- define and recognize vertical integration.
- explain commodity/fashion/seasonal goods.
- list other industries that deal with textile products.
- identify trade associations and industry publications.
- name the geographic areas for each segment of the industry.

Fashion goods evolve through many steps before they become finished garments or accessories. Many individuals and companies move products through the fashion channel of distribution from beginning to end from raw materials, to finished goods, to the end user. A ***channel of distribution*** is the route that products take from the original source, through all middle people (production, sales, etc.) to the end user. There are two ways of viewing this channel of distribution for fashion products: the soft goods chain and the four-groups approach.

Fashion merchandisers should understand the processes, timing, and practices of the individual segments or groups within the overall fashion industry. Knowing the interrelated functions of the parts affects decisions about what, when, from whom, and how much merchandise will satisfy the current market demand.

The Soft Goods Chain

The ***soft goods chain*** is the channel of distribution for apparel and home decorating textiles. It is also called the ***textile/apparel pipeline***. As shown on the left side of 4-1, the chain starts with the textile segment, moves through the apparel segment, goes to the retail segment, and finishes with end users. The end users are consumers who use the products.

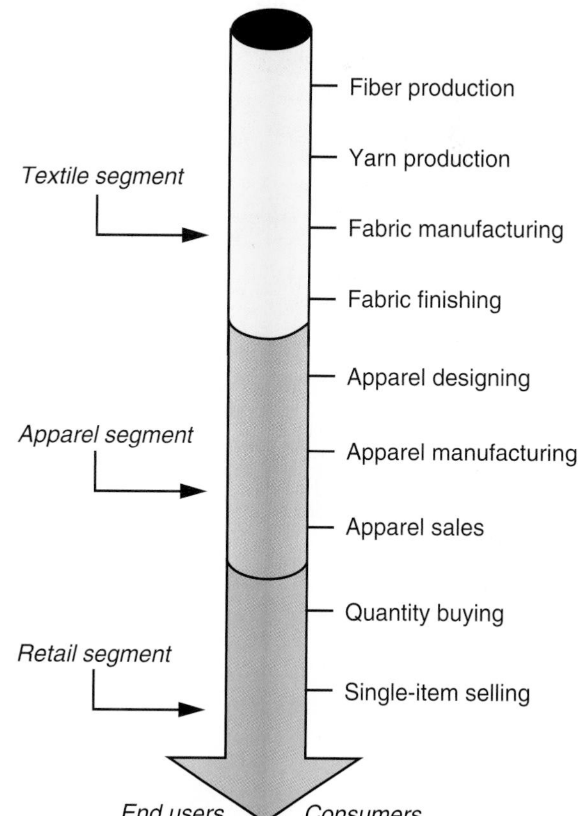

4-1 The textile/apparel product pipeline, or soft goods chain, has three main segments that feed products from beginning raw materials to finished items for consumers, who are the end users.

Elements that make up a garment evolve toward a finished product as they move through the chain. There are companies that operate at each level. Each segment buys products from the previous one and sells to the next one. Thus, for companies at the beginning and middle of the pipeline, "customers" are not end-use consumers. For them, customers are companies positioned at the next step of the overall chain.

The Textile Segment

As shown on the right side of 4-1, the textile segment of the soft goods chain starts with *fiber production*. ***Fibers*** are very thin, hair-like strands that can be quite short or very long. They are the beginning, basic units in making textile products. They originate either from naturally grown sources or from chemical mixtures, 4-2.

The next step in the textile segment is *yarn production*. ***Yarns*** are continuous strands of textile fibers in a form suitable for processing into fabrics, 4-3. They are formed by spinning, or twisting, fibers together at yarn mills. (Fibers and yarns will be discussed more thoroughly in Chapter 6.)

Next, *fabric manufacturing* is done at textile mills. The mills weave, knit, or otherwise join the yarns into ***fabrics***, which are long pieces of cloth. At this point, the fabrics, or yard goods in an unfinished state, are called ***greige*** *(gray)* ***goods***.

The final step in textile production is *fabric finishing*. This is done by bleaching, dyeing, printing, or applying special coatings to the greige goods. These processes impart color, texture, pattern, ease of care, and other characteristics to fabrics, as indicated in 4-4. They change the appearance, feel, and/or performance of each fabric to suit various end uses. (The making and finishing of fabrics will be discussed in depth in Chapter 7 of this book.)

The Wool Bureau, Inc.

4-2 Wool is naturally produced on sheep.

The Apparel Segment

The apparel segment produces finished garments and accessories. The main sections of the apparel segment are also shown on the right side of 4-1.

First, the apparel must be *designed*. ***Designing*** is the process of creating new versions of garments, accessories, or other items. Design ideas move fashion forward by creating change. The concepts that evolve during the designing process create demand among consumers to buy the new and different looks.

After the fashions have been designed, they must be *manufactured*. Almost all are mass-produced in factories, 4-5. They are cut out of fabric in large numbers and sewn along assembly lines. When they are finished, they move to apparel sales.

Apparel sales involves selling the manufactured garments in large quantities to retail stores. This serves

DuPont Company

4-3 These yarns of nylon fibers are long, continuous strands of thread, ready to be processed into fabrics.

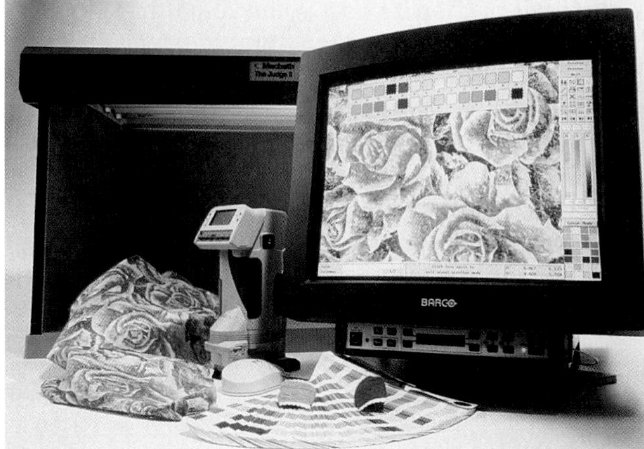

Info Design, Inc.

4-4 Excellent color accuracy can be guaranteed, even with complex print designs, because of the technology used for fabric finishing.

A and Z Industries, Ltd.

4-5 Even though modern technology is often used in apparel plants, many workers are needed to accomplish the involved tasks of garment manufacturing.

as the wholesale sales step in the chain since apparel does not have a separate *wholesale* segment the way many other industries do. Most garments are sold and shipped directly from manufacturers to retailers. The lack of a separate wholesale segment also helps to keep prices low, since fewer middle people are involved who would each take some profit. Inexpensive accessories and small, nonfashion products do go through wholesalers, often referred to as ***resellers***.

The Retail Segment

As mentioned in Chapter 3, retailing is the selling of merchandise directly to consumers. This is done through a store or other method, 4-6. As shown near the bottom of the right side of 4-1, retailers buy finished goods in large amounts from the apparel segment that precedes them in the pipeline. Retailers pay a wholesale price for this *quantity buying* of finished products. They put these items out "on the floor" of their stores for sale at a retail price, which is higher than the wholesale purchase price they paid for the items. The markup covers costs of heat, lights, taxes, sales help, and other expenses. The retail price also includes some profit for the retailer.

Retailers do *single-item selling* of the garments, accessories, and other goods to consumers. They sell one item at a time directly to the many different people who will use the products. Consumers are at the end of the soft goods chain, but satisfying their wants and needs is the objective of all the preceding companies in the pipeline.

The Four-Groups Approach

The four-groups approach is a different way of showing the same flow of goods from beginning to end. The ***four-groups approach*** separates the overall fashion industry into four main groups of businesses. They are the primary group, the secondary group, the retail group, and the auxiliary group. They are all interrelated, 4-7.

4-6 Finished goods and accessories are put on display at retail stores, where consumers can look at the choices and make purchases.

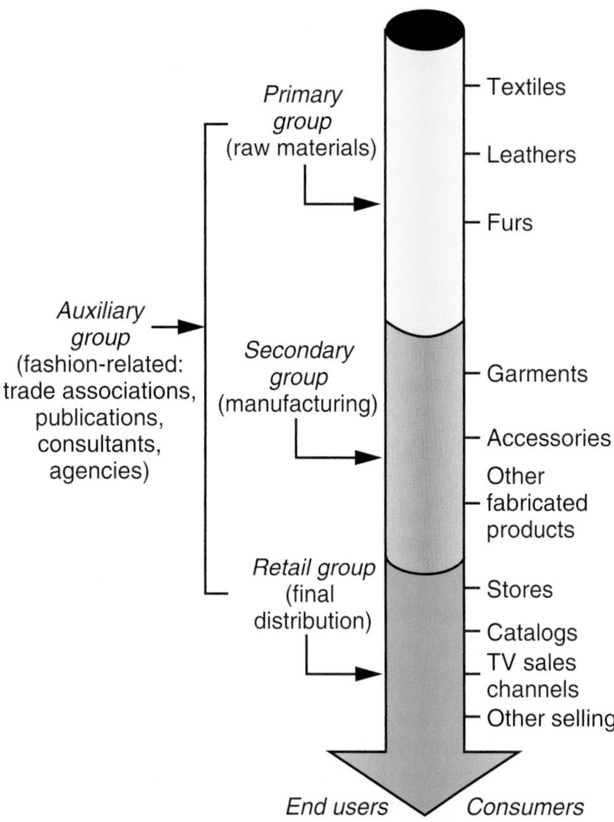

4-7 The four-groups approach to the channel of distribution is similar to the previous soft goods chain, but shows the additional auxiliary group that gives supplementary support to all other parts of the fashion industry.

Primary Group

As with the previous chain, textiles make up the first link. Combined with leathers and furs (and some plastics and metals), they comprise the *primary group* of the four-groups approach. This group provides the *raw materials* from which fashion products are made. Varying amounts of fibers, fabrics, leathers and furs are sold to apparel and accessory producers. Some of these primary products are also sold to fabric stores and production specialists who move them on for home decorating or industrial uses.

Secondary Group

The *secondary group* is the manufacturing segment, which makes finished garments from the textiles and other materials bought from the primary suppliers. This group produces sewn or *fabricated products*, which include garments, accessories, and other items.

Retail Group

The *retail group* consists of stores, mail order catalogs, TV home shopping channels, Internet retail sites, and other retail enterprises that sell the finished goods to those who want to buy and use them. Retailers are the final link between product manufacturers and consumers. They must stock adequate assortments of what consumers will buy.

Auxiliary Group

The first three groups are almost identical to the textile/apparel pipeline discussed earlier, but with different labels. The *auxiliary group* supports, or helps, the first three groups.

Fashion auxiliary enterprises function with all the other groups simultaneously. They include market researchers and forecasters who provide information about colors and other trends that are occurring in the consumer marketplace, 4-8. These consulting and reporting firms help to analyze and interpret future fashion directions. They give advice that assists manufacturers and retailers in understanding upcoming trends and satisfying consumer demand.

Other examples of auxiliary enterprises are the many fashion publications and advertising agencies that produce and disseminate fashion information and ads. Editors of fashion magazines visit the fashion markets and attend major showings to be able to report the latest fashion news. They educate both consumers and working members of the industry. Publicity and advertising agencies assist client companies in researching the consumer market and planning a total promotional campaign. The agencies often prepare and place ads in broadcast and print media, and develop selling aids and packaging.

Auxiliary businesses also include buying services in market centers that help retailers get the right merchandise for their stores. Additionally, models and modeling agencies show the new fashions in fun, exciting

ESP/Ellen Sideri Partnership Inc.

4-8 Fashion forecasters are part of the auxiliary group that offers trend advice, so companies in the other three groups can produce the right goods for market demand.

ways, 4-9. Trade associations, and their publications, are also included.

All groups in the four-groups approach depend on each other and want to satisfy the final consumers. The primary group depends on the secondary group to sell their products on down through the chain. The secondary group depends on the primary group to provide the materials for them to make their products. Both the primary and secondary groups rely on retailers to sell the merchandise to end users. All groups gain information, expertise, assistance, and promotion from the auxiliary group.

Vertical Integration

Vertical integration is the combining of two or more steps of the pipeline within one company and under one management. For instance, today many large textile mills produce their own yarn, make fabric, and perform the finishing processes which result in a finished fabric. They combine three steps of the textile segment of the pipeline rather than doing just one step. Some knitting mills start with raw fiber or yarn and knit finished socks or sweaters, 4-10. Thus, they produce a finished product ready to be sold to consumers. They combine some of the textile segment with the entire manufacturing segment of the chain.

Liz Claiborne

4-9 This fashion model does not produce fashion goods, but is important in the auxiliary group. The picture was taken by a fashion photographer, also part of the auxiliary group.

Monsanto Fibers

4-10 Knitting mills often create finished garments by knitting the shape of socks or a sweater, rather than making flat fabrics that will later be cut and sewn.

Another example of vertical integration would be an apparel manufacturer that opens one or more factory outlet stores. By doing this, the manufacturer also becomes a retailer, 4-11. The manufacturer has *integrated forward* toward the end of the soft goods chain. Two whole segments (manufacturing and retail) are combined. By doing this, manufacturers can assure a timely supply of goods into their own stores and can charge lower prices since they have eliminated a middleperson. However, they also compete with the retailers who are their own customers and who usually buy that manufacturer's goods to sell in their stores. This may cause bad feelings. Retailers sometimes refuse to buy goods from manufacturers who open their own factory outlet stores.

On the other hand, if a company takes on activities toward the source of goods, it is called *backward integration.* An example of backward integration is when

4-11 The name on this retail store is of a prominent fashion designer, showing that the company has integrated the segments of apparel manufacturing and retailing.

retail companies take on manufacturing functions. They do this by producing their own private label merchandise. ***Private label goods*** are produced only for that retailer and have the retailer's special trademark or brand name. By doing this, retailers become their own suppliers, and can assure themselves a certain level of quality, timely delivery, and lower price.

Commodity, Fashion, and Seasonal Goods

There are two main categories of merchandise with which businesses within the fashion channel of distribution are involved. They are commodity products and fashion products. ***Commodity products*** are "staple goods" that hardly ever change in design and are in constant demand. Their sales are quite predictable and they are continually produced in regular amounts. Examples of commodity goods in our industry include cotton/polyester blend fabric, and men's white business shirts and dark socks, 4-12. Other commodity items are basic types of underwear and soft-sided luggage. They are items that are always being mass produced and are always stocked in retail stores for fairly dependable, constant sales.

DuPont Company

4-12 The white business shirt and dark socks worn by this man are commodity products. They are produced and sold continuously because there is always a demand for them.

The Fashion Association/Bugle Boy

4-13 This outfit includes a fashionable vest over a commodity white T-shirt. Why is it also a seasonal outfit?

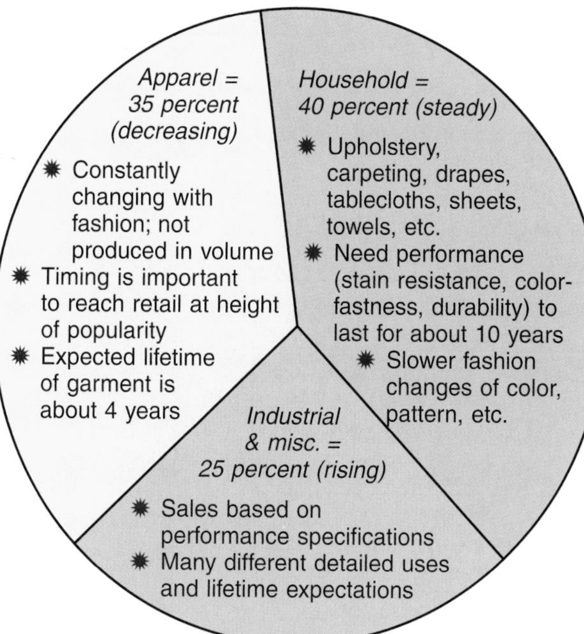

4-14 End-use markets of textile products include apparel, home furnishings, and industrial products. The apparel slice is getting smaller by percentage of the total, and industrial use is increasing.

Fashion products, on the other hand, are always changing. Last year's model or style cannot be sold this year because it is no longer in demand. It is difficult to predict what the demand for, and sales of, fashion products will be at a particular time in the market. Companies that produce and sell fashion goods are always scrambling to supply the right fashions at the right time to make a good profit.

There is a great deal of style and timing risk for companies that deal with fashion merchandise. Wrong decisions can result in huge financial losses or even force a company out of business. On the other hand, right decisions can result in huge profits. Most companies have some good years that carry them through other years that are not as successful.

Seasonal products change in popularity or demand with the seasons of the year. They include both fashion goods and commodity items, 4-13. Examples of seasonal products for summer are shorts, swimsuits, and beach towels. Winter goods include wool sweaters, heavy topcoats, and gloves.

Other Textile End-Use Industries

Commercially-produced wearing apparel is not the only end use for textiles. Other markets include household or home furnishings products, industrial textile products, and the home sewing industry. Household textile products comprise about 40 percent of the total U.S. end-use textile market, 4-14. Industrial textile products make up about 25 percent with a continual increase taking place. Apparel fabrics comprise about 35 percent and are decreasing in relation to the total U.S. market.

Household Textile Products

The household textile products industry manufactures fabrics for floor coverings, home furnishings, and domestics. *Floor coverings* include rugs and carpets. *Home furnishings* mainly include window treatments and furniture coverings, 4-15. *Domestics* include bed, bath, and kitchen textiles, 4-16. These three categories are further described in the chart, 4-17.

Household textiles, or decorator fabrics, follow fashion trends that are broader and slower moving than apparel trends. Besides the fashion aspects of color,

Burlington Industries

4-15 Home furnishings is an important market for textiles. These fabrics were especially developed for home decorating.

Revman Industries/AEON Group

4-16 These fashionable home textiles are for the household category called domestics.

Household Textile Categories	
Floor coverings	Carpeting, area rugs, oriental rugs, throw rugs, plus non-fabric floor tiles and materials.
Home furnishings	Window treatments – curtains, draperies, valances, pull-down shades, vertical blinds, etc. Furniture – slipcovers and upholstery. Miscellaneous items – throw pillows, lamp shades, artificial flowers, wall hangings, etc.
Domestics	Bed linens – sheets, pillow cases, bedspreads, decorative pillow covers, blankets, etc. Bathroom items – towels, shower curtains, seat covers, etc. Table and kitchen linens – tablecloths, napkins, kitchen towels, etc.

4-17 Household textiles are divided into logical categories for marketing, manufacturing, and retailing purposes.

pattern, texture, drape, etc., performance is an important consideration for household textiles. *Textile performance* takes into account such fabric attributes as strength and durability, colorfastness (how well the color holds its original look), and stain resistance. Household textiles should last for about 10 years.

Many household items are expensive, and their sales are dependent on the health of the economy. In bad economic times, consumers buy fewer household textile products. In an economic recovery, as employment rates and consumer confidence increase, the pent-up demand creates strong purchasing patterns. Banking interest rates also affect these purchases. With low interest rates, more new houses are built and credit cards or loans are used for "big-ticket" items, such as carpeting and couches.

Designer names have become quite important in all categories of household textiles. Designer ensembles and retail displays have emphasized the abundant use of fabrics through coordinated sheets, comforters, pillow shams, dust ruffles, throw pillows, and window treatments. An example of this concept is shown in 4-18.

Domestics are sold mainly in department stores and specialty "bed and bath" shops. Most large furniture items are sold through free-standing furniture retailers. The traditional sales method is through *gallery programs* that display actual pieces of a particular furniture company's line. Furniture is not mass-produced the way garments are because fewer of each style is sold and many are custom-covered in fabrics selected by the end-use customer.

An in-store computer design system is a new sales tool to help consumers see different, selected fabrics on various furniture frames. Such on-floor, interactive video catalogs allow shoppers to visualize different coverings for custom-covered furniture and then have photo-like mock-ups of their selections printed in color. Some of the systems are electronically linked to the factory and also serve to place the order. Retailers must allow a month or more for production and delivery of custom-ordered furniture to their customers.

Revman Industries/AEON Group

4-18 This fun image for a child's room is created with lots of bright colors, patterns, and matching textile home decorating accessories.

Industrial Textile Products

Industrial textiles are technical rather than fashionable. They are sold to commercial business customers according to industrial specifications ("specs") and performance quality, rather than a fashion look. Industrial textile marketing is done at a higher level of management because decisions often involve new equipment or different manufacturing methods that affect the entire company.

The specialized uses of industrial textiles require a great deal of continuous research and development to create the most optimum strength or other characteristics needed. Some industrial fabrics are fire-resistant or have extreme moisture absorbency. Many are used in the medical field. Others are used in road building or landfills. The major sub-categories of industrial textiles, and typical products of each are shown in 4-19.

The transportation category has the largest market for industrial textiles. They are especially used in automobile interiors and tires. ***Geotextiles***, which relate to the earth's surface, have the second largest market.

Some industrial textiles go into finished products, such as awnings, tents, and luggage. Some are consumed in processes, as filters, twine, and buffing wheels that wear out or are thrown away when used. ***Composites*** are textiles combined with other materials. Composites are used in such products as commercial hoses, belting, car fenders, boat hulls, and truck tanks, 4-20.

The Home Sewing Industry

The *home sewing industry* deals with the production and selling of non-industrial sewing machines, notions, retail fabrics, patterns, and publications. Home sewing is done for many personal reasons such as:

- for the *feeling of achievement* of having made a finished, usable item from basic raw materials.

Main Categories of Industrial Textiles
Architecture: Reinforcing domes and stadium roofs; inflatable buildings for warehousing and sports; fabric sculptures; noise control in offices, public buildings, convention halls; innovation in space, shape and design concepts; high strength of new fiber possibilities.
Agriculture: Materials used in crop production; farm maintenance, horticulture and landscaping; seed bed protection; crop covers, insect netting, shade fabrics, greenhouses; drainage systems and irrigation; animal husbandry.
Construction: Reinforcements for building materials, concrete, cement, pipe relining and/or reconstruction; insulations; bridges; roofing systems; screening.
General Industrial: Curing wraps; metalized products; netting; closure systems, tents, awnings, bags, sports and leisure; mechanical rubber goods; rope and cordage; webbing.
Filtration: Fabrics assisting in cleaning and separating and/or recovery of air and by-products; hot air/gas industrial filtration; wet filtration; milk processing.
Geotextiles: Soil stabilization and erosion prevention; reinforcement for lining waste ponds and pits; drainage systems; roadbeds for paving; hydraulic engineering; environmental protection; lining and covering landfills.
Military and Defense: Personnel protection parachutes; aerospace and electronics components; covers; chemical suits; ballistic protection; tents and inflatable buildings; medical devices; flight and tank driver garments; marine applications; rescue systems.
Safety/Medical: Textiles for protection from heat and/or fire, extreme low temperatures, impact, pressure, ionizing and non-ionizing radiation; breathable membranes; operating room textiles; special bandages; safety flags.
Papermaking: Mainly paper felts of complex weaves using monofilament yarns or for the manufacture and carrying of paper.
Transportation (for cars, buses, railways, trucks, planes, and ships): Interior materials; hose and belt reinforcement; trunk liners, air bags, gaskets and brake linings, mufflers, tires, seating, carpeting, sound dampening.

4-19 These are the major categories of industrial textiles and the typical fabric uses in each.

AKZO Nobel Twaron®

4-20 Although you might think the tank of this truck is metal, it is really a composite reinforced with a strong industrial fiber.

- for *proper fit* of a specific body shape, when ready-made clothing is only made in general sizes from standard "average" measurements for each size.
- for *creative individuality*, or to achieve fashion self-expression that is different from the garments of others who buy ready-made clothing that sometimes seems to all look alike.
- to *save money* if reasonably priced materials are available and if the person has the time and skill to make the items.
- for *quality of construction* that is better than mass produced items that sometimes fall apart sooner than expected or are unsatisfactory in other ways.
- for *relaxation* through a stress-reducing activity.

Long ago, people had to sew their own garments. Today, however, ready-made clothing is available from sources to almost all people. Commercially-produced clothing exists in a multitude of sizes, qualities, fashion levels, and price ranges. For these reasons and because busy personal schedules do not allow for time-consuming sewing projects, the home sewing industry has declined.

Additionally, the savings from sewing are less significant today. The price of store-bought garments has decreased because of low-wage production and discount retailing. At the same time, the price of retail fabrics has increased and retail fabric stores now emphasize home decorating instead of apparel fabrics. The home-sewn apparel image is sometimes looked upon as dowdy or boring, although many home sewers create very beautiful garments. There has been less teaching of sewing in schools in recent years. Possibly, if there were more industry promotion about the enjoyment and creativity of home sewing, the activity would regain its popularity.

Fashion Industry Associations and Publications

The segments of the fashion industry contain many trade associations. Various trade publications support the activities of each segment. Also, there are specific geographic locations of the industry segments.

Trade Associations

Trade associations are nonprofit, voluntary organizations made up of businesses that have common interests. The associations deal specifically with the certain industry or segment of an industry in which their members are involved. Some of the main trade associations of the soft goods chain are shown in 4-21, placed on the pipeline across from the business activity of each one.

All trade associations try to accomplish similar objectives relating to improving their segment of the industry and the success of their members. In general, these objectives include:

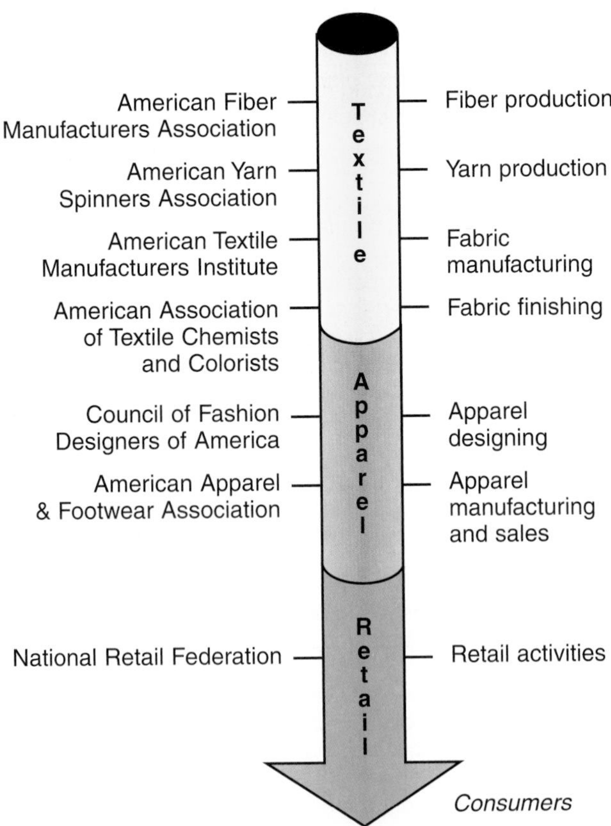

4-21 Most of these trade organizations are known in the industry by the first letters of the names in their titles. At the end of the pipeline, there are several advocate groups (not indicated) that represent consumer rights and/or protection, even though individuals may not be actual members of these groups.

- *To improve industry business conditions* through better availability of production resources, appropriate supply of finished goods, most advantageous pricing, etc.
- *To encourage the use of the industry's products* through industry marketing efforts that form more positive public opinion and promote member companies and their goods and services.
- *To promote common interests of the members* by sponsoring activities that please the members, both professionally and socially.
- *To serve as a source of market information and business development* by researching market needs and offering strategic consulting expertise to member companies.
- *To gain advantageous passage of legislation and government support* by lobbying (usually in Washington, DC) in hopes of influencing public officials toward desired action for the members and the industry.
- *To sponsor seminars, conventions/expositions, and trade shows* that disseminate new industry information among the members, such as new ideas, equipment, etc. Conventions or trade shows are usually held once a year (annually) with general sessions (meetings) to attend and commercial booths set up to show products in a large exhibit hall. Additionally, specific educational seminars, offering instruction on various subjects of interest to the members, may be held throughout the year.
- *To provide technical assistance and support* through telephone help lines and trouble-shooting services to help solve day-to-day business and equipment problems.
- *To provide networking opportunities.* During ***networking***, members exchange ideas, information, or services, forming an inter-connected or inter-related chain of communication.

One trade organization that relates to the entire pipeline is *The Fashion Group, Inc.* It is a global, non-profit professional association of women executives who represent every segment of the industry. To be eligible to be sponsored for membership, a woman must have a record of achievement and executive level success in the fashion business. Members include fashion designers, magazine editors, retail executives, and other fashion professionals.

The Fashion Group was founded to exchange information, ideas, and resources that are beneficial to member careers and the industry. It is a powerful network of women in the industry. See 4-22. The Fashion

Membership in The Fashion Group (FG) Means:

- Associating with successful women in a wide field of fashion-related businesses, as a source of information and action.
- Belonging to an organization with an educational and cultural role, as well as a social network of peers.
- Being in touch with the business, marketing, and distribution of fashion through planned programming for industry leaders.
- Viewing selected designer textiles and garments from European and American collections following the various showings.
- Joining fellow FG members who head major fashion or cosmetic corporations in their offices for business and trend talks.
- Hearing well-known speakers talk about specific markets, such as accessories, menswear, visual marketing, home fashions, etc.
- Sending regional FG officers to a New York conference each year to discuss business, exchange ideas, and review events.
- Receiving a FG newsletter about new members, major events, regional group activities, and the network calendar.
- Having access to FG members throughout the world for information and assistance when traveling.
- Presenting awards to outstanding designers, journalists, and executives at a gala international fashion dinner.
- Being listed in the FG Membership Directory, the "Who's Who" of the fashion business around the world.
- Participating on committees that develop programs, generate membership, create publications, and interact with members.
- Addressing such concerns of fashion industry women as career choices and changes, job referrals, workshops, and counseling.
- Having a say in the bylaws, guidelines, and selection of officers of regional groups and the international organization.
- Attending the Annual Meeting in New York, with working sessions, industry speakers, and interaction with FG officers.
- Having newsflashes, reports, and slide presentations from FG events available for use in a member's own business.
- Supporting FG activities, scholarships, education projects, community service, and special events.

4-22 This abbreviated list of benefits of membership in The Fashion Group, Inc. illustrates how beneficial the organization can be for those who meet the criteria to be able to join.

Group is headquartered in New York City and has regional chapters in fashion centers around the U.S. and the world. Local chapters have their own meetings and activities, and send representatives to meetings of the worldwide group.

The *American Society of Interior Designers (ASID)* is a strong and active trade association of home fashions professionals. The society tries to maintain high standards among interior designers. It has specialized groups within the overall organization, such as for commercial/office interiors.

The main trade association for industrial textiles is the *Industrial Fabrics Association International.* An annual exhibition and conference, called "Techtextil," is coproduced by *Textile World Magazine* and the *Association of the Nonwoven Fabrics Industry.*

The main trade group for the home sewing industry is the *Home Sewing Association (HSA).* A sub-group of HSA is the *Sewing Guild,* which has ongoing programs among its many local chapters of home sewers. Besides a national publication to home sewers called *Sew Business*, there are many fashion and craft sewing magazines, mainly from pattern companies. Also, fabrics are sold from swatched mailings, and mail order catalogs offer notions and gadgets of interest to home sewers.

Other trade associations will be discussed throughout this text with the specific subject matter that applies to each group.

Trade Publications

Trade publications are magazines, newspapers, and books that deal specifically with a certain industry or segment of an industry. They keep companies and employees informed about their trade. Some of the main trade publications of the soft goods chain are listed in 4-23.

Women's Wear Daily is a newspaper that reports fashion trends, design and manufacturing information, fashion events, and business and financial news of the women's apparel trade. It is not pinpointed in 4-23 because it is important to the entire pipeline, and is often called the industry's "bible." Its counterpart for the textile and menswear industries is the *Daily News Record.*

Most store managers subscribe to *STORES* magazine and/or other retail trade journals. Examples of some of the many other specialized publications are *Footwear News, Intimate Fashion News, Retail Information Systems, Apparel Merchandising, Chicago Apparel News, Dallas Apparel News,* and *California Apparel News.*

General fashion magazines are not trade publications. They show fashion direction and merchandise aimed at consumers, but also spread fashion news throughout the industry. Retailers often read these magazines, as well as official trade journals, to keep up with emerging trends and to be prepared for what consumers will be looking for in the stores.

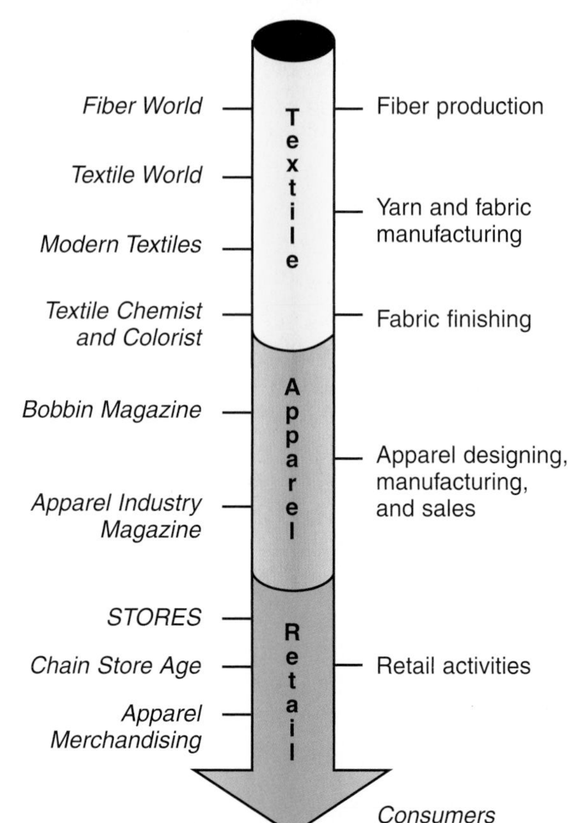

4-23 Because there are so many different types of products and markets that deal with fashion goods, a variety of trade journals provide information related to specific interests.

Geographic Locations of Industry Segments

In the 1700s and 1800s, textile production was located primarily in the New England states. After that, textile mills steadily opened in the Southeastern United States, and the ones in the north closed. In the Southeast, there were good sources of power and lower-wage labor. There was also proximity to raw materials, such as cotton. Taxes were lower. Land was plentiful and inexpensive, resulting in new, modern plants being built.

Today, the textile industry is comprised of fairly large textile companies. They are mainly concentrated in North Carolina, Georgia, and South Carolina. Other eastern states do a small amount of textile production.

Just as earlier textile production moved from the Northeast to the Southeast, much of it is now moving "offshore." Foreign textile companies are competing with American firms by making fibers and fabrics for our market. This has forced many of the U.S. mills to slow down their production. To fight this competition, U.S. mills are becoming more automated and efficient, as indicated in 4-24.

Apparel manufacturing has always been ***labor intensive***, requiring many workers to make the products. In the 1800s, the first American ready-made clothing was produced in port cities along the East Coast. Before that time, garments had been made one-at-a-time by homemakers or hired dressmakers. Men's clothing was the first to be mass produced, after the inventions of the sewing machine, a standardized tape measure, and sized paper patterns. Later, simple women's garments were manufactured in New York City lofts, using the immigrant labor that was plentiful there.

Today, there are many apparel manufacturing firms in the U.S. They are of all sizes, and each produces a particular range of products. Although the New York City area is still the center of U.S. apparel manufacturing, garment and accessory production is found in most other states as well. California ranks second in apparel manufacturing. It mainly produces sportswear, as in 4-25, and exquisite "Hollywood"-type evening wear.

The success of many U.S. apparel producers has also been badly threatened by the great abundance of imported apparel coming into this country from foreign manufacturers.

Retailing is located everywhere; it is not centered in any one part of the country. All types of retail stores exist in large cities, suburban malls, and small towns. Mail order retailers send catalogs to most people's homes. TV shopping channels broadcast into consumers' living rooms nationwide and worldwide.

CaliforniaMart

4-25 California has a strong apparel manufacturing industry, producing and selling innovative, high quality designs.

Info Design, Inc.

4-24 This advanced weaving system includes a full range of design tools, as well as connecting directly to all production machinery.

Some national retail companies have stores throughout the country, such as JCPenney, Kmart, and The Gap, 4-26. In fact, some of these companies have expanded to also have stores in other countries. Headquarters for these companies are in large cities across America. Other retailers are regionalized and have stores in only one area of the U.S., such as the Mid-Atlantic states or the Southwestern states. Many retail shops are sole proprietorships. They usually have only one location, possibly in a small town or resort area.

Many household textile products sold in the U.S. are made in the Carolinas and Georgia, as well as in California and New York. Imports are not as common in household fabrics as in apparel. The Southern Furniture Market and Design Center, located in High Point, NC, holds ongoing furnishing displays representing 1500 manufacturers. Also, it holds major exhibitions twice a year showing the latest in products,

4-26 GAP stores are located in or near most areas in the U.S., as well as in Canada and Great Britain.

display techniques, merchandising tools, and advertising aids for every aspect of the household textiles products business.

Industrial textiles that are highly specialized for certain niches are produced in many parts of the United States. Commodity industrial textiles, produced in quantity and having multiple commercial uses, are imported from other countries around the world.

Textile/apparel trade associations are either located near Washington, DC, so they can affect advantageous government action, or they are near their particular market center. Several textile trade organizations have offices in the southeastern U.S. Some apparel manufacturing, retail, and auxiliary group trade organizations are in New York City or another fashion center. Trade association directories are usually published each year that list corporate members in alphabetical order as well as separate listings under headings of the major business activities of that industry segment.

Summary

The fashion channel of distribution, also known as the soft goods chain or textile/apparel pipeline, includes the textile, apparel, and retail segments. It ends with single-item selling at retail prices to end-use consumers. The four-groups approach shows the industry with the primary group of raw materials suppliers, the secondary group of manufacturers, and the retail group of final distributors to end users. Additionally, the auxiliary group gives supplementary support to all other groups with trade associations, publications, consultants, and agencies.

Textile/apparel companies must understand different variables to satisfy the market. Some firms vertically integrate by combining two or more steps of the pipeline under one management. Commodity, fashion, and seasonal products have different demand and risk parameters.

Other textile end-use industries are not involved with commercially produced wearing apparel. Household textile goods include home furnishings made from fabrics. Industrial textiles target technical specifications and performance, rather than a fashion look. Finally, the home sewing industry deals with the production and selling of non-industrial sewing machines, notions, retail fabrics, patterns, and publications.

Trade associations are made up of businesses that have common interests. All trade associations have similar functions and objectives. Most trade publications deal with a certain industry segment. *Women's Wear Daily* reports on all news of the women's apparel trade, while the *Daily News Record* covers the textile and menswear industries. Many other specific trade journals supplement general fashion magazines that spread fashion news.

Geographically, many textile firms are located in the Southeastern U.S. Apparel manufacturing is concentrated around New York City, with California ranking second. Retailing is located everywhere from small towns, to rural malls, to large cities.

To Know

channel of distribution
soft goods chain
textile/apparel pipeline
fibers
yarns
fabrics
greige goods
designing
resellers
four-groups approach
vertical integration
private label goods
commodity products
fashion products
seasonal products
industrial textiles
geotextiles
composites
trade associations
networking
trade publications
labor intensive

To Review

1. In the textile/apparel channel of distribution, where is the original source, who are the middle-people, and who is the ultimate user?
2. Why are "customers" not always end-use consumers?
3. What is done at textile mills?
4. What step in the channel of distribution of most other products is missing from the soft goods chain?
5. Why must the retail price be higher than the wholesale price of goods?
6. Explain how the groups in the four-groups approach depend on each other.
7. Give an example of vertical integration of a company in the soft goods chain.
8. Explain the basic differences between commodity, fashion, and seasonal products.
9. Which textile end-use industry is increasing in relation to U.S. market share and which one is decreasing?
10. Compare the lifetime expectancy of apparel garments versus household textile items.
11. In household textiles, what products does "domestics" include?
12. Besides fashion aspects, what performance characteristics are important in household textiles?
13. Describe the traditional sales method for furniture retailing and a new computer sales tool.
14. Give three examples of uses for industrial textiles.
15. List five reasons why people do home sewing.
16. Briefly list the eight main functions of trade associations.
17. Name one major textile/apparel trade association and describe its purpose.
18. Name one major textile/apparel trade publication and describe its purpose.
19. List the five main reasons why textile mills moved to Southeastern states after the 1800s.
20. How are U.S. textile mills fighting foreign textile companies?

To Do

1. Starting with a fiber, describe all the steps of the textile/apparel pipeline for a particular article of clothing (sweater, jeans, etc.) in an oral or written report. Then take the same garment through the four-groups approach. Tell about what was missing from the first pipeline that was included in the four-groups approach.
2. In the library, research *The Fashion Group, Inc.* from its beginnings in the 1930s, through its development, to its activities today. Find out where the closest local group is to you and talk to a member about the activities of the group. Present your findings in a talk to your classmates, illustrated with charts or other visual aids.
3. Obtain copies of two different specialized fashion industry trade magazines from local textile, apparel, or retail businesses, or from the library. Also get copies of two fashion magazines aimed at consumers. Study the publications and show them to the class, specifically pointing out their few similarities and many differences. Then answer questions about the publications from your teacher and classmates.
4. Make three separate posters to show and discuss with your class. One should be labeled "Commodity Products" and show examples of commodity goods clipped from magazines, newspapers, or catalogs. Another

should be labeled "Fashion Products" and show clipped examples. The third should be labeled "Seasonal Products" and show examples that are seasonal commodity products on one side and seasonal fashion products on the other side.

5. Create a bulletin board display about industrial textiles. Under headings of the main categories listed in Illustration 4-19, try to find at least one picture from newspapers, magazines, or catalogs of examples of textiles being used in each category.

CHAPTER 5

Satisfying the Fashion Market

After studying this chapter, you will be able to

- distinguish between market growth, share, and segmentation.
- describe the importance and methods of market research.
- summarize the concept of product development.
- explain the latest fashion industry information technology.
- explain the efforts that are being made for overall industry excellence.
- describe how the industry is improving its image.

All parts of the soft goods chain must focus on the changing needs and lifestyles of customers. Satisfying customers in order to make a profit is the reason businesses exist. This is not easy in the highly competitive, fast-paced fashion field. However, many fashion businesses are very successful because they know their customers and they market effectively to them. They make changes in their products and selling techniques to provide merchandise that meets the wants and needs of today's consumers.

Market Growth and Share

All parts of the industry want market growth. *Market growth* is an increase in the size of the entire market; more products are sold and there are higher total dollars of sales. This usually happens because of population growth and/or good economic times.

Additionally, companies within the industry strive to have growth of their own market share. *Market share* is the part of the total market controlled by a firm. It is usually computed by sales, and indicated as a percentage in relation to the total industry, as in the size of a "pie wedge," shown in 5-1. When successful companies gain market share, that amount of increase is lost by other combined companies that sell to that market.

Stiff competition results between companies trying to increase their market share. Also, the company with the largest market share usually has the lowest per-item costs because its total costs are spread across more products. Lower costs usually lead to lower selling

Market growth and Share

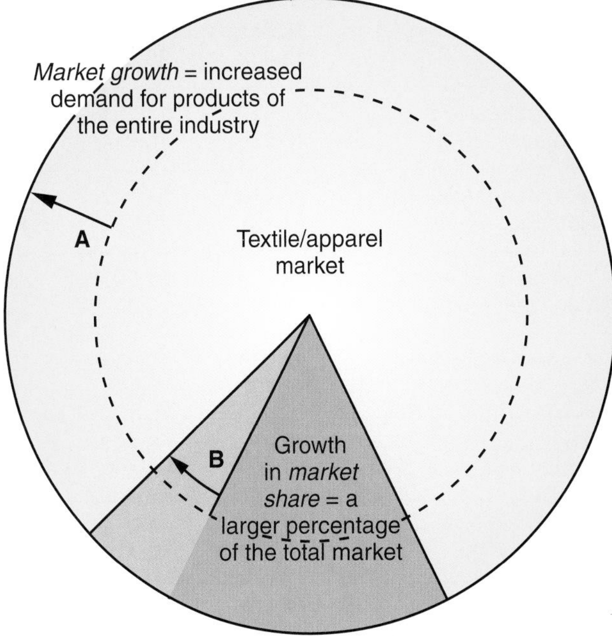

5-1 If the market for an entire industry grows, there is *market growth (A)*. If a company's percentage of a particular market becomes larger, that firm has growth of its *market share (B)*.

prices and even more sales. This, in turn, forces the less successful competitors out of the market. Thus, companies in all industries continually try to increase their market share.

Market Segmentation

Market segmentation involves dividing the total market into smaller groups that contain similar characteristics. These are *market segments.* Since no business is able to serve all consumers in a market, each business must decide which customers it can serve best to achieve the highest success. The company identifies the customers to whom it can sell the most and make the best profit. This defining of the specialized niche of the market to whom the company wishes to make its greatest appeal is called ***target marketing***.

The target market for each fashion company should be well defined. The company should make or carry products specifically directed to customers in its one or more identified market segments. For instance, a producer of children's wear might make colorful playsuits with large pockets liked by children (one target market) that can stand up to tough wear and many launderings to satisfy the parents (another target market). The retailer shown in 5-2 targets fashion boutique customers.

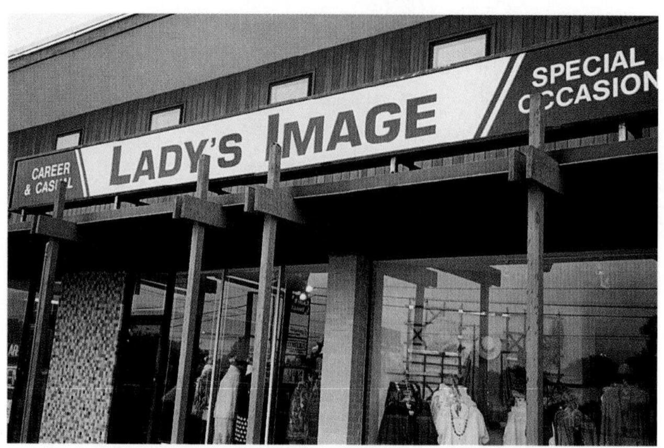

5-2 This boutique dress shop in a small city targets women who are looking for quality fashions that are a bit unusual, unlike the similar styles that are stocked by department and discount stores.

Expected U.S. Demographics for Apparel Markets Population Figures in Thousands by Years

Markets	2000	2005	2010	2015	2020	2025	%Change (2000–2025)
Children under age 5	18,986	19,127	20,011	21,174	21,978	22,498	+18.5%
Girls ages 5–14	19,506	19,593	19,380	19,894	20,904	21,881	+12.2%
Boys ages 5–14	20,471	20,554	20,340	20,901	21,978	23,006	+12.4%
Women ages 15–24	18,665	20,076	21,032	21,110	20,907	21,448	+14.9%
Men ages 15–24	19,412	20,882	21,884	21,959	21,755	22,322	+15.0%
Women ages 25–34	18,699	18,291	19,301	20,691	21,615	21,715	+15.3%
Men ages 25–34	18,535	18,014	18,991	20,393	21,319	21,405	+15.5%
Women ages 35–44	22,478	21,273	19,527	18,120	20,146	21,543	–4.2%
Men ages 35–44	22,181	20,892	18,993	18,479	19,466	20,847	–6.0%
Women ages 45–54	18,938	21,203	22,239	21,078	19,393	19,011	+0.4%
Men ages 45–54	18,093	20,304	21,325	20,118	18,347	17,878	–1.2%
Women ages 55–64	12,528	15,440	18,362	20,573	21,595	20,494	+63.6%
Men ages 55–64	11,433	14,166	16,921	19,077	20,120	19,047	+66.6%
Women ages 65–74	9,956	9,961	11,305	13,970	16,595	18,598	+86.8%
Men ages 65–74	8,180	8,409	9,753	12,273	14,791	16,826	+105.7%
Women ages 75+	10,409	11,019	11,216	11,619	12,847	15,267	+46.7%
Men ages 75+	6,167	6,779	7,135	7,705	8,986	11,260	+82.6%
Total all ages	269,470	285,983	297,705	309,134	322,742	335,046	+24.3%

Bureau of the Census, U.S. Department of Commerce

5-3 These demographics, especially the percentage trend figures in the right column, help to indicate future demand for apparel. Notice that the population is expected to increase slightly for the youth and young adult market, decrease for the middle-aged market, and increase for the senior market over age 55 by the year 2025.

Besides the right products, each firm should develop communications and services that help to sell and maintain the patronage of their selected market sectors. For retailers, location, atmosphere, image, and policies should be aimed at the desired level of style, quality, and price to correspond with the character of the segmented market of consumers.

There are several ways to segment markets, and many businesses use methods from various sources. The most popular methods are with demographics and psychographics.

Demographics

Demographics are the vital statistics of human populations, broken down by such factors as age, gender, race, education, religion, income, occupation, and geographic location. Rates of changes, or shifts, in any of these factors within a market area are especially important.

Some fashion marketers subscribe to services that report on demographic trends. Another useful source for demographic information is the U.S. Bureau of the Census, which is a national population count. Businesses use this information to find out where their customers are living, what they are doing, and the amount of money they have to spend on consumer goods. Census statistics of age demographics in the future, which can be used to estimate major apparel markets are shown in 5-3.

Recent census information indicates that population growth is slowing. To counteract this, businesses are trying to instill brand loyalty to keep their existing customers, plus find ways to gain new customers. Also, major population groups are aging. Implications of these population trends are very helpful to fashion merchandisers who try to market to, and please, the population groups.

Other demographic information, not shown in the chart, tells us that there are more women in the workforce, and with higher levels of education. This creates more need for women's career apparel, 5-4. Double-income families can also afford more expensive merchandise. However, with everyone working, consumers are very busy. Thus they need quick and convenient shopping, as well as easy clothing care. Also, with the largest part of the population passing middle age, comfort and dressing ease are prime considerations.

Recent demographics also show that larger populations are migrating to southern states. Thus, more "sunbelt" apparel is needed at the expense of "snowbelt" clothing. Minority groups are larger, resulting in more cultural diversity and market complexity. Additionally, family structures are changing, resulting in fewer "traditional" family households. Companies are figuring out how to market effectively to segments of this varied makeup of population.

Liz Claiborne

5-4 Demographic statistics that show an increase of women in the workforce can be interpreted into a growing market for outfits such as this one.

Psychographics

Psychographics are statistics that try to explain consumer behavior through such variables as lifestyle, values, attitudes, and self-concept—what people are thinking and feeling. These behaviors stem from cultural backgrounds, social groups, or personalities. By evaluating psychographics, along with demographic data, companies try to predict buying patterns. See 5-5. Certain responses to products, advertising, and other selling approaches are anticipated based on these known variables.

Recent psychographics in the U.S. show that there are more relaxed social patterns today, which means that popular clothing styles are increasingly more casual. Even in the workplace, both men and women are "dressing down." Softer fabrics and more comfortable garments that require easier care are being worn. Also, the aging population is remaining more active,

Department of Consumer Studies; University of Delaware

5-5 Discussions of psychographics and demographics, such as this one, can result in predictions of consumer economics and buying habits.

Bobby Jones of Hickey-Freeman Co., Inc./Hartmarx

5-6 Although this outfit is shown on a pre-retirement age model, the aging population is participating in active sports in larger numbers and for longer lengths of time. The demographic statistics of more older people can be combined with the psychographic indications of increased activity to show market opportunities.

requiring more apparel such as that in 5-6. People are "thinking young" and living to an older age.

There is more emphasis on saving the environment today, with people willing to spend a bit more on "green" products that are produced in an environmentally friendly way. Societal consciousness and frugality are gaining in importance, stressing quality and value in consumer products rather than emphasizing success and materialism, as in the past. Also, many people are saving toward their children's college education or their own retirement, rather than spending money on extra fashion goods.

Fashion businesses recognize and respond to these demographic and psychographic factors. Some retailers have put diaper-changing tables in men's restrooms (besides women's restrooms) to assist fathers. Some manufacturers of clothing for the many older consumers have replaced buttons and zippers with Velcro® that don't need as much manipulation with arthritic fingers. As you visit retail stores, take note of other ways the fashion industry is responding to shifts in demographic and psychographic trends.

Market Research

Market research is the process of systematically gathering and analyzing information relating to a particular market, 5-7. It studies consumer tastes and changing trends. Demographic and psychographic information is often used as a starting point. Specific age or lifestyle groups can then be targeted for more information about their shopping behavior, product preferences and needs, perceptions, and purchase motivation. Results can indicate what images, price ranges, packaging, and types of advertising certain consumers prefer. Market research findings might also show why customers choose some items and reject others.

McCall Pattern Company

5-7 Market research involves gathering data, as well as analyzing the impact of the information on the company's market and products.

Market research is an ongoing task for merchandisers of fashion goods. Fashion businesses determine more precisely who their customers are, what they want, and how much they are willing to pay for goods. Companies that are the fastest to pick up trends relating to their target market are the most successful against the competition.

Market research is done internally by large firms. Smaller companies often hire a market research organization to obtain data related to their specific needs. If a research firm is commissioned to conduct a survey for a particular manufacturer or retailer, the results belong to the company that hired the study. Market data discovered by one company that paid for gathering it is *proprietary* information, or exclusive to them and secret from others. This is expensive for industry businesses, since many firms are paying to duplicate the same work.

In other cases, a market research firm will conduct a study on its own and make the results available for a fee, or they will offer the information only to subscribing members of their ongoing market research service. Sometimes results of an industry-sponsored research study are published in a trade magazine or special report for industry members. There are also computer software packages available to guide companies through the steps of doing their own market research.

Because there are so many diverse influences that affect the acceptance of some fashion goods and non-acceptance of others, companies usually gather market predictions from a variety of sources. Besides using formal market research, they incorporate additional findings from trade journals, fashion magazines, and watching people on the streets.

Customer needs are not always easy to identify in the fashion business. Consumers find it hard to clearly state their desires for products, but know what they want to buy when they see the "right" items. Therefore, fashion firms try to satisfy lifestyle elements, such as elegance, comfort, or moderate prices. It also helps if market research can supplement the *qualitative* information (what their customers want) with *quantitative* information (how strongly they want it).

Methods of Market Research

There are many methods of conducting market research. Some are better than others in specific situations. All should be done with a sample of consumers from the company's target market, to be valid for that business. The following are examples of market research methods:

- *Surveys* are done by asking consumers questions via mail, telephone, or stopping people in malls (mall intercepts). Researchers try to profile the consumers as well as the purchases they make. This one-on-one method is time-consuming, and results can depend on quality of the questions and the skill of the interviewers. Also, results are in the present, and don't necessarily give information that can forecast future fashion trends.
- *Consumer panels* consist of participants who keep diaries. This is slow to show results for fashion products. One use for this has been to evaluate television viewing audiences. Results from consumer panels tend to show broad, sweeping trends better than specific ones.
- *Focus groups* consist of a dozen or so people in a room with a moderator or facilitator. The facilitator asks questions, shows merchandise or advertisements, or leads a discussion about a particular subject or product line. The group members often face a mirror which is a see-through window from the other side. Company representatives watch through the window and gain feedback from the reactions of the group members as they are shown or discuss various items.
- *Computer databases*, formulated from consumer actions and purchases, indicate the preferences of individuals in a target market. For instance, credit card companies place consumers into appropriate lifestyle categories when these people charge merchandise on their cards. After many purchases on credit cards, clear customer profiles emerge. Such databases, as in 5-8, pinpoint where specific consumers shop, their spending levels, recreational activities, favorite

colors and styles, garment sizes, etc. Lists of names and addresses are often sold to companies who market to particular target markets. This is very valuable information to businesses, but is upsetting to some consumers who seek privacy. The government is considering enacting consumer privacy laws to limit the selling or sharing of some computer database information without the consent of the individuals involved.

* *Electronic feedback tests* use computers to receive qualitative as well as quantitative information from those in the target market test group. An "indicator knob" can be turned by consumers in the test group, according to the intensity of like or dislike of what is seen on a screen, handled in finished form, or worn by a model. Sometimes consumers in the midwest or south are asked to react to a satellite broadcast of garments from New York or Paris and indicate the degree of like or dislike of what a retail company is considering putting into its stores. This is quick, effective, and can be *interactive*, with further immediate probing done in response to information being collected. It is quite expensive to set up and run. However, if it prevents costly mistakes, it has "good return on investment."
* ***Virtual reality (VR)*** is computer-generated and stimulates all of the user's senses to create a perception of being in another environment that responds to, or is interactive with, the user. Just as hologram images are used for realistic arcade games and jet aircraft training, fashion market research is done by giving the sensation of selecting, trying on, and buying various products. Participants can see, feel, and hear the rustling of a garment on themselves, even though it is not there. They can turn to see all sides of it, and changes can be made in the "pretend" garment according to consumer responses. Although this is very expensive, design changes can be indicated without having wasted any fabric or manufacturing time. Also, the imaginary garments never get makeup stains or broken zippers from being tried on!

The Fashion Institute of Design and Merchandising, California; Beth Herzhaft, Photographer

5-8 Computer databases accumulate a great deal of information about consumers that can be used to profile each customer's buying patterns.

Product Development

Findings from market research are used to correct current market problems and to capture new market opportunities, 5-9. Alert organizations respond quickly to market research findings. After discovering preferences of their target markets, companies fill customer desires that have been recognized for both goods and services.

Product development is the process of carrying a product idea through stages from initial conceptualization to actual appearance in the market. New products are designed, within the resource limits of a company, for specified markets. Sometimes, since most changes evolve over time, existing products are modified to satisfy changed desires of consumers. Obsolete products are replaced, and new ones are added.

Product development is especially important in the fashion industry. See 5-10. Change is always occurring, so products cannot stay the same and continue to sell. Textile firms develop new fibers or fabric characteristics to meet specific needs in the market. Apparel manufacturers design and produce lines of garments that are predicted to be in demand at the exact time they "hit the stores." Product development for retailers is

Fashion Institute of Technology; John Senzer, Photographer

5-9 Textiles and finished products can be developed specifically to satisfy the identified needs of markets.

McCall Pattern Company

5-10 Since the fashion industry must respond to changing tastes faster than most other industries, product development is an important function that is continually performed.

Department of Consumer Studies; University of Delaware

5-11 Because of information that was gathered in this computer system, these women are able to develop a customer service plan as well as calculations about implementing the plan.

stocking specific up-to-date merchandise and providing new services that will please their shoppers. Large retail companies have product development departments that oversee the design and manufacture of private label merchandise.

Fashion Industry Information Technology

Adapting to changes in the industry and the market as fast as possible has become easier for fashion-related businesses through the use of computer information systems. ***Information systems*** are computer components that work together by combining collection, classification, storage, retrieval, and dissemination of data toward a certain outcome. Pertinent information can be electronically located, gathered, processed, and used, as indicated in 5-11. Computers can show exactly what is shipped, received, selling well, or returned. Computer tracking of customer buying patterns and product preferences can help with market research and product development. As more business functions become automated, the efficiency and effectiveness of a company's operations improve through increased productivity, reduced staff, accurate stock planning and timing, and increased sales.

Technology that gives accurate, fast information helps companies make smart decisions. Data are stored and can be retrieved very quickly and as often as necessary. Technology is one of the prime elements that separates industry winners from losers. Companies that use the data wisely can develop smart strategies, gain an advantage over their competitors, and be more profitable.

With computerized information systems, companies have more accurate sales and stock records, faster check-out transactions, and fine-tuned markings for identifying all aspects of each piece of merchandise. Computer information eliminates manual stock counts and helps companies provide better customer service because they can tell quickly what pleases their customers. It is done with electronically readable codes, code printers, optical scanners, and other devices.

Codes and Printers

Almost all merchandise tags are marked with bar codes, used for fast and economical product identification and data collection. ***Bar codes*** are standardized "symbologies" of dark bars and white spaces of varying widths that are printed onto machine-readable

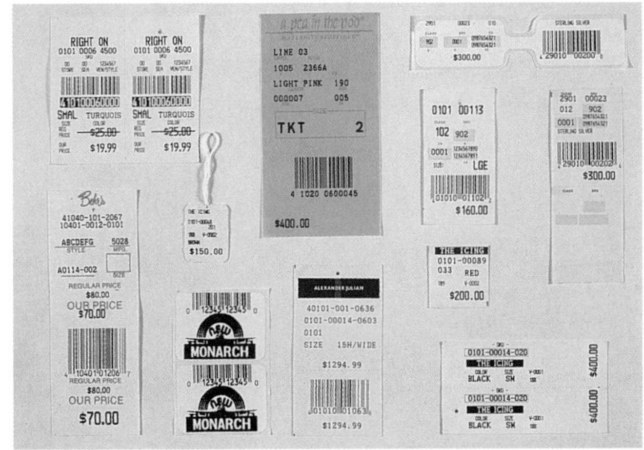

STS Systems

5-12 All of these tags contain a great deal of information, especially within the dark bars and white spaces of the bar codes.

5-13 This standard Universal Product Code consists of black and white bars and spaces of varying widths, that can be "encoded" into specific data by a computer system.

merchandise tickets or other labels. Examples are shown in 5-12. The bar and space pattern represents numbers, letters, and other data. Bar codes form a special communication language for computers that gives information about the product's brand name, style, size, color, and price.

Bar codes are used throughout the soft goods chain on raw materials, parts going through production, shipping containers, and finished products for sale to consumers. The Universal Product Code (UPC) is the most familiar bar code to most people, and has been endorsed by retailers as the preferred marking standard of the industry, 5-13. More complicated codes, increasing in use, are 2-dimensional and carry a great deal more data. More sophisticated equipment is needed to read them. Also, new codes are sometimes in squares or circles, rather than the traditional straight bars and spaces. More data can be packed into the new symbols. "Matrix codes" can even put a thousand characters or more on a small label.

Many companies that use bar codes have their own on-site bar code printer, used to create their labels or tags. One model is shown in 5-14. The company can then change bar code information, as needed, using computer software, 5-15. The computer program controls

Weber Marking Systems

5-14 Textile producers print their own bar codes for use on bales of fibers or bolts of fabrics. Apparel manufacturers and retailers have bar code printers for tags on garments.

T.L. Ashford

5-15 Computer programs that control the printer can be used to easily change bar code information.

printings of different codes at different times. Otherwise, label suppliers are paid to provide labels that are printed with the correct information.

All codes should be verified to meet industry compliance issues. ***Compliance*** involves companies using unified bar code standards that specify label printing, levels of quality, correct contents of shipments, and other identification of goods through the channel of distribution from producer to retail sale. Compliance bar code labeling helps to improve supplier-customer

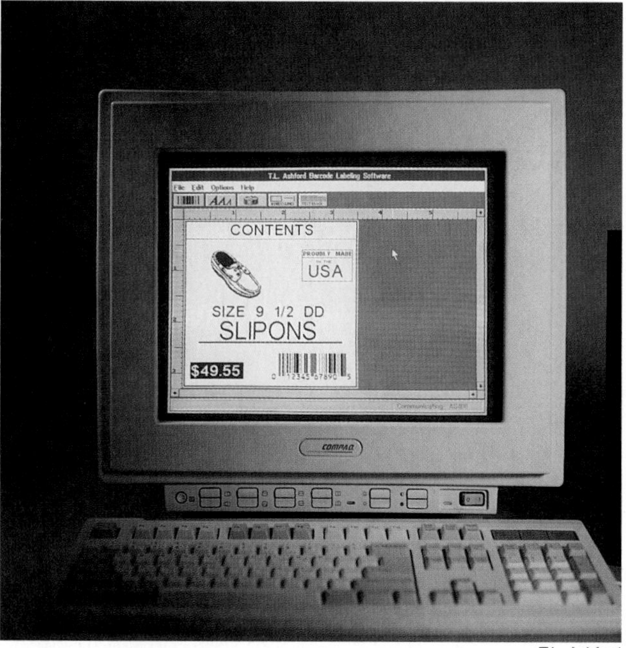

T.L. Ashford

5-16 Most compliance bar code uniformity is built into computer systems so scanners of customer companies can read the information on labels from suppliers.

relationships, so merchandise is acceptable to all companies as it moves through the soft goods chain. Guidelines coordinate the physical aspects of the labels, information content, type and symbol specification, and placement of the label on the product or container, 5-16.

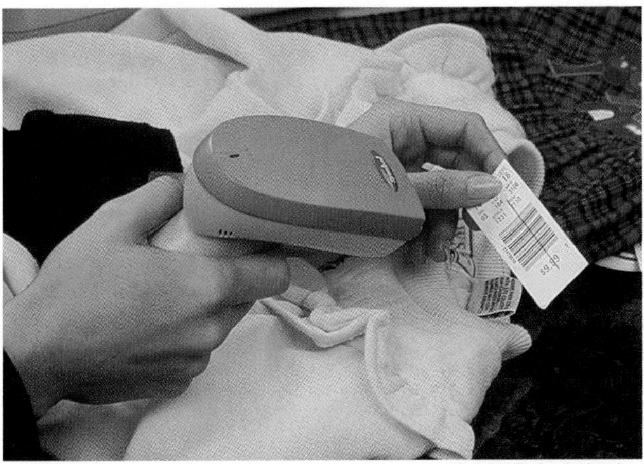

Symbol Technologies, Inc.

5-17 The red light beam, shown here as a line across the bar code, is "reading" the information contained in the code.

Burlington Industries

5-18 A fabric inspector at a textile plant can scan a bar code into the computer at her work station so the fabric can be traced from inspection to final delivery.

Optical Scanners

Bar codes are read by electronic ***optical scanners***, that feed information to the computer. The scanners send out a light beam on command. They then analyze light reflected off the surface of the bar-coded label, with dark bars absorbing the light and white spaces reflecting it back, 5-17. When the scanner "reads" the bar code, all information being received is automatically decoded and recorded in the computer system.

Most people have seen this automated data collection, or "data capture," done with stationary countertop scanners in grocery stores. Optical scanning wands and handheld laser guns are usually used at apparel retail checkout counters. Bar code scanning is also done throughout the pipeline to automatically record the movement of bolts of fabrics, garment parts going through production, or cartons being shipped or received, 5-18.

Radio frequency (RF) data communication is "wireless." It is done through air waves between handheld data collection scanners and the computer register system. This radio signal approach offers speed, flexibility, and convenience because the scanners can go where needed, rather than being attached by cable.

RF scanners are used to record information from items located a distance away from the checkout area, such as when working at store shelves along a wall, or at receiving docks, warehouse bins, or supply rooms. They can also shorten retail checkout lines during busy times by processing charge card customers out on the sales floor, thus preventing them from standing in long lines at registers. Another remote use is for special events, such as sidewalk sales outside of stores.

It is predicted that, very soon, most scanning systems will use new types of wireless systems. Also, newer "miniaturized technologies" are allowing for even more powerful, smaller, types of lightweight equipment. With more sophisticated codes, plus automatic scanning, the physical world and the computer world are talking directly–without human intervention!

This combination of printed bar codes and optical scanning automation provides fast, accurate, automatic identification for goods being received as well as being sold, 5-19. Manual, labor-intensive systems have been eliminated. A portable handheld device can now do the scanning as well as the printing of bar code labels. After scanning an item number, it can quickly print and apply a bar-coded label that is coordinated with the correct information from the main system about the particular item that was scanned. The work is done as one quick, automatic procedure.

Symbol Technologies, Inc.

5-19 Bar code and scanning technology enables products to be quickly and efficiently identified, priced, and recorded.

Other automatic identification technologies include magnetic stripes, voice recognition, machine vision, and smart cards.

- *Magnetic stripes* are common along the top or bottom of the back of credit and other financial or security cards. When the stripes are run through reading devices, information contained in the stripes is translated.
- *Voice recognition* allows computers to respond to human voices for data input and/or operating commands.
- *Machine vision* uses video cameras to read bar codes or identify a product through its "signature," such as size, shape, or color of package.
- *Smart cards* have a small microprocessor embedded in the plastic. The microprocessor provides user identification, information, or stored cash credits that can be used for purchases. Smart cards carry more extensive information than standard magnetic stripe cards. Also, the information changes with the circumstances. Similar devices are attached to merchandise for security reasons, to trip alarms at exits and alert store personnel about shoplifting.

Technology Disadvantages

As with all advancements, there are a few negative aspects to the new technology. However, the disadvantages are very minor compared to the many advantages received from the systems. Most of the disadvantages are being eliminated as time passes.

One disadvantage has been high financial cost. Companies must buy certain ***computer hardware***, or equipment consisting of keyboards, monitors, and printers. They must purchase expensive ***computer software***, or operating systems, that tell the computer to do the required procedures, such as recording what is in stock or has been sold. They must also spend money on optical scanners and bar code printers. These high costs tend to make the technology more available to large companies than small ones. Large companies can more easily afford to purchase the needed components and, thus, become more efficient. This makes it harder for small companies to compete in the industry. However, as computer costs decrease, and companies see the paybacks of electronics, more small companies will upgrade to be competitive and stay in the industry.

Another disadvantage is the inability for companies to function if there is a power failure or if the system "goes down" for any other reason. This computer downtime problem will become more significant to all users in the future as companies become more dependent on electronic information systems. At this time, most companies do not guard against this because auxiliary generator backups are very expensive.

One other disadvantage has been incorrect data entry by operators who are typing information into the computer system. This problem of human error is diminishing as more and more information is being automatically entered with scanning equipment. However, that has caused data entry jobs to be eliminated, creating some unemployment. Those who are employed, must have higher level skills in computer technology rather than just typing, 5-20.

Open Systems

A major disadvantage of computer technology in the past was the fact that hardware and software suppliers each had their own systems. There were incompatibility problems. This has been corrected today with ***open systems*** that integrate components to be mixed and matched. Computer users are no longer locked into one vendor for hardware, software, and changes or additions to the system. Parts of systems from different suppliers now work compatibly with each other electronically.

For open systems to be viable, vendors have agreed on industry data exchange standards. These allow all components to "talk to" and work with other components. Such multivendor networks allow companies, such as retailers, to get the best flexibility and value to meet their present and future needs. A retailer might now have a checkout keyboard, printer, cash drawer, and display all made by different companies, but selected in pieces that fit the best needs of the store. If one part needs to be replaced, only that part is bought rather than an entire new computer system. Since technological advances are being made at an ever-increasing rate, this also allows for incremental technology upgrades that move a company's system ahead as technology moves forward.

Open systems can save retailers, and other businesses, a great deal of money, while satisfying the most customized needs. However, managing an open system requires more knowledge of what is available, as well as how to combine, use, and maintain the system. To solve this, some textile/apparel businesses outsource this function.

Outsourcing is the hiring of independent specialists to do particular work, rather than using company employees. Information technology consulting organizations offer the services of computer experts, for a fee, to oversee the system and coordinate the automation strategy of a business. Such "third party providers" have expertise in the integration of computer components, installation, network management, employee training, and hardware maintenance. This provides a maximum return on the user company's technology investment. Then fashion company managers are relieved from knowing about and doing functions that do not specifically relate to merchandising activities. Companies often find it to be a more cost-effective way to utilize the latest technology.

Electronic Data Interchange

Electronic data interchange (EDI) enables companies to communicate information or transactions with each other through their computers. This "information

T.L. Ashford

5-20 It is important to develop good computer skills for employment in all parts of the fashion industry.

Weber Marking Systems

5-21 Software packages enable computers from different companies worldwide to communicate with each other, as if they were on the same system in the same company.

pipeline" consists of electronic linkages between companies to automatically transmit company-to-company communication of standard business transactions. Examples include advance shipping notices, purchase orders, invoices, product returns, and other standard documents.

For computers to communicate with each other, special software is used, 5-21. The software translates signals to a common "language." ***Modems***, which transmit computer data over telephone lines, send the signals between companies. After the messages are received, they print out on paper at the receiving location, in the form of the receiving company's purchase order or other official document.

EDI technology reduces the costs of clerical work, data entry, and the printing of forms, since no actual forms are manually prepared or mailed. Paperwork and postage costs are almost eliminated, while accuracy increases. It also provides the ability to track goods as they move through the chain, thus enabling companies to fully automate their order cycle. EDI improves the efficiency of all companies involved. It increases sales and profits, and it lowers costs. Almost all companies that supply merchandise to major-volume retailers are on EDI linkage systems.

As an example of how the combined technologies of bar coding, scanning, and EDI are used, the following takes place:

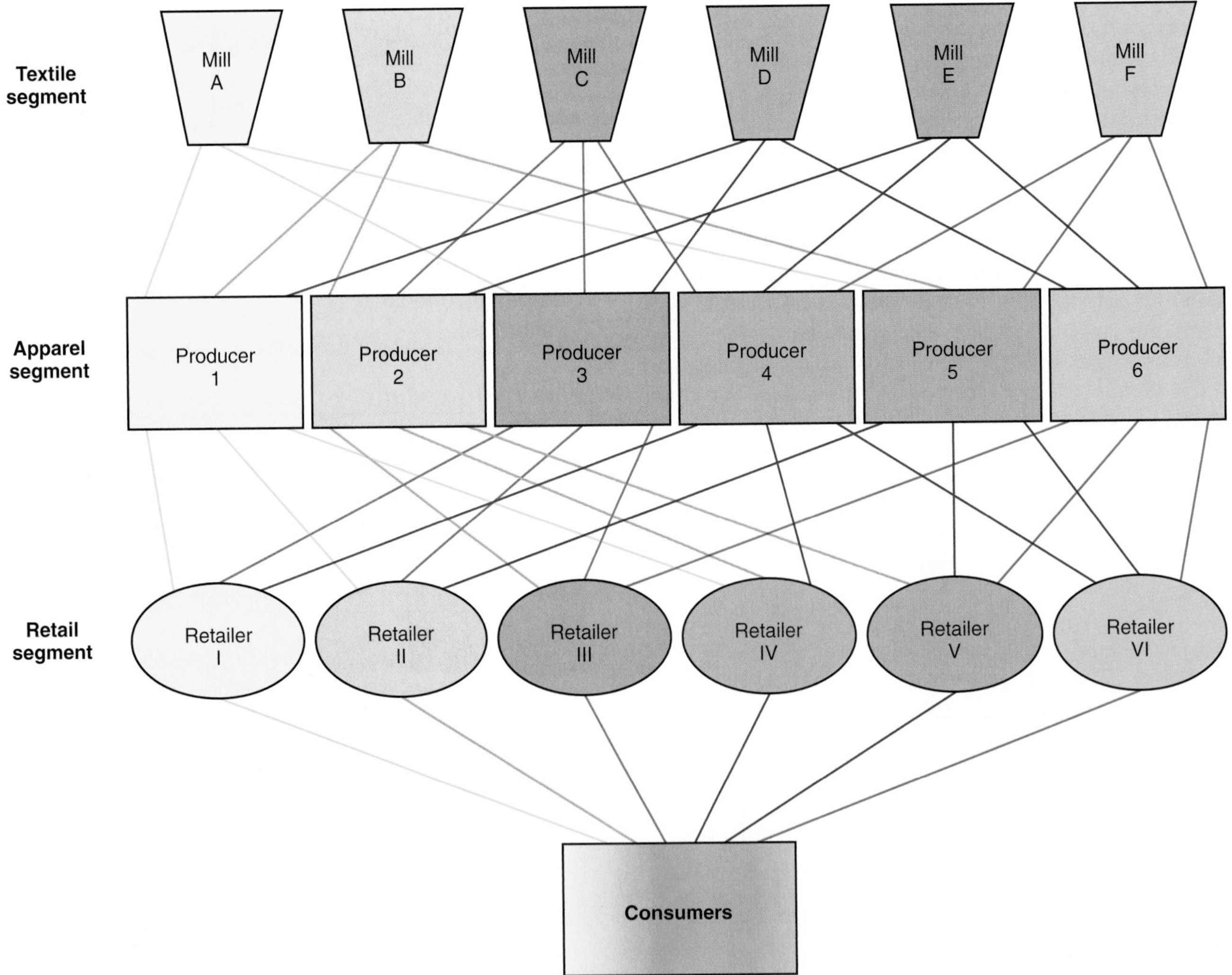

5-22 This simplified illustration shows long-term, Quick Response partnerships that link businesses from each segment into chains of suppliers and buyers.

1. Textile firms set up computer systems that measure, color code, and inspect fabric as it comes off the loom.
2. That information is transmitted to computers at apparel factories before the bolts of cloth arrive there.
3. Sewing factories only need to scan the bolt tags when the fabric arrives.
4. The fabric can move directly from the delivery truck to the cutting room for swift processing without any repetition of tasks.
5. Then, computers at sewing plants inform retail stores about production of their orders.
6. Advance shipping notices tell retailers when specific orders will leave the factory and arrive at store receiving docks.
7. Finally, *invoicing*, or billing for the materials sent, is also done automatically by computer.

Traditional EDI transmissions over telephone lines are now being supplemented or replaced by Internet communications. This business-to-business electronic commerce *(B2B EC)*, which connects companies online, is worldwide, reduces costs, and enables small companies to compete as easily as large firms because no special systems are needed. Web-based EDI business forms and appropriate data can be sent to business partners faster and more accurately. However, some security of information privacy may be compromised. Some firms establish private Web sites that can only be accessed by employees, suppliers, or business partners. Pertinent "real time" data is available and print-outs can be generated.

Cooperation for Industry Excellence

After the mid-1900s, the U.S. industry fell behind other countries in the worldwide competition of soft goods products. More foreign merchandise was sold in U.S. stores than goods made in the U.S. Many U.S. companies had failed to modernize their production plants or upgrade with technological advances. Also, some unsound financial decisions had been made, resulting in low profits.

In the 1980s,U.S. textile-apparel industry members joined together to evaluate and reverse the situation. They recognized that each segment of the pipeline (textile, apparel, and retail) was operating as a separate, independent industry. There were adversarial buyer-seller relationships between the segments. Each corporation tried to strike the best deal without concern for others or for the industry as a whole. This had created a situation of high costs, low quality, and lack of trust between companies.

To revitalize the industry, U.S. business leaders from all parts of the textile/apparel pipeline developed a plan for a course of action. They decided that if all segments could cooperate to satisfy the final consumer, the industry and all of its parts would gain strength. As a result, the unified industry is now becoming strong, efficient, and market-responsive. The industry is striving to provide quality, value-priced products to the market in a timely and efficient way. This proactive policy of cooperation has resulted in lower costs, higher quality products, faster through-put, and satisfied customers. It is good for member firms, consumers, and the U.S. economy.

Quick Response

Quick Response (QR), which transmits bar code data using EDI technology, is based on industry-wide cooperation. It streamlines the supply chain to efficiently meet consumer needs. It ties together the entire textile-apparel-retail pipeline as one unified industry rather than as individual segments. Electronic linkages are established with long-term customer-supplier partners through the entire chain, 5-22.

With QR, information flows backward through the chain for an automatic reorder system from *point-of-sale (POS)* data. As bar codes of merchandise being sold at retail are recorded through checkout scanners and computers, they trigger partner manufacturers to produce those same items to replenish the store's stock. In turn, as manufacturers run low on fabrics and sewing supplies, computers prompt their partner textile firms

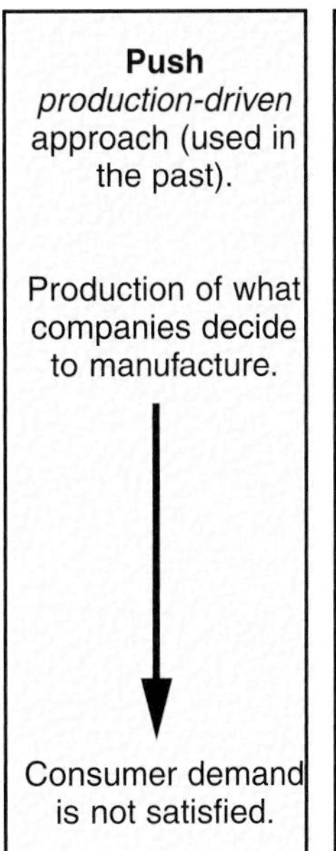

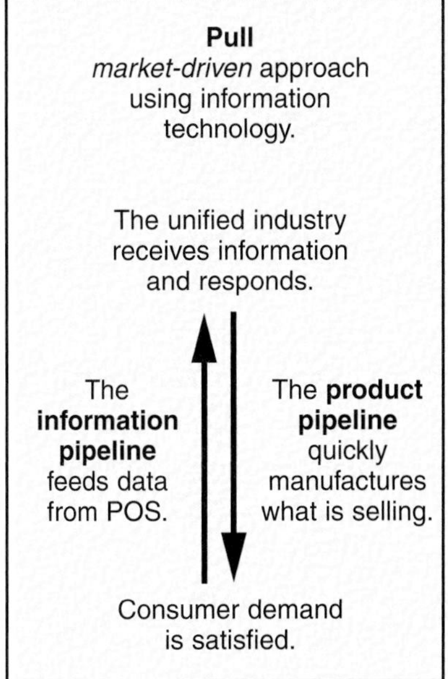

5-23 When the information pipeline feeds the product pipeline with point-of-sale data, as shown under "pull" on the right, goods and services result that satisfy consumer demand.

to automatically send more of the required goods to the apparel manufacturers.

Through such connections with suppliers, there is quicker "just-in-time" inventory replenishment throughout the chain. Inventories can be kept lower, and supply mistakes are reduced because merchandise decisions are automatically made based on demand information. Also, as part of the system, deliveries are more frequent, smaller, and correct.

As a result of QR, communications are improved and processing costs are lower. There is less duplication of functions, which means a faster response to market trends. A "pull" from the consumer end of the pipeline drives the process rather than the old "push" of mass-produced merchandise from the industry, which often resulted in products that consumers did not want. The right merchandise is available for market demand, 5-23. Retailers have higher sales and more satisfied customers. Also, to stay in the long-term partnerships, suppliers provide the promised quality and expected on-time delivery. This makes U.S.-made goods more competitive against imports by satisfying demand and shortening the time through the chain.

Quick Response is gaining widespread use throughout the industry. The needed equipment is becoming less expensive for companies to install, and it pays for itself in savings in just a few years. Also, the original fear of sharing information electronically with other companies has subsided, and standardized software programs now enable the computers of companies to communicate accurately.

General benefits of QR include:

* improved focus on consumer needs
* accuracy of communications
* higher quality standards
* more efficient purchasing, production, and distribution

Specific benefits include:

* improved shipping schedules
* lower inventories
* easier reordering
* shorter lead and response times
* improved sales forecasting
* fewer retail markdowns, closeouts, and stockouts

Results include:

* lower costs
* increased sales
* higher profit margins
* improved product flexibility through smaller orders
* higher return on investment

Industry unity among the segments stems from successful end products that are a result of combined input from each process along the pipeline. Prosperity of the partnerships perpetuates cooperative, trusting linkages, since companies share information for their own good and for the good of the chain. Bad relationships are reduced and long-term capital advancements are encouraged. The system builds strength, and spreads and reduces business risks with partnering synergies. ***Synergy*** is cooperative interaction of parts that results in a total effect that is greater than the sum of the parts added together separately. "The whole is greater than the sum of its parts" is sometimes represented as 2 + 2 = 5!

It is predicted that in the future, companies will shift their focus from doing everything, to doing only what they do best. They will link up with other companies to form networks that accomplish whole, completed processes that will serve retail customers faster and more efficiently.

Textile/Clothing Technology Corporation

The ***Textile/Clothing Technology Corporation,*** called ***[TC]²*** after its repeated initials, is a not-for-profit industry-wide organization. It is a coalition of textile, apparel, and retail firms and trade associations, government, academia (textile/apparel colleges), and labor organizations. See 5-24.

[TC]² is charged with the mission of making the U.S. soft goods industry more competitive, productive, and cost-effective. It researches high-tech innovations in apparel production equipment and processes, and helps the industry implement them. By pooling industry resources, financial responsibility and leadership are spread throughout the industry so all members can

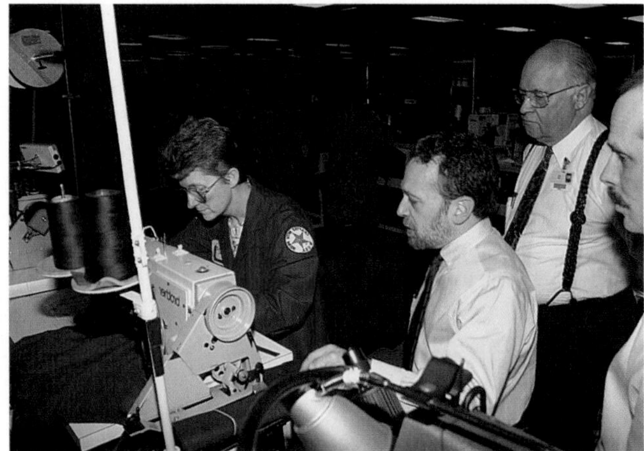

Textile/Clothing Technology Corporation

5-24 Members of government, industry, and universities are very interested in technology that is enabling U.S. soft goods suppliers to be more competitive.

keep up with the dynamic speed of change in the industry worldwide. Also, research is not duplicated because companies do not work independently from each other. Industry unity and strength are improved.

[TC]^2 operates the National Apparel Technical Center "Teaching Factory" near Raleigh, North Carolina. This industry center helps to upgrade the technical knowledge and skills of industry personnel. Its courses teach strong management skills for executives, 5-25, through basic line skills for factory equipment operators. Education and training services include courses, demonstrations, books/manuals, and videotapes to member firms at a low fee, as well as to other industry participants at a higher fee. Also, consulting services are available, dispatched to locations having problems.

Other Partnerships

The American Textile Partnership, abbreviated as AMTEX, applies government-based technologies to the domestic textile/apparel industry. It links government laboratories with the textile/apparel pipeline and academia, doing collaborative research on projects to strengthen the competitiveness of the U.S. industry. It stresses both computer information and manufacturing technologies, and contributes ideas and programs to help the environment and minimize the waste of resources in the industry.

Additional cooperative efforts are being made between businesses, government, and academia. Cooperative research is often done when industry resources provide funding for research being done in university labs. Regional collaborative networks of manufacturers, retailers, and educators exist in various parts of the U.S. to promote growth and strength of industry companies. The networks seek funding for educational outreach, research, and service to the industry.

Textile/Clothing Technology Corporation

5-25 [TC]^2 training staff members have years of experience in the industry. Courses combine some lecture and written information about new methods with hands-on equipment use.

The National Textile Center (NTC) is a research consortium of four Southeastern universities. It provides academic research to help the U.S. textile/apparel chain be strong and competitive. To this end, the schools share personnel, equipment, and facilities. They are working on several specific projects that concern the engineering of fibers, yarns, and fabrics. They are also working on garment engineering and computer systems to promote rapid response to customer needs.

Exciting innovations are occurring through partnerships to make the U.S. textile/apparel industry a world leader in the future!

Improving the Industry's Image

The consuming public has not been aware of how innovative the U.S. industry has become. Therefore, industry excellence must be supplemented with promotion to tell the story of the revived industry to consumers. Efforts are being made to communicate the industry's emphasis on technology upgrading and its concern to meet market demand challenges with top value products.

The Crafted with Pride in U.S.A. Council (CWP) was formed in the 1980s to strengthen the competitive position of the U.S. soft goods chain against imported goods. CWP sponsored national television promotions to encourage consumers to buy American-made textiles, apparel, and home furnishings. Efforts still aim at reinforcing the high image that American consumers have of goods produced in the United States, such as having quality materials and construction, dependable fit, and a broad range of styling. The importance of soft goods manufacturing to the national economy is also promoted. CWP encourages retailers and manufacturers to prominently feature "Made in USA" labels, such as in 5-26.

The industry's public image is also being improved by business efforts for higher standards of ethics and social responsibilities, as well as the environment.

Business Concerns

The way textile, apparel, and retail companies operate contributes to the excellence and image of the industry, too. Serious efforts and great strides are being made toward high standards of ethics and social responsibility, and concern for the environment. By helping to satisfy needs of individuals and communities, companies attract and keep a qualified and more productive work force, while spreading a good message about themselves and the industry. Their actions also encourage good customer relationships, other companies want to do business with them, and consumers to think highly of them and want to buy their

Crafted with Pride in U.S.A. Council, Inc.

5-26 American textile/apparel companies are encouraged to use labels, such as this one in domestically-produced apparel to help promote domestic production.

goods. It has been shown that having ethical standards also makes the business more successful—with a more profitable bottom line!

Ethics and Social Responsibility

Successful fashion firms have a corporate culture of caring. They are concerned with education, family care, health issues, and the safety of their employees. Some companies provide high school equivalency programs, continuing education courses, and college tuition assistance for their workers. Some have on-site child care centers for children of employees. Some help with tutors for school-age children of their workers, or offer free counseling services and substance abuse rehabilitation programs. Many offer flexible work hours to help employees juggle work with the demands of their family lives.

A corporate commitment to community involvement encourages employees to do volunteer work for charitable organizations and to be community leaders. Some companies allow employees to have paid time off for volunteer projects. Some sponsor AIDS benefits, support cancer research or other charitable giving, or help to build houses for the poor. A few specific examples include the following:

- A retailer helped to remodel a home for abused mothers and now has some loyal employees from that home.
- A well-known apparel manufacturer sponsors academic teams in the local high school, which helps the school and gives the company high-esteem in the community.
- A leading knitwear manufacturer put a store into a school in which students can learn how to merchandise and display products, and sell them. Products are provided at cost, and the school keeps the profits from sales to use toward educational materials.

Environment

Fashion firms have also become very concerned about preserving and improving the environment. Since textile and apparel production processes have contributed to pollution in the past, strict policies have been implemented related to environmental issues. Employee "green committees" often lead local efforts on recycling, waste minimization, planting trees, etc. Consumer concern for the environment often affects the products they buy.

Some mail-order retailers plant trees to replenish what have been used to produce their catalogs. A new, environmentally friendly, biodegradable fiber is being manufactured from wood pulp from trees that are grown in constantly replanted forests. All solvents in its production process are recycled. Cotton is now grown organically and in various colors to avoid the use of bleaches, dyes, and solvents in its finishing, 5-27.

The American Textile Manufacturers Institute (ATMI) has an "Encouraging Environmental Excellence" (E3) initiative to expand environmental awareness among textile producers. Companies can become members if they meet or exceed the program's stringent guidelines. Then they can display the E3 logo on their hangtags and printed materials. The program tries to exceed government requirements.

Recycled textiles are used in many ways, from diapers to mops to plastic wood to home insulation. On the other hand, plastic bottles are being recycled into a fiber that is used in high quality fabrics. See 5-28. The fiber is said to be physically and chemically comparable to fiber made from new material, and production costs are about the same. The material can be continually recycled so it never goes to a landfill.

National Cotton Council

5-27 An emphasis to preserve the environment is providing better processes in all parts of the textile/apparel pipeline.

The industry is trying to avoid making waste by finding substitutes for pollutants and reducing the amounts of chemicals used. It is trying to recycle existing waste whenever possible. It is striving to reduce costs while being environmentally responsible.

Wellman Fortrel®, EcoSpun™ / Larry Prosor, photographer

5-28 The fabric in this outfit, which has outstanding performance and aesthetics, is made of 100% recycled plastic bottles.

Summary

If businesses satisfy market demands, total market growth will occur, and successful companies will have larger market shares. Market segmentation identifies target niches through demographics, psychographics, and other means. Also, several different methods of conducting market research help companies gather and analyze information relating to particular markets. Products are then developed to satisfy market needs.

The technology of electronic (computer) information systems provides accurate, fast information that helps companies make smart decisions. Bar codes are printed onto machine-readable merchandise tickets, and stationary or handheld optical scanners automatically record all information into computer systems. Radio frequency and other automatic identification methods are quickly becoming popular.

Disadvantages of the technology include high financial cost, inability to function during power or system failures, and human errors of data entry. The disadvantage of hardware and software suppliers having their own systems has been corrected with open systems that offer compatible components. Additionally, standardized computer language and business transactions make electronic data interchange possible so linked companies can automatically transmit communications. Several trade shows, organizations, and journals help to spread the ideas and products of information technology.

Companies within the segments of the textile/apparel industry have joined together to strive toward industry excellence and consumer satisfaction. Quick Response pulls products through linked partnership chains from point-of-sale data that indicates actual demand in the market. The Textile/Clothing Technology Corporation, [TC]^2, is a cooperative effort to research and implement high-tech innovations. Other partnerships combine the industry, government, and academia in various ways to strive toward the U.S. textile/apparel industry being a world leader.

There are also cooperative efforts to improve the industry's image to the consuming public. This has been done with a nationwide public awareness campaign of Crafted with Pride in U.S.A. Council. Also, there are serious business efforts toward high ethics, social responsibility, and environmental concerns.

To Know

market segmentation
target marketing
demographics
psychographics
market research
virtual reality (VR)
product development
information systems
bar codes
optical scanners
compliance
computer hardware
computer software
open systems
outsourcing
electronic data interchange (EDI)
modems
Quick Response (QR)
synergy
Textile/Clothing Technology Corporation [TC]^2

To Review

1. Explain the difference between market growth and growth in market share.
2. What is the meaning of the term *proprietary*?
3. Explain the difference between qualitative information and quantitative information.
4. In market research, why is it more effective if a method is interactive?
5. Why is product development especially important in the fashion industry?
6. What is the most familiar bar code and the one endorsed by retailers as the preferred marking standard of the industry?

7. Name at least three new configurations of bar codes.
8. What do industry bar code labeling compliance guidelines coordinate?
9. How do optical scanners analyze bar codes?
10. Why do radio frequency (RF) scanners offer speed, flexibility, and convenience, and what are some examples of how they can be used?
11. What do you think are some disadvantages of using new technology in relation to fashion merchandising?
12. Why do open systems create lower costs for companies while enabling them to move forward with technology?
13. What does it mean when some textile/apparel businesses "outsource" the management of their information technology systems?
14. What do we mean by the phrase, *information pipeline*?
15. List four advantages of EDI technology.
16. In general, what occurs at information technology trade shows?
17. Explain how a "pull" from the consumer end of the pipeline is better than a "push" of merchandise from the industry.
18. Why was the Crafted with Pride in U.S.A. Council formed?
19. What are some ethical and socially responsible actions that companies take to help satisfy needs of individuals and communities?
20. What does an E3 logo indicate on a hangtag?

To Do

1. Do library and/or Internet research to discover as much U.S. Census information as you can about the demographics of your region, state, or locality. Show your findings in a written report, and combine the demographic and psychographic information into a specific fictitious market that you might target if you were an apparel retailer. Then, pretending to do product development, what kinds of products and services would you offer in your retail business? Why?
2. With five other students in the class, do extensive study on the six methods of market research described in this chapter. Present a report to the class with each student explaining one of the methods in detail. Use role-playing to illustrate the methods where appropriate. For fun, conduct a survey, consumer panel, or focus group method on the whole class. Tabulate the results and describe them to the class.
3. Visit a local supermarket, a large discount or department store, and a small apparel shop. Analyze the technology of the information systems for each type of store. Do their items have UPC bar codes, another kind of bar code, or no bar code? Ask if they print their own bar code labels. What kind of optical scanners do they use? Try to draw or explain how the scanner works. What other automatic identification technology do they use (magnetic stripe readers, security devices, etc.)? Make three large charts that show and explain your findings (one chart for each store visited). Post the charts for your classmates to see.
4. Do library research on AMTEX, NTC, $[TC]^2$, or another cooperative partnership of the textile/apparel industry. Find out how it started, how it operates, its goals, what it has accomplished, etc. Write a report about your findings.
5. Look in stores for environmentally friendly textile/apparel items. Look at labels to find products made of recycled materials, organically grown cotton, containing the E3 logo, or other indications of environmental responsibility. Explain your findings to the class, with examples if possible.

JCPenney

Companies compete with one another to increase their market share. Markets are often segmented into men's, children's, and women's clothing.

PART 2

Textile/ Apparel Building Blocks

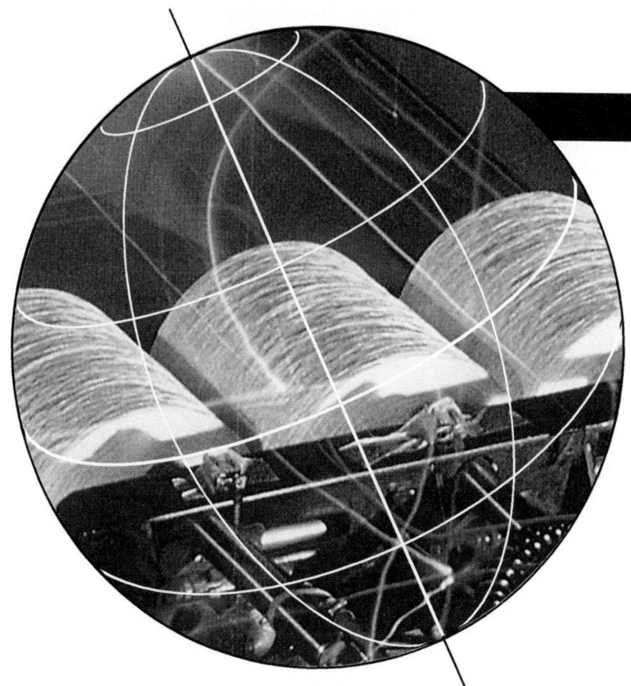

CHAPTER 6

Textile Fibers and Yarns

After studying this chapter, you will be able to

- list the main characteristics of natural and manufactured fibers.
- explain how fibers are marketed.
- summarize the role of leather and fur as primary materials in fashion.
- describe new fiber innovations.
- explain how fibers are made into yarns.

As you have already learned, fashion goods begin their creation with raw materials. The primary group of raw materials suppliers provides textiles, in the forms of fibers, yarns, and fabrics, as well as leathers and furs. These are the most basic "building blocks" that begin the process toward finished apparel, accessories, and household fashions. Fibers, leathers, furs, and yarns are discussed in this chapter. Fabric construction and finishing will be discussed in the next chapter.

The earliest planning of color and texture takes place at the primary level, 6-1. The raw material stage is the farthest from the final selling to consumers. In fact, primary-level companies sometimes work two or more years ahead of when the goods will be available at the retail level. Time must be allowed for many complicated production processes before the products are finished.

Fibers play a vital role in the design and care requirements of finished textile products. Fashion merchandisers should be familiar with fibers and understand their characteristics, to provide the right products for their target markets. Different fibers have specific properties that influence the appearance, strength, absorbency, warmth, shrinkage, and price of fabrics. These properties determine the appropriate uses and quality of the final fabrics.

Sulzer Rüti

6-1 Colors and textures must be carefully considered before fibers are produced so the fabrics and finished garments made from them are at the peak of fashion when they are eventually sold to consumers.

Some of the companies at the primary level perform only one step in providing the raw materials of textiles. Other firms are vertically integrated and perform several steps of the textile manufacturing process.

Fibers can be divided into two groups: natural fibers and manufactured fibers. Leathers and furs are not fibers, but are used in apparel products.

Natural Fibers

Natural fibers come from natural sources, such as plants, animals, and insects. Those fibers from plants are called ***cellulosic fibers***. The most popular plant fibers are cotton and linen, 6-2. Natural fibers from animals or insects are ***protein fibers***. Wool is the most popular protein fiber, and silk is another protein fiber. Most natural fibers are grown commercially by farmers or ranchers.

The Fashion Association/Sears

6-2 The garments in this outfit are made of cotton fibers. The accessories are made of leather.

Pendleton Woolen Mills

6-3 Grading is done to classify fibers according to their quality and value, such as length and fineness of fibers, strength, luster, and cleanness.

National Cotton Council

6-4 After the blossoms fall off cotton plants, cotton boll pods ripen and open. This allows the fiber to air-dry and become fluffy for harvest.

The quality of natural fibers can vary depending on the type of plant, animal, or insect and growing conditions. Price levels also vary according to the cost of producing them and their supply. Processing includes various steps of cleaning, straightening, grading, sorting and combing of the fibers after they are grown. See 6-3. The fibers are cheaper if there is a large supply, and more expensive if the supply is scarce.

Fibers vary in length. ***Staple fibers*** are short, in lengths under eight inches. Longer lengths of staple fibers are considered to be better quality than those of short lengths. Long, continuous fibers are called ***filaments***, and are measured in yards or meters. Silk is the only natural filament fiber.

Each natural fiber differs from the others, with unique characteristics that affect how it is worn and the care it requires. Most natural fibers are *absorbent*, or able to take up moisture, which allows them to be comfortable to wear and easy to dye. Without special finishing treatments, most also wrinkle when worn and shrink when washed.

Cotton

Cotton is a cellulosic fiber that comes from "bolls" (seed pods) of cotton plants, 6-4. It is grown in many of the southern states, as well as in China and other warm regions of the world.

Increasing consumer demand and use of natural fibers has caused higher production and larger supplies of cotton. At the same time, the fiber has become more competitively priced because of cost-saving production innovations. It is now fairly inexpensive and is the most popular fiber on the worldwide market, comprising almost half of the total worldwide fiber consumption.

Cotton is very comfortable to wear. It is soft and durable. It absorbs moisture quickly and dries fast,

National Cotton Council

6-5 Towels and washcloths are one of the largest end-use categories of cotton, just behind men's and boys' shirts, trousers, and shorts.

which gives a cooling effect and makes it ideal for hot, humid weather. It is used in blouses, shirts, dresses, jeans, underwear, and socks. For household items it is popular in towels, washcloths, sheets, bedspreads, curtains, slipcovers, tablecloths, and rugs. See 6-5.

New finishing treatments for cotton have reduced the fiber's tendency to shrink and wrinkle. However, washing and drying of cotton items at high temperatures is not recommended. Also, white cotton fabrics without applied finishes can usually be bleached. Bleach should not be used if a permanent press finish has been applied.

"Environmentally friendly" cotton is now grown in a range of colors, which eliminates much of the toxic waste and expense of the traditional chemical processing and dyeing usually done to the fiber. This naturally colored cotton has a luxurious feel and does not fade with washing and drying. However, it is not yet available in every color. Also, two harvests of cotton per season, rather than one, are anticipated in the future.

Wool

Wool is a protein fiber from the hair (fleece) of sheep or lambs. It is usually obtained by shearing the fleece twice a year, 6-6. Wool comes mainly from Australia and New Zealand, but is also produced in the U.S. Fiber quality depends on the breed and health of the sheep, the climate where the sheep are raised, and where on the bodies of the sheep the fibers originate. Merino sheep are said to produce the finest wool fibers.

Long staple wool fibers (over 2 inches in length) go into high quality ***worsted*** yarns and fabrics. Shorter wool fibers are used in less expensive *woolen* fabrics.

The Wool Bureau, Inc.

6-6 The fleece of sheep is removed close to the skin with large power clippers. The sheep are then put back out to pasture, unharmed, to grow another coat of wool.

Pendleton Woolen Mills

6-7 Fabrics are made from wool fibers that are used in fashionable jackets such as this one.

Silk Collection, Middleton, WI

6-8 This silk, splash-print nightshirt shows the beauty, luster, and drapability that enables the fiber to be used in luxurious apparel.

Silk Collection, Middleton, WI

6-9 Affordable silk garments, such as this summer blouse and slacks, are now widely available to consumers.

Wool is a versatile fiber with many end uses. It is a natural insulator, the warmest fiber, yet lightweight. It offers protection from changes in temperature and is used in winter clothes. Wool is slower than cotton to absorb moisture and to dry. It is popular because it is soft and *resilient*, or springy to return to its original shape when stretched or wrinkled.

In apparel, wool is most often used in sweaters, coats, suits, and accessories such as gloves, scarves, hats, etc. See 6-7. Other common uses are in blankets, rugs, and upholstery, since wool has some natural flame-retardancy. Wool will shrink and mat if machine-washed and dried, so most wool fabrics must be dry cleaned or hand-washed and laid flat to dry.

There are different categories of wool. The terms *pure wool*, *virgin wool*, and *100% wool* are interchangeable, and indicate new fibers that have never been used. *Recycled wool* fibers are recovered from previously made wool fabrics, shredded back into fibers from wool garments, cutting scraps, or mill ends. New wool is softer, stronger, and more resilient than recycled wool. It is used in fine apparel. Recycled wool is lower quality, and used in such things as camping blankets and coat interlinings.

Silk

Silk is a protein fiber from cocoons spun by silkworms. Workers soak the cocoons in warm water and unwind the long, natural filament fibers from them by hand or by machine. Approximately 1,000

International Linen Promotion Commission

6-10 The flax plant is a grass that looks like tall, slender reeds with small flowers. Linen fibers are taken from the long, wiry stem.

yards of continuous thread come from one cocoon. Threads from broken cocoons are used as staple fibers. Fabrics made from them have a rougher texture and are not as strong or lustrous as those from filament silk fibers.

Silk is known for its exceptional beauty, luster, and drapability. It is also a very strong fiber. It is "breathable" and can be worn year-round. It is used almost exclusively in luxurious apparel, such as wedding and evening gowns, blouses, dresses, and lingerie, 6-8. It is also made into suits, scarves, and men's neckties.

Silk is expensive to produce, has limited durability, and needs special care. Some silk fabrics are now washable, replacing dry cleaning with less costly, easier care. Also, silk is not commercially produced in the U.S. It is imported from silk-producing countries, such as China, Japan, and Thailand. Because of increased production, silk has become less expensive lately, which allows more consumers to purchase and wear silk garments. See 6-9.

Flax (Linen)

Flax is the world's oldest textile fiber. It is a stiff, absorbent cellulosic fiber made from the stem of the flax plant, 6-10. It is not commercially produced in the U.S., and mainly comes from Europe. The labor-intensive production of flax results in its fairly high price. Fabric made from the flax fiber is called *linen*.

Linen is known for its beauty and strength. It is durable, lustrous, and smooth. It is very cool to wear and is used for a wide variety of apparel, such as blazers, slacks, and skirts. See 6-11. Linen is also popular in fine tablecloths and bed linens. Its absorbency allows it to hold a great deal of moisture without feeling wet, which makes it ideal for dish towels, napkins, and handkerchiefs.

The Fashion Association/JCPenney

6-11 This Nehru jacket and matching pants are made exclusively of linen fibers.

A drawback of linen is its tendency to crease and wrinkle. At times, fashion trends have favored wearing wrinkled linen, but now wrinkle-resistant finishes and blends enable linen to hold a smoother finish. Linen should be dry cleaned, or laundered if it is treated to prevent shrinkage.

The specific characteristics and apparel uses of the most popular natural fibers are described in 6-12.

Other Natural Fibers

Ramie is a cellulosic fiber from the stalks of a woody, leafed plant called China grass, grown mostly in Asia. The fiber is lustrous, coarse and strong. In the past, it was mainly used for rope, canvas, and similar stiff items. Ramie is now combined with softer fibers to make fashionable, inexpensive warm-weather fabrics that resemble linen. Ramie has both apparel and household textile uses. Its care depends on the fibers with which it is combined and the final product in which it is used.

Other natural cellulosic fibers from plants include jute, sisal, raffia, and hemp.

Protein "specialty hair fibers" include camel hair, angora, mohair, cashmere, llama, vicuña, and alpaca.

Popular Natural Fibers

Fiber Name and Source	Fiber Advantages	Fiber Disadvantages	Typical Apparel Uses
Cotton Boll of cotton plant	strong, durable absorbent, cool quite inexpensive versatile uses soft, comfortable no static buildup stands high temperatures dyes and prints well	affected by mildew wrinkles unless treated or blended shrinks in hot water weakened by finishes, perspiration, sun burns readily no elasticity	underwear socks shirts jeans sportswear dresses blouses outerwear
Flax (Linen) Stem of flax plant	very strong resists dirt, stains absorbent, cool comfortable durable over time stands high temperatures smooth, lustrous lint-free	affected by mildew, perspiration wrinkles easily hard to remove creases expensive if good shines if ironed on right side burns readily ravels, shrinks	handkerchiefs suits dresses skirts shirts napkins medical cloths
Wool Fleece of sheep	very warm lightweight durable very absorbent comfortable resilient resists wrinkles creases well dyes well static resistant easy to tailor can be reused	weakened when wet affected by moths shrinks and mats with heat, moisture, and agitation needs special care, dry cleaning absorbs odors harmed by bleach, perspiration scratchy on skin pills	sweaters suits coats skirts socks slacks outerwear
Silk Cocoon of silkworm	lustrous smooth, luxurious very strong absorbent lightweight resists wrinkles, soil, mildew, and moths comfortable dyes well drapes well	expensive needs special care, dry cleaning water spots yellows with age weakens with perspiration, sun, soaps attacked by insects, silverfish	evening gowns wedding gowns lingerie blouses scarves dresses neckties suits

6-12 All natural fibers have specific characteristics that make them suitable for various types of apparel.

They are hair from animals other than sheep, such as goats, rabbits, and camels, and are available in limited quantities. They are priced higher than most other fibers.

Down is a fluffy feather undercoating of geese and ducks. It is lightweight and an extremely effective insulator. Down-filled comforters, sleeping bags, ski jackets, winter coats, and other products offer maximum warmth in very cold temperatures.

Marketing Natural Fibers

Although natural fibers have been used for thousands of years, no marketing efforts were made until manufactured fibers started to compete with them in the mid-1900s and threaten their popularity. The producers of natural fibers have worked together through trade associations to aggressively develop strategies to provide products with more desirable characteristics. They have also made extensive use of market research. This has led to blends and finishes that give natural fibers wrinkle-resistance, easier care, and closer properties to manufactured fibers to increase their popularity.

Natural fiber trade associations promote the favorable characteristics of their fibers to all levels of the fashion industry and to consumers. They disseminate information about new developments, offer color and fashion trend advice, and develop advertising and publicity kits. They prepare fashion styling reports and educational videos and posters for the trade, and for schools and consumer groups. They also help finished product manufacturers locate sources of supply of their

Cotton Incorporated

6-13 The Seal of Cotton is a registered service mark/ trademark of Cotton Incorporated.

The Wool Bureau, Inc.

6-14 The Woolmark label gives consumers the assurance of quality-tested fabrics made of pure wool.

The Wool Bureau, Inc.

6-15 The Woolblend mark assures consumers of quality-tested fabrics made predominantly of wool and blended with other fibers.

fibers. They often send out monthly newsletters and provide hangtags and labels with their logos to manufacturers of products made of their fibers. Some trade associations conduct seasonal clinics and workshops that include fashion shows along with their major promotional campaigns.

Almost all fiber trade associations provide *fabric libraries*, which contain sample fabrics for the upcoming fashion season, made of the particular fiber being promoted. Manufacturers, retailers, and auxiliary fashion professionals use fabric libraries to get information on new textile styling and color trends, locations of fabric suppliers, cost of fabrics, and new developments in fiber, yarn, and fabric production. The libraries also offer color cards, and product swatches and specifications.

Cotton Incorporated is a marketing and research organization. It acts as the product research, development, and promotional center for cotton producers, trying to increase cotton consumption and profitability. It prepares and distributes fashion forecast information to designers, manufacturers, the fashion press, and retailers. It advertises the use of cotton products, such as with "The fabric of our lives" media campaign. It also encourages manufacturers and retailers of cotton products to use the Seal of Cotton, 6-13.

The *National Cotton Council* is the central organization of the cotton industry. It disseminates educational materials about cotton. It also lobbies for trade legislation on behalf of cotton producers.

The *Wool Bureau, Inc.* is the U.S. branch of the International Wool Secretariat, which seeks to increase demand for wool. It is an association of wool growers that assists mills, manufacturers, and retailers in promoting wool and wool products. It develops special marketing and advertising programs. It researches new products and processes for economical wool production, and offers fashion forecasting and consulting to its members. Its Woolmark and Woolblend mark are shown in 6-14 and 6-15. To be labeled with these symbols, samples of the products must have passed quality testing by Wool Bureau inspectors for strength, colorfastness, and fiber content.

The *Mohair Council of America* is the promotional organization for U.S. mohair producers. It provides advice and information to users and producers of this specialty wool. It also distributes promotional materials and photographs about mohair, such as 6-16.

Mohair Council

6-16 The Mohair Council distributes promotional materials that illustrate the fashionable uses of mohair fibers to increase demand for garments made of mohair.

The Fashion Association/Willis & Geiger

6-17 The design of this leather flight jacket is inspired by those worn during World War II.

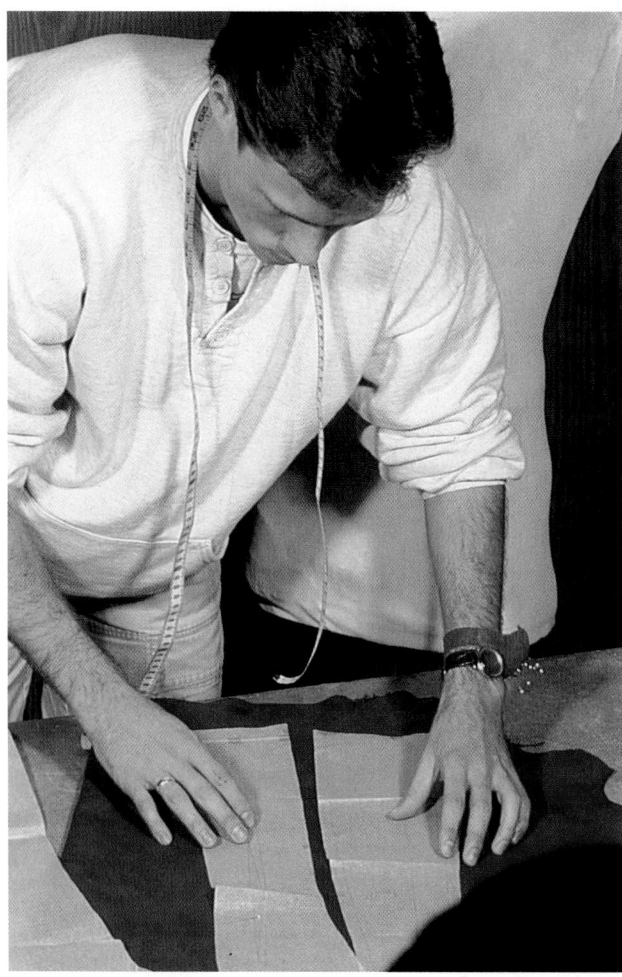

Oregon State University

6-18 Apparel design patterns for leather garments must be sized to be cut out of the hides being used.

For silk, the *International Silk Association* is located in New York City. Some marketing is carried out by individual mail-order companies that promote silk garments.

The *International Linen Promotion Commission* promotes linen fibers to all people concerned with fashion apparel and home-furnishings. It offers educational materials on the history and production of linen. It also guarantees the authenticity and quality of linen from Western Europe.

Leather and Fur

Leather, shown in 6-17, and fur are from the hides or pelts (skins) of animals. Even though they have been worn since before recorded history, their use is controversial today. Since animals must be killed to obtain hides, artificial substitutes have been developed to copy the leather and fur look. Also, real leather and fur are quite expensive since their supply is limited and their processing is complicated.

Leather

Leather is a tough, flexible material made by preserving animal hides through a process called tanning. *Tanning* converts the hides into finished, usable leather. This is time-consuming and highly

The Fashion Association/Allen-Edmonds Shoe Corporation

6-19 These hand-rubbed calfskin, four eyelet shoes are stylishly suited to complement most men's apparel.

specialized. The tanned hides come in pieces of various sizes, rather than continuous rolls of yard goods, 6-18.

The supply of leather in this country depends on the demand for meat rather than for leather. Since the hides are a by-product of the meat-packing industry, they are less expensive than those raised just for their skins. The most dominant leather in apparel is cattlehide, followed by other meat-providing animals. Reptile skins, from lizards, snakes, alligators, and various sealife are also used in fashion industry products. Some exotic types of leather cannot be used because they are protected under the Endangered Species Conservation Act, to prevent extinction.

U.S. leather producers are mainly located in northeastern and north-central states, and have sales offices or representatives in New York City. However, fewer U.S. companies now tan rawhides into leather. Cattle hides are exported to other countries worldwide, and a high percentage of finished leather and leather products are imported into the U.S. from countries such as Argentina, Great Britain, and Italy.

Specialized machinery and innovative methods of tanning have created new leather finishes, types of grains, intricate patterns, rich textures, deep colors, and other attributes. New chemical treatments have reduced the time required to transform hides into leather. Leather is priced by the square foot and is available in a variety of thicknesses and weights.

Top grain leather is the high quality "genuine leather" used in most consumer products. The largest fashion market for leather is footwear, 6-19. Leather is also used in handbags, belts, gloves, wallets, and luggage. Garments made of leather include pants, skirts, coats, vests, and jackets, 6-20. Additionally, leather is used for upholstery in the home-furnishings market, for car interiors, and other uses.

The Marketing of Leather

The leather industry must respond to consumer needs and wants, just like other fashion industry segments. Leather tanners conduct research and promotional programs. They work closely with trade associations to develop new designs and uses for leather. Because of the long processing time involved, fashion trends must be determined two years or more ahead of when the final products will reach the market.

Saxony Sportswear Company

6-20 Vests and jackets made of leather are fashionable garments that offer protection, prestige, and never go out of style.

Leather tanners and finishers do not promote their services to consumers. Advertising is done by designers and manufacturers of the final products.

The primary trade association for leather tanners is the *Leather Industries of America (LIA)*, which has its offices in Washington, DC. It lobbies the government for legislation that is favorable to leather-related companies. It also disseminates technical and fashion information to producers, retailers, consumers, and the press. It publishes an industry newspaper, offers periodic color seminars, and holds a school for people involved in buying and selling leathers.

Tanners introduce their leathers in several different trade shows around the world each year, which attract garment manufacturers, equipment suppliers, and retailers. Many trade fairs are also held for finished leather goods, such as shoes and bags. The Leather Apparel Association represents leather-goods manufacturers and retailers, as well as other companies associated with the industry. Member companies place a hangtag on their garments, guaranteeing customer satisfaction and instructing consumers about proper leather apparel care.

Fur

Fur is the soft, hairy coat of an animal. Processed fur pelts are used for "prestige" apparel and accessories. The warmth, protection, and luxurious beauty of fur has been recognized since prehistoric times. Higher status has been sought by many people in history by wearing furs.

The fur industry includes animal pelt producers, fur processors, and product manufacturers. Most are small companies with highly skilled workers. Much of this activity is done in Canada, Europe, and Asia. In the U.S. it is done in and around New York City, 6-21.

Pelt producers breed and raise the animals on fur farms or ranches. Hardly any trapping of animals is done anymore. The pelts of fur are then matched by quality and color, and auctioned in bundles to fur processors and manufacturers. Pelt prices can fluctuate sharply depending on fur supply and fashion demand.

Fur processors "dress" the pelts to make them soft, flexible, and more suitable for use in consumer products. The pelts are cleaned, stretched, and sometimes dyed to improve their appearance. Then *product manufacturers* make them into finished coats, jackets, garment trimmings, and accessories.

The U.S. is known for producing top quality furs, and many are exported to foreign markets, especially to Japan. On the other hand, the U.S. imports many lower priced fur garments. About half of the dollar amount of furs sold at retail in the U.S. is imported, mainly because of the lower costs of fur production in Asia.

The Marketing of Fur

Like the leather industry, the small companies of the fur industry rely mostly on group efforts for promotional activities. Pelt producers, fur processors, and product manufacturers work together to promote fur products through trade associations.

Fur business associations and federations are located in many countries of the world, to set standards, regulate the practices of industry members, disseminate information, and enable networking and communications to take place among members. Fur auctions are held at various times and places, during which companies sell and buy pelts. Fashion fairs and expositions are also held around the world to promote and sell finished fur garments.

The main trade journal for fur industry businesses is *Fur Age*. Its sister company, *furs.com*, is an online consumer magazine. It offers the latest fur fashion news, fur facts, tips about fur care, fur shopping advice, and other information.

Fur garments are generally sold through showrooms of furriers or through leased departments within stores, 6-22. They are also sold through consignment, mail-order catalogs, or special weekend events held in

6-21 In the fur district of New York City, fur pelts are often moved through the streets to manufacturers who make them into finished garments.

6-22 Retail stores that sell fur garments also usually clean and store the jackets and coats of consumers during the warm summer months when the items are not being worn.

hotels or convention centers. A *furrier* is a manufacturer of fur items. Furriers often have a salesroom where garments are sold to the public and usually offer cleaning and storage for fur garments. A *leased department* is an area located within a retail store owned and operated by someone else. With ***consignment selling***, the retailer accepts merchandise to sell in the store but does not own it. The store receives a percentage of the sale price. Garments not sold by a certain date are returned to the producer/owner.

In past decades, target customers for fur garments have been middle-aged women. However, now furs are worn by women or men of any age. Also, less expensive furs, such as raccoon, beaver, muskrat, and rabbit have become more fashionable, as well as fur trim on traditional cloth garments.

Because of the efforts of concerned animal rights groups, many consumers prefer to wear "faux" (artificial) furs that are made from textile fibers. Anti-fur activists have attracted media attention by protesting at trade shows, demonstrating in front of stores, and confronting people wearing fur garments. Their goal is to publicize the fact that animals are killed to obtain the fur. They want to make wearing fur unfashionable.

The *Fur Retailers Information Council* was formed to try to combat anti-fur activity and project a positive image of the fur industry. Other fur industry efforts include providing consumer information, and educational campaigns in favor of fur. Meanwhile, fiber producers are trying to duplicate the look of fur garments more closely so consumers can satisfy their personal choice of either real or artificial fur products for warmth, beauty, and an identity statement.

Manufactured Fibers

Manufactured fibers are created from various substances and chemicals through technology in laboratories. *Cellulosic manufactured fibers* are made from cellulose from plants, such as soft wood pulp, and are transformed into usable fibers by applying chemicals that "regenerate" the cellulose. Others are *noncellulosic manufactured fibers*, or "synthetic" fibers, made of various petrochemical mixtures of crude oil, natural gas, air, and water. Notice the basic origins of natural and manufactured fibers in 6-23.

Because the making of manufactured fibers is controlled by production schedules of large chemical companies, and essentially requires only raw materials, power, and labor, there can be a constant supply resulting in stable inventories. Also, there is more uniform size and quality than with fibers produced by nature. Thus, the price of manufactured fibers varies less, too.

Regardless of the raw materials and chemicals used in various manufactured fibers, they all go through the same steps to become fibers:

Basic Fiber Origins

Natural Fibers		Manufactured Fibers	
Protein (from animals)	**Cellulosic (from plants)**		**Noncellulosic (from petrochemicals)**
wool silk	cotton linen	acetate lyocell rayon triacetate*	acrylic anidex* aramid azlon* glass lastrile* metallic modacrylic* novoloid* nylon nitril* olefin polybenzimidazole polyester rubber saran spandex sulfar vinal* vinyon*

*Not currently produced in the U.S.

6-23 Natural fibers can be categorized as protein or cellulosic, while manufactured fibers are either cellulosic or noncellulosic from petrochemicals.

1. Solid raw materials are melted with heat or dissolved by chemicals to form a thick, syrupy liquid.
2. The liquid is extruded (forced out) through a ***spinneret,*** which is a nozzle with many tiny holes, similar to a bathroom showerhead. Each hole forms a filament fiber.
3. The filaments are stretched and hardened to become usable fibers.

Manufactured fibers are produced in a filament state. They are often *crimped* (curled or waved) and/or cut into staple lengths to create a similarity to natural fibers.

As with all fibers, each manufactured fiber has both advantages and disadvantages.

Categories of Manufactured Fibers

Manufactured fibers are categorized by ***generic groups***. A generic name identifies each family of manufactured fiber with similar chemical composition, 6-24. Generic names are assigned by the Federal Trade Commission. A new generic category is established only when a fiber is developed that is different in chemical composition from other fibers.

DuPont Company

6-24 Nylon produced by every manufacturer would have a similar chemical composition to this nylon fiber.

Most generic groups contain ***variants***. Each variant is a manufactured fiber modified slightly (within its generic group) during production, resulting in a change in its properties. The basic fiber is altered physically or chemically. It might be extruded from the spinneret in shapes such as round, octagonal, trilobal (three-sided), and so on. Also, certain additives put into the solution can produce different characteristics.

Variants are given *trade (or brand) names* by companies to identify the specific fibers they manufacture and sell, 6-25. Such names are always capitalized, and may have a special trademark, or symbol, that identifies them. The trade name or trademark, and the process for making the particular fiber are registered by that company with the U.S. Patent Office. No other producer can make that exact variant, or use the trade name, unless licensed to do so by the company holding the patent. Since the fiber manufacturer's identification is on the finished goods, the merchandise is almost always of a higher quality. Those businesses that use the fiber farther down the pipeline can capitalize on the publicity and promotional materials distributed by the fiber manufacturer. Sometimes fiber producers have several different variants within a generic category.

Commodity fibers are sold by generic groups and are not identified with any specific manufacturer. They are sold to anyone on the open market, with no restrictions placed on their end use and no implied or required standards of performance claimed. They have no quality assurance and are often imported into the U.S. from foreign countries. The producer of the fiber is not identified to the consumer and usually feels no obligation as to expectations for the product. Trade named variants cost more than commodity fibers.

Characteristics of Manufactured Fibers

Manufactured fibers have some qualities that are unique or superior to those of natural fibers, such as strength or elasticity. Most are versatile, nonallergenic, strong, and resistant to *abrasion* (surface wear and rubbing). Manufactured fibers usually launder well and resist moths and mildew. They are wrinkle-resistant and often require no ironing. Some are "heat-sensitive" with a low melting point that allows them to be heat-treated to set pleats, mold shape, or emboss fabric designs.

Monsanto Fibers

6-25 The acrylic fibers in this outfit have the trade name Acrilan. Acrylic fibers made slightly differently by other manufacturers have different trade names.

Some manufactured fibers feel clammy when worn because they do not absorb moisture or "breathe." Those that are nonabsorbent also build up static electricity that causes them to "spark" and cling to the wearer. They can be surface cleaned with a damp cloth since their smooth, nonporous surfaces do not hold dirt and grime. However, oil and ground-in stains are difficult to remove.

Currently popular generic categories and variant trade names are listed in 6-26. It is important for people interested in fashion merchandising to know the

Popular Manufactured Fibers

Generic Name and Some Trademarks	Fiber Advantages	Fiber Disadvantages	Typical Apparel Uses
acetate Celebrate Chromspun Estron Microsafe	Silk-like luster/feel Drapes well Does not shrink Resists moths, mildew, pilling Inexpensive Easy to dye Versatile	Poor abrasion resistance Weak Heat sensitive Special care for cleaning Dissolved by nail polish remover	Dresses Blouses Linings Lingerie Shirts Scarves Neckties
acrylic Acrilan BioFresh Bounce-Back Creslan Cresloft Duraspun MicroSupreme Pil-Trol Sno-Brite So Lara	Resembles wool Lightweight Soft, fluffy Warm, bulky Resilient, retains shape Resists weather, moths, chemicals, mildew, wrinkles Lustrous Colorfast Elastic	Low absorbency Static buildup Surface pills Heat sensitive	Sportswear Sweaters Infant wear Socks Knitted garments Pile fabrics Jackets Skirts Fake furs Bathrobes
aramid Kevlar Nomex	Strong, stretch-resistant No melting point Resists abrasion, most chemicals Resilient, supple Flame-resistant	No stretch Nonabsorbent	Protective clothing Helmets Bulletproof vests
lyocell Fibro Galaxy Lyocell by Lenzing Tencel	Soft Biodegradable/environmentally friendly Strong Absorbent, easy to dye	Tends to wrinkle	Blouses Sport shirts Dresses Jackets Slacks
modacrylic SEF Plus	Bulky, warm Resilient Easy to dye, colorfast Resists wrinkling, flames, abrasion Retains shape Dries quickly Resists chemicals, acids Soft, lightweight	Heat sensitive Static buildup Weak Surface pills Heat sensitive Nonabsorbent	Furlike fabrics Coats Trims Pile linings Knitwear Sleepwear Sportswear Fleece fabrics
nylon Anso Antron Cantrece Caprolan Eclipse Matinesse MicroSupplex Shimmereen Silky Touch Zeftron	Very strong and durable Lightweight Dries quickly Lustrous Supple Resists mildew, moths, chemicals, wrinkles, abrasion Retains shape, resilient Colorfast Easy care	Low absorbency Surface pills Damaged by sun Picks up oils and dyes in wash Static buildup Heat sensitive	Sweaters Hosiery Lingerie Skiwear Underwear Windbreakers Dresses Raincoats Swimwear Blouses

6-26 The many different manufactured fibers available today permit fabrics to be made that are right for specific end uses.

(continued)

Popular Manufactured Fibers *(continued)*

Generic Name and Some Trademarks	Fiber Advantages	Fiber Disadvantages	Typical Apparel Uses
olefin (polypropylene) Alpha Elustra Essera Impressa Innova Nouvelle Spectra Trace	Resists abrasion, chemicals, stains, mildew, pilling, wrinkles, static Not affected by weather, aging, perspiration Excellent wicking Thermal warmth Comfortable Strong, durable Very lightweight	Heat sensitive Poor dyeability Nonabsorbent	Knitted socks Sportswear Nonwoven fabrics for industrial apparel Filler in quilted goods Disposable diapers
polybenzimidazole PBI Logo	Flame-resistant Comfortable Chemically stable		Firefighters' coats Astronauts' space suits
polyester Comforel Coolmax Dacron Diolen Fortrel Hollofil Microloft MicroMattique Microselect Serelle Thermoloft	Resilient; colorfast Strong/durable Easy care Resists wrinkles, abrasion, chemicals, perspiration, mildew, moths Can be heat set Easy to dye Does not stretch or shrink Most popular manufactured fiber	Low absorbency Spun yarns pill Takes oily stains Static buildup	Permanent press fabrics Fiberfill insulation Shirts, blouses Dresses Slacks Suits Underwear Sportswear Children's wear
rayon Fibro Galaxy Viscose by Lenzing	Very absorbent Drapes well Dyes and prints well Soft, pliable Comfortable Inexpensive Colorfast No static or pilling	Wrinkles easily unless treated Low resiliency Heat sensitive Will mildew Shrinks in hot water unless treated Stretches Weak when wet	Linings Blouses, shirts Dresses Lingerie Sportswear Neckties Jackets Accessories
spandex Cleerspan Dorlastan Glospan Lycra	Very static, good recovery Resistant to lotions, oils, perspiration, sun, flexing Lightweight Strong, durable Soft, smooth Easy care	Yellows with age Heat sensitive Harmed by chlorine bleach Nonabsorbent	Swimwear Skiwear Foundation garments Support hose Slacks Exercise wear Fashion apparel
triacetate No longer produced in the U.S.	Resists wrinkles and fading Easy care Resilient Can be heat set Dries quickly Lustrous Does not shrink	Nonabsorbant Weak Static Buildup Low abrasion resistance	Blouses Dresses Lightweight knits Bonded fabrics Pleated garments
vinyon No longer produced in the U.S.	Good elasticity Resistant to mildew, chemicals, fungi,moisture	Heat sensitive	Waterproof clothing Work clothes Bonding agent in nonwovens

the fiber advantages and disadvantages, and the typical apparel uses of each of the generic groups. Also, the meaning of descriptive terms should be learned. For instance, notice that one fiber advantage of olefin is its excellent ***wicking*** ability. Wicking is the dispersing or spreading of moisture or liquid through a given area, such as pulling body moisture to the surface of a fabric where it can evaporate. That certainly relates to its uses in socks, sportswear, and disposable diapers.

Fiber Innovation

The U.S. is the world's leading innovator and producer of manufactured fibers. ***Innovation*** is the creative, forward-thinking introduction of new ideas. Fiber chemists work in laboratories to link molecules of carbon, hydrogen, nitrogen, and oxygen into long chains of chemical compounds called ***polymers***. With the polymers, fibers are engineered to meet specific needs, such as being flame-resistant, antistatic, or soil resistant. Fibers are designed for specific end-uses.

Limited quantities of a new or modified manufactured fiber are usually first produced in a ***pilot plant*** on an experimental basis. This is small-scale trial production, using commercial factory methods, to make enough fiber to check its behavior in fabrics and end uses, and to check fiber-making procedures. If research shows that both industry and consumers will accept the new product, mass production begins. New applications for the fiber are then explored and new industries are consulted and encouraged to use it.

Sometimes ***missionary selling*** must be done for a newly developed product. This is convincing customers that they need a product before trying to sell it to them, which may include helping to sell it through the rest of the chain via demonstrations, arranging displays, or planning advertising programs. The product may be so new that retailers and consumers do not yet know they should have it!

The expensive procedures of fiber research and development are carried on by many companies at the same time. The company that is first to develop a unique new variant may not have the field to itself for long. There is strong competition among the various producers of manufactured fibers, and each new product can be made specifically to match market demands. With a list of customer desires, such as for a stretchable, wrinkle-resistant fiber that provides warmth without weight, it is not surprising that several companies come up with the same answer at the same time. New trademarks appear continually as modified manufactured fibers are developed. They replace old ones that are discontinued.

Manufactured fiber producers are particularly active in helping fabric companies with new yarn ideas, developing optimum blends and constructions, improving dyeing and finishing techniques, and evaluating consumer reaction to the fabrics made from their fibers. Technical bulletins on the proper methods of processing their fibers are issued to the trade. These are supplemented by available expert advice on specific problems relating to yarn, fabric, or garment production. Swimsuit fabrics now resist fading from sunlight, saltwater, and swimming pool chlorine. Fabrics used in exercise and active outdoor wear pull moisture away from the skin to the surface where it can bead up and evaporate. The wearer stays dry and warm.

The Latest Fiber Trends

A new generic group is *lyocell,* a cellulosic manufactured fiber. It is heralded as being environmentally friendly. It is biodegradable, and made from wood pulp from trees grown in managed, constantly replanted forests. The chemical agents used to produce it are recycled. Lyocell fibers are strong, highly absorbent, and blend well with other fibers. They were originally marketed in basic garments, but are now in fashion goods. Other new fibers are being developed from renewable resources, such as corn.

A new recycling process is now turning plastic soft drink bottles into "earth friendly" fibers for apparel. After the old plastic bottles are cleaned and ground into pellets, the plastic is converted into a polyester fiber that is physically and chemically comparable to fiber made from new material. This reduces the use of new petroleum products, and trash going to landfills. It takes five 20-ounce plastic bottles to make fabric for a T-shirt in size large. Environmentalists are especially excited about the fact that the material can be repeatedly recycled. Since polyester is very durable and does not lose its performance attributes, this can be done over and over.

"Microfibers," or microdenier fibers, have become popular on the fashion scene lately, too, 6-27. ***Denier*** is the term used to describe fiber thickness or diameter. The smaller the denier of the fiber, the softer and more pliable it is. For instance, an 840-denier filament is used in truck tires, while a 15-denier filament is used in sheer pantyhose.

Microdeniers are ultra-fine; less than one denier per filament, which is about half the denier of fine silk. They are being made of polyester, nylon, and other manufactured fibers. Fabrics made from them are soft, luxurious, and drapable. The fabrics are also wrinkle-resistant, wind-resistant and water-repellent, yet breathable. They have been used primarily in rainwear

DuPont Micromattique™

6-27 These slacks are made of a soft and silky fabric of microdenier polyester fibers.

DuPont Lycra®

6-28 This cropped top, relaxed jacket, and fluid skirt are made of a polyester and nylon blended with spandex fiber that adds wearing comfort and ease of movement.

and active sportswear, but are spreading into fine garment categories.

Another trend has been the addition of spandex fiber in blends with other fibers to make stretchable fabrics. It only takes a tiny percentage of spandex to gain built-in stretch and recovery in fabrics, but which then also need special handling during cutting and sewing. The super-stretch spandex polymer fiber has been elevated from its past uses in girdles and bathing suits to today's fine sportswear, designer evening gowns, and fashionable outfits, 6-28.

Manufacturers, retailers, and consumers must be educated about how to handle, use, and care for each new fiber innovation. Most new products are first aimed at the expensive end of the market, where designers, consultants, and the trade press shape fashion trends. Later, they filter down to regular use while other new products take advantage of upscale market opportunities.

Industry experts predict that in the years ahead, new types of generic fibers with properties not even dreamed of today will be developed. In the future, fibers may be produced with built-in thermostatic molecules that will keep people warm in winter and cool in summer. Fibers may even protect against disease!

The Marketing of Manufactured Fibers

Manufactured fibers compete with each other for popularity, as well as competing against natural fibers. Companies use advertising, publicity, and market research, and extend various customer services to manufacturers, retailers, and consumers. Producers of manufactured fibers sell their fibers to fabric manufacturers as unbranded commodities or as brand-name fibers.

Trademarked variants assure consumers that the quality of the fiber has been controlled by its producer. Often, the fiber producer also requires standards of performance from the end product manufacturer. Product warranty and certification programs permit the use of the fiber trademark only to those manufacturers later in the pipeline whose fabrics or end-use products pass tests set up by the fiber producer for their specific applications and quality standards. They may specify wear testing or blend levels, and offer technical services to help correct a fabric that fails to pass a qualifying test. A warranty verifying the quality and performance is given to the consumer on a hangtag or label attached to the finished product. A replacement or refund is assured if the garment made of the fiber fails to give normal wear for a particular period of time.

Chemical companies that produce fibers maintain a steady flow of advertising and publicity to the trade and to consumer markets. Thanks to such promotional campaigns, consumer recognition of generic categories is high, and producers now concentrate on consumer recognition of their trade names. They also help to advertise the manufacturers who use their fibers. Often, ***cooperative advertising*** is done, in which the costs are shared by more than one organization, such as a manufacturer and retailer. This encourages consumers to associate the fiber with a familiar manufacturer or retailer and lowers the advertising costs of the companies involved since they are splitting the cost.

Fiber manufacturing companies belong to the *American Fiber Manufacturers Association, Inc.,* a trade organization that promotes the use of manufactured fibers. Based in Washington, DC, it carries on an active program of consumer education, government relations, and foreign trade policy on behalf of the U.S. manufactured fiber industry.

National Cotton Council

6-29 Many tiny fibers are spun together into thicker, long yarns to be constructed into fabrics.

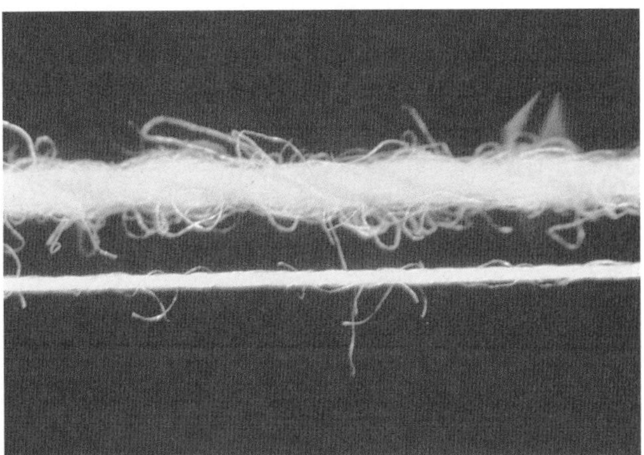

The Wool Bureau, Inc.

6-30 Spinning of short staple fibers produces a looser, fuzzier yarn (top of photo). Long staple fibers are spun into a tighter yarn with fewer fiber ends (bottom of photo). Filament yarns have no fiber ends at all sticking out from them (not shown).

Spinning Fibers into Yarns

The next step after fiber production is yarn production, which transforms the raw fibers into heavier, continuous strands of yarn. This is done through the process of ***spinning,*** which draws, twists, and winds individual fibers into long, cohesive strands, 6-29. The yarns are wound onto bobbins, also called spools. Yarns vary in size, with some being coarse and fluffy, while others are finer than sewing thread.

Filament fibers can be in monofilament or multifilament yarns. *Monofilament yarns* are simply single filaments, usually of a high denier. *Multifilament yarns* are made by twisting together many single filaments to make a thicker strand. For manufactured filament fibers, this is usually done simultaneously with fiber extrusion from the spinnerette, and called *solution spinning.*

Staple fibers (both natural and manufactured) go through a *mechanical spinning* procedure to be held into a continuous strand, 6-30. Such *spun yarns* and sewing thread are made in yarn mills.

Yarns spun from staple fibers are more irregular than filament yarns. The ends of the short fibers project out from the yarn surface to produce a fuzzy effect. Spun yarns are also bulkier than filament yarns of the same weight. Thus, they are more often used for porous, warm fabrics, with rougher surfaces, that have a more natural feeling and snag less than fabrics of filament yarns. However, spun yarns have a tendency to *pill,* or form little balls of fiber on the surface, from wearing or use.

The Fashion Association/Pronto Uomo, Div. of Mondo, Inc.

6-31 In this sweater, wool is blended with other types of fibers to offer better shape retention and easier care.

By giving varying amounts of twist during spinning, many different kinds of yarns can result. As the degree of twist is increased in any yarn, the yarn becomes harder, more compact, and less lustrous. Yarn mills produce simple yarns for classic fabrics, such as denim, and novelty yarns, as used in decorative sweaters.

Ply yarns are formed by twisting together two or more single yarns. Each yarn strand is called a ***ply***. A "four-ply" yarn would have four yarns twisted together. This is done when extra strength, more bulk, or unusual effects are desired.

Staple fibers are sometimes used without spinning to fill pillows, mattresses, sleeping bags, and comforters. This is called *fiberfill.*

Yarn Blends and Textures

Yarn characteristics can also be changed by varying the fiber content. Fiber blending brings together the best properties of two or more fibers into yarns and fabrics that offer easy care and other desirable behavior. Most often, a natural fiber is combined with one or more manufactured fibers. By knowing the advantages and disadvantages of individual fibers, the performance of fabrics containing them can be judged.

A *blend* is made when two or more fibers (usually in staple form) are put together before being spun into yarn. This uniformly mixes fibers with different physical characteristics to try to get the best performance feature of each. Different percentages of fibers in blends produce specific results. When blended properly, the positive qualities of one fiber can decrease the negative properties of another fiber. The resulting fabrics have better performance and nicer appearance, 6-31. The cost of the fabric is also lowered if natural fibers are blended with less expensive manufactured fibers.

Combination yarns contain two or more yarn plys, each of different fibers. Sometimes spun staple yarns, used for softness, are combined with filament yarns, that add strength. Another form of combination yarn might mix yarns of various fiber compositions or twist levels.

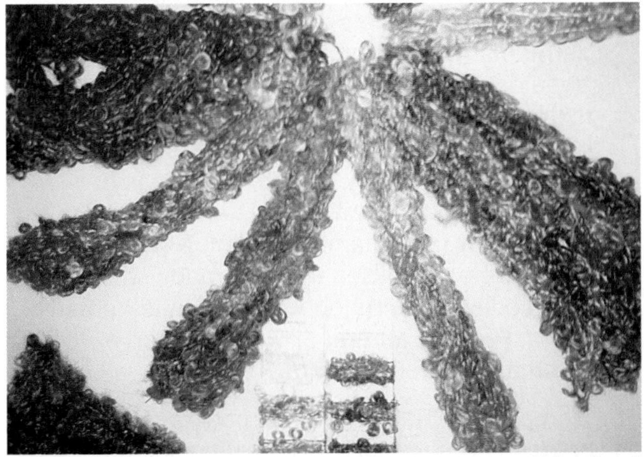

Mohair Council

6-32 These highly crimped yarns would be used in bulky sweaters. They are sometimes referred to as "novelty yarns" since most regular yarns are much straighter.

Yarns of manufactured fibers are usually ***textured*** by processing with chemicals, heat, or special machinery. This adds visual surface characteristics. Wool fibers, on the other hand, have a natural crimp, which makes them ideal for spinning into bulky yarns that trap air to form insulating barriers against the cold, 6-32.

Texturing gives bulk, stretch, softness, and wrinkle-resistance to yarns. Filament yarns are twisted and manipulated in such a way that the filaments no longer lie exactly parallel to each other. The increased space between the filaments allows the development of special qualities. When made into fabrics, textured filament yarns have more resemblance to spun yarns, but give better durability.

The Marketing of Yarn

The major trade association of this segment is the *American Yarn Spinners Association, Inc.,* located in North Carolina near the major spinning mills. The association deals with the government on such yarn-industry issues as trade laws, customs regulations, packaging and labeling, and product standards. It collects economic data to anticipate yarn production and marketing trends. It also holds seminars and workshops for its members that cover technology, strategic planning, labor relations, cost controls, and other subjects.

Summary

Raw materials, from which textile products are made, play a vital role in the design, uses, and care qualities of finished fabrics. The earliest planning of color and texture takes place at this raw-materials level, which is the farthest from the final consumer. Fibers can be divided into two categories: natural and manufactured.

Natural fibers are cellulosic or protein, from plants, animals, or insects. The most popular natural fibers are cotton, wool, silk, and linen. Other natural fibers include ramie, specialty wools, and down. Natural fibers are marketed through trade associations, that promote the favorable characteristics of the fibers and offer information to the fashion industry and consumers.

Leather and fur are also raw materials used in fashion products. Hides are a by-product of the meat-packing industry and are made into leather by the process of tanning. Fur has strong status appeal, but is controversial. The many small companies that deal with leather and fur rely on trade group efforts for promotional activities. Advertising is also done by the manufacturers and retailers of the final products.

Manufactured fibers are made by chemical companies. They are either cellulosic, from regenerated plant material, or noncellulosic, from petrochemicals. They are categorized by generic groups, and sometimes sold as commodities of those groups. Most generic groups also contain slightly modified variants, each of which is given a trade name by the company that owns the patent.

Fiber innovation is done by chemists who engineer polymers into fibers that meet specific needs. The latest manufactured fiber trends include a new environmentally-friendly generic group; the recycling of plastic bottles into polyester; microfibers; and spandex blends in fashion garments. Companies use marketing approaches of advertising, publicity, market research, and services to manufacturers, retailers, and consumers.

The process of spinning twists fibers into monofilament, multifilament, or spun yarns. Ply yarns are made of more than one yarn, and fiberfill is not spun at all. Blends and combination yarns can bring together the best properties of fibers. Yarns are also textured to add visual surface characteristics.

To Know

cellulosic fibers
protein fibers
staple fibers
filaments
worsted
consignment selling
spinneret
generic groups
variants
commodity fibers
wicking
innovation
polymers
pilot plant
missionary selling
denier
cooperative advertising
spinning
ply
textured

To Review

1. Name three raw materials in the primary group of the soft goods chain.
2. Why should fashion merchandisers be familiar with the characteristics and care requirements of fibers?
3. Name one natural staple fiber and one natural filament fiber.
4. If a fiber is absorbent, why is that an advantage?
5. What does it mean when you say a fiber is resilient?
6. Why is silk considered to be a specialty fiber?
7. What do fabric libraries contain?
8. Name one trade organization for each of three of the natural fibers that does marketing or promotion for that fiber.
9. Why are leather and fur expensive?
10. What does this country's supply of leather depend upon?
11. The fur industry includes what three main segments?
12. Why can there be a constant supply and stable inventories of manufactured fibers?
13. How does the wicking ability of olefin relate to its uses in socks, sportswear, and disposable diapers?
14. Where does a pilot plant operation fit within the development of a new fiber?
15. What is the procedure called when manufactured filament fibers are spun into multifilament yarns as they are extruded from the spinneret?
16. What are advantages of microdeniers?
17. What manufactured fiber (generic category) is used in small amounts in blends with other fibers to make stretchable fabrics?
18. Who shares the costs of cooperative advertising?
19. Describe monofilament, multifilament, and spun yarns.
20. What is the difference between blends and combination yarns?

To Do

1. In a small group, research one fiber. Prepare an illustrated oral report for the class that describes a brief history of the fiber, how it is processed, its uses, and why its specific characteristics make it a good choice for its particular uses.
2. Research one of the specialty wool fibers. Make a bulletin board display that shows the animal from where the fiber originates, in what part of the world it is produced, its most common apparel uses, and the fiber characteristics that make it unusual.
3. Visit a specialty retailer that only sells leather goods and one that only sells fur garments. If possible, talk to the store managers to find out the profiles of their target customers, the range of products they carry, how and where their products are made, how the stores advertise or promote their businesses, etc. Write an essay that describes your findings.
4. Visit a department store to check the fiber content on the labels of five different kinds of garments (fancy, casual, sport, diapers, socks, sweater, etc.), or find five advertisements for textile products in magazines and newspapers. Note the type of garment, its intended uses, level of fashionability, and its generic fiber content. Also notice if there is any promotion of a particular trade named variant. Notice the price levels of articles that are made with commodity fibers as opposed to trade named fibers. Prepare an oral or written report summarizing your findings.
5. Find a cooperative advertisement for textile products in a magazine or newspaper. Mount the ad and prepare a written report that explains who the advertisers are, what their products are, brand names they are promoting, and why it is advantageous to advertise together.

Chapter 7
Textile Fabrics and Finishes

After studying this chapter, you will be able to

- identify the most common fabric constructions.
- describe the main fabric finishing procedures.
- recognize the importance of quality and performance standards.
- summarize important aspects of the textile industry.
- explain how finished fabrics are sold down the chain.
- cite textile industry trade information.
- tell about future predictions for textiles.

After fibers and yarns have been produced, yarn is sold to textile mills where fabrics are constructed. If fabrics are going to be made with previously dyed colored yarns, they may be ready to sell as yard goods after textile production, 7-1. Fabrics that are produced as greige goods are dyed, printed, coated, or otherwise finished to make them fashionable and functional to be sold for their desired end uses.

Pendleton Woolen Mills

7-1 Fabrics made with colored yarns are often woven into stripes, plaids, or checks and do not need further dyeing after being constructed.

Fabric Design and Construction

The appearance and performance of fabrics depends on their fiber content, type of yarn, fabric construction, and finishing. These factors can be varied to make millions of specific textile products with different characteristics. The two major forms of fabric design are structural and applied design.

Structural design is achieved by "building in" texture or interest to fabrics when they are manufactured, 7-2. The most common ways to construct apparel fabrics

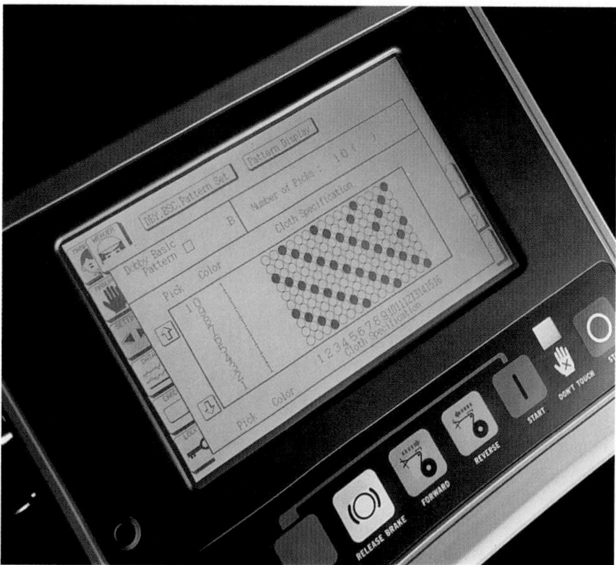

Sulzer Ruti

7-2 This touch screen computer terminal allows a weaving operator to control the machine that does the structural design and construction of the fabric.

are by weaving and knitting. Other methods are used less often. Within the weaves and knits, the types and sizes of yarns can be varied in interesting ways.

Applied design is accomplished by adding color, pattern, or other design features to the structural design after the basic fabric has been made. An example of this is shown in 7-3.

Weaving

Weaving is the procedure of interlacing two sets of yarns at right angles to each other, usually done on a loom, 7-4. The lengthwise yarns are called *warp yarns*, and are threaded onto the loom side-by-side and pulled tight. They must be strong and durable to withstand the strain of the weaving process.

The crosswise yarns are called *weft (*or *filling) yarns.* A "shuttle" on the loom pulls them back and forth, from side to side, over and under the warp yarns to form the fabric. A ***selvage*** forms where the filling yarns turn at the fabric's edge to go back the other direction. The selvage, which is strong and will not ravel, is along both edges of the fabric.

Grain is the direction the yarns run in the fabric. Warp yarns form the *lengthwise grain.* They run parallel to the selvages. Weft yarns run along the *crosswise grain.* In woven fabrics, the crosswise grain stretches more than the lengthwise grain. The grain is important in apparel, since garments need to stretch more around the body than up and down. The warp yarns should go up and down in garments for strength and stability.

Bias grain is diagonal on the fabric. ***True bias*** runs at a 45-degree angle, or halfway between the lengthwise and crosswise grains. The greatest amount of stretch in a woven fabric is along the true bias. Note the selvage and grain lines shown in 7-5.

Fashion Institute of Technology

7-3 Applied design goes onto the surface of fabrics after they are in yard goods form.

The Fashion Institute of Design and Merchandising, California

7-4 This hand loom shows the same procedure of weaving that is done with huge industrial weaving looms at textile mills.

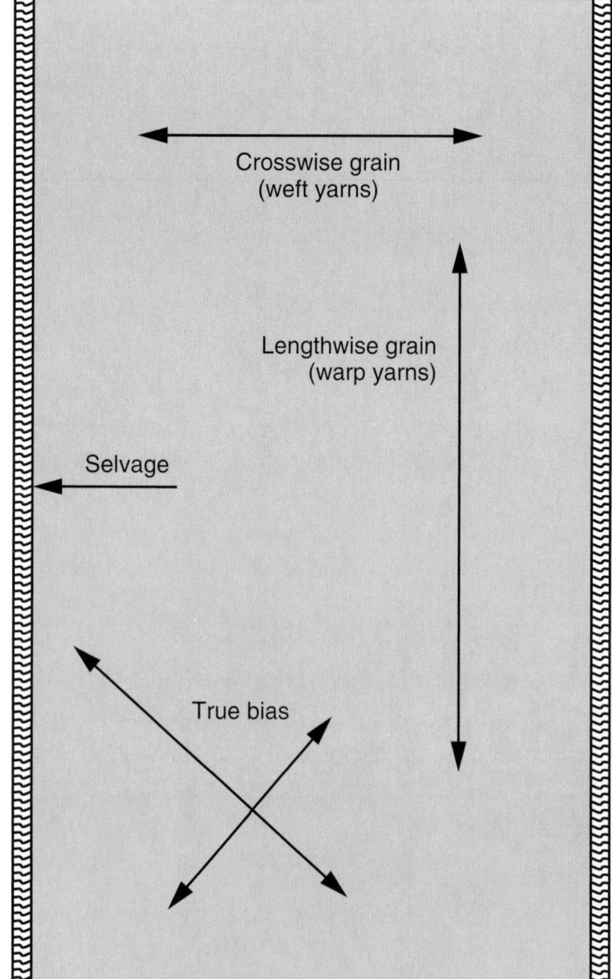

7-5 The way the lengthwise, crosswise, and bias grains of a fabric are used in garment construction determines where there is strength, stability, stretch, or other design or fit considerations.

Types of Weaves

The three basic weave types are plain, twill, and satin. They differ by passing the weft yarns over and under different numbers of warp yarns. They also have different appearance and durability characteristics. Other weaves are variations of one or more of the three basic weaves.

The simplest and most common weave is the *plain weave*, 7-6. Usually the lengthwise and crosswise threads are the same denier, passing alternately over and under each other, similar to a tennis racket, but much closer together. This creates a fabric that is strong, reversible, and durable.

Plain Weave

7-6 The plain weave is simple and is used in more fabrics than other weaves.

The appearance of a plain weave can be changed by using large yarns with small ones, textured yarns, or a special finish. The *basket weave* is a common variation of the plain weave, formed by using two or more yarns as one. In the common two-by-two basket weave, two weft yarns pass over and under two warp yarns.

In the *twill weave*, a yarn in one direction "floats" (passes) over two or more yarns in the other direction at regular intervals. Each float usually begins one yarn over from the last one. This causes a dominant yarn to be seen on the surface of the cloth, creating a diagonal rib pattern, 7-7.

Most twill weave fabrics are very firm and tightly woven, which produces strong, durable fabrics. Twill weave fabrics resist wrinkles and hide soil. Variations have floats that might be long or short. Large, high-twist, or textured yarns also create different looks. The angle of the diagonal pattern may vary from a reclining slope to a very steep slope.

The *satin weave* has long yarn floats on the surface in one direction, 7-8. They go over four or more yarns and under one, and each float begins two yarns over from where the last one began. This produces a very shiny fabric surface of yarns running almost entirely one way.

Twill Weave

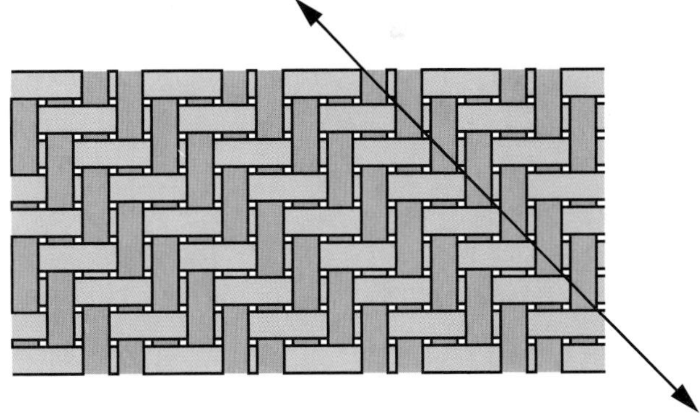

7-7 The fabric surface of twill weave fabrics has a diagonal wale.

Satin Weave

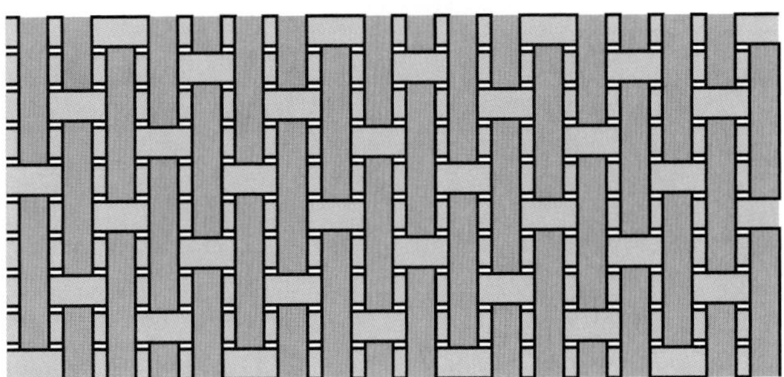

7-8 The long floats on the surface of the satin weave cause light to reflect, resulting in a shiny appearance.

Weaves

Examples of ***plain weave fabrics*** *include:*

muslin	percale	gingham
chiffon	broadcloth	taffeta
organdy	poplin	seersucker
sailcloth	chambray	shantung

Basket weave fabrics, a variation of the plain weave, include:

hopsacking	monk's cloth	oxford cloth

Examples of ***twill weave fabrics*** *include:*

denim	gabardine	serge
surah	ticking	

Herringbone designs in fabrics are made with a twill weave with wales that change directions at regular intervals to produce a zigzag effect.

Examples of ***satin weave fabrics*** *include:*

satin, with the floats running in the warp direction
sateen, with the floats running in the filling direction.

Satin usually has more luster than sateen.

7-9 The three basic types of weaves are used to create a variety of fabrics.

The satin weave is smooth, slippery, and drapable. It is good for formal wear and linings. When the yarns are woven tightly, the fabric is stiff and strong. When the yarns are loosely woven, they resist wrinkles and are more pliable. However, in general, this type of weave is the least durable because the floating threads tend to catch on other surfaces when worn. This causes snagging, pulling, and friction, resulting in pills and a duller sheen.

Study 7-9 to see examples of fabrics constructed with the three basic types of weaves.

Variations

Variations of the three basic weaves can create interesting structural designs in woven fabrics. Stripes, checks, plaids, and other patterns are made with different colors of yarn woven in specific patterns.

Large, intricate designs are woven on a *Jacquard loom.* The loom is programmed to raise and lower specific warp yarns for each passage of the shuttle. Damask, tapestry, brocade, and fabrics with an inserted woven name are made in this way. See 7-10.

Sulzer Ruti

7-10 This sophisticated, Jacquard-pattern mattress ticking has eight different weft yarn colors. Beautiful brocades are also made this way for evening gowns.

Sulzer Ruti

7-11 This looped terry cloth has extra design characteristics built in by changing the pile height for a "wavy effect" and adding different colored yarns.

Pile fabrics have loops or yarn ends projecting from the surface. Terry cloth in towels is a good example of loops, 7-11. Corduroy, velvet, and fake furs have clipped yarn ends. Extra weft yarns usually form the pile.

Cut pile fabrics have a *nap*, which is a layer of fiber ends raised from the surface. Nap appears different when the fabric is viewed from various directions because fiber ends lying at diverse angles reflect different amounts of light. The nap must run the same direction throughout an entire finished product or the different parts will have inconsistent color, shading, or pattern.

Knitting

Knitting is a fabric construction method of looping yarns together. One yarn can form the entire fabric by interlocking a series of loops together, done a row at a time, back and forth, or in a continuous, circular pattern. The knitted fabric or garment becomes longer as rows of loops are interlocked into the previous loops. The loops, or stitches, can be varied to create numerous patterns and textures. The number of stitches, or loops, per inch is the *gauge*. A higher gauge number indicates a closer and finer knit, 7-12.

Knitted fabrics have natural flexibility and stretch built in by the knitting process. They tend to move with and fit the body shape comfortably, and are versatile and wrinkle-resistant. They are very popular for use in active sportswear, sweaters, and travel wardrobes. They do not ravel, like woven fabrics, but can get lengthwise "runs" from broken yarns, as seen in nylon stockings. They can also snag or come unknitted if the yarn is pulled.

Almost all knitting for garments sold in retail stores is done on commercial knitting machines. The West

Nicklaus for Women/Hartmarx Corporation

7-12 The body of this shirt has a textured pattern in a lower gauge than the fine, smooth, higher-gauge knit of the collar.

Coast, especially California, has the largest concentration of knitted fabric producers.

Types of Knits

Circular knitting machines make knitted fabrics in tube form, 7-13. Flat knitting machines make flat knitted fabrics, 7-14. The two basic methods of knitting fabrics are weft knitting and warp knitting. Their structures and characteristics are shown in 7-15.

Weft (or *filling) knits* have one yarn strand that forms a horizontal row of interlocked loops. The

National Cotton Council

7-13 Yarns feed into this circular knitting machine that makes a tubular fabric.

Hong Kong Trade Development Council/Fang Brothers Knitting Ltd.

7-14 This flat knitting machine in Asia uses the same procedures as similar machines in knitting mills throughout the world.

commercial process is essentially mechanized hand knitting, done on either circular or flat machines. Specially designed circular knitting machines can make properly-sized tubes for such items as hosiery, underwear, and socks. Large circular widths are also cut open and used as flat fabric.

Basic Knits and Their Characteristics

Type of Knit	Structural Drawing	Fabric Names	General Characteristics
Weft Yarns run across		Single knits Jersey Purl knits Ribbed knits Double knits Interlock knits Sweater knits	Made on circular or flat machine Can be full-fashioned Stretchy May run if snagged Cut edges may curl Great versatility
Warp Yarns run lengthwise		Tricot Raschel knits	Made only on flat knitting machine Stable and durable Do not ravel; have selvage edges Quite run-proof Limited stretch Versatile

7-15 Weft knitting yarns form interlocking loops in horizontal rows across the fabric. Warp knitting yarns are interlocked in a lengthwise zigzag pattern.

With flat machines, the number of stitches can be automatically increased or decreased to shape the finished garment. This reduces the cutting and sewing of garment parts, and makes a finer garment. Sweaters and dresses often have this *full-fashioned* shaping.

Single knit fabrics are made on single needle, weft knitting machines. Single knits will often run if snagged, and cut edges may curl or roll. Also, they stretch in both directions and may stretch out of shape. They are lightweight, soft, and drapable. They are most often found in formal wear, lingerie, and T-shirts.

Double knit fabrics are made on double needle, weft knitting machines. Loops of two yarns are drawn through from both directions to knit two layers interlocked as one. Plain double knits look the same on both sides. They have "give," but are more firm and stable than single knits, and will not sag or stretch out of shape. They are used in dresses, slacks, suits, and coats.

Purl knits have prominent crosswise ridges. They are reversible since both the back and face are the same. They have superior stretch and recovery in both directions. Rib knits have pronounced lengthwise ridges. They have excellent crosswise stretch, which makes them good for waistbands, neckbands, and cuffs, rather than for whole garments.

Sweater knits are very stretchy and are usually loosely knitted. Their large denier yarns resemble hand-knitting, 7-16. *Textured knits* are made from filament yarns that have been permanently crimped, coiled, curled, or looped.

Other knitted patterns are made by changing the placement of smooth and bumpy stitches. A Jacquard knitting machine makes complex designs and textures. Tremendous pattern variety can be achieved with combinations of these stitches.

Warp knits are only made on flat knitting machines, with many yarns and needles. Each yarn is controlled by its own needle, forming long lengthwise rows in a zigzag pattern. This is the fastest way to make fashion fabrics.

Warp knits are stable, durable, and relatively run-proof. They are usually lightweight, tightly knit, and stretch only in the crosswise direction. Large quantities can be produced inexpensively. In yard goods form, they can be recognized by their straight selvage edges.

Tricot is the most familiar warp knit. It does not run or ravel, but cut edges have a tendency to curl. It is used for drapable or clingy dresses, shirts, and lingerie.

Raschel knits are made on the raschel knitting machine, which can make fabrics from heavy crochet-like knits to sheer net or lace effects. It knits stripes, checks, and diagonal patterns. Raschel knits usually have lots of texture and limited stretch.

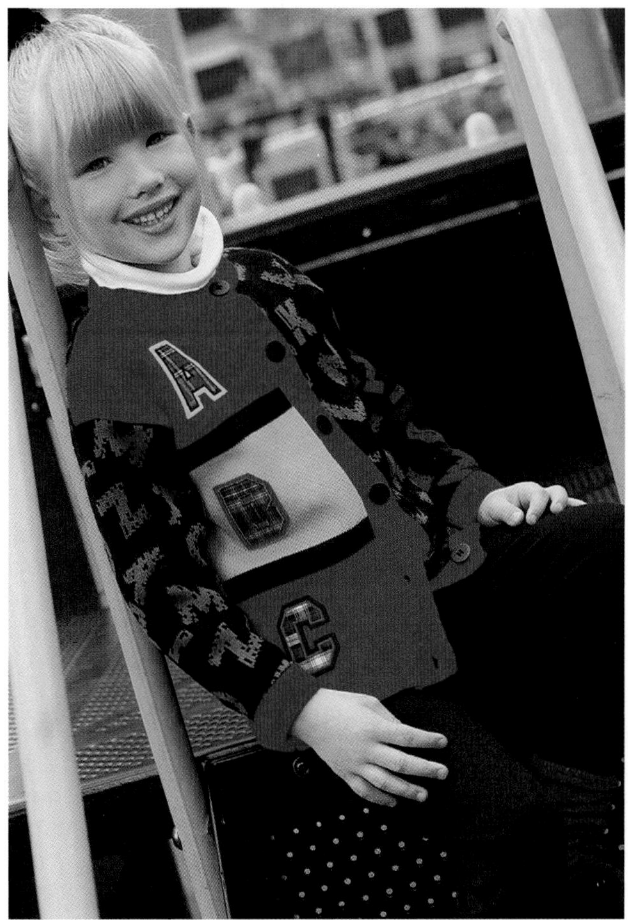

Monsanto Fibers

7-16 Sweater knits imitate the look of knitting that can be done by hand with knitting needles.

Other Construction Methods

Although weaving and knitting are the most popular ways of making fabrics, several other methods can also be used to produce yard goods or to permanently join more than one layer of fabric.

Nonwoven fabrics

Nonwovens are made from a compact web of fibers, not yarns, held together with a combination of moisture, heat, chemicals, friction, and/or pressure. Sometimes a glue-like chemical "binder" is added, or manufactured fibers can be melted together because of their chemical makeup. Also some nonwoven fabrics are made by machines that mechanically tangle the fibers into a mat. They are used for padding or as batting in quilts.

Nonwoven fabrics have no grain line. They have minimum stretch, and their cut edges do not ravel. Since they are relatively inexpensive, many are used for industrial and medical purposes where they are *disposable* (thrown away after use, rather than being laundered and re-used).

Other nonwovens are used in garment interfacings, such as in collars and cuffs, to give strength and support.

Vinyl and urethane *films* are thin, nonwoven "sheets" that are not made from fibers, but can be finished to look like leather or woven fabrics. Often they are used to coat other fabrics. The coated fabrics are used for raincoats, umbrellas, purses, shoes, and household textiles, such as tablecloths.

Artificial suedes are nonwoven fabrics made by combining polyurethane with fine polyester fibers. When made into garments, their raw cut edges can be left exposed like real suede or leather, since they do not ravel or fray. Also, their surfaces can be stamped, embossed, painted, or perforated for unique textures.

Laces and Nets

Laces and nets are openwork fabrics made by crossing, twisting, or looping yarns into designs. Knots often hold the threads together, or continuous coils of thread may loop through each other to form a mesh. See 7-17. Laces and nets can be fine or coarse.

Braided Fabrics

Braided fabrics are made by *braiding*, also called *plaiting*. Three or more yarns are interlaced to form a regular diagonal pattern down the length of the resulting cord. Braided fabrics are usually narrow. They are used for decorative trims and shoelaces, and are sometimes joined together to make rugs.

Bonded Fabrics

Bonding is a method of permanently laminating together two layers of fabric that are already constructed. Sometimes a chemical adhesive is used, or the layers may be fused with a web of fibers that melts when heat is applied. Bonding provides stability, strength, body, or opacity (inability to see through). Sometimes bonding serves as self-lining to eliminate the need for a separate garment lining.

Bonded fabrics have more body and wrinkle less than single fabrics. They do not fray or ravel. They are warm without being heavy, which makes them popular for skiwear and winter coats.

Fusible web is a sheet of binder fibers that can act as an adhesive between two layers of fabric because it has a relatively low softening point. For home sewing, it is used for hemming or other garment construction processes when a heated iron is placed on fabrics that have web between them. Iron-on patches and interfacings have a fusing substance only on the wrong side so they can stick to other fabrics when a hot iron is applied.

Quilted Fabrics

Quilted fabrics consist of a layer of padding (or batting) sandwiched between two layers of yard goods. The three layers are usually held in place by machine stitching around decorative areas or shaped spaces. Sometimes fabrics are quilted by *pinsonic thermal joining*, which is done by a machine that uses ultrasonic energy

7-17 Lace is crocheted into this open work poncho for a vintage look.

to join layers of thermoplastic materials. The ultrasonic vibrations generate localized heat, which results in a series of "welds" that fuse the materials together in the chosen "quilted" design.

Fabric Finishing

Fabric finishing is done by applying colors, designs or surface treatments that change the look, feel, or performance of fabrics. Businesses that convert greige goods to finished fabrics, and distribute those fabrics, are called ***converters.*** Textile converters anticipate demand and fashion trends to create finished fabrics that satisfy consumer needs. They are positioned between greige goods, textile mills, and apparel manufacturers on the pipeline, at the end of fabric production.

The plants that handle the various textile production stages, including converters and print and dye plants, may or may not be owned by one company or be geographically near each other. Some companies that were independent converters in the past, have been acquired by textile mills to become an integrated part of the mill. Converters usually do not handle woolen or worsted fabrics, industrial fabrics, or knit goods because those are produced as finished textiles or products.

Small, independent converters fill particular fashion niches and can offer "fashion-forward" goods in small yardages. They usually employ one or more fabric designers to create end products that suit the needs of their soft goods customers. The independent converters buy greige goods and contract with various dyers, printers, and finishers as needed. They are very flexible in their design possibilities because they do not own production equipment, but take advantage of the specialized machinery of others. They can quickly change their fabric styles to adjust to customer demands. They can sell a wider range of fabric types and can be more "risk-oriented" with their products.

There are many possible processes in fabric finishing, including bleaching, dyeing, printing, and adding finishes.

Bleaching

Bleaching is a chemical process that removes any natural color from fibers or fabrics. It is done to create white yard goods, or as a process before dyeing or printing a fabric. Bleaching removes impurities (sizings, oils, and waxes) that may have accumulated during the manufacturing process so that applied colors will be "true." It is also done to intentionally fade products, such as in "stone washed" jeans. See 7-18.

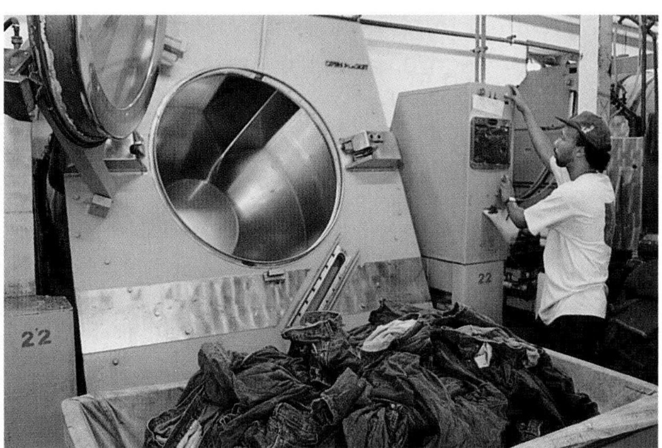

Universal Denim Services

7-18 Although bleaching is often done to "purify" greige goods before dyeing or printing them, it has become a popular process to intentionally fade blue jeans.

Dyeing

Dyeing is a method of giving color to textiles using coloring agents called *dyes.* Dyes of natural or chemical origin react differently with various fibers. Some dyes that color one type of fiber are useless on others. Colors have traditionally been developed in laboratories where dyes are skillfully blended to match specific colors, 7-19. Today, computers are programmed to mix dye colors, which gives speed and uniformity to the process. Dyeing penetrates textiles so the right and wrong sides are the same color.

The term ***colorfast*** implies that the color in a fabric will not fade or change with normal expected use and care. This should include laundering, dry cleaning, sunlight, perspiration, and rubbing. Colorfastness depends on the chemical makeup of the dye, the fiber content of the product, and the method of dyeing.

Textile products are dyed at the fiber, yarn, fabric, or garment stage of production. Dyeing later in the pipeline gives more accurate responses to fashion market demands.

PANTONE® TEXTILE Color System®/Pantone, Inc.

7-19 Color standards are available for companies to match their yarns, fabrics, and sewing notions. The same color can then be matched by everyone throughout the fashion industry.

Fiber Dyeing

Fiber dyeing involves adding color to fibers before they are spun into yarns. The dyes penetrate the loose fibers, resulting in uniform color and good colorfastness. Colored fibers can be mixed in yarns and fabrics for almost unlimited patterns and effects. Natural fibers are said to be *stock-dyed*, or "bale-dyed," at the fiber stage. Manufactured fibers can be *solution-dyed*, in which the color is part of the fiber-making solution that is extruded through the spinneret. Clear, rich colors result, since the pigments are a structural part of the fibers.

Yarn Dyeing

Yarn dyeing is done by placing the yarns into a dye bath after they have been wound onto spools, but before being made into fabrics, 7-20. This gives good color absorption, and an opportunity to design fabrics with woven stripes, checks, plaids, and Jacquard patterns with different colored yarns. Plain fabrics, in a coordinating color, can be woven or knitted for related apparel separates.

Burlington Industries

7-20 After being wound onto spools at the spinning mill, uncolored yarns are put onto holders and submerged into a dye bath until the color has penetrated thoroughly. After drying, the yarns are made into fabric.

Piece Dyeing

Piece dyeing is a process where fabrics are dyed after they have been woven or knitted into greige goods, 7-21. Rollers pass lengths of fabric through the dye bath or over rolls of applied dye. Piece dyeing is the most common, least expensive, and fastest method of dyeing textiles. Less complete dye penetration is achieved, but large amounts of greige goods can be stored. They are then dyed in the latest fashion colors just before the fabric is sold to apparel manufacturers for cutting and sewing into garments.

Most piece-dyed fabrics result in solid colors, except those that are cross-dyed. In *cross dyeing*, a fabric is made of two or more fibers that take dyes differently. When such multifiber fabrics are placed in dye baths containing different compositions of dyes, the fibers are colored in various predictable ways. This can result in plaids, checks, heathers, or other patterns.

Garment Dyeing

Garment dyeing is gaining popularity because it gives manufacturers flexibility late in the pipeline, after fashion demand has been determined. Used mainly for knitted garments, it enables producers to make fast, market-responsive deliveries of orders to retailers. Apparel is manufactured of undyed yarns or greige goods, in various styles, but without buttons or labels. When specific orders are received, often through Quick Response linkages, the garments are dyed in the requested colors, and promptly labeled and shipped.

Printing

Printing is a process for adding color, pattern, or design to the surface of fabrics. It is done on the "right" side, with the "wrong" side being unprinted or much

National Cotton Council

7-21 In piece dyeing, lengths of greige goods are colored by one of several methods. "Pad-batch" dyeing, shown here, is similar to printing on paper.

lighter than the right side. It is most successful on fabrics made of absorbent fibers so the dyes in the print can penetrate deeply into the fibers.

Overall prints are the same across all of the fabric. They are the most common, and the easiest for apparel manufacturing. *Directional prints* have a specific direction to them, such as with animals or cars that must be used in a certain direction. *Border prints* have a distinct border design, usually along one or both sides of the fabric. They are used artistically in apparel, such as with the border running along the bottom of a skirt. Fabrics printed with a border around all sides of a large square are used for scarves.

Even or *balanced plaids* are the same in both the lengthwise and crosswise directions. The design matches if a corner is folded back across the center of any repeat. A checked design is an example of an even plaid. *Uneven plaids* are different in one or both directions. For instance, they may be different to the right and up than they are to the left and down, 7-22. This makes it harder for apparel manufacturers to "match" the lines of the plaid at garment seamlines.

There are several basic methods of printing textiles, including roller, screen, rotary screen, heat transfer, and ink-jet printing, as well as other methods.

Roller Printing

Roller printing, a simple, high-speed method, applies color directly to fabric as it passes between a series of metal rollers that are engraved with the design. A different roller is used for each color. The engraved part of each roller is full of dye paste and transfers the color directly onto the fabric.

Sulzer Ruti

7-22 Although this plaid is woven rather than printed, it is easy to tell that this is an uneven plaid since it has yellow stripes in the lengthwise direction that are not present in the crosswise direction.

Roller printing produces large quantities of designs inexpensively, but is being replaced with newer technology. The printing quality can vary according to how well the design was etched on the rollers and how carefully the fabric was fed through the rollers. When the design is printed crooked or looks blurred, the print is "out of register."

Screen Printing

Screen printing is an old art done by hand on flat screening frames, similar to stenciling. Each color requires a separate stretched screen made of a sheer fabric with some areas painted to resist dye. The untreated areas of the screen allow dye to pass through onto the fabric being printed. Screen printing gives better quality designs than roller printing, and is used for logos, symbols and large repeats.

Rotary Screen Printing

Rotary screen printing is a combination of the first two methods and has become widely used. It is accurate, fast, and efficient. Dye is transferred through separate cylinder-shaped, design treated, nylon screens that roll over the fabric. Dye colors go through the open sections of each screen, printing the design.

Heat Transfer Printing

Heat transfer printing is increasing in popularity as an efficient and economical method in which special dyes in the desired colors and patterns are placed onto paper using a rotary screen printer. The paper is placed on the fabric and, with heat and pressure, the colors and patterns are transferred from the paper to the fabric. Since paper is smooth, complicated designs with a good deal of depth and color can be produced. T-shirts are often printed with small heat transfer designs.

Digital Printing

Digital (electronic) *printing* is the newest method for printing small lots of fabric fast, more cheaply, in finer detail, and with an extremely wide range of colors. It is like ink-jet printing with an office computer, but rolls fabric through an extra-wide printer. Huge, computer-driven ink-jet textile printers have arrays of micronozzles that spit droplets of colors onto fabrics moving through them. Computerization allows for efficient design setup (eliminating the preparation of printing plates), a greater variety of design options, and electronic storage of designs. It gives flexibility for short runs, greatly reducing response time to fashion trends. It prints small samples or long yardages on demand at low cost. Additionally, this electronic printing method is environmentally safe, using much less water than traditional printing methods, and the dyes lie on the cloth's surface. This, in turn, allows printing to be done onto many different fibers, with the colors matching exactly. Some computer-controlled printing is also being done with photocopying machine technology.

Flocking

Flocking is a specialty procedure that prints a design onto fabric with an adhesive (glue substance). Then small pieces of fluffy material are sprinkled over the fabric. They stick to the glue in the desired pattern to produce design with texture.

Finishes

The appearance, feel, and performance of fabrics can be improved by applying *finishes.* These coatings specifically impart wearing advantages, ease of care, or other desired characteristics for the end use of products. See 7-23. Less desirable characteristics of fibers can often be controlled. However, finishes cannot improve the basic quality of fabrics, which depends on the particular fibers, yarns, and method of construction. Fabric finishes may also reduce the absorption and coolness of a fabric.

DuPont Teflon

7-23 These coats manufactured by Newport Harbor are treated with a fabric protector for water and stain resistance.

Most textile finishes are *permanent,* lasting the life of the garment, or *durable*, lasting through several launderings or dry cleanings before losing their effectiveness. A *temporary* finish lasts only until the fabric is washed or dry-cleaned. Starch is an example. A *renewable* finish is temporary, but can be replaced or reapplied. Some stain- or water-resistant finishes on such items as trench coats and upholstery fabrics are renewable.

A term that ends in *proof*, such as waterproof, means complete protection. A term with *resistant* or *repellent*, such as water-repellent, means that the finish provides partial protection.

A combination of fabric construction and finishing creates the hand of fabrics. ***Hand*** is the way fabrics feel to the touch. Characteristics such as drapability, thickness, softness, firmness, crispness, elasticity, and resiliency can be judged by feeling a fabric carefully. The hand of a fabric can determine how appropriate it is for a certain type of garment or end use.

There are many separate finishes for fabrics. They all fall within two main categories: mechanical and chemical finishing processes. Fabrics can receive finishes from one or both categories, as well as being bleached, colored, and/or printed.

Mechanical Finishes

Mechanical finishes affect the size and appearance of fabrics. They can give the fabric surface a smooth and flat look, or a napped or brushed texture. They are done by mechanical methods, rather than with chemicals.

Heat, moisture, drying, and stretching are used to give fabrics their correct length and width. Preshrinking is also done with heat and moisture. A lustrous, smooth, polished surface, or embossed designs, result when fabrics are passed between heated cylinders or rollers. If the rollers revolve at different speeds, rubbing occurs for a soft surface, such as for polished cottons. Some fabrics are singed with heat or flame to give a smooth, flat finish.

Corduroy undergoes cutting to create rows of cut pile. Some fabrics are brushed with stiff, metal-bristled brushes to remove loose fibers, threads, and lint, as well as to produce a napped finish. Shearing is done to trim fiber or yarn ends. Pressing and pounding give a flat, harder surface. These are all examples of mechanical finishes.

Chemical Finishes

Chemical finishes usually affect fabric performance. They enable fabrics to better serve their intended purposes. The finishing agents chemically react with the fibers to become part of the fabrics.

Various chemical finishes make polymer manufactured fibers more absorbent and softer. The luster, strength, and dyeability of cellulosic textiles is increased with a process called *mercerization.* Antistatic finishes prevent garments from clinging to the body of the wearer. There are also chemical finishes to make fabrics crease-resistant, mildew-resistant, moth-resistant, and stain-resistant. Children's sleepwear is often given a flame-retardant finish.

Fabric Finishes

Finish	Results
Antistatic	Prevents buildup of static electricity so clothes do not cling to wearer
Bleaching	Whitens cellulosic fabrics
Brushing	Removes short, loose fibers from fabric surface, giving a soft, even pile
Calendering	Makes the fabric surface smooth and polished
Crease-resistant, wrinkle-resistant	Reduces/prevents wrinkling of fabrics
Flame resistant	Prevents fabrics from burning easily by reducing oxygen supply or chemically changing the fibers
Mildew resistant	Prevents mildew on fabrics
Mercerization	Improves luster, strength, and absorbency of cellulosic fabrics
Moth-resistant	Repels moths and carpet beetles from attacking wool fibers
Napping	Produces a raised, fuzzy fabric surface by pulling up fiber ends
Permanent press, durable press	Eliminates ironing after laundering and reduces wrinkling during wear
Preshrunk, Sanforized®	Prevents fabrics from shrinking more than a small amount
Scotchgard®	Surface protection against oil and water
Sizing	Provides extra body and weight to fabric with a starch solution
Soil release	Helps fabrics release stains and dirt during laundering or cleaning
Waterproof	Prevents water from soaking into fabric
Water-repellent	Helps fabrics resist water

7-24 Compatible finishes are applied to particular fabrics depending on the fiber content and intended end use.

A *permanent press* finish is a resin applied to certain fabrics (especially cotton/polyester blends) to help them retain their original shape and resist wrinkling during wearing and after laundering. Since spots and stains are sometimes hard to remove from blends that have a permanent press finish, a soil release finish can also be added.

New wrinkle-resistant finishes are now popular for 100 percent cotton fabrics. They are especially popular in men's dress shirts and casual pants. Chemical finishes can also reduce shrinkage, add glazing, and make fabrics stiffer and heavier. See the description of specific finishes in 7-24.

Quality and Performance Standards

Quality is the degree of excellence of a product. Textile grading helps to determine the proper market for specific goods. Customers relate the quality and price of products to indicate value for their needs. ***Quality standards*** rate textiles and other products according to levels of defects. See 7-25. ***Performance standards*** rate their suitability for specific end uses.

Burlington Industries

7-25 Companies inspect their fabrics as they are woven. If a defect is detected, the loom can be stopped immediately and the problem corrected.

Textiles are tested with specialized equipment to measure them against the standards and to evaluate their characteristics and properties. For example, laboratories might try to measure the resistance of fabrics to abrasion, snagging, and flammability. Colorfastness during laundering is tested, and woven and knit fabrics are measured for their elasticity. The added cost of testing textiles is cost-effective if problems are discovered and corrected that would have prevented satisfactory use. Being *cost-effective* means the benefits outweigh the expense.

The *International Organization for Standardization (ISO)*, representing about 140 nations, has developed "ISO 9000" standards to certify the quality of goods and services internationally. Rather than focusing on product standards, companies must have systems in place to scrutinize quality. Registered companies are evaluated for design, development, production operations, service, and other business categories. Certification implies consistently high quality and usually helps companies have better business methods as well as increased sales in the global marketplace. Many companies in Europe and other countries will not buy products from firms that are not ISO certified.

Sulzer Ruti

7-26 State-of-the-art CAD systems can create both intricate structural and applied designs for fabric construction.

The Textile Industry

Specialized companies of different sizes perform the various stages of the textile segment of the chain, but many have merged together to create fewer, stronger companies. They offer many different products that occupy large markets. Many textile mills are located in the southeastern part of the U.S., where labor and land costs are low. Most have sales offices in New York City.

Some textile firms are vertically integrated to include the processes from buying fibers to selling finished fabrics or garments. For instance, pantyhose producers often knit filament nylon yarns directly into the finished product that is distributed to retail stores. Most knitwear is produced by integrated companies.

Textile companies must coordinate technology, fashion, and marketing skills to be successful. The three areas are interdependent.

Technology

Technology involves new manufacturing machinery and procedures to match production with market demand for fabrics that have the desired characteristics. Constant research and development have brought innovations in computerization to make textile design and manufacturing faster and better. Automation reduces the amount of labor needed in production processes, giving more uniform quality to the goods produced, as well as lower costs. New machines combine higher production speeds with lower energy usage. Environmental damage from chemicals and wasted textile materials have also been reduced.

Computer-aided design (CAD), designing with computer equipment, has shortened product development cycles since both structural and applied designs can be created electronically. Many previously time-consuming hand manipulations are done quickly and accurately today with CAD systems, 7-26. CAD is now a necessary business tool.

By combining CAD with *computer-aided manufacturing (CAM),* production controlled electronically, woven and knit patterns are developed on computers which also automatically control the looms and knitting machines. Besides sending messages to production machinery directly from a computer, images can be printed out for

Info Design, Inc.

7-27 The ability to combine technical design and perfect simulation enables all people involved to see the expected results and make changes before the actual fabric is made.

merchandising decisions, 7-27. Computers also enable firms to calculate production costs and figure the selling prices of fabrics before they are knitted or woven. CAD/CAM technology increases the capacity to innovate and lowers overall costs for textile designing, construction, and finishing. With today's automation, mills are more flexible and less dependent on labor and can track all procedures through the production line.

Applied textile patterns are designed on computers by writing with a wand on an electronic tablet. Scanners can also input designs that already exist, such as logos. Computers can brighten or fade colors, reduce or enlarge motifs, and combine multiples of the same motif. See 7-28. They can also give related printing specifications. Designs can be saved in the computer and called up for later use.

Fashion

Fashion involves early projections of colors, textures, weights, and finishes that will meet public fashion acceptance when the fabrics finally reach consumers. Since the textile segment of the pipeline must work far ahead of consumer demand, it must lead in recognizing new fashion directions, 7-29.

Textile designers act on fashion trend predictions about 18 months before products made with the fabrics will hit the market. The weight and construction of the fabrics must complement the styles of garments that will be manufactured. Firm fabrics are needed if predictions show structured clothing trends; lightweight fabrics are needed for soft looks. Identifying trends becomes more important each year, with keener worldwide competition.

Fashion Institute of Technology; John Senzer, Photographer

7-29 Trends must be carefully predicted, with textile development that coincides with the colors, textures, and other characteristics that will be in demand by consumers when fashions reach retail stores.

PRIMIVISION DESIGN SYSTEM BY CADTEX

7-28 By doing creative work on a specialized textile/apparel industry computer system, a motif can be extracted from the original water color design, resulting in perfectly coordinated fabrics.

To predict future fashion trends, many textile producers employ fashion staffs. They use logic, market research, and "gut feel" to predict fashion. They coordinate trend information from fiber, yarn, and apparel companies, and from textile shows throughout the world. They analyze the fashion press, visit the world's fashion centers, and observe fashion leaders. They also use outside sources, such as ***forecasting services***, which are highly skilled consultants that specialize in predicting future fashion trends. Forecasters provide their clients with reports and newsletters, color swatches, examples of weights and textures, and sketches of silhouettes all geared to appropriate apparel markets, such as women's, men's, or children's.

Marketing

Marketing skills combine product planning, pricing, promoting, and distributing so the right fabrics are available to satisfy demand. Fabric manufacturers help those down the chain who use their fabrics. They maintain fabric libraries in their showrooms for their clients to use, and make up small amounts of their fabrics for promotion and selling aids. Also, sample garments are often made in the new fabrics.

Fabric manufacturers provide hang-tags and care labels for apparel manufacturers to attach to the finished garments. They often stage seasonal fashion shows for retailers and the fashion press in market areas. They assist with store promotions featuring their products, and help retail buyers locate merchandise

Mohair Council

7-30 Finished fabrics are presented to prospective buyers as actual samples. Information on the card includes the name and address of the company selling the fabric, name or style number of the fabric, fabric width, fabric color, and selling season.

made from their fabrics. They also conduct in-store sales training programs. They supply informative materials to the trade press, schools, retail sales personnel, and consumers.

Sometimes fabric manufacturers run cooperative ads with apparel manufacturers that use their fabrics, or retailers that sell the products. Many of the ads are in "print media," such as magazines and newspapers. They feature the brand names of their products, and make consumers aware of new fabrics and apparel styles, as well as the retail stores where they can be purchased.

Selling the Finished Fabrics

Fabrics are sold to apparel manufacturers, home furnishing manufacturers, and other end users as "piece goods." Samples are mounted with descriptions to show customers, 7-30. Often the apparel industry requests the production of fabrics with certain characteristics to satisfy market demand. Other times developments in the textile industry inspire new apparel designs.

Fabrics end up as either staple fabrics or novelty fabrics. ***Staple fabrics*** are commodity textile products made continuously each year with little or no change in construction or finish. Many staple fabrics are imported from other countries. ***Novelty fabrics*** are fashion fabrics that change with style trends. They are coordinated with apparel and accessory designs and are previewed by retail stores and the press to publicize upcoming trends. Most novelty fabrics are made and finished in the U.S.

Large fabric companies have offices with showrooms in New York City staffed with knowledgeable salespeople. Fabric buyers and designers from apparel manufacturing companies visit the showrooms to gain firsthand information about each season's fabrics, 7-31. Salespeople from fabric companies also call on designers at apparel firms to sell their piece goods.

Other people or companies that deal with fabrics after they are finished are textile jobbers, brokers, or retail fabric stores.

Textile jobbers are wholesale distributors who buy textiles at low prices from companies that can't use them. Fabric sources for jobbers include mills, converters, and

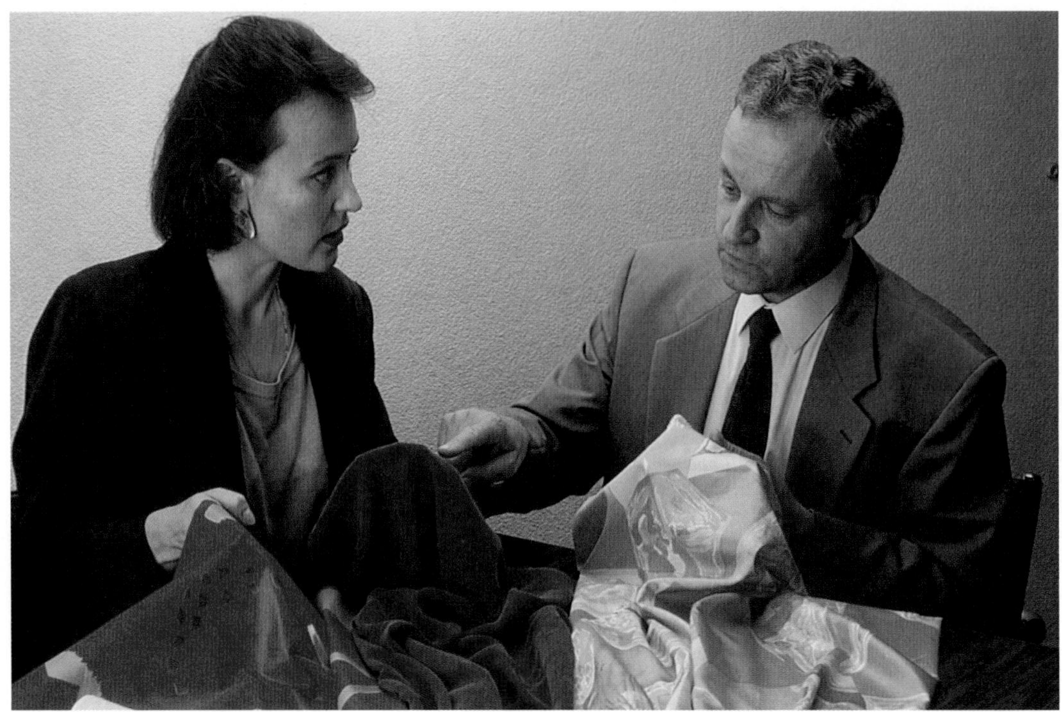

Sulzer Ruti

7-31 Fabric companies try to serve as competent and reliable partners with their customers. Their salespeople offer customer support services to try to solve problems and offer advice.

Taken at Fabrications

7-32 Although retail fabric sales are important to consumers, only a small percentage of finished fabrics are sold this way. Most finished fabrics are sold directly to apparel or other end-use manufacturing companies.

apparel manufacturers. As resellers, they take ownership of the fabric and sell it in various size pieces to companies that can use it or to fabric retailers.

Jobbers usually deal in small lots. Sometimes they buy in anticipation of future fashion demand or buy discontinued colors, styles, or prints. They help dispose of mill ***overruns*** (when a mill makes more fabric than was ordered by its customers). They can supply small apparel manufacturers that do not need the large quantities of fabric that mills and converters require their customers to buy. However, those who buy from jobbers may not be able to reorder if they need more of the same fabric.

There are fewer textile jobbers in existence today than in the past. They are located in cities where fabrics are marketed to the apparel manufacturing industry, such as New York City.

Textile brokers never own the fabric. They act as liaisons between textile sellers and buyers, trying to match the needs of both. They are paid a certain percentage of the price of each sale, known as a *commission*. Small mills that do not employ a sales force use brokers. However, with recent acquisitions and mergers in the industry, there are fewer small mills and only a few remaining textile brokers. Brokers also deal with imported textiles.

Other small lots of fabrics are sold through retail fabric stores for over-the-counter sales, 7-32. Some of the fabrics are for home sewn apparel. More and more are now for home decorating.

Trade Information

There are many trade groups associated with the textile segment of the pipeline. The most comprehensive is the *American Textile Manufacturers Institute, Inc. (ATMI)*. It is large and influential in industry marketing, government relations, trade policy, and related matters. Other specialized trade organizations are listed in 7-33.

The *American Printed Fabrics Council, Inc.* is a trade organization that recognizes creative achievements

Specialized Textile Trade Organizations	
American Association of Textile Chemists and Colorists (AATCC)	Is concerned with the "wet processing" aspects of textile finishing, such as bleaching, dyeing, and printing.
American Textile Machinery Association	An organization of companies that supply equipment and services to textile producers. Members are located around the world and the annual directory of members, products, and services is published in several languages.
Association of the Nonwoven Fabrics Industry	Emphasizes industrial applications since about half the textiles used industrially are nonwovens.
Computer Integrated Textile Design Association	The trade association for textile and apparel CAD/CAM makers and users.
Institute of Textile Technology	A cooperative, privately funded education, information, and research organization to keep the textile industry apprised of global research findings, especially through the *Textile Technology Digest*.
International Textile Manufacturers Federation	A global organization of textile industries.
Textile Quality Control Association	Concentrates on instruments and procedures for textile testing.

7-33 There are separate trade organizations for most parts of every industry, including textiles.

American Printed Fabrics Council, Inc.

7-34 Creative achievements in printed fabrics are recognized with "Tommy" Awards. Here, an award is earned by the designer of the two prints in the girl's dress.

in printed fabrics, 7-34. The organization has also encouraged companies to register for copyright protection of textile designs. Additionally, Cotton Incorporated holds annual *Cotton Textile Designers Awards* to honor both aesthetic creativity and functional effectiveness of 100 percent cotton fabrics. Both organizations announce winners for many specific awards within the apparel and home fabrics categories.

Textile companies subscribe to such magazines as the *Textile Research Journal*, *Textile World*, *America's Textiles International*, and *American Dyestuff Reporter*. These, and other such trade journals, report the latest textile-related developments.

New fashion trends are introduced at trade shows and sourcing fairs held throughout the world. Fabric producers show new designs and fabric textures for the following year's fashion apparel and accessories. They inform designers, manufacturers, and retailers about new merchandise developments. The most important shows for the apparel fabric industry are the *Interstoff Textile Fair* held in Germany, and Premiere Vision held in France. Other major events are held in Italy, China, New York City, and other fashion centers.

The Future of Textiles

In the midst of global competition, the U.S. textile industry is innovative and progressive, with a competitive spirit. Its pace of change will accelerate with advanced technology, moving it from a labor-intensive industry to a capital-intensive one with a high degree of automation. The higher speeds of new equipment will result in lower costs, better quality, and faster responses to market needs. Additionally, U.S. firms are already partnering with each other, as well as with firms in other countries, to compete in the global economy. The Internet is helping these efforts.

To prosper in the international market, the industry will close outdated plants and totally automate newer ones. Companies will restructure to have fewer levels of workers and management, and become larger and stronger through mergers. They will be more service-oriented toward their customers all the way through the pipeline. Those with quality products and good management will grow stronger.

Flexibility and versatility for shorter production runs of different fabrics will be needed to quickly satisfy changing market trends. The mass-production methods of the past will be replaced with computerized methods that allow for fast changes for smaller, more customized orders of unique products. Automated equipment will create job losses at lower skill levels. Workers currently in the industry will need to be retrained for other positions. More skilled workers will be needed to achieve top production quality and quantities. Ambitious, young workers can become leaders in the industry's new progressive environment.

The consumption rate of textiles will continually increase as worldwide standards of living go up. Experts predict that polyester will be the predominant fiber, with cotton also remaining popular. There will be more modifications to existing generic fibers, resulting in a higher number of "high performance fabrics" than totally new fiber categories. Nonwovens and disposable textiles will be very common, and textile imports from other countries are expected to continue to increase.

Predictions also indicate that the production of knits will grow, with fewer wovens produced. Less energy is consumed in producing knits than wovens, and energy efficiency is a prime area to cut costs for the industry. Knitting mills have lower equipment costs than weaving mills. New automation is expected most for circular knitting, which is very flexible and fast, plus raw material waste is being eliminated. Consumers will also see more seamless garments in the future, knit to specific sizes with built-in stretch. Additionally, new developments in yarn production will create greater popularity of novelty yarns.

Successful textile firms of the future will use industry change to their advantage. They will have to learn to cope with imports. More sophisticated marketing techniques will give more attention directly to retailers and consumers. Orders will be filled faster and more accurately with computer data communications through the entire pipeline.

Summary

Fabric design is achieved when textiles are manufactured or applied with added designs. Textile mills produce fabrics by weaving, knitting, or holding yarns or fibers together in other ways. Types of weaves include plain, twill, and satin weaves, or variations of those three basic types. Knitted fabrics include weft knits, warp knits, and variations of those two basic types. Other construction methods produce nonwoven fabrics, laces and nets, braided fabrics, bonded fabrics, and quilted fabrics.

Fabric finishing is done by converters that change the look, feel, or performance of fabrics. Finishing treatments include bleaching, dyeing, printing, and adding finishes. Dyeing can be done at the fiber, yarn, piece goods, or garment stage, with a faster, more accurate response to market demand if done later in the pipeline. Printing applies design to the surface of fabrics with rollers, screens, heat transfer, or other means. Final finishes are done by mechanical methods or chemical reactions.

Quality and performance standards determine the value of textile products for customer needs. Production technology includes computer-aided design and computer-aided manufacturing, which allow product development to be done electronically with more flexibility and lower costs. Fashion projections and marketing skills must also be incorporated into developing fabrics.

Finished fabrics are sold to apparel manufacturers, home furnishing manufacturers, and other end users. Most staple fabrics are imported, while most novelty fabrics are made in the U.S. Besides the salespeople employed by large fabric companies, selling of finished fabrics is done by textile jobbers, brokers, and retail fabric stores.

Many trade groups are organized within various areas of the textile segment. For these segments, there are also specific trade journals and shows that address the latest developments and sources in the industry.

The future of textiles will be fast-changing, involving new technology and globalization of the industry. Companies will become flexible and versatile to satisfy their customers. Polyester and cotton fibers will remain popular, as will novelty yarns and the production of knits.

To Know

structural design
applied design
weaving
selvage
grain
true bias
knitting
nonwovens
converters
bleaching
dyeing
colorfast
printing
hand
mechanical finishes
chemical finishes
quality standards
performance standards
forecasting services
staple fabrics
novelty fabrics
overruns

To Review

1. What four factors determine the appearance and performance of fabrics?
2. What is the difference between structural design and applied design?
3. Describe warp yarns and filling yarns in woven fabrics, and relate them to lengthwise and crosswise grain.
4. List the three basic types of weaves.
5. Describe pile fabrics and nap
6. In knitted fabrics, what is the gauge, and what does the gauge number indicate?
7. What are the two basic types of knitting machines?
8. Name, and briefly describe, the two basic methods of knitting fabrics.
9. How are nonwoven fabrics held together?
10. What is fabric finishing?
11. Where are textile converters positioned on the pipeline?
12. Why can independent converters be so flexible in their design possibilities?
13. What is the difference between stock-dyed and solution-dyed fibers?
14. What is the most common, least expensive, and fastest method of dyeing textiles?
15. Explain why garment dyeing has gained in popularity.
16. List the four basic methods of printing textiles.
17. Describe permanent, durable, temporary, and renewable finishes.
18. What do the initials CAD and CAM represent, and how have they helped the product development and production of textiles?
19. Briefly describe how textile jobbers, brokers, and retailers are alike and how they are different.
20. Why is the consumption rate of textiles expected to increase in the future?

To Do

1. Make a bulletin board display that illustrates the following about textiles: fiber, yarn, woven fabrics in each of the three basic weaves, various knitted fabrics, dyed fabric, and printed fabric. Explain the samples with clear, brief labels.
2. Obtain a one-yard piece of woven fabric and a one-yard piece of knitted fabric. In an oral report to the class, show and explain the following: warp yarns, filling yarns, selvage, lengthwise grain, crosswise grain, bias grain, stretch versus stability of various grains, gauge, formation of loops, roll when pulled, stretchiness, best apparel uses for the fabrics, and tendency to run, ravel, or curl.
3. Examine four fabric samples. Note the appearance and feel of each. Then unravel the yarns to determine how the fabric was constructed. Analyze the construction of each fabric. Mount the fabric pieces on paper, along with your written descriptions of them.
4. In a small group, take on the role of a fashion forecasting service. Use logic, research, and "gut feel" to predict fashion colors, silhouettes, and other trends for two years in the future for women's, men's, or children's apparel. Prepare an oral report for the class that includes visuals (drawings, pictures, swatches, color "storyboards," etc.) to show your predictions. Try to substantiate the reasoning for your choices.
5. Research one of the trade organizations discussed in the chapter. Write a report about your findings.

Fashion Institute of Technology; John Senzer, Photographer

This textile designer applies a surface design to fabrics.

PART 3

Designing and Producing Apparel

CHAPTER 8

Using Design in Fashion

After studying this chapter, you will be able to

- explain the importance of each element of design in relation to fashion.
- apply the principles of design to apparel.
- describe how harmony is achieved in garment designs.
- discuss how to use design to create illusions that enhance appearance.

Design is the plan used to put an idea together. It is used in garments and accessories, as well as buildings, cars, paintings, landscapes, and other created products. By studying about, observing, and experimenting with design, fashion professionals can develop good taste and advise people how to look their best.

The ***elements of design*** are color, shape, line, and texture. These elements are put together in different ways to form designs. The ***principles of design*** are balance, proportion, emphasis, and rhythm. They are guidelines for using the elements of design. When the elements of design are used effectively according to the principles of design, harmony results, 8-1.

Using the Elements of Design

In fashion, the design elements are combined according to current trends. They are combined a bit differently each season to move fashion forward. The way they are used distinguishes garments from each other and allows consumers to express themselves. Sight and touch affect the emotions of consumers and can influence the sale of garments. Retail employees must be able to interpret the way the fresh new looks of each season are designed.

Color

Color is the most exciting design element. When people see apparel or other items, color is noticed first and is often the prime factor when a retail customer selects a garment. All colors are beautiful, but they must be used wisely and combined well to make apparel look its best on the wearer.

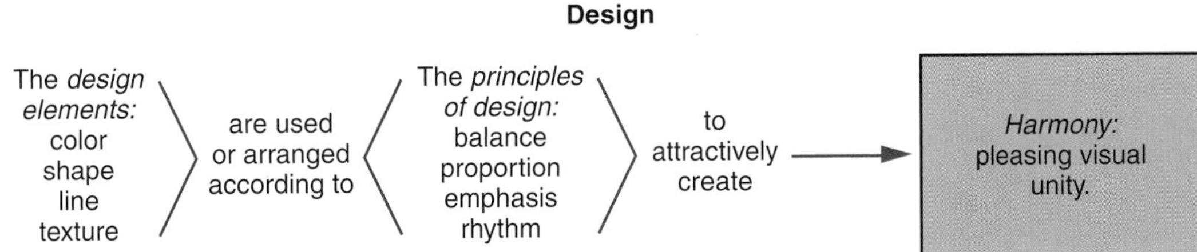

8-1 When the elements of design are used successfully according to the principles of design, pleasing harmony is created.

Color has three dimensions or descriptive qualities:

- ***Hue*** is the name given to a color, such as blue, red, or green. It distinguishes one color from another with a descriptive title.
- ***Value*** is the lightness or darkness, ranging on a gradation scale from almost white to almost black. A ***tint*** is toward white, or lighter than the pure hue, 8-2. A ***shade*** is toward black, or darker than the pure hue. For example, navy blue is a shade of blue, and baby blue is a tint of blue.
- ***Intensity*** is the brightness or dullness of a color. Pure, clear, strong colors are bright with high intensity, 8-3. Dull, dusty, or "muddy" colors have low intensity.

Monsanto Fibers

8-2 The pastel colors in the design pattern of this sweater are tints of hues.

Black, white, and gray are ***neutrals.*** They have no hue and can be used alone or with almost any colors. White reflects light and feels cooler in hot climates and the summer season. Black absorbs all light and brings warmth to the wearer. Beige is also usually considered to be a neutral in apparel, since it can be used with most colors.

Several common guidelines for the use of some specific colors in clothing are given in 8-4.

Jeanswear Communications/Boss by I.G. Design

8-3 The vivid yellow of this shirt illustrates an attractive use of color in high intensity.

Guidelines for Using Color in Apparel

- Black is good for formal wear. It tends to be sophisticated.
- Brown is casual, natural, and informal.
- Navy looks good on almost everyone. It is good for sportswear or classic styles.
- Beige and gray give a professional or tailored image. Both of these colors are quiet and unassuming, and they can be accessorized well.
- White looks good with all other colors. Off-white is better for most people than pure white.
- Red, green, and blue have many tints, shades, and intensities that make these hues suitable for almost all occasions.
- Yellow is good for casual, fun clothes, but it is not pleasing with many skin tones.
- Bright colors are fun for active sportswear or as accents with neutrals.

8-4 Although fashion often bends the rules, colors in apparel are usually best used according to these accepted guidelines.

Using the Color Wheel

The ***color wheel***, 8-5, is used to show hues, how they are related to each other, and how they can be created by mixing dyes or paints together. The color wheel shows:

- *Primary hues* of red, yellow, and blue. These basic colors need their own pigments. They cannot be made from any other colors, but all other colors can be made by mixing them. They are placed equal distance from each other on the color wheel.
- *Secondary hues* are orange, green, and violet (purple), made by mixing equal amounts of two primary hues together. On the color wheel, they are found halfway between the two primary hues that are used to create them.
- *Intermediate hues* are between each primary and secondary color, made by combining equal amounts of the adjoining colors. When naming them, it is customary to state the primary hue first. Intermediate colors are yellow-green, yellow-orange, red-orange, red-violet, blue-violet, and blue-green.

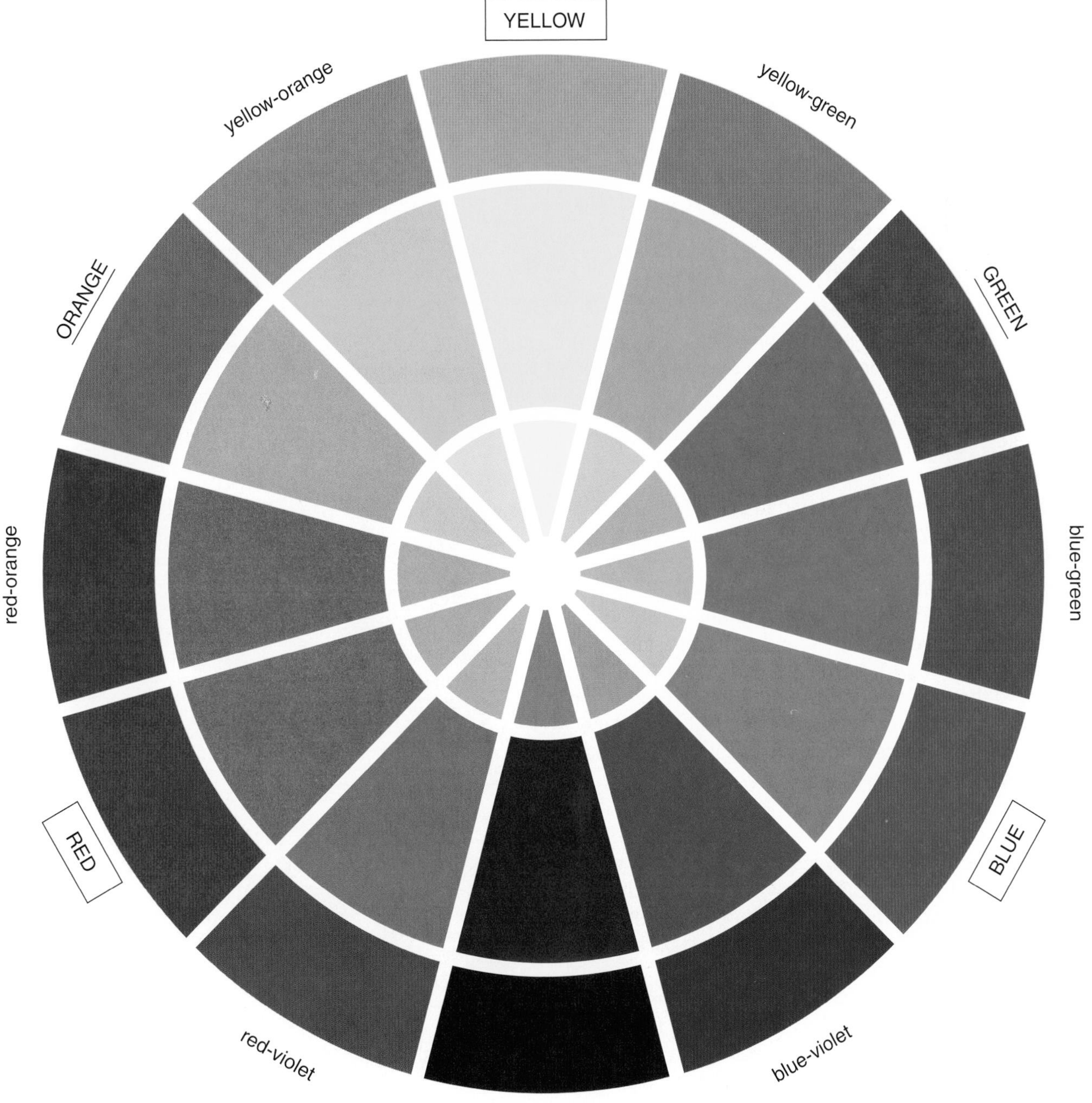

8-5 The color wheel shows how hues are related. The names of the primary hues have boxes around them. The names of the secondary hues are underlined. Intermediate hues have their names written in lowercase letters.

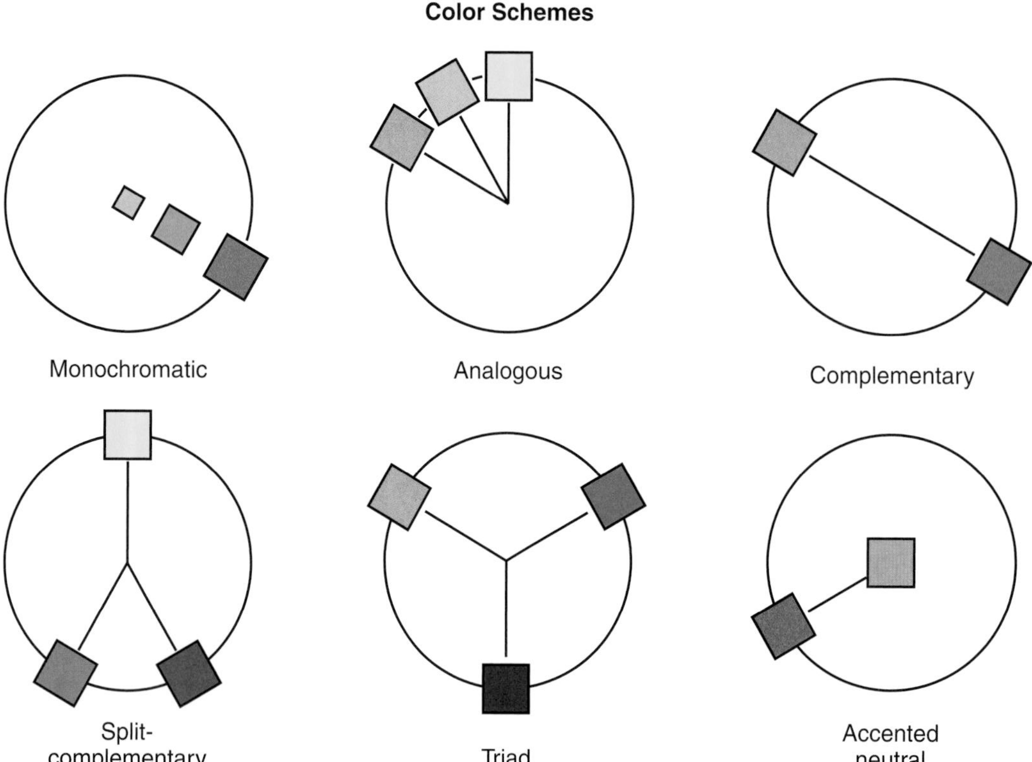

8-6 These six color schemes show the relative positions of the hues on the color wheel that are used together as pleasing combinations in various values and intensities.

The color wheel can be divided into warm and cool sides. *Warm colors*, representing fire, sun, and brilliance, are from red to yellow on the color wheel. Orange is the warmest color. Warm colors give a feeling of activity and cheerfulness, and set an outgoing, lively mood. However, if they are overdone, they can give a nervous impression. *Cool colors*, representing water and the sky, are from green to violet. Blue is the coolest color. Cool colors give a restful, calm, quiet, relaxing feeling suggesting a subdued mood. If overdone, they can be depressing.

Color Schemes

Color schemes are ways that colors can effectively be used together. The most widely used color schemes are shown in 8-6. Different results are achieved by combining various colors in textile prints or parts of garments and accessories.

A *monochromatic color scheme* uses different tints, shades, and intensities of one color. It tends to appear restful because of the unity that results from using just one hue. A pale green shirt with darker green slacks is an example of a monochromatic color scheme. Neutrals are sometimes added to a monochromatic scheme for contrast and interest, 8-7.

Monsanto Fibers

8-7 Blue is used monochromatically in this outfit, with a tint (baby blue), shade (navy blue), and the addition of a neutral (white).

An *analogous color scheme* uses adjacent, or related, colors on the color wheel. To avoid monotony in apparel, different values and intensities give some contrast. This plan uses such colors as blue and green, or pink and violet together. The combination of yellow, yellow-green, and green is an analogous scheme with three hues. See 8-8.

A *complementary color scheme* uses hues that are directly across from each other on the color wheel. This creates the greatest contrast, with the colors looking even brighter and more intense when used side by side. This scheme is often used for school colors so uniforms and banners look vivid and exciting. However, in apparel, complements are rarely used together in full strength. In tints and shades, they can be sophisticated and pleasing. For instance, a soft tint of one is usually attractive with a deep shade of the other, or a large area of one may be accented with a small amount of the other. Examples of complementary color combinations are red and green, and blue and orange, 8-9.

A *split-complementary color scheme* uses three colors. It combines one color with the color on each side of its complement. For instance, blue might be used with yellow-orange and red-orange. This is also a bright color scheme and must be carefully coordinated in apparel.

Bobby Jones of Hickey-Freeman Co., Inc./Hartmarx Corporation

8-8 The print of this blouse contains pink, violet, and blue. The three hues are analogous on the color wheel.

Wrangler Hero

8-9 A cheerful orange shirt worn with blue denim shorts is a good example of a complementary color scheme.

A *triad color scheme* combines three colors equidistant on the wheel, such as red, yellow and blue, or violet, green and orange, 8-10. Triad color schemes have a great deal of contrast that can be softened with pleasing values and intensities. A large area of one of the colors in a tint or shade is often used with small amounts of the other two for fashion accents.

An *accented neutral color scheme* combines white, black, gray, or sometimes beige, with a bright color accent. An example would be a gray and black striped suit and white shirt with a red necktie or scarf. The accented neutral color plan is pleasing to the eye and very versatile in clothing. The color that looks best on the wearer can be used as the accent and might be advantageously placed near the face, at the shoulders, or around the waist.

Using Color in Fashion

The effects of color can be used to advantage in fashion. For instance, extreme contrast makes colors

The Fashion Association/Gene Meyer, Div. of Mondo, Inc.

8-10 The forest green corduroy suit is combined with a vibrant orange shirt and violet necktie for a triad color scheme.

seem more exciting because they look brighter. A combination of black and white is the most extreme, 8-11. Using a color with a neutral makes the color look brighter. Colors with medium or dark value look even darker when used next to a light area, and light colors look even lighter next to a dark area.

Outfits are generally more attractive if they do not have equal areas of light and dark. They might be mostly dark with an accent of light, or vice versa. In most cases, colors in clothes seem better balanced if light ones are used above dark ones. Also, it is usually not recommended to use more than three major colors in one outfit. It is best to use one color for a large area and another color or two for smaller areas.

Colors can appear to change the size and shape of the person wearing them. For instance, light, warm, and bright colors appear to advance, or to come toward the observer. Thus, white, yellow, orange, and red make a form look larger. On the other hand, dark, cool, and dull colors appear to recede, or to back away from the observer. They make a form look smaller. Such slimming colors are black, navy blue, dark blue-violet, charcoal gray, chocolate brown, and burgundy. Garments in large sizes are often made in these colors so the wearers look smaller.

If a person wants to minimize attention to certain sections of the body, dark, dull colors should be worn. Light colors could then be placed on other areas of the body. Bright colors are best used in small amounts, and can be very effective to play up good body features since they catch the eye. For instance, others will notice a person's face if a brightly colored scarf, tie, or collar is worn near it.

A single color, or all close values, for an entire outfit makes a person look thinner and taller because the appearance of an unbroken line is created. When two colors are combined in an outfit, it may seem to be broken into separate parts. Sharply contrasting colors appear to shorten the body because the eye stops at a line of contrast instead of moving up the figure in a vertical direction. Strong contrasts call attention to where the space has been broken. Thus, a wide belt

Liz Claiborne

8-11 Although black and white are not considered to be colors, the sharpest contrast is achieved when these two are used together.

Monsanto Fibers

8-12 A white collar on a dress or other garment draws the attention of viewers to the face of the wearer.

of a bright or contrasting color makes a person look shorter. If someone is too tall, the outfit can be broken up with different colors on the top and bottom.

To emphasize the best physical features, a small amount of a light or bright color can be used in an advantageous location on an otherwise subdued outfit. A white collar or pearl or shiny necklace is often placed on a dark dress to draw the eye of others there, 8-12. A light or bright stripe is often knit across men's golf shirts to broaden the appearance of the chest.

When considering colors for clothing, try to reflect the personality of the wearer. A quiet, shy person is usually more comfortable wearing "quiet" colors, such as pale, cool, and neutral colors. Bright colors would overpower his or her personality. On the other hand, a dramatic, energetic, outgoing person is better suited to bolder colors, such as warm, bright hues, often with striking contrasts.

Fashion professionals are also aware that bright colors are more easily remembered. Bright articles of clothing cannot be worn as often as more subdued outfits. Less intense colors are also easier to combine into multiple outfits in the wardrobe.

From a distance, the colors in narrow stripes and small plaids blend together. For instance, small red and white stripes look pink from across the room. This may or may not be favorable, depending on the desired effect with other parts of the outfit and the accessories.

It should also be noted that colors appear to change when viewed under different lights. In retail environments, it is often hard to match colors, since fluorescent and incandescent lights give different effects than natural light. Fluorescent lights make colors look bluer, while incandescent lights give a yellow cast and tend to pale the look of some colors. To get a true color match, it may be necessary to view items near a window with natural light.

Shape

Shape is ***silhouette***, or the overall form or outline of an outfit. It results from the cut and construction of a garment. It projects a quickly noticed image from a distance and can be a major factor in people's opinions of other people's size. Thus, the way shape is used to reveal or disguise body contours can enhance or hide much of the body form underneath. Clothing silhouettes that are most flattering emphasize and accent people's good features and hide the less attractive ones. They draw attention away from areas that should not be noticed.

Full, wide, flaring clothing shapes add width, making people look larger. They are best worn by slim people. Trim, compact silhouettes make people look smaller. Straight, tubular shapes give an appearance of added height and slimness, 8-13. Tightly fitting clothes reveal body contours, and are best for people with "ideal" shapes. Also, if clothes are too tight, they appear to have been outgrown and can make people look overweight.

Shape also reveals whether or not apparel is in fashion at any given time, and it is more accentuated in high style design than in garments for the mass market. Fashionable silhouettes of the past have had huge, padded shoulders, excessively tight or full skirts, or skirt lengths down at the ankle or up at mid-thigh. The most lasting fashions have been the ones that have complemented the natural contour of the human body.

Facial shapes should also be considered in relation to apparel neckline designs, which should try to create the illusion of an oval face. If the shape of a person's face is extreme in any way, that shape should not be repeated in the neckline, which would strengthen the shape. Rather, a contrasting neckline balances the face. For instance, people with long facial shapes should wear wide, horizontal neckline designs. People with pointed chins should avoid V necklines, while those with full, round faces are flattered by V necklines. People who have an oval face can wear any neckline shapes.

JCPenney

8-13 The long, narrow silhouette of this outfit gives a tall, straight appearance to the person wearing it.

Saxony Sportswear Company

8-14 This leather jacket has many structural lines.

Line

Line is a distinct, elongated mark as if drawn by a pen. Lines lead the path of eye movement up and down, side to side, or around an object. In fashion, lines outline the inner and outer spaces, and connecting parts, to form details of garments. The popularity of various lines and details moves with fashion.

Structural lines are formed when garments are constructed, such as at the seams, darts, pleats, tucks, and edges. Notice the structural lines in 8-14. Structural lines are assembly details that also create visual interest. They are especially noticeable if the fabric of the garment is plain.

Decorative lines, or applied lines, are created by adding details to the surface of clothing. They include the fabric design and trims added simply to decorate the outfit to add style and personality. Decorative lines result from applied edgings, top-stitching, lace, tabs, flaps, or buttons. They can also be created with accessories, such as scarves and necklaces.

Decorative lines often accentuate structural lines. For instance, a row of top-stitching down the front of a shirt emphasizes the long straight structural edge of the shirt. However, too much detail causes competition between the lines and is confusing and unattractive. The more elaborate the structural and decorative lines are, the more attention will be drawn to the body.

Line Types and Directions

Lines can be straight, curved, or jagged. Also, they can go different directions in apparel, such as vertically, horizontally, and diagonally.

Straight lines are bold and severe, suggesting dignity, power, and formality. They give an appearance of steadiness or stability, but can look stiff if overdone. All clothes have some straight lines in them, for instance along the edges of pant legs or the bottom of a hemmed skirt. Notice the lines created in the design of 8-15.

Curved lines can be very rounded and circular, or flatter with a gentle curve. They are less conservative,

JCPenney

8-15 The straight lines in this dress are accentuated by the contrast of black and white.

formal, and powerful than straight lines. They add interest and smoothness, and they appear to be soft, gentle, and youthful. They give a charming, graceful, flowing feeling.

Curves accent the natural lines of the body. However, they give the illusion of increased size to the human shape, so they look best on slender bodies. In apparel, curved lines should be used sparingly. Too many of them used in one outfit can become confusing. Somewhat flattened curves are the most flattering. Circles are closed lines, so they stop the eye entirely.

Curved lines are found along rounded collar edges, scoop necklines, and scalloped edges. Fabric prints sometimes contain them. The stronger or more abrupt a curve is, the more powerful and moving it seems. Long, sweeping curves create a smooth and pleasant feeling.

Jagged lines change direction abruptly in zigzag patterns. They are very noticeable and can create a jumpy, confused feeling. They should be used sparingly. See 8-16.

Vertical lines are those that go up and down. In apparel, they give the impression of added height and slimness, making the body look taller and thinner. They also give a feeling of dignity, strength, poise, and sophistication. They are found along the front of shirts, and the outside and inseam edges of pants.

Horizontal lines go from side to side like the horizon, carrying the eye from side to side. They suggest rest and gentleness, giving a relaxed, calm feeling. They give the impression of less height and more width and, if emphasized, make the body look shorter and wider. A tall, thin man could use horizontal design lines to make himself look more filled out. Horizontal lines are found where a belt goes around the waistline and at the bottom edge of a jacket or skirt.

Diagonal lines are on a slant. The degree of slant and length of the line determine the visual effect in clothes. Shorter, more horizontal diagonals create the effect of width. Longer, more vertical diagonals create a leaner, taller effect. Diagonals are versatile and interesting, but are strong and draw attention to the area where they are used. They can give a feeling of action and strength, and appear dramatic and eccentric. They are found in V necklines, along collar lapels, and along the outer edges of flared skirts. Notice the diagonal lines in 8-17.

Monsanto Fibers

8-16 The jagged lines within the horizontal stripes of this sweater create an unusual and fun pattern.

Texture

Texture is the tactile quality of goods, or how the surface of a material feels and looks. It is the hand, surface interest, or "character" of fabric. Texture can be described with such words as smooth, rough, dull, shiny, stiff, firm, crisp, fuzzy, bulky, nubby, soft, shaggy, flat, harsh, sheer, loopy, furry, scratchy, pebbly, delicate, sparkling, and fine. Texture can also be referred to as lightweight, medium-weight, or heavyweight.

Texture is partially determined by the fibers, yarns, and method of construction of a fabric. This is called *structural texture*. See 8-18. Finishes and designs applied to the surface are *added visual texture*.

Texture, like the other design elements, can also create illusions in apparel. Garments made of fuzzy, heavy, bulky fabrics add visual size to the areas over which they are worn. However, they also can disguise figure irregularities. Smooth, flat textures tend to make people look smaller, and are suitable for most body shapes.

Shiny textures make people look larger because they reflect light and emphasize body contours. They make fabric colors seem lighter and brighter. On the other hand, rough textures have the opposite effect. They tend to subdue colors because light hits their uneven surfaces at different angles. Dull textures make a person look smaller because they absorb light. The same hue would look different in satin than it would in corduroy or gabardine, because of the way light is reflected from the surface of the fabric.

Sheer fabrics also subdue colors because the skin of the wearer is seen through the fabric. Sheer fabrics reveal the body shape and soften it when the fabric is used over a soft lining. Clinging, soft textures especially reveal the body's silhouette. On the other hand, stiff, crisp textures make the total shape look bigger, because they stand away from the body, which also helps them conceal figure faults. They require seams and other construction shaping to give form to garments, since they cannot be draped.

Combinations of textures can be very interesting in apparel, if not too many are combined in one outfit.

Saks Fifth Avenue

8-18 This Polo Ralph Lauren outfit is rich with structural texture. It includes a velvet shirt and striped wool pants.

Monsanto Fibers

8-17 Diagonal lines are located along all sides of the diamond shapes in this sweater, as well as forming the diagonal stripes across the entire front.

Often one main texture is used with trim or an accessory having an accent texture. For instance, a rough tweed coat might have a smooth leather belt or large shiny buttons. Notice the textures in 8-19.

Textures chosen for various outfits must also be suited to the occasions for which they will be worn. Rich, luxurious velvets and brocades are dressy. Glossy satin and fine silk are usually for fancy clothes. Plain corduroy and fleece are casual. Heavy fabrics are for hard work or for warmth.

Added visual texture is often more noticeable than the structural texture of a fabric, and can affect the apparent size of the wearer just as structural texture does. For instance, printed fabrics can give an overall vertical, horizontal, diagonal, curved, or jagged feeling. The print can, then, add to an illusion of height or width of the wearer. Added prints can be small, medium, or large, quiet and subtle, or loud and bold. They diminish the appearance of structural lines. The more interesting the added texture is, the simpler the structural lines of the garment should be.

Large, bold added visual patterns emphasize the area where they are used and increase the apparent size of the wearer. This is compounded if the print has bright colors or sharp color contrasts. Small, subdued, overall prints tend to make a person look smaller, especially if they are in closely related colors.

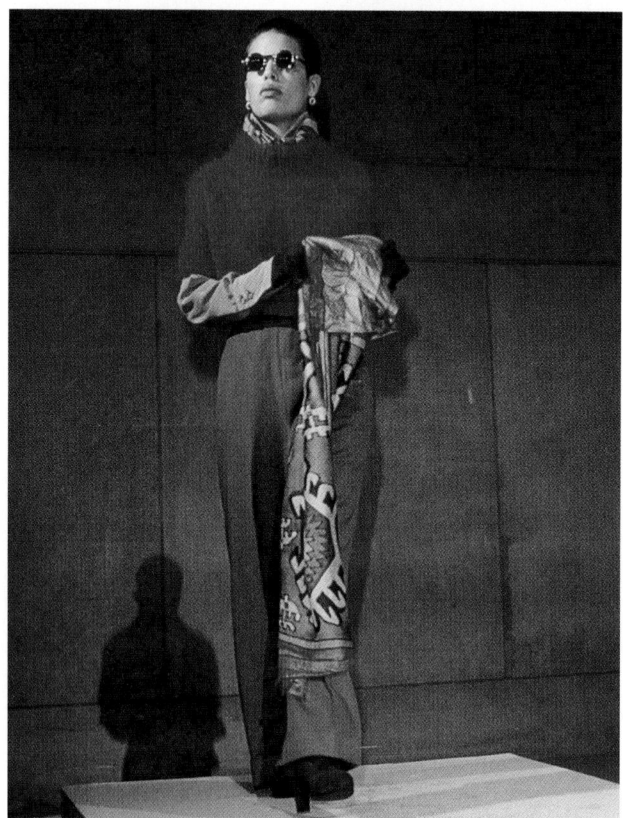

Fashion Institute of Technology/John Senzer, Photographer

8-19 What words would you use to describe the several interesting textures in this outfit?

Using the Principles of Design

A garment with good design is pleasing to the eye. It makes the wearer look his or her best. It has a good combination of design elements according to the principles of design. As you have discovered, the elements of design (color, shape, line, and texture) tell *what* is included in design; the principles of design (balance, proportion, emphasis, and rhythm) tell *how* the elements are combined. If this is done well, harmony (the goal of design) is achieved.

Balance

Balance produces equality among the parts of a design or outfit. It implies equilibrium or steadiness among the parts, with equal interest on either side of an imaginary centerline.

A well-designed garment will display pleasing balance, not only from side to side and top to bottom, but also from front to back. When all sides of a design appear equal in weight or power of attraction, the design seems to have stability.

Balance in garments is produced by structural parts and added decoration. Structurally, the draped neckline of a dress might be balanced with softly gathered folds in the skirt. Added decoration might include shoulder buttons to balance waistline piping. Balance should also be present in the fabric design.

In balancing the design elements, one long line balances two short ones, and one wide stripe balances two thin ones. A larger area of fine or soft texture balances a smaller area of heavy or coarse texture. Warm and dark colors appear heavier than cool and light ones. A small amount of a bright color balances a large amount of a dull one. A small area of a warm color balances a larger amount of a cool color. Large amounts of tints or neutrals balance smaller areas of shades or bright colors.

The two main types of balance are often represented with a seesaw, 8-20. They include formal and informal balance.

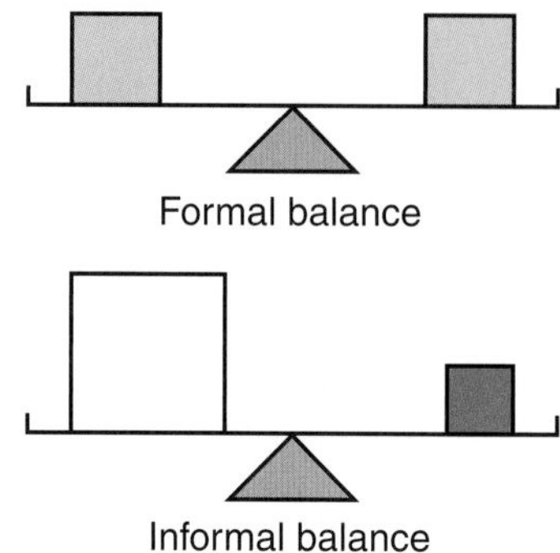

8-20 Formal balance is identical on each side of the center, while informal balance does not have the same features but still has the same "weight."

Formal Balance

Formal balance is symmetrical, with one side just like the other. Identical details are arranged the same distance from the center on the right and left sides. Examples of formal balance are one pocket on each side of a jacket or two rows of tucks on each side of a blouse. Most garments are designed this way, since it is easiest and the least expensive to produce. See 8-21.

Formal balance is dignified and formal. If overdone, it can look stiff and monotonous. However, since the human figure has formal balance, clothing necklines, waistlines, and skirt and slacks hemlines almost always are designed to hang evenly all around.

Informal Balance

Informal balance creates equilibrium with an asymmetrical arrangement of design details. Parts are placed unequally from the center in a way that achieves balance. An arrangement of colors, shapes, lines, and textures on one side balances a different arrangement on the other side. This is often achieved in garments with diagonal lines and off-centered closings. In accessorizing an outfit, a scarf or decorative pin can be used to balance a draped side opening. A small area of dark or bright color can balance a large area of light or dull color. Informal balance is more subtle and casual than formal balance, and usually is more interesting and dramatic.

Proportion

Proportion is the spatial, or size, relationship of all the parts in a design to each other and to the whole. This is sometimes called *scale.* Proportion is determined by how the total design is divided and the inner lines arranged. When all the parts work well together, the garment is well-proportioned rather than out of proportion.

Proportion is most pleasing when areas are divided unevenly. This creates an interesting balance of unequal, but similar, areas. This explains the use of short jackets over long skirts, long tops over short skirts, and so on. Also, an odd number of parts, such as three, is more interesting than an even number, such as two or four.

Garment designs should be related to the structure and proportion of the human body. The ideal body is said to be "8 heads tall," with 7/8 of it below the head, 8-22.

The Fashion Association/Brian McKinney Designer Collections

8-21 This outfit has formal balance because the right side is just like the left side. The only exception is the buttons which must be on one side and the buttonholes on the other.

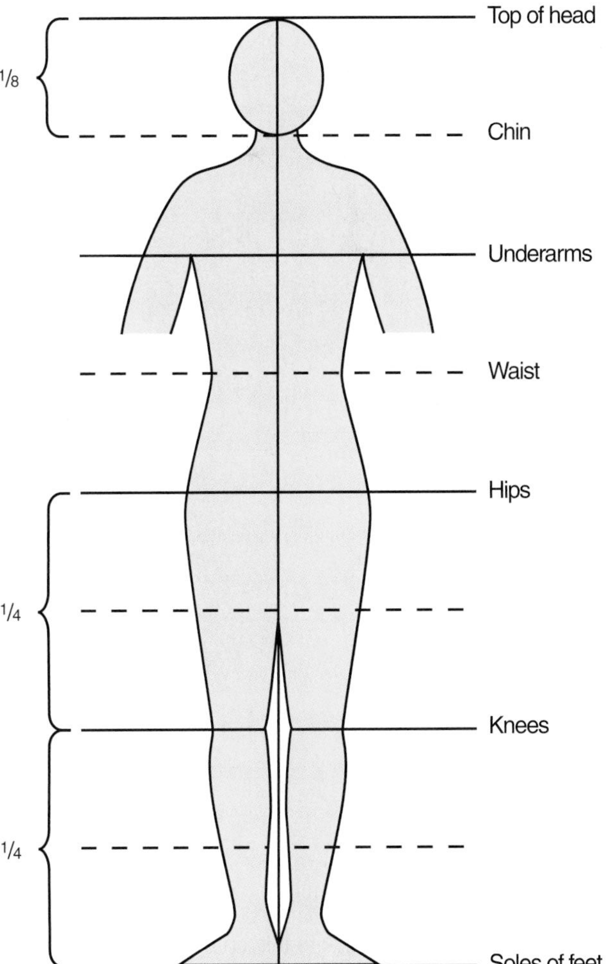

8-22 The ideal body is said to total eight times the height of the head, or quarters at the underarms, hips, and knees.

The proportions have 3/8 of the total figure from the waist to the top of the head. The remaining 5/8 of the body is from the waist to the soles of the feet. To coordinate with this, most outfits divide unequally, usually with the top area smaller than the bottom area.

Determining pleasing proportion for each fashion requires relating the garment, print, or accessories to the correct proportion of the person wearing it. Details, such as buttons and trimmings, should also be related to the overall size of a garment. For instance, a tiny pocket would look out of proportion on a large, heavy overcoat. A woman with a large frame wouldn't look right carrying a tiny purse. A large plaid design in a shirt might be attractive on a tall man, but would overpower a small girl. See 8-23.

Garments that bring out the natural proportions of the body are usually flattering and pleasing. They also remain in style for a long time. Those that make the body look distorted or out of proportion usually appear only as fleeting fads.

The Fashion Association/Sears

8-23 The size of the check in this shirt is pleasing (not too tiny and not too huge) in relation to the size of the man wearing it.

Emphasis

Emphasis is a concentration of interest in a particular part or area of a design. It is the center of interest, or what is seen first. All other parts of the design are subordinate to the area of emphasis.

Without a main focal point, an outfit looks unplanned and monotonous. In fact, a secondary emphasis may be included if done carefully, 8-24. However, too many areas of interest create a cluttered, confusing design.

Emphasis can be used in apparel to draw attention to an attractive personal feature or draw the eye away from an undesirable feature. For instance, a colorful belt emphasizes the waistline. For a shorter appearance, emphasis should be at the waistline or hemline. A bright necktie places the emphasis high on the body, drawing the eye of the viewer upward to create a taller feeling, 8-25. Emphasis is most commonly used to call attention to the face.

Emphasis can be created with contrasts of colors or textures. Light, bright colors and shiny textures attract attention. Structural lines, decorative trimmings, and the unusual shape of an area will also attract

Saks Fifth Avenue

8-24 This outfit, by designer Sonia Rykiel, has its primary emphasis at the neckline with secondary emphasis at the two wrists.

Hart, Schaffner & Marx/Hartmarx Corporation

8-25 Emphasis is up at the neckline, created by the light-colored shirt and bright necktie customarily worn with men's dark business suits.

attention. A center of interest can be achieved with one large item or a group of small ones. An appliqué on a contrasting background, or jewelry, can add emphasis to otherwise plain outfits.

Rhythm

Rhythm is the pleasing arrangement of the design elements to produce a feeling of continuity or easy movement of the observer's eye. Rhythm encourages

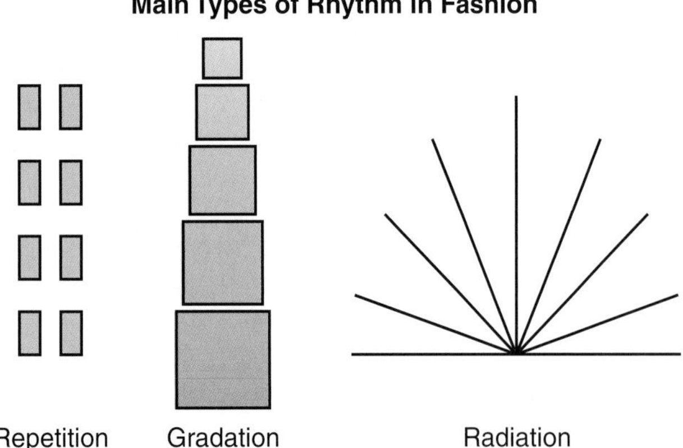

8-26 The eye moves through the lines and spaces when rhythm is created by repetition, gradation, or radiation.

the viewer's eye to move steadily and smoothly through the lines and spaces of the design, from one part to another. The main ways to create rhythm are by repetition, gradation, or radiation, 8-26.

Repetition repeats lines, shapes, colors, or textures in a garment. This can be done with all parts having the same shaped edges, such as squared, rounded, or scalloped. It is also achieved by repeating buttons, tucks, pleats, or trim.

Gradation is a gradual increase or decrease of similar design elements, also called progression. Colors might go from light to dark, textures from fine to coarse, lines from thin to thick, and shapes from small to large. The gradual changes provide continuity while giving a feeling of movement.

Radiation is created by lines emerging from a central point like rays, resulting in the parts being an equal distance from that point. It is created when gathers, tucks, seams, darts, flowing lines, or colors fan outward from an area.

Harmony

Harmony is pleasing visual unity of a design created by a tasteful relationship among all parts within the whole. Garments that have harmony are pleasing to the eye and suit the wearer. When a total design is good, the overall effect is harmonious. Every part looks as if it belongs, with nothing out of place. On the other hand, if elements of the design clash, confusion results.

Accessories often tie outfits together visually and create harmony. When several different patterns are used in an outfit, the result may look confusing. Patterned garments usually look best with solid-colored ones, especially when the solid color is included in the pattern. Repeating colors from a garment by adding a belt, tie, or other accessory is also often attractive.

A harmonious outfit has enough variation to be interesting, but does not have excess variation that displeases. A judgment must be made to decide if harmony has been achieved. Some people have more natural aptitude for this than others. However, through observation and experience, most people can recognize apparel that is harmonious and that flatters the person wearing it. Analyze the harmony that is achieved in 8-27.

Saks Fifth Avenue

8-27 Think about how the elements of design have been used according to the principles of design to create harmony in this Bill Blass wool top and cardigan with a satin skirt.

Illusions Created by Design

As you have learned in this chapter, by using the elements and principles of design cleverly, the good features of people can be accentuated, and their less desirable features can be hidden. With effective use of design, people can look shorter, taller, heavier, or thinner in various areas of their bodies. To help others achieve "personal style," fashion professionals must understand how to enhance the appearance of particular body shapes. Charts 8-28 and 8-29 summarize ways to utilize design in apparel.

The shape of a female's body is called her ***figure***. The shape of a male's body is called his ***physique***. Body size is usually measured at the chest, waist, and hips. However, the proportion of the parts gives a better indication of shape. This relationship among the different areas of the total human form is called *body build*.

Creating Height and Width Illusions	
For a Taller, Thinner Look	**For a Shorter, Wider Look**
Straight silhouettes	Wide silhouettes
Vertical lines	Horizontal lines
Shaping with seams or darts	Shaping with gathers or pleats
Smooth, flat textures	Bulky, heavy textures
One-color outfits	Contrasting colors (top/bottom)
Small, matching belts	Wide, contrasting belts
Fit that skims body easily	Tightly fitting clothes
Dark, dull, cool colors	Bright, light, warm colors
Subtle prints, plaids, etc.	Bold prints, plaids, etc.
Simple, uncluttered looks	Full sleeves, wide pants
Emphasis leading the eye up	Emphasis leading the eye down

8-28 Fashion experts can create body shape illusions by following these suggestions.

Think about how to use certain styles for desired illusions to flatter various body builds. For instance, for women, an A-line silhouette can hide wide hips. It can also balance a full bust or wide shoulders. High or low-waistline styles can balance a figure or conceal problem areas at the chest, waist, or hip levels. To hide a woman's large waistline, a tubular dress could be worn that intentionally falls straight from the shoulder to the hem. On the other hand, if a waistline is especially small, a garment with a close fit at the waist and a full skirt would emphasize its smallness.

Attention Getters and De-Emphasizers	
To Avoid Attention to Areas	**To Attract Attention to Areas**
Dark, dull colors	Light, bright colors
Cool hues	Warm hues
Minimum structural design	Structural accents there
Minimum applied decoration	Applied decoration there
Flat, dull textures	Shiny textures
Soft fabrics	Clingy fabrics
Plain, unpatterned fabrics	Large, busy prints

8-29 Fashion professionals can help people highlight their best physical features and camouflage the areas they feel are less desirable.

Fashion professionals know how to help others with their clothing selections. Every aspect is important for an entire visual effect from head to toe. For instance, wide feet look best in simple, one-color shoe styles. A buckle or other decoration on a shoe may make the foot look shorter or wider. Ankle straps cut the illusion of body height and call attention to heavy ankles.

The rules of creating height and width, or emphasizing or de-emphasizing areas, are the same for all parts of an outfit, as well as the total effect.

Summary

Color has hue, value, and intensity. It is often the most important design element. It communicates in various ways, and is used in apparel according to accepted guidelines. Color schemes can be chosen, and certain color effects can be achieved.

The shape, or silhouette, of fashions influences the illusion of the size of a person. Fashion silhouette can enhance or hide much of the body shape. Silhouette also reveals whether or not apparel is "in fashion" at any given time.

Lines lead the eye of the observer around the spaces, parts, and details of garments. Structural and decorative lines combine for an overall effect. Straight, curved, or jagged lines can be used vertically, horizontally, and/or diagonally to create predictable illusions.

Structural texture and added visual texture also add interest to apparel and can be used to increase or decrease the apparent size of the wearer. Texture should be suited to the occasions for which it is worn, the overall design of the garment or outfit, and the person wearing it.

Balance gives equilibrium to a design, with all sides appearing equal in weight or power of attraction. Formal (symmetrical) balance is the most common, with identical details arranged the same distance from the center. Informal balance is asymmetrical, with parts placed unequally from the center.

Proportion relates parts of a design to each other and to the whole. This is most pleasing when garment areas are divided unevenly and coordinate with the structure and proportion of the person wearing the outfit. The ideal body height can be drawn with eight equal areas to which design can be attractively related.

Emphasis is created with a center of interest, or focal point, which is seen first. Emphasis is used in apparel to draw attention to an attractive personal feature or away from a less desirable feature.

Rhythm produces a feeling of continuity of movement through the lines and spaces of a design. The main ways to create it are by repetition, gradation, or radiation.

A garment with good design is pleasing to the eye and makes the wearer look his or her best. When the elements of design are used effectively, according to the principles of design, pleasing visual harmony results. A harmonious outfit has enough variation to be interesting but does not have excess variation that displeases. It flatters the person wearing it.

With effective use of design, people can look shorter, taller, heavier, or thinner. Fashion professionals must understand how to enhance the appearance of female figures and male physiques. Certain styles can be used for desired illusions to flatter various body builds.

To Know

elements of design
principles of design
hue
value
tint
shade
intensity
neutrals
color wheel
color schemes
silhouette
line
structural lines
decorative lines
texture
balance
proportion
emphasis
rhythm
harmony
figure
physique

To Review

1. How can fashion professionals develop good taste and advise people how to look their best?
2. Name the elements of design.
3. Name the principles of design.
4. What design element is noticed first when a retail customer selects a garment?
5. Why does white feel cooler and black bring warmth to the wearer?
6. List the primary hues, then the secondary hues.
7. Distinguish between warm colors and cool colors.
8. Which color scheme combines three colors equidistant on the wheel?
9. What types of colors appear to advance, or come toward the observer to make a form look larger? What types of colors appear to recede, or back away from the observer, to make a form look smaller?
10. What color would small blue and yellow stripes look from across a room?
11. How do fluorescent and incandescent lights affect colors?
12. Which lines give the impression of added height and slimness, making the body look taller and thinner?
13. Why do shiny textures make people look larger?
14. What effect do large, bold visual patterns have in a design?
15. What are the two main types of balance?
16. What is another term for proportion?
17. With ideal body proportions, how much height is above the waist and how much is below the waist?
18. What can happen if there are too many areas of interest or emphasis in a design?
19. What must fashion professionals understand in order to help others achieve "personal style"?
20. List at least one way to accomplish each of the following:
    a. To make a body look taller and thinner.
    b. To make a body look shorter and wider.
    c. To avoid attention to areas.
    d. To attract attention to areas.

To Do

1. On the dull side of white poster board, make a complete color wheel using only red, yellow, and blue paints, mixing the secondary and intermediate hues with those primary hues. Also, make a value scale of tints to shades for one of the hues and show a gradual dulling of the intensity of a hue by adding increasing amounts of its complement. Label your work.
2. Use six pieces of white paper to illustrate each of the six color schemes described in this chapter (with different hues than those in 8-6). Find apparel pictures from magazines or mail-order catalogs that show at least three of the color schemes and mount them on the paper and label them according to color scheme.
3. Find and clip at least six pictures of outfits that show straight, curved, jagged, vertical, horizontal, and diagonal lines. Mount the pictures on paper and write an analysis of the effect of the lines in each. Also identify each of the lines as structural or decorative.

4. In an oral report to the class, analyze the elements of design in at least four actual garments or clear pictures of garments. Compare the relationship between outer shape and inner structural and decorative lines. Describe the structural and added visual texture. Tell what illusions might be created by the color, shape, line, and texture in each garment. Also be prepared to answer questions from the class.
5. Write a report that analyzes a hypothetical figure or physique, describing the good and less desirable features of the person. Then explain what design illusions should be created for that person's best look and how to accomplish it in his or her apparel. Find pictures or draw sketches of at least two outfits that would achieve the best look for that person.

JCPenney

The elements and principles of design were combined to create this fashionable outfit.

CHAPTER 9

The Fashion Design Segment

After studying this chapter, you will be able to

- explain the price market categories of apparel.
- define designer collection showings.
- describe how designers capitalize on their name recognition.
- summarize the designing process for fashions.
- identify the world's fashion centers and their specialties.
- recognize some influential fashion design names and labels.
- cite U.S. fashion associations and awards.

Before apparel manufacturing can take place, the fashion design process must occur. Fashions are designed and produced at various price levels. Collection showings enable designers to capitalize on their name recognition to extend their profit-making opportunities. The designing process is based on needs of the market combined with creative inspiration. Highly acclaimed designers are located in many fashion centers throughout the world, 9-1.

Council of Fashion Designers of America/Patrick McMullan, photographer

9-1 U.S. womenswear fashion designer Victor Alfaro is shown here after winning an award presented by the Council of Fashion Designers of America.

Price Market Categories of Apparel

All new fashions start as designs. Each design is created for a specific price range, design level, and target customer. The price of garments to consumers depends on the quality of the materials, the type and amount of labor used, the complexity of the style and construction, and the reputation of the designer or manufacturer.

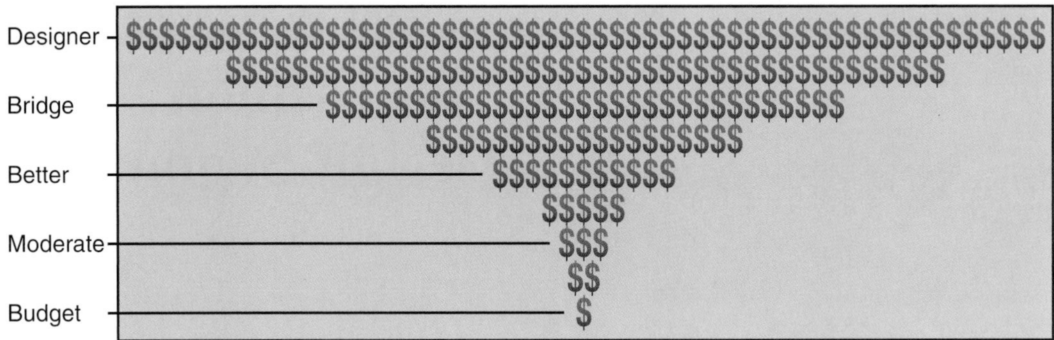

9-2 There is no longer a distinct delineation between the price levels of apparel. Each one runs into the next one, forming a continuous price slide from top to bottom.

Fashions, particularly women's garments, are grouped around five main price levels. They are:

- designer
- bridge
- better
- moderate
- budget

Although the levels have been quite distinct in the past, they are now blending together into one continuum. There is less separation of the categories, 9-2. Many designers and manufacturers are providing goods to a wider span of the market. Their different fashions are included in several of the categories at one time. Also, design firms are buying ownership interests in other design firms, forming multinational corporations to combine forces and capitalize on their synergies.

Designer

At the designer price level, this almost extinct ***couture*** (koo-tur') segment provides original, high priced fashions for the tiny "class" market (as opposed to lower-priced apparel for the "mass" market). The garments have distinctive styling and emphasize top quality. These "prestige" fashions are created by name designers, such as Oscar de la Renta, Bill Blass, and James Galanos. The garments are ***custom-made***, or made-to-order for the client. This provides individual fit to the client's measurements and one-of-a kind exclusiveness. Couture fashions are offered to customers at many thousands of dollars through the designer's salon.

Most successful high fashion designers have had help getting started from financial backers or business partners who also share in the profits. The creative talent of the designer is recognized and combined with the money and promotion of benefactors to establish international influence. It is also important for designers to have the support of the press and other media to spread their fashion ideas and build their name recognition.

Bridge

Bridge lines are "secondary" lines of well-known designers. Their high prices are between the couture and better categories, with garments selling for many hundreds of dollars. These limited-edition garments of expensive fabrics and fine details are produced in small

Hong Kong Trade Development Council

9-3 This outfit by designer Cary Tang gives an elegant, casual look. Like other designer fashions, it is of quality materials and construction.

quantities. They contain a status designer label and have a small, profitable market. They are usually sportier and more career oriented than couture clothes, 9-3. Often they are designed by talented, unknown design assistants with the approval of the name designer. Some of the best design assistants branch off into businesses of their own.

Bridge lines offer the most expensive ready-to-wear apparel produced. ***Ready-to-wear (RTW)*** refers to garments, especially women's apparel, produced in factories according to standard sizes, as opposed to being individually custom-made. Examples of bridge lines are Anne Klein II, DKNY (Donna Karan New York), and Joan Vass. Bridge lines are retailed through fashionable dress shops or special designer sections of upscale department stores.

Better

Better dresses and other better garments have high quality, but a more reasonable price. They are designed by talented experts who are unnamed on the label, but who are vital to the success of a firm. The larger numbers of these RTW garments are more accessible to consumers and retailers than high fashion designs. They are retailed in selected specialty and department stores and have such labels as Evan Picone, Jones New York, and Liz Claiborne, 9-4.

Moderate

The moderate category is made up of medium-priced merchandise with well-known brand names, such as Jantzen, Gap, and Wrangler, 9-5. This apparel is widely available and worn by most Americans. Some labels are sold through department and chain stores, and others through specialty apparel stores. This category employs the most fashion designers. They work on the design staffs of manufacturers, designing thousands of garments and accessories to be mass-produced under a manufacturer's trade name. Many of the designs are *adaptations* of designer creations, with certain distinguishing features of the style that inspired them, but not exactly the same.

Some moderately priced apparel is produced in the U.S., some is made overseas, and some manufacturing companies supplement domestic (U.S.) production with offshore manufacturing. Retailers sell higher

Liz Claiborne

9-4 Fine quality better apparel can be found in many good retail stores.

Wrangler Hero

9-5 Well-made moderate apparel represents good value to consumers and is widely available through retail stores.

volumes of this level than the more expensive categories and have lower ***margins*** (profit per item). However, the total profits are higher.

Budget

Budget is the lowest priced category of apparel. It is found on retail racks and shelves for the mass market. Almost no original designing is done at this level. Instead, copying is done of other garments. This results in downscaled ***knockoffs***, or direct line-for-line duplicates of designs, usually of higher priced garments or accessories, 9-6.

Budget manufacturers employ *design stylists* to create the knockoffs. They simplify garments or accessories that are popular in the higher priced categories. The knockoffs are created in less expensive materials and with fewer details and cheaper trims. Stylists copy updated versions of widely popular styles that will sell immediately in great quantities. Because of photos, fax machines, next-day air deliveries, and worldwide computer connections, knockoffs sometimes reach the stores before designer originals are available. This is unfortunate for the original designers!

Budget garments are manufactured inexpensively in large numbers. The volume production is mostly done overseas, in low-wage countries. Low priced chain and discount stores sell budget apparel as unbranded or private label merchandise. Common labels include the Gitano and Donkenny brands.

Collection Showings

The garments shown in a designer's or apparel manufacturer's specific seasonal presentation is called a ***collection***, especially for more exclusive garments. See 9-7. In a large manufacturing company, the collection may be made up of several different lines. A ***line*** is a group of styles and designs that are produced and sold as a set of new selections for a given season. A line especially refers to moderate and lower priced garments. A collection or line might contain from 60 to 200 garments.

The Fashion Association/Brian McKinney Designer Collections

9-7 This double-breasted suit with matching vest and drawstring pants, worn with a striped collarless shirt, is only one outfit in an entire designer collection for a particular fashion season.

9-6 These knockoffs, sold for far less than the original designs, are made of less expensive materials.

At the top designer levels, showings are glitzy runway extravaganzas. They are like stage productions, with high fashion models parading to music. Each outfit precisely fits the model who wears it in the show, 9-8. At the end of the show, the designer makes a traditional walk down the runway to cheers and applause from the invited guests.

The exclusive audiences at the collection showings include private customers, fashion journalists, retail store buyers, celebrities, and friends of the designers. Photographs and video footage are allowed for press releases, which give the designers publicity in newspapers and magazines. However, no sketching or picture taking is allowed by others in the audience.

The cost of preparing for and producing high fashion couture showings is exorbitant. The fine fabrics and trimmings, as well as the custom construction of each of the many designs, makes them extremely expensive, and hardly any garments are sold as a result of

Fashion Institute of Technology

9-8 Outfits presented in collection showings are made to perfectly fit the models wearing them.

Fashion Institute of Technology

9-9 Collection showings are exciting and informative fashion trade events that create publicity.

the showings. Additionally, there are modeling fees and costs for hairdressers, makeup experts, lighting, and music. In fact, most of these showings are no longer profitable, losing money due to rising costs and declining sales. They are held strictly for publicity and prestige. They allow the designer to show his or her creativity and gain a great deal of publicity. See 9-9.

Designer RTW collection showings are the most important fashion events. They are held as giant trade exhibitions. They take place in New York, Paris, and other cities. To cut costs, top design firms stage their shows at one common site. Corporate sponsors donate money and products, such as beverages, cars, and cosmetics, in return for publicity. The shows are attended by hundreds of retail store buyers, press people, celebrities, and sponsorship guests. Design firms try to keep retail buyers at their events long enough to make deals and take orders. Depending on retail orders, only about half of the designs of each collection will be put into production.

The major showings are held twice a year for a week to 10 days. Couture collections are shown about three months ahead of the fall-winter and spring-summer fashion seasons. Ready-to-wear collections are shown earlier, to give retailers time to place orders and manufacturers time to produce and ship the lines to stores for the retail selling season. Thus, the fall-winter women's RTW collections are shown worldwide in February/March, and spring-summer collections are shown in September/October. The usual calendar includes New York followed by London, Milan, and Paris in close order. Some overseas designers like to show in New York because it is first! Menswear collections are shown about two months earlier in a different order.

The individual showings are spaced so important clients, retail buyers, and the press can attend each one. Scheduling for shows is arranged by industry organizations in each fashion city, resulting in a different collection shown every hour all day long. In the evenings, there are parties, exhibitions, dinners, and other VIP events.

Videotapes of showings are now sometimes sent to the firm's best clients, or to retailers, so they can order without attending the showing. A new, low-key trend for collection showings is to invite selected guests to a breakfast, brunch, or lunch with models walking around the tables wearing the designs. One designer recently mailed hundreds of 3-D View-Masters to clients, retailers, and the media to look at his collection "at their leisure" on slides. Many RTW firms show their lines in their own corporate showrooms.

Capitalizing on Name Recognition

Today, consumers have access to an abundance of mass-produced fashions of excellent quality in all sizes and price ranges. Also, their lifestyles and attitudes toward clothes have changed, creating a desire

JCPenney

9-10 Today almost everyone wants lots of pants, tops, and accessories that are popularly priced, rather than expensive one-of-a-kind garments.

for more clothes that are moderately priced, 9-10. Almost no expensive couture fashions are sold.

Top fashion designers, however, continue to have specific creative reputations and personal trademarks for which they are known. These give the products a perceived difference. ***Perceived difference*** is the idea that, in customers' minds, the items stand out from others, usually because of image and quality. Each designer strives to have his or her signature, initials, logo, or type of garment instantly recognized. A ***logo*** is a symbol that represents a person, firm, or organization. Logos are sometimes used on clasps of purses. They are embroidered onto chest pockets of shirts or jackets or woven into lining fabrics to show the designer's distinctive image.

Though couture collections lose money, the publicity from designers' showings keeps their names famous, and helps them maintain demand for other business opportunities. Designers capitalize on this name recognition to make a good profit with ready-to-wear lines and house boutiques and by entering into agreements for licensing, franchising, and sewing patterns. Designer labels in RTW clothes, accessories, and other products indicate to retail buyers and consumers that the items should be of fine quality and in good taste.

Secondary Lines

The ultra-expensive market for couture fashions has dwindled. Designer secondary lines have almost completely replaced custom-made fashions, which require fittings, take a long time to be made, and are inconvenient for today's fast-paced schedules. Therefore, renowned designers now promote their secondary lines as the garments of choice for the upper echelon of society.

Designer RTW (bridge) garments feature top quality fabrics and construction. They are produced in small quantities at selected manufacturing plants that are usually not owned by, or geographically near, the design firm. Then they are carefully distributed around the world so only a few items are available in the same consumer market. Customers can try garments on in exclusive dress shops, and wear them instantly if no alterations are needed. The fashions have the look, feel, and label of the prestigious designer.

House Boutiques

House boutiques are small retail shops owned by the designers. They used to be only in or near the designer's headquarters, but now they are also located in fashionable areas of other cities. They feature RTW designs as well as high priced, high quality accessories, such as handbags, lingerie, shoes, jewelry, and scarves. The merchandise is designed by the designer or a design assistant and manufactured by outside producers. Items bear the designer's prestigious label. The design company pays the rent and hires the salespeople.

Licensing

Licensing is a legal arrangement whereby manufacturers are granted the exclusive right to produce and market goods that bear the famous name of a designer. The designer, in return, receives a percentage dollar amount of wholesale sales. Licensing provides designers with a method of promoting their names, while having limited risk or liability. The designer gives a personal "stamp of approval" to someone else's products, for a specific period of time, in return for royalty fees.

For manufacturers, the status symbol of a designer's name is very profitable because of the image

Council of Fashion Designers of America/Corina Lecca, photographer

9-11 Calvin Klein, a designer of womenswear and menswear, has many licensing agreements for nonapparel products. He is shown here with his wife, Kelly.

of fashion quality and prestige it provides. For retailers, these name products sell well to consumers who want to identify with particular designers. For well-known designers, licensing is extremely lucrative, with large royalties received annually in this "name game." Major designers license their names or logos to different manufacturers on a large variety of products, including bed linens, shoes, eyeglasses, perfume, luggage, chocolates, and car interiors. Many designers have multiple licensing agreements for noncompeting products, 9-11. Some are restructuring their firms to concentrate on international licensing growth.

Smart designers take an active role in assuring that the design and quality of licensed products meet the expected standards of their label, especially to eliminate the chance that the famous name could be compromised with unacceptable products. Designers who find it hard to keep tabs on the level of design or quality of all their licensed products establish license directors and design studios. These employees arrange the licensing deals and check to be sure that the products are worthy of the designers' labels.

There are other types of licensing besides designer licensing. Celebrity licensing associates the name of movie stars, famous athletes, and other celebrities with products. Character licensing is tied to cartoon characters, such as Disney or TV cartoon heroes, and is prevalent in children's wear and toys. See 9-12. Corporate licensing results in clothing that outwardly features logos or depictions of copyrighted products, such as soft drinks, candy, or other commercial products.

9-12 Licensing of well-known characters, such as cartoon personalities, helps to sell articles of clothing to certain consumer groups.

9-13 Although home sewing is not as popular today as in the past, some designers still offer fashions for the home sewing market.

Franchising

Top designers also supplement their businesses with franchises in cities around the world. ***Franchising*** is a contract arrangement in which the designer grants a retailer the right to use his or her famous name and trademarked goods within a particular trading area. In return, the designer receives a set amount of money (an original lump sum plus a monthly royalty payment on goods or services sold). The designer or a manufacturing firm *(franchisor)* has no direct ownership of the franchise and does not help run the business, but supplies the goods that the retailer sells. The *franchisee* is the owner (person or group) of the business that benefits from the expertise and reputation of the franchisor. All the franchise stores with the same name might be owned by different people.

Franchise stores of designer fashions are often located in exclusive shopping areas of major cities or in boutique areas within large department stores. Benetton, Esprit, Liz Claiborne, and Lady Madonna Shops are a few of the many fashion franchises. Other types of franchises with which you might be familiar include fast-food restaurants, convenience stores, and automobile dealerships.

Franchising allows store owners to get their businesses off the ground quickly with instant name recognition, although they have no control of the parent firm's products or distribution reliability. On the other hand, franchisors can control the design and distribution of their products, have limited liability, and need less capital to expand quickly into many market areas, thus increasing their profits. To continue their franchise demand, franchisors must satisfy their franchisees and consumers.

Sewing Patterns

A few designers add to their incomes by selling the patterns of some of their creations to commercial pattern companies, such as Vogue, McCalls, and Simplicity. Such ***designer patterns*** are reproduced and featured in pattern catalogs at fabric stores where the patterns are sold. See 9-13. Skilled home sewers can use the patterns to make their own designer clothes.

The Designing Process

The previously discussed business opportunities apply to famous up-scale fashion designers. However, most designers in the fashion industry are not well-known to the general public. They work for more moderatly priced apparel manufacturers' firms, creating the lines that are sold with their firms' labels.

Ready-to-wear designers start work on their company's lines about a year before the apparel will be bought by consumers. The lines are ready to be shown to retailers six months ahead of the retail season. Notice where fashion design falls on the time chart of the textile/apparel pipeline in 9-14. When the designs of one collection go into production, designing plans start for the next season.

Besides including some new garment designs in each RTW line, styles that are selling well in one season are modified into fresh interpretations for the next season. A fashionable summer design in lightweight fabric, pastel colors, and short sleeves might be continued for the winter collection in a wool blend, darker colors, and long sleeves. Presently, trends move through the fashion cycle more slowly, with updates providing fresh looks rather than extreme fads that come in and go out of fashion quickly.

U.S. firms generally have conservative business strategies that try to minimize financial losses and maximize short-term profits. Thus, they make "safe" decisions with designs that are known to be popular and that will be accepted by the majority of consumers, rather than taking risks with far-out concepts. Designers have the challenging task of creating new, exciting, fashion-forward ideas that will also be accepted by enough consumers to make a good profit. The majority of fashion change is gradual.

To stay in business, designers must be attuned to consumer lifestyles and be able to predict upcoming fashion trends that will be popular. The real challenge is in evaluating trends and their timing in relation to a firm's specific target market. Fashion changes are no longer dictated by designers "pushing" new designs on consumers to make money. Fashion designers and manufacturers respond to what they think are the changing needs and wants of consumers. They produce new and different styles from which consumers select their actual choices.

Fashion piracy is the stealing of design ideas without the permission of the originator. It is always a threat to creative work, but is extremely common in the fashion business. The U.S. has no legal copyright protection against it. Most copied designs are toned down by manufacturers to meet the mass production capabilities of their factories, price ranges of their customers, and to have a wider appeal at retail.

Copying saves money for manufacturers and dominates the lower price markets of the industry. It enables producers to immediately get out fast-selling styles with the latest trends, while the popularity of the styles still exists. Since firms are specialized by apparel type, size, and price range, many different firms must produce versions of a design idea for it to reach all potential customers. By providing a similar style at

Textile/Apparel Timing

Time ahead of retail selling	Activity Taking Place
4 years	Innovations of new fiber variants
2 years	Color projections and fabric development
18 months	Trend projections
12 months	Fabric manufacturing
7–9 months	Apparel designing
3–6 months	Retailers order from manufacturers
2–4 months	Apparel manufacturing
—	Retail selling to consumers

9-14 This simplified chart shows the approximate timing of activities through the distribution chain. Timing has been shortened with electronic linkages and manufacturing within close proximity to the market, but is longer for overseas production.

Design Intelligence

9-15 Forecasting services monitor the "pulse" of all major fashion centers and predict trends that designers can incorporate into their fashions.

Hong Kong Trade Development Council

9-16 Do you remember the trickle-up theory from Chapter 2? The designs in this Mega Advance Limited collection were influenced by young or lower income groups into high fashion garments.

several price levels, different consumer market segments are satisfied.

Sources of Inspiration

When creating new fashions, designers use many different sources for inspiration. Forecasting services are very influential for early predictions, 9-15. They even offer private design work and consultations, including sketches with exact details and measurements, for a fee. Forecasters also cover the major fabric fairs, apparel markets, and "hottest" retail shops throughout the world to see what is gaining in popularity. Besides early predictions, they give advice on how to modify trends for immediate use to the general public.

Past fashion movement can give clues for future fashion designs, since some styles reappear with predictable regularity. For instance, skirt widths and lengths, and waistline emphasis move in and out of fashion. Historic costume collections are studied for silhouette, detail, and fabric ideas.

Designers also look at art movements, new stage plays, and popular movies and television shows. News events, new living patterns, and nature contribute to some designs. Designers notice prestigious people with unique looks, such as royalty or rock stars, who sometimes set fashion trends. "Fashion forward" young people on the streets sometimes invent their own extreme looks that designers notice, 9-16. Designers are keen observers of people and the way they put outfits together.

Designers get some inspiration from foreign and American fashion magazines and fashion shows. Fabrics often give creative impetus, 9-17. New fabrics from textile firms or unusual textiles from other cultures are especially helpful. Successful designers have a feel for changing economic, social, and political conditions that affect fashion.

Current trends in consumer attitudes and purchasing patterns are analyzed to ensure that goods are produced that customers want. *Winners* from the previous

Fashion Institute of Design and Merchandising, California/BethHerzhaft, photographer

9-17 Fabric pieces can provide design inspiration, since ideas evolve when swatches are handled and placed next to each other.

season are recut for production the next season. Winners are the best-selling items in a manufacturer's line. Also, designers talk to retail store owners and buyers about the kinds of garments their customers would like. Even so, many of the new designs introduced each season fail to become popular. Some are too extreme, or appear too early, before consumers are ready to accept them.

Styles that are identified early as future best-sellers in many price ranges are called *prophetic fashions*. By pinpointing prophetic fashions early, fashion businesses can design, produce, and sustain them as long as they are popular.

Fashion Institute of Technology/John Senzer, Photographer

9-18 Some designers get inspiration as they use a sketch pad, with new fashions evolving from the end of their pen or pencil!

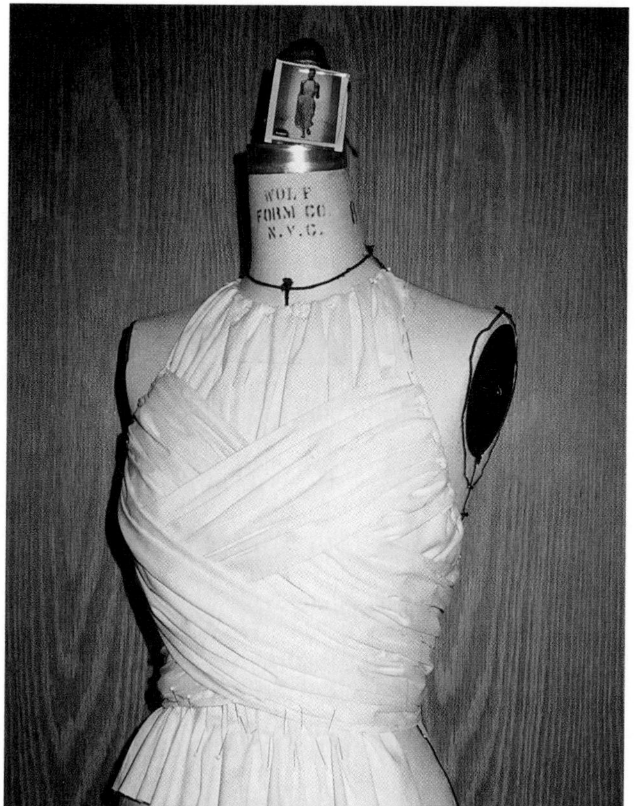

Dept. of Apparel, Interiors, Housing & Merchandising/Oregon State University

9-19 Draping fabric onto a mannequin to design fashions is often done for higher priced gowns and dresses, especially in Europe.

Using Technology in Fashion Design

Traditionally, designers have either made sketches of their ideas, as shown in 9-18, or draped them in muslin on a dressmaker's form, as in 9-19. A pattern was then made manually for that design idea. Some designers still work in these ways. However, the methods are very slow for high volume production.

Today, most companies use CAD systems for fashion design, with increasingly user-friendly systems. CAD terminals can include sketch pads with electronic pens for drawing images into the computers, 9-20. Also, existing images, such as previous drawings or actual fabric patterns, can be scanned into the system with equipment that can read an image on paper and put it into the computer. All work can be saved and retrieved on command for updating. Seasonal color palettes can be incorporated, with hundreds of thousands of color options (including tints and shades), 9-21.

Through global telecommunication networks, computer-generated designs can be transmitted via "electronic file transfer" of digital images. Other members of the firm can give their reactions almost instantly. Also, cameras can give photographic replicas of designs for test-marketing or to show retailers the upcoming collection. The opportunity to view the line with major customers before buying fabrics, making samples, and starting production saves manufacturing costs and ensures marketable delivery.

If a seam or other detail is changed in one part of a garment, other affected parts are automatically adjusted by the CAD system. When the design is finalized, the computer can digitize the sketch to print out a pattern of it for production.

CAD enhances the creative process and shortens product development time to make changes to achieve the final design. Hundreds of design options can be built

Ball State University-Indiana

9-20 CAD equipment can combine many different options to accommodate the needs of different designers.

Info Design, Inc.

9-21 Computer systems used for design work offer almost unlimited color selections, as well as the ability to do storyboard presentations that display all aspects of designs.

into the software, to be combined according to the final goal of the designer. *Electronic graphics interchange* allows garment parts, colors, and prints to be changed with a computer command. Designers can experiment with a vast array of shapes, colors, textures, and fabrics.

"3-D imaging" enables a designer to create a three-dimensional design that shows depth and form. The image can be manipulated and viewed from all sides. Costly mistakes are avoided since the design is not made up in fabric until it is finalized.

CAD systems work best for sportswear, children's clothes, and tailored apparel. These garments are regularly designed with flat patterns and do not contain draped, flowing lines. CAD is also good for knitwear. The knitwear is designed and then, in a matter of hours, the computer automatically programs the knitting machines to produce it. Manually, this would take days or weeks to do.

World Fashion Design Centers

Most major cities of the world have several talented, exclusive fashion designers. Besides New York and other U.S. fashion cities, foreign centers include Paris, Milan, London, Tokyo, Hong Kong, and others. Countries are eager to export their fashions to other countries and have their own semiannual exhibits and trade fairs. Designers and apparel companies have promotional trade offices in other major fashion cities around the world where they show their collections.

European womenswear collections are shown just before the New York showings. Retail buyers watch the trends presented and purchase merchandise to sell in their stores. Today, fashion is totally global, with important fashion cities in many countries of the world.

United States

The United States has gained worldwide recognition for fashion creativity. New York City is still the U.S. fashion capital, especially for higher priced lines. In New York City, designer fashion week shows are held twice a year in tents at Bryant Park in Manhattan. Over 50 shows are staged. Supermodels work several shows per day. Retail buyers, celebrities, and the media attend. It is a glamorous and hectic time for all. California, especially Los Angeles, is known for innovative styling in sportswear and "Hollywood" evening wear. The cultural opportunities and lifestyle activities of these cities offer constant sources of inspiration and new ideas.

Dallas is known for dresses and moderately priced lines. Other fashion hubs include Atlanta, Miami, Seattle, San Francisco, and Chicago. The fashion press, movie stars, political figures, and international visitors help to support the fame of U.S. designers. U.S. market centers will be discussed further in Chapter 16.

France

The world's high fashion industry originated with the superior French dressmaking industry, with exquisite construction and luxurious materials. The city of Paris is an international cultural center and is still considered to lead world fashion with the purest creativity, 9-22. French collection showings immediately precede those in the U.S. Many top designers from other countries choose to show their collections in Paris.

Haute couture (pronounced oat koo-tur′) is the name for the high fashion designer industry of France. Paris haute couture businesses are located in city "fashion houses" rather than in modern commercial buildings. Also, many designers from other cities have branch salons in Paris. Several fashion houses bear the name of their originator who has retired or is deceased. These businesses continue with new designers.

The trade association for top designers of the Paris couture is the ***Chambre Syndicale*** (pronounced shom′br sin-dee-kall′). It was formed to determine qualifications for couture houses, requirements for their showings, and to deal with their common problems and interests. A *couturier* (high fashion designer) must be recognized as talented and successful to become a member. He or she must abide by a set of rules that include a code against copying and a minimum number of original outfits per collection. The rules also govern minimum numbers of staff models and production workers, dates of showings, shipping dates, and so on.

The Chambre Syndicale sponsors a school to educate apprentices for the couture industry. It also represents its members in relations with the French government, arbitrates disputes, and regulates working hours and uniform wage arrangements. It coordinates the dates of the showings and registers those who will attend. Individual customers and the press are admitted free.

Trade buyers, such as apparel manufacturers, retailers, and pattern companies, must pay a ***caution*** (kaw-see′-on) fee to attend French designer showings. This fee is usually quite a large payment, intended to deter free copying, and may be applied toward purchases of collection garments. Sometimes it is an agreement to purchase at least a certain amount. Since RTW trade buyers

9-22 Many names of Paris designers make that French city famous for fashion creativity.

are essentially buying copying rights, they are charged more for a garment than a private customer is charged.

The French designer ready-to-wear industry is called ***prêt-à-porter*** (pret-ah-por-tay′). The "pret" collections are shown at the same time as mass produced RTW lines. The showings are at different locations during "Fashion Week" (lasting about 10 days) in Paris. Womenswear, menswear, childrenswear, and knitwear are shown at separate times.

Italy

Italy is known for beautiful fabrics, sophisticated prints, sportswear, knitwear, and menswear. It is a fashion leader in the design and manufacture of leather accessories, such as shoes, handbags, and gloves. Many Italian fashion houses are family-run, with the skills passed on from generation to generation.

The high fashion design industry of Italy is called ***alta moda***. Couture is centered in Rome, with high quality RTW in Milan. Cheaper RTW, menswear, children's wear, and knitwear is from Florence.

The Italians promote their fashion collections often, with fashion fairs showing different categories at different times. The main collections are shown just before the French showings, so foreign buyers and press can cover both markets in one trip. Milan has the largest exhibits, showing womenswear and knitwear. Accessories are shown at a different time. Florence has major exhibitions for childrenswear and menswear. Italy even has fashion fairs devoted to uniforms and work clothes.

Great Britain

London is Britain's major fashion center. London is famous for custom-made "Savile Row" menswear of top quality and elegant women's apparel for royalty. Today, London's strength lies in high quality ready-to-wear men's tailored apparel, fine rainwear, and far-out "punk" fashions, as in 9-23. Carnaby Street is known for uninhibited fashions. Bond Street is now the creative area, with designer shops and upscale retailers.

British fashion is promoted by the British Fashion Council (BFC). The BFC sponsors and schedules the London Fashion week twice a year, where designers show their lines. Top RTW designers belong to a cooperative association called the London Designer Collections.

The fabrics and apparel products of England, Scotland, and Ireland include top quality tweeds and woolens, as well as lamb's wool and cashmere, in both woven or knitted creations.

Other European Fashion Centers

Germany's fashion design segment is small, but the country is a large producer of well-made, conservatively styled, high to moderately priced RTW for women and men. The excellent construction and detailing of German-made apparel is very dependable. German textiles provide worldwide inspiration for new fabric and apparel designs. Fashion fairs feature different categories of apparel at various times and in different German locations.

The Scandinavian countries of Denmark, Norway, Sweden, and Finland are renowned for woolens, especially their native patterned ski sweaters and other knitwear. They are also known for furs, leathers, and innovative fabric designs. Their gold and silver jewelry has clean-cut designs. The four countries form a consolidated market center. They also hold major trade fairs and maintain permanent showrooms together in Copenhagen, the center of the Scandinavian fashion world.

Spain excels with leather, suede, and beading. The fairly young fashion industry is centered in Madrid, with menswear in Barcelona. A government-backed effort to modernize, unite, and promote Spain's fashion industry is leading to more international recognition of the country's goods. Most fashion houses are small, but trying to grow by creating manufacturing and financial relationships. Many firms show merchandise at European fashion fairs outside their country, as well as in Spanish cities.

Canada

Canada should not be considered a shadow of the U.S. It has a wonderful fashion personality of its own, mostly at the high and moderate price levels. The industry, centered in Montreal and Toronto, is growing fast, with design confidence and innovative products. Besides apparel, especially outerwear and furs, Canadian

Underground Shoes—Great Britain

9-23 Shiny fabrics, imitation furs, and unique footwear are some of the fashion forward looks of Great Britain.

designers create decorative household linens. The trade groups, Fashion Canada and the Fashion Designers Association, offer fashion scholarships and foster international marketing programs to promote Canadian fashion designers and an international fashion image. The annual Festival of Canadian Fashion spotlights the country's fashion industry for the world.

Central and South America

The fashion markets of the major cities of Rio de Janeiro, Buenos Aires, Sao Paulo, and Bogota represent the emerging fashion industries of this part of the world. Latin America provides close proximity and cheaper sources of supply for U.S. retail buyers, with design and production capabilities for reliability. With ready supplies of cotton, wool, leather, and cheap labor, governments of the countries have marketed their apparel products to the world. Their status in the world marketplace is increasing.

Some of the fashion products of Central and South America revolve around each country's national ethnic heritage of crafts. Other products are made to North American manufacturers' specifications, using cheaper production costs of that area of the world.

Japan

Several talented Japanese designers have fashion businesses in Paris and are members of the Chambre Syndicale. Others design, manufacture, and sell their clothing lines themselves, all over the world. They own retail outlets, lease space in department stores, and train the employees who work in them. Japanese fashion firms have the ability to produce goods quickly, and often provide merchandise ahead of other fashion centers.

Japan sends some medium to high priced clothing to other countries. The strikingly unusual shapes and fabrics do not lend themselves to volume production or the lower priced mass market. Many designers do innovative and experimental work, emphasizing a Japanese flair for mobility and comfort. They pay little attention to waistlines, rarely emphasize any certain body part, and consider hem lengths irrelevant. Also, the exchange rate between the Japanese yen and other currencies has made Japanese goods expensive in some countries.

The semiannual Tokyo Fashion Week introduces Japanese designers to buyers, the public, and the press. It operates through a central information office and gives the designers a structure for scheduled showings. Designers join together to help make their city and country important in the fashion world. Japanese design talent is recognized at "The Best" annual fashion awards presentation.

China and Hong Kong

China is a huge country by size and population. It is considered to be a "sleeping giant" and a future major force in the fashion world. Although it has been slow to acquire modern technology, it produces large amounts of textiles and does high volume mass production of many lower-priced apparel items found in U.S. stores. Much of the work is low-wage contract manufacturing for U.S. and European RTW firms. China also has a huge population that will become an important market for apparel as its consumers gain discretionary money to spend.

Hong Kong is a tiny, prosperous part of China, and a very important trading center for the world. Known in the past for cheap production of other country's designs, Hong Kong now also produces its own designs. It offers exotic fabrics, especially beautiful silks, and original dress creations, 9-24. However, its strength continues to be in production more than in the introduction of new designs. Its sewing factories manufacture lines for U.S. apparel firms and retailers. Hong Kong is the world's largest exporter of fashion apparel.

Fashion collections are shown during the annual Hong Kong Fashion Week, which promotes Hong Kong's overall image and established designers, 9-25. It also fosters new talent, with young hopefuls presenting their designs to compete for a cash prize and a trip to the Paris collection showings. The Fashion Week is organized by the Hong Kong Trade Development Council, which also promotes the designers in trade shows around the world and arranges for their personal appearances in stores.

Hong Kong designers have also formed their own group, the Hong Kong Fashion Designers Association, which sponsors shows of its members' designs.

Taiwan

Taiwan has textile and apparel factories, especially making sportswear of manufactured fibers. The country has been an important source of low-priced, medium quality, high volume apparel for America's mass retailers. Recently, Taiwan has upgraded the quality of mass production work that it does for other countries, with improved variety and innovation of technology. Good fashion design training is now also available in Taiwan, and the industry has organized to showcase Taiwanese products to the rest of the world.

South Korea

Korea has some young designers who create fashions for their country's fashion-conscious market. Most of them concentrate on RTW, such as volume-priced knitwear, menswear, and sportswear. Much of the production in South Korea is done to specifications of companies in other countries because of low labor rates.

Other World Locations

Fashion designers from Singapore, Indonesia, Thailand, Malaysia, and the Philippines show their creations in the "Best of the Asian Designers" show each year in Singapore. Some Asian designers also present their collections during Australian Fashion Week. Australia's fashion industry is centered in Sydney, with many talented designers.

India is a strong location, with textiles and fashions of cotton and silk. Its industry conducts promotions and fashion events with major retailers. It also assists American and European designers in developing sourcing contacts in India. India has a specialized college of design and technology to educate and train fashion professionals.

Eastern Europe and Russia have become producers of apparel through contracts with design firms in the West. Shortages of raw materials and machinery are being rectified. Some countries now have good designers and are learning how to market their fashion products internationally. Russia's fashion industry has an organized fashion week with showings of designer collections. Israel has achieved prominence with quality beachwear and leather goods.

Hong Kong Trade Development Council

9-24 A great deal of originality is shown by many Asian designers, such as Flora Cheong Leen of Hong Kong.

Hong Kong Trade Development Council

9-25 Hong Kong designer Allan Chiu has fastened fabric at the waistline of this dress, showing contrasting layers at the front bodice and skirt hemline.

Some Influential Fashion Designers

Many popular American and foreign couture and RTW design names are listed in 9-26. Some are individuals, and some are business names.

Most designers and their firms are known for particular specialties. In some cases, the well-known name of a designer is maintained for the fashion house after that person has died or retired. A new designer is hired

Names in Fashion Design
Joseph Abboud—New York designer of menswear, women's RTW, and accessories.
Adolfo—Cuban-born American designer of men's and womenswear, now concentrates on licensing agreements.
Victor Alfaro—Mexican-born U.S. womenswear designer.
Azzedine Alaia—Tunisian-born designer of close-fitting, black, campy RTW apparel from Paris.
Linda Allard—See Ellen Tracy.
Hardy Amies—British couturier for men and women, noted for tailored suits, coats, and evening dresses.
Giorgio Armani—Italian designer of relaxed, refined apparel.
Laura Ashley—Continuing business of deceased British designer of romantic flowered prints and lace for apparel and home fashions.
Badgley Mischka—New York collections, often beaded, designed by Mark Badgley and James Mischka.
Jhane Barnes—American designer of upscale men's clothing.
John Bartlett—New York designer who expanded from menswear into womenswear.
Geoffrey Beene—Award-winning American designer of all kinds of apparel with a relaxed, elegant look, superb cut, unusual details, and beautiful fabrics.
Benetton—Italian family business known for sweaters and many franchise stores worldwide.
Antonio Berardi—British designer who now shows his collections in Milan.
Manolo Blahnik—Spanish-born, London-based designer of exquisite shoes.
Bill Blass—American who has done elegant creations for rich and famous people, now also has RTW line and licenses.
Nicolas Bosch—Award-winning fabric designer of Spain.
Hugo Boss—German fashion firm, showing collections in Milan.
Dana Buchman—See Liz Claiborne.
Byblos—Italian firm with non-conformist designs of John Bartlett.
Pierre Cardin—French designer of "unisex" apparel for men and women who has many licensing agreements.
Oleg Cassini—Does classic womenswear in New York; now many licenses.
Jean-Charles de Castelbajac—European (Morocco, France, Italy) designer of rugged-looking men's and women's apparel, often of quilted cotton, canvas, and plaids; collections shown in Paris.
Nino Cerruti—Italian knitwear, womenswear, and licenses worldwide; shows RTW in Paris.
Lulu Cheung—Creates feminine womenswear in Hong Kong.
David Chu—Taiwanese designer of New York-based Nautica classic sportswear.
Liz Claiborne—Retired New York designer who originated the firm with her name. Dana Buchman and Karen Harman now design the bridge lines.
Comme des Garcons—See Rei Kawakubo.

9-26 Outstanding design talent exists throughout the world, with fashion influence that affects apparel globally. *(continued)*

Names in Fashion Design (continued)
Sybil Connolly—Irish dress designer in Dublin.
Jasper Conran—British designer of bright, youthful looks.
Andres Courreges—French designer of superbly tailored garments.
Oscar de la Renta—Spaniard who designs men's and womenswear collections in New York (with his name) and Paris (for the house of Pierre Balmain), and has many licensing agreements.
Louis Dell'Olio—New Yorker who used to design the Anne Klein lines, but now has his own company.
David Dixon—Canadian designer with fine tailoring in menswear and womenswear.
Dolce and Gabbana—Italian design team, popular with entertainers, does collections for men and women, designs the Complice line for the Italian firm Genny, and has several licenses.
Randolph Duke—American designer of graphic, bold, striking apparel.
Escada—German label on elegant tailored sportswear, now uses a team of international designers.
Fendi—Italian family business known for furs, excellent construction, expensive RTW, and handbags; now designed by Karl Lagerfeld.
Salvatore Ferragamo—Italian designer of shoes and RTW.
Gianfranco Ferre—Italian designer who creates an architectural look with clean lines and complex construction for his own firm (Milan) and the house of Dior (Paris).
Andrew Fezza—American who does designer and RTW lines that have a clean, relaxed, casually elegant appearance.
Katia Filippova—Russian who designs bright avant-garde mixtures of Soviet and Western "pop" in Moscow.
Tom Ford—American designer of the many Gucci and Yves Saint Laurent lines.
James Galanos—U.S. couture designer, especially of women's gowns and dresses.
John Galliano—British RTW designer of eccentric, romantic fashions. Now designs Christian Dior lines.
Jean-Paul Gaultier—French designer of avant-garde creations that are new, daring, and controversial for men and women.
Genny—Italian label for fine womenswear and eveningwear.
Ghost—British label with soft fabrics and feminine styles.
Romeo Gigli—Italian designer of muted styles in strange colors; shows collections in Milan and Paris.
Hubert de Givenchy—Firm of retired French designer of elegant, beautifully made daywear and evening gowns, now designed by Alexander McQueen of London.
Gucci—Italian "GG" label of fine leather goods; now owns design firms of Yves St. Laurent (Paris) and Alexander McQueen (London).
Hermes—French lines of leather handbags, scarves, ties, apparel, fragrances, and gifts sold in exclusive shops around the world.
Stan Herman —Award-winning U.S. designer and president of the Council of Fashion Designers of America.
Carolina Herrera—Venezuelan-born New York designer of elegant evening gowns, little black dresses, RTW, and jewelry and fragrance licenses.

9-26 *(continued)*

Names in Fashion Design (continued)
Tommy Hilfiger—U.S. designer of popularly priced sporty menswear.
Isani—Label of Soyon and Jun Kim, Korean brother/sister team known for youthful shirt dresses and Chanel-inspired suits.
Akira Isogawa—Design talent of womenswear in Australia.
Marc Jacobs—New York designer known for attention to fit, drape, and detail in relaxed, creative designs.
Betsey Johnson—American designer of original, anti-establishment dresses and sportswear.
Alexander Julian—New York designer, mainly of menswear, with artistic interpretation of color.
Gemma Kahng—Korean designer of classic suits in bright colors and large jeweled buttons.
Norma Kamali—New Yorker known for sweatshirt fashions, the "ra-ra" skirt, and paper-like apparel.
Donna Karan—Practical, wearable women's career apparel, including the popular DKNY bridge line and other lines.
Kasper—U.S. designer of suits and professional separates.
Rei Kawakubo—Japanese founder of Comme des Garcons in Paris; she drapes the body with asymmetrical emphasis.
Kenzo—Japanese designer in Paris doing clean lines of quilted cotton or knits with traditional Japanese influence.
Anne Klein—Firm started by, and named for, now-deceased American, known for quality sportswear and interchangeable garments. Designing is now done by others.
Calvin Klein—"All-American" sportswear designs with sophisticated simplicity.
Michael Kors—New York designer of garments with clean lines and imaginative touches, plus licensing agreements.
Krizia—Italian firm of Mariuca Mandelli and Aldo Pinto (wife and husband) that pairs unlike fabrics and introduces a different animal theme each year; now designed by Belgian, Jean-Paul Knott.
Christian Lacroix—Paris designer of elaborate wedding gowns and fanciful patterned apparel; also does RTW for Italian label, Genny.
Karl Lagerfeld—Legendary German designer for several international labels, including the houses of Chanel and Fendi.
Helmut Lang—Of Austrian descent, designs sleek, urban, wearable womenswear, menswear, and accessories in New York.
Eddie Lau—Designer in Hong Kong.
Ralph Lauren—Classic American "Polo" fashions for men, women, children, and homes. Has many licensing agreements and retail stores worldwide.
Bob Mackie—Californian known for dramatic, glamorous gowns for TV stars, as well as day wear and swimwear.
Matsuda—Traditional Japanese inspiration in men's and womenswear, as well as boutiques and franchises.
Pat McDonagh—Canadian fashion designer.
Mary McFadden—American designer uses beautiful fabrics and low-key looks.
Nicole Miller—New Yorker known for little black dresses, whimsical silk print dresses, scarves, and men's ties.
Nolan Miller—California glamour designer for stars in movies and TV shows.
Antonio Miro—Leader of Spain's men's elegant, sporty lines.

9-26 *(continued)*

Names in Fashion Design (continued)

Missoni—Italian family firm with simple, sophisticated knitwear; daughter Angela has given the label a sexier look.

Issey Miyake—Japanese designer in Paris and Milan who does sculpted creations of silk and unusual materials, and layered and wrapped looks.

Trafico de Modas—Family-run Spanish firm that emphasizes children's wear.

Mondi—German RTW label of graceful knits, a wide range of accessories, and many boutiques.

Claude Montana—Paris designer of strong, rugged, masculine looks, outlandishly bold knitwear, and leather.

Pedro Morago—Designs loose, relaxed men's styles in Spain.

Hanae Mori—Japanese designer in Paris of fine apparel with beautiful colors and innovative beading.

Thierry Mugler—French designer of high style, sexy apparel, and far-out accessories.

Jean Muir—British designer of soft, tailored, classic apparel of top quality construction.

Josie Natori—Philippine designer who mainly does high style, elegant lingerie; now in New York.

Margarita Nuez—Spaniard who does clothes for professional and executive women.

Manuel Pina—Spaniard internationally renowned for elegant, sexy women's clothes.

Jesus del Pozo—Spaniard who designs colorful womenswear with simple, austere lines.

Miuccia Prada—Italian designer with innovative fabrics and computer-enhanced patterns.

Lilly Pulitzer—Has designed "Florida prints" and cotton dresses for decades in the U.S.

Mary Quant—British designer who popularized miniskirts and youthful "mod" looks in the 1960's.

Zandra Rhodes—British designer who uses beautiful fabrics of silk, chiffon, and rich hand-prints based on history and art.

John Rocha—British designer known for experimental uses of fabrics and colors, layered textures, and simple silhouettes.

Christian Roth—New York design talent who does simple shapes in bright colors.

Cynthia Rowley—New York designer creates fun designs for women of all ages.

Sonia Rykiel—Paris RTW designer of clean-lined knit apparel in neutrals, offered in many boutiques worldwide.

Yves Saint Laurent—Famous Paris design house now owned by Gucci; elegant, artistic eveningwear; theater costumes; accessories; home furnishings; Rive Gauche boutiques.

Jil Sander—German design house now partnered with Prada

Arnold Scaasi—American designer of glittering ball gowns, ruffled dresses, gala cocktail suits for TV stars and others.

Ronaldus Shmask—New York designer of menswear with simple dramatic shapes and off-beat solid colors.

Crystal Siemens—Canadian designer with a knack of combining colors and textures.

St. John—Firm that creates classic knitwear designed by Marie Gray and her staff.

Anna Sui—American (of Chinese descent) does free-spirited, mod, avant-garde, bohemian fashions.

Alfred Sung—Highly respected Canadian couturier.

9-26 *(continued)*

Names in Fashion Design (continued)
Sybilla—U.S.-born designer who does creative, youthfully original apparel in Spain.
Zang Toi—Malaysian-born designer who uses bright colors and reasonably priced fresh looks; now in New York.
Yuki Torii—Japanese designer now in Paris.
Ellen Tracy—Several lines of RTW women's apparel designed by American Linda Allard.
Pauline Trigere—Long-time U.S. designer and CFDA Lifetime Achievement Award winner.
Richard Tyler—Australian, based in Los Angeles and New York, uses sophisticated styling and expert tailoring for actresses; also designs for Byblos.
Patricia Underwood—British milliner (hat designer) in the U.S.
Emmanuel Ungaro—European (French/Italian) designer in Paris of soft apparel with great colors and patterns; also has many licensing agreements.
Valentino—Italian couturier in Rome of elaborate gowns, with RTW shown in Paris.
John Varvatos—Designs for own label in New York, plus Nautica menswear.
Gianni Versace—Firm started by, and named for, now deceased Italian with creativity in knits, leathers, colorful prints, and complete look of menswear outfits; designs now being done by his sister, Donatella Versace.
Vitorio & Lucchino—Two Spanish men who design colorful, adaptable womenswear together, often with fringe, mantillas, and lace.
Adrienne Vittadini—Hungarian-born American designer of bridge lines, often uses knits in designs.
Diane Von Furstenberg—Creates upscale women's dresses in New York.
Karen Walker—Popular Australian designer of fun, youthful womenswear.
Vera Wang—U.S. designer, of Asian descent, especially known for exquisite bridal gowns.
Vivienne Westwood—British designer inspired by ongoing pop culture trends; shows collections in New York and Milan.
Yohji Yamamoto—Japanese designer in Paris who uses layers and knits to wrap and conceal the body, rather than seeking sexy looks; minimalist elegance.
Slava Zaitsev—Russian designer of womenswear.

9-26

to continue the tradition of high fashion with new creations. A few examples of this are the fashion houses of Chanel, Dior, Nina Ricci, and Anne Klein.

U.S. Fashion Awards and Associations

The most prestigious U.S. fashion awards were known as the Coty Awards from the 1940s through the 1970s. Voting was done by a national jury of newspaper and magazine fashion editors. Many of today's designers were named to the Coty Hall of Fame, the highest fashion honor of the past. It was achieved by winning a Coty Award in three different years. Awards were given to fashion designers recognized as the most creative and outstanding in womenswear, accessories, menswear, and other categories.

These same awards were continued as the Cutty Sark Awards through the early 1980s and were then discontinued. Another important recognition of design talent through the years has been the Neiman Marcus Award, given by the Dallas retailer. Fashion magazines also recognize fashion talent, such as the Harper's Bazaar Trophy.

Recently, the most important fashion awards have been presented by the *Council of Fashion Designers of America (CFDA),* the trade association of top U.S. designers. Awards are given for designers of the year in several categories, as well as special awards for other fashion achievements. Early in a designer's career, being named the "Best New Fashion Talent" is a great honor. The fashion industry's highest honor today is the CFDA Lifetime Achievement Award, 9-27. Awards are controlled by CFDA's approximately 230 member designers. West coast designers are recognized with California Designer Awards.

Various independent awards are also given by well-known businesses and professional groups. The International Association of Clothing Designers and Executives (IACDE) for designers who work for tailored clothing manufacturers, holds their International Design Awards Fashion Show each year. VH1 Fashion Awards as well as the MTV awards, combine fashion and entertainment in annual televised award shows. Also, Gold Thimble and Silver Thimble Awards are given to students in schools of design, with a panel of renowned designers judging the Annual Designer Critics Award Show.

Council of Fashion Designers of America/Corina Lecca, photographer

9-27 Designer Pauline Trigere, shown here, and several others have received a Lifetime Achievement Award for making an outstanding contribution to American fashion and style over their lifetimes.

A trade show that is attended by many fashion designers and manufacturers is the International Licensing and Merchandising Conference, held annually in New York City. It brings together over 10,000 *licensees* (manufacturers of products) and *licensors* (designers or owners of well-known labels) from all over the world. Attendees try to coordinate profitable licensing agreements among the opportunities presented.

Summary

New fashions are produced at different price levels, with less distinction between each level as time goes on. The couture level does original high fashion custom designs. Bridge lines are designer secondary lines of expensive, limited edition ready-to-wear items. The moderate category includes medium-priced merchandise with well-known brand names. Budget apparel includes downscaled knockoffs for the mass market.

The most important collection showings are held twice a year introducing the spring-summer and fall-winter lines. These are often expensive extravaganzas, attended by wealthy private customers, journalists, retail store buyers, and celebrities. Ready-to-wear showings are the most important fashion events now, held as giant trade exhibitions.

Since couture lines now lose money, collection showings are mainly for publicity, to be able to capitalize on the designer's famous name. Demand is created for upscale secondary lines. Designers also have house boutiques to sell their goods. Licensing is a lucrative way of capitalizing on the designer's fame. Franchising has become popular to expand market coverage with many retail locations. Also, designers might sell the patterns of some of their creations to commercial pattern companies.

Designing for RTW starts about a year before the apparel will be bought by consumers. The lines are shown to retail buyers six months ahead. Besides new designs, popular styles of one season are modified into fresh versions for the next season. Fashion piracy is common, saving money for manufacturers who get fast-selling styles out immediately. This results in similar styles that satisfy different consumer market segments at several price levels simultaneously.

Designers respond to consumer lifestyles to predict fashion trends for their target market. They produce many styles, from which consumers select their choices. Ideas are from forecasting services, past fashions, as well as art movements, stage plays, and movies and TV. Designers also respond to news events, famous people, and how people on the streets coin outfits. High-tech companies use CAD systems to design and market the lines.

Important world fashion cities are Paris, New York, Los Angeles, Milan, London, Tokyo, and others. They hold trade fairs and exhibits in hopes of exporting their fashions. Haute couture originated in France, which has led world fashion for hundreds of years. Major cities throughout the world make significant contributions to the fashion design industry.

There are many well-known American and foreign design names. Some are individuals and some are business names, often known for particular specialties. The Council of Fashion Designers of America has a membership of top U.S. designers and presents annual fashion awards in several categories.

To Know

couture
custom-made
bridge lines
ready-to-wear (RTW)
margins
knockoffs
collection
line
perceived difference
logo
house boutiques
licensing
franchising
designer patterns
fashion piracy
haute couture
Chambre Syndicale
caution
prêt-à-porter
alta moda

To Review

1. What variables determine the consumer price of garments?
2. Describe where each of the price market categories of apparel is available to consumers.
3. Through what means do designers get free publicity in newspapers and magazines?
4. Name two ways that top RTW design firms have cut costs of collection showings.
5. Why are RTW collections shown earlier (farther ahead of the selling/wearing season) than couture collections?
6. Describe three new, lower-key ways that designers show their collections to clients and retailers.
7. What do designer labels in RTW fashion products indicate to retail buyers and consumers?
8. What advantages does licensing provide for the manufacturers, retailers, and designers that are involved?
9. Name and describe three other types of licensing besides designer licensing.
10. Briefly describe the main advantage and disadvantage to franchisees in a franchise arrangement.
11. Name three advantages to franchisors in a franchise arrangement.
12. Name at least three reasons why fashion piracy is so common in the U.S. fashion industry.
13. Name at least four sources of inspiration for new fashion designs.
14. Describe electronic graphics interchange and 3-D imaging.
15. Name five major fashion cities of the world.
16. Name at least three criteria that couturiers must meet to be members of the Chambre Syndicale.
17. Name at least two types of textile/apparel goods in which the following countries excel: Italy, Great Britain, Germany, Spain, and Canada.
18. Give two reasons why Japanese fashions are *not* usually sold to the lower priced mass market.
19. What is the trade association of top U.S. fashion designers?
20. In licensing agreements, who are the licensees and who are the licensors?

To Do

1. Visit stores to view examples of better, moderate, and budget price market categories of apparel. Try to evaluate why they fall into certain categories. Analyze their cost of materials, where they were made (cost of labor), complexity of style, quality of construction, and profit the company can expect because of a well-known name, label, or other attribute. Prepare a written report of your findings.
2. Collect from newspapers, fashion magazines, and store flyers, two or three examples of each of the five main price market categories of apparel. Assemble them into a booklet that includes designer names and possible design inspiration. Try to find similar styles at several price levels. Note the design inspiration if it is evident.
3. Choose a top-quality fashion designer who has achieved well-known status. Find newspaper articles and/or advertisements showing the designer's collection showing, logo, location of house boutiques, licensed products, franchises, or sewing patterns. (A designer will not be involved in all of these business categories; just some of them.) Prepare a bulletin board display

with concise explanations of how the designer is capitalizing on his or her name recognition to increase profits.

4. Pick one of the main fashion design countries mentioned in this chapter. Study its culture and standard of living. Also study its fashion industry in more depth than what was included in this chapter. Prepare an oral or written report that explains how and why the country's textile/apparel expertise has evolved.

5. Choose one of the designers identified in 9-26. Research how the designer got started in the industry, what his/her particular specialties are, what lines are offered at what price levels, and why that designer is so popular. Does the designer belong to a fashion design trade association or has he/she received any fashion awards? Include pictures of the designer's clothes or magazine/newspaper articles about the designer in a written or oral report.

Fashion Institute of Technology; John Senzer, Photographer

Fashion designers from throughout the world feature their collections in fashion shows.

CHAPTER 10

Ready-to-Wear Manufacturing

After studying this chapter, you will be able to

- summarize the business aspects of apparel manufacturing.
- explain inside and outside shops.
- describe preproduction procedures from costing and editing the line to cutting the garments.
- discuss the process and methods of apparel production.
- explain employee concerns of health and safety, as well as equitable pay.
- describe offshore production.

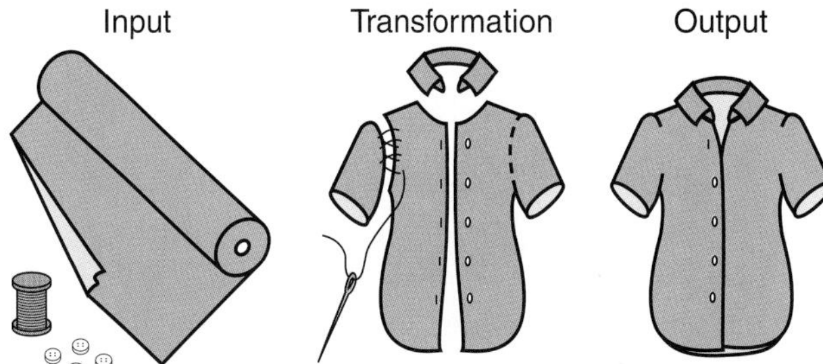

10-1 The apparel conversion process transforms basic materials such as fabric, thread, and buttons into the desired finished garments or accessories.

As was discussed in Chapter 4, the apparel segment of the soft goods chain consists of the main steps of:

1. apparel designing
2. apparel manufacturing
3. apparel sales

These are interrelated parts of apparel production businesses, each dependent on the others. This chapter will concentrate on apparel manufacturing, also known as production.

Production is the transformation of resources into a form that people need or want. It is a "conversion process" that transforms input (materials) into output (finished goods), 10-1. It uses ***factors of production*** which include the resources, labor, capital, and business leadership to manufacture goods, 10-2. It is important that production volume be related to market demand.

The apparel industry is called the *rag trade* and is made up of many various *needle trades*. Apparel manufacturing companies, commonly referred to as *cutters*, mass-produce large quantities of garments that are made and sold in dozens (groups of twelve). They serve both the retail market and the consumer market. There is always fashion excitement in the business, with the possibility of high profits some years and devastating losses other years. Highs and lows result from design risks, economic conditions, and cyclical trends.

Factors of Production
Resources—land and materials
Labor—workers
Capital—money and equipment
Business leadership—ideas and organization

10-2 Factors of production are used to manufacture apparel and accessories as well as to make all other physical goods.

The Business of Apparel Manufacturing

Apparel manufacturing is totally global, spread throughout the world with many millions of employees. It has always been labor-intensive, giving low-wage manufacturing locations a great advantage. However, it is becoming more technical, requiring higher skills to use computerized equipment, 10-3.

The apparel industry is crucial to the U.S. economy, through the materials and services it buys, the wages and taxes it pays, and the goods it produces. The industry is dominated by production workers, traditionally providing employment for many women and minorities. Pay has been low compared to other U.S. manufacturing jobs, but high compared to labor rates in developing countries. To be competitive, American companies have had to cut costs. Many low-skilled U.S. manufacturing jobs have been lost to automation and foreign manufacturing.

The apparel industry consists of firms ranging in size from small privately-owned enterprises that specialize in one apparel category, to large, corporate conglomerates. Business failures have closed some companies, while acquisitions have merged small firms into larger ones. The competitive nature of the industry and the necessity of costly automation has resulted in fewer, but larger, apparel firms.

To expand and diversify, growing firms often open new divisions with different lines and labels at various price levels. The separate divisions of multiproduct companies usually operate quite independently, with their own production and marketing procedures. The divisions gain financial support and guidance from the larger corporate parent. Fewer firms are privately owned now, resulting in more public corporations that sell stock to gain capital for technology upgrades and expansion.

A and Z Industries, Ltd.

10-3 More specialized knowledge and training is required to use today's methods and equipment for apparel manufacturing.

Sulzer Ruti

10-4 Many new fabrications are available for each fashion season from which manufacturers can choose.

Automation is the use of machinery to perform physical tasks that were previously performed by humans. Automated equipment can perform tasks quickly and accurately, and reduce labor and material costs. Automation is often done to achieve greater productivity. ***Productivity*** is a measure of how efficiently or effectively materials and the factors of production are used. Improved productivity gives higher amounts of output in relation to the amounts of input. Productivity usually improves as companies shift from labor-intensive to capital-intensive (automated) manufacturing. Then they are able to compete better in world markets.

To be successful, apparel manufacturers must keep costs low, quality high, and selling prices in line with those of competitors. Apparel companies' costs include fabrications, findings, and trimmings, as well as wages, equipment, and overhead (electricity, rent, taxes, etc.). *Fabrications* are fabrics, 10-4. They can also be leathers, furs, or other materials used in making the garments or accessories. *Findings* are the functional parts of the garments, such as linings, zippers, hooks, snaps, thread, and labels. *Trimmings* are the decorative buttons, laces, belts, and braids that are added to garments to enhance the designs.

Any profits made are usually used to expand and improve the company. This is done with new equipment, market research, product development, bonuses for valued employees, pay for new employees, and dividends to stockholders.

Competitive Strategies

Fashion manufacturers (and retailers) try to gain success with at least one of the basic competitive approaches shown in 10-5. The strategies include either being the low cost source for products, offering differentiated products, or satisfying a narrow market niche.

The Basic Competitive Approaches

1. Striving to be the industry's *low-cost source,* thereby aiming for a cost-based competitive advantage over rivals. Imported commodity products, which are manufactured in large numbers (using economies of scale) with low wage rates, are placed here.
2. Pursuing *differentiation* based on such advantages as fashion styling, quality, performance, service, or technological superiority. Designer brand names compete nicely this way if they maintain high standards of the necessary elements.
3. Focusing on a *narrow market niche,* winning a competitive edge by catering to specific buyers' needs and tastes better than rivals.

10-5 The U.S. textile/apparel supply chain mainly follows the strategies of offering fashion products (#2) and focusing on market segmentation (#3) to be globally competitive. If technology can reduce production expenses in the future, it will help the U.S. to compete with lower costs (#1).

For companies to be the low-cost source, they must run a more efficient operation than their competitors. Their managers must be driven to achieve lower expenses, questioning all expenditures. The company might be in an old facility, with no mortgage or rent payments, plus have other low overhead. A new lighting system may cut electricity costs. More efficient production equipment may lower the total costs of wages since fewer workers are needed. At retail, more consumer self-service reduces total wage costs because less sales help is required. However, chances are the low-cost company manufactures goods overseas where labor rates are cheap. In general, it is difficult for U.S.-made goods to compete with similar imported goods.

Some U.S. manufacturers try to be low-cost sources for retailers by lowering their prices. If the manufacturer reduces an item by 50 cents to the retailer, it can be a large total cost decrease for retailers that order many dozen of that item. The manufacturer will make $.50 less profit than the equal-cost competitors for each pair, and the same expenses must be covered, but the lower price should attract more sales. By selling many more of the item than competitors, the company may be able to make a larger overall profit. This is difficult for U.S. companies to accomplish on a long-term basis.

To pursue differentiation, companies might try to obtain more profits by offering higher quality goods, better service, or distinctive design features that set them apart from their competitors. For instance, a manufacturer might offer jeans with a better fit, unusual styling, and faster delivery response to orders. A retailer might have helpful salespeople, a more convenient location, or a more prestigious shopping bag for which customers are willing to pay an extra amount.

Businesses that differentiate with more upscale goods usually attract fewer customers. However, consumers who do buy goods from those companies spend more money per item. Thus, those businesses may end up with an equal or larger total profit than high-volume, low-margin companies. This provides an incentive for businesses to maintain high standards, and increases the choices available to consumers. It also ties in with the marketing triangle discussed in Chapter 3.

To focus on a narrow market niche, innovation is used to satisfy specific market opportunities better than any other company. Firms that are successful with this take advantage of changes in the desires of their target markets, production and sales technology, economic conditions, and the competitive environment. They are continually first to offer something with a special appeal to the group of customers with whom they have proven themselves as expert providers.

U.S. manufacturers are more successful at satisfying niche markets with fashion merchandise than being the low cost source. American companies have developed flexibility for shorter runs and faster style changes, while foreign companies do economical long (high

Monsanto Fibers

10-6 The market niche for this cheerful knit outfit is probably grandparents who can afford to buy it and who are eager to get special items for their grandchildren.

volume) production runs of commodity items using low-wage labor. Certain womenswear manufacturers, childrenswear producers, or other "focused" product lines satisfy certain market niches, 10-6. Sporting goods and electronics retailers are especially good with this strategy.

Fashion Seasons and Lines

Manufacturers produce lines according to particular types of apparel, price ranges, sizes, and/or geography. They design, produce, and sell their lines for separate ***fashion seasons***, which are distinct retail selling periods.

There are two main fashion seasons: *Spring/Summer,* which is sold at retail February through July, and *Fall/Winter,* which is sold at retail August through January. However, most manufacturers have four or more production seasons, depending on the merchandise category. While tailored menswear and women's shoes and purses follow the two main seasons, women's RTW usually has four to six seasons. See 10-7. Women's RTW seasons include:

- Spring
- Summer
- Fall I (transitional)
- Fall II (winter)
- Holiday (party attire)
- Resort/cruise wear

The greatest fashion changes take place for the fall lines. Each line contains a group of similar or color coordinated garments that are for the same time of day or type of occasion. Large manufacturers might have several related lines.

Today, a new constant merchandise flow is phasing out the older, seasonal approach. Manufacturers constantly add and subtract garments from their lines, doing shorter production runs with more frequent style changes. They also ship smaller orders of goods more often to their retail customers. With electronic linkages, the entire pipeline tries to satisfy changing market demands that are indicated by point-of-sale statistics. If some garments in the line

Fashion Institute of Technology/John Senzer, Photographer

10-7 Menswear lines are usually only designed for the two main fashion seasons. These "storyboards" show the designers, colors, and fabrics for one seasonal line.

are selling poorly at retail, no more of them are produced. Other garments, that are selling well, are produced in more quantity, with new versions or colors being added to the line. However, the potential to produce more than the market can absorb causes intense competition for manufacturers to keep their retail accounts.

Garment Districts

Most fashion cities have a ***garment district***, or garment center, which is the area where most of the apparel companies are located. It is usually divided into clusters according to merchandise type and price range (textiles, men's/boys' wear, budget dresses, women's sportswear, furs, bridals, etc.). Lines are developed in garment district design rooms, and finished items are displayed in their showrooms. Manufacturing is done in lofts or factories nearby, or in other parts of the country or world.

On garment district sidewalks, "pushboys" thread through the crowd with bins of fabrications or racks of finished garments that they move down the avenue, 10-8. Cross streets are crowded with trucks being loaded and unloaded. The New York garment district is located on both sides of Seventh Avenue in Manhattan, mainly between 26th and 42nd Streets. The district is called *Seventh Avenue (SA)* and the street has been renamed "Fashion Avenue." The Los Angeles garment district is between 7th and 11th Streets, from Main to San Pedro Streets. San Francisco does not have a garment district concentrated in one area. Apparel companies are spread throughout the Bay area.

10-8 Fur coats and other finished garments are moved on racks through garment districts during all hours of workdays.

Universal Denim Services

10-9 Most jeans manufactured in the U.S. are produced in Southern states.

Since the apparel business is labor-intensive, factory locations depend on the availability and cost of labor. New York's garment district developed as a manufacturing center over a century ago because it had available immigrant workers. However, fewer manufacturing facilities exist in New York today, because rent, labor and utility costs have gone up drastically. Many design workrooms still remain, but production has moved out of the city. U.S. manufacturing of high-fashion and tailored apparel is mainly located in the Mid-Atlantic states and California. Factories that produce jeans and casual slacks are concentrated in the South. See 10-9. More and more manufacturing is being done overseas.

Inside and Outside Shops

Not all apparel firms actually do the cutting and sewing of their garments. Firms that do all stages of production, from design concept and fabric purchasing, through all sewing procedures, to the shipment of finished garments, are called *inside shops.* They employ their own cutting and sewing workers. Firms that handle everything but the sewing, and sometimes the cutting, are *outside shops.* They send those parts of production to other, independently-owned sewing factories called ***contractors***. Contractors produce goods according to the apparel firm's designs and specifications and sew in the apparel company's label or brand name. See 10-10.

Fewer American apparel firms now own their own factories, with contract production responsible for a large portion of RTW apparel. Outside shops that never

A and Z Industries, Ltd.

10-10 The contract factory that promotes itself with this logo and advertisement makes better quality sportswear for companies that have upscale labels.

produce any of their own goods are referred to as *apparel jobbers*. They buy raw materials, hire contractors to manufacture all of their products, and then sell the finished goods.

The contracting system enables a variety of products to be made by the apparel firm. An outside shop may contract many different sewing factories at the height of its production season. An inside shop may also contract-out some of its sewing for extra capacity during busy times. By doing this, apparel firms can meet changing consumer demands without making large financial investments in new equipment. Also, newcomers to the industry, who have design ideas but limited capital, can go into production quickly.

Contractors hire workers and operate sewing factories to produce garments to specifications. They use the fabrics and designs of the apparel company that hired them. They are paid for the number of items they complete, without ever taking title to the goods. Sometimes they produce private label merchandise for retailers.

Sourcing is the investigation, identification, and development process of determining how and where manufactured goods will be procured. When retailers select apparel firms from whom to buy their goods, it is called sourcing. When apparel companies seek out contractors to produce goods to their specifications, it is also called sourcing. Apparel companies consider the price, quality, timely delivery, and capabilities of providing product variety when deciding on which contact plants to use. For many apparel companies, worldwide sourcing strategies are basic to their operations, with different items being manufactured in the most advantageous countries.

Pros of Using Contractors

There are definite *advantages* to using contractors. They include the ability to specialize, flexibility, lower costs, and faster delivery of orders.

Specialization

The contracting system allows for specialization of manufacturing expertise, since different contractors concentrate on narrow niches, such as knitted garments. Contractors have the right equipment and trained workers to do their certain type of work. A contractor may do sewing work for several different companies or rely on just one apparel firm to keep it busy. As fashion trends change, an apparel company can change to the contractors that specialize in the type of work the company needs to have done. Contracting is especially prevalent for women's and children's wear, in which fashions change the fastest.

Flexibility

By hiring contractors, apparel manufacturers gain flexibility for varying market demands. If one season's line is extremely successful, with large production needs to meet requested orders, several contractors can be hired to satisfy sales order volumes as they are received. In a slow year, only one contractor might be used. This relieves the apparel company of the burden of production peaks and valleys. An inside shop, with it's own factories, might have idle plants in a slow year. Plus, if trends change significantly, an inside shop's factories may not be able to diversify to manufacture those different types of goods.

Lower Costs

By using contractors for their production, apparel companies have hardly any labor or capital equipment needs. Large investments are not needed for sewing equipment that may soon become obsolete. New apparel firms, with limited capital, can produce garments in large quantities without having manufacturing space, equipment, or worker payroll. The hired factory must deal with labor costs and machinery maintenance. The contractor is the production expert, while the apparel firm specializes in merchandise designing and marketing.

Faster Delivery of Orders

By adding more contracting plants during peak demand, orders can be completed in a timely way. This eliminates difficulties in hiring and training extra suitable workers for busy times or keeping a large company factory busy year-round.

Cons of Using Contractors

There are also *disadvantages* of apparel firms using production contractors. The main drawback is the limited control the company has over the quality of work and inspection of the contractor's work. Often no individual has full responsibility for the finished product. Also, unreliability may be a problem. Other apparel firms that regularly use a contractor may need work

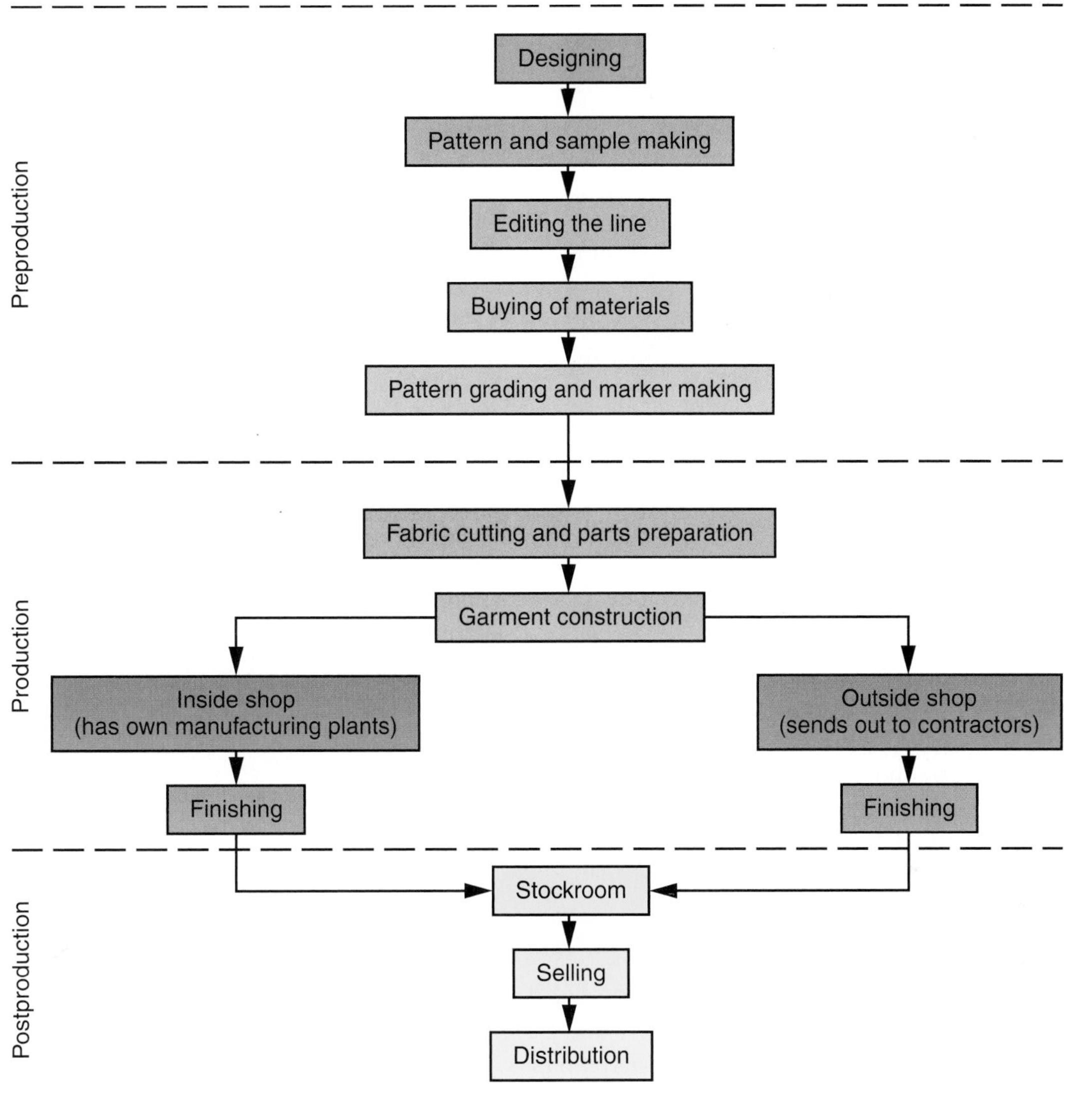

10-11 The process of apparel manufacturing moves through these steps from the original design conception to the finished products that are shipped to retail accounts.

done and be given preferential treatment, thus postponing the work of the first company.

Preproduction Procedures

Many production steps turn the design ideas into finished wearing apparel. A breakdown of RTW production is shown in the "Flow Chart of Apparel Manufacturing," 10-11. You may want to refer to it as you study this chapter. It is a continuous process, with overlapping steps. As one line is being sent through the manufacturing flow, additional designs are considered for that line, and development of the next season's line is started.

Companies try to establish a cohesive, profitable line through customer targeting and fashion planning. "Merchandising the line" starts with a plan that estimates demand for various colors, styles, sizes, quality, and price in the company's market. Companies look at the kinds of clothes the consumers in their primary markets prefer and study their computer data about past sales to identify last season's winners and losers. Changes in customer preferences are noted, as well as hot items in the higher-priced market that might be adapted to the company's price level or toned down for a wider appeal.

Fashion Institute of Technology/John Senzer, Photographer

10-12 Pattern making takes precision and concentration to get all parts of designs to go together perfectly.

Selecting and Costing the Designs

Designs that had high sales volumes in the previous season may be retained for the next season, with only minor changes. These items are *refabricated*, which is using the most acceptable parts of the design for a new version to make it suitable for another season. The fabric is changed, and some adjustments may be made to a detail or trim to make it slightly different.

Based on the merchandising plan, correct amounts of supplies must be acquired for production. Timing must be planned so the finished garments are delivered for the selling season. Details of promotion and sales must be coordinated. Also, while a new line is being developed, the line that is currently being sold in stores is still being perfected by changing or dropping poor sellers and adding new options.

The fashion designer probably starts with a sketch of an idea. Then the designer or a pattern maker makes the first pattern of each design from a sloper, 10-12. A *sloper* is the company's basic pattern for particular body measurements from which fashion patterns are created. It has a basic sleeve, bodice front, bodice back, skirt front, and skirt back (or pants front and back). If CAD equipment is being used, the computer program contains the sloper and can print out a hard copy of the fashion pattern from a sketched design on the monitor screen. A few exclusive designers drape and pin fabric onto dress forms to create their garment ideas.

Style numbers are assigned to designs to identify them for manufacturing, selling to retailers, and distribution. Manufacturing details are calculated. ***Costing*** is done to figure the expenses of producing each item, 10-13. Design and production personnel tabulate the costs of fabrications, findings, and trimmings. They figure labor costs and production capabilities of company plants and contractors, calculating costs to sew design details such as pleats, tucks, yokes, and topstitching. Products must be made with the right quality at the price that customers are willing to pay.

Apparel Production Costing

Category	Calculation Considerations	Approximate share of wholesale selling price	
materials			
fabric	price-per-yard × yardage needed	36%	**Variable costs**
other	findings and trimmings; the more used, the higher the cost		
direct labor	# minutes to produce the garment × cost-per-minute = labor cost per garment	11%	
overhead	rent, maintenance, utilities, promotion, shipping, packaging, taxes, and *indirect* labor (salespeople, management, clerical)	33%	**Fixed costs**
profit	income from sales after all expenses are deducted	20%	
wholesale price		100%	

10-13 Costing results in the wholesale price from the manufacturer to retailers who buy the goods. If materials, labor, and/or overhead costs increase, the amount of profit decreases.

Costing and product specifications are often calculated by computer. Their accuracy can make the difference between a profit or loss at the end of the season, since success or failure depends a great deal on manufacturing cost and selling price.

Editing the Line

Only a small fraction of the designs first intended for a line are actually produced. Manufacturers *edit*, or change and revise the line at several points. After the costing process, some designs are eliminated. Details of others may be simplified, resulting in fewer seams, no pockets, and cheaper materials to stay within the price limits of the firm. Each preliminary design of the line is worked on until it looks just right and is suitable for the company's production.

The approved style numbers for the preliminary line are then produced as sample garments. ***Samples*** are trial garments, or prototypes, made up exactly as they are intended to look when sold. Expensive garments are first made in muslin to finalize the design and fit before cutting into the real fabric. Fabrics for samples are from small cuts from mills that hope to sell large amounts of production fabrics to the company later.

Oregon State University

10-14 Sample garments are finalized with the exact design and fit that they will have when produced to be sold through retail stores.

Sample garments are used to check design aspects and fit, 10-14. They are shown to top management and the firm's key retail accounts, who respond with specific remarks about strong and weak points in the line. Since styles that are produced, but don't sell, cause large financial losses, unpopular styles are eliminated. Other designs are altered. The samples are then used to promote sales and as examples for production.

After the lines are openly shown to all retail buyers and initial orders are taken, the amounts of each style to be manufactured are determined. The line is edited again. If sufficient orders are not received to support profitable production and sale, those items are also dropped from the line. Firms usually have policies about the minimum number of pieces to be produced. Some require many thousands to be ordered before production begins. Lines are continually reedited according to changing trends and acceptance of the style numbers. By concentrating on best sellers, final profits are maximized. Also, new items called *sweeteners* are usually added to a manufacturer's line between design seasons.

Apparel companies also sometimes try to get market feedback with samplings. *Samplings* (not sample garments) are small quantities of garments that are made up and placed in retail stores to test the designs. At the first indication of consumer reaction, popular styles are ordered by retailers and made by manufacturers in larger numbers. Unpopular styles are discontinued. Consumer reaction is the most important input.

Precutting Processes

The sample pattern must be graded for production. ***Grading*** is the process of making garment patterns into the complete range of smaller and larger sizes that will be produced. This is usually done by computer, 10-15.

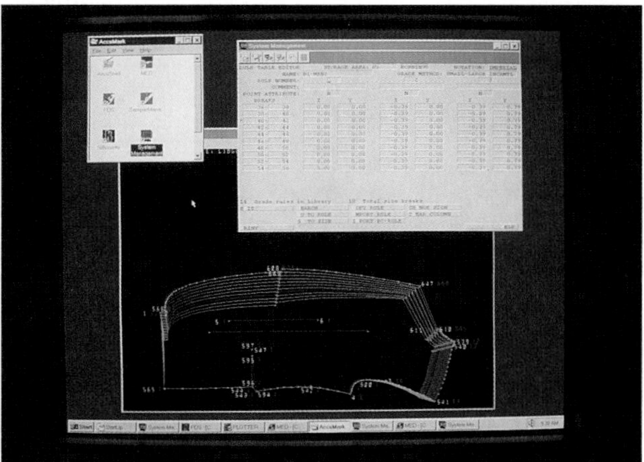

Gerber Garment Technology, Inc.

10-15 The many lines around the pattern piece represent the edges of that same garment part in different sizes. When each garment part is reduced or enlarged similarly, the final garment becomes considerably smaller or larger.

Fashion Institute of Technology/John Senzer, Photographer

10-16 With training on patternmaking computer programs, design and manufacturing employees can create markers electronically.

Investronica, Inc.

10-17 All parts of apparel manufacturing are becoming computerized, including cutting procedures.

Final fabric selections are ordered from textile firms, and the needed fasteners, thread, and trims are ordered in volume. Preferred suppliers offer trusted quality, fair prices, on-time delivery, options for returns, and are able to supply more materials at a later time if production is increased. Manufacturers usually have a limited number of reliable suppliers. They have more than one for each supply need (in case one has a problem), but not so many that it is confusing. New suppliers are added periodically and some old ones are dropped.

The layout of pattern pieces is drawn onto a marker. A ***marker*** is a long piece of paper, the width of the fabric to be cut, with all of the pattern pieces, in all sizes, laid out for cutting. It is the plan of how the pattern for every garment part needed for manufacturing will economically fit onto the fabric, as shown on the computer screen in 10-16. Pattern pieces are fit as closely together as possible to eliminate waste. With patterned fabrics, cutting must be planned to coordinate or match adjoining parts. The marker is used as a guide for the cutter.

CAD equipment is used to make markers by displaying miniature pattern pieces and their layout arrangement on the monitor. The layout is calculated for the fabric width and where the end of one bolt and beginning of the next one falls. The system can match plaids and stripes, avoid flaws (fabric defects), and minimize waste. When the best layout is determined, it prints out the marker in full size, with the pattern number and size printed on each pattern piece.

Higher efficiencies are being added to CAD software packages all the time, as well as "artificial intelligence" to make basic decisions. ***Data integration*** is the combining of several steps into one continuous computerized process, for instance, designing through preproduction. Also, some systems have a telecommunication feature that allows a company to do the design and pattern work at its main location and electronically send markers to a manufacturing operation elsewhere for production. These features are especially necessary with the market responsiveness needed for electronic partner linkages, such as the Quick Response program.

Cutting

Finally, cutting is started. In traditional factories, layers of flat fabric are unrolled onto long cutting tables by large machines, called *spreaders*, that move bolts of cloth back and forth. High stacks result that might have 100 layers of fabric. Then the long paper marker is placed across the top so workers can cut along the outlines of the drawn pattern pieces.

Rather than cutting with large shears, electric cutting machines are used that are similar to power saws, cutting all layers at once. The number of garments cut at one time varies, depending on the type and thickness of the fabric, the cutter's skill, the price of the garments, and the number of orders. With the entire thickness of the stack being cut at once, fabric stacks of garment parts result.

Computerized factories (with CAM) do electronic cutting, using knife cutters, water-jet cutters, or lasers. Computers can preset the cutters to accurately cut around the garment parts automatically, eliminating the need for a marker. The shapes and sizes of the garment parts are programmed into the computer, 10-17.

Computerized knife cutters, like manual cutters, cut multiple layers of fabric and may even sharpen themselves automatically. *Water-jet cutters* cut smaller stacks of fabric layers with a thin stream of very high-pressure water. *Laser-beam cutters* vaporize a single layer of fabric almost instantaneously with an intense, powerful beam of light. Even though only a single garment is cut a piece at a time, the speed and accuracy of laser cutters make them economical. They can cut as many garments, in the same amount of time, as a human operator with a manually controlled multiple-layer cutter. They offer great style flexibility for short production runs, since they can cut many different styles in a short period of time and are very precise in cutting intricate shapes.

Apparel Production

After cutting, the garment parts go step-by-step through the assembly line. Since production costs are high, every unnecessary procedure is eliminated. More time is needed to produce tailored clothing because of the detailed steps in constructing a suit or coat.

Several different methods have been used in factories to manufacture garments since mass production began about 150 years ago. Older methods, that are being used less as time passes, include the tailor system and progressive bundle system. Newer computerized methods include the unit production system and modular manufacturing.

Traditional Tailor System

The *tailor system* of apparel manufacturing uses one person to do all sewing tasks to make a garment, 10-18. Today it is only used for very high-priced, custom sewing jobs. It can provide top quality, but is slow and expensive. The person constructing the garment must be skilled in all sewing and tailoring tasks. Much handwork and extensive pressing are done.

Faster methods have been developed for suits and coats, such as "section construction" done by workers who are each proficient at assembling one section of the garment. More built-in shaping is provided by the pattern, rather than from hand sewing or steam pressing, and some garment parts are fused together.

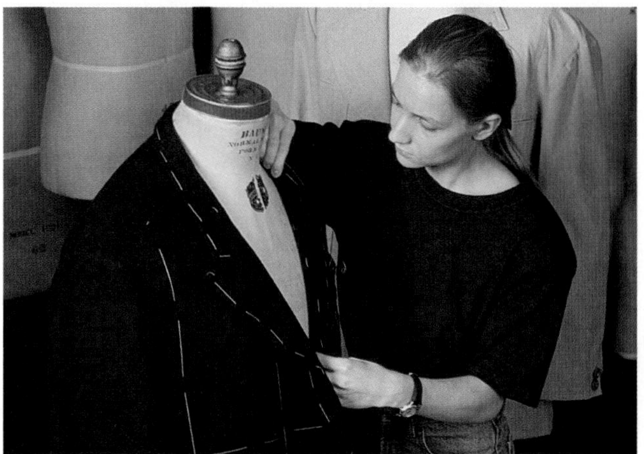

Fashion Institute of Technology/John Senzer, Photographer

10-18 This jacket is being tailored, incorporating fitting techniques and hand sewing methods for a top-quality garment.

Unstructured styles are offered in sizes such as small, medium, and large, which are less precise than an exact range of specific sizes.

Progressive Bundle System

Piecework manufacturing assigns one specific task to each person along an assembly line. This division of labor divides the total manufacturing process into small, individualized jobs, with each sewing machine operator repeatedly doing only one job on a specialized machine. This procedure attempts to make production time per item as short as possible while the work moves along.

Piecework has been done by the *progressive bundle system* since mass production began. In this system, the cut garment parts are sorted and tied into bundles of dozens, and tagged with work tickets to go through the sewing operations. Outside shops send them to a contract factory, and inside shops put them into rolling canvas bins ("handling trucks") to go to the different production stations in their factory. Collars go to one station for sewing, sleeves to another, and so on. The bundles move through the assembly line, eventually coming together to be joined into the completed garment. The work is inspected periodically during the production process.

Unit Production System

The *unit production system (UPS)* is a computerized piecework system, 10-19. Computer-aided manufacturing (CAM) methods integrate production

Apparel Manufacturing Methods

Manually Monitored and Controlled Equipment	***Tailor system:*** all sewing tasks done by one person; obsolete.
	Piecework system: one specific task done by each person along the assembly line. 1. *Progressive bundle system:* tied dozens of parts are rolled to production stations through the line.
Computer Monitored and Controlled Systems	2. *Unit production system* (UPS): CAM application that routes cut pieces to production stations via overhead conveyor.
	Modular manufacturing: employee teams arrange own work assignments for better efficiency, productivity, quality, and flexibility; CAM application.

10-19 The progression of the main apparel manufacturing methods used in the industry, from older to newer is shown here. The top ones involve manually monitored and controlled equipment and the bottom ones are computerized.

Investronica, Inc.

10-20 Unit production is a computerized system that carries unconnected garment parts to the proper sewing machine operators until manufacturing is completed.

procedures into *systems* that combine all elements of information and technology to achieve the best results.

In the unit production system, the cut pieces of each garment are loaded (hung) together onto an overhead product carrier that moves them from operator to operator in the assembly line with a computerized conveyor system. See 10-20. Time is saved since bundles do not need to be untied, retied, ticketed, or manually moved along as work is done. Also, operators can better see how the overall garment design looks.

With UPS, each workstation has a computer terminal. When a task has been completed, the operator presses the "send" button on the terminal or scans a bar code on the garment holder to automatically direct the items to the next station. This routes work so the sewing line is continuously balanced. Garment parts are fed to workstations with full consideration of the skill and speed of each operator. Each terminal provides information to the main system, which tracks operator efficiency, piece rate and payroll data, total operating costs, and style data—for better production planning. Supervisors can continually monitor the production line with a central computer, and make changes when needed. Also, the quality of garments can be tested between operators without interfering with line efficiency.

Modular Manufacturing

Modular manufacturing, sometimes referred to as *flexible manufacturing*, divides the production workers into separate, independent teams, or module work groups. The teams carry out all production tasks. The modular system is gaining in popularity. It is mostly used by large manufacturers who can afford to

Textile/Clothing Technology Corporation

10-21 This team of workers is producing apparel in a manufacturing module. Module members stand to work, hand garment parts to each other, and may take care of the operations at more than one station.

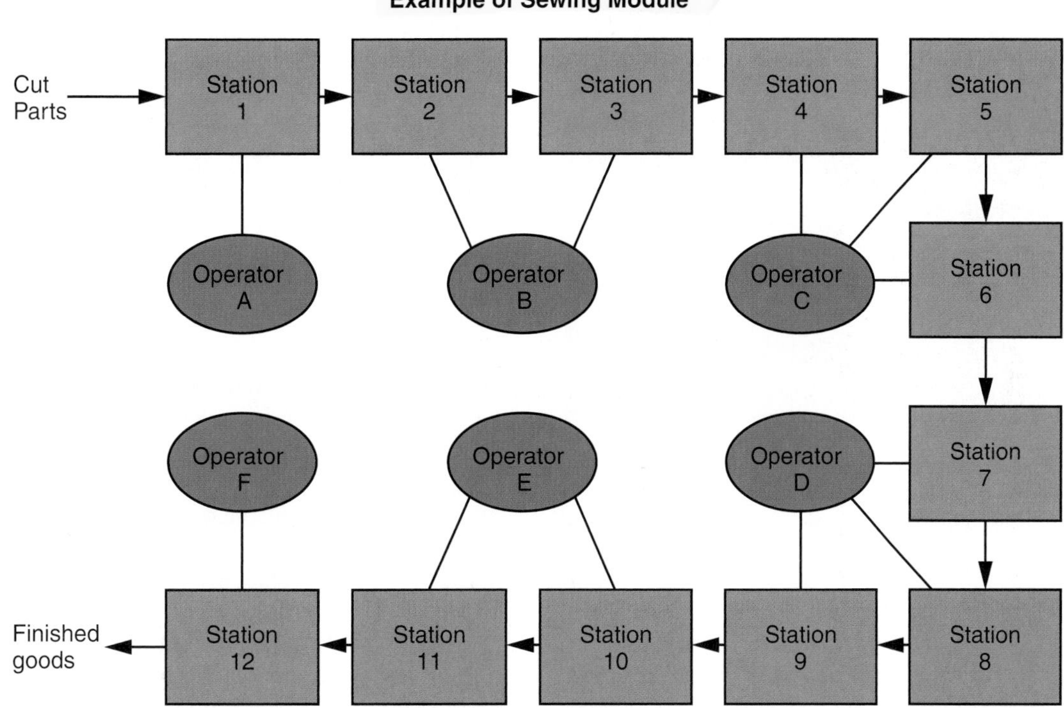

10-22 Six operators have been empowered to run this sample module of 12 workstations. Fewer employees, but with more skill and responsibility, are used. Procedures at some stations are more complicated and take more time than others.

implement it. It requires a strong commitment from all levels of employees, as well as ongoing training.

With the modular system, employees are taught to strive for high performance and ongoing improvement. The teams sort out their own problems and agree on work assignments and schedules of the members. Many modules feature stand-up, hand-off sewing with team members moving between stations. See 10-21.

Modular manufacturing offers increased productivity, and lower costs, even though higher standard pay is given to the multiskilled operators. Often, operators are responsible for alternately loading three or four automatic, programmable machines that perform several functions, as indicated in 10-22. Also, since all members of the group are trained with higher skills to do all jobs, rotation within the module offers more job diversity and less likelihood of injury from repetitive tasks.

Modular manufacturing also *empowers* the workers. In other words, company managers give module employees the authority, responsibility, and autonomy to make decisions and take actions needed for the highest group output. Workers feel a "sense of ownership" in the performance of their tasks. This improves product quality and production through-put time. Peer pressure reduces absenteeism and encourages nonperformers to leave on their own. There may also be problems within team modules if one member holds back the team's work progress, earnings or causes other conflict. Advantages of flexible manufacturing are listed in 10-23.

Benefits of Flexible Manufacturing
Reduction of inventories
Improved customer service
Shorter through-put times
Lower costs
Greater flexibility
Increased productivity
Healthier/safer workstation design
Improved quality of products
Better space utilization
Balanced production flow
Higher job satisfaction for workers
Less tardiness and absenteeism
Lower employee turnover
Company unity through teamwork
Encourages domestic production

10-23 Although the development and training process of modular manufacturing is time-consuming and expensive to initiate, all these benefits result from a successful program. This, in turn, enables manufacturers to gain the competitive advantage to compete globally.

Hong Kong Trade Development Council

10-24 At this knitted garment plant in Hong Kong, finishing of garments includes blocking the items while they are being pressed.

Bevco Precision Manufacturing Company

10-25 This industrial strength chair offers height and tilt adjustments, padded swivel seat, and a sturdy five-legged base. These features help relieve back and neck strains, improve circulation, and aid in prevention of repetitive motion injuries.

Finishing

To finish sewn garments at the end of production, hems and fasteners are put in by machine, and a final pressing is done, 10-24. Labels and hangtags are attached, and the garments are inspected. If flaws or mistakes are found, they are either returned to be fixed or sold cheaply as seconds. The finished inventory of manufacturers is stored in stockrooms or sent to regional distribution centers for delivery to retailers that place orders.

Employer Concerns

Apparel companies are increasingly concerned with employee health and safety issues. One example of this is the emphasis in today's production plants on reducing or eliminating cumulative trauma disorders (CTDs). Examples of CTDs are carpal tunnel syndrome, tendinitis, and shoulder and back pains that result from jobs that involve repetitive motion.

Ergonomics, or human engineering, matches human performance to the tasks performed, the equipment used, and the environment. It makes sure the job requirements are suitable for the capabilities of the workers. To prevent motion injuries, occupational health problems, and worker fatigue, equipment is designed and arranged for the most effective and safest interaction with those using it. For instance, the height of sewing machine stands and chairs is adjustable, 10-25. Worktables can tilt, lighting adjusts, and footrests have been added at workstations. Some workers wear noise protection for their ears, or back or wrist braces, 10-26. At the same time, workers must be trained to use the equipment properly and effectively. Often pre-work warm-ups and periodic stretches are encouraged. Job rotation is also scheduled to relieve fatigue by using different muscles and body parts.

By paying attention to ergonomics, and spending time and money on proper equipment and training, production company costs decrease. Because fewer employees become sick or disabled, medical insurance costs go down and disability compensation payments are reduced. Also, workers have a better mental outlook about their jobs and lives.

Another employer concern is how to equitably pay employees for work done. The question of equitable pay for production employees stems from the differences between piecework manufacturing tasks and flexible team systems. With the apparel manufacturing process undergoing change, new incentives are needed to motivate employees. Apparel manufacturing workers have traditionally not received a straight hourly wage or flat salary.

The piecework system is based on individual incentives to work as fast as possible. Workers are paid according to a rate based on the difficulty and time

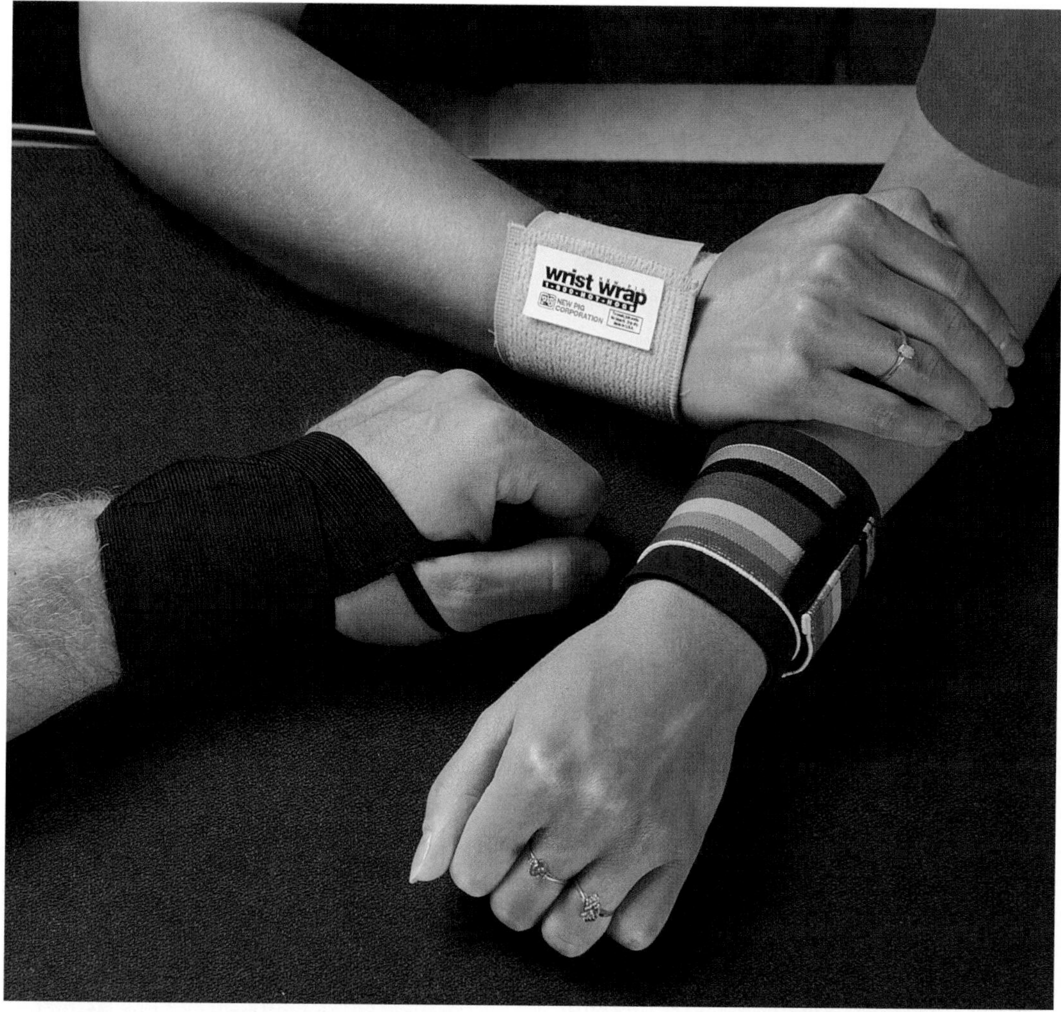

New Pig Corporation, 1-800-HOT-HOGS®

10-26 Wrist braces strengthen and steady the wrist, helping to prevent injuries to workers.

required to do each specific sewing task, determined by time studies. That rate is multiplied by how many times the operator does the task. This motivates operators to accomplish as much as possible, but also sometimes results in high worker stress and injuries.

The new system is based on group incentives to do the best work possible. In modular manufacturing, individual piece rate pay is replaced by group payments based on total module production. It also includes *gainsharing*, in which all members share in extra group incentive rewards when the team exceeds work expectations. Gainsharing rewards high group productivity and quality performance with bonuses, without boosting general wage rates.

Various wage plans offer different employee earnings potentials. They need certain amounts of company planning and supervision. Some plans even de-emphasize money and appeal to the personal needs of employees. Each plan should consider worker performance, earnings, and morale. Product quality is important, as well as a sense of cooperation. Also, company management must take into account the roles of planning, training, supervision, and indirect labor (support employees) needed.

The area of ***work design*** encompasses the ergonomic matching of jobs and equipment to employees, the companies' output requirements, compensation plans, and worker behaviors that are reinforced. It has gained importance since good work design not only benefits companies with higher profits, but also provides workers with financial and psychological well-being. Successful apparel manufacturers know that their employees are their most valuable assets, 10-27.

Offshore Production

Apparel companies and retailers often have their products manufactured outside of the U.S., at lower costs. Labor is a large component of apparel production,

Gerber Garment Technology, Inc.

10-27 Since good employees are extremely important company assets, work design strives to keep employees safe and well matched with their jobs.

and similar construction details take about the same amount of time to accomplish in any part of the world. Low-wage producers, therefore, have a competitive advantage. To use this cost advantage, U.S. apparel companies sometimes own, and often contract with, factories abroad.

The lower wages overseas usually include no overtime pay or fringe benefits. Additionally, foreign government incentives (tax exemptions, rebates, preferential financing plans) further reduce the production costs in those countries. On the other hand, U.S. manufacturers must comply with government regulations regarding high standards of safety and benefits for workers. This raises the costs of producing apparel in the U.S.

Textile and apparel industries have been among the first to set up operations in developing countries. Manufacturers who do *offshore production*, with overseas sewing shops, are constantly looking for countries with lower wage rates, good innovations, and unrestricted quotas. Today, the fact that a garment has the name of an American designer or firm does not mean that it was made in the U.S. Manufacturing done in one's own country is called *domestic production*.

Imports, or goods that come into the country from foreign sources, have risen because of the intense competition in the apparel industry. In some cases, imports fill certain voids in the U.S. for unusual or low-priced commodity items. Garments that require extensive handwork, such as beaded sweaters or embroidered jackets, are almost always sourced offshore.

American apparel producers ***export*** some goods, or send them out of the country. However they have not been able to match exports with the rising tide of imports. Instead of exporting goods from the U.S., some major apparel producers have set up licensing agreements with foreign producers. Apparel is made overseas with the American firm's label and specifications. It may be sold overseas without coming to the U.S. In return, the firm receives a percentage of sales.

Apparel manufacturers who use cheap foreign labor for their production may own or contract facilities in developing countries. Large firms may have an American supervisor stationed there to keep tabs on all of the company's production in that country or in that particular area of the world. *Sourcing consultants* have evolved to guide companies in identifying countries and factories that give the best opportunities for their apparel production. However, company representatives should still go there to check on the situation before making final production decisions.

Offshore sourcing in this hemisphere, such as production in Latin America, provides close proximity to both the home office and the market. When sourcing from distant locations, such as Asia, ***lead times*** (for ordering ahead) and ***response times*** (for factories to produce and deliver goods) are much longer. This is a disadvantage for fashion accuracy and market responsiveness.

Most merchandise travels across the oceans via container shipping freighters. Air freight shipments shorten delivery times, but increase costs.

Summary

Apparel production is global, labor-intensive, and becoming more technical and automated. The industry is crucial to the U.S. economy through the materials and services it buys, the wages and taxes it pays, and the goods it produces. Fashion companies compete on cost, differentiation, or market niche focus. They constantly add and subtract designs from their seasonal lines. They are traditionally concentrated in garment districts of cities, however, more manufacturing is now being done overseas.

Inside shops sew their own products, while outside shops use contractors. This enables them to have more specialization, flexibility, lower costs, and faster delivery of orders, even though some control and reliablilty is lost.

Companies plan garments in response to estimated market demand. Style numbers are assigned to designs, costing is done, and the line is edited. Samples are made to check design aspects and fit, and to get feedback from company management and key accounts. After retail orders are taken, production quantities are decided and materials are ordered. The pattern is graded, a marker is made, the fabric is spread, and cutting begins.

New technology is changing today's apparel production. The traditional tailor system is being phased out. The progressive bundle system is being replaced by the computerized unit production system. Modular manufacturing offers flexibility. Employee concerns involve health and safety, as well as equitable pay. Ergonomic equipment and training are stressed. Piecework pay is changing to systems based on group incentives.

Since labor is such a large component of apparel production, manufacturing in low-wage countries gives a competitive advantage. Offshore production has caused rising imports that have longer lead and response times.

To Know

production
factors of production
automation
productivity
fashion seasons
garment district
contractors
sourcing
costing
samples
grading
marker
data integration
piecework
modular manufacturing
ergonomics
work design
imports
export
lead times
response times

To Review

1. What three main factors impact apparel companies' high profits some years and devastating losses other years?
2. Why are there fewer but larger apparel firms now?
3. Why do public corporations have an advantage over private companies in achieving technology upgrades and expansion?
4. How do apparel manufacturing companies use their profits?
5. List three competitive approach strategies of fashion manufacturers.
6. Why are U.S. manufacturers more successful at satisfying niche markets than foreign companies?
7. What are the two main fashion seasons?
8. What is the difference between inside shops and outside shops?
9. What do apparel companies consider when deciding on which contract plants to hire?
10. How does "merchandising the line" start?
11. What is a sloper?
12. Why are style numbers assigned to apparel designs?
13. What do manufacturers do when they "edit" a line?
14. What are samplings?
15. What attributes do preferred suppliers usually have?

16. Describe how water-jet and laser-beam cutters work.
17. In the unit production system, what moves the cut pieces of each garment from operator to operator?
18. Why do companies' costs decrease when they pay attention to ergonomic equipment and training?
19. What is gainsharing?
20. Differentiate between offshore production and domestic production.

To Do

1. Gain a further understanding of CTDs and ergonomics in garment manufacturing through research. Explain the latest efforts for ergonomics in the apparel industry and how the effective application can help a company improve productivity, profits, and employee health.
2. With two other students in your class, expand the three main sections of the "Flow Chart of Apparel Manufacturing" shown in 10-11 (with one student taking preproduction, one taking production, and one taking post-production). Add subheadings and short descriptions of the specific activities done at each stage. Put your work together as three large posters in a row, for a bulletin board display of the entire "Ready-to-Wear Manufacturing Flow."
3. Cut out a picture of a garment from a magazine, catalog, or advertisement. Write a report on its production. List all the different steps you think took place to produce the garment. What different skills and specialized machines or attachments do you think were needed? Is it suited to domestic or offshore production? Why?
4. Cut out a picture of an expensive suit or dress from a fashion magazine. Do a costing estimate for the garment, assuming certain prices for the materials, direct labor, overhead, and profit. Then redesign the garment to have fewer details and less expensive materials and labor rates. Explain your costing comparisons to the class in an oral presentation, and answer questions about how you reached your conclusions.
5. With a classmate as a "business partner," pick a general category of apparel—such as ladies suits, men's sportswear, bridal attire, etc. Cut out pictures of several garments of that category as part of a line. Tell what other garments might be in the line, the colors, fabrics, etc. If possible, create sketches to illustrate your ideas. Where might the items be produced and why? Edit the line and show your final selections.

CHAPTER 11

Wholesale Apparel Marketing and Distribution

After studying this chapter, you will be able to

- discuss inventory management of goods.
- explain benchmarking and quality programs.
- describe trademark protection.
- identify technological advances in apparel manufacturing.
- explain how and where apparel producers sell their finished goods.
- describe the distribution of fashion items.
- summarize apparel industry trade information.

Ongoing considerations of apparel companies involve managing various amounts of production materials, garment parts, and finished goods as fashions are manufactured. Programs must be implemented and maintained that monitor the quality of goods produced, as well as protecting company trademarks. Technological advances in apparel manufacturing are helping companies achieve higher efficiencies in all of these areas.

Finally, apparel lines are sold and transported to retailers. Many industry trade groups relate to the design, manufacture, sale, and distribution of fashion goods.

Inventory Management

Inventories are goods held on hand for the production process or for sale to customers. Manufacturers have three main groups of inventory:

- *raw materials*, which are preproduction fabrics, trimmings, and notions. Some of these are shown in 11-1.

Gerber Garment Technology

11-1 Bolts of fabric, ready to be spread and cut, make up the primary raw materials for apparel manufacturing.

- *work-in-process* (WIP), which includes partially completed garments, in parts or sections that have not yet been joined together.
- *finished goods*, which are completed, post-production items.

Retailers are different from manufacturers because they offer a service of selling only finished goods. Thus, their inventories only involve the finished goods category.

Both manufacturers and retailers also have inventories of business support goods. These include computers, office supplies, display props, and cash registers.

Inventory control is the process of maintaining inventories at a level that prevents stockouts and minimizes holding costs. Keeping large or wrong inventories is expensive. Fashion goods lose their appeal, becoming obsolete as time passes. Costs have already been incurred for their materials and the labor to construct them. However, no cash has been received if the goods are still in inventory.

To store extra goods, higher insurance premiums must be paid to cover possible physical loss of the goods from theft, fire, or flood. Sometimes taxes are assessed. Warehouse space must be owned or rented as well as lit and heated. (A *warehouse* is a "holding facility" for storing backup stocks of supplies or finished goods.) Because of these added expenses of maintaining inventories, companies sometimes have to borrow money. This, in turn, results in loan interest costs. Notice the repercussions of various types of inventories in 11-2.

Materials handling includes all activities of the goods not involved in actual production processes. Examples are the moving, storing, packing, and transporting of the raw materials, semifinished parts, or final garments. Most of this is done manually. Company profits are lost with extensive materials handling procedures, and these activities consume most of the time from product beginning to product completion.

It only takes a certain amount of sewing production time to make a garment, but it takes several months for a garment to pass through the pipeline. For instance, it now takes about 10 months for a fashion item to be made from the fiber stage to being offered for sale at retail. However, each item averages only about 18 "value-added" hours of actual production time. The rest of the time the inventory is sitting somewhere.

Manufacturers are trying to automate the record keeping and reduce this materials handling time as much as possible. They are using newer, more efficient methods and equipment that give faster through-put time. Computerized production applications reduce materials handling time by balancing the work flow more efficiently and bypassing some human contact with the work. This can result in higher material utilization, productivity, and quality control.

Importance of the Right Inventories

Too little inventory	causes	lost manufacturing and sales, because materials and goods are not available when needed.
Too much inventory	causes	extra handling, product obsolescence, and excessive carrying costs for storage space, heat, lights, insurance, interest on money, etc.
The wrong inventory	causes	both lost sales and high costs, since no one wants to buy the goods but they have already been paid for.

11-2 Inventory control is a complicated, but very important, function for all businesses, especially for apparel manufacturers and retailers because of the timeliness of fashion goods.

Inventory Planning and Execution

Technology has enabled the functions of inventory planning and execution to become much more accurate and efficient. The "material requirements planning" methods of the mid 1900s were aimed at manually getting correct materials where needed for production–on time and without unnecessary stockpiling. This was replaced in the late 1900s by *manufacturing resource planning (MRP II),* a computerized system of planning production materials and levels of inventory. Still used, it coordinates data from all company departments to maintain small but sufficient inventories and smooth production processes. Computerized manufacturing methods show when and what materials are put into products as soon as they are used. These systems determine when materials should be ordered and when they should be delivered, based on when they will be needed.

The *just-in-time (JIT)* inventory system is a continuous process of inventory control that, through pipeline teamwork, seeks to deliver small quantities of materials precisely where and when they are needed. If done well, this system eliminates waste by utilizing small inventories that require less storage space, accounting, and investment. Materials arrive at the manufacturing plant just in time for production, and finished goods arrive at retailers just in time to be sold, 11-3.

Apparel companies have found that the strength of MRP II is planning, while the strength of just-in-time is execution. Both utilize bar codes and electronic scanners that automatically enter information into the computer system. Apparel producers are trying to combine the two processes to operate concurrently for a simplified process and increased quality. This should enable companies to keep satisfied customers and fend off competition.

Companies are now implementing enterprise resource planning (ERP), which allows them to manage their entire global production supply chain, from materials providers, manufacturing, and delivery to retailers. This seamless integration of all operations through one database has dramatically slashed response times and back orders. It incorporates accounting/financial applications, advanced planning, purchasing, receiving,

11-3 Finished goods are ideally delivered into the back doors of retailers at just the time they are needed to be sold to consumers who are entering through the front door.

human resources, order entry, and distribution. Users at all levels of the enterprise can specify and manipulate the information that is important to them, allowing for smoother and less time-consuming business practices. Information is available for management to run "what if" scenarios and make decisions about sales forecasts, back orders, unpaid bills, and other matters. ERP, combined with electronic linkages through the rest of the chain, helps all companies keep lean but timely inventories for market demand. More profits result for all firms involved. Materials providers automatically replenish supplies for manufacturers, and manufacturers accomplish automatic inventory replenishment for retailers.

Apparel companies compete with others not only on cost, but also on design, time, quality, and flexibility. Inventory control is a primary competitive advantage that U.S.-based manufacturers can use to combat imports. Goods produced in the U.S. may cost more than those produced offshore in low wage countries. However, producers can be faster and more responsive to retailers' orders. In turn, retailers can have higher sales and more satisfied customers.

Benchmarking for Quality Products

Benchmarking is the continuous process of measuring a company's goods, services, and practices against world-class firms that are renowned as leaders. Then the company's performance is changed to meet or beat those methods. The best ideas of the apparel and related industries are identified and improved.

Benchmarking results in change that brings about better processes. For example, one company might have an innovative method for efficiently distributing their finished goods. Other companies notice that "benchmark" and adopt it. Another company might have the best flow-charting of a manufacturing process or the most efficient self-managed work teams. Others notice and try to emulate these ideas. Each company strives to do the best job in each operation, so the total process is as efficient and effective as possible, 11-4. Also, industry training opportunities are available to workers who want to learn the latest techniques.

This is a *proactive* approach to make processes better, to do everything right the first time. It is better than a *reactive* approach that fixes problems after they occur. Benchmarking builds in high-quality work for error-free goods. This saves the costs of inspection, doing work over, or having items returned by unhappy customers. American business has discovered that improved quality is not an expense. Instead, it generates profits.

Quality Programs

Programs that emphasize high standards of product quality are being stressed in order to achieve top customer satisfaction. Three different quality programs are used by many apparel firms. They are quality control, quality circles, and quality assurance, as summarized in 11-5. A newer total emphasis is total quality management.

Total quality management (TQM) is a concept that has been implemented and used successfully in apparel manufacturing and other industries. The ongoing process focuses on internal requirements needed to deliver the right products in the very best way. It is a long-term commitment for continuous improvement of service and satisfaction beyond customers' expectations. This, in turn, increases company profits.

TQM encompasses the concepts of empowerment of employees, work teams, and benchmarking, 11-6. It requires the commitment of, and communication among, all employees from top to bottom. The quality process must start at the highest level of senior management

Pendleton Woolen Mills

11-4 If one company develops a good way to apply pockets during apparel manufacturing, others will try to incorporate that benchmark process into their manufacturing.

Traditional Quality Programs

Program	Description
Quality control	Routine checking and testing of products is done against a standard to find and correct defects. (A work process.)
Quality circles	Small groups of workers meet regularly to identify, analyze, and find solutions to work-related problems. They try to suggest and implement consistently high-quality methods. (A team effort.)
Quality assurance	Company practices and procedures are identified and followed that promise to meet customer specifications and expectations. (A guarantee to customers.)

11-5 Different quality programs are effective for different products and companies. The programs are run company-wide, involving all employees at every level.

and permeate every employee in the organization. Empowerment allows all workers to participate in the solutions of problems and to help develop new ideas and concepts. Additionally, recognition of good ideas and improved work processes motivates others and improves the TQM process. It spreads to suppliers to improve the quality and cycle time of their products. It also offers an unconditional guarantee to customers.

Because of technology and business conditions, staffs have been cut in many companies. This makes it even more critical that each employee's work be superior and valued. Besides quality and performance standards, apparel companies are also now using the metric system of measure, for global uniformity.

Trademark Protection

A reputation of quality and style is highly valued in today's competitive fashion market. A distinctive trademark can support this message and provide consumers with a sense of purchasing confidence. A ***trademark*** is any word, name, logo, device, or combination of these that is used to identify and distinguish goods of one company from others. See 11-7.

Companies legally protect their trademarks by registering them with the Patent and Trademark Office of the federal government. The trademark registration system exists, in part, to prevent other companies from counterfeiting a company's products. Federal registration

How to Achieve Top Quality
(Adapted from Dr. W. Edward Deming's TQM work)

1. Create consistency and constancy of purpose—set the organization's goals and focus on achieving them.
2. Adopt a new philosophy toward top quality.
3. Cease dependence on inspection; instead, do it right the first time.
4. Stop awarding lower price tags—lower costs will result with top quality automatically.
5. Constantly improve.
6. Institute on-the-job training about how to do things right.
7. Institute leadership of action at all levels (empowerment).
8. Eliminate fear so leadership and creativity can result.
9. Break down barriers within the organization for synergy instead of conflict.
10. Eliminate slogans, exhortations, and zero defect targets that are trite or can't be attained.
11. Eliminate production quotas that cause corners to be cut to meet them or stop progress of going beyond them.
12. Give positive reinforcement for pride of workmanship (such as giving proper credit when/where it is due).
13. Institute a program of self-improvement (with incentives).
14. Put everyone to work actively participating in the process (no "observers").

11-6 TQM is a tool that tries to achieve total quality in all that is done. Although it may initially cost money and cause frustration, there are big payoffs in company profits and worker pride.

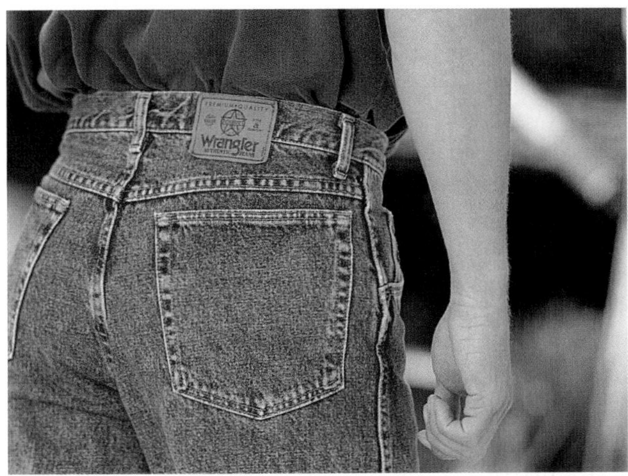

Wrangler Hero Men

11-7 A well-established trademark is recognized by consumers and reinforces the message of guaranteed quality.

gives companies exclusive ownership and privilege to use the mark. It provides the right to sue in federal court for trademark infringement.

Counterfeiting of fashion goods, including a duplicated label and logo, is a serious problem. *Counterfeit fashions*, with false producer labels or designer logos, are sometimes sold in flea markets or by disreputable discount retailers. With counterfeit fashions selling for less than the real products, and usually of inferior quality, a substantial threat exists to the reputation and sales of legitimately trademarked items.

Once a trademark is registered, the company must police it, to preserve its strength. First, the company should make sure that its customers and competitors are aware of the registration. Giving such notice includes using the registration symbol (®) with the mark. Companies can also give notice of trademark ownership rights by using the trademark symbol (™), if they decide not to register or until registration is issued.

Company employees should be educated about the trademark and what it signifies. All should be informed to report a counterfeit product if one is spotted. New companies or competitors sometimes try to pass their products off as one with an established high reputation.

To protect trademark profits, distinctiveness, and reputation, companies should challenge others in court who use the mark or a closely similar one. This helps to remove the counterfeiters from the market, minimize damage of counterfeit products to the company's reputation, and deter other companies from copying that tradename's products, labels, and logos. It alerts other potential infringers that the company will protect the mark.

If an apparel manufacturer sues, the company may name both the manufacturer of the counterfeit goods and the retailer that is selling them. This can provide strong future deterrence throughout the pipeline. It is a good reason why retailers should check out their vendors. It is also an argument in favor of long-term supplier partnerships.

Technological Advances in Apparel Manufacturing

High-tech computer technology and equipment is revolutionizing the entire apparel production industry. The trend is to integrate companies, goods, and services into comprehensive systems that continuously communicate and interact. See 11-8 and 11-9.

New computerized programmable sewing machines are faster and more flexible than older, manually controlled machines. Automated workstation units perform multiple sewing tasks without the need to add new equipment. This allows the U.S. apparel industry to compete against cheaper foreign labor. Manufacturers have lower production costs, higher quality goods, and quick turnaround time. Computerized machines are being used more universally now. This is because the price is coming down, the systems are more user-friendly, and there is a larger pool of technology-literate workers to operate them.

Unlike machines that must be retooled to change, computer-controlled automation is very flexible. The programming is changed on software rather than having to manually alter the machinery. This reduces set-up costs and time, and allows smaller quantities of apparel to be produced economically. Forecasting mistakes are corrected faster. Fewer design and financial risks are taken. More innovative designing can be

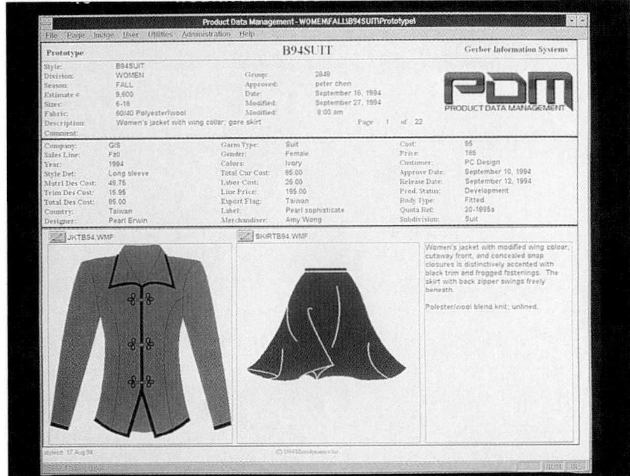

Gerber Garment Technology

11-8 This "Product Data Management" tool organizes fabric, sketch, pattern, and labor information in a central database. It enables authorized users to view or modify fabric, trim, pattern design, and assembly and costing information.

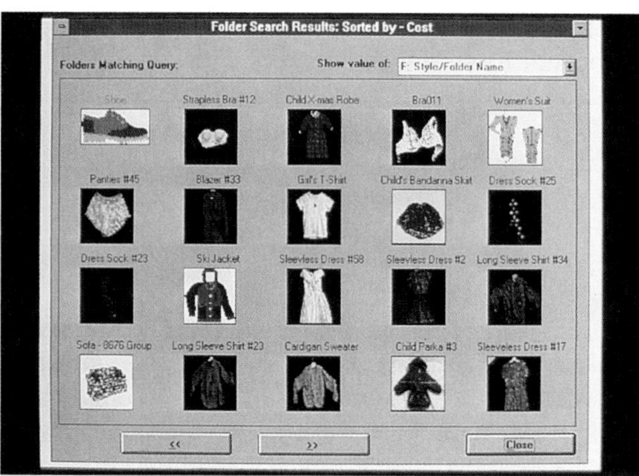

Gerber Garment Technology

11-9 To organize, store, and retrieve images, this system catalogs and files thousands of designs. Thumbnail sketches enable users to visually browse through collections and to access an enlarged picture or drawing of each design that includes all relevant data.

done with a sewing system that can rapidly produce small quantities of garments in various styles.

Robotics involve machines that can be programmed automatically to do mechanical tasks. They are being linked together to do whole piecework operations, with little or no human intervention. Robotic workstation machines pick up a garment part, align it, sew it, trim it, and move it to the next station. The best application for robotics is in repetitive procedures, in which the same process is done constantly. These "steel collar workers" can also work 24 hours a day!

Fully integrated systems are linking computerized units, communication data, and "artificial intelligence." This enables the machines to make decisions by themselves, including detecting product defects. Also, voice-activated sewing machines are controlled through speech recognition.

Computer-Integrated Manufacturing

Computer-integrated manufacturing (CIM) is a combination of many electronic steps in an apparel or other production system. As indicated in 11-10, CAD, CAM, and other systems are tied together. With all functions computerized, bottlenecks at certain points of the chain are prevented. All of the computer commands used to design, manage, and manufacture goods communicate with each other. For some products, this achieves "hands-off" production. Presently, for example, a pillowcase is totally made and packaged by machine. Also, a cowboy boot machine just has to be loaded with

Computer-Integrated Manufacturing (CIM)
ties together CAD, CAM, and other company data
and machines to work toward "hands-off" manufacturing.

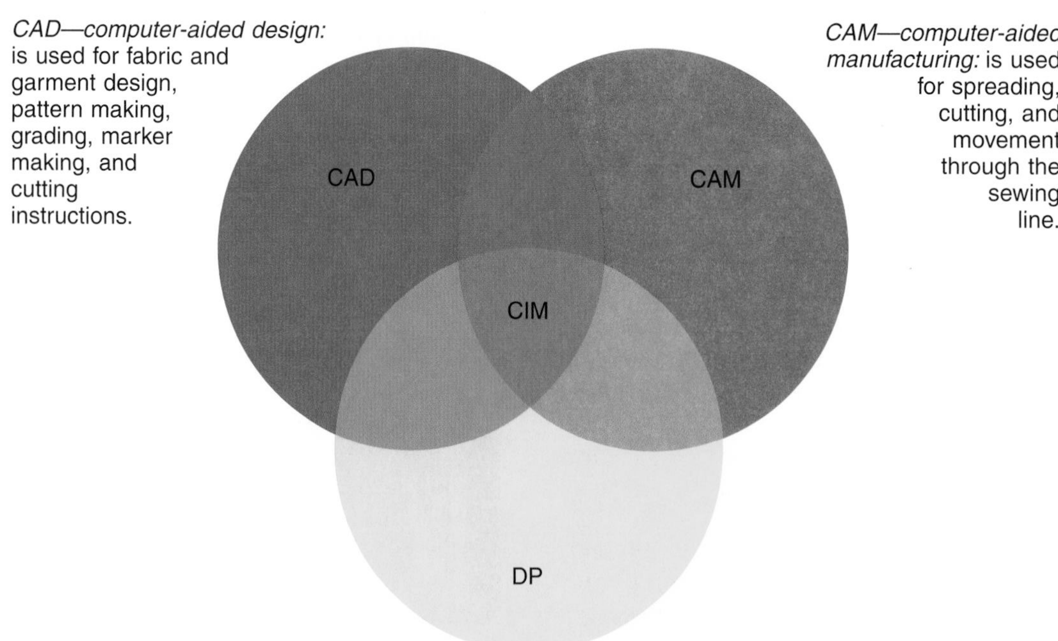

DP—data processing: computerized transformation of data into more usable forms by sorting, summarizing, or storing; includes invoices, bills paid, inventory records, payroll, etc.

11-10 Apparel manufacturing is becoming more technical and more automated as time passes.

leather; decoratively stitched boots are unloaded at the other end.

The main advantage of CIM is that it allows maximum coordination and centralized control of production operations. Duplication of data entry is reduced, lowering chances for error. Changes in design and technical specifications can be instituted quickly. Job status can be noted at any time to better predict delivery dates for customers.

Planners foresee fabric, trimmings, and notions entering one end of an automatic assembly line and emerging at the other end of the line as finished garments. Fashion designers will create their designs on computers, laser cutters will swiftly cut one garment at a time, and robotic machines will do the rest. This will give companies total responsiveness to customers, with the product constantly moving forward to eliminate wasted materials handling time.

CIM standards, coordinated with the American National Standards Institute (ANSI), are being developed to enable communication between all apparel industry entities. Work will be able to go straight through a line with programmable machines controlled by automatic information exchange. Suppliers of machinery and software will offer complete coordination of graphic interface for four-color images, plotter data, marker exchange, materials handling and conveying, and robotic sewing.

Future directions and the level of intensity of these CIM standards and standards-based equipment will depend on the demands of apparel manufacturers. Equipment suppliers constantly try to develop new technology that improves apparel production processes. Preventative maintenance programs have also become more important. These are needed for less downtime, better product quality, and lower expenditures for replacement machines.

Ideas About the Future

Going further with electronic linkage partnerships and CIM, ***demand flow manufacturing (DFM)*** may eventually be reached. Individual affordable garments will be produced quickly, responding to consumer demand. Computers will capture order information remotely and use it directly to manufacture customized garments ordered one at a time. Customization may replace mass production. Key ingredients are valid, timely data collection and communication.

This customized production will reduce trend forecasting risks, while meeting specific needs of individual consumers. See 11-11. Standard sizes may even disappear, resulting in totally computer-produced garments from beginning to end, ordered from retail. A non-contact, 3-D video camera will be pointed at a person to scan body measurement and shape data directly into a computer. Then a single garment will be cut and produced exactly for that person's dimensions, in the fabric and design of the consumer's choice. This marks a return to made-to-measure custom apparel!

To accomplish this, production facilities must be able to make any design at any time, which might be accomplished by downloading electronic information to different plant sites. It is a total "pull" concept; a consumer-oriented system that treats the entire chain as one organization. It is also anticipated that no entity in the pipeline will receive payment until the consumer buys the finished product.

Other possibilities for future apparel production include "stitchless" electronic injection sewing. This uses thread in a polymer (chemical) liquid state that later solidifies. It is done with ultrasonic "sewing machines" that have no needle and thread. They operate four times faster than conventional sewing machines, and trim the edge of the seam at the same time. Pattern wheels can simulate stitches in solid lines, dots, single stitches, double stitches, zig-zags, ropes, flowers, or other patterns. For fabrics that are hard to bond, a bonding tape may be put between the garment part layers.

Fused seams might be heat-sealed with ultrasonic energy. Future technology may also fabricate apparel automatically in the form of seamless garments that are tubular molded, rather than sewn. Another possibility for the future is apparel that will contain heat-sensitive body coils to heat or cool the wearer. Climate-controlled suits could be powered by solar cells.

Efficient factory and retail store layouts will be designed with virtual reality so companies can evaluate how they work before they are built or equipped. Characteristics such as lighting requirements, number and locations of production stations, and aisle widths will be modeled. The system will show optimal production line balancing, as well as needed management information, 11-12.

Technology transfer is the spread of technological knowledge. As time passes, technology transfer moves at a faster pace on a global scale. All segments of the industry have a faster learning curve, and the industry is totally integrated throughout the world. U.S. companies contract with foreign producers and vice versa. International data networks provide global access to information. Telecommunications systems enable close worldwide ties for production and marketing. Additionally, international students attend universities known for world-class curriculums in certain specialties and take information back to their countries. Thus, technological development must be continuous for companies to maintain a competitive edge.

Selling the Finished Apparel

After the garments are manufactured, apparel companies must decide when, where, and how to

A

B

Computer Design, Inc.

11-11 (A) A photograph of people wearing garments without decoration can be inserted into the computer. (B) Design work, done directly on the computer, can show infinite different designs imposed onto the previously plain garment in the photo.

Textile/Clothing Technology Corporation

11-12 Simulation of a flexible manufacturing line can be done by computer, showing a worker moving from one station to another.

profitably sell the lines to retailers. Should they be shown in several cities? Should road salespeople take the lines around to retail buyers individually? Should advertising be done in trade publications to retailers? Much of this is determined by the price/quality category of the lines.

Apparel producers present their lines to retail store buyers about six months ahead of the wearing season by showing them sample garments. Most apparel is sold directly from producer to retailer. This direct-order system gives faster response and helps to keep prices as low as possible, since no middle people have to be paid.

One meaning for the term *market* is a meeting place for buyers and sellers of goods, usually with many sellers in close proximity to each other. During the period known to the fashion trade as ***market weeks*** (or *fashion weeks*), retail store buyers from all over the country go to fashion market cities. They look at the new collections in fashion shows and/or in manufacturers' showrooms, 11-13. Spring showings feature fashions for the next fall/winter. Fall showings sell

Chicago Apparel Center

11-13 Fashion shows are staged during market weeks to present manufacturers' lines to retail buyers.

fashions that will be sold by retailers the following spring/summer.

Selling Locations

As stated earlier, New York City is the major U.S. fashion city. Los Angeles is the fashion center on the West Coast. All fashion cities worldwide hold scheduled fashion weeks during which they show their new lines, and retail buyers visit to make purchases for their stores. Manufacturers' sales offices in the fashion cities are also available all other times of the year for buyers to select additional items and place reorders.

Sales presentations are formal, well-prepared showings of a company's goods to potential customers. These are done in showrooms or other places where potential customers are gathered. Selling staffs answer questions and take orders, 11-14.

11-14 Manufacturing company representatives give sales presentations to retail buyers to try to influence their buying decisions in favor of that manufacturer's goods.

Showrooms are company-owned sales areas where merchandise is displayed and sales presentations are given, 11-15. A company's main showroom is often part of the corporate office facility. Large manufacturing companies maintain additional showrooms in one or more major apparel markets.

Apparel marts are large buildings or complexes that house permanent showrooms, 11-16. They enable

11-15 Companies use showrooms as an effective way to feature and promote their fashion merchandise.

many apparel manufacturers to be in one convenient location for retail buyers. Apparel marts cater to smaller, regional retailers. They particularly attract specialty store buyers.

Many apparel firms have permanent leased showrooms in marts, so buyers can see their lines at any time. Other companies might show their lines during market weeks at these regional marts, held on particular dates. Elaborate multicompany fashion trend shows, retailing seminars, and other special activities are held at that time, too.

Apparel marts are located in several cities. Major marts include the Atlanta Apparel Mart, California Mart (Los Angeles), Dallas Apparel Mart/Menswear Mart, and Chicago Apparel Center, 11-17. Other regional sales centers are located in Seattle, San Francisco, Denver, Minneapolis, Miami, Charlotte (NC), Kansas City (MO), and Woburn (MA). Marts usually show lines

Seattle International Trade Center

11-16 Apparel marts are almost like shopping malls, but at the wholesale level. Only authorized retail buyers are allowed to enter and go from showroom to showroom to purchase goods for their stores.

Chicago Apparel Center

11-17 Apparel marts house many showrooms, plus personal conveniences for retail buyers, within large buildings devoted only to wholesale fashion activities.

that are popular in their part of the country. Dallas is quite representative of the whole U.S.

Apparel producers hope to accomplish many objectives in showroom or mart settings. Mainly, they want to sell their goods. They get input to determine which items to mass produce, drop, or change. They also get ideas for new products and designs.

Apparel companies try to show their goods in the most effective and efficient ways. This is done to impress retail buyers, make a fashion statement, and gain media exposure. Some firms hold press previews for fashion reporters and editors in hopes of getting positive publicity. Others produce videos of their lines. Manufacturers strive to establish better relationships with retail decision makers and train their sales representatives. Specific ways of achieving their objectives are shown in 11-18.

Some manufacturers show their collections accessorized and professionally modeled in their showrooms. Others hang their garments on walls and racks to show to retail buyers, 11-19. All companies hope the buyers will place orders before they leave the showrooms. As orders are taken, production schedules are revised upward for strong sellers and downward for items less desired by retail buyers.

If apparel manufacturers are not big enough to open their own corporate showrooms, they might use an established representative in a mart. The representative has a showroom where several different lines are shown.

Sales Expertise

Besides having selling staffs in their showrooms, some apparel firms have traveling sales representatives (reps) showing and selling their lines around the country. The manufacturers preview the new styles to their sales representatives at home office fashion shows and sales meetings. The reps then travel within their assigned territories with sample lines to show to retailers.

All sales reps may be expected to be at their company's showroom during market weeks. After market weeks, the company reps serve as customer service personnel to help their retail accounts maintain low and effective inventory levels that bring good profits. They also show retailers the new style numbers that are introduced mid-season.

Sales managers supervise the sales force and lead sales forecast planning. ***Sales forecasting*** is predicting the quality of each item that will be sold during a particular future fiscal time period. A ***fiscal period*** is a financial accounting period, usually 6 months or one year. A fiscal year may coincide with the calendar year (January 1 to December 31) or may be different, such as from July 1 to June 30.

Retail sales statistics reveal what has happened in the past, but sales forecasting tries to predict future demand. It is important for manufacturers to anticipate the right amounts of goods that will be ordered by customers. Resources and production capacity must meet expected manufacturing needs.

The forecast is also used to evaluate the success of the company's sales performance after a fiscal period is finished. Actual sales are measured against the forecast figures. Additionally, results of the past forecast are used to develop the sales forecast for the next period.

Manufacturers that are too small to have their own company reps use independent sales reps that work on a commission basis. Independent reps sell collections of several different manufacturers' lines that are not in competition with one another, but that are sold to similar target consumers. For instance, items of a small manufacturer of women's slacks might be sold to retail accounts by a rep who also sells another small company's skirts, another's knit tops, and another's women's sweaters. Manufacturers and independent salespeople can purchase annual directories of retail buyers, that list buyers' names, their merchandise specialties, company names, locations, and phone numbers. Some manufacturers sell directly to consumers via Internet Web sites, but risk losing some of their retail accounts that become upset by this practice of bypassing the retailers.

When sales transactions are finalized, a ***contract*** is drawn up. A contract is a written agreement between a buyer (retailer) and seller (manufacturer), detailing all conditions of the sale. People from both the selling and the buying companies sign the contract and get a copy of it. Most contracts are quite similar, with standardized clauses that describe delivery, payment, and other details.

Manufacturers Show Merchandise at Markets	
To:	**How Accomplished:**
Sell their goods	From samples and salesmanship
Determine which items to mass-produce, drop, or change	From customer orders and input
Get ideas for new products and designs	Through conversation and viewing other manufacturers' lines
Show their goods in the most effective/efficient ways	On models, accessorized, in an attractive showroom, etc.
Establish better relationships with retail decision makers	Personally meet and talk to retail buyers and managers
Make a fashion statement and gain media exposure	Project design creativity and business image to targeted customers and press
Train sales representatives	On-the-job talk about new merchandise, actions that follow company policies, networking, etc.

11-18 Manufacturers can achieve many objectives by showing their merchandise in showroom or market settings.

Chicago Apparel Center

11-19 Each type of apparel is shown in the best and most cost-effective way to help retail buyers understand the company's lines.

Sales Promotion

After retailers accounts have placed orders, some apparel producers do cooperative advertising with the stores that sell their lines. They might advertise their merchandise to consumers in national fashion magazines and include a list of the regional stores that carry their lines. At other times, retailers advertise in local newspapers and promote a particular manufacturer's products. Either way, the businesses share the advertising expenses and both benefit.

Manufacturers sometimes provide retailers with selling aids, such as large photographs for store displays, 11-20. Other selling aids might include counter cards, newspaper advertising mats, and customer mailing pieces or bill enclosures. They may have in-store programs that provide training talks to salespeople, to explain new merchandise and demonstrate how new fashions can be worn and combined. They might also offer personal appearances by the firm's designer, videotapes of collections, fashion shows, or trunk shows.

During a ***trunk show*** a complete collection of samples is brought into a retail store or exhibition hall by a manufacturer for a limited amount of time. There is heavy local advertising, and orders are taken directly from customers by a key company designer or representative for later delivery. Customers can see and buy from the producer's entire line, ordering any style, color, or size of the garments presented. This would probably be too many items for the retailer to stock under regular conditions, since retailers edit their purchases from manufacturers to only the number of styles and colors

11-20 The manufacturer of these fashion items has provided the framed picture for the retailer to display on the wall in the retail selling department.

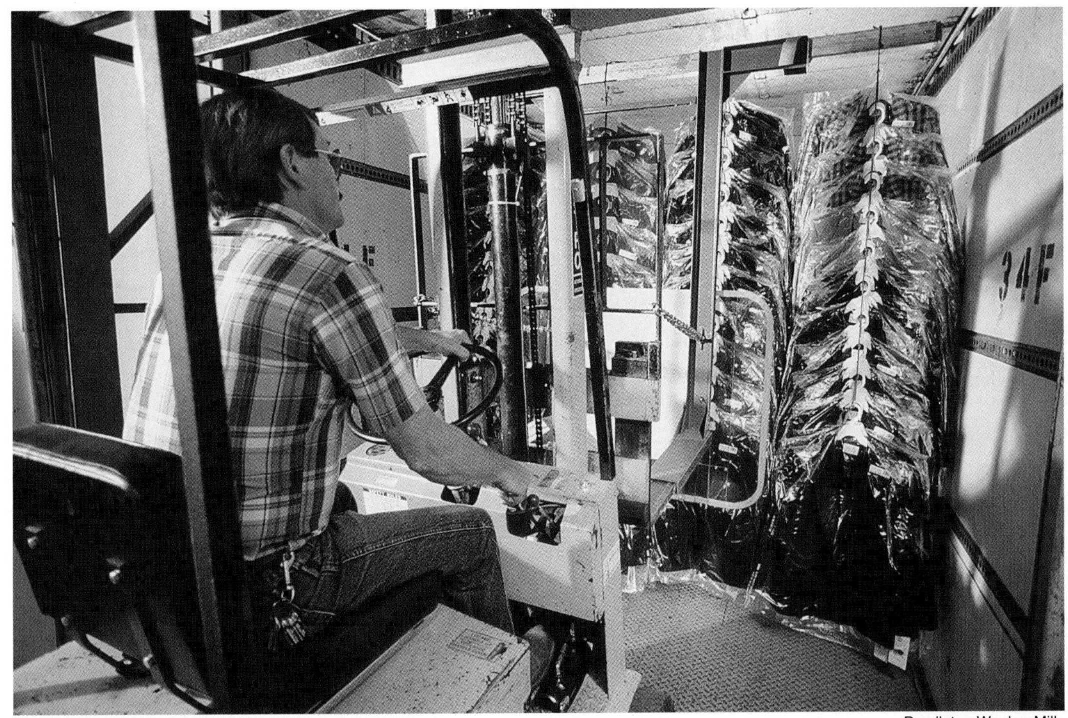

Pendleton Woolen Mills

11-21 Distribution involves the logistics of controlling inventories of goods within warehouses and sending the right orders to the correct locations.

they can afford and that will sell to their customers. Trunk shows give retailers a chance to sell the merchandise without taking the risk of carrying the items in their inventory.

Trunk shows also enable manufacturers and retailers to evaluate consumer feedback about the line. Manufacturers can incorporate customer desires into future style numbers. They listen and respond to customers' preferences, and decide which items are destined to be best sellers or unsuccessful "dogs." Then, changes in production can be made as early as possible to keep costs down. Production must be increased for popular items, since reorders provide the biggest profit margins for manufacturers.

Customers enjoy meeting a designer or company representative at trunk shows. Interested consumers ask questions about the garments, and how to wear and accessorize them. At the same time, manufacturers and retailers enhance their image by associating with each other.

Distribution of the Finished Apparel

As discussed in Chapter 3, distribution strives to move fashion goods to their proper destinations to coincide with market demand timing. It includes planning, implementing, and controlling the physical flow of goods from points of origin (manufacturers) to points of use (consumers). It involves both sales and logistics. ***Logistics*** include the handling details of storing and physically moving merchandise to the proper locations, 11-21.

Apparel producers of less expensive lines often use an *open distribution policy*, in which they sell and ship goods to any retailer that can pay for the merchandise. Sometimes manufacturers control the mass-distribution of lower-priced products by setting a high minimum order requirement. Higher-priced producers usually use a *selected distribution policy*, selling and shipping only to a limited number of stores per area. This helps to maintain their exclusivity.

If a certain label of goods from a manufacturer is ***confined,*** it is sold only to one retailer within a certain geographic trading area. It may be sold only to a particular chain of retail stores nationally. On the other hand, some apparel companies are ***dual distributors***, offering their products through both regular retail accounts and their own company-owned retail outlets.

The vertical integration that combines production and retailing for manufacturers' outlet stores causes the producers to compete with their own customers. This is a disadvantage since it may anger the retail customers who stock their items. However, having their own retail locations does help manufacturers control ongoing production and provide fast deliveries to their outlet stores, since they are their own suppliers. See 11-22. Outlet stores also have one less cost layer between producer and consumer. They can, therefore,

11-22 The merchandise for manufacturers' outlet stores comes directly from the manufacturing plant without being sold to retail buyers.

Pendleton Woolen Mills

11-23 In distribution facilities, orders are put together according to the amounts of each item that have been ordered.

offer lower prices to consumers and create a better profit margin for themselves.

Order Processing

As previously described, electronic data interchange (EDI) is used to send and receive orders between trading partners. When the manufacturer receives electronic information, such as a purchase order from a retailer, or point-of-sale data showing depleted inventory at retail, an order is triggered. The system also automatically sends a confirmation back to each retailer that specific purchase orders have been received by the manufacturer.

Then bar-coded "pick tickets" are sent to the stockroom or distribution center. The orders are "picked" with the right styles, colors, and sizes by scanning garment tags and/or box labels. The picked items are then moved to the packing area, usually with a conveyor system. See 11-23. There folded items are packed flat in corrugated boxes with bar codes on the ends to identify the contents. Hanging garments are put onto hangers and hung on bars in stand-up boxes. The finished-order cartons are sealed and addressed with bar-coded "ship to" information to the receiving departments of the retailers.

It is important that merchandise container bar code labeling and scanning systems comply with standardized requirements. *Shipping container marking (SCM)* facilitates the identification and shipping of containers among vendors and retailers. It also supports the flow of merchandise through retailers' distribution centers. The marking can be read by a variety of optical scanners.

Warehouse picking of orders and shipment tracking, with bar code and scanner distribution technology, is required for the fast, ongoing demands of Quick Response replenishment. With increasing customer expectations, improved logistics provides superior service to retail customers, better management of inventories, and shorter supply cycle times.

EDI and SCM can tell retailers how and when shipping will take place. This is done with *advance ship notices* that detail the number of cartons in each shipment and the contents of the cartons for the receiving stores. Also, manufacturers often ship orders directly to the specific stores of a national chain. This eliminates the retail step of dividing merchandise into smaller lots and moving it to individual stores from company distribution centers.

The use of bar-coded carton labels and trusting vendor partnerships eliminates the need for retailers to check the contents of shipments when they are delivered. Instead, receiving employees at stores can simply scan the bar codes to verify the contents of cartons. Retail inventories are automatically updated accordingly. The needed goods can immediately be unpacked and put out onto the selling floor of each store.

Merchandise Shipping

To ship garments to other cities and states, modern transportation systems move merchandise to stores in fast, dependable ways. Depending on the needed speed of delivery or merchandise price category, transportation might be by highway (truck), air (plane), ocean (ship), or rail (train). Often it is a combination of these methods.

Within the U.S., most fashion goods travel by truck, 11-24. This method allows for flexible routing and time schedules. It can move goods door-to-door. Trucks are especially efficient for fast service of short hauls containing high-value merchandise.

Goods that are sourced offshore come by ship into U.S. ports or are flown in on cargo airplanes. Large containers of standard sizes can be stacked on ocean freighters, placed on flat railroad cars, or put onto truck trailer beds. They can travel long distances without being unpacked. *Consolidated shipping*, in which two or more shippers put together a truckload, lowers transportation costs. Air freight is fast for long distances, but is expensive.

When large shipments arrive near their geographic destinations, they are divided and transferred to trucks for delivery to retailers. Satellite shipment tracking is being used to keep track of merchandise at all times. Store managers know exactly when shipments will arrive so employees can stay busy with other tasks until a truck is arriving at the unloading dock. See 11-25. This technology puts freight carriers, such as highway trucks, into the Quick Response pipeline. The trucks contain computers that can send messages to instantaneously route them to where the goods are needed. Home office dispatchers know where the trucks are at all times. Trucks are even equipped with a signal that allows them to be scanned while driving by weigh stations, and to automatically be billed for tolls without having to stop.

Some companies outsource their physical distribution to third-party experts. These logistic specialists know the best methods and have the right equipment to be especially efficient in maximizing the flow of goods. An example is shown in 11-26. This can result in faster delivery and financial advantages for companies that hire them. Such contract warehousing and transportation can reduce fixed overhead expenses and eliminate the need for seasonal employee hiring.

The soft goods chain is moving toward retailers managing the distribution process. Retailers are "bringing in" goods rather than manufacturers "sending out" goods. Efficient logistics enable small- and medium-sized retailers to survive against today's large retail corporations.

As time passes, distribution facilities are expected to become smaller and more dynamic. They will be totally automated with bar codes and advanced scanners. Most received goods will be electronically identified, sorted, routed, and shipped in an uninterrupted

11-24 Finished goods are loaded into the backs of trucks to be driven to retail warehouses or stores that ordered them.

11-25 Trucks back into loading docks that are the same level as the floor of truck trailers. Boxes and racks of apparel that are unloaded can go directly into the store from the trucks.

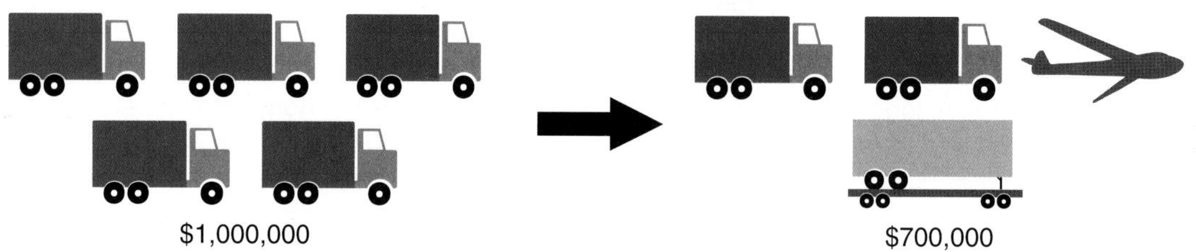

11-26 Instead of simply shipping all goods by truck, logistic experts can redesign a company's distribution network to get items to the right places at the right times with a lower cost.

flow. This will be more accurate and very cost effective, with faster throughput and reduced labor costs. The decision on how to ship will be based on reliability, time, price, distance, size, and weight rather than by mode (train, plane, ship, or truck).

Apparel Industry Trade Information

The American Apparel and Footware Association (AAFA) is the national trade association representing all types of U.S. apparel producers. Most U.S. apparel and footware manufacturers are members. AAFA's goal is to maintain the economic well-being of the industry and its companies in hopes that its members can offer high quality goods at competitive prices. It has strong programs in business strategy, education, technology, marketing, communications, and relations with contractors and retailers. It is concerned with health and safety issues, and environmental concerns. It helps to develop compliance and CIM standards. It also does extensive government lobbying in Washington, DC, giving industry input on domestic legislation and trade negotiations.

The Fashion Association (TFA) used to be another trade group of retailers, apparel manufacturers, and textile firms. To eliminate duplication of memberships, this organization has now joined with the AAFA as its public relations arm. The TFA supports the AAFA membership and the apparel production and retailing industries through an ongoing program of fashion and business promotion. Another trade group, the International Apparel Federation (IAF), promotes common business interests and support for its worldwide membership of apparel manufacturers.

The AAFA holds a convention in conjunction with the ***Bobbin Show***, the apparel industry's largest annual event. The show is sponsored by *Bobbin Magazine*, a leading trade journal for apparel industry executives and decision makers. The Bobbin Show introduces a multitude of new technology, with hundreds of equipment exhibitors selling their products, 11-27. It displays new materials and fashions, and includes many seminars, conferences, and special events, 11-28.

Many other trade publications are important to the industry. One widely-read trade journal is the *Apparel Industry Magazine*. *Women's Wear Daily* and the *Daily News Record* (described in Chapter 4) report all new apparel trends. They have photos, fashion illustrations, and stories, as well as business and financial news of the womenswear and textile/menswear industries respectively. The *Apparel Marketing Digest* summarizes articles that have appeared in other magazines and newspapers on apparel industry subjects.

The two previously prominent labor unions of the textile/apparel industry merged in 1995 to become the Union of Needletrades, Industrial and Textile Employees (UNITE). It has over 250,000 individual members. The merger has consolidated employee bargaining resources and broadened the geographic reach and political clout of the workers.

The union is cooperating with management of U.S. companies, to try to keep as many jobs as possible in the U.S. Its members are encouraging modular manufacturing, Quick Response strategies, and advanced

Bobbin, a Miller Freeman Inc., Company

11-27 New machines for commercially cutting and sewing garments are shown to apparel manufacturers at the Bobbin Show in hopes that the manufacturers will want to put them into their factories.

Bobbin, a Miller Freeman Inc., Company

11-28 Fabrics in new fiber combinations, methods of construction, and colors are shown to apparel manufacturers at the Bobbin Show for them to order to produce their lines.

technology. They opposed these in the past because of loss of jobs. However, UNITE members now realize that if these advances are not put into place in U.S. factories, all U.S. textile and apparel production jobs will disappear to offshore locations.

Summary

Manufacturers have inventories of raw materials, work-in-process, and finished goods, while retailers sell only finished goods. It is important to maintain the right inventories, with proper planning and execution. Electronic linkage partnerships help companies keep lean, but timely, inventories for market demand.

Benchmarking causes change that brings about better processes. Quality programs emphasize high standards to achieve top customer satisfaction. Total quality management is a long-term commitment for continuous improvement of service, and satisfaction beyond customer expectations. A distinctive trademark can support a reputation of quality and style. Companies register and police their trademarks to discourage counterfeiting.

High-tech computer technology and equipment is revolutionizing apparel production. Computer-integrated manufacturing allows maximum coordination and centralized control of operations. Demand flow manufacturing reduces trend forecasting risks, while meeting specific needs of individual consumers. Many different possibilities exist for technology of the future.

Most apparel is sold directly from producer to retailer. Selling is done with sales presentations at market showrooms or marts. Some firms also have traveling sales representatives, or use independent sales reps. Manufacturers may also help retailers promote their lines to consumers.

Distribution of the finished apparel might involve an open or selected policy. Order processing between trading partners may be done electronically. Standardized bar code labeling and scanning systems are used. Shipping is done by truck, plane, ship, train, or an optimum combination of these methods.

Many trade associations and journals, as well as industry shows, keep members informed about the latest technology. The major labor union has over 250,000 individual members.

To Know

inventories
inventory control
materials handling
benchmarking
trademark
robotics
computer-integrated manufacturing (CIM)
demand flow manufacturing (DFM)
market weeks
showrooms
apparel marts
sales forecasting
fiscal period
contract
trunk show
logistics
confined
dual distributors
American Apparel and Footware Association (AAFA)
Bobbin Show

To Review

1. Describe apparel production raw materials.
2. What does a condition of too much inventory cause?
3. What is manufacturing resource planning (MRP II)?
4. Differentiate between proactive and reactive approaches to quality.
5. What costs are saved when benchmarking is used to build high quality work for error-free goods?
6. How can companies legally protect their trademarks?
7. Why is computer-controlled automation very flexible?
8. For what specific apparel production operations is computer-aided manufacturing used?
9. For production equipment, what are the results of preventative maintenance programs?
10. How might seams be produced in the future?
11. What is the meaning of the term *market* in this chapter?
12. What are sales presentations?

13. As apparel manufacturers take orders from retail buyers, in what way are production schedules revised?
14. How is a sales forecast used to evaluate the success of the company's sales performance after a fiscal period is finished?
15. What kinds of orders provide the biggest profit margins for apparel manufacturers?
16. With whom do manufacturers compete when they have outlet stores?
17. When manufacturers ship orders directly to the specific stores of a national chain, what retail step is eliminated?
18. Name the main advantage and disadvantage of air freight.
19. Who is most likely to read *Bobbin Magazine*?
20. Why do UNITE members now encourage modular manufacturing, Quick Response strategies, and advanced technology which they opposed in the past?

To Do

1. With another student, visit a small store. Write down all of its types of inventories (such as computers, display props, women's skirts, men's neckties, etc.). Ask the store manager (or an employee) if there are more goods in a storage area, ready to be put on the floor when needed; how often shipments arrive and how much merchandise is usually in a shipment; if the shipments come from a retail distribution center or directly from manufacturers; if the store sometimes has too many or too few of some items; etc. Prepare an oral or written report about your findings.
2. Study MRP and just-in-time inventory control with a classmate. Do library or computer Internet research in business journals, books, and listings. Then describe to the class the details of what you learned. Hold a discussion about the importance of these inventory control methods in relation to apparel manufacturing.
3. Identify four different apparel company trademarks. Make a bulletin board display with a photo or drawing of each trademark, the name of the company that owns it, and the image it projects to consumers.
4. Do a study of how apparel manufacturers help retailers with sales promotion. Find examples of cooperative advertising in national publications or local newspapers. Visit retail stores to look for various types of selling aids provided by manufacturers. Make a booklet that shows or describes at least four different examples that you discovered.
5. Review this chapter's section on "Distribution of the Finished Apparel." Write a short story, with the main characters being a group of finished shirts that take different distribution paths to the end users. Tell the adventures of each one as you try to use all the terms and situations described in the text, including order processing and merchandise shipping.

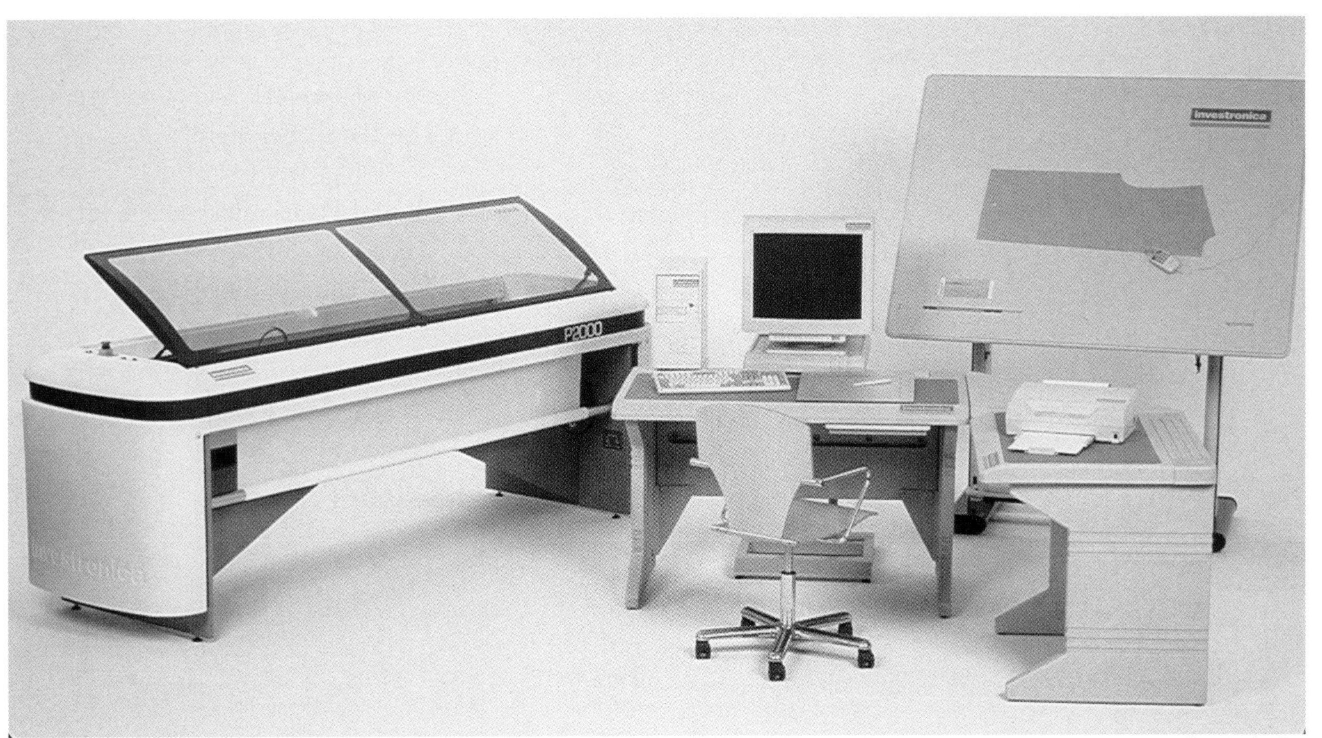

Investronica, Inc.

New technology plays a vital role in producing apparel.

PART 4

Retail Business Fundamentals

CHAPTER 12

The Retail Segment

After studying this chapter, you will be able to

- list the functional areas of retail firms.
- explain the main types of apparel retailers.
- describe store ownership groups.
- summarize retail trade information.

You have already learned that retailing is the service business of selling products directly to final consumers for their personal use. It is the exchange of merchandise for money or credit. Retailing is the link that moves finished goods from manufacturers to consumers—the last step in the channel of distribution.

Retailing is America's fourth largest industry. It is a major employer, providing far more jobs than manufacturing and other types of businesses. Retailing includes such entities as grocery stores, car dealerships, and many thousands of stores that sell clothing. It involves the basic steps shown in 12-1. In addition, retailers provide product information and stimulate demand for merchandise. Retail businesses try to minimize operating expenses while maximizing sales and customer satisfaction.

Fashion retailing is very competitive and constantly changing. If the retailing effort is not effective, all levels of the pipeline are impacted because the products are not sold. The companies do not make money, and everyone in the chain suffers. Therefore, retailers must listen to consumers and respond to their preferences. Since retailers deal directly with consumers and are often the first to recognize changing consumer demand, they should share this information with producers. They must also react to a constantly changing and often unsettled economic climate.

Basic Steps of Retailing
1. Planning the types and quantities of goods to sell
2. Buying the goods from suppliers
3. Receiving the goods
4. Arranging the goods for sale
5. Selling the goods

12-1 These basic steps form the process that retailers go through to run their businesses.

To encourage sales, the presentation of items in stores must educate consumers on how to wear or combine articles of clothing. Retailers need to show how to put together and accessorize outfits, thus creating consumer demand. See 12-2. Advertising tells consumers where specific goods are available. However, if the public is not ready for certain styles, those styles will not sell.

Retailing is undergoing major changes, with some highly specialized stores catering to narrow niches and others trying to provide all types of goods and services. For instance, grocery stores now house bank branches, prescription pharmacy departments, and videotape rental counters. All retailers are experimenting with new ways to appeal to consumers. Retailers try to maintain a balance between the correct merchandise to meet the needs of targeted consumers and the ability to operate effectively and efficiently.

12-2 Retailers increase sales by helping customers gain confidence in combining garments into coordinated outfits.

Functional Areas of Fashion Retail Firms

Retail businesses generally have five key functional areas of responsibility. The functional areas include merchandising, financial control, store operations, personnel, and promotion. The goal of each of these areas is to manage resources in the best possible way to satisfy customers, while helping the company make a good profit. Large companies often have separate divisions for handling these functions. The owners of small companies may do all functions themselves, or hire outside accountants, advertising agencies, and other specialists to help them. The following is a brief description of each of the five functional areas:

- **Merchandising.** Fashion merchandising involves the activities of planning, buying, and selling apparel and accessories. It is the central function of apparel retailing, and the main subject of this book. Retailers buy large quantities of finished garments and other goods at wholesale prices, and sell single items or small quantities of goods to many different people at retail prices, 12-3.
- **Financial control.** The financial control function deals with supervising the budget and overseeing the spending activities of the store or retail firm. It manages such activities as credit and collections (incoming money), paying bills and

12-3 This retailer has purchased quantities of various colors of shirts that are folded on the merchandise display table. The shirts will be sold individually to many different consumers.

wages (outgoing money), getting loans if needed, and inventory control.

- **Store operations.** This function is concerned with physically managing and maintaining the store. One activity is housekeeping—maintaining a clean, functional, and attractive building. Other activities include customer service, protection and security, and receiving and marking of the merchandise.
- **Personnel.** The personnel function deals with hiring, training, scheduling, and rewarding employees with raises or bonuses. It is concerned with all benefits provided to store employees, such as health insurance. It formulates human relations policies, keeps records on employees, and does job performance evaluations. This includes "outplacement" if someone must be terminated from his or her job.
- **Sales promotion.** This involves advertising, display, public relations, publicity, and special events.

These five key functions will be more fully explained in other sections of this book. They are briefly summarized in 12-4.

Main Types of Apparel Retailers

Retail stores are located everywhere, from large cities to small, remote communities. Although large multi-unit chain stores account for a large percentage of total retail sales, many stores are small family-owned businesses. They are independent owner-operated stores, run by a husband and wife or a proprietor and a few employees. These *"mom and pop stores"* are located throughout America and generally offer consumers more convenience and personal service than the retail giants. However, the independent stores are finding it hard to compete with the giant superstores that, because of large-volume sales, can offer greater selections at lower prices. Many stores of all sizes have changed hands, either merging with other stores or becoming part of large conglomerates. Other stores have reorganized for greater efficiency, or expanded to compete more equally with the conglomerates.

Retail stores, also referred to as retail outlets, can be classified into two main categories. These categories, general and specialized, are based on the merchandise the stores carry.

- ***General merchandisers*** market all types of goods in multiple price ranges and try to satisfy the many needs of a broad range of customers. An example of a general merchandiser is Sears, 12-5. General merchandisers range from rural general stores to midsized department stores to huge mass merchandisers.

Functional Areas of Responsibility in Retail Firms
Merchandising: merchandise planning, quantity buying, single-item selling
Financial control: accounting and bill paying, credit and collections, buying/selling statistics, budget and expense control
Store operations: building maintenance, business supplies, inventory receiving/marking/warehousing, protection and security, customer services (wrapping, delivery, exchanges, complaints, etc.)
Personnel: employee hiring, training, scheduling workers, benefits (health insurance, pension plans, etc.), job evaluations, promotions, transfers, and dismissals
Promotion: planning and executing advertising campaigns, window and floor displays, interior signs, public relations, media publicity, special events (fashion shows, art contests, etc.)

12-4 These functional areas of responsibility might all be done by one person in a very small store and exist as separate divisions of a large retail organization.

12-5 Although Sears has concentrated more on apparel sales recently, it also sells electronics, appliances, and other general merchandise.

12-6 This specialized merchandiser sells only classic ladies fashion goods at moderate and better price levels.

- ***Specialized merchandisers*** offer limited lines of related products targeted to more defined customers. They are "focused merchandisers" that market only certain categories of goods to particular age groups, size categories, or lifestyle/taste levels. See 12-6. The customers of specialized merchandisers are more alike than those of general merchandisers.

Even though retailers can be categorized as either general or specialized merchandisers, they can be further classified by specific types. These main types of retailers, which sell at least some fashion merchandise, are listed in 12-7, along with examples of each type. Each of these main types of apparel retailers is explained in detail in the sections that follow.

Types of Retailers	A Few Examples
Department stores:	Bloomingdales, Dillard's, Emporium-Capwell, Filenes, Foley's, Macy's, Marshall Field's, J.W. Robinson's
Specialty department stores:	Bergdorf Goodman, Mervyn's, Nieman-Marcus, Nordstrom, Saks Fifth Avenue
Chain stores:	Sears Roebuck, JCPenney, Kohl's, Victoria's Secret, Gap, Limited
Discount chains:	Ames, Caldor, Kmart, Target, Wal-Mart, Zayre
Off-price discounters:	Designer Depot, Loehmann's, Marshalls, Ross Stores, Syms, TJ Maxx
Factory outlets:	aileen, Bass, Cape Isle Knitters, Manhattan Shirts, Maidenform, VanHeusen
Wholesale warehouse clubs:	BJ's Wholesale Club, Price/Costco, Sams Wholesale Club
Supercenters/Hyper Markets:	American Fare, Hypermarket USA, Super Kmart, Wal-Mart's Super Center Store
Specialty stores:	Geary's Beverly Hills, Tiffany's, David's Bridal, American Eagle, Talbots
Spin-off stores:	Aeropostale (from Macy's), Express (Limited), Old Navy (Gap)
Franchise stores:	Benetton, Charles Jourdan, Lady Madonna, Mothercare, Ralph Lauren's Polo Shops
Designer boutiques:	Giorgio Armani, Givenchy, Sonia Rykiel, Valentino
Specialty chain stores:	Casual Corner, Foxmoor, Lane Bryant, Paul Harris, The Limited, Gap, Victoria's Secret
Category killers:	Circuit City, Hechinger, Office Depot, The Sports Authority, Staples, Toys "R" Us
Licensed merchandise stores:	The Disney Store, The Hollywood Store
Mail-order retailers:	J. Crew, Lands' End, L.L. Bean, Silk Collection, Spiegel
Variety stores:	Ben Franklin, M.H. Lamston, M.E. Moses, Dollar/Closeout chains: Dollar General, Family Dollar, Pic N Save
Dollar/Closeout chains:	Dollar General, Family Dollar, Pic N Save
Personal selling:	Amway, Doncaster, Mary Kay, Tupperware, The Worth Collection, Avon
Catalog showrooms:	Consumers, Service Merchandise
Television retailing:	Home Shopping Network, QVC Network, ValueVision International
Computer retailing portals:	fashionmall.com, itsybits.com, outletmall.com, shoppinglist.com

12-7 Retail companies are often included in more than one retail category. For instance, many chains are discount specialty or department stores. Thus, they fall within three of the categories. The lines between many store types have blurred.

Department Stores

Department stores are large-scale general merchandisers that offer many varieties of merchandise grouped into separate departments, 12-8. Department stores usually have a fashion orientation, selling almost all clothing and household needs in a wide range of colors, sizes, and styles. The goods are categorized into such areas as menswear, juniors, infants, jewelry, and shoes. The departments may also define various quality and price ranges. For instance, there may be a "ladies better dresses" department and a "budget sportswear" area. Each department within the store has salespeople and a place to pay for the goods being purchased. Departments are usually separate profit centers for record-keeping purposes.

Department stores have traditionally enjoyed a prestigious reputation of higher quality, fashion, and customer service. They almost always offer credit, liberal payment plans, and return or exchange privileges. Other conveniences may include gift wrapping, service desks, home delivery, and one or more restaurants. They often have bridal registries, wardrobe consultants, and personal shopping assistants, as well.

Department stores strive to maintain an image of quality and integrity. They want customers to regard them as being dependable. They have traditionally had a full markup policy on nationally branded merchandise. However, in order to be competitive, they have had to lower their markups in recent years. Many have also reduced their selections of hard-line goods, such as furniture and major appliances, to concentrate on more profitable fashion merchandise.

Department stores sell to many income levels because of their wide range of products. However, most department stores target the majority of their merchandise toward people in the middle to upper-middle income brackets. They also have somewhat higher operating expenses than most other stores because they must cover the costs of having more personnel and extra services. They advertise heavily and have many promotional activities. However, they also have large buying and sales volumes that help to lower their expenses.

12-8 Dillard's has been a successful department store for many decades. The company has branches in many areas of the U.S.

Branch Stores

When an established department store opens "satellite" stores in other locations, the new ones are called branch stores. ***Branch stores*** are usually smaller retail units owned and operated by a parent store and located in suburbs or other metropolitan areas. They have the same name and receive their merchandise and business direction from the original flagship store.

The ***flagship store*** is the "parent," or main store, that was probably originally located in a central business district. See 12-9. The flagship usually houses the executive, merchandising, and promotional offices for the entire operation. The buying, advertising, and control of

12-9 The Macy's flagship store in New York City is the majestic home office for all the Macy's branch stores throughout the country.

all branches is done centrally to save on operating expenses. Also, if merchandise is not available at a branch store, it can usually be obtained on short notice from the flagship store. Some department stores have closed their old downtown flagship stores and moved their administrative offices elsewhere.

Retailers first established suburban branches in widening circles around a main downtown flagship store. Now branches are frequently located far away from the home base. Some companies even have *twigs*, which are very small branch stores that carry narrow selections of the parent store's merchandise. These stores usually target specific customers. They are specialty-type shops, often located near university campuses, in hotels, or in airports. They carry limited items for niche consumers, such as college students or tourists.

Junior Department Stores

Junior department stores are smaller than conventional department stores and do not carry as wide a range of goods. See 12-10. They carry limited assortments of apparel, housewares, gifts, and household textiles. Major appliances and furniture are not offered, and the merchandise is usually moderately priced. Small, locally owned department stores fall into this category. These stores are having problems competing today because of their lower sales volume. They cannot purchase their inventory at low enough prices or sell goods at high enough prices to attract customers and make a profit.

Chain Stores

A ***chain*** is a group of stores (usually twelve or more) that is owned, managed, merchandised, and controlled by a central office. All the stores of a chain handle similar goods at similar prices, including a great deal of their own private label merchandise. The stores of a chain look very much alike, as in 12-11. No store is considered to be the main store.

Decisions of chain-store companies are made at the central headquarters. These offices are usually not located at any one of the stores. This differs from department stores where branches are merchandised and controlled from the parent store. Employees at the central offices

- decide on the chain's product assortment
- place orders to get quantity discounts
- send goods out to individual stores
- set pricing, advertising, promotion, and other policies for all units.

Chains may be general or specialized merchandisers. Some offer discounted prices, while others sell exclusive designs at high prices. Some apparel chains focus on a special size, age, or income group. Certain chain organizations may be local or regional, while others operate nationwide. National chains may be big enough to have regional offices as well as the central home office to which all report.

Prices in chain stores are often lower than those in department stores. Since large chains have enormous buying power, manufacturers can afford to produce merchandise to the chain's specifications. Thus, private label merchandise may be styled and made exclusively for them at lower prices. However, department stores are also sourcing private label goods. The volume-buying methods of chain and department stores are becoming very similar to each other.

Major chain and department stores often serve as ***anchor stores*** that provide the attraction needed to draw customers to shopping centers and malls. Anchors are the "destination stores" that support the many small "me too" stores located in shopping centers. The simplified mall layout shown in 12-12 illustrates this concept.

Discount Stores

Discount stores are retail establishments that sell merchandise at lower than recognized market-level

12-11 Most JCPenney stores are similar. They are merchandised and regulated by a central office in Texas.

12-10 Many towns throughout the U.S. have junior department stores started by local families many years ago.

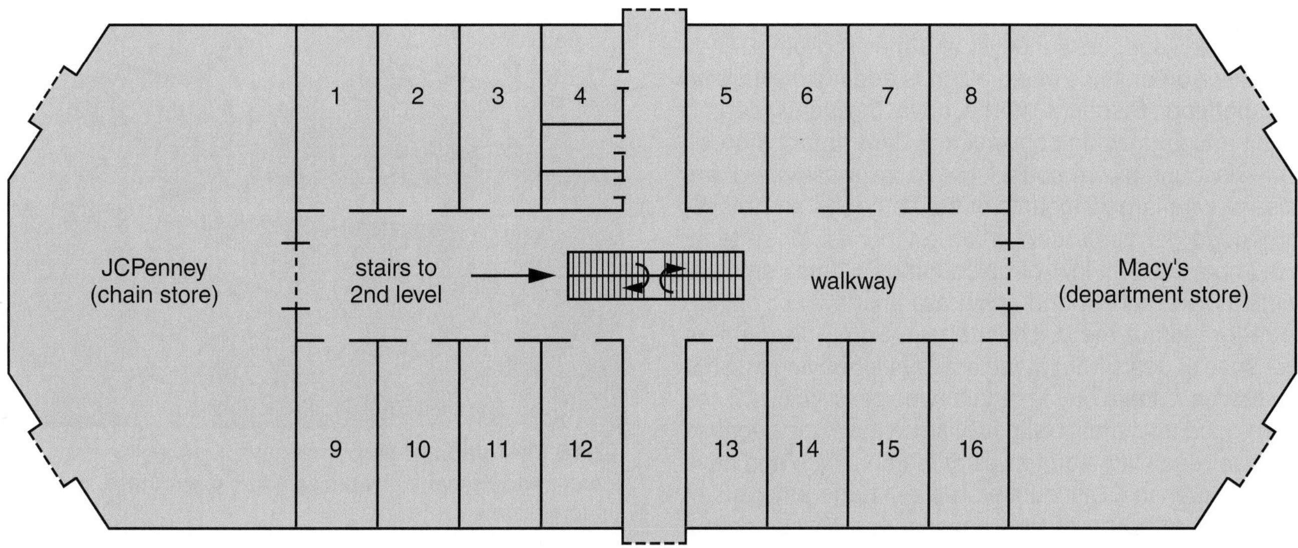

12-12 This simplified mall layout has a two-story general merchandise anchor store at each end that draws shoppers to the mall. The specialized stores between the anchors might include a greeting card shop, shoe store, fast-food restaurant, kitchen-gadget store, and costume jewelry shop, as well as restrooms and a mall office.

prices. Recently, discount stores have shown the strongest growth of all retail firms, achieving large increases in market share.

Discount stores are located in large, simple buildings in heavily traveled areas. They offer minimal services, expecting customers to serve themselves with little assistance, as shown in 12-13. Merchandise from all departments is paid for at checkout counters near the store's exits. Generally, no extra customer services, such as telephone orders, gift wrapping, and home deliveries, are offered. They strive for high volume to make good profits. The basic operational strategy for discount stores is shown in 12-14.

Discounters have generally been fashion followers rather than leaders. However, many have recently made an effort to be more current in their fashion inventory. More name-brand merchandise and customer services are offered than when the discount concept began. To try to combat intense competition, many discounters have "traded up," now accepting credit cards and offering some assistance on the selling floor. Discount stores have gradually become more like department stores, which experts describe as the "wheel of retailing" theory.

The *wheel of retailing* is an evolutionary process in which stores that feature low prices gradually upgrade themselves with more elaborate facilities and services to broaden their appeal. However, higher prices are then required to survive, and the new level appeals to different shoppers. The store's previous price slot is replaced by lower-priced competitors. Some upgraded stores do not survive after losing their price advantage or deviating from their original strategy and identity.

Symbol Technologies, Inc.

12-13 Like most general merchandise discount stores, this retailer supplies shopping carts so customers can serve themselves.

Basic Strategy of Discount Retailing

- consistently low selling prices
- "no-frills" facilities with low operating costs
- customer self-service
- high sales volume with fast turnover rates
- low profit margins

12-14 Even though individual items sold by discount stores have low profit margins, the huge volumes of products sold result in large total profits for discounters that successfully carry out the strategy.

Most discounters are chains, 12-15. They are open in the evenings, on Sundays, and most holidays. They undersell other kinds of stores, thus adding to stiff retail competition. Discount stores have frequently forced retail prices down in conventional department stores.

Discounters are considered to be *mass merchandisers*, with large amounts of staple goods and mass-produced garments selling for low prices. Most items are imported from low-wage countries. Some items are well-known brands, and some are unknown or private label brands of the discount chain. Some discounters get special deals from manufacturers for buying in large quantities. Others buy at regular wholesale prices. They earn good total profits with only small markups because they sell such large quantities of merchandise and have lower expenses. Discount stores sell huge amounts of lower-priced apparel and accessories to customers with modest clothing budgets.

12-16 This off-price discounter buys high-quality merchandise at very low prices and passes these savings on to customers.

Off-Price Discounters

Off-price discounters sell brand-name or designer merchandise at lower-than-normal prices. See 12-16. They focus on higher-fashion goods at moderate prices. They tend to carry a changing and unstable collection of goods, bought at below-wholesale prices. Items sometimes have the labels cut out to protect the manufacturers' regular items sold elsewhere in upscale shops.

Off-price discounters do not place advance orders with manufacturers for specific merchandise to be produced. Instead, they make low-cost special purchases during the season when most other stores are thinking about the next season. They stock up on production overruns (too many items were produced), end-of-season goods (surplus stock), closeouts (discontinued items), samples, and irregulars. Off-price discounters buy whatever is available. Most pay promptly rather than asking for credit. They put the goods on the floors of their stores as soon as they are received. Since off-price discounters have limited return privileges, they keep slashing prices until the items are sold. They also receive no promotional help from the manufacturers.

12-15 Kmart is a national chain discount store with central offices in Troy, Michigan.

Factory Outlets

Factory outlets are manufacturer-owned-and-operated discount stores that sell only the merchandise the company makes, at reduced prices. See 12-17. The goods include overruns, canceled orders, and discontinued items. This vertical distribution system eliminates the cost of a middle person and provides the company with more control. It assures the manufacturer an outlet for its products and assures that the stores will have merchandise to sell. However, manufacturers' brand-name images can be damaged if their first-quality goods are commonly discounted. As

12-17 Most factory outlet stores are owned by the manufacturing companies of the goods they sell.

a result, full-price retailers may not stock that manufacturer's goods, since they compete against the factory outlets with the same goods, but at different prices.

Factory outlets were originally single, small stores near factories that sold manufacturers' surplus or unsellable goods. Recently, however, manufacturers are operating chains of outlet stores and producing extra garments specifically to sell through them. New factory outlet malls have opened that house stores from many name designers and manufacturers. Stores located in these malls must be careful not to compete closely with the full-price retailers that stock their items.

Outlet malls are usually located in outlying areas. Many are now upgrading and competing directly with traditional malls.

Wholesale Warehouse Clubs

Wholesale warehouse clubs specialize in bulk sales of a limited selection of nationally branded staple merchandise. Their strategy is to pare costs to the bone, offer almost no services, and sell large-quantity lots of popular items at rock-bottom prices, often 20 to 40 percent below discount store prices. Customers are not offered credit, shopping bags, or home delivery.

Most warehouse clubs charge an annual membership fee to customers who then make up the cost in year-long savings. The "clubs" are basically large, bare warehouses with concrete floors that cost little to build and almost nothing to maintain. Merchandise is bought with volume discounts and stacked high in packing cartons on industrial metal shelving. Almost no advertising or promotion is done. Currently, only a few apparel and home textile items are sold in these clubs, but more may be added in the future.

Hypermarkets

Hypermarkets are huge "supercenters." They sell individual items of almost every type of popular goods, including brand-name apparel, groceries, furniture, appliances, and general merchandise, at low prices. They operate out of spartan facilities and function as combination grocery and discount stores. They target time-stressed consumers who want to do all of their shopping in one place. The concept, which started in Europe, also features a very high volume of sales at low prices. See 12-18.

Jusco Co., Ltd./AEON Group

12-18 This hypermarket, which sells almost every type of merchandise, is located in Japan.

Specialty Stores

Specialty stores carry large selections of limited classifications of merchandise. They usually have lower volume and higher prices than discounters. Stores in this category vary in their degree of merchandise specialization. They might handle only toys, sporting goods, books, jewelry, or clothing. Examples of specialty clothing stores are maternity shops, shoe stores, bridal boutiques, children's apparel, and accessory shops. See 12-19. *Sub-specialty stores* specialize even further, such as carrying only neckties.

Specialty stores target specific consumers by offering unusual merchandise, more personalized service, convenience, and ambiance. They are often known for a certain level of design or quality of merchandise. Specialty stores feature customer service and can give advice about the selection of goods within their specialties. Returns are usually accepted, but customers are sometimes given credit toward other purchases rather than cash. Because two-income couples have higher incomes but less time to shop, these consumers are attracted by the quality products, nearby locations, good store hours, excellent service, and quick entry and exit of many specialty stores.

Many specialty stores are now franchise stores or national chains with well-known retail names. They are

Claire's Nippon

12-19 Stores that only sell accessories are very specialized. They know their line of products and offer the most up-to-date fashion looks in their price range.

12-20 This small children's store is privately owned. It is located in a group of upscale suburban shops that attract shoppers who might be looking for special outfits for their children or grandchildren.

12-21 The Sports Authority, headquartered in Fort Lauderdale, Florida, operates stores nationally that sell all types of goods to sports enthusiasts.

often located in shopping centers or malls, which help them draw in customers. Some small, local specialty stores are independently (privately) owned, as is the store shown in 12-20. They have lower sales volumes and must therefore charge higher prices than larger stores. Most provide good customer service and personal contact. Also, the personal preferences of regular customers are acknowledged.

Specialty Chains

Specialty chains are specialty stores that are part of a regional or national chain. Each company's stores are all alike throughout the entire geographical area. Specialty chains have rapidly grown in popularity in recent years. Large, discount specialty chains are called ***category killers***. They carry such huge selections of merchandise in a single product category at such good prices that they practically destroy the competition in their specialty area. An example of such a specialty chain is the one shown in 12-21.

Boutiques

Boutiques are small, stand-alone shops or distinctive areas within larger stores that sell unusual, few-of-a-kind apparel, accessories, or decorative items. Sales associates give individual attention to their clients, who enter to browse and buy. The merchandise of these specialty stores is selected for special-interest customers, and is usually fashion-forward.

Boutiques have unique images. Many sell new, artistic, or handmade items presented in attractive, creative ways. Some cities have areas where many boutiques are located along with art galleries and restaurants.

Licensed Merchandise Stores

Another category of specialty retailers is *licensed merchandise stores* or "concept shops" built around licensed merchandise, as shown in 12-22. These stores sell items, such as clothing and collectibles, that are adorned with licensed logos, names, and pictures from TV shows, movies, the recording industry, sports teams, and commercial products. Stores sell T-shirts, sweatshirts, accessories, stuffed animals, figurines, and other items that show such licensed entities as Mickey Mouse, Star Trek, the Dallas Cowboys, Hershey Chocolate, or Pepsi. The stores are decorated to accent the theme of their merchandise.

Non-Store Retailers

Although most apparel and other items are still sold through retail stores, non-store retailing has grown about 20 percent faster per year recently than conventional store retailing. ***Non-store retailing*** is selling without a conventional store facility. It includes mail-order catalog sales, telecommunication retailing, and personal selling.

12-22 This is the marquee over the entrance to The Disney Store located on Fifth Avenue in New York City. All of its merchandise has Disney characters and logos.

12-23 Items in mail-order catalogs are shown and explained for consumers in hopes that large sales volumes can be achieved.

Mail-Order Retailing

Mail-order retailers sell merchandise through catalogs that they distribute to consumers, such as the ones in 12-23. Customers select items by looking at pictures or illustrations and reading accompanying descriptions. Mail-order retailers offer shopping at home for customers who cannot (or prefer not) to go out. Orders are placed either by mail, toll-free telephone numbers, computer or fax. In some cases, orders can be placed in person at a company facility designed for that purpose. Merchandise is usually paid for by credit card and shipped directly to customers' homes. Catalog firms often have extended order-taking hours, sometimes 24 hours a day, seven days a week. Mail-order retailers sometimes sell apparel and other items at low prices because they purchase goods in large quantities, have low overhead, and sell to a mass market.

Mail-order retailing is also known as ***direct-mail marketing***. Billions of catalogs are mailed to American households each year, 12-24. This retail method especially satisfies the shopping needs of two-career families and affluent singles, whose busy schedules leave them little time to shop. They can browse through the catalogs and order during their spare moments. The appeal of mail-order shopping has also been related to shopper dissatisfaction with crowded stores and malls, inadequate parking, and lack of service and personal safety in conventional retail locations. Also, catalog descriptions of items are often more complete than what salesclerks in stores provide. However, customers cannot evaluate the texture, weight, or color of the garments or try them on to check the fit.

Some mail-order retailers offer a full line of items similar to department store selections. Others specialize in a single line of merchandise, which might be practical, low-budget items or unique, luxurious ones. The trend in mail order is toward specialty catalogs aimed at narrow niches of the consumer market. Computerized mailing lists provide companies with names of people in particular market niches, such as consumers at certain income levels or with particular hobbies.

Lands' End Direct Merchants

12-24 In direct-mail marketing, seasonal mail-order catalogs are sent directly to consumers.

Catalogs are prepared with the target audiences in mind. Those that show inexpensive, basic items for a general audience may have many small items per page on newsprint paper. Expensive merchandise may be sold with one elegant item shown on each colored catalog page of glossy magazine quality. Some catalogs from the same company have different covers or personalized messages for each household receiving the mailing. Family names and crests shown in the catalog are applied to products with inkjet printing. Some catalogs have entertaining story-telling copy. Clever marketing ideas are used by many of the companies.

Some retail department stores and chains offer catalog shopping in addition to their regular store selling to expand their market area and increase company sales, 12-25. Such stores might attract customers' attention with bill inserts, mailed circulars, or newspaper inserts. They often distribute their full-size catalogs through the mail or send catalog users a card with instructions to pick up a catalog at their nearest store. On the other hand, large mail-order houses sometimes also have retail stores.

Computers and bar code scanners are used in mail-order distribution centers to track inventory and to control warehousing. Although direct-mail marketers

12-25 Double exposure to consumers results when retailers operate stores as well as mailing out catalogs. Victoria's Secret has slightly different merchandise in their stores and catalogs.

Lands' End Direct Merchants

12-26 Successful mail-order retailers, such as Lands' End, have developed efficient methods of shipping merchandise to their customers.

have low overheads, increasing postal rates have made catalog mailings more expensive. Consequently, many companies have tried to pare down their mailing lists to include only the best prospects. In addition, merchandise shipping costs have increased. These costs have been passed through to consumers who must pay higher handling fees when they order merchandise.

Direct-mail marketers have improved their customer service recently. They offer fast order processing and shipping, better inventory management, and higher merchandise quality, 12-26. They have educated their order-taking associates to give expert help to customers. Careful packaging techniques are used when the merchandise is shipped. Additionally, they have made return procedures easier. Mail-order retailers have gained the respect of consumers.

Telecommunication Retailing

Telecommunication retailing allows consumers to use communication devices to place their merchandise orders. It includes television retailing and computer retailing.

Television retailing uses certain television channels to show and describe merchandise available for purchase, 12-27. Sometimes celebrities sell their own signature lines of merchandise. Consumers can control what they view. Viewers order by telephone, often speaking with an order operator. See 12-28. Sometimes orders are placed automatically by entering information through push-button phones. Customers pay by credit card or other means, and the merchandise is shipped to them.

When television shopping channels first started in the 1980s, the medium was used to unload leftover merchandise that would no longer sell in stores. Now it is used to introduce and test the market for new products to see if there will be consumer acceptance of the products before they enter the regular distribution chain into retail stores. For new styles or concepts, television reaches a national audience and gives the equivalent of free advertising. Thus, risks are minimized for new products that are featured. However, it is hard to get most product lines onto the home-shopping channels. Using an agent is the best way. Fresh, exciting merchandise is desired for TV sales.

Computer retailing, also called electronic retailing or "e-tailing," combines computer and telephone technologies with marketing and merchandising. It allows shoppers to view merchandise on their computer monitors at home and order via the modem connection. Consumers can use an online *portal* (a starting Web site with links to many specific sites for a certain subject, such as shopping) or go directly to specific store sites. The Web addresses for retail stores with Internet sites are usually "www.companyname.com." Consumers can look at "electronic catalogs" to see three-dimensional pictures or other visuals and read detailed descriptions of items. Shoppers are able to comparison shop between several retail companies for various features and prices. To order, they key in the item numbers of products they want to buy and enter their credit card numbers. The merchandise is delivered to them within a few days.

E-tailing is now more mainstream, as online shopping patterns normalize. Computer users can shop on any site at any time of the day or night. Internet sales are increasing rapidly, but companies must make it easy for consumers to shop, in order to retain customers for repeat purchases. Digital images must present the goods as close as possible to what they really are. However, just as for mail-order and television retailing, computer retailing has much higher merchandise return rates than traditional retail stores. Besides taking care of order fulfillment, telecommunication retailers need "reverse logistics" expertise to handle the returns.

Personal Selling

Personal selling is done without a retail store. It moves cosmetics, jewelry, clothing lines, and other

QVC, Inc.

12-27 Television retailing requires a sophisticated television production studio to sell merchandise.

merchandise to customers through either door-to-door sales or selling parties (showings) in private homes or work environments. Orders are taken by a company representative, and the items are delivered to the customer later. The merchandise is often of high quality or unusual design, but may be higher in price.

QVC, Inc.

12-28 Many operators, who are familiar with the merchandise and trained in customer relations, accept telephone orders from television-viewing customers.

Other Types of Fashion Retailing

Upscale fashion has traditionally been sold through department and specialty stores, with moderate and budget lines sold by chains and discount stores, and through mail-order. There are a few other types of fashion retail outlets, including variety stores, kiosks and carts, catalog showrooms, and leased departments.

Variety Stores

Variety stores offer a few items in many classifications of lower-priced merchandise. They started as "five-and-ten" or "dime stores" in the small towns of America. Variety stores stock inexpensive clothing, stationery, housewares, and toys, often displayed on open counters. Clothing items are basic, such as underwear, T-shirts, and simple accessories. Their checkout counters are near the exits. Many small-town variety stores have gone out of business because they could not compete with large discount and other stores that have opened up near them.

Kiosks and Carts

Kiosks and *rolling carts* are open sales pavilions, usually situated in central areas of shopping malls. See 12-29. Kiosks have an interior area for one or more salespeople, but carts have no interior area. Often kiosks and carts sell jewelry or small gift items meant

12-29 Kiosks in mall aisles give retailers high exposure to consumers, plus add excitement for shoppers who may see new or small items to buy.

12-30 Catalog showrooms, such as Service Merchandise, sell a great deal of jewelry as well as nonapparel items.

for impulse purchases. With minimum lease commitments, they can be used seasonally such as for holiday items. Even some permanent mall tenants, such as department stores, use kiosks and carts for "outposting" seasonal products or unique items into mall walkways. Some new kiosks feature computer terminals from which electronic sales are made for traditional retailers that do not have stores in that mall.

Kiosks require low capital expenses because they are small, although the rent-per-square-foot is more than for a traditional store. Often only one salesperson is required during hours the mall is open. Sales can be good because kiosks have great exposure to consumers, usually in high-traffic aisles for shoppers to walk past and view the merchandise.

Shopping mall owners like the extra rent received from kiosk and cart tenants, as well as the shopping interest for consumers. These mini-businesses also foster new types of retail ideas and may become tenants in permanent store sites in the future. With this as a low-risk way to nurture new businesses, the owners can test the salability of their products as well as their merchandising and marketing skills.

Catalog Showrooms

Catalog showrooms display sample items in the stores that are also shown in their catalogs, 12-30. Customers either browse through the catalog or around the sales floor to select the items they want to buy. Merchandise is then ordered by catalog number on a special telephone or computer within the store. In a short while, the order arrives on a conveyor belt from the warehouse area to the pickup location.

Not much fashion merchandise is handled by catalog showrooms. Although low overhead at such stores enables prices to be low, the price in the printed catalog must allow a profit to be made for the duration of the use of that catalog. This is usually six months to one year.

Leased Departments

As mentioned in Chapter 6, a leased department is a department within a store, operated by an outside firm. The host store supplies the space and essential services (electricity, janitorial services, use of restrooms, etc.) in return for a fee or percentage of the sales. The leasing firm owns the merchandise, pays for the advertising, and hires the staff. The leasing firm must, in turn, abide by the store's rules and policies.

Department leasing enables stores to offer merchandise and services to customers that might be too expensive to provide otherwise. The arrangement is convenient for the leasees (merchandise owners) since they do not have to own and maintain a store to sell their goods. However, it may be hard to maintain the store's fashion image with outside organizations managing various departments.

Leased departments are especially suited for expensive merchandise or products that require specialized knowledge or skills. Fur departments, beauty salons, and shoe repair centers are often leased. Fine jewelry departments and restaurants are other examples of

Sensormatic

12-31 A combined store name is one way of telling shoppers that a merger has taken place.

leased space. The firms of name designers sometimes lease a department within a retail store. Generally, shoppers are unaware that certain departments are leased.

Store Ownership Groups

Store ownership groups, also called retail corporate ownership groups, are corporations formed by individual stores joining together under a central ownership. This is an example of ***horizontal integration***, with several chains or companies at the same location on the distribution pipeline combining under common ownership. Each retail entity retains its previous local identity, name, philosophy, and ambiance, but all share the information and expertise of the corporation.

Such corporate ownership groups continue to acquire more stores, consolidate, or merge with other retailers, 12-31. They can then use centralized volume buying for larger-quantity purchases at lower prices. They can take advantage of special private label or import programs available to all in the corporation. The group can afford to hire corporate specialists to concentrate on such areas as pricing, promotion, merchandising, inventory control, and sales forecasting. They can combine functions to operate more efficiently with fewer levels of management than if they were all separate entities.

Today, most department stores are no longer independently owned, but are owned by these large corporate ownership groups. Mergers and acquisitions have caused the creation of fewer, larger corporations for survival. Member stores are centrally owned and controlled for broad policy-making, but are operated and merchandised autonomously. Each store division of the corporation has its own branches, as well as its own buyers and merchandise mix. It presents itself to customers as if it is still an independent company. The general public is usually unaware of stores being owned by these groups.

Retail Trade Associations and Publications

The ***National Retail Federation (NRF)*** is the world's largest retail trade association. It strives to represent and promote healthy and prosperous retailing and to unify the entire industry. Membership in the organization includes department, specialty, discount, mass merchandise, and independent stores. The NRF logo is shown in 12-32.

The NRF has affiliate associations in all 50 states and in many other countries. Its international members operate stores in over 50 nations. The NRF has its headquarters in Washington, DC, where it lobbies for government legislation in favor of retailers. It works toward more open international trade with sources and markets throughout the world. Also, it monitors government mandates that require companies to comply with rules that raise costs.

The officers and directors of the NRF are top executives of major retail firms. The National Retail Federation publishes *STORES* magazine, as well as various publications, books, periodicals, and checklists. The NRF has developed job skills standards for retail sales

National Retail Federation

12-32 The official logo of the National Retail Federation represents the shadowed side and top (with curved handles) of a shopping bag, which also looks like an arrow pointing toward the future.

associates, and promotional materials spotlight the career opportunities of retailing.

The NRF holds an annual convention where retailers can learn about the latest strategies, ideas, and technologies of the industry. Industry leaders, suppliers, educators, and analysts from around the globe present the latest goods and services. Informative sessions help retailers update, streamline, and evaluate their operations. Many specialized conferences are offered for professional growth at other times of each year, too.

The International Mass Retail Association (IMRA) is for all mass retailers and discounters. Publications read by these members might include *Discount Store News (DSN), Apparel Merchandising,* and *Chain Store Age.* The International Association of Department Stores publishes and distributes the *Retail Newsletter.*

The Direct Marketing Association is a trade group for mail-order companies. Industry publications geared toward mail-order businesses include *DM News, Direct Marketing Magazine,* and *Catalog Age* magazine. For specific retail information, some industry consultants publish reports and newsletters to which retailers can subscribe.

Summary

Retailing involves planning, buying, receiving, arranging, and selling goods. This competitive and constantly changing industry is the liaison between manufacturers and consumers. The key functional areas of retail firms include merchandising, financial control, store operations, personnel, and sales promotion. Retailers strive to manage resources in the best way to satisfy customers, while making a good profit.

All retailers are either general merchandisers or specialized merchandisers. More specific categories include

- department stores, probably with a flagship store and some branch stores;
- chain stores that have a central headquarters office and (with department stores) are often anchor stores in malls;
- discounters or mass merchandisers that offer low prices and minimal services in stores with low overhead, including off-price discounters, factory outlets, wholesale warehouse clubs, and hypermarkets;
- specialty stores that carry limited classifications of merchandise, including chains that may be category killers, as well as boutiques and licensed merchandise stores;
- non-store retailing, such as mail-order marketers, telecommunication retailers, and personal selling;
- and variety stores, kiosks and carts, catalog showrooms, and leased departments.

Store ownership groups have become larger and more common, with continued mergers and acquisitions. They use centralized volume buying and effective merchandising techniques to operate efficiently for their store divisions.

The National Retail Federation (NRF) is the major trade association of the retail industry. It provides the latest strategies, ideas, technologies, and services for its members. Other professional associations and publications are available for specific parts of the industry.

To Know

general merchandisers
specialized merchandisers
department stores
branch stores
flagship store
chain
anchor stores
discount stores
off-price discounters
wholesale warehouse clubs
specialty stores
category killers
non-store retailing
mail-order retailers
direct-mail marketing
telecommunication retailing
store ownership groups
horizontal integration
National Retail Federation (NRF)

To Review

1. Is retailing a service business or a manufacturing business? What does it exchange?
2. Why is fashion retailing so important to all levels of the pipeline?
3. Which of the five functional areas of fashion retail firms is considered to be the central function?
4. Briefly describe the retail functional area of store operations.

5. Briefly describe the retail functional area of sales promotion.
6. Why do independent stores have a hard time competing with giant superstores?
7. Name at least five customer services or "conveniences" that might be offered by department stores.
8. Describe "twig" stores.
9. Are chain stores general or specialized merchandisers?
10. What are "me too" stores and where are they located?
11. What type of retail store has shown the largest growth in recent years?
12. What is mass merchandising?
13. Regular discount stores sell inexpensive goods that they buy at wholesale prices. Explain the goods that off-price discounters sell, and at what price level they buy them.
14. Name a benefit of the vertical integration of a factory outlet from the manufacturing side and from the retail side.
15. What type of people are targeted by hypermarkets?
16. Why do some consumers prefer catalog shopping?
17. Although direct-mail marketers have low overheads, what expenses have increased for them?
18. Describe electronic retailing.
19. What types of products are especially suited for leased departments?
20. List three benefits of membership in the National Retail Federation.

To Do

1. Form a group with five other students in your class to "become" The Gap, The Limited, or another major specialty chain. Assign each person to one of the basic steps of retailing as listed in Chart 12-1. Do research to gain more information about each area and the chosen store. Present a report to the class that illustrates specifics of each of the steps.
2. Research one of the types of retailers listed in Chart 12-7. Write a report about how this type of retailing got started, how popular it is today, and other information that you find to be interesting.
3. Make an appointment with the manager of a small, independent store. At the meeting, ask well-planned questions about how the retail functional areas of responsibility are accomplished for the business. Write a report about the information you learned, with a section for each of the areas of responsibility. Also, write a thank-you note to the manager for having met with you, and include a copy of the note with your report.
4. From the advertisements in a pre-holiday newspaper, or another day for heavy retail advertising, pick out ten retailers. Decide which retailers are general merchandisers and which are specialized merchandisers. Then tell what types of stores they are, such as discount, specialty, chain store, etc. Make a chart of your findings.
5. Select a mail-order catalog and present an illustrated report to the class. Include such information as the merchandise selection, price level, probable target market, ordering methods, guarantees offered to customers, and any other interesting features or services.

Retail Positioning

After studying this chapter, you will be able to

- explain how to target a specific retail market.
- analyze consumer buying motives.
- describe how stores differentiate themselves from competitors.
- summarize merchandise and service product strategies.
- interpret various pricing strategies.
- explain place strategies of site location and facility design.
- summarize promotion strategies.
- identify changing trends in retail positioning.

Strategy of Retail Positioning

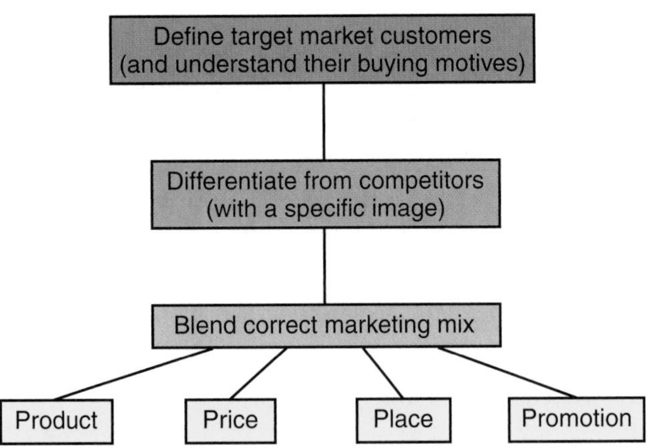

13-1 Retail companies should try to position themselves at a certain place in the market that will enable them to achieve the highest possible success.

Business success depends on building a growing body of satisfied customers. To do this, retailers must first define their target markets and decide how they will be positioned in those markets.

Retail positioning relates to where a store situates itself in the consumer market. This positioning guides all other decisions about how the retailer satisfies its target customers while differentiating itself from competitors. This is done with a marketing mix that blends variables of product, price, place, and promotion into an overall strategy for retailing success. Some stores are positioned with the lowest possible prices and least amount of service. Others are positioned for the best values for fashion forward career apparel. Still others coordinate the variables to position themselves in other ways. This strategy of retail positioning is illustrated in 13-1 and will be described in detail in this chapter.

Targeting a Specific Market

If retailers do not define their target markets clearly, for themselves and their customers, they usually end up satisfying no market at all. This can happen when a retailer tries to offer something for everyone. As you learned in Chapter 5, market segmentation enables a company to define a target niche of customers with similar characteristics. It can be done with demographics, psychographics, and other information. Each segmented group responds in a similar way to various goods and services, sales promotion activities, and advertising.

Ongoing market research of actual and potential retail customers is needed, gathering and analyzing information about the chosen market's tastes and

Department of Consumer Studies, University of Delaware

13-2 Target market analysis can be done by computer, enabling marketing strategy and implementation plans to be made.

changing trends, 13-2. Stores often use computerized credit data to fine-tune their customer knowledge. Large companies can further segment their customer base electronically using customer purchase data contained in their computer systems. Companies use the information to better satisfy their customers' needs and desires through database marketing. Also, if research shows that the chosen market is not being satisfied, the store can either change its target market or redesign its marketing mix to once again satisfy its target market.

Retail managers regularly talk about "their customer." This singular term, "customer," represents the store's ideal targeted consumer. However, it must be determined if that ideal customer is the actual customer that is shopping at the store. One challenge for retail managers is the constant adjustment to this ever-changing customer base. Various ways for managers to stay in touch with the customer include working on the selling floor, listening to customer feedback from the store's staff, working with a focus group, and doing customer surveys.

To better satisfy their customers, retailers develop and follow ***merchandising policies***. These are specific management guidelines the company follows to keep their inventory choices on track. Merchandising policies are adjusted regularly based on current trends and the needs of the target market. Retailers also have ***operational policies***, which are designed to make customers feel good about shopping in their stores. These policies make the store appealing for the target market through physical appearance and customer services.

Stores' merchandising and operational policies complement each other to maintain the optimum marketing mix of product, price, place, and promotion. The policies are monitored carefully in relation to changing retail patterns, economic conditions, and the buying motives of target customers.

Understanding Buying Motives

Purchasing behavior is the way consumers act in the market. It is influenced by cultural, social, and psychological factors. To set it into action, consumers must have a want or need to be satisfied, and a desire to fulfill that want or need in a certain way. The response is a purchase based on ***buying motives***, or the reasons why people buy what they buy.

Buying motives fall within the extremes of rational and emotional responses. *Rational behavior* is a response to conscious reasoning. It is based on logical thinking and decision making. Important factors in a rational decision might be a garment's durability, comfort, quality, economy of use, and price. See 13-3. A totally rational consumer will evaluate effective use of resources according to

- how badly an item is needed
- how often it will be worn

Nicklaus for Men/Hartmarx Corporation

13-3 A consumer might use rational behavior to pick this outfit since it is comfortable and well-suited for its intended use.

- how long it will last
- its quality for the price
- its affordability in relation to other wants

13-4 As shoppers walk past this retail display, they might be emotionally drawn to the cheerful colors and designer name on the merchandise.

Emotional behavior is based on feelings. A consumer who reacts emotionally will see a fashionable item in a favorite color and buy it just because he or she likes it. See 13-4. Factors contributing to an emotional decision include imitation, emulation, desire for status and prestige, sex appeal, desire for distinctiveness, ambition, fear, and personal pride. Consumers are generally unaware of the role these factors play in their choices.

Sometimes consumers have rational reasons for going to certain stores. They may shop where they know they are getting the best price. Other consumers have emotional reasons for preferring particular retailers. Perhaps they get an ego boost from shopping in a store that has a prestigious reputation. Most purchases fall somewhere between the two extremes of rational and emotional behavior, as shown in 13-5. Some of each type of behavior is combined in varying degrees for different people, at different times, and for different products. However, fashion purchases usually involve higher amounts of emotional motives than rational ones. Thus, fashion marketers most often appeal to emotional buying motives in their advertising, visual merchandising, and sales training.

There are also product and patronage motives involved in consumer purchases. ***Product motives*** involve consumer purchases based on qualities or images of certain products. These product qualities might be materials, construction, style, fit, or guarantees associated with trade names or reputations. Manufacturers try to instill this loyalty in customers to encourage them to continue to buy their products.

Patronage motives involve customers who consistently buy from certain retailers or favor particular stores. The reasons why customers choose to shop at one store rather than another may be based on reputation, image, merchandise assortment, or price. Other

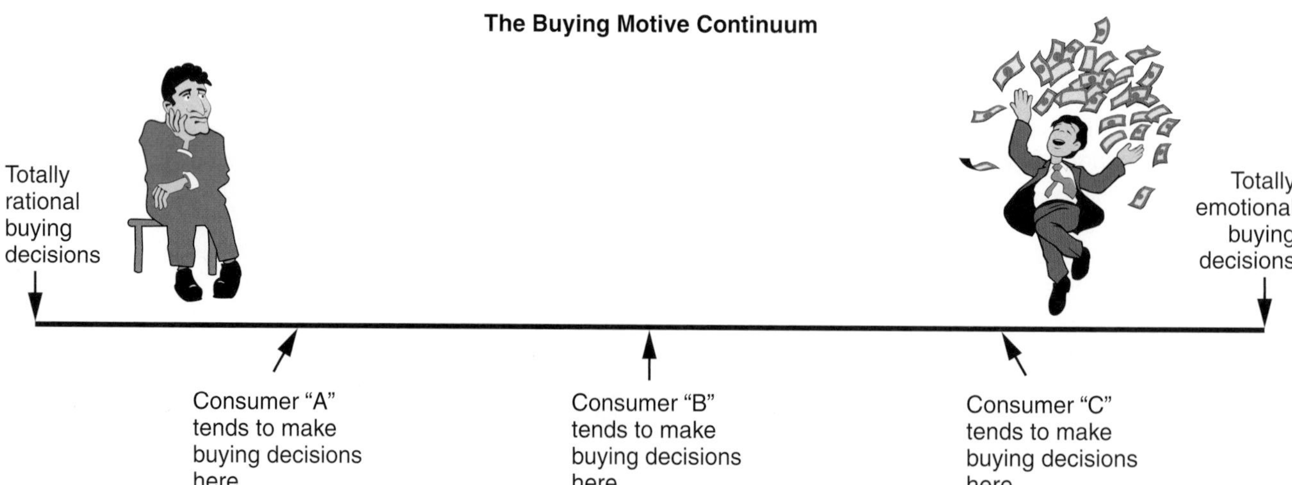

13-5 This scale shows various degrees of rational and emotional responses that people might use when making purchasing decisions. Also, the same consumer will fall at different places along the continuum at different times and when buying different products.

Talbots/AEON Group

13-6 Loyal customers shop at Talbots stores because of the merchandise assortments and customer services that satisfy the company's target market.

factors include convenience of location and customer services, 13-6. Retailers try very hard to gain loyal patronage from their customers. However, less long-term store loyalty exists among shoppers today. Patronage decisions now seem to be based on where consumers think they are getting the best value at the time.

Product and patronage motives are based on a combination of rational and emotional buying motives. Different consumers prefer different kinds of products and stores. It is important for retailers to evaluate what customers think about their stores, as well as the products carried. Also, different market segments might see or use a particular store differently.

Differentiating from Competitors

Because of the vast number of retailers in existence, there is strong competition among individual stores for customers' time and dollars. There are four types of apparel retail competition:

- ***Direct competition*** is between two or more retailers using the same type of business format. For instance, the Gap and The Limited are in direct competition because of their similar merchandise, customer service, prices, and locations. The retailers shown in 13-7 and 13-8 are in direct competition with each other. Regional drugstore chains are often in direct competition with each other, as are small, independent dress shops.
- ***Indirect competition*** is between two or more retailers using different types of business formats to sell the same type of merchandise. For example, supermarkets and department stores compete in selling women's pantyhose, but they are very different types of retailers.
- ***Vertical competition*** is between businesses at different levels of the supply chain. The best example is apparel manufacturers who sell their apparel lines to retailers, as well as to the retailers' customers through factory outlet stores.
- ***Lifestyle competition*** does not involve similar stores or products, but rather a fight for consumers' pastimes. This is a fairly new concept. Whereas consumers sometimes went shopping as a form of leisure activity, spending discretionary income in the process, they now may use that time and money to dine out or watch a movie. Although restaurants, video/DVD rental stores, and movie theaters are also consumer retail establishments, they are not apparel retail stores. See 13-9. Thus, they present a completely different type of competition.

13-7 American Eagle Outfitters sell sporting apparel, accessories, and equipment for outdoor activities.

13-8 Trail Creek Outfitters sell very similar merchandise at similar prices to American Eagle Outfitters. The two stores are in direct competition with each other.

13-9 Restaurants compete with retail stores for consumers' time and money.

Since shoppers have more choices today, retailers must select their target markets and marketing mixes very carefully. They should look at which competitors are satisfying which market segments. Possibly several stores are going after the same consumers, while other consumer groups are being ignored. Also, retailers can no longer count on higher sales and profits by just opening new stores, since the rate of population growth has slowed and people are spending less money on material goods. To gain more profits, retailers must tighten their operations and try to lure customers away from competitors.

There will always be competitors with similar products. Since stores of similar types offer mostly the same merchandise, they must convince consumers that they have beneficial differences. Retailers must set themselves apart or differentiate themselves from competitors. To win customer loyalty, companies try to offer the desired merchandise, services, and atmosphere preferred by their customers. Some stores have repositioned themselves in the market, such as going from full-line general merchandisers to limited-line apparel merchandisers.

Retailers can set themselves apart from others in many ways, as shown in 13-10. Differentiation can be achieved with unique merchandise, such as private labels or confined national brands that a retailer sells exclusively. Stores can feature goods from other countries, "surprise" merchandise, or very narrowly targeted products, such as large or petite sizes. They can differentiate with extended hours, such as being open 24 hours a day, or with special sale events. Distinct images can also be developed.

Ways Retailers Can Differentiate from Competitors
Merchandise: variety of choice, quality, fashion taste, sizes, price, etc.
Value: highest level of merchandise for least amount of money.
Convenience: easy location, one-stop shopping, organized store layout, etc.
Services: ample sales help, alterations, personal shoppers, bridal registries, etc.
Store atmosphere: pleasant, clean, cheerful, efficient, etc.
Others: advantages change over time as consumer attitudes change.

13-10 Retailers can use these factors as advantages over their competitors.

Presenting an Image

A store's *image* is how the store is perceived by the public. It is like a personality, different for each retail company. An image can be powerful in attracting and satisfying consumers. It is very important for stores to develop and maintain individual identities to set themselves apart from competitors. The store's image should realistically project the kinds of merchandise and operations it offers for particular types of customers. Its image of itself should match the customer's impression of the store.

A store's unique fashion image is formed by a combination of its merchandise fashion level, services offered, physical environment, employees, and promotion. These components should be carefully combined to project a store's image to the public, and should be developed to appeal to the target customers, 13-11.

The merchandise fashion level is the emphasis of presenting goods in the early (introduction or rise) or later (peak and beyond) stages of the fashion cycle. Prestigious retailers that target affluent and fashion-conscious customers usually offer fashion goods earlier in the cycle. Discount stores emphasize fashion styles much later in the cycle.

Services offered also contribute to the image. Stores with an upscale image offer a wider range of services than discount retailers. Higher price/quality stores might include credit (charge) privileges, generous return policies, telephone ordering, home delivery, well-appointed rest rooms, gift wrapping, in-store restaurants, free parking, alterations, and jewelry repair. Discount "bargain" stores might operate strictly on a cash-and-carry basis, and have limited refund policies.

The appearance of a store's physical environment is very important. How stores please customers' senses forms an ***ambiance***, or atmosphere, that has a great influence on fashion image, 13-12. Upscale stores usually have luxurious surroundings, mid-priced stores have pleasing surroundings, and low-priced discount stores may not try for any particular ambiance at all. These physical environments match the image being projected.

The number of employees, and their appearance and attitudes, also contribute to image. Upscale stores are expected to have plenty of sales assistance available for shoppers. Employees should be courteous, knowledgeable, helpful, and dressed at a similar fashion level to the merchandise for sale in the store. If an image is correctly interpreted by a company's

13-11 The outward image presented by this entrance to a Saks Fifth Avenue branch store in a resort community appeals to the upscale customers of the retailer.

13-12 Describe the fashion image indicated by the entrance to this shop.

own employees, it spreads to the customers and reinforces itself in the marketplace. Bargain-image stores have limited numbers of employees, who may wear plain, company-provided smocks. They are not expected to provide individual help on the sales floor since that is one way that prices are kept low.

Promotion, such as advertising, should project the image appropriate to attract desired target customers, 13-13. If a store attracts shoppers at a certain fashion level because of its advertising, but stocks merchandise different than projected, shoppers will likely leave without buying anything. Advertising and promotional messages should clearly define the store image to the target audience.

Sometimes it is necessary or desirable to change a store's image. This might be done to adjust to changing demographics, the desire to attract additional customers, or to differentiate itself from increased competition. Stores want to keep old customers and add new ones, which might be done by changing the merchandise assortments, services, ambiance, and promotion over time.

Customers patronize retailers who treat them fairly and honestly. Retailers at all price levels are interested in building both reputation and image. By carrying out targeted policies through their actions, retailers build the correct image, whether it is budget, upscale, or somewhere in between.

13-13 This poster at the mall entrance of an Eagle's Eye store does more than promote one type of shirt. It also tells passersby that the store has multipurpose, classic items in natural fibers at good prices.

Product Strategy

You learned in Chapter 3 that products are either goods (merchandise) or services. A company's *product mix* is its entire selection of goods and services. Retailers differ in terms of the product assortments they sell. Besides selling goods (shirts, slacks, suits, and accessories), they also offer services, such as advice from sales clerks, convenient parking, and clean rest rooms. Both goods and services must be considered when retailers evaluate their product strategy. Shoppers are more demanding than ever these days, seeking the highest quality merchandise, at the lowest prices, with the best service.

Merchandise Selection

A store's array of goods is called its assortment. *Assortment* refers to the range of stock, or total selection, a retailer carries, whether it is full, limited, or specialty, 13-14. Customers buy from retailers

13-14 This specialty shop carries only tennis products, including apparel, rackets, and balls.

offering the merchandise assortments they want. Included in assortments are the variety and types of styles offered; the colors, sizes, fashion, and quality level; and the price ranges of the goods. Retailers study their target markets in order to anticipate the assortments their customers will expect them to have. Their goal is to successfully compete against other retailers.

Assortment breadth (width) is the number of different item categories or classifications offered by a store or department, regardless of how many of each category is stocked. An assortment is said to be "broad" or "wide" when many different varieties of goods are available. For instance, there may be many different types, brands, and price-ranges of dresses or suit styles offered for sale.

Assortment depth indicates the quantity of each item available in the assortment of goods offered to customers. An assortment containing an item in great numbers, in many sizes and colors, is said to be "deep." Thus, there might be multiple dresses and suits of the varieties offered. An assortment with only a few of each item is said to be "shallow."

Three different approaches to stock depth and breadth are (A) broad and shallow, (B) narrow and deep, and (C) moderate breadth and depth. These are illustrated in 13-15. Stores that carry a broad and shallow assortment stock small amounts of many different styles. Upscale, prestige retailers tend to stock broad and shallow assortments. They offer small stocks of many styles in limited sizes and colors because their customers desire exclusivity.

Stores that carry a narrow and deep assortment stock relatively few styles, but offer them in many sizes and colors. Mass merchandisers focus on narrow and deep assortments of proven goods that are in the culmination stage of the fashion cycle. They stock the latest fast-selling items in large quantities and have high inventory turnover rates.

Stores that cater to mid-range fashion and quality might stock moderate breadth and depth. These tend to be department and specialty stores. However, these stores usually stock broad and shallow assortments early in the season when new styles are being tested. When demand for styles has become clear, they concentrate on narrow and deep assortments of the most popular styles. Since retail space and inventory costs must be considered, stocking a broad assortment may limit the depth to which those items can be carried. Conversely, if depth is desired, space and costs often limit the variety that can be offered.

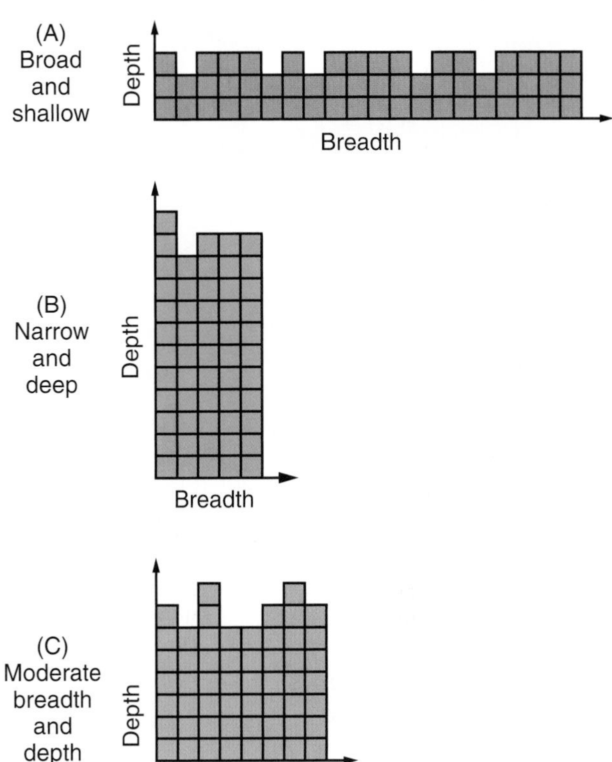

13-15 A long horizontal line of representative squares indicates many categories of goods (A). Tall vertical columns of squares show that many items in each category are stocked (B). A compromise approach (C) shows equal consideration of breadth and depth.

Service Selection

Customers shop in retail stores that provide services comparable to the prices they are paying. The amount of service corresponds with the price/quality level, whether self-service, limited service, or full-service. The services mix is one of the key non-price tools for setting stores apart from each other. For instance, retailers might decide to lengthen their credit payment terms or extend their evening hours to differentiate their store from their competitors.

Discount stores, featuring low prices, offer only basic customer services, such as free parking, credit, and merchandise return privileges. Traditional department stores provide additional customer services, such as gift wrapping, repair services, and alterations. Exclusive stores might provide special services, such as a store employee delivering an evening dress and making sure it fits the customer properly, or helping a customer coordinate a dress, shoes, and jewelry.

Services encourage customers to stay in the store as long as possible. The store provides all the needed services to keep customers there to make more purchases. They don't have to leave to put money in a parking meter or use a restroom elsewhere. Customer services will be discussed more completely later in this textbook.

13-16 Some retailers use their name to indicate to consumers that their price level is low.

Price Strategy

Pricing policies determine the price levels at which retailers sell their merchandise. A store's pricing policy must be coordinated with its image since the price level of goods plays an important part in determining the kinds of customers a store will attract and keep. See 13-16. Retailers' "price points" indicate the amount of money at which items are offered for sale. Pricing is a key positioning factor and must be decided in relation to the target market, competition, and other marketing mix factors. It is imperative that retail companies select the most appropriate competitive pricing strategy for their market. Choosing the correct approach to pricing has a large effect on profits.

Currently, most retailers emphasize low price as a major appeal to customers. The price-value relationship has become a powerful buying incentive, with price-conscious consumers actively comparing prices at several stores to obtain the best possible "deal." Also, with malls and shopping centers housing many stores in one location with duplication of merchandise, it is easy for consumers to do comparative shopping. Most retailers mark down some items, or run sales on slow-moving goods, 13-17. This attracts customers into their stores to buy additional higher-profit items.

There are usually market constraints on pricing, with certain price ranges for particular items in various market segments. General price levels can be categorized as popular (low or budget), mid, or high. The "right price" is the amount consumers are willing to pay for certain products and retailers are willing to accept. It is

13-17 Signs that indicate a lowering of prices are used to attract shoppers into stores.

the price that is satisfactory to the customer both before and after the sale. In summary, it is a price that brings about the sale, generates a profit, satisfies customer expectations, and meets competitive situations.

The Price/Quality Relationship

Quality and price usually, but not always, correlate. Consumers generally equate high prices with high-quality goods, and low prices with low-quality goods. Upscale retailers offer high-quality goods at moderate to high prices, and stores that target a wider customer base offer lower-quality merchandise at lower prices.

Prestige pricing is a policy of setting high prices on items to attract customers who want quality goods or the status of owning expensive and exclusive merchandise. Retailers price products to be consistent with consumers' expectations. Some retailers set prices above those of competing stores to convey an image of superior product quality or prestige. This also differentiates the products and stores in the minds of potential customers. Retailers who use this pricing policy usually have a very good location, a high level of service, and carry exclusive brand names.

Items of relatively low quality may be highly priced if there is a reason, such as a designer's name or styles in the introductory phase of the fashion cycle. However, most retailers do tie their price ranges to quality standards. A store policy of stocking only top-quality merchandise permits high price ranges, whereas a store that features intermediate quality usually sets some bottom limits that it will not go below. Stores that emphasize lower "serviceable" quality tend to also emphasize their low prices.

The class distinctions that have previously distinguished various price/quality retailers from each other are now eroding somewhat due to constant price promoting. ***Price promoting*** is advertising special price reductions of goods to bring in shoppers, 13-18. This builds traffic to buy other items as well. Shopping traffic has been shown to move up and down in direct relation to promotion pricing of merchandise. Shoppers have been exposed to so much price promoting that they have developed sophistication in seeking low prices.

13-18 This television commercial is a good example of price promoting to a large general audience of consumers.

Upscale stores seem less compelled, and less inclined, to indulge in price promoting to the same degree as the mainstream stores because they continue to enjoy their own prestige and attraction. However, upscale stores have recently engaged in more price promoting than has been customary for them in the past.

Specific Pricing Approaches

All retailers would like to sell large volumes of goods at high prices for huge total profits. However, the marketing triangle has shown that price and quantity sold are inversely related to each other. Most retailers either seek high unit markups on low volumes of goods, or low markups on high sales volumes. The overall profits of each might be similar, but they are selling to different target markets and offering other differences in the total marketing mix. In developing a pricing strategy, the retailer must price merchandise low enough to generate sales but high enough to cover costs and make a satisfactory profit.

Pricing below the market is a policy in which retail prices are set below those of the competition. Price-cutting policies were originally introduced by supermarkets, and then spread to apparel and other product sectors. Retailers may use this below-market pricing policy if they

- are in an inconvenient location
- are a self-service organization
- concentrate on volume sales
- stock private label merchandise
- lower their costs by using innovative technology to receive floor-ready merchandise from manufacturers
- forego some promotional efforts

Original (list) retail prices are often higher than actual selling price points. ***Value pricing*** is the selling of items below the price suggested by vendors of the goods. This price-cutting policy is used by discounters, especially on national brands. However, some vendors and retail stores imply that list prices for merchandise are higher than they really are. The goods are then marked down to a normal level, but with value pricing implied. This practice can cause retailers to loose credibility with consumers.

To ensure price competitiveness, some retailers promise to match the lowest advertised price that shoppers show them from ads. In fiercely competitive situations, competing stores might engage in a *price war.* That is when they drastically lower their prices to try to undersell each other. The theory is that the store with the lowest prices will attract customers from the other competitors, and ultimately force them out of business.

Some retailers use a "price line" selling policy, in which they offer their merchandise for sale at a limited number of predetermined price points. For example, a store may offer women's sweaters at $29, $39, and $49 only. The store's buyers actively seek out merchandise that can be sold to consumers at these prices.

Everyday low pricing (EDLP), another strategy for retail positioning, promotes the idea that consumers can shop in the store at any time, knowing that they will get a fair price that gives good value for the money. This strategy has been used recently by some discount chains. It tries to instill a sense of trust and consistency toward pricing, while providing a reasonable profit to the retailer. High seasonal markups are eliminated, as well as bargain prices during promotional sales. Stores that use this strategy may enjoy more credible pricing, reduced advertising costs, a steadier flow of sales, and better partnerships with vendors. However, higher sales volumes and lower operational costs may not match the overall reduction of prices. Also, the many shoppers who shop sales events and enjoy "the thrill of a bargain" are disenchanted by this approach.

Place Strategy

Place strategy relates to site location and physical store design, which should complement each other. These are very important determinants of retail success. They directly relate to retail positioning for particular target markets, establishing store images, and differentiating from competitors.

Site Location

A prime store location is key to attracting enough customers to make a good profit. The market area from which a retailer draws might encompass several blocks to several hundred miles of its site. Customers often choose a store because it is situated near work or home, or with a group of other stores where they can complete all of their purchases.

When considering site locations, large retailers will first evaluate a wide area, such as a certain part of the country. For instance, national chain retailers evaluate market growth and needs for their stores in various regions of the country before deciding to expand into those areas or open more stores in the region.

Regional retailers must determine the right state or town in which to locate. A certain population base, with target-market composition, is needed to support different types and sizes of stores. For some retailers, small, local markets of their target-market segment, which have less competition, are better than heavily populated areas that have more competition. On the other hand, mass merchandise "mega stores" draw from a larger area of heavy population. Even if there are already similar stores in that area, they may be able to take business away from the competition and be very successful.

13-19 If retailers that serve the same or similar target markets locate together, they can attract more customers.

Once the right local market has been chosen, a decision must be made about the most suitable shopping center, mall, or street location. Large retailers sometimes stand alone, able to draw customers by themselves. Other retailers depend on the pulling power of a cluster of stores grouped together for more convenient one-stop shopping, 13-19. A *tenant mix* is the particular assortment of different types of stores grouped together in a cluster, shopping center, or mall.

The site should be visible to passing traffic and easy to approach, enter, and exit, 13-20. It should be

13-20 The best retail sites are along major roads that are heavily traveled with clear entrance and exit routes.

13-21 Enclosed shopping malls, such as this one, are often decorated like outdoor gardens, but they allow customers to shop in indoor comfort year-round.

safe from crime and other consumer problems. It should also be compatible with customers' shopping needs. For instance, office supply stores are usually not located near residential neighborhoods, and garden centers are usually not found in downtown business districts. Retailers try to place their stores for the convenience of their target markets.

Types of Store Clusters

Various types of store clusters should be evaluated as a part of place strategy. Some site locations are in planned shopping centers and malls, while others have evolved as unplanned clusters of stores. In most store clusters, especially those that were planned and have a unified appearance and common areas (parking lot and sidewalks), the stores act together for promotional purposes. Some centers are enclosed into protected malls to make shopping more pleasant for consumers in any type of weather, 13-21.

There are five types of store clusters. These include the following:

- *Central business districts.* These areas of cities or towns, that contain high concentrations of stores and offices, usually evolved over time without a plan. The location of individual stores is often based on what spaces were available as the area matured. Most central business districts now have a hard time competing against newer, planned, suburban shopping areas. Some downtown sections are plagued with traffic, parking, and crime problems. In recent years, many communities have tried to revive the appearance and safety of their downtown areas. They have done this with parking garages, security patrols, and closing streets to make mall-like settings, 13-22. However, most still mainly serve consumers who live in the city, downtown workers for lunchtime shopping, and tourists or business visitors to the city.
- *Neighborhood shopping centers.* These are small shopping centers with usually 5 to 15 stores. They serve about 7,500 to 40,000 local

13-22 The downtown area of Denver, Colorado, has been transformed into a mall, with only limited public transportation vehicles running through it.

13-23 This factory outlet mall has hundreds of stores, eateries, and a motel that houses visitors who come by tour bus or car.

consumers in surrounding neighborhoods who can drive to the center within ten minutes. Older neighborhood shopping centers generally do not have the esteem or variety of newer, better-planned malls and shopping centers. As communities have grown, "shopping strips" have developed along major roads, usually selling convenience products. This type of center might have a supermarket and several family-owned service stores (dry cleaner, beauty shop, hardware store, etc.).

- *Community shopping centers.* These medium-sized centers usually have 15 to 50 stores. They normally contain a primary store, such as a department store branch or variety store, a supermarket, specialty stores, restaurant(s), professional offices, and a bank. Most selling is of convenience products to a market of 40,000 to 150,000 people within a five- to six-mile radius.
- *Regional shopping centers.* These are large centers that are often enclosed malls with several shopping levels. They serve at least 150,000 people and draw customers from a radius of more than 10 miles. They feature many stores and multiple products, including one or more full-line department stores and often 70 or more smaller stores. Although regional shopping centers usually have suburban locations, a few are "vertical shopping centers" located in large cities. In these, the stores are contained in one tall building, usually with an enclosed parking garage. Many factory outlet malls are also considered to be regional shopping centers. They target budget shoppers who are willing to drive longer distances for an assortment of value-priced goods, 13-23.
- *Super-regional centers.* These are the largest malls and shopping areas, also referred to as "power centers" or "mega malls." They often cover an area of 100 acres or more. Their millions of square feet of selling space usually includes six to eight anchor stores and at least 150 specialty stores, plus eateries. They draw from 25 miles or more, often attracting travelers from out of state. In fact, bus trips are sometimes scheduled to bring groups of people to these centers because they have such drawing power. They evolved in the late 1980s, built by commercial real estate developers to take advantage of the "retailing revolution."

In many locations, shopping centers and malls have reached their saturation point, with too many stores competing for too few sales dollars. Sales and profits have dropped, vacancy rates have increased, and some centers have gone out of business. Older malls are being renovated in order to compete, and few new ones are being built. The current trend is toward huge category killer power centers or smaller, less expensive

13-24 Strip malls are less expensive to build, and the stores are convenient for shoppers to enter after parking their cars in the adjoining lot.

13-25 Gap stores have selective coverage of most market areas with stores scattered among major shopping centers.

strip malls. Strip malls are comprised of a line of stores connected by a walkway, which runs along the front of the stores, 13-24.

Another factor that has a major impact on company profits is the cost of building, buying, or leasing facilities. Small retailers may have to settle for whatever locations they can find and afford, while large retailers can employ site-location specialists. From all potential site alternatives, they evaluate what sites are available for rent or purchase, which are most suitable in structure and size, and which are the most affordable based on the retailer's operating budget.

Market Coverage in Site Selection

Site selection strategy for some retail companies also includes *market coverage*, or how concentrated a presence the retailer wants to have in a specific geographic area. The main market coverage strategies include the following:

- ***Intensive market coverage***, which involves selecting and utilizing as many retail outlets as are justified to obtain blanket coverage. This approach tries to serve all customers of an entire market area. A typical example is convenience stores.
- ***Selective market coverage***, which involves choosing enough locations to ensure adequate coverage of selected target markets. Chain apparel retailers and department stores often do this by locating a store in each of the major shopping malls of a metropolitan area, 13-25.
- ***Exclusive market coverage***, which involves using one location to serve either an entire market area or some major segment of that market. Prestigious specialty retailers can use this approach since customers will travel farther for their goods.

Facilities Design

After the site location has been determined, the store should be designed to create a strong visual identity with

Talbots/AEON Group

13-26 A distinctive red door with shiny brass hardware visually identifies every Talbots store to consumers and indicates the level of merchandise inside.

13-27 Once an identifiable nameplate is established and becomes well known, shoppers are automatically aware of the types of goods and services that each branch store offers.

the right ambiance for the target market, 13-26. Stores can visually distinguish themselves from competitors using a unique physical environment. A store's image is influenced by both its exterior and interior appearance.

Store Exterior

A customer's first impression of a store is often created by the store's exterior. Store exteriors can help bring in new customers and retain existing ones. The best store exteriors attract, stop, and "invite" customers to shop. Considerations about store exteriors include their position on the site, architecture, and signage.

A store's position is how and where it is placed on the site. The best store position offers visibility, compatibility, and convenience. The following affect a store's position:

- The store is clearly visible to vehicle and/or pedestrian traffic, using the most advantageous setback, angle, and elevation. A visible store becomes part of a consumer's mental map of where to shop for certain products. It attracts impulse shoppers on first visits, as well as long-term customers who are reminded of its products by continually noticing the store. The following affect a store's position:
- The store is compatible with its surroundings, fitting the contour of the land and natural habitat. The design and construction materials are harmonious with the environment. The size of the facility is also in proportion to the size of the lot.
- The store is convenient for consumers, offering ample parking that is easy for vehicles to negotiate, safe for pedestrian movement, and accessible for people with disabilities.

A store's architectural design should appeal to the targeted consumers. The design can reflect a retailer's size, prestige, product mix, and affiliation. Also, a store's architecture should be functional and allow the store to operate efficiently. Functional considerations include construction and maintenance costs, energy use, security, and customer convenience. Operational efficiency encourages easy movement of customers and sales personnel, and maximum merchandise exposure.

A store's *signage* is the total of all the signs that attract consumers' attention and identify the store and its offerings. The main store identification sign should indicate who the retailer is, with an identifiable name, logo, or other symbol, 13-27. Exterior signs also may inform consumers about the store's type (department store, supermarket), its product line (food, greeting cards), its service and price levels, and when the store is open, 13-28. Signage should

13-28 The creative name for this store is further identified by a brief explanation of the types of goods carried. Store hours are listed on the door plaque.

13-29 An entire store cannot be devoted only to merchandise stock (selling areas). The store must also have sales support areas such as rest rooms and payment desks.

reflect the image of the store, generate interest, and invite consumers to try the store.

Store Interior

Interior space is divided into selling areas and sales support areas. Selling areas, where merchandise is available for customers, take up most of the interior space. Sales support areas are devoted to customer services, merchandise processing, and staff activities. They include dressing rooms, rest rooms, checkout counters, receiving and stock areas, offices, and employee training areas, 13-29.

Good interior store design minimizes operating expenses while maximizing sales and customer satisfaction. Selling space should have a friendly, welcoming atmosphere that is inviting and convenient for customers. It should also provide a functional and safe atmosphere that boosts employee morale and allows for smooth store operations. Appropriate layout, fixtures, lighting, color, and space utilization all play a role in designing selling space. Well-planned stores always sell more than stores that are not well thought out.

Shopping is encouraged with good traffic flow through the store. Good sight lines allow for customer viewing of various departments and merchandise. The walls, fixtures, ceilings, and flooring are a backdrop for the merchandise. They should define and accentuate the environment without detracting from the merchandise presentation. Interior decor should be psychologically pleasing to the store's target market to put customers into a buying mood.

For upscale stores, decor really matters since customers expect a retailer with expensive fashion merchandise to have an elegant facility. The decor may be traditional, with wooden fixtures and oriental rugs, or very contemporary with chrome and glass. It usually has expensive lighting and chandeliers, and dressing rooms that are large and private. On the other hand, stores with bargain prices usually have a bargain look, with simple fixtures, small or open dressing rooms, and few decorations.

13-30 Retailers and malls employ workers to maintain a high level of cleanliness for a pleasant shopping environment.

Careful planning of store environments should be an ongoing process. Store interiors must be updated frequently to keep the stores fresh and appealing. Trends of store decor change, just as fashions change. A store that looks out-of-date with old, worn furnishings and fixtures suggests to customers that the merchandise is also out-of-date.

Cleanliness, sometimes referred to as housekeeping, is also very important for store and mall interiors, 13-30. A clean, neat, and well-maintained retail environment imparts an image of caring for the customers.

Promotion Strategy

Sales promotion involves any activities that encourage consumer interest in the purchase of goods or services. Promotion activities include such things as advertising, publicity, visual merchandising, and special events. Special events may include fashion shows, trunk shows, personal appearances, and in-store art shows. All stores make use of some sales promotion, choosing the most appropriate methods for their type of store and target market. Promotion has become more important today because of increased retail competition.

The right message to the right group of consumers tells how the retailer will satisfy customers' wants and needs. The types of advertising and promotional activities chosen are the ones preferred by the store's target market customers. Advertisements in newspapers and magazines, and on radio and television should sound and look like the image that appeals to those customers. Specific sales promotion activities will be discussed in more detail later in this book.

In summary, stores attract customers with good image and location that is promoted effectively. They pull customers into the store with attractive storefronts, windows, and signage, and lure them through every aisle with the right products and services. They offer competitive prices and leave a lasting impression with professional salesmanship. This results in high profits because customers return for repeat purchases.

Recent Trends in Retail Positioning

Shopping has been an American pastime with the mall being the place to go to spend extra time. However, a day out for shopping is not common for consumers lately. New studies show that there are two different ways for retailers to attract shoppers now. They are (1) retail efficiency to quickly and painlessly satisfy shopping chores and (2) entertainment as the destination point, with shopping included. Stores are repositioning themselves toward one concept or the other to respond to these findings.

Efficiency for Shoppers

Almost everyone is on the run these days, trying to get as many things done as quickly and easily as possible. Although shopping has always been necessary, in the past it was done for more pleasure and psychological satisfaction than today. Leisure time today is less likely to be spent shopping. Most people are in a hurry and are more focused on accomplishing their shopping tasks efficiently.

Mall shopping has been criticized by consumers because it is too time consuming. It may take a long time for shoppers to find a parking place and to get from the car to the store where they want to shop. This is why smaller strip centers and specialized stores have become more popular. Customers also want to spend less time in line at the checkout counter and have faster payment processing of their credit card or check.

The retailers who realize that shopping is a chore for many consumers, and try to make it more efficient, are showing success. This also requires rethinking the notion of customer service. Customers want stores to offer them organized shopping. They want quick information on how to find products in the store, they want those products to be in stock, and then they want to be left alone to make their own shopping decisions. Also, more men are shopping these days. They especially like a clear, organized atmosphere with no surprises, 13-31. Retail technology is also enhancing this. Traditional retailers that have established Web sites in addition to their traditional selling, are trying to achieve "consumer intimacy" to satisfy all their customers' desires, rather than just following a low-cost strategy.

Entertainment Plus Shopping

The second drawing card for shoppers is entertainment as the destination activity during more leisurely times. A consumer survey has shown that most people are bored with shopping in stores that all seem to look alike and carry similar merchandise. Many customers seek activities that provide a combination of socialization, recreation, entertainment, and shopping. If shoppers are going to make a purchase, they want to have fun doing it! Even TV cable shopping now has entertainment, good fashion, plus Hollywood celebrities and big name designers.

Studies suggest that people desire a more positive experience when shopping, with more enjoyment. They want to go away with memories of a good time. The next generation of successful stores will offer more than just merchandise and services; these stores will ensure that their customers are entertained. This concept has been dubbed "shoppertainment."

Retailers are responding to this new concept, resulting in an increase in the number of entertainment-oriented stores. The idea is to draw people for the entertainment value, with shopping resulting from the entertainment. Some of the newest shopping malls have built images around theme park atmospheres. This also provides a focus in planning the image and physical facilities of a store or mall. Consumers expect to find some combination of restaurants, game arcade, and multi-plex theater where they shop.

Some stores and shopping centers are now marketing themselves as tourist attractions, with high-tech computer simulations and virtual-reality experiences. They offer interactive play with different action outcomes based on user input. Some malls feature indoor amusement centers where people can go on rides or become "virtual characters" in their favorite films or TV shows. The entertainment areas are also helping to fill vacant mall spaces of stores that have closed.

Additionally, if retailers cannot make shopping fun, they are considering moving the shopping to where the fun is. Retailers that are planning to open new stores might consider locating near a movie complex, restaurant area, casino, or in a mall where entertainment is being added. The entertainment areas and retail stores do not compete for sales of merchandise, but do compete for some consumer time and money. To bring in sales, the entertainment and retail store segments do *joint cross-marketing* to draw consumers to the site. Consumers take advantage of both the entertainment and shopping while they are there. If the experience is satisfying, they will return.

13-31 The existence of wide aisles, clear intersections, and good signage provides for efficient shopping.

The two basic retailing philosophies of efficiency and entertainment do not compete with each other since they fill different consumer needs at different times. Shoppers regularly visit local shopping centers for their immediate needs, and shop as pleasurable entertainment during leisure times.

Summary

Retail positioning enables stores to market effectively. Retailers must define their target markets clearly and conduct ongoing market research about the changing tastes of their customer base. To better satisfy their customers, stores develop and follow specific merchandising and operational policies. They try to understand the rational and emotional buying motives of their customers, as well as the product and patronage motives that might affect customers' buying decisions.

Competition affecting retailers might be direct, indirect, vertical, or lifestyle competition. To differentiate from competitors, each retailer should present a well-defined image. This can be done with a combination of its merchandise fashion level, services offered, physical environment, employees, and promotion.

Retail product strategy involves a store's entire selection of goods and services. Different approaches to assortment breadth and depth, and levels of services, should be considered.

Price strategy involves using price to attract customers. It must also be based on a store's image and target market. The relationship of price to quality should be considered, and the option of price promoting. Other specific pricing approaches are pricing below the market, value pricing below suggested list price, entering into a price war, using a price line selling policy, or following an everyday low pricing strategy.

Place strategy relates to site location and facilities design. Location might be in a central business district, neighborhood shopping center, community shopping center, regional shopping center, or super-regional center. Market coverage might be intensive, selective, or exclusive. Important considerations in facility design are the store's exterior position, architecture, and signage. Store interior space is divided into sales support and selling areas.

Sales promotion activities should be appropriate for the type of store, image, and target market, to draw the right people into the store to make purchases. A combination of all these positioning strategies should result in high profits with customers returning for repeat purchases.

New trends in retail positioning include two different drawing cards for shoppers that should now be addressed. One emphasizes retail efficiency to painlessly satisfy necessary shopping that consumers consider to be a chore. The other is based on entertainment as the destination for consumers, with shopping included in the experience.

To Know

retail positioning
merchandising policies
operational policies
buying motives
product motives
patronage motives
direct competition
indirect competition
vertical competition
lifestyle competition
ambiance
assortment breadth
assortment depth
prestige pricing
price promoting
value pricing
everyday low pricing
intensive market coverage
selective market coverage
exclusive market coverage

To Review

1. What must stores do if research shows that their chosen market is not being satisfied?
2. Who are retail managers referring to when they talk about "their customer?"
3. Describe rational behavior.
4. Why can retailers no longer count on higher sales and profits by just opening new stores?
5. What is meant by merchandise fashion level?
6. Why might it be necessary or desirable to change a store's image?
7. What is a company's product mix?
8. How do retail space and inventory costs relate to breadth and depth of merchandise assortments?
9. Summarize what is meant by the "right price" for a product.
10. What attributes do retailers usually have who use a prestige pricing policy?
11. Give at least five reasons why some retailers might be able to adopt a price cutting policy of pricing below the market?
12. How have some downtown areas tried to revive their appearance and safety?
13. What are vertical shopping centers?
14. What is meant by the statement that shopping centers and malls have reached their saturation point?
15. What is the meaning of market coverage?
16. What is the basic objective of good interior store design?
17. Name four types of sales promotion activities.
18. Contrast the needs satisfied when shopping in past years with recent trends in shopping.
19. Name three ways stores can provide shopping efficiency for customers.
20. What is meant by "joint cross marketing" of the entertainment and retail store segments of malls?

To Do

1. Pick a prominent local retail store. Write a report that identifies the store type (department store, specialty store, etc.) and explain where the store has positioned itself in the consumer market. Illustrate the report with a chart (similar to Figure 13-1) that provides a definition of the store's target market, differentiation from competitors, and specific marketing mix blend.
2. Hypothetically define what you think the target market customer characteristics might be for one of the following: upscale department store, chain department store, discount store. Make a chart showing what you think the following general characteristics might encompass: age range, gender, family structure, income range, education level, typical occupations, lifestyle/hobbies, geographic locations of homes or apartments, attitudes, and types of advertising that would bring the best response.
3. In a small group, prepare an oral report for the class that explains the four main types of competition discussed in this chapter. Name two specific companies in each category and explain why they compete in the way you have them categorized. How do you think they could differentiate themselves better from their competitors?
4. In 13-15, showing different stock assortment strategies, options A, B, and C each have the same amount of total inventory (count the squares to check that out!). With two classmates, redraw the diagrams on a larger scale. Fill in the squares with names of categories of apparel, as well as specific items, colors, sizes, and any other information you feel helps to explain the concept. For each different inventory approach (A, B, and C), tell what type of store would probably use that type of assortment strategy and, if possible, name an actual store of that type that exists in your local area.
5. With another student, formulate the place strategy for a certain *fictitious* retailer that is about to move into your area. Prepare a report that explains what you believe would be best for the retailer concerning each of the following: site location, type of store cluster, type of market coverage, and exterior and interior facility design features.

CHAPTER 14

Retail Merchandise

After studying this chapter, you will be able to

- explain how women's apparel is sized and classified.
- describe the production and sizing of men's apparel.
- explain how infantswear and childrenswear is promoted and sized.
- name various accessory groups.
- describe fashion-related cosmetics industry products.

You have learned that "goods" are a store's articles of merchandise and that "lines" are groups of related products. Merchandise items can further be divided into hardlines and softlines. ***Hardlines,*** or hard goods, are nontextile items. They include major appliances, tools, and other items that are not made of fabrics. ***Softlines,*** or soft goods, are products made from textiles. (An older term for soft goods is "dry goods.") Softlines include yard goods, apparel, household textiles, and miscellaneous softlines (stuffed toys, sleeping bags, backpacks).

The chart in 14-1 outlines the main softlines groups and their merchandise categories. The main merchandise categories of apparel are womenswear, menswear, and infants' and children's apparel.

Apparel is further divided into merchandise classifications. Womenswear, for instance, will include sportswear, dresses, evening and bridal, maternity, outerwear, suits, etc. The final identification of goods is by individual *merchandise items.* Individual items are distinguishable by specific, unique characteristics. These unit items are known by a certain brand, style, size, color, material, price, or other features. An example of a merchandise item would be a particular blue VanHeusen cotton shirt with a button-down collar in size 16/33.

Manufacturers assign style numbers to merchandise items so they can plan and execute production, take orders, and ship the right items. Retailers use these same style numbers when placing orders for the goods. Inventory records are updated with the style numbers when the goods are received at the store and sold to consumers. By dividing and subdividing merchandise, retailers can more easily target certain consumer groups, allocate store space, develop inventory control systems, and create a unique image.

Merchandise Groups and Categories

Softlines Groups:	Yard goods	Apparel	Household textiles	Miscellaneous soft goods
Merchandise Categories:	Sewing fabrics	Womenswear Menswear Infantswear Childrenswear	Draperies, upholstery, carpets Domestics (bedding) Linens for table and bath	Stuffed toys Sleeping bags Backpacks Tents

14-1 There are four main softlines merchandise groups. The apparel merchandise group includes four merchandise categories.

Consumers do comparison shopping at the merchandise classification level, with products being directly comparable and substitutable. ***Substitutable goods*** can be used in place of each other. For instance, a head scarf might be used instead of a hat, or mittens might be bought instead of a pair of gloves. Consumers' final selection is at the merchandise item level, when they decide which particular item to buy.

Women's Apparel

Womenswear includes all apparel for females aged 14 years and over. It is the largest, most important segment of retail merchandise, accounting for about 60 percent of all apparel sales. The multi-billion dollar industry employs hundreds of thousands of people around the world with varied skills and abilities. It reacts to an increasingly global economy and to ongoing technological innovations. It is glamorous and exciting, as well as risky and competitive.

Fashion movement results from continually evolving fashion tastes and varied lifestyles. With about five merchandise seasons a year for new womenswear lines, there is a great abundance of new merchandise produced and sold every year. Each season's lines are in retail stores for about ten weeks or less before the lines for the next season replace them on the sales floor. See 14-2.

Except for a few dominant apparel manufacturing companies, the womenswear industry is made up of thousands of small to midsized companies. Some are divisions of larger corporations, but many are family-owned producers. The companies and divisions have a high degree of specialization, limiting their production to only one or a few related size categories, price ranges, and merchandise classifications. However, some companies have expanded recently, becoming stronger and more successful and encompassing wider product mixes. They are forcing some smaller companies out of business because the smaller firms cannot compete. Larger firms have separate divisions for their various size categories, price ranges, and merchandise classifications. (The price categories of designer, bridge, better, moderate, and budget were discussed in Chapter 9.)

14-2 When the merchandise for one fashion season has been offered at retail for a certain length of time, stores must sell it to make room for new, incoming merchandise.

Women's Apparel Sizes

Women's apparel is divided into several size categories, depending on figure types (body structures) based on the shape of a woman's figure. The categories group women according to a relationship of height to weight and bone structure, and also with the chest, waist, and hip measurements. Numbered sizes are within the categories of misses, womens, and juniors.

The *misses* category is for fully developed women of average height, weight, and proportions. The sizes within the category are in even numbers from 0 to 20. Very few of the smallest and largest sizes are stocked at retail, with deep stock offered in the middle range or most common sizes.

The *women's* category is for females with larger proportions and is offered in even sizes from about 14 to 46 or higher. *Half-sizes* are for heavier, short-waisted females and are followed by "$^{1}/_{2}$," such as size $18^{1}/_{2}$.

Junior sizes are for fully developed, small-boned and short-waisted females. They are offered in odd-numbered sizes from 3 to 15.

Most of these sizes are also offered in petite and tall sizes. *Petites* are for shorter females, which is sometimes indicated with a "P" after the size number, such as 10P. See 14-3. *Tall* sizes for taller females often have the size number followed by a "T," such as 10T.

In the past, the petite and women's half-size categories were mostly ignored by apparel manufacturers, and were considered unfashionable and unimportant

14-3 Retail stores usually subdivide their women's apparel departments into body types so consumers can more easily find garments that fit them.

14-4 When a retail store or department includes the term "plus" in its name, it usually carries half-sizes and larger-cut garments.

market segments. However, they have now been recognized as important niches and good profit generators. Some entire specialty stores cater to them, and department stores devote space to merchandise that satisfies these market niches. The popular larger sizes are referred to as the women's "plus size" business. See 14-4. Stylish, classic options are now offered in the plus size market, which makes up over one-third of women's apparel sales.

Some womenswear companies ***double-ticket*** their sizes by marking them with two combined sizes, such as both junior and misses sizes. Actually, there is no such size category, but this is possible with less-fitted styles that companies market to customers in both the junior and misses categories. Examples of double-ticketed sizes are 9/10 and 11/12. Some companies also combine sizes into extra small (XS), small (S), medium (M), large (L), extra large (XL), and extra-extra large (XXL).

Even though women's apparel sizing is divided into several general categories with specific numbered sizes, sizing has not been standardized within the industry. Since each company has a different "idea" about the proportions of its target customer, the same size from different manufacturers may fit consumers differently. This is because the slopers (basic patterns) and dress forms used by manufacturers to develop their designs are made for the fit of a particular target customer.

All styles from the same manufacturer should fit the same person the same way. They may not, however, fit other women of the same size if they have different body shapes. For instance, one woman who wears a certain size may have a smaller bust and larger hips than another woman who wears that size. The first woman may have the "model figure" of producer A, while the second woman has the "model figure" of producer B. If a woman finds a manufacturer that makes garments that fit her figure, she will probably continue to buy that company's garments season after season.

Also, manufacturers of expensive fashions often *downsize* their lines so that a dress that is a size 10 or 12 from a budget manufacturer is a size 8 in a more expensive label. Therefore, the same woman may be able to wear a smaller size in a more expensive line than in a less expensive line. Often the more expensive the apparel line, the more generous the sizing. This causes the customers of expensive womenswear lines to feel more fashionably slender since they wear a smaller size in that line of clothing!

The industry has not been very interested in creating a universal sizing policy. Although body measurements are said to be standardized for each of the categories, discussions and preliminary work have not accomplished universal fit. The technology is available to standardize all sizes, but the industry is so segmented that this may never be done.

Women's Apparel Classifications

Besides size ranges, apparel merchandise categories can be broken down further into merchandise classifications. Illustration 14-5 shows the basic merchandise classifications of women's apparel, as well as the types of garments included in each class.

Women's apparel companies usually specialize in producing particular classifications of garments in specific size and price ranges. For instance, swimwear producers almost never make dresses, and dress manufacturers usually do not produce items in both women's and girls' sizes. Additionally, producers usually do not make both expensive and low-priced lines because different construction details and qualities of fabrics are used. High-priced apparel is made with expensive fabrics from upscale fabric lines, and low-priced apparel is made of inexpensive fabrics.

Retail buyers also think and work like specialists. They shop one group of producers for intimate apparel, a different group for suits and coats, and still others for sportswear or accessories.

Women's Apparel Merchandise Classifications

Sportswear separates:
- tops: blouses, shirts, sweaters
- bottoms: slacks, shorts, skirts
- sports attire: for tennis, golf, etc.

Dresses: one- or two-piece styles from casual to dressy

Evening and bridal: cocktail dresses, wedding gowns and bridesmaid dresses, other dressy/formal attire

Maternity: all types of apparel for pregnant women

Outerwear: coats, outdoor jackets, rainwear

Suits: indoor jackets with pants, skirts, walking shorts

Activewear: leotards and dancewear, jogging suits

Swimwear/beachwear: swimsuits and cover-ups

Intimate apparel:
- foundations: bras, garter belts, girdles, "shapewear"
- lingerie: daywear—slips, panties, camisoles sleepwear—pajamas, nightgowns, negligees
- loungewear: robes, housecoats, at-home lounging attire

Accessories:
- scarves
- gloves
- handbags/purses
- belts
- neckties
- hosiery
- handkerchiefs
- hats
- jewelry
- umbrellas

Footwear: shoes, boots, slippers

Miscellaneous wearing apparel: uniforms, aprons, smocks, etc.

14-5 This chart lists the merchandise classifications, or classes, for women's apparel and the specific types of items typically included in each classification.

Men's Apparel

Throughout history, men have been slower and less willing than women to accept fashion changes in their wardrobes. Recently, however, men have become more interested in having added variety in their wardrobes and selecting more unusual sports and leisure wear. ***Active sportswear***, consisting of garments for sports participation, is also worn during leisure time. Sportswear has been the fastest-growing segment of the menswear industry, offering a variety of styles with emphasis on color, fabric, design, and comfort, 14-6.

Bobby Jones of Hickey-Freeman Co., Inc./Hartmarx Corporation

14-6 Since men's apparel trends have become more casual, sportswear is worn for sports activities as well as for some business and social occasions.

Special-purpose apparel is available for fashion-conscious males who want to make a "statement" about themselves and their lifestyles. Men's apparel now allows for different wardrobes for work, sports, evenings out, and relaxing. Also, business attire has become more casual. The industry has responded with more varied merchandise to satisfy the market demand created by this increased fashion interest, 14-7.

A decline in sales of structured suits has been offset by increased demand for ***suit separates***. These are jackets and trousers worn the way tailored business suits used to be worn. Suit separates mix and match various jackets with different pants, taking the sport coat and trouser look a step further, as shown in 14-8. In many locations these separates are now worn for office work and other fairly dressy occasions.

The Fashion Association/Brian McKinney Designer Collections

14-7 Designer menswear lines show creative fashion flair, which has received more interest in the market lately.

Hart Schaffner & Marx/Hartmarx Corporation

14-8 The jackets and trousers of suit separates are not of the identical fabric as suits are. They are dressy but can be mixed and matched in different combinations.

The jackets and pants of suit separates are bought individually by consumers. Separate tops and bottoms allow for more accurate fit, requiring fewer expensive alterations. Also, this extends men's wardrobes since the same garment may be worn for both business and casual occasions. Tailored sport coats can be worn with dress slacks and a necktie for business, or worn over jeans and a T-shirt for a contemporary casual look. See 14-9. Men who buy and wear suit separates are often considered to be fashion-forward rather than conservative dressers.

The Fashion Association/Lands' End

14-9 This look is more casual than it would be with a dress shirt and necktie.

The trends of fashion movement for men have been influenced by an emphasis on healthy, fit bodies. This has resulted in a demand for jogging suits, tennis and running shorts, and workout attire. See 14-10. Also, the fit of men's tailored suits and coats has changed to accommodate body shapes that have wider shoulders, larger chests, and narrower waists.

Since classic tailored menswear lines have slow, subtle fashion changes and long, complex production methods, they are presented only twice a year.

The Fashion Association/Lands' End

14-10 Layering of garments can provide comfort for active lifestyles. Here, a fleece jacket is worn over a rollneck sweater and tan denim shirt, combined with canvas shorts.

Fall/winter lines are considered to be the most important, followed by spring/summer lines. The primary difference between seasons is fabric weight and fiber content, although many suits are constructed of lightweight wools or wool blends that are considered to be all-season fabrics. As more fashion emphasis has entered menswear, especially in sportswear lines, some menswear firms have shifted to four seasons a year.

Production of Menswear Lines

Officially, menswear includes all apparel for males aged 17 and older. However, many producers of menswear also make garments for boys.

The menswear industry is responsible for billions of dollars of factory output, spread among many areas of the United States and the world. Different production segments of the industry require different skills. Sewing of tailored jackets and coats is complicated, requiring highly skilled operators. Sizing is complex, and fashion emphasis is on fabrics (tweeds, checks, plaids, pinstripes, etc.) rather than on new styling designs, 14-11. Tailored suits and coats have been primarily made in New York, New Jersey, and Pennsylvania where there are skilled tailors. Production is now moving south where both land and labor are less expensive.

On the other hand, men's shirts, underwear, work clothing, and jeans provide employment to people with minimal sewing machine skills. For men's sportswear, style and design features are emphasized rather than the exact fit and meticulous workmanship of tailored garments. Manufacturing facilities of casual men's garments are located in San Francisco, Chicago, Philadelphia, and the South. States in the Pacific Northwest and the Southwest are gaining in the amount of men's sportswear and casual attire produced. Northern states across the country produce sports outerwear

Hart Schaffner & Marx/Hartmarx Corporation

14-11 The main fashion emphasis of classic men's sport coats and suits is the design of the fabric.

and activewear, such as ski clothes, parkas, and hunting and fishing gear, 14-12.

While most womenswear firms have traditionally been small, the menswear industry is dominated by large firms. Many menswear firms have grown large by opening new divisions, acquiring other companies, or both. Also, menswear companies have done a good job of marketing their brand names.

Menswear manufacturers usually specialize in clearly definable categories of garments. Designer labels are available at the upper price levels. These upscale collections feature complete groups of merchandise that are produced, displayed, and sold in retail stores as coordinated lines. The largest number of menswear garments, however, are mass-produced at lower price points and contain popular or private labels.

The Fashion Association/Willis & Geiger

14-12 This men's fishing vest is rain-resistant and has 31 different pockets of all shapes and sizes to hold fly fishing needs.

Some menswear producers have expanded into women's apparel, either by creating or by acquiring women's divisions. This is especially true for tailored women's apparel. Additionally, some female consumers buy and wear men's apparel because they like to have oversized shirts or sweaters, hip-fitting jeans, or a man's business look with a necktie and jacket. Consequently, there is currently less separation between the womenswear and menswear segments of the industry.

Less contract manufacturing has been used for menswear than for women's apparel production. The complex tailoring requires more quality control, which encourages companies to have inside shops. However, contract production is increasing as men wear more casual separates and have faster-moving fashion cycles.

Contracting is also a way for firms to beat the competition and to achieve growth. Menswear companies are emphasizing marketing and responsiveness to customers' needs, rather than just production. This has encouraged the use of contractors who will do short runs of styles quickly and inexpensively. A *short run* is the production of a limited number of units of a particular item, fewer than an average production run.

The two-tier system of dual distribution is fairly common with menswear companies. Manufacturers sell bulk quantities of their lines to retailers at wholesale prices, as well as selling directly to consumers through their own retail stores.

Men's Apparel Sizes and Classifications

Men's tailored apparel has ***dual sizing*** with different chest measurements combined with different body types. The body types are categorized as short, regular, long, and extra tall regular or long, that fit various heights and builds. Men's suits and sport coats are sold by chest sizes and body types, such as 42 long, with the deepest stock offered by retail stores in mid-range sizes. Producers must provide all of these sizes for each of the styles in their lines to satisfy consumer needs. However, menswear sizing is much more standardized than womenswear sizing, running truer to measurement specifications.

Men's slacks also have dual sizing, with a waist measurement combined with an inseam (inside leg) length on hemmed pants. See 14-13. The waist measurement is listed first, with the inseam following, such as trousers in size 36/32. In this instance, the waist measurement is 36 inches and the inseam measures 32 inches. Expensive menswear retailers sell unhemmed trousers, often with suits. The leg length is measured and marked at the proper length for the customer. The pants are then custom-hemmed by an alterations tailor. With many stores discounting merchandise and others charging for alterations, fewer trousers are currently being custom-hemmed.

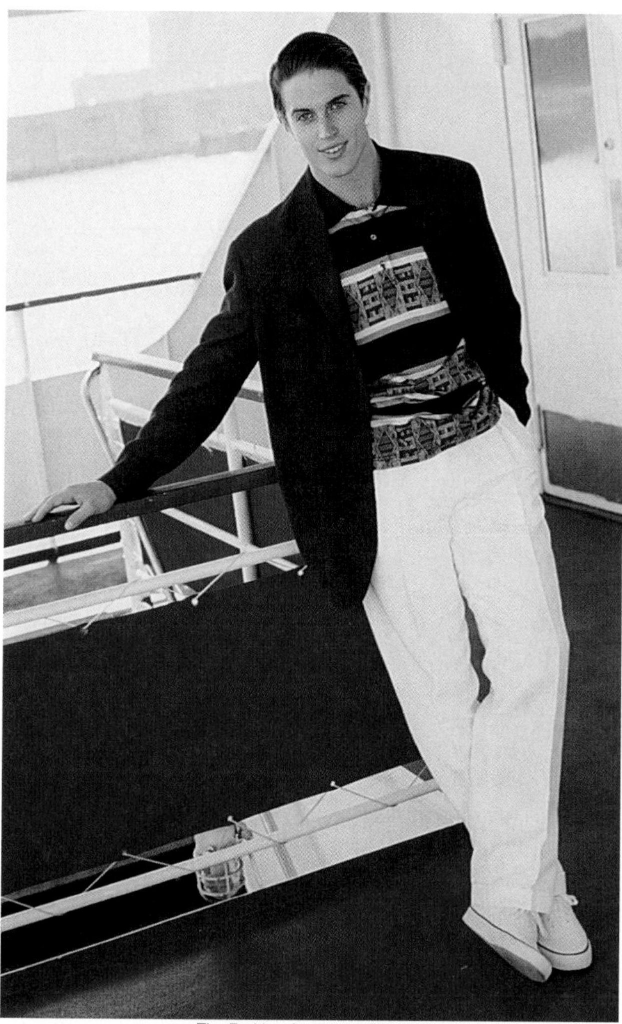

The Fashion Association/Mondo di Marco, Div. of Mondo Inc.

14-13 These white trousers are produced and sold in various combinations of waistline sizes and inseam measurements to offer the exact fit required for different men.

Because many jackets and pants are now sold as separates with many sizes available, men can mix and match the pieces into a suit or coordinated sport coat and slacks outfit. However, the large variety of sizes required to be stocked by retailers in this market has necessitated huge investments of capital for slow-moving stock. Some menswear manufacturers have changed their styling to "softly tailored" designs that have a looser fit, thus requiring fewer sizes. Also, some retailers have discontinued their men's tailored apparel departments because of high inventory costs.

Men's long-sleeved dress shirts are sized by neck measurements at one-half-inch intervals and sleeve lengths at one-inch intervals. See 14-14. The sleeve length measurement is from the center of the back yoke at the neck, across the top of the shoulder, around the bent elbow, to the bottom of the sleeve at the wrist. Shirts are either tapered (slim) or regular (full) cut. Once again, the dual sizing and many size ranges offered cause a slow production process for manufacturers and inventory problems for both manufacturers and retailers.

Some men's sportswear sizing has been simplified. For instance, most men's sweaters and sport shirts are sized small, medium, large, and extra large. Neck measurements and sleeve lengths are standard for each size. Combined with this, shirt producers have tried to pay less attention to fit and more attention to fashion. They produce a large percentage of their styles with average measurements. However, since this has not been well received by some customers, major menswear retailers carry both types. They carry fashion shirts in sizes using average measurements and classic dress shirts in the customary collar and sleeve-length sizing. A specialty size niche that has gained success lately is the "big and tall" market.

The Fashion Association/Gene Meyer, Div. of Mondo Inc.

14-14 An example of a men's shirt size is 16-34. The first number is the neck (collar) measurement and the second number tells the measurement from the center back neck to the wrist.

Men's Apparel Merchandise Classifications
Tailored clothing: suits, overcoats, topcoats, sport coats, dress trousers, formal wear
Furnishings: dress shirts, neckwear (ties, scarves), underwear, hats, socks, sleepwear, robes
Sportswear: sport shirts, knit shirts, sweaters, shorts, slacks, exercise wear, swim trunks
Heavy outerwear: parkas, snowsuits, ski pants and jackets
Work clothing: work shirts and pants, overalls, jeans
Footwear: shoes, boots, slippers
Miscellaneous wearing apparel: raincoats, uniforms, caps

14-15 Just as womenswear has specific classifications of apparel, the menswear category has its own classifications.

Men's apparel is grouped into several merchandise classifications. Illustration 14-15 shows the different classifications of menswear apparel.

Infants' and Children's Apparel

Infants' apparel is for babies and toddlers younger than three years old. *Children's apparel* is for girls and boys in preschool and grade school. Preteen and teen sizes provide the transition to adult apparel.

The childrenswear industry has become increasingly important to our economy in recent years. A few childrenswear companies are large, but the majority of producers are small companies. Many are in New York's garment district, but others are moving farther south to reduce their costs. Secondary concentrations exist in the Miami and Los Angeles areas. A great deal of childrenswear is imported from Asia, Europe, and Central and South America. Menswear firms have been longtime producers of boys' apparel, with womenswear firms less likely to produce children's apparel.

Most childrenswear producers typically sell three seasonal lines. They are spring/summer, fall, and holiday. Fall is the most important season because it features back-to-school wear, 14-16. New fashion looks are introduced then, and the lines are promoted heavily by manufacturers and retailers. Fashion advertising activities at other times of the year are generally less for childrenswear than for women's apparel. Children's apparel lines are designed a year ahead and shown to retail buyers six months ahead of the consumer wearing season.

The childrenswear industry incorporates some of the same color and style trends as adult apparel. Childrenswear fashion is becoming more responsive to new trends as soon as they are recognized. Smaller manufacturers are quicker to incorporate new styles and fashions than larger ones.

Childrenswear producers usually specialize by type of merchandise, size, and price level. Many manufacturers concentrate on a specific age segment of the market, such as infants, toddlers, children, or preteens. Others do several age segments in only casual or dressy attire, or only upscale lines with a well-known label. Many manufacturers make a single type of product in several size ranges. A firm might specialize in dresses, sportswear, or sleepwear, and produce them in sizes for infants, toddlers, and children. The same design and production methods are used in childrenswear as for adult apparel, although children's garments are usually simplified.

Price levels for children's apparel include budget, moderate, and better, with an additional small designer market at very high prices. Most budget-level items are produced offshore, with U.S. producers concentrating at the moderate price range. Some U.S. apparel companies have discontinued their childrenswear lines because domestic production was not profitable.

Attitudes Related to Childrenswear

The way parents dress their children shows how the parents view the children. For instance, some parents see a child as a mini-adult and select clothing that is a scaled-down version of their own wardrobe. Other parents put their children on display by buying the latest fashions, usually with prestige labels. Still others feel that children should be dressed comfortably so they can play and not worry about getting their clothes dirty. Childrenswear producers and retailers must try to please all of these varied children's clothing markets.

As children get older, their apparel becomes an important means of self-expression. A sense of identity and self-worth is gained by children when their outfits are noticed and complimented. From about age three, they want to dress like their friends.

Monsanto Fibers

14-16 Parents usually buy new wardrobes for their children in the fall for the new school year.

Children also form opinions about how they want to look because of television shows and commercials. Movies, TV, and videotapes have had a great influence on children, and have promoted various apparel looks. Also, advertising is geared toward them, since children have become more involved in shopping for their clothes and deciding what they will wear each day.

Children want to be included in the decision-making process concerning their clothes or to totally make their own choices. Young children often accompany their parents on shopping trips. They freely express their desires about what they want, often reflecting their desire to fit in with their peer groups. They are happier when they can select something themselves, rather than having it picked out for them. In this way, they also practice making choices and learn about making wrong decisions. However, parents usually make the final purchase selection, keeping in mind that the child's apparel preferences are the ones that will be worn the most and enjoyed.

Infantswear Sizes and Desirable Features

Like other apparel markets, childrenswear has special size categories with numbered sizes within them. The categories correspond with average heights and weights that relate to children's ages, 14-17.

Infant sizing is for babies from birth to when they start to walk (at about one year). These garments allow room for diapers. Two different sizing systems are used. Numerical sizes are in increments of 3 months, from 3 to 24 months. The other system uses the sizes of newborn, small, medium, large, and extra large. A tag on infant garments or a chart placed on the outside of each garment package should specify the heights and weights of the sizing system used. Shoppers should be encouraged to buy infant apparel according to a baby's actual height and weight, not age.

14-17 Apparel for infants is in a separate department of most retail stores.

Infants grow fast and wardrobe needs change quickly. Slightly larger sizes can accommodate a growing baby, with the garments being worn longer. However, garments that are far too big are dangerous since they can become tangled. Also, with climate changes, parents should only buy what is needed for each season as the baby grows.

Infant apparel purchases are usually based on comfort and practicality rather than on fashion trends. Soft garments are best for a baby's delicate skin, but fabrics that are extremely fuzzy can irritate the nose and throat. Fabrics should be absorbent and let moisture evaporate, as well as being shrink-resistant and durable. Knit garments provide warmth and ventilation and often have built-in stretch that "grows" with the infant.

Practicality in infant clothing includes ease of changing. Front openings and snaps down the legs provide easier dressing and changing of diapers. Also, most infants dislike clothing that has to be pulled over the head. Washability provides easy care, and fewer garments are needed if they can be laundered frequently. Safety considerations include the flammability of materials, especially for sleepwear. Buttons, snaps, and trims are dangerous if they can be pulled off and swallowed, or poked into a nose or ear by the baby. They should be securely fastened to the fabric.

Toddlers' Sizes and Features

Toddlers are children who are actively moving around and walking. Toddlers are usually between the ages of one and three years. They have short bodies and legs and still have their baby roundness. Toddlers' sizes are from 1T to 4T. Sizes are generally based on age, but are established according to measurements of height, chest, waist, and approximate weight. See 14-18.

Toddlers' garments should be made for comfort, constant action, and easy care. These garments are made to go over diapers or training pants and usually

14-18 The toddler category of children's apparel is arranged in retail departments for toddler girls and toddler boys.

have a snap crotch. Adequate fullness is needed at the armholes, pant legs, and seat/crotch for freedom of movement. Shoulder straps should be wide, and criss-cross in the back or insert through shirt shoulder tabs to keep them from slipping down.

Childrenswear Sizes

Preschoolers' sizes are for young children who are taller and more slender than toddlers, and starting to have defined waistlines, 14-19. These garments are generally for girls and boys between the ages of three and six years. Sizes for these young children are 3, 4, 5, 6, and 6X or 7. They are based on weight, height, chest, and waist measurements. Often there are two versions of each size—slim or regular. Some corresponding toddlers' and children's sizes are based on the same chest and waist measurements. They differ in the diaper allowance, length, and width through the shoulder and back.

Sometimes young children's clothing sizes are labeled small, medium, and large. In such cases, small relates to a combination of sizes 2 and 3, medium is sizes 4 and 5, and large is sizes 6 and 7. Elastic-waist garments will fit waistlines approximately one inch smaller to one inch larger than shown in the size chart.

Apparel for Older Children

Girls sizes 7 to 16 are for girls of those corresponding ages. Regular sizes are supplemented with slim and girls plus categories. Corresponding *preteen* sizes parallel girls sizes but offer more sophisticated styling, similar to the junior size range in women's apparel.

Boys apparel sizes range from 8 to 22, with slim and husky categories. Additionally, "young men," "student," "teen," or "prep" labels are sometimes used to suggest more sophisticated styling. Sizes 14 and higher are usually manufactured by menswear companies.

Additional Features of Childrenswear

When young children show an interest in dressing themselves, they develop greater independence and responsibility if their clothes have self-help features. ***Self-help features*** make it easier for children to get into and out of clothes by themselves. Such features include large armholes, well-marked backs and fronts, and easy-to-fasten front closings. With practice, small hands can manipulate grippers, zippers, medium-sized buttons, and Velcro® tabs. Also, elastic waistlines enable children to pull pants on and off by themselves.

Children's clothes are more practical if they have built-in ***growth features***, which allow garments to "expand" as children grow. Garments with growth features have simple designs, usually with large necklines. Raglan or kimono sleeves, or sleeveless armholes, allow for expansion since there is no defined end to the shoulder. Elastic waistbands, stretch fabrics, and wrap styles adapt to growth.

Monsanto Fibers

14-19 Preschooler sizes have a taller and more slender shape than toddlers' sizes.

Length adjustments are the most important, since children grow taller much faster than they grow wider. To allow for this, garments might have wide hems and cuffs that can be let down, no definite waistlines, and adjustable shoulder straps.

Although grandparents sometimes purchase more fashionable children's garments at higher prices, parents mainly choose garments that are economical. Children's casual outfits that stress comfort, durability, and easy care are preferred, 14-20. Sturdy fabrics and reinforcements at points of strain (pocket corners, placket ends, knees, and elbows) stand up to hard wear and repeated launderings. Corduroy, textured fabrics, and prints help to hide wrinkles and soil.

Children generally like pockets large enough to hold the treasures they collect. Many like strong, bright colors. Prints and garment details should be in proportion to the size of the child. Children's apparel should also not catch or cause tripping, such as with tie belts, long skirts, drawstrings, or very full sleeves. Trim should be firmly attached and placed where it does not hamper the child.

Monsanto Fibers

14-20 The circular knit construction of this fleece top is comfortable for a child to wear. The bright colors are cheerful, and the Acrilan fiber is washable.

Jockey International, Inc.

14-21 Many accessories are shown here, including hosiery, two pairs of shoes, jewelry, and a handbag/briefcase.

Children's outerwear must provide protection from severe weather, which includes water-repellency and warmth without weight. Heavy, bulky clothes are tiring for children and place strain on the shoulders.

Accessories

Accessories, or articles added to complete or enhance outfits, are the secondary items that dress up or set off garments. They are needed to achieve a complete fashion look, 14-21. Most fashion accessories are softlines, such as scarves and gloves, but some are not made of textiles. These include jewelry. Since they are fashion items and accompany soft goods, they are categorized with them for easier retail classification.

Retailers generally have accessories available to coordinate with the apparel fashions that are being sold. This enables customers to achieve a total look. Accessory producers watch the same forecast trends about colors, textures, and silhouettes as garment producers do since the success of accessory sales is dependent on apparel fashions.

Fashion merchandisers should know how to create the latest fashion looks using accessories, showing customers how to turn mediocre outfits into terrific ones. Customers can be shown how to bring out their best features or personalities with accessories. Accessories can extend wardrobes and add variety by pulling different garments together and updating old ones. The same outfit can be accessorized to look dressy or casual, as if a person owns more clothes. Since accessories are small and usually do not cost as much as garments, consumers can buy more of them to extend and update their wardrobes. The importance of accessories also increases when consumers do not like the styles being offered in retail stores. In that case, they update their existing garments with new accessories.

Accessories are often ***impulse purchases***, bought on the spur of the moment without much planning. To encourage such sales, retailers place them in high-traffic areas, such as at a main intersection of store aisles or near check-out counters. See 14-22. Accessories are also sometimes placed within ready-to-wear departments so they can be coordinated with the garments being sold.

Accessory items become more important in poor economic times because they are used as inexpensive extenders for consumers' wardrobes. ***Extenders***, or multipliers, can be mixed and matched within a wardrobe for more outfits. They can be used to update garments that are already owned.

Accessory companies present at least two new seasonal lines per year—spring/summer and fall/winter. The small and medium-sized firms that dominate the industry have not become larger with mergers and consolidations as in other parts of the textile/apparel pipeline. However, many have signed licensing agreements with well-known apparel designers to create upscale designer accessory lines. On the other hand, import competition is hurting the U.S. accessories industry, with less expensive items coming from offshore sources.

14-22 A display along a main aisle can attract the attention of shoppers, encouraging them to buy scarves, hats, handbags, shoes, jewelry, and other accessories.

The Fashion Association/Allen-Edmonds Shoe Corporation

14-23 These "spectator" style brown and white shoes have a cap toe with medallion design.

Footwear

Footwear includes dress shoes, casual shoes, boots, slippers, and athletic shoes, 14-23. Most footwear is quite expensive and is carefully selected by consumers. Shoes and boots should provide support, as well as comfort and durability. They should not dominate a person's outfit and should most often blend with the pants or skirt. Men's shoes usually coordinate with the color of the man's belt.

Hosiery

This category includes panty hose, tights, socks, knee-highs, leg warmers, and all other stockings. Most are stretchy for good fit, 14-24. The texture and color of women's nylon hose should relate to the shoes and natural skin color. Sandlefoot hose are worn with shoes that have open toes or heels.

Men's socks are almost always dark for dress and white for sports. Argyle, striped, and decorated socks gain fashion popularity periodically. Hosiery of various styles, fibers, colors, and qualities are sold at different prices and through various types of retail stores.

Monsanto Fibers

14-24 Socks are knit for comfort and to fit feet of several different shoe sizes.

Handbags and Small Leather Goods

Handbags should coordinate with shoes, either being of a matching or lighter color value. Basic handbags are in neutral shades or in the basic colors of a person's wardrobe. They should be scaled to the body size of the wearer. Straw bags are often for warm weather use, and canvas bags are sporty. Smaller purses and clutch bags are used with dressy attire. The term *small leather goods* or flatgoods relates to such items as wallets, billfolds, coin purses, and small cases for business cards.

Belts

Belts are sold in various widths, colors, and materials, such as metal, leather, fabric, macramé cord, or others, 14-25. Buckles may be plain or elaborate. Some depict an animal, theme, or designer's logo. Buckles may be detachable so different strips of belting can be inserted into them for versatility. Reversible belts have combinations of two colors or textures, such as a black side and a brown side.

Jewelry

Jewelry includes pins, necklaces, earrings, bracelets, cuff links, and other items. It is sold at three price levels. ***Fine jewelry*** is the most expensive and is usually retailed by jewelry stores. It is of very high quality; made of genuine gold, silver, or platinum; and may contain gemstones. ***Bridge jewelry*** is of excellent quality and is made to look like fine jewelry, but is less expensive. It is made of good metals or other materials and may have semiprecious gems, 14-26. ***Costume jewelry***, also called fashion jewelry, is the least expensive. It may be made of plastic, shells, wood, plated metals, artificial stones, or unusual materials. Some costume jewelry is made to look like better jewelry, only with cheaper materials. There are often costume jewelry fads that create inexpensive fashion fun!

The amount of jewelry worn with an outfit should not be overdone, and it should be appropriate for the occasion. Certain pieces of jewelry are considered classics and remain in style for many years. These include simple chains, hoop earrings, pearl necklaces, and circle bracelets.

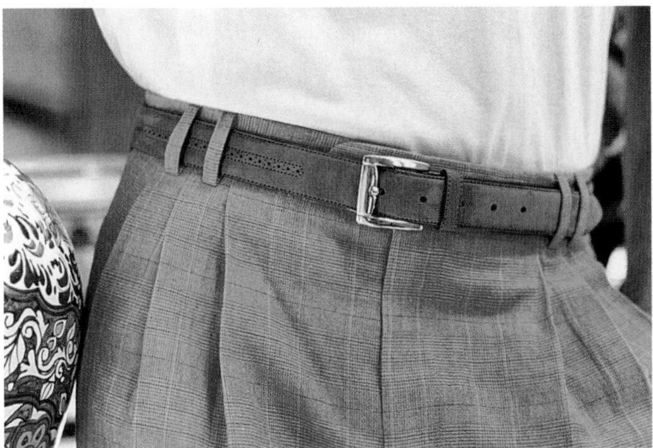

The Fashion Association/Mondo di Marco, Div. of Mondo Inc.

14-25 Belts are both functional and decorative accessories.

Saks Fifth Avenue

14-26 These sterling silver rings by Marina Schiano contain semiprecious gemstones.

Headwear

This category includes all hats and caps. An older term for women's hats is "millinery." Hats and caps add fashion to outfits, keep the head warm in winter, and offer protection from the sun in summer. Various headwear fashions are classic berets, knit caps, visors, felt hats for winter, and straw hats for summer.

Scarves

Scarves come in many sizes, colors, fabrics, and designs. They are versatile accessories, used for warmth or strictly for decoration. They can be worn around the neck, on the head, or in other ways. Fashion trends change the sizes of scarves and how they are worn. Fabric designs can add color near the wearer's face. Scarves can also tie together all the separate colors of an outfit.

Neckties

Neckties are sold in many fabrics and surface designs, 14-27. They can express the personality of the wearer with either conservative or bold patterns, textures, and colors. The width of neckties swings between narrow and wide as fashion changes. Sometimes bow ties or string ties are in style. Also, neckties may be complemented with a tie tack or clasp when those items are fashionable.

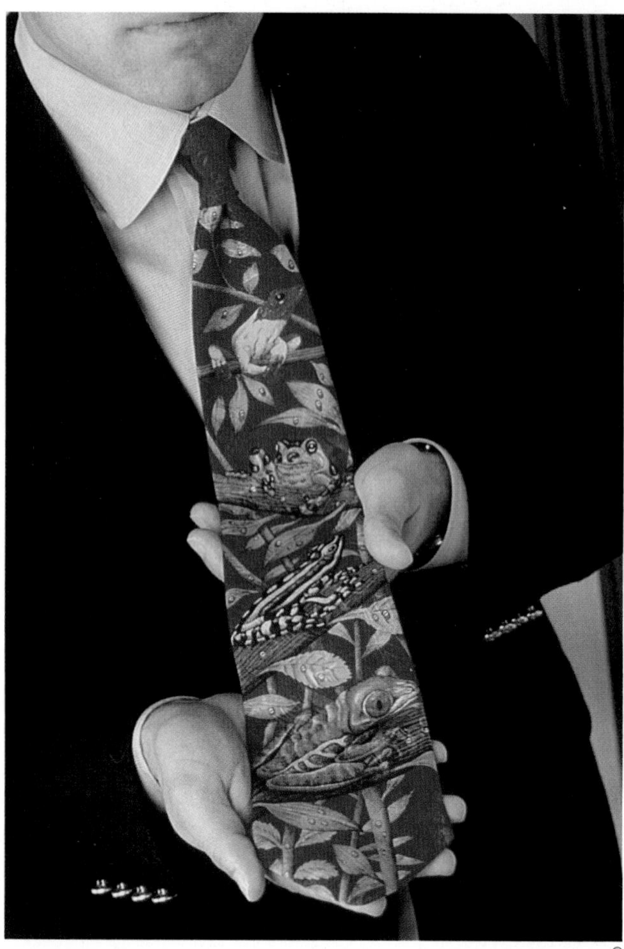

Wemco®

14-27 This is just one design among the wide choices of necktie patterns offered by menswear and department stores.

Handwear

Gloves can be practical to keep hands warm in cold weather, or high-fashion items of fancy fabrics or trendy colors. Simple, basic gloves of cloth or leather can be worn with almost any outfit. Gloves with leather or vinyl palms are best for driving a vehicle. Mittens are primarily for children.

Cosmetics Industry Products

The cosmetics industry provides products designed to be used directly on the body, rather than as apparel. The products coordinate with a total fashion look by adding color, cleanliness, and scent to the wearer. They contribute to a good self-image.

The overall cosmetics industry has three main segments.

- ***Cosmetics*** are products to be applied to the face, skin, or hair to improve appearance. The main example is makeup.
- ***Toiletries*** are personal care products used in grooming. Examples of toiletries are toothpaste, shampoos, and deodorants.
- ***Fragrances*** are products which add a pleasant scent. Examples are perfume, cologne, and scented bath products, 14-28.

Cosmetics industry goods are primarily produced in the U.S., especially in New Jersey where major pharmaceutical companies have operations. Some domestic firms manufacture a portion of their products overseas. Also, imports come from French and Japanese companies. Most cosmetics companies have their main headquarters and marketing offices in New York City. The trade group–Cosmetic, Toiletry and Fragrance Association–is in Washington, DC.

A small number of large manufacturers hold the major share of the cosmetics industry market, especially in the more expensive lines. Mergers and acquisitions have resulted in a consolidation within the industry. Giant corporations offer several major brand names aimed at different customers. Their products represent a huge market with good profits.

14-28 An important part of the cosmetic market is that of fragrances. *Eternity* is one of the well-known fragrance names.

14-29 Brand-name cosmetics, toiletries, and fragrances are featured at individual counters of many retail stores.

There are two major price levels of cosmetics industry products: prestige lines and mass market lines. *Prestige lines* are sold by department and specialty stores, and account for the highest sales volume of fragrance and skincare products. They have limited distribution through a carefully controlled number of upscale stores, which enables them to maintain a high-quality, exclusive image. Prestige lines are given their own counter space in department or upscale specialty stores, usually near a main entrance, 14-29. ***Brand-line representatives***, hired only to sell that brand, are specially trained and uniformly dressed.

Mass market cosmetics lines are sold by lower-priced retailers. These products constitute the bulk of cosmetics sales. They are often sold in "health and beauty aids" sections of discount and variety stores, supermarkets, and drugstores. They are presented in informational packages so customers can make their own selection without assistance. Many large chain stores have their own private label brands that are sold at lower prices because of minimum packaging and lack of promotion.

Since consumers view most cosmetics brands as similar in content and benefits, clever marketing is the key to success. Of the various fashion businesses, the cosmetics industry is one of the largest spenders on advertising and sales promotion, especially for launching new products. Elaborate special events, backed by multi-million dollar television and print ads, are the norm for major fragrance introductions. Perfumes have had increased celebrity brands and name licensing. For ongoing cosmetics marketing, advertising campaigns in newspapers, magazines, and television stress product benefits or lifestyle images. Promotion is needed because of strong competition, as well as the impulse purchasing nature of the products.

Some cosmetics companies have placed computerized displays in retail stores to increase sales by helping customers choose which of the company's products are best-suited to them. Computers create a video image of the customer's face on which various makeup applications are demonstrated. A different system has consumers key in their own coloring and skin type, and the computer responds with a personalized selection of products and shades from the company's cosmetic line.

Market predictions can be made for cosmetics products from economic and demographic statistics. When income levels are down, fragrance sales decrease because scents are a luxury item bought with discretionary income. As the baby-boomer population ages and seeks to look younger, skincare products that feature anti-aging benefits are experiencing market growth. Sun-screen elements are being added to moisturizers and makeup to help consumers guard against sun-caused wrinkles and skin cancer. Makeup sales have also increased as women continue to try to enhance their natural features. Additionally, more cosmetics products are being made for the important markets of darker skin tones, and the small but growing men's market.

Summary

Merchandise items are first divided into hardlines and softlines with apparel being part of the latter. Apparel merchandise is further broken down into categories (womenswear, menswear), classifications (sportswear, dresses), and items (style, size, color, brand). Producers assign style numbers to merchandise items for identification through production, ordering, and shipping. Retailers evaluate, buy, and sell specific merchandise items. Also, consumers make their final selections at this level.

Womenswear is the largest softline segment. Size categories by figure types have numbered sizes within them. However, there are no industry standards for uniform sizing. Women's apparel merchandise classifications include sportswear separates, dresses, outerwear, intimate apparel, etc.

Men have traditionally been slower to accept fashion changes. They have recently increased their interest in sports and leisure wear. Individual expression is obtained with different wardrobes for different activities and more casual business attire. Dual distribution is common with menswear companies. Production requires skilled workers for tailored suits and coats, and minimal sewing machine skills are required for casual attire. Sizing for menswear is quite uniform, with specific measurements for tailored garments and more simplified sizes for some sportswear.

Children's fall lines promote back-to-school wear and incorporate some of the same color and style trends of adult apparel. Producers usually specialize by type of merchandise, size/age segment, and price level. Manufacturers and retailers must satisfy parents who dress their children in scaled-down versions of their own clothes or desire prestige labels. Most parents look for comfortable and practical clothes for their children. Children often have opinions about how they want to dress. Size categories of infants, toddlers, children's, girls, and boys correspond with average heights and weights that relate to children's ages. Self-help features and growth features are important considerations for independence and practicality.

Accessory trends coordinate with apparel fashions. Fashion merchandisers should know how to create the latest coordinated fashion looks with accessories. Since accessories tend to be impulse purchases, retailers place them in high traffic areas and often feature them as wardrobe extenders.

The cosmetics industry makes products used directly on the body. Cosmetics, toiletries, and fragrance products enhance a total fashion look. Prestige lines and mass-market lines are sold differently, with clever marketing as the key to success. Market predictions can be made for cosmetics products from economic and demographic statistics.

To Know

hardlines
softlines
substitutable goods
double-ticket sizing
active sportswear
suit separates
dual sizing
self-help features
growth features
impulse purchases
extenders
fine jewelry
bridge jewelry
costume jewelry
cosmetics
toiletries
fragrances
brand-line representatives

To Review

1. What are the main categories of softlines?
2. What does it mean when it is said that the womenswear industry has a high degree of specialization?
3. What is the women's "plus size" business?
4. For womenswear, why does the same size from different manufacturers fit consumers differently?
5. What is meant by manufacturers of expensive fashions downsizing their lines?
6. Why do men's suit separates allow for more accurate fit?
7. Contrast the skills required for sewing men's tailored jackets and coats with the skills needed for sewing men's sportswear.
8. In apparel production, what is a short run?
9. What constitutes the dual-sizing measurement combinations for men's hemmed slacks? For men's long-sleeved dress shirts?
10. What specialty size niche has gained success in menswear lately?
11. Name the three seasonal lines for childrenswear.
12. Describe the two different sizing systems for infant apparel.
13. Why are knit garments popular for infants?
14. What are the two main considerations of safety for infant clothing?
15. How does the styling of preteen sizes differ from girls' sizes?

16. Describe three self-help features in children's clothing.
17. Merchandise items that are bought on the spur of the moment without much planning are called _____.
18. What is the main fashion change for men's neckties?
19. Describe the types of stores that sell prestige lines of cosmetics and mass-market lines of cosmetics.
20. Why can private label brands of cosmetics products be sold at lower prices?

To Do

1. With a classmate, visit a discount store, department store, or chain store. Write down the major categories of hardlines and softlines carried by the store. Note what merchandise classifications of apparel softlines are carried, and give examples of at least three merchandise items within each classification. Compile the information into a booklet.
2. With a classmate, locate and visit a women's "plus size" store or a men's "big and tall" store near you. Study the merchandise and, if possible, interview the store manager. In a written or oral report, answer the following questions:
   - What sizes are offered?
   - What manufacturers are represented and where are the items produced?
   - What promotion is used by the producers and by the store?
   - What types of accessories are offered for a total look?
   - What other information did you learn that is important?
3. Cut out, mount, and label pictures of childrenswear from advertisements or from catalogs of children's apparel that
   - imitate an adult look
   - have a prestige label
   - stress comfort, durability, and easy care
   - illustrate growth features
   - illustrate self-help features
4. Present an oral report about recent trends in one of the main accessories categories listed in this chapter. Show photos and/or actual examples of the latest looks. Tell how each is promoted and situated in retail stores for the highest sales.
5. With two other classmates, do a study of one of the segments of cosmetics industry products. Include a prestige line and a mass-market line in your category. Gather information about the products, their ingredients, promotional activities, promises of results to consumers, where the products are available, prices, etc. Especially note any details about how they are retailed. Give an oral report to the class about your findings.

CHAPTER 15

Planning to Buy

After studying this chapter, you will be able to

- describe the merchandise planning function.
- outline internal and external sources of planning information.
- explain factors to be considered in preparing financial and merchandise assortment buying plans.
- describe ongoing inventory management planning.
- explain the variables in selecting merchandise sources.

As discussed previously, merchandising mainly involves planning, buying, and selling of the right merchandise blend to optimize profits. It consists of the following three steps:

1. *Merchandise planning* involves estimating, as correctly as possible, consumer demand and how it can best be satisfied.
2. *Merchandise buying* is done through vendors, such as apparel producers, to obtain the merchandise decided upon during the planning phase.
3. *Merchandise selling* involves two different aspects. One is ***indirect selling***, or nonpersonal promotion aimed at a large general audience. The other is ***direct selling***, or the exchange of merchandise to individual consumers in return for money or credit.

These three steps make up a ***merchandising cycle*** of ongoing activity, as illustrated in 15-1. When the planning and buying for the current season are accomplished by retailers, selling takes place. The merchandising cycle continues with the planning and buying of new merchandise to replenish goods being sold and for the next season. This ongoing replenishment also moves fashion forward with styles that reflect the trends that have occurred since the last merchandise was bought. It is a continuous cycle.

This chapter will explain the planning stage of retail merchandising. The other two steps will be discussed in later chapters.

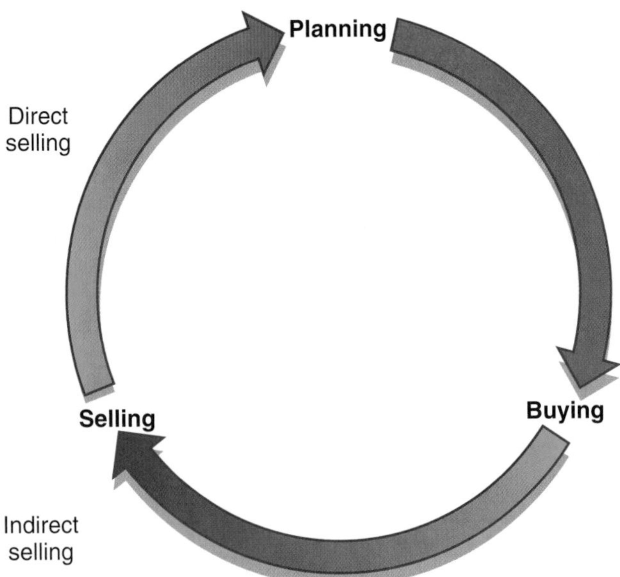

15-1 The merchandising cycle illustrates the continuous planning, buying, and selling activities of merchandising.

The Merchandise Planning Function

An extraordinary amount of planning goes into the merchandising of fashion products. The planning is more complex than most people realize. Fashion merchandisers must decide when a style becomes a fashion. Then the fashion's suitability for the particular retail operation must be determined.

Retail buyers are merchandising professionals who are responsible for selecting and purchasing goods for their companies. Their goal is to make a profit for the company when the goods are sold. Retail buyers must estimate future demand for merchandise for the target clientele of their stores. Planning the merchandise involves determining quantities and timing for various styles, colors, sizes, prices, and fashion emphasis, 15-2. The store image must always be considered, and the activities of competitors must be watched. Buyers follow store policies as to breadth and depth of stock, while trying to make the highest possible profit.

All buyers must be able to recognize what people want, when they will want it, and what they will be willing to pay for it. They must also be able to predict the quantities that the market can absorb. Buyers must notice changes in people's living patterns, preferences, and tastes. Correctly "reading" customers' tastes involves skill and practice. The actual success of the buyers' choices are decided by customers who accept or reject the merchandise offered for sale to them. Consumers make the final decisions about what will or will not sell.

The planning function varies with different sizes and types of retail organizations. For instance, the owner or manager of a small shop may also be the buyer of all the goods sold in that shop, 15-3. This buyer has the responsibility for planning every piece of merchandise to be stocked, as well as for buying and selling it.

Sulzer Ruti

15-2 Thorough planning is necessary before buying merchandise or making other business decisions.

For larger stores or chains, a buyer might be in charge of planning the goods for a group of departments, one specific department, or just one classification. In other words, these buyers specialize in certain types of goods. Buyers who work for department stores usually purchase merchandise for only their own departments. This is referred to as ***departmental buying***. Chain store buyers typically buy only one category classification, such as men's sweaters or women's better dresses. This method of buying is increasing in popularity and is called ***classification buying***. These specialized buyers do not have the responsibility of overseeing the selling of the merchandise.

Gathering Planning Information

Because buyers must place orders months in advance of the selling season, they need to accurately forecast what merchandise will appeal to their customers. A great deal of information is available to help buyers anticipate customer demand and fashion trends. Internal information can be found within the retail company or store. External information exists outside the store.

Availability of Internal Information

Some of the best merchandising information is obtained within the store itself. Internal sources include past sales records, customer feedback to salespeople, want slips, consumer polls, and store merchandising bureaus.

In Cooperation with The 410 Shoppe

15-3 The buyer for a small shop must plan and purchase all the merchandise, keeping track of information from all vendors.

Department of Consumer Studies; University of Delaware

15-4 With computerized sales records, fashion merchandisers have more information at their fingertips when they need it.

Past Sales Records

Sales records indicate what merchandise has sold in the past. These records also show what goods are unwanted because they have been returned or marked down. Sales records do *not* show what stock could have been sold if it had been available.

The use of computers has made the collection and analysis of such records faster and more accurate, 15-4. Small stores sometimes hire computer services to analyze data about customer purchases. Both sudden and gradual changes in consumer preferences can be detected. Records can also show the results of advertising and promotional events. They can relate sales results to the media used, publicity received, or weather conditions.

Salespeople

Personal selling provides a valuable source of product and customer information, 15-5. Salespeople should register their observations about customers. If a means of communication exists between salespeople and buyers, important customer feedback can be directly acted upon. Since few buyers spend much time on the sales floor, direct contact between buyers and customers is rare, especially in large businesses where the buying is done from a central office.

Want Books or Want Slips

Want books or *want slips* are forms salespeople can use to record customer inquiries or requests about products not carried by the store or that are out of stock. These forms can identify potential new products, preferred product assortments, and current stock deficiencies. They can keep retail buyers informed about changing customer wants.

Consumer Opinions and Behavior

Consumer opinions and behavior can be formally collected by using surveys, panels, customer counts, and sample products to determine preferences. Information-gathering surveys about merchandise, promotions, and services can be completed with interviews or questionnaires. Questions can be customized to gain the desired information. Focus groups and customer advisory panels can also be very helpful, 15-6. Observing and counting what customers, fashion leaders, young people, and other groups are wearing can help determine important trends. Results are compared from one period to another, and change is calculated. Also, a retailer can stock a small sample order of new products to observe customer responses before placing a full order for certain items.

Western Kentucky University

15-5 Employees who interact with the store's customers gain a great deal of feedback about customers' merchandise likes and dislikes.

Fashion Institute of Technology/John Senzer, Photographer

15-6 The opinions of others can be sought for valuable consumer information. These fashion merchandising students are learning to present material and collect useful feedback.

In-Store Merchandising Bureaus

Larger companies often have in-store information departments, such as a fashion bureau or testing lab, that are good information sources. Fashion bureaus specialize in forecasting fashion trends so each buyer does not have to do it independently. Fashion bureaus of large stores work closely with their buyers to assist with coordinating and projecting the store's fashion image. Additionally, standards and testing labs are sometimes operated by retailers to check that merchandise meets company standards.

Availability of External Information

Buyers use several forms of merchandising information from outside their stores. Some external information sources are vendors, trade information, comparison shoppers, resident buying offices, and fashion forecasters.

Vendors

Vendors, from whom goods are purchased, can be good sources of product information. Vendors have extensive exposure to the marketplace and interaction with other retailers. However, retailers should verify the information, since it is biased toward the vendor's goods. (Vendors are also referred to as suppliers and resources.)

Trade Information

Information from trade associations, shows, and publications can be very useful in planning. Trade associations specialize in various segments of the market. At trade shows, manufacturers come together in one place to network and exhibit their merchandise, 15-7. Trade publications, such as newspapers and magazines, can be studied for industry statistics, vendor advertisements, and market news and trends. Consumer publications also show fashion trends and availability of goods, especially in ads of retail competitors.

Bobbin, a Miller Freeman Inc., Company

15-7 At trade shows, fashion merchandisers can feel fabrics, see finished goods, and have face-to-face discussions with vendor representatives.

Comparison Shoppers

Comparison shoppers are hired to check and report back to their employers the depth of merchandise assortments, prices, ambiance, and services offered in competing and noncompeting stores. They also note the advertisements, displays, and knowledge and demeanor of salespeople. This helps to determine what products are being sold and what merchandising tactics are being used to sell them. In general, the products in higher-priced stores tell what is coming and should be ordered for stores featuring lower-priced merchandise.

Resident Buying Offices and Reporting/Consulting Services

These hired services provide all types of planning and buying information for a fee. They will be discussed in depth in the next chapter.

Preparing Buying Plans

Merchandise planning for the future is based on data from past seasons. It tries to determine such factors as how much the store expects to sell, how much merchandise will be needed to make those sales, and how much merchandise can be stocked efficiently in the store. Buying plans are subject to ongoing revision as actual sales results are tabulated.

Retail buyers must try not to order less than what will be sold. Reorders of the items that sell quickly may not be available later in the season because manufacturers may already be working on the next season's line. That causes the store to lose the opportunity of additional sales, as well as creating unhappy customers who are not able to find the goods they desire. Buyers must also try not to order more than consumers will purchase because inventory is a financial investment for a business. Overstocking lowers profits since leftover goods must be sold at reduced prices, 15-8.

Retail buyers try to establish an expected rate of sale. They base their quantity and timing of orders to realistically support that. ***Stock turnover***, or *inventory turns*, is the number of times the average inventory on hand is sold and replaced in a given period, or how fast merchandise goes in and out of the store. The calculation, shown in 15-9, is used in planning the total size of the inventory for a given period, such as six months or a year. Fine tuning the buying "works the inventory harder" by increasing the turnover rate for a better return on the investment.

15-8 After the primary selling period of a fashion season, prices are lowered to attract more customers to buy the remaining goods.

Consumers patronize stores that have the widest, deepest, and most current merchandise assortments. However, with high inventory investment and carrying costs, there is tremendous pressure on retailers to work the inventory harder, or increase the turnover rate to maximize profits. The objective of retail planning is to provide sufficient stock to make most sales, but with a controlled dollar investment in inventory. Because fashions and fads change so quickly, retailers try to be well stocked while an item is in high demand, and try to be low in inventory when the demand drops off.

The decision about inventory level and depth of stock involves several variables. For instance, when the cost of working capital (interest rate on borrowed money) is high, it is prudent to reduce inventory levels. However, when vendors offer special quantity discounts, retailers may decide to increase their stock to take advantage of the good deals. The extra goods can either generate more profit with a regular markup or be more competitively priced. However, if a store has limited stockroom space, renting additional storage space increases inventory carrying costs. Also, fashionable and seasonal goods lose their value as the selling season progresses, and if future prices will be lower, quantity orders should be held back. On the other hand, if a price increase is anticipated, larger early orders might be placed.

Calculating Stock Turnover

$$\text{Stock turnover} = \frac{\text{\$ retail sales for the period}}{\text{\$ average inventory for the period at selling price}}$$

(Total the levels of inventory for each month of the period and divide by the number of months in the period to determine the average value of the inventory.)

Example: If retail sales for the entire period were $1,000,000 and the average value of the inventory during that time was $100,000, the stock turnover rate would be 10. This means that the inventory is completely sold and replenished 10 times during that period of time.

$$\text{Calculation: } \frac{\$1{,}000{,}000}{\$100{,}000} = \text{Stock turnover of } \mathbf{10}$$

15-9 Stock turnover, also called inventory turnover, is usually calculated for a one-year period. Fashion merchandising businesses strive for the highest possible stock turnover rates.

In Cooperation with The 410 Shoppe

15-10 No matter how perfectly buying plans are calculated, stock must be constantly checked and inventory adjustments made.

Since planning work is based on estimated numbers for the future, a very important factor is flexibility. The plan is a forecast. It must anticipate such factors as economic conditions, market strength, new styles, store policy changes, promotional plans, and events that might affect future selling. Thus, the plan must include provisions for constant adjustment based on actual inventory and sales results, 15-10. The buyer constantly checks these factors against the merchandising plan and makes needed changes.

All information must now be translated into a plan to satisfy anticipated demand, sales, and profit. Buyers prepare ***buying plans*** that describe the types and quantities of merchandise to purchase for their departments or stores for a specific time period and for a set amount of money. Written plans include both financial estimates and merchandise item estimates, projecting sales in terms of both dollars and merchandise units.

Financial Planning and Control

Financial planning results in a ***dollar merchandise plan***. This is an estimated dollar amount, or budget, for planned stock, sales, and profit for the department for a six-month period. The two periods of the year are February through July, and August through

Calculating Stock-to-Sales Ratio

$$\text{Stock-to-sales ratio} = \frac{\text{\$ value of stock at retail at beginning of the month}}{\text{\$ projected sales for the month (based on past monthly sales)}}$$

15-11 By planning the inventory for a store or department according to the stock-to-sales ratio, the right amount of merchandise should be available to sell.

January. The plan projects the dollar amount of merchandise needed for each month of the time period. It is based largely on an analysis of last year's plan and results. The objective is to guide the buyer in purchasing the right dollar amount of merchandise to meet consumer demand at a given time.

Besides forecasting sales dollars by months, dollar merchandise plans also forecast stock values at the beginning of each month to cover sales. An important guideline for this is the ***stock-to-sales ratio***, shown in 15-11. Based on past sales figures of how fast the particular items of a department or category sell, the ratio is calculated to determine stock needed at the beginning of each month (stock BOM). For instance, if the stock-to-sales ratio is 2.7 and sales are estimated at $10,000 for the month, $27,000 of stock should be planned for the beginning of the month.

The stock-to-sales ratio is related to stock turnover. While stock turnover indicates an average figure for a certain time span (six months or a year), the stock-to-sales ratio is a figure for a specific point in time (beginning of each month). Stock turnover and the stock-to-sales ratio are guides to help estimate the amount of stock required in relation to sales. Stock-to-sales industry norms can also be used for reference. Although stock-to-sales ratios were previously above 4, recent ratios for apparel and accessory stores have averaged between 2 1/2 and 3 because of efficiencies in the distribution channel.

Retail companies also limit buyers to a certain open-to-buy (OTB). ***Open-to-buy*** is the dollar or merchandise unit amount that buyers are permitted to order for their stores, departments, or apparel classifications for a specified time period. The OTB is a control device, calculated weekly or monthly. Its purpose is to maintain the proper mix and level of goods. *Available OTB* is what can be spent or number of items that can be purchased at the current time. Present inventory and goods on order are deducted from the original allocation of planned purchases to arrive at its amount. Software systems are now available to calculate this data.

Fashion Institute of Technology/John Senzer, Photographer

15-12 When planning the merchandise needed for a handbag or leather goods department, many styles and sizes of bags should be considered, as well as colors and textures.

SKU: 512052
GENDER: MENS/REGULAR
STYLE: 10089C
SIZE: LARGE
COLOR: OLIVE HEATHER
VENDOR: 637
CUT: 66828

15-13 An SKU (often pronounced "skew") number is assigned to each type of item in stock.

Assortment Planning

After obtaining an approved dollar plan, buyers plan balanced proportions of styles, colors, sizes, and other variables, 15-12. An ***assortment plan*** projects the variety and quantity of specific stock-keeping units to be carried by a store or department to meet customer demand. A ***stock-keeping unit (SKU)*** is the smallest unit for which sales and stock records are kept. These units have item numbers for inventory control and identification. See 15-13. A fashion assortment lists each item by SKU number, including size, price, color, etc. The assortment plan for a store with branches indicates what specific items are allotted to each branch store.

A buyer's goal is a *balanced assortment*—an "ideal" stock situation. A balanced assortment has sufficient items to meet demand, with breadth and depth to satisfy all customers, while maintaining a reasonably low investment in inventory. It times merchandise deliveries with customer demand and the store's ability to stock, display, and promote the goods. A balanced assortment usually includes some new styles, some that have been evolving, and some classic items. This

Jockey International, Inc.

15-14 Men's boxer shorts are kept in stock by men's departments all the time because they are basic items with constant demand.

Liz Claiborne

15-15 Fashion merchandise constantly changes. An elegant, long-sleeved evening cardigan over a satin dress might be in extreme demand at one time, but have minimum demand shortly thereafter.

provides customers with sufficient choice. It also allows for adequate reserve. It spreads out purchases so some open-to-buy is available to buy newer items, place reorders of fast-selling goods, and take advantage of special buying opportunities.

The two main methods for developing merchandise assortment plans are the basic stock plan and model stock plan. A *basic stock plan* is a proposed purchase list composed mostly of commodity goods, such as blue jeans, underwear, hosiery, and men's dress shirts, 15-14. These are basic merchandise items with consistent demand and dependable sales. Buying levels are quite predictable, based on selling history. These items are always kept in stock and the basic stock plan can be very specific. Included on the plan sheet are the item names, brand identifications, physical descriptions, cost and retail prices, and other information that precisely identifies the goods.

A *model stock plan* is composed mostly of fashion merchandise, 15-15. It includes items that have strong customer appeal for a limited time. These items are always changing as fashions rise and then fall out of favor. Demand is harder to predict for these goods.

A model stock plan for fashion items deals with unpredictability and higher risk. It is more likely that the goods will have to be lowered in price to clear the inventory before the end of the fashion's popularity, 15-16. Because of this unpredictability, the model stock plan is less specific than the basic stock plan. It does not have exact descriptions of items to be purchased. However, it does include specifics such as classification, cost, color, size, and retail selling price.

Many retailers also maintain a *never-out list*, which contains key items or best-sellers that should always be on hand and on display. The goods might include fast-selling staples, key seasonal items, and best-selling fashion merchandise. If these items of high demand are ever out of stock, a permanent loss of sales results.

By doing assortment planning, retailers try to have sufficient inventory of a balanced assortment of merchandise. Most retailers try to adjust the breadth and depth of their merchandise assortment as the season progresses. They plan a broad, but fairly shallow, assortment for early in the selling season. This offers customers a greater choice when they are more

15-16 Retailers mark down the prices of fashion goods much more than staple items since fashion merchandise must be cleared from the stock.

particular, so fewer sales are lost. During the peak selling time, retailers tend to stock an assortment that is both broad and deep. Late in the selling season, the assortment should be narrowed to only a few of the most popular items. This can reduce the number of final markdowns.

To maximize sales volume, stores must offer sufficient breadth to satisfy discriminating customers and also carry enough depth to prevent stock-outs. A *stock-out* is when the store is out of a particular item. Even though stock-outs late in the selling season may produce a broken assortment, "holes" in the inventory usually are not restocked.

Additional Planning Considerations

There are a number of additional factors a buyer considers in preparing a buying plan. How many different brands to stock is a dilemma faced by most retailers. Consumers obviously want an adequate selection, but adding more substitute products may not significantly increase retail sales. In some cases, substitute products only take sales away from existing products. For instance, stocking additional lines of socks would probably not increase total sales. Instead, some customers would merely switch from brands regularly stocked to the new brand, 15-17.

Whereas substitute products can be used in place of each other, complementary products increase store sales without negatively impacting other products. ***Complementary products*** are items purchased to supplement or accessorize other products. Stocking them provides customers with one-stop shopping convenience. For instance, gloves and hats are usually part of the assortment that accompanies winter jackets, 15-18. For retailers, complementary products often provide additional, unplanned sales of goods with above-average profit margins.

Monsanto Fibers

15-17 There is only a certain level of consumer demand for socks. If a department store offers a new line of socks as well as the usual line, sales will be split between the two lines but total sales may not be larger.

Specification buying is when a retailer submits definite specifications to a manufacturer rather than looking for goods already produced. The quality of materials, workmanship, style, and fit of items are specified, 15-19. This procedure includes private label production for chain stores that purchase large quantities of goods. At other times, manufacturers will confine certain goods to stores that order large volumes.

Planning might be done for some *consignment buying* in which the supplier retains title to the merchandise until it is sold. The goods are shipped to the retailer

DuPont Company

15-18 L.L. Bean offers this rugged parka and bomber jacket, as well as gloves, hats, and sweaters that are worn for the same activities.

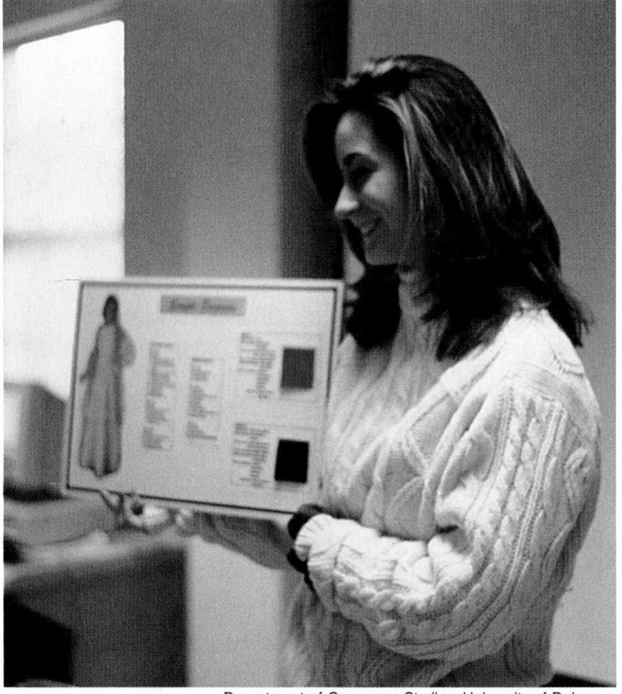

Department of Consumer Studies; University of Delaware

15-19 Specification buying gives all details of what is desired by the retailer, and the goods are produced accordingly.

to sell, but the retail company does not own the goods. The retailer displays and sells the goods and deducts an agreed-upon commission (percent of sales dollars). The remainder of the sales money is returned to the supplier. Unsold merchandise is also returned to the supplier after a specified time. Consignment sales enable producers to control the terms of the sale and help overcome retail resistance to new products. Retailers can test goods without risking investment, but it also lowers their profit. Consignment buying is common for jewelry.

Memorandum buying is an arrangement in which the retailer takes title to the goods when they are received, but unsold goods may be returned to the vendor after a specified time. It is similar to consignment buying, but the retailer has more control in setting the selling price. Also, the retailer may have the right to pay for the goods as they are sold, which allows for better cash flow and does not affect open-to-buy dollars.

Regular price-line buying involves the writing of purchase orders for merchandise from vendors at regular price during market times, as well as later reorders. The vast majority of merchandise is purchased in this manner. If *advance buying* is done well ahead of the desired shipment date, the retailer usually pays a lower price for the merchandise. Manufacturers lower prices to encourage business during these slack periods. On the other hand, *promotion buying* is the purchase of items at special low prices to be offered at reduced prices to the store's customers. These orders are often placed late in the ordering calendar and are sometimes referred to as *clearance merchandise*. They are usually featured in off-price discount stores or as promotional sale items in regular retail stores, 15-20. Promotional orders are almost always for very large quantities of merchandise for a planned promotional event.

Clearance merchandise might include job lots, irregulars, seconds, or closeout goods. A *job lot*, or odd lot, is a broken or unbalanced assortment. The vendor reduces the price for quick sale to get rid of it. *Irregulars* are items with imperfections, such as slight mistakes in manufacturing. However, they are not as imperfect as *seconds*, which are factory rejects with defects that may affect their wearability. *Closeout goods* are selected, discontinued goods, usually of various sizes and colors. They are sold at a low price because of slow sales, a broken assortment, overstock, or the need to make space for a new season.

Ongoing Inventory Management

Inventory management activities insure a flow of merchandise from vendors to stores to consumers. The desired result is stock levels that are consistent with demand.

15-20 Late in a buying season, clearance merchandise might be purchased at low prices to be offered to store customers as promotional "clearance sale" goods.

Accurate inventory management has increased in importance. Since retailing has become so competitive and consumer credit so available, stores must carry assortments of goods that fulfill the immediate wants of consumers. If retailers have stock-outs on items, consumers can probably find the items at nearby stores. This satisfies the *instant gratification* of consumers, which is the unwillingness to defer fulfillment of their wants to some future time. Ordering items for customers to have next week does not work. Besides losing immediate sales, the store may lose the customers, who will not return because the store seemingly cannot satisfy them.

Two older methods to record sales of specific items are stub-ticket control and card-control systems. With *stub-ticket control*, the salesperson removes a specific portion of the price ticket when the item is sold. These stubs are periodically counted, and the items sold from inventory are reordered. The *card-control system* has a separate card for each item stocked. At the end of each business day, information from sales slips are tallied, posted to the cards, and deducted from the listed inventory. This gives a perpetual count of merchandise on hand and a dated history of increases and decreases in demand. When the inventory level drops below a preset minimum stock amount, the item is reordered. These methods are still used by small stores. For medium-sized retailers, they may be satisfactory for commodity goods. In general, they do not provide information fast enough for seasonal and fashion merchandise.

Most retailers now use faster and more accurate *computerized inventory-management* systems that include electronic scanners, 15-21. With computerized tallying, the moment items sell, they are electronically deducted from the inventory counts. Retail buyers can use recent point-of-sale data from checkout computers to tell them what items are increasing or decreasing in popularity. If inventory limits are set, the system automatically reorders through electronic data interchange (EDI) replenishment and Quick Response linkages. This in-season replenishment provides a considerable advantage in the fashion business, where timing is always important.

Today's stock control technology, called *electronic point-of-sale (EPOS) equipment*, offers improved inventory cost reduction without sacrificing customer goodwill. EPOS equipment can print out information every few minutes, daily, or weekly. This allows retail buyers to make more informed merchandising decisions. EPOS equipment is also used to record markdowns, layaways, and transfers to other stores.

Retailing is now at the point of ***vendor-managed inventory (VMI)***. Retail buyers and their suppliers establish specific stock level and replenishment criteria so EPOS data that goes to the suppliers' computers calculates what and how much new inventory is needed for each store. Manufacturers are responsible for replenishing merchants' supplies of merchandise. Replenishment goods are shipped within a day, directly to the specified store, and immediately put onto the selling floor. Sales and inventory turnover rates have increased, and carrying costs and markdowns have decreased.

Selecting Merchandise Sources

Activities of buyers include locating and selecting the right vendors, or merchandise suppliers, for the merchandise they are planning for their stores. Different types of merchandise sources are available. Specific vendor attributes should be analyzed in order to choose the best sources.

Types of Merchandise Sources

Vendor sources include manufacturers, wholesalers, sales catalogs, importers, foreign resources, and company-owned manufacturing facilities. The last two, foreign resources and company-owned manufacturing facilities, will be discussed later in this chapter.

Symbol Technologies, Inc.

15-21 Computerized inventory management systems keep tabs on inventory so stock levels and consumer demand for each item can be continually monitored.

Manufacturers

Retail buyers usually plan to order quantities of fashion goods directly from manufacturers. This is done either by visiting vendor showrooms or by manufacturers' representatives visiting the buyers at their stores, 15-22. With fewer small independent stores in existence, increasingly merchandise is flowing directly from producers to large chain organizations. The following are advantages of buying directly from producers:

- The goods are usually the latest styles.
- Prices are lower (with fewer middlepeople).
- Goods can be made to the retailer's specifications.
- Merchandising support is usually available.

Wholesalers

Wholesalers purchase large quantities of goods from manufacturers and sell small quantities to retailers. They are also called middlepeople, resellers, or distributors. Wholesalers stock great breadth and depth of merchandise from many producers. Small retailers buy from them to reduce their inventory investment. These retailers get quick delivery and can place small orders for goods that are usually only available from manufacturers in large lots. However, the prices are higher to cover wholesalers' upcharges.

Wholesalers are used mostly for convenience goods rather than fashion items. *Convenience goods* are necessities that consumers purchase regularly from the most accessible retail outlets. Examples of convenience goods are food and toiletries. Besides replenishing stores at frequent intervals, wholesalers may provide retailers with market information and selling advice about the products. Sometimes they have fashion goods with imperfections or a broken variety at the end of the season.

Sales Catalogs

Another way to source goods is through sales catalogs. These are usually for basic items. Sales catalogs contain photos or drawings of items, and often fabric swatches. Buyers can consider merchandise selections at their leisure without pressure from the manufacturer's representative.

Importers

Importers' merchandise is produced overseas, usually in countries with low wage rates, and brought into the U.S. The goods are sold through showrooms in American market centers and distributed the same

15-22 A clear idea of a vendor's merchandise and the terms of each sale can be obtained by meeting with company representatives.

as domestic products. Foreign producers sometimes have agents in this country that take orders for private label styles to be made abroad and delivered directly to the store. Mass merchandisers buy a great amount of foreign goods from overseas manufacturers.

Evaluating Vendor Attributes

When analyzing sources for goods, several vendor attributes are evaluated. They include merchandise offerings, practices and policies, services, and past performance.

Merchandise Offerings

Retail buyers first consider vendors' merchandise offerings. The producer's goods must be suited to the retailer's customer group, price, quality, fit, and fashion level. Producers should also continually offer new products to benefit their retailers. Vendor pricing must be low enough to markup for retailers to achieve good profits.

Practices and Policies

Retail buyers consider the practices and policies of vendors when deciding where to place their orders. These include the following:

- Payment and credit terms.
- Reorders. Some manufacturers produce only ordered amounts of merchandise and then move on to producing new styles. Generally, lower-priced goods can be reordered, but not higher-priced lines.
- Retail pricing rules. Vendors may allow discount stores to price their goods below normal retail levels.
- Distribution practices. Some vendors have their own factory outlets that compete with stores that carry their goods. This discourages retail buyers from purchasing their merchandise.
- Minimum required purchase policies.
- Policies about accepting returns.
- Policies against selling clearance merchandise at large discounts.
- Confinement of goods practices. Since vendors want to sell as much as possible, they do not like to confine goods so one retailer has exclusivity in a trading area. However, large or upscale retailers seek this. Exclusivity may be limited to a period of time, a part of a line, or to retailers who order very large volumes.

Vendor Services

Many producers offer help to stores that sell their goods. Such services might include training of salespeople and promotional assistance through cooperative advertising, selling aids, bill inserts, and trunk shows. Other services include accepting returns and offering markdown insurance. Some producers will do *vendor preticketing* in which they attach labels and price tags to merchandise as specified by the retailer.

To maximize vendor services, the concept of ***floor-ready merchandise (FRM),*** shipped to the store in a condition to be put directly onto the selling floor without any additional preparation by retail employees, is gaining in use. This merchandise includes price tags, labels, informative hangtags, and items prepackaged or already placed on hangers, 15-23. This practice saves the retailer considerable time and expense. FRM, combined with automatic vendor replenishment, is providing optimum merchandising efficiency for retailers. Industry FRM standards are being written, and some large retail firms penalize vendors who do not comply.

Past Performance

Finally, retail buyers consider the past performance of vendors when making merchandising plans. They consider their own experience with each vendor, or they talk to others who have dealt with the vendors. Considerations include the vendors' fairness, accuracy in filling orders, delivery timing, and product quality. *Turnaround time* (how soon the vendor can deliver after

A and Z Industries, Ltd.

15-23 Manufacturers often put labels and retail price tags on goods they produce, thus eliminating the need for retailers to do so.

goods are ordered) is an important consideration. The shorter the turnaround time, the lower the required inventory level.

Buyers keep files on the resources they use through the years. A "sourcing notebook" is an invaluable tool when it contains the names, addresses, and phone/fax numbers of vendors used. It also should note the purchases made and the performance of the vendor, such as reliability of delivery and quality of products. A sample resource evaluation form is shown in 15-24. The retail company's statistics on stock turnover, sales, markups, and markdowns provide the best information about the goods of previously used vendors.

Selecting Specific Sources

Key resources are developed for each category of goods to be purchased. These are preferred vendors with whom the store has had excellent past dealings and has consistently placed large orders. Merchandise from these key resources is profitable, has the proper image, and meets the needs of the store's customers. Buyers divide most of their open-to-buy among the key resources.

Buyers also have *classification resources.* These are vendors that specialize in given classifications, such as swimsuits, leather jackets, or other items. Retail buyers use these as resources for specific items for which they are especially good.

An important question when selecting sources is how many are necessary to achieve merchandising goals. It is unwise to depend on only one or a few vendors. If they cannot fill the orders for some reason, the store would lack products. Even if the one major supplier is always reliable, the store might miss changes in the market, such as new items. On the other hand, using more vendors than necessary can be confusing. Advantages of both options are listed in 15-25. It is better to use a medium number of suppliers, spreading commitments on the basis of profit opportunity or the broadening of merchandise assortments. Buyers should establish a well-selected group of vendors while being alert for new sources.

Buyers should regularly determine if their vendors are keeping pace with ever-changing customer buying patterns. Besides the vendors that have had good performance in the past, new resources should be sought to supplement them. This enables the store to have an evolving "new" fashion look and to replace some of the sources that become less desirable. Buyers often select only a few items from each new vendor that represent the best of the vendor's lines. New vendors are discovered through the trade press, consumer magazine articles and advertisements, fashion buying consultants, market directories, networking with other fashion professionals, and looking at other stores' merchandise. A new, efficient method is sourcing through global online networks, to which vendors and retail buyers subscribe. Buyers can send bulk e-mail requests to many manufacturers of specific types of goods. Digital images and complete descriptions can be enlarged on the computer monitor for better evaluation. Buyers who want to see goods before buying, can arrange for samples to be sent from vendors. Price quotes and orders can be negotiated confidentially, without other online members knowing the details.

Brand Names Versus Private Label Merchandise

Retailers also must decide if they should emphasize designer names, national brands, their own private label goods, or some combination of these to enhance their market share. Labels differentiate products from each other, offering perceived differences through distinct images, 15-26. Consumers seek labels on products that they have found stand for value.

Many designer names and manufacturer brands have come to represent prestige and quality to consumers. Some names are so popular, in part as a result of national advertising, that they enjoy brand preference or even brand insistence from consumers. For some stores, stocking popular national brands helps to attract new customers as well as keep old ones. Retail advantages of stocking brand-name merchandise include known quality, proven specifications, reliable sources, and ample markup.

Name-brand producers often place requirements on retailers who carry their goods. For example, stores may have to stock a certain amount of brand merchandise each season. This sometimes causes retail overstocking

Sample Resource Evaluation Form

Company name: ______________________ Dept. #: ____________

Address: ______________________ Classification: ____________

____

Phone #: ______________________ Fax #: ______________________

Contact names and titles: ______________________

____

Company position in industry: ______________________

Dun & Bradstreet rating: ______________________

Vendor importance to store: ______________________

Store importance to vendor: ______________________

Suitability of merchandise: (purchase cost, retail selling price, quality, fit, fashion level)

____

____

Company practices/policies: (reorders, quantity requirements, discounts, pricing rules, payment/credit terms, etc.)

____

____

Services offered: (returns, markdown insurance, staff training, promotional assistance, preticketing or FRM, etc.)

____

____

Fairness/ethics: (truthful dealings, deliver as promised, etc.)

____

____

Historical data: (goods ordered, results of sale—% markup, markdowns, returns, other feedback)

____

____

Additional remarks: ______________________

____

Evaluator's name: (printed) ______________________ Signature: ____________

Title: ______________________ Date: ____________

15-24 An evaluation of vendors can be done effectively by using a form such as this one that summarizes the merchandise, services, past dealings, and other information of each source being considered.

and limits OTB money available to purchase other goods. Also, name brands are widely distributed, which sometimes results in the same goods being sold through higher-priced and lower-priced stores even though the producers try to maintain retail price levels. This hurts the prestige of upscale stores, and lower-priced stores benefit from the brand image established by upscale competitors. To combat this, producers of many top brands now offer lines at different price tiers with multiple trade names to retailers at various market levels.

Choosing the Number of Suppliers

Advantages of buying from a single supplier:

- Quantity discounts may be available since orders are probably larger.
- "Favored customer" treatment, such as promotional help, is often received.
- The store becomes associated with a certain trade name that customers recognize.
- There is cooperative effort in developing new, exclusive products for the store.

Advantages of buying from several suppliers:

- Less dependence on a single supplier who, due to a mishap, may not be able to provide goods.
- Greater access to market information through conversations with many vendors.
- Better service since the supplier is competing with other vendors for the retailer's business.
- Wider selection of products to buy since vendors offer different styles, colors, fabrics, fit, prices, etc.
- Total credit extension is greater since orders are charged among many vendors with varying payment terms.

15-25 Most retailers use several key resources, with new sources always being considered.

Kmart Corporation

15-26 Kmart's Jaclyn Smith apparel is intended to impart a stylish image associated with the well-known actress.

Private label (house brand) merchandise is produced specifically for a retailer and contains the store's own trademark or brand name, 15-27. The merchandise is produced exclusively in the colors, patterns, styles, and fabrics the retailer specifies. The store becomes known for that brand and controls the manufacturing as well as the retailing functions.

As mass merchandisers have captured a larger share of retail sales, private label goods have gained in popularity. Private labels are priced below manufacturer brands, which allows the stores that have them to be more competitive. House brands also have higher markups, and they give better profits to stores than manufacturer brands.

In the past, private labels were low-priced knock-offs of higher-priced designs. They suffered from a low-quality image. Recently, however, upscale stores have been producing private labels with original fashion flair, geared toward their target customers. Quality materials are used, and workmanship is excellent. Many stylish specialty chains produce and sell their own brands exclusively. The major advantages and disadvantages of private label programs are listed in 15-28.

For private label manufacturing, retailers provide specifications ("specs") and samples of the designs they want produced by the contract sewing shop. Sometimes they supply the fabrics. Often the goods are very similar to national brands and made by the same factory. Sometimes retailers purchase a manufacturer's line and have it labeled for them when made. Some retail firms even have their own manufacturing plants.

By having private label goods manufactured to specifications, retailers are integrating backward into the softgoods chain to become apparel producers. To do this, buyers are assisted by *product development directors* who have a thorough knowledge of fabrics, apparel design, and manufacturing methods. See 15-29. Buyers are becoming production experts!

Offshore Sourcing

Offshore sourcing is the term used when goods are bought from overseas producers or when private label goods are contracted with foreign manufacturing plants. There has been rapid growth of apparel imports with most large retailers doing some direct importing. Retail buyers source goods globally, seeking the best deals from each of many countries.

15-27 The Worthington trade name is a well-known private label of the JCPenney Company.

Most buyers plan a great deal of offshore sourcing since goods produced overseas are often cheaper for retailers to buy. They can be sold to consumers at about the same prices as domestic goods. This allows retailers to have higher markups and bigger profits. Also, sometimes retailers can import new and different merchandise that no one else has or garments that require lots of handwork that are not produced in the U.S. If retailers want these items, the goods may have to be imported.

However, there are also risks in offshore sourcing. Fashion timing is difficult, with long lead and response times required. Having supply sources far away from retailers necessitates early buying decisions since orders are placed much farther ahead of when they will be received and sold. Retailers are forced to order next year's seasonal merchandise before they know what is selling well this year, making it hard to order the right merchandise or the right amount. With early ordering, imports must also be financed for a longer time than domestic products. This leaves less money available for retailers to buy other goods for their stores, and can cause lost profits if exchange rates between currencies of different countries fluctuate. (An *exchange rate* is the price at which one country's money can be converted into another's.)

Additionally, imports limit the ability of retailers to respond quickly to the market, such as with reorders. There may be shipping delays, magnified by customs inspections, or quota uncertainties that result in late merchandise arrivals. Surprises often occur with the quality of goods delivered, or the fit of garments is not right for U.S. customers. Communications may be difficult between the retailer and offshore producers because of geographic distances and language barriers. Also, staff travel costs are high. These advantages and disadvantages of offshore sourcing are summarized in 15-30.

Retailers are being nudged by U.S. apparel producers to seek domestically sourced goods to save American jobs. To encourage retailers to source domestically, U.S. manufacturers are striving for more efficient production and faster response time, more

Private Label Programs

Advantages of private label programs:

- Retailers have design control and can specify the quality, fit, price, and packaging of their goods.
- Retailers can build a specific image of style and quality for the store.
- Retailers pay less for the goods because the producer's designing and selling expenses are eliminated.
- Retailers have more control of the channel.
- Lower-priced knock-offs can be made of fast-selling, higher-priced styles, with slight changes to update them for each season if they stay popular.

Disadvantages of private label programs:

- Retailers have a large financial investment that ties up money that could be used to buy goods from other manufacturers.
- Much of the manufacturing is done overseas, causing long time spans between design, production, and delivery.
- There may be slow customer acceptance of products until the labels are recognized and trusted.
- No markdown money or warranties are available from manufacturers if there are problems with the merchandise, causing retailers to absorb those losses.

15-28 The advantages and disadvantages of private label goods should be considered carefully by each retailer.

Oregon State University

15-29 Fashion merchandisers may also now serve as product development directors, formulating the designs and specifications for private label goods.

Offshore Sourcing

Advantages of buying from foreign sources:

- Lower cost and/or higher markups for bigger profits.
- Opportunity to buy unique, distinctive products.
- Consumers are not able to compare goods/prices at different stores.
- The merchandise may add status or prestige to the store.
- Smaller orders may be accepted, allowing for more production flexibility.
- Provides goods that U.S. manufacturers do not produce.
- Gives jobs to poor/developing nations.

Disadvantages of buying from foreign sources:

- Buying trips are longer, requiring extended time away from the home office.
- International travel, food, and accommodations add to costs.
- Long lead/response times make it harder to respond to market trends.
- Reorders are often unavailable.
- Communication is difficult due to distance and language barriers.
- Potential problems with quality, sizing, or fit.
- Greater legal complications with no universal legal system.
- Higher financial risks due to political instability; currency rates.
- May be delays in shipping and border entry.
- Takes away U.S. manufacturing jobs.

15-30 Although offshore sourcing may give larger profits to retailers, there are important disadvantages that should be considered when merchandise planning is done.

accurate fashion timing, and flexibility for reordering. However, international sourcing has become the norm for most retailers.

Summary

Merchandise planning is one of the main functions of the merchandising cycle. Fashion merchandisers must analyze fashion trends and their suitability and timing for the particular retail operation. Buyers must consider the store image, activities of competitors, and policy about stock breadth and depth in seeking the highest possible profit. Buyers in small stores do all functions, while buyers for larger stores or chains do departmental or classification buying.

Planning information for buyers can be found inside and outside the store. Internal information is gained from past sales records, customer feedback to salespeople, want books and slips, consumer opinions and behavior, and in-store merchandising bureaus. External information comes from vendors, trade shows and publications, comparison shopping, resident buying offices, and reporting/consulting services.

Retail buyers must try not to order less or more than needed. They try to base the quantity and timing of orders on an expected rate of sale. Buying plans include both financial planning and control, and merchandise assortment estimates. A balanced assortment is reached with a basic stock plan and/or a model stock plan.

Additional planning considerations include an evaluation of the effects of substitute products, complementary products, specification buying, consignment buying, and memorandum buying. Buyers might do regular price-line buying, advance buying, approval buying, and promotion buying of clearance merchandise. Clearance merchandise might include job lots, irregulars, seconds, or closeout goods.

Ongoing inventory management planning tries to insure a flow of merchandise from vendors to stores for stock levels that are consistent with demand. Although stub-ticket control and card-control systems are used by small stores, most large and medium-sized retailers use computerized inventory management systems. Electronic point-of-sale equipment and vendor-managed inventory systems have made inventory management more efficient and have changed the way buyers work.

Activities of buyers also include the search, evaluation, and selection of the right sources for their stores' merchandise. Types of merchandise sources include manufacturers, wholesalers, importers, or company-owned manufacturing facilities. When evaluating vendor attributes, retail buyers consider vendors' merchandise offerings, practices and policies, services, and past performance. Retailers evaluate whether to emphasize designer names, national brands, their own private label goods, or a combination of these. Offshore sourcing is also an option.

To Know

indirect selling
direct selling
merchandising cycle
retail buyers
departmental buying
classification buying
comparison shoppers
stock turnover
buying plans
dollar merchandise plan
stock-to-sales ratio
open-to-buy (OTB)
assortment plan
stock-keeping unit (SKU)
complementary products
specification buying
vendor-managed inventory (VMI)
floor-ready merchandise (FRM)

To Review

1. How does the merchandising cycle move fashion forward?
2. Why might a buyer for a small shop know customer preferences better than a buyer for a large retail firm?

3. What important information do past sales records *not* show?
4. Why are want books and want slips important?
5. Why can vendors be good sources of product information?
6. In the planning process, if buyers look at merchandise in higher-priced and lower-priced stores, what conclusions might they draw in each case?
7. What is meant by "working the inventory harder?"
8. Since retail planning is a forecast for the future, what factors must be anticipated?
9. How are stock turnover and the stock-to-sales ratio related to each other and to sales?
10. In general, what is a balanced assortment?
11. Why are buying levels more predictable for a basic stock plan than for a model stock plan?
12. Describe how most retailers try to adjust the breadth and depth of their merchandise assortment from the early season, to peak selling maximum time, to late in the selling season.
13. Give an advantage for the producer and an advantage for the retailer of a consignment arrangement.
14. How does advance buying benefit both the retailer and the manufacturer?
15. Why has accurate inventory management increased in importance?
16. List four advantages of buying directly from producers.
17. Describe three vendor policies that might discourage a retailer from buying from them.
18. How do retail buyers discover new vendors?
19. State two advantages and two disadvantages of stocking national brands.
20. What are U.S. manufacturers doing to encourage retailers to source domestically?

To Do

1. In a small group, meet with an apparel buyer of a local fashion retail store. Before the interview, prepare a list of questions so the interview can be done as efficiently as possible. Give an oral report to the class that includes visuals to illustrate your information. Remember to write a thank-you note to the buyer after the interview.
2. With permission of the retail department's selling staff, carefully look at the merchandise in an apparel department of a general merchandise store. Notice if the department carries brand or private label names and if they were produced in the U.S. or offshore. Evaluate the breadth and depth of the assortment according to the type of store and time in the selling season. Determine if complementary products are available. Note other observations and prepare a written or oral report that tells your findings.
3. In a small group, do comparison shopping in two stores that are fairly similar, as well as one noncompeting store. Make three charts (one for each store) for a bulletin board display. Each chart should describe the following:
   - depth of merchandise assortments
   - prices
   - ambiance/atmosphere
   - displays
   - services offered
   - types and amounts of advertising
   - knowledge and demeanor of salespeople
   - other findings (special events, convenience of location, etc.)
4. Research general merchandise planning and sourcing or ongoing inventory management in current books and/or trade publications. Select a specific topic and write a report that adds to the information that was provided in this chapter. Relate the information to fashion merchandising.
5. With one or two classmates, pretend that you have assumed product development duties for a very small, private label line of sportswear separates for a women's or men's specialty chain. Include the following:
   - description of target customer (age, lifestyle, etc.)
   - goal, such as a coordinated line of shorts and tops
   - fabric story, such as medium-weight cotton knits
   - color/texture story, such as specific solids, prints, trims, etc.
   - garment choices (show with pictures, drawings, etc.)
   - ideas about production (U.S., offshore, combination)

   Describe and show to the class the final private label line that has evolved. Use fabric swatches, examples of colors, and pictures from catalogs or advertisements or your own drawings to illustrate your ideas. Explain how the line will satisfy the target customer and how it meets the original goal.

CHAPTER 16

Merchandise Buying

After studying this chapter, you will be able to

- summarize the activities of market weeks and trade shows.
- list domestic fashion market centers and apparel marts.
- state factors involved in buying foreign goods.
- describe the market resources available to buyers.
- summarize strategies of market trips and merchandise selection.
- explain the process of writing orders.

Retail buyers place their main orders for merchandise from three to six months ahead of when the goods are needed by the store. This enables manufacturers to know what quantities to produce and to have enough time to make and ship the garments. Planning for promotion and advertising to consumers about the new merchandise is started about three months ahead.

Buying at the wholesale level for resale at the retail level is also called ***procurement***. Each buyer specializes in a certain type of merchandise with a targeted customer audience in mind. To place their orders, buyers visit major apparel market centers.

Market centers are concentrated geographic areas where goods are bought and sold at wholesale prices. They are locations where manufacturers and their representatives show and sell their fashion goods, or lines, to retail buyers. Fashion market centers may be either the garment districts of cities, or regional marts located in areas around the United States. Some market centers are in fashion cities around the world.

Market Weeks

The most common method of doing major buying, as well as making contacts with new sources, is by visiting market centers during market weeks. ***Market weeks*** are scheduled periods of time during which producers introduce their new lines of merchandise and retail buyers shop the various lines. These mutually rewarding events may last from less than a week to about two weeks in some major markets.

Market weeks are held periodically in each market center. This is the best way for buyers to see and talk to the largest number of vendors in the shortest amount of time, 16-1. The widest variety of goods from vendors big and small, old and new, can be seen and compared. Also, because of the competition of many

Chicago Apparel Center

16-1 During market weeks, discussions are held between buyers and sellers of fashion merchandise to answer questions and write orders.

Seattle International Trade Center

16-2 Producers have their own spaces to sell their goods to buyers who visit the market center.

suppliers located in close proximity to one another, buyers can often get the lowest prices.

Retailers say they "go to market," referring to visiting a market center or mart, usually during a market week. Retail store buyers from all over the country visit New York City, foreign fashion cities, or regional U.S. apparel marts to place orders for their stores. Individual market centers often feature a type of merchandise or "look" from their part of the country or world, though they also sell goods in most other categories and price ranges. Retail buyers look at new collections in showrooms in the producers' sales offices, 16-2.

Keeping buyers comfortable and interested so they will write orders is the primary goal of showroom employees. Vendors encourage buyers to make appointments to view their lines during market weeks. The showroom staff give buyers as much assistance and support as they need. Many provide refreshments for buyers in hopes that they will spend more time in their showrooms.

During market weeks, producers exhibit their new lines with as much flair as possible. Some show their collections accessorized and professionally modeled in their showrooms. Others hang their garments on racks in their showrooms and show them individually to retail buyers. Some designers and manufacturers produce videos of their lines. Press previews for fashion reporters and editors are held in hopes of getting publicity.

Fashion shows are presented during market weeks by the major designers and manufacturing firms to show their goods to buyers and the press. These create publicity that result in media exposure. The shows are extravagant productions, staged to music. See 16-3.

Chicago Apparel Center

16-3 Since many retail buyers are present during market weeks, elaborate special events showcase some of the merchandise.

Often they are the combined work of many different designers, all of whom enter their most beautiful or interesting designs. To achieve coherence, combined shows are often organized around a theme, such as a particular color or a new fashion trend.

Advantages of Market Weeks for Retail Buyers

Some buyers visit markets once or twice a month to keep up with new developments, while others only go during market weeks. When and how often a buyer visits the market are determined by a number of factors. The size and price range of the department or store and the distance of the store from the market are two factors. In addition, the speed with which a market develops new styles and the lead time a market requires for delivery are considered.

Besides the main purpose of buying goods for their stores, there are many other reasons that retail buyers attend market weeks. These are as follows:

- *Gaining a sense of the market.* This occurs through calculated observation. Fashion trends are "absorbed" by retailers, providing a broad base of information about colors, styles, and fabrications, that is used for buying. An

Seattle International Trade Center

16-4 This market center showroom features the largest selection of licensed silk-screened T-shirts in the Northwestern U.S.

awareness of the economic conditions that affect the market enables buyers to make decisions with greater confidence. These market conditions include such factors as current availability of goods, prices, delivery schedules, and terms of sale.

- *Seeing entire lines of vendors' latest merchandise.* This gives buyers a chance to finalize their buying plans for a balanced assortment of goods. Buyers can view samples of merchandise from the wide selection of the latest goods available and compare goods of different vendors, 16-4. This is a much better way of making the main purchases for the store than ordering from photos or swatched sketches.
- *Discovering new sources of lines from previously unused manufacturers.* During market weeks, all of the manufacturers are represented with their new goods. By viewing these lines, store buyers can purchase merchandise that their local competition may not have, thus gaining the advantage of being on the "leading edge" of the market. They can add some new looks to their inventory and delete some older looks to acquire assortments they feel are appropriate.
- *Meeting and consulting with manufacturing-firm management.* These meetings enable buyers to hear about industry trends and to discuss their special needs and concerns with principals of supplying companies. Face-to-face discussions create better working relationships and a sharing of information. Buyers might learn what noncompeting stores are buying this season. After these market week meetings, buyers can call vendors and speak to people they met during market week.
- *Getting special terms and purchases, including lower prices.* Special terms might be available if large quantities, broken sizes, or imperfects are ordered. The buyer might learn about the availability of some end-of-season items from the previous line available immediately and negotiate a special purchase for a retail sale event. Also, an advantageous payment schedule or good discount terms might be negotiated for new items.
- *Gaining promotion or selling help from manufacturers.* Buyers who attend market weeks can often make arrangements with vendors for cooperative advertising in newspapers or magazines, 16-5. They may be given sample ads to run with their store's name added. Sometimes point-of-sale selling aids are given out by vendors, such as posters showing their goods. In-store training assistance might be provided through brochures and videos. A visit from an employee of the manufacturing firm might be

16-5 Bergdorf Goodman and Neiman Marcus stores arranged for this cooperative advertisement in fashion magazines with sales representatives of the Steve Fabrikant Collection.

arranged to show retail sales employees how to combine or accessorize various garments.

- *Networking with other buyers.* Networking includes observing how other retailers shop the market and meeting other buyers, often from other parts of the country. Much can be gained from sharing ideas and experiences with new and old acquaintances during market weeks. These fellow buyers can be called to discuss merchandising activities at other times of the year.
- *Getting ideas for merchandise displays.* Buyers can observe how garments and outfits are combined, accessorized, and displayed in vendors' showrooms. Worthwhile observations are also made by visiting market-area stores that "put their best foot forward" when retail buyers are in town for market week, 16-6. These retail stores usually are in tune with the most fashion-forward ideas. Visiting buyers learn by viewing their creative displays and merchandise arrangements. See 16-7.
- *Attending educational seminars, meetings, and other planned events.* These events are sponsored by market groups, apparel marts, trade associations, vendors, or universities. Some offer information about market trends or new products, such as computer software systems. They may be educational, such as how to establish Quick Response partnerships or how to do certain new accounting procedures. Association meetings are often held during market weeks since most members are in town. Marts often treat buyers to breakfasts, luncheons, cocktail parties, and fashion shows, adding interest and excitement that will encourage attendance.

16-6 When in New York City during market weeks, out-of-town retail buyers often try to visit top stores to see how the latest merchandise is presented.

16-7 Out-of-town retail buyers who walk through the Nordstrom store in Seattle would see many displays featuring the latest garments and accessories.

Advantages of Market Weeks for Vendors

Apparel producers also benefit from market weeks. They can show their latest merchandise to the most retailers in the most effective and efficient manner. Often they can make a fashion statement and gain publicity from fashion shows and other events. Also, from the response of the retail buyers, the vendors determine which styles to manufacture and in what quantities. They will manufacture only those style numbers that have enough store orders to make production profitable.

Manufacturers can train their sales representatives during market weeks because they need the efforts of all of their employees. New reps can work alongside seasoned company staff members. All staff members can meet the buyers from their retail accounts. Additionally, vendors learn about retailers' needs during market weeks and listen to their ideas for new products. Suggestions about styles or requests for new versions might include a different jacket length, width of pants, or coordinating blouse. The manufacturer might add these in mid-season, or put them into next season's line.

Trade Shows

Besides market weeks, there are other industry events for retail buyers, often sponsored by trade associations. *Trade shows* are periodic, temporary exhibits

International Apparel Mart, Dallas Market Center

16-8 The "Great Hall" of the International Apparel Mart in Dallas is the site for many fashion shows and award ceremonies.

that are scheduled throughout the year in various trading centers. Smaller than market weeks, trade shows usually last two to four days and are typically attended by buyers from only one region of the country or that deal in one specific type of product. Trade shows might be held in hotels, civic centers, or small exhibition halls.

An advantage of trade shows is that they cover areas of fashion that might otherwise be lost at major market weeks, such as tennis or golf wear, or big and tall men's apparel. Trade shows also display the work of unusual or small designers who cannot afford to exhibit at major marts. Trade shows often cater to small stores that want unique merchandise.

There are fewer exhibitors at trade shows, so major buying is harder to do. Because they are temporary events, they cannot provide the ongoing service that year-round marts offer.

Apparel Marts

Apparel marts, in a single large building or complex of buildings, enable manufacturers and buyers to come together in one convenient location. The marts are usually arranged by fashion category, concentrating the same type of merchandise in one area. They also include auditoriums for fashion shows and meeting rooms for workshops, seminars, and conferences, 16-8. Newer marts even have office space where buyers can relax and review their buying progress. Marts also offer assistance with secretarial and legal work, check-cashing, fax transmissions, messenger services, and printing.

Some major apparel marts are open year-round and manufacturers have permanent showrooms so buyers can see their lines at any time. The marts also rent out temporary spaces for other manufacturers to use just during market weeks. Those with permanent showrooms hire temporary employees to increase their sales staff during market weeks.

As expenses have increased in New York City, many manufacturers have moved their headquarters and production facilities to other regions of the U.S. As they establish themselves in new regions, they support and attend regional marts. This has helped to spur the development of new marts. Regional apparel marts save retailers the time and expense of going to New York City for buying trips. This is especially important to small, independent retailers who may be located far from New York. It is physically less exhausting, and usually less expensive, to visit showrooms in one or two buildings than trying to make appointments with vendors that are blocks apart, 16-9.

Store buyers from around the country and the world visit apparel marts located in such cities as Los Angeles, Dallas, Chicago, Miami, and Atlanta. Each has its own unique "personality." Apparel marts have regional trade shows or market weeks for each fashion season.

International Apparel Mart, Dallas Market Center

16-9 When all vendor showrooms are under one roof like a large shopping mall, it is easier and more comfortable for retail buyers to go from showroom to showroom.

Individual marts have from eight to twenty market weeks during a given year, each featuring specific types of goods.

Four or five market weeks are held each year for women's and children's apparel, three to five for men's and boys' wear, and two to five for shoes. Separate market weeks are held in many marts for accessories, infantwear, lingerie, bridal apparel, and other classifications. See 16-10. In general, markets for

- spring apparel are held in October/November,
- summer goods are shown in January,
- fall items are shown in April,
- winter/holiday lines are shown in June/July,
- resort markets are held in August/September.

Apparel marts have ongoing promotion to attract as many vendors and retail buyers as possible for their market weeks. Flyers and brochures go out to stores and their buyers several times a year, 16-11. Buyers are sent materials about special airline packages, hotels with special rates, shuttle services to and from the mart, and screening procedures. Retailers must meet the apparel mart's requirements before they can buy. Only authorized manufacturers and buyers are admitted to market week, and high security precautions are taken.

To prepare for mart fashion shows held during market weeks, the mart's fashion director contacts firms about having some of their items in a combined show. Such shows are staged during evening hours when formal mart selling is not taking place. Several fashion extravaganzas might be staged during a mart's market week.

Each mart has a *market directory*, which is a showroom guidebook, 16-12. It lists locations and phone

16-11 Apparel marts, as well as individual merchandise vendors, have mailing lists of buyers. Promotional mailings are sent out to inform buyers of upcoming market weeks.

16-10 Each apparel center has specific market weeks for different types of merchandise. Buyers attend only during the times that apply to the inventory their stores carry.

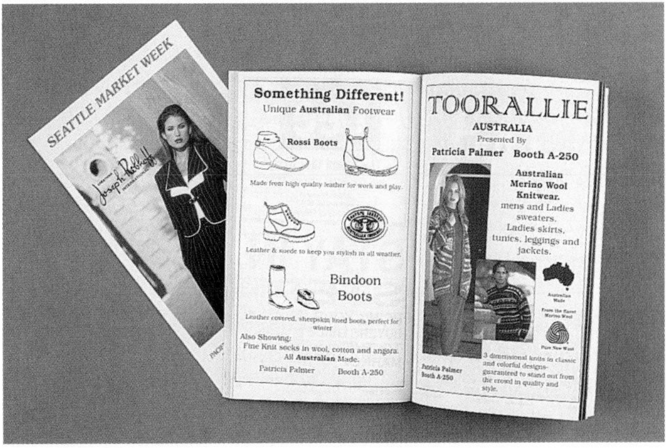

16-12 This market directory of the Pacific Northwest Apparel Association lists all vendors alphabetically and has a classified directory of those same vendors by product category.

numbers of all the representatives and showrooms, along with the merchandise lines and sizes they carry. A market directory is given to retail buyers when they register to make it easier for them to find specific manufacturers and classifications of goods.

During market weeks, buyers usually attend a mart orientation program. They receive a program of scheduled events and tickets. Mart consultants are available to assist buyers as needed. Also, a steady flow of daily publications, including trade newspapers, flyers, brochures, and newsletters, keeps buyers well informed. The advantages and disadvantages of buying at regional marts are listed in 16-13.

Regional Apparel Marts

Advantages of Regional Marts for Retail Buyers

* Save money: Generally lower costs for transportation, lodging, meals, and shipping.
* Save time: Less time away from the store and more efficient buying in one convenient location.
* Provide convenience and comfort: Many showrooms are under one roof, along with restaurants, parking, and support services.
* Good merchandise offerings: Suited to the area's climate and lifestyle; national and international vendors.
* Services cater to smaller retailers: Easier to reorder; smaller orders are expected; seminars/workshops are helpful.
* Enjoyable, personal atmosphere: More relaxed, comfortable, and friendly.

Disadvantages of Regional Marts for Retail Buyers

* Timing of market weeks may precede producers' final line decisions: Used as test markets so some orders may never be delivered.
* Temporary, inexperienced sales help is hired to work market weeks: They have limited merchandise and operations knowledge; no lasting relationship can be built.
* New, small manufacturers may not be there: Unusual items may not be offered.
* Lack of special-purchase goods: Items for promotional sales not available.
* Few resident-buying offices: These services are mainly available in major markets.

16-13 Regional marts have many advantages, especially for small, independent stores, and some disadvantages for buyers.

Domestic Fashion Markets

Domestic market centers are the major fashion areas in the United States. These include New York City, Los Angeles, and Dallas. In addition, many important regional markets have developed for the buying of fashion goods. Buyers for medium or large-sized stores may visit New York and Los Angeles twice a year. They generally make short trips to smaller, local marts during specific market weeks to fill in with new mid-season items.

New York

As you have learned, New York City is the historic center of the U.S. garment industry. Early apparel production was concentrated there where business and theater lifestyles created a need for fashion. The communications industry evolved there as well, providing advertising, publishing, radio, and television to promote fashion news through words and pictures.

Today, New York remains the U.S. fashion capital, 16-14. Many fashion designers choose to work there because the theater, opera, art galleries, and museums provide continual inspiration for new ideas. Key designers preview their new collections with fashion shows in large tents set up in Manhattan's Bryant Park during the twice-yearly fashion weeks. Retail buyers who go to New York also gain ideas about new ways to promote the coming fashions.

Although New York may seem crowded, expensive, and inconvenient to some manufacturers and buyers, it has more merchandise selection than any other fashion market. Buyers consider it to be the most dynamic and creative market center, with more of the newest fashions than anywhere else. Many buyers believe that New York continues to have the most resources for the best merchandise for their stores.

Fashion Institute of Technology/John Senzer, Photographer

16-14 New York City maintains its fashion lead in the U.S. with the most designers, manufacturers, and showrooms of any city.

They shop New York for the bulk of their needs and supplement their goods from other markets. Most major companies in the textile/apparel pipeline maintain showrooms in New York City, even though rent, taxes, and other costs are high.

New York has no permanent central fashion facility, such as an apparel mart. This makes it challenging for buyers since thousands of showrooms are located in buildings along the streets of the garment district. However, similar categories and qualities of goods are generally located close to one another. Retail buyers trek from showroom to showroom in and around the garment district in all types of weather to see the manufacturers' lines. Time, planning, and a comfortable pair of shoes are required to shop the New York market! The pros and cons of making buying trips to New York City are listed in 16-15.

Los Angeles

Los Angeles, California, is second only to New York City as an apparel market center. Its atmosphere and merchandise are very different from New York. Its fashions are often innovative and trend-setting. Los Angeles focuses on relaxed and casual California-style sportswear and swimwear, as well as "Hollywood glitz" evening wear. Fabrics are lightweight. Some fashions have an oriental look.

Retail Buying in New York City
Advantages
✷ It is considered to be the U.S. fashion capital.
✷ It has the greatest selection of merchandise of any fashion market.
✷ It is the main U.S. port and business center.
✷ Trade associations, publications, retail companies, advertising agencies, TV networks, etc., have offices there to promote new ideas and trends.
✷ Its fashion-forward people make it exciting and stimulating.
Disadvantages
✷ It is expensive to visit due to high transportation costs and expensive hotels and restaurants.
✷ Its fashion market can be overwhelming and confusing for some people.
✷ Some buyers consider it to be a dirty and dangerous city.
✷ Buyers must go from building to building in all kinds of weather to visit the many showrooms.
✷ Freight and shipping costs are high if the store is located far from New York.

16-15 The New York market is considered the best place to do retail buying, even though it has some drawbacks.

CaliforniaMart

16-16 This modern market facility in Los Angeles is considered to be a "vertical mart" because it is tall rather than low and spread out.

The CaliforniaMart is the most established mart in Los Angeles, 16-16. It is the major downtown apparel center, housing over 10,000 lines in 1,500 showrooms under one roof. It has showrooms of manufacturers from other parts of the U.S. and world, as well as California.

Dallas

The apparel market in Dallas, Texas, is known for sportswear and "western wear." It is the center of the southern apparel industry. Retailers from south-central and southwestern states, as well as other areas, do some or all of their buying at the Dallas Market Center. This center is the largest wholesale complex in the world, and it features all types of merchandise. It is comprised of eight buildings, two of which are devoted to apparel. They are the International Apparel Mart and a separate, but connecting, Menswear Mart, 16-17. Together, they contain showrooms for tens of thousands of apparel and accessory lines.

Dallas market week trends are known to be representative of the entire U.S. If mainstream fashions are successful there, they will probably be popular throughout most of the country. Thus, vendors listen carefully to feedback about their lines from retail buyers during Dallas market weeks. Often they then change their merchandise to be more "on target" for selling in other market centers.

Chicago

Chicago, Illinois, is not a major apparel production center, but it is the home of a few women's and men's apparel manufacturing companies. It is an

International Apparel Mart, Dallas Market Center

16-17 The International Apparel Mart is just one of the specialized market centers within the Dallas Market Center complex.

Atlanta Apparel Mart

16-18 Businesses show all their lines during market weeks since buyers represent a wide variety of retail stores.

important wholesale market and also houses the headquarters of some giant retail chain stores including Sears. Its Market Center attracts buyers from midwestern states, as well as Canada.

The Market Center is in downtown Chicago. It consists of the 25-story Chicago Apparel Mart building, as well as the Expocenter exhibit hall. Buyers from small and medium-sized midwestern stores often source completely from vendors in the Chicago Market Center. Buyers from large department stores may call on the showrooms only for reorders or mid-season fill-in orders.

Miami

Miami, Florida, is known for reasonably priced childrenswear and "sunshine sportswear," such as cruise fashions, swimsuits, and lightweight activewear. It services retail buyers of Florida. It is also the important link between U.S. apparel firms and low-wage offshore production in the Caribbean Islands and Central and South America. Much of the growth of Miami's apparel manufacturing is attributed to the quality labor of Cuban immigrants, many of whom have risen in the garment industry to become business owners.

The Miami International Merchandise Mart contains both apparel and giftware showrooms that are open all year. However, most of its activity occurs during its periodic, scheduled trade shows.

Atlanta

In Georgia, AmericasMart—Atlanta serves major markets for home furnishings, floor coverings, apparel, and giftwares. The center includes the Atlanta Merchandise Mart, the Atlanta Decorative Arts Center, and the Atlanta Apparel Mart. The latter is mainly visited by buyers from the surrounding southeastern states, in search of all categories and classifications of apparel. See 16-18. It offers a well-balanced selection of merchandise, especially better apparel and sportswear lines. The mart also contains a large, multistory theater which is used for fashion shows and other market meetings.

Other Domestic Market Centers

Other fashion markets have developed throughout the country that serve stores in their surrounding states. These markets save retailers the time and expense of a trip to a major market center. San Francisco, California, and Seattle, Washington, distribute a great deal of Asian merchandise. Seattle is considered the fashion center for the Pacific Northwestern states. Boston, Massachusetts, Kansas City, Missouri, and Minneapolis, Minnesota, also have apparel showrooms within general merchandise marts.

Las Vegas, Nevada; Charlotte, North Carolina; Denver, Colorado; and Portland, Oregon; as well as communities in Michigan, Ohio, Indiana, and Wisconsin, have small regional markets. While some of these showrooms are occupied year-round, most buying and selling activity occurs during periodic planned and promoted market weeks. Local store owners and buyers can visit these showrooms in a day or less to supplement their stocks between market weeks at larger markets. These regional marts especially meet the needs of small stores and emphasize local apparel design and production.

Buying Foreign Goods

Foreign market centers are buying areas outside the United States. They are increasingly competing with American markets for retailers' business, offering a wide variety of goods, often with different cultural or ethnic influence. International sources of supply are important for many retailers with buyers traveling to foreign fashion markets to observe design trends and buy goods for their stores. Large retailers send experienced buyers to source from these markets.

As the world's fashion capital, Paris is considered to be the home of the latest high fashion ideas. Buyers for renowned upscale stores consider it necessary to travel to Paris for at least a portion of their buying. Some buy designs which they then adapt and produce for the American market. Buyers also visit Milan, London, Hong Kong, and other fashion centers for total global sourcing. See 16-19.

Foreign fashion centers hold fairs in their countries for buyers to attend, as well as scheduling fashion fairs in America. The latter enable buyers of smaller stores, who cannot afford to hire foreign representatives or travel to foreign markets, to buy foreign goods. There is also increased international representation at U.S. market weeks. Most marts now devote special sections to imported merchandise.

The simplest way to source internationally is to buy from an import agent based in the U.S. Importers have established contacts overseas and can save store buyers the time and expense of making foreign buying trips. Importers shop in overseas markets either to find and buy specified goods that a certain store is seeking or to source their own "lines." They then sell to retailers who like what the importers have selected. This makes imported goods available to small retailers, but retailers cannot order their own customized or exclusive goods. Retailers benefit from shorter delivery terms and have no added international transportation costs or responsibility for the goods.

Many American retailers do direct importing, often through commissionaires in foreign countries. ***Commissionaires*** are independent buying agents, hired around the world by retailers. They are usually natives of the countries where the goods are produced. They know the customs, laws, and production capabilities of their countries. They also know the

Hong Kong Trade Development Council

16-19 Buyers can make selections from these Goland Fashion Ltd., mix-and-match separates shown in Hong Kong.

tariff and quota schedules of the United States. They shop for new resources in their countries, often for many firms. They help buyers make contacts, negotiate transactions, and follow the goods through to delivery. They do the actual buying of goods for stores if authorized to do so.

For private label goods, bought on the basis of specifications, commissionaires locate available textiles, find manufacturers, and try to ensure the best deals. They also follow up on orders to check quality and delivery dates. They are paid on a percentage commission basis of the first cost. ***First cost*** is the wholesale price for goods in a foreign country of origin, exclusive of shipping costs and duties.

Large stores might maintain their own foreign corporate buying offices in major international cities. These are usually located in fashion capitals, from which their buyers can also travel to smaller markets in that region of the world. Permanent employees who work in these store-owned foreign buying offices survey the market for new trends, advise the store's U.S. buyers, make purchases, and follow up on deliveries. (Specific methods of offshore sourcing are discussed in Chapter 24.)

The Doneger Group

16-20 Since RBO employees work in the market center, they are familiar with products being offered by the various vendors. They can then match the right merchandise with the needs of their clients.

Helpful Buying Resources

Besides getting information from fashion and trade publications about coming trends, a variety of enterprises act as advisers and sources of information for retail store buyers. Among these are resident buying offices, merchandise brokers, reporting/consulting services, and manufacturers' traveling sales representatives.

Resident Buying Offices

Resident buying offices (RBOs) are service businesses that employ buyers who daily scout fashion markets to provide their client stores with advance market information and buying help. Buying offices operate in the major fashion market centers. They report on what products are available from suppliers, and they select merchandise for their member retailers. Retailers contract with them for service help during market weeks to locate desirable goods and for additional support throughout the year, 16-20.

Resident buying offices are either independently owned businesses that receive payment from the stores they serve or store-owned offices. The independent RBOs are also called fee or salary offices. Stores contract with them on a yearly basis, paying according to the services provided. Independent RBO client groups consist of noncompeting member stores, often from many parts of the country. The two types of buying offices are described in 16-21.

Many RBOs maintain offices and display areas in New York City, which helps to strengthen that city's fashion marketing leadership. A few RBOs are located in or near regional apparel marts. Some have branch offices in several U.S. market centers and many foreign countries.

RBOs are the eyes and ears for their retail clients, assisting, but not replacing, the store staff. They are market researchers that cover specific wholesale markets and present news about upcoming trends to their member stores, 16-22. They usually serve a certain type of store based on size, target customer, merchandise categories, or price points. A summary of the services provided by RBOs is given in 16-23.

Most stores belong to a buying organization. The information and assistance that RBOs offer helps all types of retailers compete in the marketplace, especially small merchants that have fewer resources of their own. Group buying, with many stores combined through such offices, can offer lower prices through quantity discounts and more reliable deliveries. Group buying also leads to more clout in the marketplace.

Although RBOs work for retailers, they also perform an unpaid service for manufacturers. They bring producers' merchandise to the attention of buyers when the items meet particular store needs and standards. Because of this, apparel manufacturers try to cater to the buying offices.

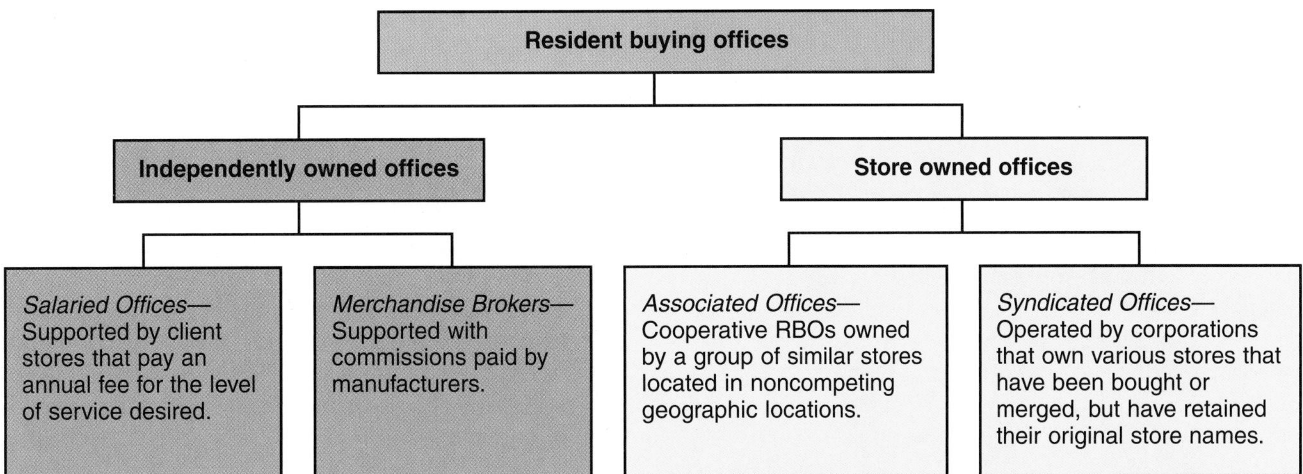

16-21 The ownership of resident buying offices differs even though the services they provide to their retail stores are similar.

Other Buying Resources

Merchandise brokers work on a commission basis, paid by producers when retail buying is arranged for that vendor's goods. There are fewer merchandise brokers today due to the strengthening presence of regional marts and the large retail organizations created by mergers and acquisitions.

Reporting/consulting services collect, tabulate, and report information on product lines and/or merchandising

The Doneger Group

16-22 Resident buying office employees show their member retail buyers what the trends are for the upcoming fashion season.

Services Provided by Resident Buying Offices

- Evaluate economic trends and consumer behavior.
- Send out news bulletins about market information (trends, new items, price changes, best sellers, supply conditions, etc.).
- Hold trend clinics and product seminars for clients.
- Locate and recommend vendors.
- Set up appointments for buyers with vendors.
- Accompany buyers on calls.
- Assist with vendor negotiations and special deals.
- Provide office space, clerical help, and mail/phone/fax service for visiting buyers.
- Place orders for stores on request.
- Arrange delivery and payment schedules.
- Follow up on shipments of orders.
- Place reorders and fill-in orders for fast delivery.
- Arrange merchandise adjustments and returns.
- Provide promotional assistance with sample ads, direct mail pieces, etc.
- Put together group buying for quantity discounts and more reliable deliveries.
- Do product development work for private label lines.
- Assist with international sourcing.

16-23 Resident buying offices provide many services for their retail clients.

The Doneger Group

16-24 Portfolios featuring upcoming merchandise are prepared by reporting/consulting services to inform their members of the colors and styles that will be in the stores.

activities, charging fees for their reports. They report upcoming trends for retail merchandise, 16-24. They project consumer demand and list best-selling items and where to source them. These reporting services are similar to the fashion forecasting services used by textile and apparel producers, but they report closer to the retail buying season instead of far in the future. They do not help stores make actual market contacts.

Sometimes *manufacturers' traveling sales representatives* visit buyers at their stores. These "reps" sell their lines by making calls on various retailers. The manufacturers first show the new styles to their sales reps at sales meetings. The reps then travel within their assigned territories with samples to show to retailers. This saves buyers travel time and expense. It also helps buyers to make more informed decisions, since they have the in-store resources of sales records, plans, current merchandise, and store personnel to draw from. Additionally, buyers feel they have more control in their own environment than in a manufacturer's showroom.

Market Trip Strategies

Buyers must learn to think like their customers when they go to market, rather than basing buying decisions on their own personal likes or dislikes. The customer is the one who will make the final purchasing decision and determine the ultimate profitability of the department or store.

Although most retail buying takes place during market weeks, buyers may visit most markets at any time. Buyers for small stores tend to go to market less often than buyers for large chains, department stores, or fashion-oriented stores. Buying trips are taken to purchase fashion goods, but not commodity goods, which can be ordered by phone, fax, or EDI connections.

To get the most out of a market in the least amount of time, the buyer must be well prepared. The buying plan approved by store management will have established guidelines about how much money to spend and how much merchandise to order (see Chapter 15). However, plans should be flexible in case market conditions or unexpected trends require changes. Decisions about specific styles, colors, and fabrications are made when the actual items are viewed. Buying is done by classifications, price lines, sizes, colors, and quantities, up to the dollar figure that has been approved.

Since most stores use the services of a resident buying office, a copy of the buying plan should have been sent to that office, along with any requests for specific help that will be needed. When buyers arrive at the market center, they visit their RBO. There they meet with the merchandise representative of their classification of goods, 16-25. Buyers verify any appointments that have been made for them, gather the latest information, and set up additional appointments if needed.

Resident buying offices often hold preliminary seminars, clinics, or fashion shows for visiting buyers to familiarize them with trends and what they should seek from vendors. Buyers also look at market-area retail advertisements and visit local stores. Out-of-town buyers try to get a feel for new merchandise and promotional techniques before visiting vendors.

Visits to Vendors

Visits to vendors are organized according to merchandise classifications and price lines. Buyers may first view better price lines to establish standards of fashion and quality to strive to match. They may then view the lower-priced lines to establish a range to work between. Styling, value, and knock-off comparisons can be made.

Vendors most often used by stores are visited early in the week, but generally no commitments for goods are made at that time. Major purchases will usually be spread among the key resources, since they are the most reliable and provide the most profitable goods for the store. The RBO will probably also recommend some new resources to visit if time permits. Conversations with executives of vendor firms, or trips to their plants and shipping rooms, provide additional information about the quality and supply of goods and the manufacturing capabilities of the firm. This is especially necessary for specification buying. Knowing the right

The Doneger Group

16-25 The first order of business after a retail buyer arrives in the market center should be to meet with the staff at the store's resident buying office for information needed before visiting vendors.

people in firms can also be advantageous for better terms or delivery dates.

Buyers are their stores' agents in dealing with vendors, which is an important responsibility. They must be ethical in their dealings, following store policies. They should try to develop good relationships for long-term mutual benefits. Good buyer-vendor relationships build long-term profit success.

Viewings of collections are booked in showrooms from early morning until the market closes at five or six o'clock. In the showrooms, a sales representative usually works with one retailer at a time. A showroom model may be available to try on merchandise at the buyer's request. Vendors provide buyers with order pads that list style numbers and often include sketches of the items. This helps buyers remember the fashions. Top designers might have fashion shows for groups of buyers.

Vendors hope that buyers will place orders before they leave their showrooms in case they change their minds later or see better lines to buy. However, buyers hardly ever make purchases when they first see the goods. They must try not to be overwhelmed with the wide number of choices and enthusiastic sales pitches. They should resist pressure and learn to say *no.* Buyers need to view and deliberate about the many lines of similar goods being offered by vendors. Then they can make wise choices for only the exact merchandise they planned to buy, 16-26.

With new advances in technology, computer design systems are being made available in showrooms. Vendors can customize designs for buyers while they wait. Computer printouts are made of the designs, enabling vendors to produce individualized story boards for various stores. This allows for immediate satisfaction of buyers' desires. Via Internet Web sites, buyers who do *not* go to market can peruse vendors' electronic catalogs that show digitized images of apparel, including the ability to rotate goods on the screen. (Some buyers who *do* go to market preview lines this way prior to visiting vendors.) After ordering, B2B Internet messages report on purchase order status, specifying real time manufacturing progress and delivery information. Retailers also know as soon as possible about delays, substitutions of goods, and incomplete shipments. This system helps to equalize the buying for small and medium-sized independent retailers, giving them the same selection and prices as large chains.

An even more revolutionary method uses virtual reality. Apparel lines are shown in three dimensions on

16-26 If a buyer has planned to order only certain styles and colors, that plan must be kept in mind while viewing the many other tempting fashions available in the market.

computer-generated models on runways with lighting, music, and even the rustling of fabric. Buyers can participate using computer terminals in their own offices, which have connections to a manufacturer's design system. Buyers view the garments and request changes on-line, facilitating a design dialogue without face-to-face contact or actual merchandise being produced. This results in minimal garment samples, plus more design originality. Printable orders follow on-line, making the dialogue complete.

Making Merchandise Decisions

After buyers have visited the showrooms of the various vendors, they are ready to make their merchandise decisions. They review their volumes of notes that contain item descriptions and their impressions about what they have seen. They organize the information and evaluate it. To *edit the line*, they prioritize the goods, with the best quality, fashion level, and price values for their buying plan listed first. They eliminate items that are not needed, are the wrong price, or are otherwise incorrect for the store's target customers. The remaining merchandise is rated, often with a simple system of checks, pluses, or other rating to determine the exact goods that they will purchase.

Buyers write the orders later in market week. Experienced buyers may ***leave paper***. That is the industry term for writing completed orders with vendors, usually during market week. Sometimes orders are left with the RBO, to combine with orders of other stores into quantity purchases that qualify for discounts and other special terms. Other buyers wait until they get back to their retail offices to write their orders. There they can check store sales records, merchandise on hand, and committed orders. Some buyers must get approval from higher management before submitting orders to vendors.

When all orders are ready to be placed with the selected vendors, they are compared with the buying plan. This ensures proper matching of classifications, price lines, units, dollars, colors, sizes, and other important factors. Buyers are responsible for the completeness, accuracy, and legibility of orders. They should not let vendors write the orders for them.

Prices of regular-line garments are firm, as stated on vendors' price sheets. However, negotiations between buyers and vendors are necessary for agreement on the terms of sale, delivery schedules, services to be included, and other options. ***Terms of sale*** are the conditions governing a sale, as set forth by the seller. These terms are fairly standard within the apparel industry. They include the following:

- any discounts allowed
- the payment period
- transportation arrangements
- date of delivery
- point of transfer of title to the merchandise
- allocation of transportation costs
- other specific conditions of the sale

Bargaining on price may be done in foreign buying or in some domestic situations, such as for job lots, irregulars, and closeout goods. Buyers who know the market conditions and understand production methods and costs are the most qualified to negotiate terms with vendors. Asking for unfair prices, discounts, or services does not help to build ongoing relationships with vendors.

Writing the Orders

A ***purchase order (PO)*** is a written document authorizing the manufacturer to deliver certain goods at specific prices and times. It is the paper or form with an identifiable PO number that finalizes the merchandise purchase from a vendor, 16-27. Most buyers use their own PO forms. When filled out at the store, each form may be faxed to the respective vendor to be reviewed and signed. When order forms are completed, with the terms and conditions of the transaction and signed by both parties, they become legally binding contracts. Buyers and vendors should both strive to meet the agreements as specified on the purchase order.

Older types of purchase orders are filled out by hand. Newer Quick Response orders are longer-termed, more open and flexible, and based on trust between electronically linked partners. Purchase order and invoice data are transmitted via telephone lines, with computer-to-computer interchange. Retailers' orders and vendors' invoices are in on-line files or in electronic mailboxes that can be accessed with codes.

Chicago Apparel Center

16-27 Buyers must make sure all purchase orders are filled in correctly and completely.

The ***completion date*** is the specified date when the goods are needed by the retailer. If the merchandise has not left the manufacturer by that date, the order is subject to cancellation. Most orders have a lead time of several months. The manufacturer can ask the retailer for an extension of time if the completion date cannot be met, but may lose the sale if the retailer does not agree to the extension. However, the retailer will not have the goods to sell at any time if the extension is rejected.

The term *as ready* denotes that the manufacturer promises to ship orders when they are completed, rather than by an exact date. This can lead to later controversy if goods are not received at the store for the optimum retail selling time. How firm or open the agreement is depends on the relationship between vendor and retailer.

Types of Orders

There are several different types of orders that buyers place. ***Regular orders*** are stock orders for line merchandise. They specify style numbers, quantities, delivery dates, sizes, and colors. ***Advance orders*** list the same specifics as regular orders, but have a longer lead time before the delivery date. Advance orders might be placed for specification goods that have style characteristics requested by a particular retailer. Foreign goods often need more time to complete or receive. There are also certain “long production goods,” such as men’s suits or ladies’ knits, that require longer planning and production time. Additionally, promotional goods for a special sale that is planned for November might be ordered with a key resource well in advance of the sale date.

Reorders are additional orders of the same merchandise as ordered previously. Reorders are used to replenish those items that have sold well. These orders also list full details, including style numbers, quantities, delivery dates, sizes, and colors. They are usually placed for immediate delivery to maintain current stock. ***Back orders*** are orders that have not been fully or even partially filled within the time specified due to a stockout. They are still in the vendor’s files to fill and have not been canceled by the retail buyer.

When a close relationship exists between a buyer and a producer, the buyer may send an ***open order*** to the manufacturer that does not detail styles or colors. The manufacturer fills and delivers what is deemed best for the retailer at the time. Open orders may also be sent to resident buyers who decide which vendors to use and what items to buy. Although open orders may be used to get new hot-sellers, it can be a dangerous practice for both retailers and manufacturers. Retailers can end up with different goods than expected, and manufacturers can lose favor and be pressured to take return goods.

Special orders are placed to satisfy individual customers’ requests. The customer’s name and an order number are attached for later identification. Sometimes special-purpose orders are placed to meet the requirements for window displays, fashion shows, or other special events.

Blanket orders are promises to buy from favored vendors over a period of time. Large companies imply this with Quick Response partnerships, and resident buying offices do this in anticipation of receiving orders from their client stores. There is no specification of colors, sizes, or shipment, all of which are ordered later against the total blanket amount. The retailer or RBO gives an estimate to the vendor of a needed amount for an entire season or year, which the vendor agrees to supply. Several partial orders with specific delivery dates are placed at various times to eventually complete the entire blanket order amount.

Approval buying is an arrangement in which merchandise is shipped to the retailer’s store for inspection before the final purchase decision is made. However, before the retailer can sell the goods, ownership must be secured.

After all buying is completed with purchase orders, buyers set up a schedule for checking on delivery of orders. This enables them to make sure that merchandise is received on time. Items that are not received may be canceled. Buyers also hold instructional merchandise meetings with selling departments as the new fashion items arrive at the store.

Summary

Retail orders are placed several months ahead of when they are needed to allow for production and promotion. Most buying activity is done in vendor showrooms during market weeks. There are many advantages of market weeks for both manufacturers and retail buyers besides the selling and buying of goods. Industry trade shows are smaller, more specialized market events held periodically in various regions of the country.

Apparel marts enable manufacturers and buyers to come together in one convenient location. The major domestic market centers are New York City, Los Angeles, and Dallas, the center of the southern apparel industry. Regional centers also include Chicago, Miami, Atlanta, and others that save retailers the time and expense of trips to distant centers.

Foreign markets offer retail buyers a wide variety of goods with different influence and design trends. Global sourcing is also done through U.S. importers, commissionaires, or foreign corporate buying offices.

Helpful buying resources, such as resident buying offices, act as advisers and sources of information and buying help for retailers. They are either independently owned fee offices or store-owned organizations. Buyers can also be assisted by merchandise brokers, reporting/consulting services, and traveling sales representatives.

Buyers must think like their customers when they go to market. Buyers must be well prepared and follow their buying plans and a sound strategy. Buying decisions are usually not made until after all merchandise has been evaluated.

Finally, purchase orders are negotiated, written, and signed. There are various options of delivery dates and types of orders. Follow-up assures timely receipt of the items.

To Know

procurement
market centers
market weeks
commissionaires
first cost
resident buying offices (RBOs)
leave paper
terms of sale
purchase order (PO)
completion date
regular orders
advance orders
reorders
back orders
open order
special orders
blanket orders
approval buying

To Review

1. Why is it important to manufacturers that retail buyers place their main orders for merchandise several months ahead of when they are needed by the store?
2. Why can retail buyers often get the lowest prices during market weeks?
3. Name three types of promotion or selling help manufacturers might provide buyers who attend market weeks.
4. Name two advantages of trade shows.
5. What type of retailers especially attend regional marts?
6. Who is admitted to mart market weeks?
7. What fashion market has more merchandise selection than any other?
8. List two advantages and two disadvantages of shopping the New York fashion market.
9. Why do vendors listen carefully to feedback about their lines from retail buyers during Dallas market weeks?
10. What is the simplest method to source internationally?
11. What are resident buying offices?
12. What three advantages does group buying offer?
13. Are small store buyers or large chain buyers likely to go to market more frequently?
14. How are commodity items usually ordered?
15. How can out-of-town buyers get a feel for new merchandise and promotional techniques before visiting vendors?
16. What effect does virtual reality selling and on-line buying have on garment samples and originality of design?
17. When editing the line, what items do retail buyers eliminate first?
18. List three terms of sale buyers and vendors negotiate.
19. What are four situations in which advance orders might be placed?
20. Why are open orders sometimes risky for both retailers and manufacturers?

To Do

1. Contact the regional apparel mart nearest you or another mart of interest to you. Request any available materials, including a market directory and/or promotional kits. Using the information received, write a report about the mart. Put the report and materials from the mart into a booklet to share with other students.
2. Make an appointment to meet with the buyer of an apparel shop. Before the interview, prepare a list of questions about where and how the shop's buying is done. Ask about market buying trips, buying foreign goods, helpful resources used, editing the line, writing the orders, and other questions that interest you. Present a report to the class.
3. Contact the sales office or nearby showroom of an apparel manufacturing firm. Ask the company to send you a press kit about its latest line, other information that is available to prospective buyers, and an order form that a buyer might use. Also ask what local stores in your area carry the firm's merchandise so you can look at some actual garments. Prepare an oral or written report that analyzes the information you have gathered.

4. To study this season's new merchandise and display techniques, view current advertising being done by major retail stores in your area. Visit the stores to observe how garments and outfits are combined, accessorized, and displayed. Notice any creative merchandising ideas. Make a bulletin board display that shows the latest trends in merchandising.
5. Contact a resident buying office near you or in New York City (corporate offices may be more responsive to students). Ask them to send as much information about their company and services as possible. Also do library and/or Internet research about resident buying offices. Organize the material and write a report.

PART 5

Strategies for Retail Success

CHAPTER 17

Communicating Information

After studying this chapter, you will be able to

- discuss internal business communicating.
- describe how the communication process works.
- explain nonverbal communication.
- summarize how human verbal communication skills are used in business.
- list basic communication aids and technologies for business.
- lead a discussion about communication technology advancement in the world of fashion marketing.

In business situations, *communication* might be defined as exchanging information for results. The ability to communicate may be the most important factor in a person's success in the workplace. Communication is also vital to the success of entire companies. Most business dealings rely heavily on the accurate exchange of information, 17-1.

Whether employees communicate only with other personnel within the company, or with people outside of the firm, all communications follow the same process. Some communicating is done nonverbally, but most is done using verbal skills. Communication technology has made information management easier, and advancements are improving the methods and speed of business communications.

Fashion Institute of Technology/John Senzer, Photographer

17-1 Explaining, showing, listening, and looking are all included in the important process of communicating information.

17-2 Employees of companies meet to discuss specific concerns, formulate business strategy, or view design ideas that have been developed on the computer.

Internal Business Communication

For businesses to operate smoothly, communication must take place between and among all employees. There are several important areas of internal communication for businesses. For instance, there are meetings with various groups of employees, 17-2. A weekly staff meeting might be held to discuss

Department of Consumer Studies; University of Delaware

17-3 Communication skills are studied and practiced in college courses that emphasize the importance of communications in the business world.

policy changes, evaluate recent sales results, and announce new merchandise and trends. The success of meetings is dependent on the ability of the participants to communicate with each other, 17-3. One-on-one communication is also vital for employees within a company. All reading, listening, speaking, and writing skills are used on a daily basis.

Lines of Authority

Internal communications generally follow specific ***lines of authority***, or levels of responsibility within the company's structure. Each level of responsibility may consist of one person or a group of people. Each group works to achieve the organization's objectives, with members having certain tasks to perform. The coordination of this differs with each company's organizational structure, and often changes over time.

In the early stages of a company's development, top-level managers and bottom-level employees work closely together. They may communicate with each other directly. As companies become larger and more complex, they go through organizational transformations in which workers have less contact with top managers. There are more defined levels of work and jobs become more specialized. More rules and policies are established and written down. As a result, communication becomes more standardized and formal.

An ***organization chart*** shows a company's official structure, indicating lines of authority. It is a visual representation of the organization's hierarchy, showing how employees are grouped and the lines of formal communication.

An organization chart is usually shaped like a pyramid, as shown in 17-4. Numerous lower-level employees report to supervisors, leading up to fewer middle managers, and finally to upper management and one top executive. Communication is expected to move officially through these levels, or "chain of command." Each level serves as the communication conduit between the levels above and below it.

Every company also has an informal organization, which is the network of interactions that are not part of the formal structure, but that influence how the

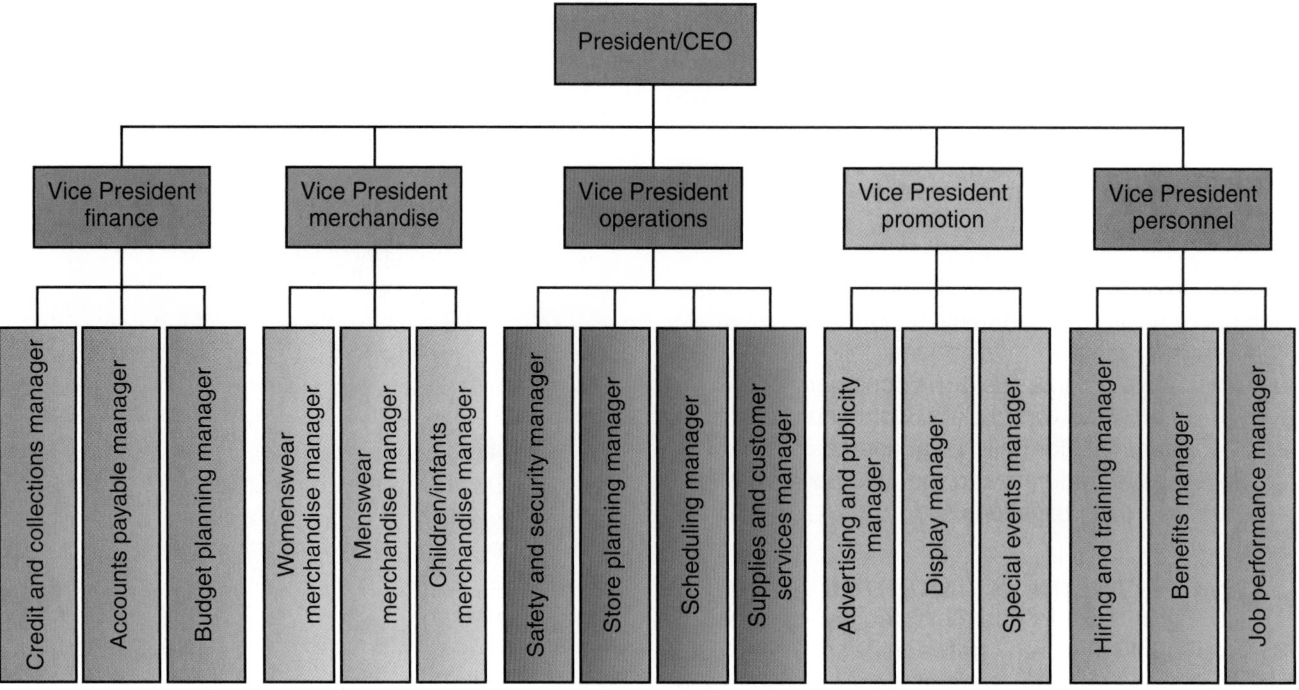

17-4 In a corporate organization chart, the chief executive is shown at the top with lines leading to lower levels of authority and responsibility.

Fashion Institute of Technology/John Senzer, Photographer

17-5 New fashion silhouettes, colors, textures, and other information must be communicated for profitable results in the marketplace.

organization accomplishes its goals. This involves knowledge of company operations because of longevity, even at lower job levels, and social relationships that develop on a personal level. These may be either beneficial or harmful in varying degrees.

The Communication Process

Communication of information is one of the primary resources for every business. It is crucial for competitive success. For effective communication, data must be turned into information that can be used to make decisions. ***Data*** consists of numbers, statistics, facts, and figures that may be meaningless without interpretation. When the data are processed, the result is ***information*** that is relevant, accurate, timely, and complete.

The best communication of information effectively conveys the right knowledge to the proper audience. In fashion marketing, it delivers the desired impact to others inside and outside the company, and to the target market. Fashion marketing involves an intense need for information, to constantly identify, digest, and react to new fashion ideas and market trends, 17-5. Electronic linkages have encouraged better and faster communications throughout the softgoods pipeline.

The ***communication process*** involves transmitting meaningful messages between parties that are clearly understood. The communication process always involves the same elements, which are illustrated in 17-6.

The two major parties in the communication process are the sender and the receiver. The *sender* of a message is the source, or the party sending the message to another party. The *receiver* is the destination of the message, shown at the other end of the illustration. The receiver might be a coworker, supplier, potential customer, or an entire target market. The receiver evaluates the message and the source of the message in terms of trustworthiness and credibility.

The potential for problems exists between the sender and receiver. Some problems arise from encoding and decoding. *Encoding* is the process of the sender putting thoughts into symbolic form, such as words, pictures, or hand gestures. It is how the source makes the message meaningful for the receiver. *Decoding* is the process by which the receiver assigns meaning to the symbols encoded by the sender. For instance, an advertiser attempts to send a particular fashion message in a TV ad. Consumers who watch TV receive and interpret the words, people, music, and apparel the ad contains. The receivers translate the message according to their attitudes and experiences. Consequently, senders and receivers need a common frame of reference, or mutual understanding, to communicate effectively.

The ***message media channel***, in the middle of the process, includes various approaches for transmitting the message. The message might be carried via face-to-face

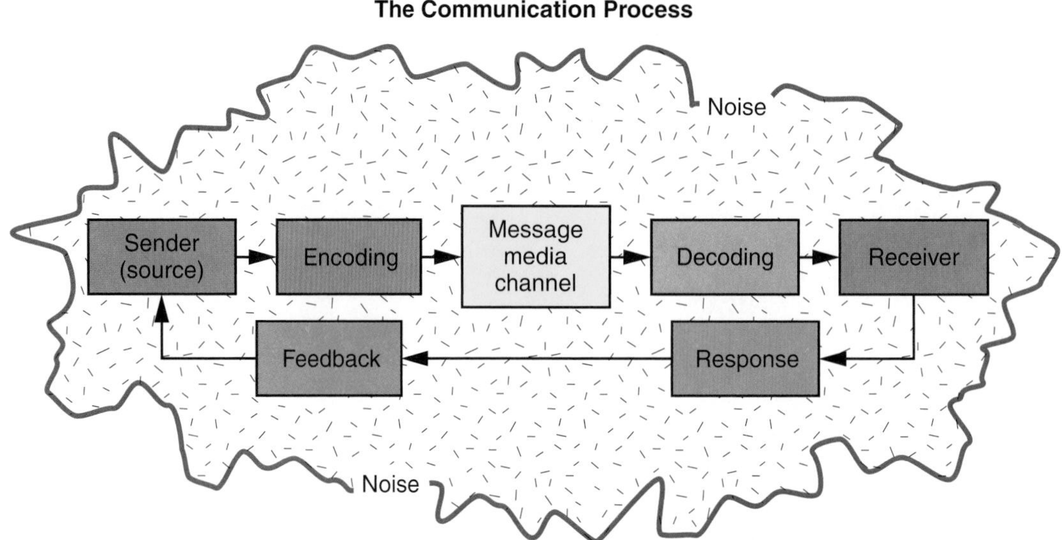

17-6 The communication process is indicated by the arrows and elements shown in this illustration.

conversation, business memo, electronic mail, telephone, newspaper, radio, or other medium. The receiver would probably attach more credibility and value to a product message described in a well-respected trade magazine article than from a high-pressure sales telemarketer.

Arrows going back toward the sender show response and feedback. *Response* includes the reactions of the receiver after being exposed to the message. *Feedback* is the part of the receiver's response communicated back to the sender. This returned information helps the sender judge how the message is being received and if the message needs to be changed.

In the message media channel, a salesperson might deliver the message personally, with voice and action. This face-to-face communication gives immediate response from the receiver and feedback to the sender. On the other hand, general advertising delivers messages impersonally. This only produces feedback after a period of time. The feedback is discovered through market research or sales figures. Whenever possible, clear, fast feedback is preferred.

"Noise" permeates all parts of the communication process, as depicted in 17-6. Noise is the unplanned static, distortion, or interference that occurs during the process that might result in the receiver getting a different message than the sender sent. It is comprised of any distraction that reduces the effectiveness of the correct message being received. It might be loud renovation construction work in a retail store when a salesperson and customer are trying to communicate about merchandise. At home, a family member might walk into the room while an ad is running on TV.

Those who communicate well know they must consider the audience they want to reach and what responses are desired. They try to create simple, relevant, and complete messages that take into account how the receivers will interpret the messages. They send messages through media that reach the target audience. They also develop response channels to get accurate feedback about their messages.

Nonverbal Communication

Communication can be nonverbal or verbal. ***Nonverbal communication*** is the sending and receiving of messages without using words. Nonverbal communication is most commonly sent and received through hand gestures, facial expressions, eye contact, and other body movements. *Body language* is the name given to communication through body movements. It can send many clear signals and messages, 17-7.

Pendleton Woolen Mills

17-7 Explain how self-assurance is communicated by the body language of this woman.

17-8 This store display in Saks Fifth Avenue in New York City communicates the upscale image and fashion leadership of that retailer.

People's appearance is a way of communicating nonverbally. In the fashion industry, it is especially important to be well groomed and to wear appropriate clothing. Fashion marketers send positive visual messages by being neat, clean, and well dressed.

Nonverbal communication can also be effective through such media as pictures, drawings, flags, musical instruments, and other nonword signals. Retail window displays and in-store floor displays are a means of nonverbal communication, 17-8. Many business presentations use slides or charts to reinforce spoken words. Nonverbal and verbal forms of communication are very effective when used together.

Verbal Communication Skills

Verbal communication involves the use of words. Verbal skills include reading, listening, speaking, and writing. These skills also relate to effective telephone and computer use. A conscious effort should be made to learn, practice, and improve all of these skills in order to communicate more effectively. All of these skills are needed to be successful in the fashion field.

Reading Skills

Reading skills are very important to do fashion marketing and other jobs effectively. In work situations, people are expected to read and understand many types of printed materials. Memos, letters, instructions, requests, reports, books, newspapers, trade publications, and other written information must be read and understood.

Good reading skills can enable people to organize their thoughts and analyze problems, 17-9. Understanding and interpreting what they read helps people determine the best actions to take. As people read, their general knowledge and vocabulary also increase.

By improving your reading skills, you will be able to read faster and remember more of the content of the material. To do this, you should "read with a purpose." Know why you are reading something so you can focus on the information you really need. Look over the material first to decide how to read it. Then read it quickly if you only need the main ideas. You may just read the first paragraph, main headings, and last paragraph. If you must "digest" the content or remember detailed information, read more slowly and go over important parts more than once. To retain the information, think about or mentally visualize the main ideas after reading each section.

To improve your vocabulary, look up any words in the dictionary that you do not know. Reinforce these meanings by noticing how the words are used in the sentences you are reading. Also, businesses and industries have their own special vocabularies to describe products or operations, which may need to be explained by coworkers. These words and phrases are used in technical or job-related materials and should be understood. They make communication among employees more efficient.

Department of Consumer Studies; University of Delaware

17-9 Being able to read instructions and other information is necessary to accomplish tasks throughout the textile/apparel pipeline.

Listening Skills

For communication to take place, receivers of messages must open their minds to consciously understand messages that are being sent. Many words that ears hear are "tuned out" or not remembered because the mind interprets them to be unimportant. Sometimes messages are not understood because different meanings are transmitted by the speaker's voice inflection or body language. Correct interpretation of these factors is also involved in listening.

For effective listening, people must pay attention to the speaker and stay focused on what is being said with genuine interest and concentration, 17-10. Patience is often needed to listen quietly and thoughtfully rather

17-10 When listening to someone speak, look at the speaker and try to understand everything that is being said.

than interrupting the speaker or taking over the speaking role. The speaker's background, experiences, or point of view should be respected as points or opinions are being expressed. Also, details should be clarified if not understood.

Active listening is recommended in business settings where communication is important. ***Active listening*** is the process of giving the speaker some type of feedback that indicates the message is being received and understood. A nod, a smile, or direct eye contact offers nonverbal feedback. The feedback may be a short verbal response such as saying *yes*. In addition, the listener may ask further questions to probe more deeply and clarify confusing points. This helps the participants respond effectively to all issues under discussion.

Open-ended questions bring the most information. ***Open-ended questions*** require multiple-word answers, rather than merely a *yes* or *no*. Examples of open-ended and closed-end questions are shown in 17-11. Retail salespeople who use open-ended questions with their customers can draw out valuable information from them. At the same time, they are showing that they are genuinely interested in learning what their customers really want. Understanding and sensitivity are also created between the two parties which, in turn, establish credibility and trust.

Speaking Skills

The way people speak has a large influence on their personal and professional lives. Speaking skills are used in one-to-one conversations, group situations, and presentations to large audiences. For most people, the speaking situation becomes less comfortable as the receiving group becomes larger, 17-12. In all cases, speaking clearly helps individuals express their thoughts and ideas to others. People's quality of speech influences the impressions others form of them and how effectively they communicate.

Contrasting Types of Questions

Closed-end Questions	Open-ended Questions
Do you like this shirt?	Why do you like this shirt?
Do you like to shop here?	Where do you like to shop?
Do you like this color?	What colors do you like?
Is this length okay?	What length do you prefer?
Are you happy with this pin?	Why do you like this pin?

17-11 Closed-end questions, which can be answered with a yes or no, do not provide much useful information. For better communication, use open-ended questions.

In cooperation with The Fashion Association

17-12 This retail fashion director addressing the press seems comfortable speaking to a large group.

Fashion employees must often present ideas verbally to groups of customers or coworkers. Sometimes they must make sales presentations to buyers, give media interviews, conduct training sessions for retail sales staffs, or moderate fashion shows. The ability to speak in front of a group is easier when the speaker knows the topic well and has prepared for the presentation.

When preparing a speech, these suggestions might help. Decide on the main items to be discussed. Organize these points in a logical order into the outline of the talk. Experts say that effective speakers first tell the audience the main topics of the upcoming talk. To catch their attention, a funny story or personal experience might be used to lead into the subject. Next, they go through the actual content they have prepared. In closing, speakers summarize the main points they have made.

Visual aids are instructional display items that are used to enhance a presentation. They are especially important in the fashion industry, which depends on communicating the subtleties of design and new trends. When making presentations, visual aids can greatly increase the understanding of what is being discussed because information in pictorial form is often easier to grasp, 17-13. Many illustrations, charts, graphs, maps, diagrams, and 3-dimensional models are used to reinforce points made in presentations.

Newer computers often come with "graphics packages" that can be used to easily create visual aids, often in color. ***Computer graphics*** refer to computer-generated drawings and designs. Also, CAD systems

Sensormatic

17-13 The concept of a retail anti-theft tag can be explained much easier with the visual aids of a graphic chart and an actual garment than with only words.

can print out designs that have been developed on them. This information is often put onto slides or transparencies. Some computer systems allow graphics to be projected directly onto a screen for large-group presentations. Information included on graphics and visual aids should be clear and well organized. Often major headings are shown in large type as "bullet statements."

When planning a speech or presentation, keep your listeners in mind. Be aware of their situations or feelings, carefully phrasing your ideas. This shows that you respect your audience, and it helps to gain their full attention. Practice giving your speech. This will increase your self-confidence and reduce your reliance on notes. Time your speech to make sure it is not too long. Also, plan to dress appropriately for the group to whom you will be speaking.

When delivering your speech, speak slowly and distinctly. Project your voice so everyone can hear you clearly. Use proper grammar and words the receivers can understand rather than trying to impress them with long cumbersome words. Being brief and to-the-point is most effective. Also, try to sound upbeat and positive, using a pleasant tone of voice. Make eye contact with your listeners. To obtain feedback on whether or not your messages are being received accurately, ask your listeners what they think about what you have said.

Writing Skills

Writing skills are needed to transfer information to others, such as giving directions or sending messages. Writing memos, progress reports, policy statements, job descriptions, and computer messages are common ways to communicate within the company. At the same time, written communication is essential to present the organization to the outside world through letters, faxes, press releases, sales brochures, advertisements, and annual reports. It is important to be able to compose coherent correspondence, directions, descriptions, and explanations that are geared to the appropriate audience.

Writing skills include the ability to spell correctly and use proper grammar. They also involve knowledge of sentence structure and paragraph formation. Successful business people work to improve their writing by proofreading what they have written. They look for errors in spelling, sentence construction, how ideas are explained, and overall organization. This is followed by revising the work to correct the mistakes. A dictionary or computer "spell check" program should be used to check spelling. A language reference book may be needed to check grammar and punctuation. Written work should be simple, clear, and adhere to the conventions of standard English.

Business Letters

Business letters should be brief, clear, and thorough. Every business letter should contain certain standard parts, 17-14. The following are the eight parts of a business letter:

- *Return address or printed letterhead* of the person or company where the letter originates. A letterhead displays the company logo and lists the company name, address, phone and fax numbers, and Web site or e-mail address.
- *Date* that the letter is written.
- *Inside address*, which is the complete name, business title, and address of the person to whom the letter is written. This is the same address that will appear on the envelope.
- *Salutation*, or beginning greeting, such as "Dear Ms. Smith" or "Dear Bob," depending on how well the receiver is known by the sender. If you do not know the name of the person who is to receive the letter, use "Dear Sir or Madam," "Dear Fashion Professional," or other descriptive and polite salutation. This is followed by a colon (:).
- *Body content* of the letter contains the full message being sent.
- *Complimentary close*, or sign-off, such as "Sincerely" or "Yours truly," followed by a comma (,).

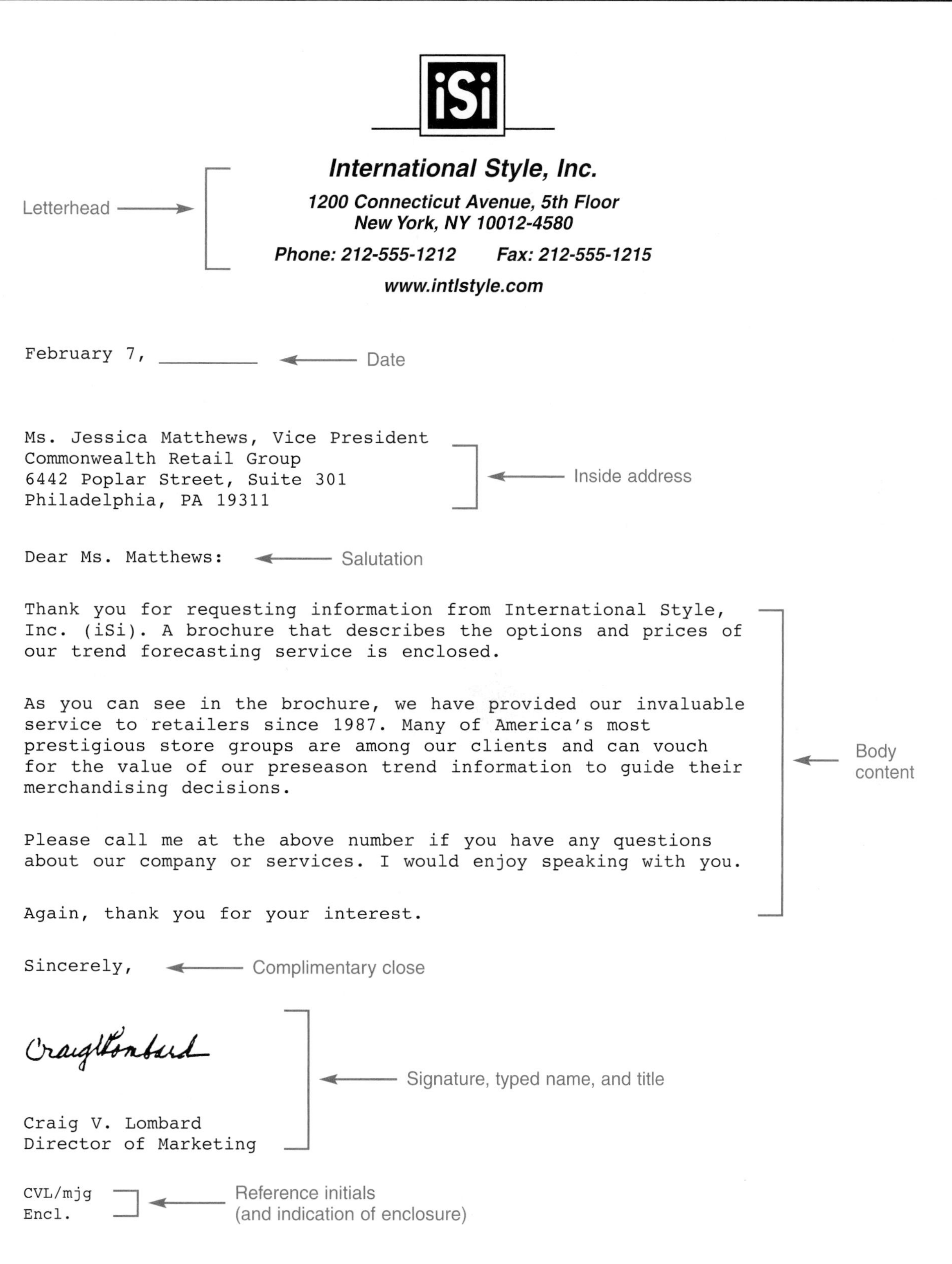

International Style, Inc.
1200 Connecticut Avenue, 5th Floor
New York, NY 10012-4580
Phone: 212-555-1212 Fax: 212-555-1215
www.intlstyle.com

February 7, ________

Ms. Jessica Matthews, Vice President
Commonwealth Retail Group
6442 Poplar Street, Suite 301
Philadelphia, PA 19311

Dear Ms. Matthews:

Thank you for requesting information from International Style, Inc. (iSi). A brochure that describes the options and prices of our trend forecasting service is enclosed.

As you can see in the brochure, we have provided our invaluable service to retailers since 1987. Many of America's most prestigious store groups are among our clients and can vouch for the value of our preseason trend information to guide their merchandising decisions.

Please call me at the above number if you have any questions about our company or services. I would enjoy speaking with you.

Again, thank you for your interest.

Sincerely,

Craig V. Lombard
Director of Marketing

CVL/mjg
Encl.

17-14 Business letters have certain parts that should be presented in a standard form.

- *Signature*, followed by *typed name and title of sender.*
- *Reference initials* if the letter was typed by someone other than the person who wrote it. The writer's initials are usually capitals, followed by the typist's initials in lowercase letters. The two sets of initials are divided by a slash (/) or colon (:). As more people write their letters on computers, reference initials are being used less often.

If you find it hard to start a business letter, first make an outline of the ideas, facts, or order of events to be communicated. Write about the most important topic first and the least important last. Thank-you letters, which should be sent as soon as possible after a favor or event has taken place, should tell why you are thanking the person and why it was appreciated. If you are requesting information, explain your needs and when the information is required. Thank the party in advance for any help they might provide. When responding to a request, start by thanking the person for requesting the information, provide the information, and close the letter by stating that you were happy to help.

A copy should be kept of any letter sent. If written on a computer, the letter can be stored on a disk or in the computer's hard drive. Commonly used letters can also be stored and customized as needed.

Business Memos

Business memos are used to send messages to people within a company. A ***memorandum***, or ***memo***, is an informal written message from one person or department to another person, group, or department in the same company. Memos are easier to write than letters because they tend to be short and deal with only one subject. Often they are written on a company form, which may be a part of the computer word processing system. Memo forms have areas to fill in the date, to, from, subject, and body of the message. A sample memo format is shown in 17-15.

Business Reports

Business reports usually present results of studies, new ideas, information about situations, or problems that need action. They are most often written to help with decision making and can be either formal or informal.

Formal reports analyze complex issues, often resulting in lengthy presentations. They start with a cover, title page (listing title, authors, and date), and table of contents. The title is a brief description of the topic of the report. The next page is an "executive summary" that gives a synopsis of the report's content, including any conclusions reached. It is written after the report is finished, but is inserted before the body of the report in the final presentation. Then the report has a short introduction that briefly states the subject,

International Style, Inc.

Inter-Office Memorandum

Date:

To: (Name(s) to whom it is being sent)

From: (Name(s) from whom it is being sent)

Re: ("Reference" or subject of the memo)

C: (Names of people who should receive a copy)

The body of the message would be filled in here . . .

17-15 This memo is within the company's computer software, so the person writing it only has to fill in the proper spaces, add the body of the message, and print it.

research methods used, and nature of the content. The body of the report usually includes graphs, tables, and illustrations to explain certain points. Finally, an analysis of the situation by the author, giving practical and specific recommendations is included. A bibliography and appendices with data, notes, and sources conclude the formal report.

Informal reports are shorter and may be typed on specially printed company forms. Several types of report forms are often included in computer software programs. Examples of informal reports are sales reports, work progress reports, market research reports, and records of business calls.

Telephone Use

Telephone use is one of the fastest and most effective ways to communicate in business, 17-16. How employees answer the phone, help callers, and call other people influences the impressions others form of the employees and their company. Telephone manners are important. Words and tone of voice should convey friendliness, sincerity, and interest in the caller. Companies often have written telephone guidelines for employees.

When the phone rings, it should be answered within the first three rings, if possible. A pleasant "good morning" or "good afternoon" is usually followed with the name of the company. Hold the phone about one inch from your lips and speak directly into it. Speak clearly and distinctly, never chewing food or gum. Always be courteous to the caller, even if it is a wrong number.

Full attention should be paid to the caller. A message pad and pen should be kept close to the phone to write down messages. Each message should include

- the date and time of the call,
- who the message is for,
- who the message is from,
- the caller's telephone number and extension, and
- the message.

After writing the message, it is best to review it with the caller to make sure the information is correct. If you are not sure how to spell a person's name or company, ask the caller. Close by thanking the person for calling. When messages are left for you, always return phone calls as soon as possible.

Telephone orders for merchandise, along with credit card information, must also be written accurately. Customers should always be thanked for their business. Expressing appreciation will encourage them to continue doing business with your company.

When calling others, plan your call in advance and have all the needed facts in front of you. Know what you want to say and how you want to say it so your call can be brief and concise. State your name, the name of your company, and why you are calling. Allow the other person to ask questions and repeat information. At the end of the conversation, thank the other person for his or her assistance or cooperation.

Computer Skills

It is essential to have well-developed computer skills in today's business world. You have learned that CAD, CAM, and CIM systems are used in designing and manufacturing. Computer systems are important in speeding product development, 17-17. Computers keep track of production and inventory, providing immediate knowledge about the availability of items. They process customer orders for vendors and quickly activate distribution and shipping.

At the retail level, computers indicate percentage markups for pricing and markdowns on sale items.

17-16 Business people rely on the telephone as a primary means of communication.

Prima Vision Design System by CADTEX

17-17 After a product is designed using the computer, a paper "hard copy" can be printed to show the results of the computer design work.

Scanning systems record point-of-sale statistics, providing communication feedback from consumers to the fashion industry. Specific software can keep tabs on customers' accounts and instantly check a customer's credit through electronic hookups. Computers generate billing statements each month showing the accounts payable, detecting overdue accounts, and automatically figuring interest charges. They also help with management decisions by processing data into usable information.

Many firms today have personal computers (PCs) for each of their employees, allowing many communications to take place electronically. This has become possible because costs of computer systems are lower, the systems are easier to use, and more people are now "computer literate" (know how to use computers). More jobs are available for people who have computer skills. Fewer jobs will be available in the future for people who do not have these skills.

Employee use of computers allows for greater productivity. A higher quality of work is being accomplished. Correspondence, buying plans, and other business documents are now produced more efficiently. There is better efficiency, with lower costs per unit of work being done, because work is composed directly at the computer. Support staffs are not needed for these functions, thus lowering processing costs. The work is more accurate because it is entered by the originator, rather than a data-entry person who may not understand the information passed along from someone else. This gives workers more control and reduces the size of organizations, with fewer levels of employees.

Telecommunication is the transfer of information from computer to computer using telephone lines. Telecommunication is allowing more people to work out of their homes. In *telecommuting*, a computer terminal in the home is connected through a modem and phone lines with the company computer system or another network. A ***computer network*** is an interconnection of computing equipment using data communications circuitry. Information within a network can be accessed at a company, in the home, or from other sources connected to the network.

Technology for Information Management

Information traveled slowly in the past, which also resulted in slower fashion movement. Today, however, advances in communication technology spread ideas and business transactions rapidly. So many facts and figures are transmitted that there is an explosion of information. The abundance of fashion merchandising data is a result of more powerful computers, automated capture of SKUs, and customer-tracking programs. Almost everyone in the pipeline has communication overload!

All fashion businesses communicate information internally within the company. They also communicate externally with suppliers, the financial community, customers, competitors, government, labor, the local community, and stockholders. Every business has a great deal of interaction with others and can react quickly to market needs. Fast responses occur for placing retail orders or reorders, taking markdowns, and spotting trends.

Information Management

Good information management can give a company a competitive advantage—an edge over other companies in meeting customers' needs. Information management is comprised of the activities that generate an orderly and timely flow of relevant information to support business activities. It is done with productivity-enhancing tools, such as computer systems. *Information technology (IT)* departments in corporations and independent IT consultants specialize in management information systems, e-commerce, and strategic technology directions for firms, 17-18.

Communication technologies are constantly being developed. "Office automation" was originally directed at secretarial and clerical activities. Now it is used at all levels of operations to help make business communications more effective and efficient and provide a better basis for decision making. Such automation supplements the traditional interpersonal communications of face-to-face meetings, telephone conversations, and notes jotted on memo pads. These technologies include electronic communication techniques and other communication aids.

Lands' End Direct Merchants

17-18 Information technology employees support the activities of all other functions of a business with top computer knowledge and skills.

Electronic Communication via Computer Technology

There are more and more electronic communication techniques used in business today, and more are being developed all of the time. The most common ones currently in use include word processing, desktop publishing, spreadsheets, electronic mail, electronic calendaring, and on-line services.

Word Processing

Word processing is the entering, editing, storing, and printing of words using a computer. A computer system is used to generate documents, replacing the old method of typing on a typewriter. It combines computer hardware and word processing software as a unit. The material typed at a keyboard is shown on the computer screen. Errors are easily corrected, 17-19. Changes can be made to the material, such as adding and deleting words, moving sentences or paragraphs around, and adjusting margins and spacing, before it is printed onto paper.

Word processors can check spelling, provide help with word meanings, and sometimes even correct grammar. Some software is designed to incorporate the contents of a database (stored facts, figures, addresses, etc.) into written documents. On command, the work is automatically printed, saved for the future, or otherwise processed. Word processing contributes to more effective and efficient written communications.

Desktop Publishing

Going beyond basic word processing, *desktop publishing* uses computers to create, edit, and produce documents that are of a similar quality to that produced by typesetters. The attractive, professional appearance of the documents adds to their communication effectiveness.

17-19 Word processing is the writing and editing of text on a computer and printing the document when completed.

For desktop publishing, copy is entered at a keyboard and arranged on the computer screen as it will appear on paper. The computer system can be used to create and insert colored charts, graphs, symbols, borders, unusual page layouts, and text in various sizes and letter styles. Photographs and logos can be put into the system with special scanning equipment. When the user is satisfied with each page as it appears on the computer screen, it is printed using a high-quality printer. Sometimes the computer disk containing the document is taken to an outside printing company for use with the printer's equipment if a more professional-looking product is desired.

Desktop publishing is convenient and easy to use. It uses one system for the entire publishing process from creation to printing. The user can see what the finished pages will look like before they are printed. Newsletters, business reports, and office publications are often prepared this way.

Spreadsheets

Spreadsheets are financial management programs that can be used for financial planning, analysis, and reporting. Numbers are entered and automatically placed in rows (across) and columns (up and down). Examples are ledger sheets on which a company's financial statements or sales reports are written. An advantage of spreadsheets is their power to project changes in a financial situation based on a set of numbers. Certain mathematical expressions exist in the software or can be entered as desired. This allows the user to see how a change in input data can affect the end result. When one number is changed, all the other numbers in the spreadsheet are automatically adjusted according to the mathematical formula established. For instance, in a spreadsheet of department store sales, the updating of a single department's figures can automatically change the total sales for the company, percentage of total company sales for that department, and future sales forecast.

Spreadsheets are often used to experiment with various scenarios of events to help in making business decisions. For instance, a retailer might consider spending an increased amount of money on advertising, which is anticipated to bring in extra sales. When the anticipated expenditure is entered into the computer, numbers in the rows and columns change according to predetermined formulas. These figures can then be analyzed to help make the decision as to whether to run the advertising or not.

Electronic Mail

Electronic mail, often called ***e-mail***, is a method of sending and receiving messages using networked computers, telecommunication software, and modems.

An e-mail message is typed at a computer terminal and then transmitted to an electronic mailbox, or several mailboxes on a distribution list.

An *electronic mailbox* is a computer holding file where messages are held until they are retrieved at the convenience of recipients by entering their personal passwords. Other people's electronic mailboxes cannot be accessed. If a message needs to be sent to a group of people, it can be placed on an electronic bulletin board that everyone can access. Though messages can be efficiently distributed in this manner, the "tone" of the message may be missing with this form of impersonal communication.

For businesses, e-mail requires a fairly low investment in comparison to the benefits received. It increases employee productivity and is convenient for contacting people who are difficult to reach by telephone. If employees have computers at home that are connected to the company's network, they may read and answer their e-mail messages in the evening. When employees are traveling, they may take a laptop computer and routinely check their e-mail messages.

E-mail systems are also capable of sending documents from one company to another. Examples include forecasts, purchase orders, production schedules, shipping information, and POS data. To complement QR/EDI partnering, the industry is trying to get as many trading partners as possible onto compatible e-mail network systems. Day-to-day business can be transacted between sales offices, manufacturing plants, distribution centers, and branches of retail companies. Communications, such as technical guidelines or policy information, can flow to everyone at the same time. For example, using an electronic bulletin board, a retailer might post a message for any trading partners who want to respond.

Electronic Calendaring

Electronic calendaring uses a networked computer to store and retrieve employees' appointment calendars. The computer can be programmed so only certain people can review the calendar and enter appointments using a keyboard terminal. To schedule a meeting involving several people, the software can check each person's calendar and pick a mutually convenient time. Some people like this system because it eliminates the time spent setting up appointments and meetings. Others dislike it because they feel they are not in control of their personal schedules and lose some of their privacy.

On-Line Services

On-line services use a computer to present material on the screen and print it on a printer, if desired. An ***on-line service*** is an interactive electronic system in which data and graphics are transmitted from a computer network, over telephone lines, onto a subscriber's computer screen. There are a number of commercially available services that enable subscribers to access any information from the many categories offered. Users are able to get encyclopedia information, stock market quotes, or airline flight availabilities. They are also able to take part in interactive "real-time" discussions by joining a forum or "chat room" and typing in comments and responses to other users.

On-line services also typically provide users with access to the Internet (a global network connecting millions of computers that all work together to share information). The Internet enables the World Wide Web (WWW) to exist. The Internet and individual Web sites are accessed through Internet service providers by paying a monthly or annual service fee.

Individual locations of the WWW (Web sites) have specially formatted "pages" of information that might be presented in words on the screen, still or moving pictures, and even sound. These pages, which may be sponsored by an organization, a university, or a commercial firm, are known as *Web sites.* The basic location or first page of a Web site is called a *home page.* Text on these pages will typically include highlighted words (called "links") that allow the user to access related information by "clicking" on them with a computer mouse. This feature makes the World Wide Web a very useful tool for research and information-gathering.

The interactive capabilities of on-line services provide many opportunities for business. For example, apparel merchandisers can put their merchandise on-line, similar to catalog sales, so consumers can use their home computers to comparison shop and make purchases. It is predicted that this technology will be a major mail-order sales medium to private homes. Most mail-order and traditional store retailers now have Web sites, 17-20.

Other Communication Aids

There are many other communication aids that also contribute to the efficiency and effectiveness of business operations. Some of these are voice mail, automated conferencing, and facsimile transmission.

Voice Mail

Voice mail uses recording devices to accept telephone messages from callers when the recipient is not available to answer the phone. The inflection in the voice can be transmitted, rather than just the words as in written messages. A computer can also be used if it features voice mailboxes that can store audio messages in digital form and then convert them back to audio form upon retrieval.

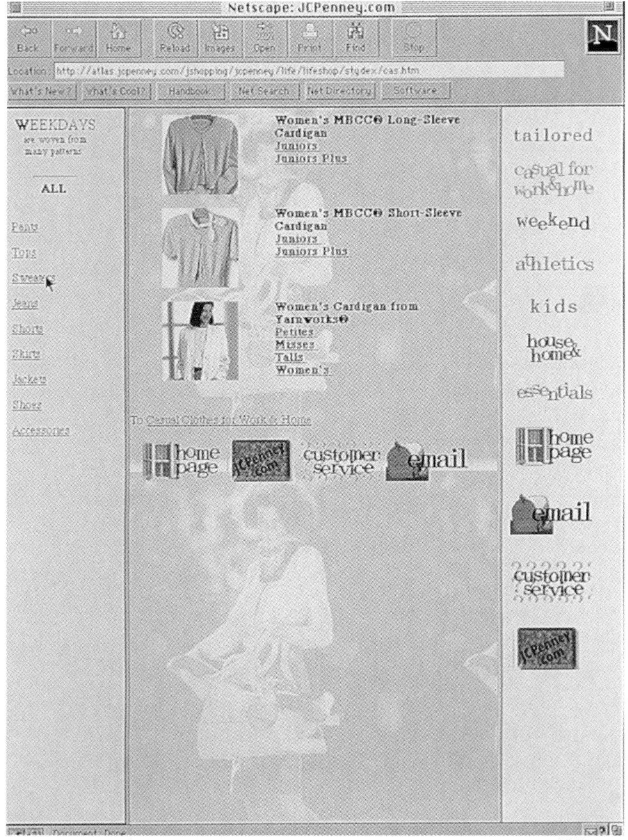

JCPenney

17-20 This "menu" enables the user to choose to see a variety of JCPenney merchandise items, to communicate with the company's Customer Service Department, or to leave an e-mail message.

Automated Conferencing

Automated conferencing, also called teleconferencing, allows for simultaneous communication between people who are in different locations. It saves the time and expense of traveling to other locations for meetings. It increases the number of people who can participate in decision making, allowing for better information and agreement on decisions. Problem-solving can be done by exchanging information and coordinating activities as a group. Automated conferencing also improves turnaround time for design and other decisions, thus also improves turnaround time for design decisions, thus satisfying customer needs promptly. Conferencing can incorporate audio, video, computer, or all three mediums.

- *Audio conferencing*, or "conference calling," allows more than two people to participate in telephone conversations. Many firms have private, high-quality audio communication circuits between sites that can be activated with the flip of a switch.
- *Video conferencing* is done with television equipment to send and receive audio and video signals. People can both hear and see others in various locations as a conference is conducted. This allows some face-to-face communications, but it is an expensive method of communicating. Large firms may have their own video conference set-ups, or rental arrangements can be made through some telephone companies and large hotel chains.
- *Computer conferencing* uses a networked computer system to allow people to exchange information. It is similar to electronic mail, but the information exchange is confined to a well-defined group. This is often used with a large number of participants who may not all be on-line at the same time, but who add their input at their convenience.

Facsimile Transmission

Facsimile transmission, commonly called ***fax***, uses special equipment to electronically transmit visual images. The sending fax machine encodes a document image at one end of a communication channel (usually a telephone line). The receiving fax machine decodes it at the other end and prints a copy of the original image. Some computers have fax boards that can be activated to send or receive faxes. However, most faxes are sent through special machines that only send and receive faxes, 17-21.

This communication method sends documents quickly and easily, regardless of the geographic location. Anything that can be photocopied can be transmitted by fax. It has become a popular means of transmitting messages and business documents. Most computer software for businesses contains a fax form that is automatically printed after information has been entered by the sender. An example is shown in 17-22. Faxes are also popular with people who work from their homes.

17-21 A written message can be sent or received immediately using a fax machine.

Facsimile Cover Sheet

To:	Jessica Matthews
Company:	Commonwealth Retail Group
Phone:	215-555-2830
Fax:	215-555-2840
From:	Craig Lombard
Company:	International Style, Inc.
Phone:	212-555-1212
Fax:	212-555-1215
Date:	2/10/(year)
Pages including this cover page:	2

Re: ("Reference" or subject of the fax message)

Comments:
Per our telephone conversation today, here is a copy of a page from our most recent monthly bulletin. You can see how timely the information is for retail merchandise planning . . .

(content of message continues here)

Thanks for your interest in our valuable service.

17-22 A fax form built-in to the computer software enables employees to quickly fill in the necessary spaces, add a message, and print the document to send through the fax machine.

Communication Technology Advancement

Changes in the communications field are fueling competition in the time-based fashion industry. Everything is speeding up, and those businesses that can respond the fastest are the winners. To gain success, a company needs to be networked through telecommunications. With constant improvements in computer technologies, the costs will continue to drop. Also, the number of units of information being transmitted will increase dramatically. There will be a common set of international communications standards that will enable all computers and telecommunications systems to "talk" to each other. This will speed the implementation of technology worldwide.

Communication technologies in the fashion pipeline have expanded the industry's "information loop." More people are involved in the decision-making process because they can readily access the needed information and add their input. In the "paperless environment" of computer communications, the flow of information is becoming smoother with fewer errors. Additionally, information is on hand when it is needed.

The ability to respond to sales by placing a reorder, taking a markdown, and spotting trends all occur at a much faster pace for today's fashion retailers. Fast, accurate communications enable more timely merchandise decisions to be made. Instead of tracking weekly sales at the style level, as was laboriously done years ago, retailers can now accurately track daily sales at the SKU level. Companies that have not invested in the needed technology to do this find it difficult to compete.

As a result of communication technology, business people can make better and faster decisions, but they also have more data than needed. A tremendous amount of detailed data is available, much of which can get in the way unless it is converted into meaningful information, 17-23. Thus, new systems are being developed that can analyze and summarize large masses of data to identify what is important.

Business managers are using computer systems to help implement their business plans in running their companies. This can be done using either prepackaged or customized software programs. Information is organized to achieve company goals, such as to carry specific stock quantities or to improve turnover. By coordinating data with business objectives, the information is helpful rather than confusing.

A key question for upper management is how to weigh the company's investment in technology with its return in higher creativity, increased productivity, and better planning and control of merchandise. Studies have shown that expenditures on communication technology are cost-justified, yielding a competitive advantage to those companies that make the investment. Even though it is hard to put a dollar value on the benefits, successful companies aggressively seek out new technologies. With the speed of technological change, they feel it is critical to stay up-to-date. Also, as more computer-trained employees enter fashion-related industries, the importance of advanced systems for business functions will increase.

Artificial intelligence (AI) is when computer systems simulate human thought and reasoning. They display behavior that would be regarded as intelligent if it were observed in humans. AI involves both "expert" and "neural" systems. Expert systems must be set up by an industry expert to go through specific processes. Neural systems learn internally from previous activities. *Neural computing* involves such activities as perception, learning, automatic programming, and problem solving. Such a system can go through a speedy trial and error procedure that finally takes it through the right path to the correct solution, learning as it goes.

17-23 Spreadsheets filled with data must be translated into meaningful information.

In retailing, neural computing is expected to become important in target marketing, credit applications, and recognizing patterns of credit card fraud. For sales forecasting, it compares former forecasts to actual results, continuing to learn, adjust, and become more accurate. It can predict sales that will result from specific promotional activities, determine the optimal SKU mix for a store, or calculate markdowns that will enable a certain amount of inventory to be sold by a certain date.

Summary

Business communication involves the exchange of information for results. Internal business communicating is done through lines of authority as well as informally. In the communication process, the sender encodes a message and transmits it via a media channel to a receiver who decodes it. The receiver's response gives feedback to the source, and all of this takes place among interfering noise.

Nonverbal communication is done in many ways, including body language, personal appearance, pictures, and other non-word signals. Verbal communication skills include reading, listening, speaking, and writing. Good reading skills can enable people to organize their thoughts, analyze problems, and increase their general knowledge and vocabulary. Listening includes paying attention and concentrating to consciously understand messages that are sent. Speaking skills are used in individual conversations, group situations, or presentations to large audiences. Writing skills are used in business letters, memos, reports, and other messages. All of these skills combine into effective telephone and computer use.

New technology for information management is constantly being developed. Electronic communication techniques include word processing, desktop publishing, spreadsheets, electronic mail, electronic calendaring, and on-line services. Other communication aids are voice mail, automated conferencing, and facsimile transmission.

Communication technology is fueling time-based fashion industry competition. Costs are decreasing, and the number of units of information transmitted is increasing. Communication technologies expand the information loop, reduce errors, and allow for faster decision making. Problems are data overload and evaluating the company's investment in technology versus its return.

To Know

lines of authority
organization chart
data
information
communication process
message media channel
nonverbal communication
verbal communication
active listening
open-ended questions
visual aids
computer graphics
memorandum (memo)
telecommunication
computer network
information management
word processing
electronic mail (e-mail)
on-line service
facsimile transmission (fax)
artificial intelligence (AI)

To Review

1. As companies become larger and more complex, what happens to their internal communication?
2. What does an organization chart show?
3. Explain the relationship between data and information.
4. Describe response and feedback in the communication process.
5. What is body language?
6. Describe the reading procedure that can be used if you quickly need only the main ideas in written material.
7. Give your own example of an open-ended question that you might use with a customer if you were a salesperson.
8. List at least three situations in which fashion employees must verbally present ideas to customers or coworkers.
9. If you find it hard to start writing a business letter, what should you do?
10. What types of subjects do business reports usually present?
11. In telephone use, what three attributes should a person's words and tone of voice convey?
12. Why has it become possible for most firms to now have personal computers for their employees?
13. List at least six types of groups that fashion businesses might communicate with externally.
14. What is information management?
15. When one number is changed in a spreadsheet, what happens to other numbers in its rows and columns?
16. What kinds of documents might be sent between companies on an e-mail system?
17. How can on-line services benefit apparel retailers?
18. Describe the main advantages of automated conferencing.
19. How have communication technologies in the fashion pipeline expanded the industry's information loop?
20. What are at least five ways that neural computing is expected to become important in retailing?

To Do

1. Select a magazine advertisement and explain how it uses the communication process. What messages do you think might have been sent and received? How were any messages encoded and how might various receivers decode them? What types of noise could distort the messages? What types of responses would give feedback to the source?
2. To illustrate nonverbal communication, do the following:
   - Without talking, have the class guess a "pictionary" phrase by drawing a set of pictures on the blackboard or a chart pad.
   - Act out a charades message, given to you by the teacher, for the class to guess.
3. To illustrate verbal communication, do the following:
   - Describe a fashion outfit to your classmates, including colors and accessories, without using any visual aids, hand motions, or other body language. Have your classmates sketch and color the outfit you described. Post the sketches for comparisons.
   - As a follow-up, discuss how body language and visual aids can work together to make a verbal message clearer and more meaningful.
4. Prepare a short speech on the subject of communication technology in the world of fashion marketing.
5. Review the communication aids and technologies described in this chapter. Select one technology application and write a short business report that analyzes why it would or would not be good for use in a home fashion consulting business. Include all parts of a business report (an objective analysis, recommendations, and bibliography).

CHAPTER 18

Concepts for Successful Selling

After studying this chapter, you will be able to

- describe all aspects of the direct selling function.
- explain how to create a selling environment with stock preparation and merchandise knowledge.
- demonstrate the selling steps.
- explain how to perform various types of merchandise sales transactions.

You have learned that merchandising involves planning, buying, and selling, as shown in 18-1. The planning and buying functions have been studied. The selling function has two different aspects—indirect selling and direct selling. Both should increase sales and promote the image of the store.

Indirect selling is general promotion to the public, such as advertising, publicity, and special events. It will be discussed in the next unit. ***Direct selling,*** often called *personal selling,* is the exchange of merchandise to individual consumers in return for money or credit. It is based on personal communication, with both the salesperson and consumer sending and receiving information during the process. Face-to-face, personalized interaction takes place between the customer and salesperson. Direct selling is the subject of this chapter.

The Functions of Merchandising

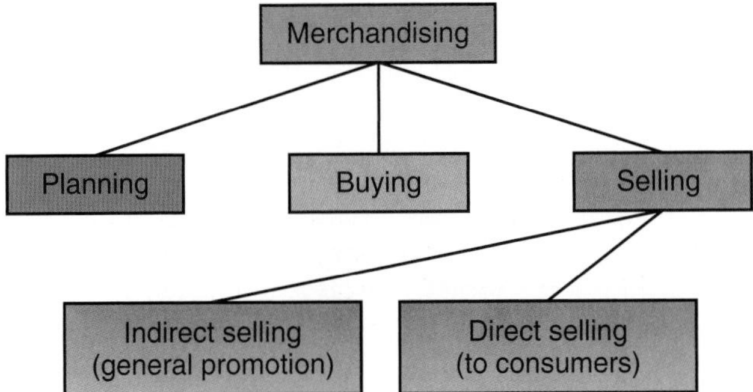

18-1 The selling function of merchandising is done in two different ways: as general promotion to the public and personally to individual consumers.

The Direct Selling Function

Fashion retailing is a people business. To customers, the salespeople *are* the store. They represent the store by developing relationships with the customers. Sales personnel are the only people with whom customers have contact. The caliber of the selling staff is an important way that stores can differentiate themselves from other stores and gain a competitive edge, 18-2.

Successful salespeople know how to help their company and its customers. Good selling skills give mutual benefit to both seller and buyer. The retailer benefits from higher sales and greater profits while the buyer benefits from better service. Happy customers are likely to return for future purchases, and they spread the word to others about the store and its products. Word-of-mouth endorsements are the best form of advertising for any firm, and repeat business with the same customers is an essential element for success.

A good balance of the right number and kind of salespeople is important for retail success because salespeople's salaries comprise one of the largest operating expenses. If a firm has too *few* salespeople, some important selling tasks may not be done properly or at all. Having too *many* salespeople wastes money. Store managers and personnel directors must work together to decide how many salespeople are

18-2 When the sales staff is helpful to customers and appreciative of their patronage, a store can shine above its competition.

needed at various times to meet demand. They must establish guidelines for selecting salespeople, as well as training, supervising, and motivating the sales staff.

Good personal selling can set stores apart from the competition and bring them success. Good service is especially the hallmark of upscale retailers, as well as retail firms with smart management. Customers say there is no replacement for a salesperson's extra effort to find a particular item or to express a sincere thank you, 18-3.

Salesclerks Versus Sales Associates

Almost all retail sales work is responsive selling. ***Responsive selling*** is done in response to the customer's presence in the store, rather than going out to find customers, as is done in some other industries. This form of selling is done by salesclerks and sales associates.

Salesclerks usually only facilitate routine sales transactions. They are said to be "order takers" since they stand behind a counter to ring up sales, 18-4. They are generally employed by stores with lower-priced merchandise. Salesclerks usually receive lower pay, and are given little training beyond the basics of operating a checkout terminal. This may leave them less qualified to help customers solve problems.

Sales associates use more formal or creative selling skills. They are considered to be "order getters." High-service retailers, such as department and specialty stores, employ and train more professional sales associates. These employees have the

Sears

18-3 Well-trained salespeople are always pleasant with their customers and thank them after they make purchases.

18-4 Order-taking salesclerks have an important job of making correct transactions, but do not help customers select merchandise.

knowledge and skills needed to attract customers into the store and help them find merchandise that meets their needs, 18-5.

Not only must good sales help be found, but sales employees must be properly trained and rewarded for good performance. Some stores post signs or run classified advertisements to find sales help. Some large retailers have kiosks in their stores, used to recruit shoppers to be salespeople by applying via computer on-the-spot. Others use recruiting firms to find and pre-screen job candidates. These pre-hiring specialists know the laws and procedures of the hiring process, and can more easily check each job applicant's education, previous employment, record of theft or criminal activity, etc. Employee retention has also been improved, with trained sales personnel staying longer with companies.

Some retail companies have tried to lower their operating costs by reducing their number of sales employees and cutting back on formal sales training for employees. This has caused the direct selling function to deteriorate in these stores. This practice is generally associated with discount stores, but it can happen in any store that is not profitable.

Customer-Oriented Selling

Customers are happy when they feel salespeople care about them and are doing their best to fulfill their needs, rather than just "pushing" the store's products on them. The slick, high-pressure sales-oriented approach of the past has been replaced with a customer-oriented sales approach. It involves making customers feel important, identifying their needs, and finding the best solutions. It assumes that customer needs provide sales opportunities, that customers appreciate helpful suggestions, and that customers will be loyal to salespeople and stores that have their interests at heart, 18-6.

Consumers like salespeople who have credibility, honesty, problem-solving capabilities, and product knowledge. Stores also like their employees to display self-confidence, leadership, and stress tolerance. Store policy, hiring, and training should encourage these positive selling attributes.

It is up to sales management to be sure that salespeople know what their job duties are and how to perform them. A written job description is essential. Training new sales personnel can be a challenge since

Talbots/AEON Group

18-5 The sales associates employed by Talbots and other high-service retailers are trained to answer questions that customers might ask about their merchandise needs.

In Cooperation with The 410 Shoppe

18-6 Customer-oriented selling tries to meet the needs of each individual customer rather than selling items to people whether they need them or not.

people are hired with different backgrounds, skills, and abilities. Some trainees are hired with no knowledge of the company or its products, and little knowledge of selling. Others may come with lots of experience, but also some bad habits developed elsewhere. Still others may have good selling skills, but need to know more about the store's customers. Ongoing training brings success.

The National Retail Federation has released voluntary, industry-based skill standards for retail sales associates. They were developed in conjunction with leading government, education, and training representatives. The new standards are designed to help prepare workers for sales floor success, as well as reducing turnover and trimming training costs. The standards cover a broad area of duties and tasks of sales associates, including

- customer service
- selling and promoting products
- monitoring inventory
- maintaining the appearance of the department or store
- protecting company assets
- working as part of a department or store team

Sales Goals and Rewards

Some salespeople will do their best without any special urging from management. They enjoy people, like the products they sell, and consider selling to be a fascinating job, 18-7. They are ambitious self-starters. However, the selling job can also involve frustration when dealing with difficult customers. Thus, salespeople often need special encouragement to work at their highest levels.

For high-service retailers to hire and motivate quality salespeople, the company must offer attractive compensation. ***Compensation*** is payment and benefits for work accomplished. The level of compensation should be at the "going rate" for the same job elsewhere. To pay less than the going rate will attract too few quality salespeople; to pay much more is unnecessary. Management can also boost morale and performance through a good organizational climate, realistic sales quotas, and positive incentives.

The ***organizational climate*** describes the feeling that employees have about their opportunities, value, and rewards for good performance. Some companies treat salespeople as if they are unimportant to the success of the business. If salespeople are held in low

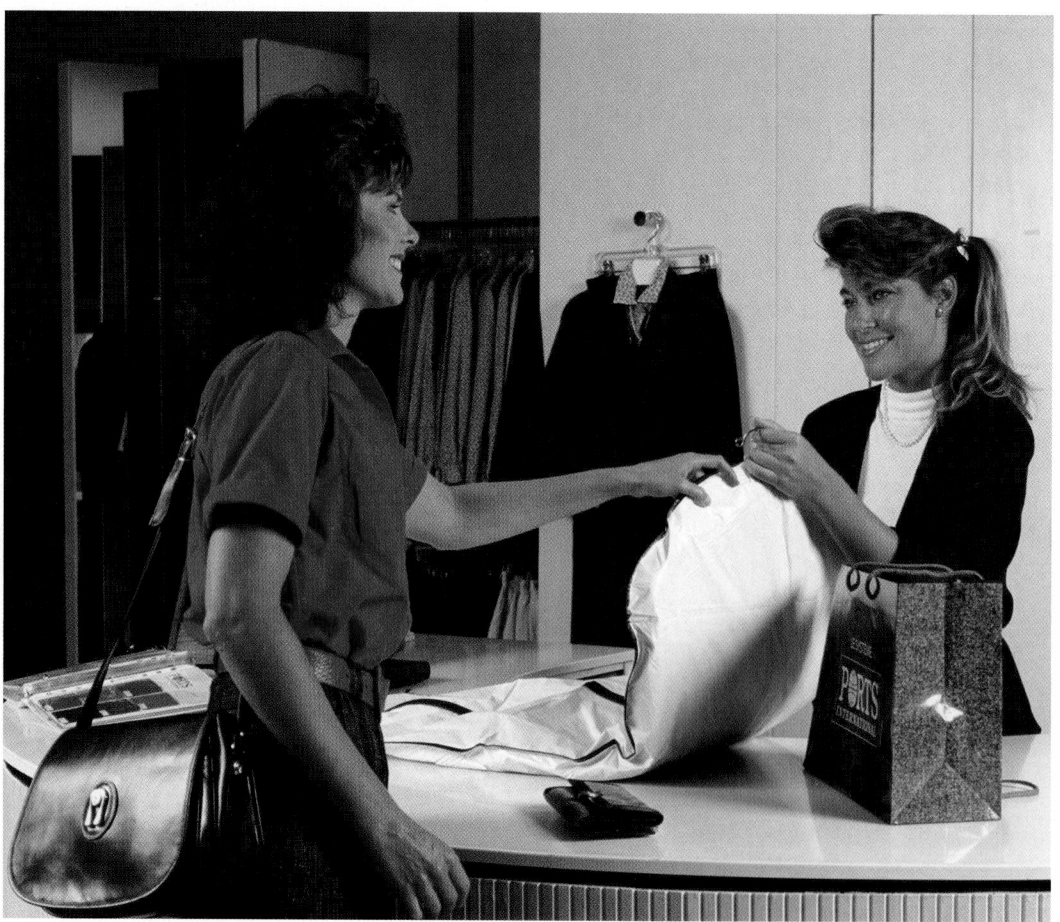

18-7 Many people enjoy selling fashion merchandise, have the perfect personality and drive to succeed, and would not want to do any other type of work.

esteem, there is usually a higher turnover rate (more people quit and have to be replaced) and poorer job performance. Other companies treat their salespeople with high esteem, creating little turnover and top performance. The company's attitude toward its salespeople affects their behavior.

Sales quotas are projected volumes of sales (units or dollars) assigned to a selling department or person for a certain time period. Employee compensation is often tied to how well salespeople meet these quotas, which indicate successful sales efforts. Sales quotas are intended to encourage salespeople to do their best.

Incentives are also used to stimulate salespeople to achieve higher sales. Greater effort is encouraged because a prize or reward is offered as an incentive. Sales contests sometimes spur a better selling effort. Incentives might also include honors, merchandise and cash bonus awards, days off, trips, and profit-sharing opportunities.

Pay incentives are often used to reward good sales results. Commission-based pay does this automatically. A ***commission*** is payment based on a percentage of the dollar amount of sales made by a salesperson. For instance, a 30 percent commission would be payment to the employee of $30 for every $100 dollars of merchandise sold by that employee. Often a low hourly wage is combined with a small commission. This assures an income to the employee, but enables a higher amount to be earned with higher sales.

Another incentive used by some retail companies is to base the hourly pay on sales productivity during the previous 12-month period. For instance, sales associates who have averaged $100 per hour in sales may be paid $6 per hour, while those who have averaged $300 per hour in sales are paid $18 an hour. This also encourages successful salespeople to stay with the company for a long time.

Some retailers hold daily or weekly sales meetings to encourage better sales. In the meetings, information is shared about new merchandise and special events and promotions. Also during these meetings, recognition is given to those sales associates who have achieved the store's highest dollar sales and the highest units per transaction for the previous day or week. They might receive a congratulatory compliment, certificate, or bonus.

Managers may also tie rewards to customer service, recognizing salespeople who go out of their way to help customers. Excellent selling should be rewarded and poor-quality service corrected in order to prosper in these competitive times. To revive or maintain good personal selling in stores, trained salespeople must hone their skills with daily practice. Managers should visit the sales floor to observe sales associates so their skills can be appropriately recognized. Encouraging employee satisfaction can motivate salespeople to take responsibility for making decisions that will keep customers coming back.

Creating a Selling Environment

In a retail organization, besides serving customers, salespeople also have duties concerned with handling merchandise. Some merchandise activities must precede the direct selling steps. Many involve *stockkeeping,* which includes receiving, preparing, protecting against damage or theft, and controlling the merchandise before it is sold. These tasks are often done by salespeople. Other activities that lead to successful selling include keeping the selling floor in order and gaining merchandise knowledge.

Stockkeeping Duties

Once the goods are purchased, they must be received at the store, checked, marked, and prepared for sale, 18-8. *Receiving* is the actual exchange of goods between the vendor's transporting agent and the retailer. Merchandise is usually received by truck at the rear of the store, where it is also inspected for possible shipping damages. Shipments are then verified as being correct as ordered, with the right styles, fabrics, sizes, colors, qualities, and quantities. If all is as ordered, the shipment is recorded, or "logged in," and invoices are authorized for payment.

Receiving and preparing goods for sale also involves transferring items between branches of a multi-store company and handling returns. In large retail companies, with many stores in a geographic region,

Tandem Computers

18-8 Retail salespeople often have some stockkeeping duties in preparing goods for sale.

Weber Marking Systems

18-9 Labeling software is available for most computer systems, which allows retail employees to write and print labels using on-site printers.

an item might be available in one store but desired by a customer in a different store. In that case, the item is sent (transferred) to the other store. ***Returns to vendors (RTV)*** are goods that are shipped back to a supplier by a store. Returns may result from errors in filling the order, unacceptable substitutions, late delivery, defective merchandise, or other breaches of the contract. Before making the return, the store should contact the vendor to discuss return arrangements.

Sales tickets may need to be added to some merchandise. Tickets are printed with appropriate store system bar codes, as well as information for shoppers to read, such as price and size, 18-9. After the tickets are attached, the garments are properly folded or placed on hangers. Often they must be steamed to remove wrinkles after being unpacked, 18-10. They are then distributed to the appropriate departments that will sell them.

Keeping the Selling Floor in Order

Part of fashion selling is presenting the goods effectively to customers so they will want to buy the items. Consumers respond best to a convenient and attractive display of goods, 18-11. The presentation of items in the store should also educate consumers about ways to

In Cooperation with The 410 Shoppe

18-10 Before putting items on the retail floor for sale, they should be made to look their best.

18-11 When merchandise is clearly displayed and items are easily accessible to customers, more sales will be made.

wear or combine articles of clothing. Retailers can show how to put together and accessorize an outfit, creating consumer demand for the merchandise.

Basic department stocking of merchandise is usually done by salespeople, 18-12. This includes the following tasks:

- putting out goods to maintain stock levels
- sorting and arranging by color, size, and/or classification
- using appropriate hangers or shelf arrangements
- straightening merchandise during hours of low traffic
- setting up and cleaning merchandise selling fixtures

When not doing direct selling with customers, salespeople should use their initiative to see what tasks need to be done in their department or store. Although these duties are important in retailing, they should not receive more attention than helping customers. The customers' needs should always come first.

For some products, such as health and beauty aids, rack jobbers take care of the merchandise displayed in a section of the store. ***Rack jobbers*** are wholesalers that sell specialized goods, especially through self-service retailers. They provide, set up, and maintain the fixtures for their product lines. They mark their own prices and stock their inventory, which the store then sells. Rack jobber companies are paid only for goods sold, with a percentage going to the retailer.

Gaining Merchandise Knowledge

Before effective selling can take place, salespeople must also learn about the special features of the items they sell. Constant updating is necessary to know what new merchandise has been received, what items are on sale, what items have been relocated, and what store procedures have changed.

With direct selling, the salesperson has the opportunity to emphasize the advantages of merchandise. Salespeople must be able to answer customers' questions and discuss the merits and costs of goods, 18-13.

Symbol Technologies

18-12 While salespeople do stockkeeping duties, they are still available to help customers find the items they are seeking.

Kmart

18-13 Salespeople should not only know the colors in which various shirts are offered, but might also have to answer questions about required care.

With complete product knowledge, the sales message can be modified to meet the specific needs and circumstances of each shopper. Salespeople have an opportunity to overcome objections that customers have about merchandise by showing the attributes of goods and answering questions. Even when a sale does not result, the salesperson has formed a relationship that will likely bring the shopper back to the store in the future. Nothing can take the place of developing and maintaining personal relationships with customers.

Understanding Labels, Hangtags, and Packaging

Merchandise knowledge includes understanding sizing, which was explained in Chapter 14. Additionally, required information on labels, hangtags, and packaging should be understood.

Labels are small pieces of ribbon or cloth that contain printed information. They are permanently attached to the inside of garments where they do not show during wear, such as at the back neckline or side seam of shirts, blouses, and dresses. Labels are usually at the center back waistband of skirts and slacks. On suits, jackets, and coats, they may be on the inside pocket at chest level or on the front facing below the waistline. Labels may be any color or style as long as they do not ravel. The information may be on both sides of the label if the label is attached to the garment so it can be turned over. Sometimes label information is stamped onto shirttails or neckbands with indelible ink, or glued or fused onto fabrics.

Certain label information is required by law, 18-14. A garment label must state the generic name of all fibers used in the garment and the percentage of each fiber used. The label must identify the producer or distributor, and name the item's country of origin. A label must also be included that describes the care requirements to maintain the appearance of the garment. Other information, not required by law, may include the fabric construction, special finishes, performance standards, and brand name.

Garment Label Information Required by Law

Fiber content	Generic names of fibers in the item
Percentages of fibers	Listed in order by weight from most to least
Identity of responsible part	Registered number of producer or distributor (RN)
Country of origin	Where item was assembled
Permanent care requirements	Clear/complete instructions and warnings about care/maintenance

18-14 The items listed in this chart are required by law to appear on all labels. Label information helps consumers decide what merchandise to buy.

Hangtags are removable "signs" that are attached to the outside of garments with strings, plastic bands, pins, staples, or adhesives. They are made of heavy paper or cardboard, and often hang from buttons, buttonholes, zippers, belt loops, or underarm seams, 18-15.

Hangtags are not required by law and are meant to be removed before garments are worn. They are a form of advertising or promotion to help sell products. In general, hangtags tell consumers what manufacturers want them to know about their products. Although some information from inside labels may be repeated on hangtags, the content may include any of the following:

- brand name/trademark
- size
- suggested retail price
- style number
- special features, such as fabric finishes, reinforced pockets, adjustable button cuffs, reversibility, etc.
- symbols and logos to identify designers, manufacturers, or sellers
- a certification or seal of approval, telling of good test results from a lab
- guarantees of replacement or refund of money if items do not perform satisfactorily

Packaging is the covering, wrapper, or container in which some items are placed. Usually, much of the information that is on a garment's inside label is repeated on the outside of the package. If information

18-15 Hangtags can provide useful information that customers can read and salespeople can use as helpful background for selling the goods.

that is required by law on labels cannot be seen through the packaging, it must be repeated on the package so consumers can read it before purchasing the item.

Salespeople with knowledge of textiles and apparel can help their customers to understand the information on labels, hangtags, and packaging. Fibers, yarns, fabrics, finishes, and design elements/principles were discussed in Chapters 6 through 8. By understanding the characteristics of certain fibers or design features, salespeople should be able to instruct consumers about how garments will look, wear, and clean.

Using the Selling Steps Effectively

With the merchandise arranged and knowledge of products complete, the selling steps can be accomplished. To achieve effective selling, salespeople must show that they like people. They should also display a desire to help people as efficiently as possible. Customers must not go unhelped or leave angry because they were rudely treated!

People who sell fashion should wear what is being sold. They should be recognizable to customers with a name badge, special smock, or other identification, 18-16. Showing courtesy and attention to customers includes avoiding distracting mannerisms, such as making remarks to other salespeople, biting fingernails,

In Cooperation with Kmart

18-16 Successful retailers, who want customers to know who they can go to for assistance, identify their employees in specific ways.

The Selling Steps
1. Approach and greeting
2. Classifying customers
3. Presentation of merchandise
4. Overcoming objections
5. Closing the sale
6. Supplementary suggestions
7. Maintaining relationships

18-17 If these selling steps are followed, satisfied customers will return again, allowing the selling steps to be repeated.

or staring at customers. Straight posture and friendly body language indicate interest and sales assurance.

In other types of sales jobs, salespeople *prospect*, or search for customers who have the willingness to buy and the ability to pay for the company's products. They learn how to spot good prospects and turn them into customers. However, most retailing involves only responsive selling. The selling steps are shown in 18-17. Each step depends on the success of preceding steps.

Approach and Greeting

Salespeople must meet and greet customers to get the relationship off to a good start. It is sometimes hard to approach shoppers who are strangers, probably because of fear of rejection when brushed off by the potential customer. Some salespeople lack the skills to accomplish the approach and greeting process successfully. However, all shoppers should be acknowledged and approached. The approach and greeting are critical to establish a relationship that enables the selling process to proceed.

Approaching customers includes getting their attention and recognizing them as an important guest in the store. Some stores ask their salespeople to introduce themselves to customers and to shake their hands, if appropriate. Merely asking from afar "May I help you?" usually gets the response, "No thanks, I'm just looking." The salesperson has implied that the customer looks lost or bewildered. Also, the salesperson has quickly gained and lost the customer's attention, and has missed an opportunity to establish a productive relationship.

The initial hello or personal introduction might be followed by a question or statement that is related to the situation. The easiest is to refer to a piece of merchandise the customer might be handling. The greeting should also provide some information that is not obvious to the shopper, such as the wrinkle-free qualities of the cotton shirt being considered. The point is to let the shopper know that he or she has been noticed and is important, and that the salesperson has information and assistance to offer.

Some retailers suggest that their salespeople use a compliment or a conversational greeting that links them to the customer and puts the customer at ease. To keep a compliment or conversation on track, the subject might be a color the customer is wearing that looks especially good (that is also a favorite of the salesperson) or the school mentioned on the T-shirt the customer is wearing (which the salesperson's nephew also attends). This comfortable chatting relaxes defenses and establishes common ground. However, it must be sincere—not obviously contrived.

Some stores have a policy of greeting every customer within 30 feet of the salesperson within 30 seconds or less. If this is not done carefully, it can seem as if an overeager salesperson is trying to force a sale immediately or to get the customer out of the way. Asking fast questions while pushing merchandise toward them will put customers on alert rather than at ease. It will then be difficult to establish the desired rapport.

The approach and greeting is not intended to result in an immediate sale, but to get the customer to agree to see and hear more about the merchandise. An effective salesperson uses an easygoing style that makes the customer feel comfortable and proceeds at the customer's pace.

Classifying Customers

The greeting might be followed by some key questions to learn more about the customer's needs. Some customers want no assistance until they have made a selection. Others need and want a great deal of help. Most shoppers fall somewhere between these two extremes.

Casual lookers might simply be browsing or killing time while waiting for a ride or meeting a friend. These customers may just want to see what kind of merchandise the store stocks. Being left alone after a cheerful greeting will encourage this type of customer to return in the future.

Undecided customers may need an item for personal use or for a gift. More time might need to be spent with these shoppers. They are interested in hearing pertinent information and getting ideas. They look at labels, care instructions, and other printed materials. Salespeople should display patience with customers who are evaluating the choices.

Decided customers should be helped efficiently. They know exactly what they want and why. They prefer to quickly make their purchases and be on their way. Extra conversation about superficial subjects might aggravate these shoppers.

Classifying customers should be coordinated with buying motives (studied in Chapter 13). Every customer falls between the extremes of rational behavior (based on conscious reasoning) and emotional behavior (based on feelings). Also, product motives, based on loyalty to certain brands, and patronage motives, which bring consumers back to the store, should be determined. Successful selling approaches evolve according to these factors.

To classify customers, good salespeople use open-ended questions. These encourage customers to do most of the talking while the salesperson listens and thinks about possible solutions. Customers' wants, needs, likes, and dislikes are best determined through active listening. Open-ended questions may confirm what the salesperson already knows, draw out new information, and get at underlying customer attitudes.

There will always be some customers who are in a bad mood, and may be abrupt with salespersons. The salesperson's natural tendency is to return that attitude. However, a negative response only makes the salesperson feel worse and reduces the chance of getting a sale. Thus, successful salespeople face such encounters as challenges. They try to stay friendly and pleasant, and do everything possible to make customers happy. This does not always work, but salespeople who try this will be successful more often than those who return the anger.

Presentation of Merchandise

For a successful merchandise presentation, the customer should be actively involved. A salesperson can then adjust the presentation according to the customer's feedback. Since each customer's needs are different, each presentation should be tailored to the individual person and the in-store circumstances at the time. Such presentations make customers feel they've been assisted rather than convinced to buy an item.

Good presentations include an explanation of ***product features***, or physical characteristics of items, 18-18. Consumers don't buy products, they buy the benefits and solutions that product features provide. Therefore, salespeople should try to discover the combined benefits/solutions customers are seeking. Benefits and solutions include such things as comfort, saving money or time, safety, ease of care, higher social status, or sex appeal. Certain product features can provide these benefits and solutions. For instance, someone who has limited cash needs value-priced items; a person who dislikes ironing needs wrinkle-free slacks; and a customer whose waist and hips are two different sizes needs an elasticized waistband. Salespeople must translate the many varied features of mass-produced products into the few personalized customer benefits and solutions being sought.

A salesperson should ask the customer about the benefits he or she seeks from a product. The salesperson

Mega Sports

18-18 Some products, such as athletic footwear, require salespeople to have more knowledge in order to help customers make their selections.

can then provide information that arouses the customer's interest. The salesperson might recommend particular garments that satisfy the customer's needs. Getting the customer to touch or try on the merchandise is important. Above all, the shopping experience should be made enjoyable for the customer.

As a salesperson, you should try to present the advantages of goods based on the customer's needs. This reduces any perceived risk in making the purchase. Mention the strongest benefit first in order to build interest. For impulse buyers, that may be all that is needed. For hesitant customers, one very strong benefit might be saved for the end of the presentation. While the benefits of certain features may be obvious to salespeople, customers often need help to make the connection.

Customers may understand their general wants and needs, but require help in satisfying them. They may know that they need shoes, but must be helped with size, color, style, price, and other variables. These many small decisions require salespeople to be both knowledgeable and creative.

Interaction of salespeople with customers moves sales toward completion. Salespeople should have comfortable eye contact with customers. Generally, salespeople should look toward the product when telling about features and reestablish eye contact when presenting benefits and solutions.

Sometimes customers want to be left alone to ponder the purchase decision. In that case, salespeople should do other things, but be available in case they are needed. They can re-approach the customer later if necessary. If and when the consumer indicates the merchandise choice is a good one, the salesperson should be available to close the sale.

Overcoming Objections

Customers who do not buy merchandise immediately after the sales presentation often have spoken or unspoken objections to certain aspects of the products. These objections can be logical or psychological. They might relate to the product, price, store, timing, or salesperson. They might occur at any point in the presentation, or they may surface if the salesperson tries to close the sale.

Objections are a natural part of the selling process. They give the customer time to think and evaluate the alternatives. The customer can also ask for more information or clarification about the product. In fact, shoppers who are silent are the more challenging customers. Salespeople must guess what their objections might be. For the salesperson, spoken objections indicate where to go next in recommending solutions or to slow down the sales pace.

Salespeople should use a positive approach when handling objections. They should try to seek out hidden objections or ask customers to clarify their objections. This is an opportunity to provide more information. Salespeople should strive to turn the objections into reasons for buying. If not handled well, objections can be stumbling blocks to making sales.

Experienced salespeople learn to expect certain types of objections about products and try to prevent them. If objections must be dealt with, salespeople should handle them tactfully and clearly.

Closing the Sale

Closing the sale refers to getting a commitment from the customer to buy the merchandise. Asking for the sale is designed to get action as a result of the previous steps. It should not seem like the salesperson is manipulating the customer, or that this is the end of the customer-salesperson relationship. It can be hard for the salesperson to know when and how to seek a commitment. Getting a commitment is a learned skill, resulting from training and experience.

Some salespeople dislike this phase of the selling process because they fear rejection if the customer decides not to buy the product. Even though salespeople are told not to take rejection personally, negative decisions seem personal and may be hard to accept. Fear of rejection can be so strong that some salespeople omit this step, and they lose sales because they did not ask the customer to finalize the purchase.

A ***trial confirmation*** can be used to get an indication of what needs to be done to close the sale. For instance, a question might be asked to see if the product's benefits and solutions are understood. Another approach is to offer the customer several options and note the response. Also, the salesperson should mention if the item is on a one-day sale or is the last one in stock, if that is truly the case. Salespeople must learn to adapt to individual customers and selling circumstances.

A customer's decision about a large purchase, such as an expensive winter coat, might result in a long silence while the customer weighs the pros and cons. The silence may seem endless to the salesperson, but the longer the silence, the more likely the sale will take place. Inexperienced salespeople often interrupt the silence, causing them to lose the sale. Silence places pressure on the shopper to commit to the purchase, and the salesperson should let it continue.

At the right time, the salesperson may suggest that the customer make the purchase. Experience is a great teacher about recognizing the right moment to close a sale. A commitment should be sought when the shopper gives signals of being close to making a decision, such as physical actions, comments, and questions. This might be when the customer agrees with the value of a benefit or solution, or agrees with the salesperson's response to a concern. A smile of approval, or a final holding up of a garment to check it again, are signals of a positive decision. Other signals include the customer soliciting another person's opinion or appearing more relaxed. The salesperson might then ask to ring it up, 18-19. The salesperson can ask whether the customer wants certain items, get the customer to make minor choices such as color or style, or indicate that the customer will lose out on the sale price or the merchandise if the purchase is not made now.

Sears

18-19 Positive discussion about the good choice can continue, if appropriate, as the salesperson rings up the customer's purchase.

The salesperson should keep trying to close the sale as long as the concerns expressed can be handled effectively and the customer does not show signs of resentment. Pushing the sale after the customer has decided against the product may cause the shopper to never return to the store. Instead, the salesperson should thank the shopper for coming in and invite him or her back again soon.

Supplementary Suggestions

Sales can often be increased by directing customers to other merchandise, additional services, or referring them to other departments or company-owned stores. ***Suggestion selling*** is a method of increasing sales by adding to the customers' original purchases. It should be done to help customers, rather than to force more sales. It is *not* done to push random products onto customers, though more sales do result in a higher profit for the company.

Suggestion selling requires knowledge of the store's products combined with an understanding of the customer's needs. Salespeople who want to provide benefits and solutions for their customers are very successful with suggestion selling. Suggestion selling includes the following:

* add-ons
* trading up
* more than one
* special offers

Add-ons are additional related merchandise items that create complete outfits, 18-20. For example, a woman buying a suit might be encouraged to purchase a coordinating scarf or pin.

Trading up, also called *upselling,* is suggesting a substitute item that is higher-priced, of better quality, or more economical for the customer. It can be a larger size container of items that offers a lower cost per item. Other examples of trading up would be a newer style dress that the customer might like better, or a larger package of socks that is more economical for the customer in the long run.

As the name implies, *more than one* is selling more than one of the same or similar item. Customers who find one item they like might be encouraged to buy a second one in a different color. *Special offers* are when an additional item can be obtained as a result of purchasing an item. For instance, if one necktie is purchased, the second one may be half price. Salespeople should make their customers aware of such special offers.

In Cooperation with The 410 Shoppe

18-20 One of the hats available from this store or a pair of cowboy boots might be fun add-ons to the items available on this rack of fashion garments.

Some salespeople hesitate to make supplementary suggestions, thinking customers with sizable purchases might not want to spend any more. Salespeople may relate customers' spending habits to their own, but they are not in a position to decide what customers can afford to buy. If customers' needs have not been satisfied, they will spend their money in other stores. Salespeople should not force unneeded items onto customers, but they should try to define and satisfy all their needs.

Salespeople should be encouraged and trained to do suggestion selling properly, and rewarded for doing it well. It is an integral part of the selling process, and a substantial opportunity for increased sales and good customer service.

Maintaining Relationships

Closing the sale is really the beginning of a relationship rather than the end of the sale process. By deliberately establishing closer ties with customers, relationships are strengthened and maintained. Some stores refer to their customers as "guests."

When a sale is finalized, the salesperson should reinforce the customer's purchase decision with an approving statement. A sincere thank you and the use of the customer's name are common courtesies. Credit card sales can remind salespeople of customers' names. Learning and using their names makes customers feel special and encourages them to return to the store. A handshake is recommended in appropriate instances to let customers know they are important to the salesperson and the store. If available, the salesperson's personal business card can be given to the customer. The salesperson should also ask the customer to please return soon.

If a customer has made a risky or expensive purchase, the reinforcement process is even more important since the customer may have doubts about having made the right decision. A feeling of dissatisfaction may cause the merchandise to be returned. On the other hand, reassurance and doing everything possible for the customer encourages the customer to enjoy the item and feel good about owning it.

Bonding is the process of salespeople doing everything possible to strengthen relationships with customers. Emphasis should not be on the most contacts, but on developing loyal, repeat customers. In turn, sales are increased and repeat business encouraged.

Salespeople with high-service retailers keep ***client books,*** in which customers' names, addresses, phone numbers, sizes, and important dates are recorded. A similar method is keeping a card file. After all, current customers are also future prospects. When customers return to the store or department, client books enable salespeople to remember their names. When additional purchases are made by these customers, the client book is updated with information about the purchases, as well as any comments about their satisfaction with previous purchases.

Follow-up is important to ensure customer satisfaction with purchases and repeat business. Good salespeople increase future store traffic by contacting current and prospective customers with legitimate reasons to invite them to shop at the store. This might be a special thank-you note or a call to make sure a garment was altered properly or delivered on time. Such actions show commitment and concern for customers.

Contacting previous customers when special sales are scheduled or new merchandise arrives is called *preselling.* Salespeople contact those customers who might be interested. This starts the selling steps all over again in a never-ending cycle. Sometimes birthday cards are sent to remind customers that they have not been forgotten and are important to the store. High-service stores provide the necessary phones, stationery, and postage to salespeople to encourage customer follow-up, 18-21.

Salespeople not only represent the store and its merchandise to customers, but also communicate customers' needs, desires, and concerns back to management. They are the communication feedback link between consumers and merchandise buyers and store managers. Salespeople interact with customers daily and are the firm's best-informed people about what customers think and expect. POS statistics can tell management what has and has not sold, but only the salespeople can explain why.

Retail Sales Expertise

To continue strong customer relationships and maintain a loyal clientele, responsive sales professionals do the following:

- Respond to personal needs of customers, but also honor manufacturers' warranties
- Follow through on commitments made to customers
- Adhere to the company's return policy while handling customer complaints cheerfully
- Maintain key information on customers
- Balance phone queries with in-store customer service
- Complete special orders
- Schedule personal appointments with shoppers and select merchandise in advance, if requested

18-21 To maintain the best relationships with customers, these practices become automatic for professional salespeople.

Merchandise Sales Transactions

Transacting sales by salesclerks or cashiers may seem somewhat mechanical, since they often scan bar codes on merchandise tags at a checkout counter. However, cashiering duties also include collecting and recording customers' payments that are made with cash, checks, and credit cards. A *checkout counter* or *checkstand* is the table or station where customers bring merchandise to pay and to have the merchandise bagged or wrapped. It is sometimes referred to in retailing as the cash/wrap area, 18-22. It contains a *cash register* or *checkout terminal* that performs mathematical operations, calculates tax, and records payments. It also generates a *sales slip*, which is a cash register receipt that shows prices for items, any tax, and the sales total of the transaction.

Salespeople and cashiers are sometimes required to remove a stub from the price tag of each item they ring up on the checkout terminal. These stubs contain SKU information. They indicate what inventory has been sold and are used to calculate reorders. However, most stores now use computerized point-of-sale (POS) registers for all checkout procedures, 18-23.

Sales tax is charged on various purchases and services in most states. Each state determines its own sales tax rate and uses the money to provide governmental services. Computing sales tax at checkout used to be done with a sales tax table placed near the cash register. Now the tax is automatically calculated by POS registers when items are scanned.

POS registers are connected to a central computer. The registers tabulate total sales by department,

Tandem Computers

18-22 The cash/wrap area is where customers bring merchandise for salespeople to ring up the purchases.

Symbol Technologies

18-23 Fashion merchandise, as well as most other types of items, are now checked out through computerized retail POS systems.

update inventory records, and identify low stock conditions. The central computer also provides information to registers about the existence of merchandise at other stores that can then be requested for customers.

Because electronic POS registers are connected to a central computer, prices can be adjusted automatically as needed. When prices change, such as when items go on sale, new prices are entered into the master computer system. Then, the ***price look-up (PLU)*** feature automatically adjusts the prices to the correct amount when the appropriate bar codes are scanned at checkout. This avoids reticketing or hand marking sale items for temporary promotional events.

Methods of Payment

For cash payments, most checkout computers calculate the amount of change due after the transaction price and money tendered have been entered. The cashier does not need to compute how much change to give, but merely counts out the proper amount for each customer. At the end of the day or the employee's shift, the amount of money in the cashier's drawer should match the amount calculated by the machine. If there is a discrepancy, the cashier may have to explain and make up the difference.

For payments by personal check, identification is required, such as a driver's license that contains a photo of the customer. Certain identification information is filled in on the back of the check for later reference if needed. There are also check verifying companies that can be connected to stores through phone lines. They electronically approve or disapprove personal checks, and guarantee the money for those that they approve.

For credit card sales, the cashier swipes the card through a machine that reads the magnetic stripe and sends information over phone lines to a credit bureau or verification service. The credit processing service checks to see that the card has not been reported stolen, the account is not overdue, and the amount of the purchase does not take the customer's account

Tandem Computers

18-24 Salespeople know how to facilitate credit transactions and to ask the customer to sign the credit card slip.

above the approved credit limit. An authorization denial implies that the charge will not go through.

If the credit charge can go through, an authorization number is shown on the machine. This is added to the credit card sales slip and the customer signs the slip, 18-24. At that point the cashier or salesperson should check that the signatures on the sales slip and the back of the credit card match. The credit card should not be given back to the customer until the charge procedure is finished.

Sometimes a "paperless signature capture" system is used. Instead of signing a paper credit card receipt, customers sign using a pen-like stylus directly on an electronic screen. The screen can also display a multiline message to the customer with advertising or promotional messages.

Once the transaction is complete, cashiers and salespeople carefully remove items from hangers and fold the merchandise. Bagging merchandise is not difficult. Some stores require bags to be stapled shut at checkout so additional items are not stolen and placed into the bags later. Cashiers may offer to place smaller packages of items already purchased inside a larger bag to consolidate the customer's packages. All of these duties should be accompanied by a smile and a sincere thank you to customers for shopping in the store. Showing genuine customer concern and service is a very important part of merchandise sales transactions.

Returns, Exchanges, and Other Adjustments

Salespeople and cashiers are also required to handle merchandise returns, exchanges, and other adjustments. When handling these transactions, sales slips are requested to verify prices. Some stores do not refund money when merchandise is returned. Instead, they give an exchange-credit toward other items in the store.

Sometimes rain checks, layaway purchases, and C.O.D. sends must be handled. A ***rain check*** is a certificate that entitles the customer to buy an out-of-stock advertised special at a later time at the same advertised price. These are offered when sale items are sold out before the end of the sale period. A ***layaway*** is a deferred purchase arrangement in which the store sets aside a customer's merchandise until the customer has fully paid for it. To put an item on layaway, the customer may have to make an initial deposit. Ongoing partial payments are made toward the total amount until the item is completely paid for. If the purchase is not completed by a certain time, the deposit may or may not be refunded, depending on store policy. A ***C.O.D. send*** is a sale which is to be delivered to the customer. The letters C.O.D. represent the words "cash on delivery." Payment for the merchandise is made to the delivery person by the customer when it arrives. The delivery company gives the money to the originator (sender) but charges a fee for that service.

Summary

For the direct selling function of fashion merchandising, salespeople represent the store to customers. The caliber of the selling staff is an important way that stores can differentiate themselves and gain a competitive edge. Salesclerks generally work for lower-priced retail stores and sales associates are employed by high-service retailers. Customer-oriented selling has replaced the old sales-oriented approach. Salespeople need definite goals and rewards to work at their highest level.

Salespeople usually also have merchandise handling duties. When goods are received at stores, they must be checked, marked, and prepared for sale. The selling floor must be kept in order to present the goods attractively to customers. Also, before effective selling can take place, salespeople must gain product knowledge, often from labels, hangtags, and packaging.

By using the selling steps well, better sales performance can be achieved. Salespeople must meet and greet customers to start a good relationship. By asking open-ended questions, salespeople can classify customers and determine their needs. Presentations of merchandise should be tailored to individual people and circumstances, indicating advantages of goods. Salespeople might have to overcome objections in order to close the sale. Supplementary suggestions may increase sales and satisfy customer needs more completely. Good relationships should be maintained after merchandise sales are finalized by taking steps to bond with customers.

Merchandise sales are transacted at checkout terminals using electronic POS registers. Payments for merchandise are made by cash, personal check, or credit card. Sometimes returns, exchanges, adjustments, rain checks, layaway purchases, and C.O.D. sends must also be handled.

To Know

indirect selling	product features
direct selling	trial confirmation
responsive selling	suggestion selling
compensation	add-ons
organizational climate	trading up
sales quotas	client books
incentives	price look-up (PLU)
commission	rain check
returns to vendors (RTV)	layaway
rack jobbers	C.O.D. send

To Review

1. How do good selling skills benefit both the company and its customers?
2. In what two ways do satisfied customers cause future sales?
3. Distinguish between the jobs of salesclerk and sales associate.
4. Briefly describe both the older sales-oriented selling and the newer customer-oriented approaches.
5. What positive selling attributes do consumers like salespeople to have?
6. What are the National Retail Federation retail sales skill standards designed to do?
7. Name three examples of incentives retailers can use to motivate their salespeople.
8. Why might merchandise be returned to the vendor?
9. What tasks are included in basic department stocking?
10. Define hangtags.
11. What does the greeting "May I help you?" imply to the customer? What might be a better opening remark after the inital hello?
12. Rather than resulting in an immediate sale, what is the approach and greeting intended to do?
13. What two techniques can help a salesperson classify a customer?
14. Describe how a salesperson should handle an objection.
15. What is meant by the term, "closing the sale"?
16. Name and define at least three specific types of suggestion selling.
17. In the selling process, what is bonding?
18. Name at least four of the functions that point-of-sale registers perform.
19. What do credit processing services check when a card is "swiped" through a machine?
20. Why do some stores require bags to be stapled shut at checkout?

To Do

1. Role-play a salesperson using the features-benefits-solutions selling approach. Have another student play the role of a customer. Include approach and greeting, open-ended questions, successful handling of objections, several closing techniques in assisting the customer to commit to the purchase, and suggestion selling. After making the imaginary sale, also explain what follow-up might be done to maintain the relationship.
2. Study the booklet "Raising Retail Standards" from the National Retail Federation. Prepare an oral report that includes visual aids to illustrate your points.
3. Do library and/or Internet research about government legislation concerning labels, hangtags, and packaging. Choose a law to report on and explain why the law exists and what government agency is charged with enforcing it. Choose from the following:
   - Textile Fiber Products Identification Act
   - Permanent Care Labeling Rule
   - Wool Products Labeling Act
   - Flammable Fabrics Act
   - Fur Products Labeling Act
4. With permission of department or store managers, observe and take notes in both a high-service apparel store and a discount store. Notice the customer service, stockkeeping duties, and check-out routine of employees. Try to classify particular customers as casual lookers, undecided, or decided about purchases. Note any of the selling steps that stand out in certain instances. Prepare a written or oral report about your findings.
5. Read a book about the art or skills of selling. Write a report that relates the information to fashion goods. Also tell how retail sales differ from other types of selling, such as industrial sales.

CHAPTER 19

Calculating for Best Results

After studying this chapter, you will be able to

- identify various business financial records of firms.
- describe the parts of an operating statement.
- summarize comparative analysis of operating ratios and other performance indicators.
- evaluate pricing considerations and strategies.
- complete various merchandise pricing calculations.

Careful planning and control of finances is necessary to establish and maintain a firm's financial health. First, retailers must keep good financial records. Then, certain calculations of sales, costs, and profit create the operating statement. Specific ratios are used to make smart marketing and pricing decisions. Many company decisions are largely influenced by the results shown on accounting statements. It is important for all fashion merchandising employees to have a basic knowledge of the financial aspects of retail operations. This knowledge begins with an understanding of financial records.

Financial Records

A system of financial recordkeeping includes constant updating of various ledger accounts. A *ledger* is a book or computer program containing ongoing accounts of the company. *Accounts* are records of debits (subtractions of money) and credits (additions of money) as a result of business activities. The complexity of the accounts depends on the size and type of company.

For most fashion merchandising firms, ledger accounts include

- *cash receipts*, which show money received from cash sales;
- *cash disbursements*, or money that has been paid out;
- *sales*, which indicates the financial income over a certain period of time, such as a day, week, month, quarter (three months), or year;
- *purchases*, or merchandise bought for resale, usually categorized by classification or department;
- *payroll*, which shows employee wages and deductions, such as social security and taxes;
- *equipment*, which lists capital assets, such as delivery trucks, office furniture, and computer hardware;
- *inventory*, or the value of the company's merchandise;
- *accounts receivable*, which shows the balances customers owe to the company; and
- *accounts payable*, which shows the balances the company owes to others, such as vendors (suppliers), advertising media, banks (loans), etc.

The Operating Statement

The factors that contribute to a fashion merchandising firm's profit can be shown in the following multiple formula:

merchandise price × volume sold = sales
sales – cost of goods sold = gross margin
gross margin – operating expenses = net profit (or loss) before taxes

A company's ***operating statement,*** sometimes called the *income statement,* is a summary of the financial results of the firm's operations over a specified period of time. A series of monthly operating statements is valuable for managing the business. By comparing the operating statement from one time period to the next, the firm can spot favorable or unfavorable trends and take the appropriate action. Trends in sales, costs, profits, or losses can spur needed action.

Formal operating statements, released to shareholders and the public, usually summarize results for three months (one quarter), six months, or a full fiscal year. A *fiscal year* is an accounting period of one year, which might or might not coincide with the calendar year (January 1 through December 31). The specific time period covered is written at the top of each operating statement. Most retail companies use a fiscal year of February 1 through January 31 because inventories are low and activities are slow a month after the holiday selling period, so this accounting can be accomplished.

The main purpose of the operating statement is to determine the net profit (or loss) figure. The statement presents data in a clear and concise manner to support that figure. A simplified operating statement for a retail company is shown in 19-1. You may want to refer to this example as you read this section. The amount of information included in formal operating statements varies among companies. Most statements contain more information than the sample shown.

The main parts of an operating statement are:

- *sales* – money received from merchandise sold (money in);
- *cost of goods sold* – amount spent purchasing the stock (money out);
- *operating expenses* – expenditures to sell the goods and run the company (money out);
- *profit (or loss)* – the amount of money remaining after costs and expenses are deducted from sales. A loss (or negative number because more money went out than came in) is indicated...

The major summary items are shown in dollar amounts on the right side of the operating statement. They support the basic components of sales, cost of goods sold, operating expenses, and profit (or loss). Other items on the statement provide details of explanation.

A-B-C Company		
Operating Statement **For the Year Ending December 31, (year)**		
Gross sales	$5,300,000	
Less: Returns and allowances	300,000	
Net Sales		$5,000,000
Cost of goods sold:		
Beginning inventory, January 1, at cost	$ 600,000	
Purchases at net cost (less discounts; plus freight)	2,900,000	
Cost of goods available for sale	$3,500,000	
Less: Ending inventory, December 31, at cost	500,000	
Cost of goods sold		$3,000,000
Gross margin		$2,000,000
Less: Operating expenses:		
Selling expenses	$ 750,000	
General expenses	300,000	
Administrative expenses	550,000	
Total expenses		$1,600,000
Net profit or loss before taxes		$ 400,000

19-1 This basic operating statement contains all the major categories required, with a small amount of supporting detail.

Some firms have large net sales, but also have large expenses that ruin their "bottom line."

Although an operating statement is not the only financial statement prepared by companies, it gives the most pertinent ongoing financial information. It establishes the relationship of sales to the cost of goods sold, expenses, and profit. Opening and closing inventory figures are shown, as well as expenditures to purchase goods during the period. Operating expenses are listed to make it easier to compare them with previous statements and to help control these expenses.

Net Sales

At the top of the operating statement is the gross sales figure, also called gross revenues. The *gross sales* figure is the total dollar amount received from sales. It is determined by multiplying the individual prices of all items sold by how many of each were sold. It is the money taken in before deductions are made, but after sales taxes have been taken out.

Deductions from gross sales are a result of customer dissatisfaction. Deductions include returns and allowances. *Returns* are when customers are given a full refund or credit for items they bring back to the store. Customers return items because they change their minds, or they find that the merchandise is damaged. *Allowances* are price reductions on items that may be slightly damaged, but that customers decide to purchase anyway at a lower price.

When returns and allowances are deducted from gross sales, the resulting number is *net sales,* or the actual dollars earned and kept from sales during the accounting period. On the operating statement shown in 19-1, it appears as

Gross sales (total selling price of all items sold)	$5,300,000
Less returns and allowances	– 300,000
Net sales	**$5,000,000**

Inventory Cost Calculations

The cost of inventory is calculated in the "cost of goods sold" section of the operating statement. ***Cost of goods sold (COGS)*** indicates the dollar amount spent on goods that have been sold to customers during the period. It is a combination of the cost of the inventory at the beginning of the fiscal year, plus the money spent acquiring new inventory, minus the inventory still available for sale at the end of the year.

To verify inventory, a physical count of goods is taken at the start of the fiscal year. It gives the exact inventory for both the end of the previous year, such as December 31, and the start of the new year, which would be January 1.

Adding together the cost of the inventory at the beginning of the fiscal year (January 1) and the costs of new purchases made January through December gives the total cost of goods the store has *offered for sale* during the year. However, COGS is the cost value of what has *sold,* not what is on hand at any given time. Since a store has a certain amount of inventory that is *unsold* at the end of the year (December 31), that must be deducted since it will be inventory carried over for the next year. The final number is the cost of goods sold during the year. In the operating statement shown in 19-1, it appears as

Beginning inventory at cost	$ 600,000
Plus cost of purchases	+2,900,000
Cost of products offered for sale	$3,500,000
Less ending inventory at cost	– 500,000
Cost of goods sold	**$3,000,000**

A physical inventory count is not taken to arrive at daily, weekly, monthly, or quarterly inventory levels. These figures are usually established by "perpetual inventory" records, which subtract items sold and add amount purchased. This is quite accurate because of ongoing computerized point-of-sale statistics.

Gross Margin

Continuing down the operating statement, the final cost of goods sold is deducted from net sales, which then shows the company's gross margin. ***Gross margin*** is the sum of money available to cover expenses and generate a profit. It is a merchandising term that means the same as *gross profit*—the term used more often in the manufacturing sector.

Gross margin can also be calculated for product lines or specific SKUs. For instance, if a retailer pays $40 each for 100 jackets, and prices each jacket at $72, the anticipated gross margin (if sold at full price) for each jacket is $32 ($72 selling price – $40 cost = $32 gross margin). The anticipated total gross margin on the entire jacket line is $3,200 (100 jackets × $32 gross margin) if all sell at full price.

This can also be shown as

Total sales (100 jackets × $72 selling price)	$7,200
Less COGS (100 jackets × $40 purchase cost)	4,000
Gross margin	**$3,200**

If 50 of the jackets sell at full price, 40 sell at a marked-down price of $60, and the remaining 10 sell at a clearance price of cost, the actual dollar gross margin is $2,400. This can be shown as

50 jackets × $72 full price	$3,600
40 jackets × $60 marked-down price	2,400
10 jackets × $40 purchase cost	400
Total sales	$6,400
Less COGS	4,000
Gross margin	**$2,400**

Expenses

Expenses are listed below the gross margin in the operating statement. They include selling, general, and administrative (SG&A) expenses of operating the business. They may be listed in any order or grouped in the most useful way for analysis. Selling expenses include payroll (wages) for the sales staff, advertising costs, delivery costs, etc. Administrative expenses include management salaries, office supplies, postage, and other miscellaneous administrative costs. General expenses include rent, utilities, and other operating overhead.

Profit/Loss

When expenses are deducted from the gross margin figure, the resulting number shows ***net profit*** (or loss). This may also be called operating profit (or loss). It is the figure upon which each company's income tax is based, but tax calculations are not necessarily shown on the operating statement. After taxes have been deducted, the final number shows the after-tax profit (or loss) from sales.

Comparative Analysis

Comparative analysis is the periodic examination and company's overall strategy. It can also be used to evaluate sales performance of specific employees and departments. It should be done by all retailers. Today, with computerized marketing information systems, sales analysis can be done easily.

It is important in business to compare current sales performance with previous periods. Comparisons should also be made with competitors and the industry as a whole. Figures showing sales, profits, and various financial ratios of individual companies and industry averages are readily available. They are published annually by private consulting firms and trade organizations, such as the National Retail Federation. Such comparisons enable a company to make a constructive evaluation of its performance. Analysis is commonly done using operating ratios and other comparison figures. Growth in sales, gross margin, and profit are good barometers of corporate health.

Operating Ratios

Operating ratios are mathematical relationships of income and expense figures that measure a firm's effectiveness in generating sales and managing expenses. They are calculated from the operating statement and can be shown with another column to the right of the dollar figures on the statement. See 19-2. This column contains percentage figures, using net sales as 100%.

The basic operating ratios are computed by dividing net sales into the various operating statement items that are listed below the net sales level in the statement. Net sales is used as the denominator in calculating operating ratios because that figure shows the sales that the firm actually made. Then change the answer calculating to a percentage by shifting the decimal point two places to the right.

The *ratio of cost of goods sold to net sales* is calculated as follows:

$$\text{Cost of goods sold ratio} = \frac{\text{COGS}}{\text{net sales}}$$

For example, if COGS is $3,000,000 and net sales are $5,000,000, the COGS ratio is 60%.

$$\text{COGS ratio} = \frac{\$3{,}000{,}000}{\$5{,}000{,}000} = 0.6 = 60\%$$

This COGS ratio shows that 60% of the dollars that were taken in for net sales were spent on the cost of the inventory that was sold. This cuts down the income considerably, plus operating expenses have not yet been deducted.

To calculate the *ratio of gross margin to net sales,* use this formula:

$$\text{Gross margin ratio} = \frac{\text{gross margin}}{\text{net sales}}$$

Operating Statement with Operating Ratios

Net sales	$5,000,000	100%	
Cost of goods sold	–3,000,000	60%	COGS ratio
Gross margin	2,000,000	40%	gross margin ratio
Expenses	–1,600,000	32%	expense ratio
Net profit	$ 400,000	8%	profit margin

19-2 Operating ratios, shown as percentages for each main category of the operating statement, indicate relationships of those categories to net sales.

For example, if the gross margin is $2,000,000 and the net sales are $5,000,000, the gross margin ratio is 40%.

$$\text{Gross margin ratio} = \frac{\$2{,}000{,}000}{\$5{,}000{,}000} = 0.4 = 40\%$$

The 40% ratio of gross margin to net sales means that 40% of the net sales dollars are available to cover the expenses of sales and administration, plus a profit. These are the items that fall below the gross margin level of the operating statement.

The *ratio of expenses to net sales* (expense ratio) is calculated as follows:

$$\text{Expense ratio} = \frac{\text{operating expenses}}{\text{net sales}}$$

For example, if the operating expenses are $1,600,000 and the net sales are $5,000,000, the expense ratio would be 32%.

$$\text{Expense ratio} = \frac{\$1{,}600{,}000}{\$5{,}000{,}000} = 0.32 = 32\%$$

This ratio indicates that 32% of the net sales revenues have been used to cover the overhead costs of the business during the period. These include selling, administrative, and general expenses.

The net ***profit margin,*** also known as *return on sales* (ROS), measures profit as a percentage of net sales. This ratio is considered by many to be the most important for evaluation and planning purposes because it shows how well the firm is managing its costs in relation to its sales revenues. To determine the net profit margin, use this formula:

$$\text{Profit margin} = \frac{\text{net profit}}{\text{net sales}}$$

If the net profit is $400,000 of the net sales of $5,000,000, then the profit margin is 8%, as shown below:

$$\text{Profit margin} = \frac{\$400{,}000}{\$5{,}000{,}000} = 0.08 = 8\%$$

The profit margin, or net profit ratio, shows that 8% of the net sales dollar (8 cents of every dollar) is left for taxes and profit. Also note that the expense ratio (32%), added to the profit margin (8%) equals the gross margin ratio (40%).

Because these operating statement categories are interrelated, only a few pieces of information are needed to figure the others. For example, knowing the gross margin ratio and net profit ratio makes it possible to figure the COGS and expense ratios. Also, knowing just one dollar amount and the percentages enables all the other dollar amounts to be calculated.

A company's operating ratios are best used by comparing the same ratios over time. Percentages are much easier to compare for results than dollar figures. If the company grows to a different size, numbers change but ratios show the same relationships of dollar income and outgo. This indicates improvements or problems. Also, the performance of competitors of different sizes can be compared on an equal basis with percentages, gathered from annual reports or published industry averages. Knowing how other companies are doing helps retailers make meaningful judgments about their own operating efficiency and financial situation. Companies can identify conditions that deviate from established norms.

Operating ratios have gained wide acceptance within the business community. They have become standards by which retailers judge their performances. The ratios serve as reference points rather than absolute guidelines.

Selling Space Performance

Another important figure for comparing performance from year to year or with other companies is dollars of ***sales per square foot*** of selling space. This is calculated by dividing the total sales volume by the total square feet of selling space. Sales per square foot is a common performance objective in most types of retailing.

For instance, if a department store has 25,000 square feet of selling space and its annual net sales are $5,000,000, then its sales per square foot for that year would be $200. This calculation would look like the following:

$$\text{Sales per square foot} = \frac{\text{total sales volume}}{\text{total square feet of selling space}}$$

$$\frac{\$5{,}000{,}000}{25{,}000 \text{ sq. ft.}} = \$200 \text{ Sales per square foot}$$

Sales per square foot can be calculated for whole chains, individual stores, different product lines, or specific SKUs. Retailers set yearly goals of a certain number of dollars per square foot. They try to increase this figure each year. In recent years, many major specialty stores have outperformed department stores in dollars of sales per square foot. Estimated overall averages by product category are shown in 19-3.

A similar calculation is *gross margin return on selling space* (GMROS), or gross margin per square

Estimated Retail Sales Per Square Foot

Specialty Shops	
Consumer electronics/music	$900
Photo/books/cards/gifts	700
Jewelry	550
Convenience/specialty food	400
Drug/health care	350
Apparel	300
Toys/sporting goods	250
Furniture/appliances	200
Department stores	$150

19-3 Stores that stock large amounts of small items that sell quickly and are not regularly reduced in price (such as card shops) have higher sales per square foot than stores that carry fewer large items that are often offered at reduced prices (appliance stores).

foot of selling area. It also measures the utilization or return achieved from the selling space. The figure is obtained using this formula:

$$\text{GMROS} = \frac{\text{gross margin}}{\text{selling space}}$$

For instance, if a retail store with a gross margin of $500,000 has a total of 20,000 square feet, its gross margin return on space is $25, as shown below:

$$\text{GMROS} = \frac{\$500{,}000}{20{,}000 \text{ sq. ft.}} = \$25$$

A retail company can determine which of its branch stores are doing the most effective jobs per square foot, even though some of the branches may be large and others small. Also, the profitability of a line of sportswear might be calculated according to how much floor space is allocated to it. To determine the number, the gross margin for that store or product line is divided by the store or line's square feet of selling space.

Stores with many lines of merchandise calculate a ***profitability range*** for product lines. This is a range of figures showing the most profitable to the least profitable lines of merchandise, based on the profit per square foot of selling space. A decision might by made that the lines with the lowest profitability be dropped and replaced with new merchandise that could yield higher profitability. Highly profitable lines might be expanded.

Other Sales Analysis

Stock turn rates (stock turnover) and stock-to-sales ratios are important retail figures. They were explained in Chapter 14 of this textbook. In general, high inventory turnover and low stock-to-sales ratios increase profits. Besides higher sales levels, the advantages of high turnover and low stock ratios include fewer markdowns and lower inventory expenses, such as for insurance, storage space, property taxes, and stockroom workers.

Same-store sales growth is another indicator of retail success. After a store has been in business for at least a year, this calculation compares the results of each succeeding year. It is usually shown in a percentage increase or decrease in sales. Every store tries to increase its sales growth each year to improve upon its own past record. Stores also try to show more growth than other branch stores of the same company, as well as competitive stores and industry averages.

Comparable-store sales is considered one of the best measures of performance. Retailers like to compare their sales to comparable stores. These stores would be close competitors of similar corporate or store sizes, expense structures, merchandise lines, departmental structures, and ways of operating.

There are still other measures of *sales productivity* of stores, employees, or product lines. These include the following:

- average sales per hour
- items per transaction
- dollars per transaction
- total sales per employee

These figures can be calculated and compared to previous periods or other companies. To calculate these figures, certain numerators are divided by appropriate denominators. For instance, for the *average sales per hour*, the formula would be

$$\text{Average sales per hour} = \frac{\text{Total sales}}{\text{Number of hours}}$$

Both the total sales and number of hours should relate to the same factor. For instance, if analyzing a store's average sales per hour, the store's total sales for a period (week or month) would be divided by the number of hours the store was open during that period. If analyzing an employee's average sales per hour, the employee's total sales for the period would be divided by the number of hours that employee worked during the period.

For the *average items sold per transaction*, the total items sold is divided by the total number of transactions. This can tell a retailer how many items each employee, department, or store averages per transaction. To calculate the *average dollars per transaction*, the total dollars of sales for a store, department, employee, or product line is divided by the total number of transactions.

Total sales for each employee is often tabulated to evaluate the performance of individual salespeople. This figure is sometimes used to award incentive bonuses or other prizes. Totaling all sales that each salesperson has made does not require a mathematical equation or long addition problem. Usually there is an employee number entered into an assigned POS terminal or the number is punched in by the employee when sales transactions are made. Then the computer system can automatically total the number of sales during a given time period (day, week, or month) for each employee.

Expense Management

Since two major factors, money coming in (sales) and money going out (costs/expenses), interact to determine profit or loss, expense numbers must be analyzed as well as sales revenues. ***Expense management*** is the process of planning and controlling operating expenses. To make a profit, operating expenses must be less than the company's gross margin. Expenses include fixed and variable costs, as well as controllable and uncontrollable costs.

Fixed costs are those costs that remain the same regardless of sales volume. These overhead expenses usually last over an extended period of time, such as mortgages or fire insurance on buildings. ***Variable costs*** increase or decrease with the volume of sales. For instance, the purchase cost of twenty dresses to sell will be twice as much as the cost of ten dresses to sell. The fixed costs are then spread across more sales if twice as many dresses are sold. *Total costs* are the sum of the fixed and variable expenses.

Controllable expenses are those expenses over which the company has direct control. These expenses can be adjusted as needed to respond to operating conditions, such as increasing the selling staff for holiday sales. *Uncontrollable expenses* are those over which a company has no control and which, in the short run, cannot be adjusted to current needs. They result from such conditions as bad weather or a changing economy.

Major department stores have shown good expense management by operating with lower *debt levels* than most discount and specialty stores. In other words, they borrow less money. This lowers their expenses since they do not have to make high interest payments on loans. Higher debt levels affect improvements, such as renovations and investing in new technology. Consequently, even if retail sales are high, interest payments may impact profits and long-term growth.

With comparative analysis, if some expenses are rising, those particular costs can be singled out for special attention. Resulting cost-cutting efforts might affect every employee in the firm. Cost controls, or a high level of cost consciousness, improve retailing success, but require the cooperation of each employee.

Pricing Considerations

Price point is a merchandising expression for the dollar amount at which an item is offered for sale. It is the amount of money that customers are willing to pay and that companies are willing to accept for goods or services. Simply stated, *price* is the amount of money charged for products. Today's shoppers are value and price conscious. They plan purchases carefully, looking for quality products at the best price.

The main objectives of pricing strategies are

- overall profitability
- optimum sales volume
- deterrence of competition
- presenting an image

Overall profitability is evaluated from the gross sales, net profit, and gross margin shown on the operating statement. Good financial performance raises the value of a company's stock and business image. Although retailers may set their prices to achieve a specific gross margin dollar amount, they are usually more interested in gross margin as a percentage of sales.

A store's *sales volume* is heavily affected by prices, since price strongly influences the number of units sold. More sales volume (from lower prices) also translates into increased stock turnover and market share, but may decrease gross margin and profits. Various price level strategies affect the amount of consumer traffic that a retailer attracts. Sales volume goals can be expressed in either dollars or units. They can be calculated for individual product lines and SKUs, or for entire retail stores or companies.

Deterrence of competition is accomplished with low prices, since other firms may not have the operating efficiency or volume to match these prices. Low prices may keep a company's sales volumes up, keep current customers from going elsewhere, and prevent competitors from increasing their market shares.

The pricing strategy of some retailers is to remain comparably priced with competing businesses, changing prices only to reflect price changes in competing stores. Another strategy is to sustain a certain profit margin, with price changes calculated according to increased or decreased costs. Sometimes retailers modify their pricing based on supply and demand.

Federal and state governments may scrutinize pricing practices. For instance, retailers that charge very high prices might be unfairly gouging customers. Retailers with very low prices may be viewed as trying to drive competitors out of business. *Sales-below-cost laws* are state laws that attempt to preserve competition by restricting unusually low pricing.

Since price says something about products and the stores that sell them, *image* is another objective of pricing strategies. Prestige-sensitive consumers use price to judge quality. They consider a high price to indicate quality and a low price to signal an inferior product. Thus, fashion items of different price levels are usually separated from each other and sold in different departments.

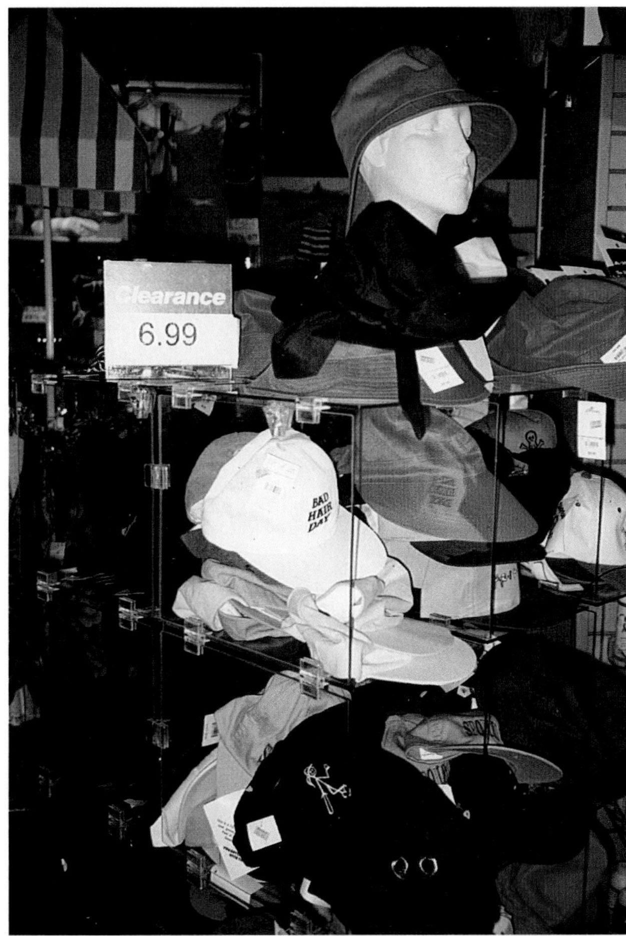

19-4 Odd-figure pricing is being used to sell these hats at less than $7.00.

Other Pricing Strategies

Some specific pricing strategies include odd-figure pricing and loss leaders. ***Odd-figure pricing*** is the retail pricing of merchandise a few cents less than a dollar denomination, such as $1.99 or $199.95. See 19-4. Psychologically, it is hoped that customers will consider the items to be priced much lower than the next higher dollar amount, thus seeming less expensive.

Loss leaders are low-priced articles on which stores make little or no profit. They are popular items that are promoted at a reduced price to attract shoppers into the store. Retailers hope that shoppers will then buy other goods at regular prices while they are in the store, from which good profits will be made, 19-5.

Repricing includes both price increases and decreases on goods that are in stock. The price of goods might be lowered for special sales and to move slow-selling goods. The price of goods might be increased if the replacement cost of items from vendors has gone up. The latter enables current merchandise to correspond with the new prices.

The Cost of Overbuying

To allow for customer choice, extra goods have traditionally been purchased by apparel retailers, offered for sale, and later marked down if they have not sold. This increases store traffic. *Overbuying* is the purchasing of unneeded merchandise in excess of anticipated sales.

This overbuying strategy does not necessarily maximize profits since it increases costs (stockkeeping, advertising, employees, debt service, etc.). Thus, many retail buyers are now purchasing less in their original orders to achieve higher final profits. Quick Response EDI linkages are now used to replenish low stock of best-selling items as the season progresses.

Some overbuying is needed to offer a good choice to customers and to allow for merchandise that is not received as ordered. Therefore, overbuying is done when there is a good chance to increase sales. Stores might cautiously overbuy only in their strongest categories and sizes.

Some products in stock may be marked down and still not sold. Companies must eventually dispose

19-5 The shoppers who come into the store to buy the popular khaki trousers may also purchase shirts, belts, and other apparel that have higher profit margins.

of unsold goods. Liquidators buy leftover retail inventory, often called *closeouts*, for cash payment. Although the payment may be only a fraction of the original cost of the goods (such as 10 or 15 cents on the dollar), it is better than receiving no cash at all. Sometimes the remaining items only have fiber or rag value. Other times they are donated to charity or shipped to underdeveloped nations. When old inventory is cleared, there is room for new goods. Also, carrying costs on the old goods are then eliminated.

Pricing Calculations

Fashion retailers do certain pricing calculations continually. They add markups to goods received to sell. They reduce the price of some items to try to sell them faster. They consider various markdown strategies, while trying to maintain a certain ongoing average markup.

Markups

A *markup*, sometimes called a *markon*, is the amount added to the cost of merchandise to determine the selling price. The ***initial markup*** refers to the difference between merchandise cost and the selling price originally placed on merchandise. It is the "first markup" on items, and is what the retailer hopes to receive in payment from customers.

For instance, if a retailer buys jackets for $40 each, they must be sold for more than this cost to make a profit. If $32 is added onto the cost to cover expenses and profit, $32 is the initial dollar markup and $72 is on the price tag. The $32 is also the gross margin from that item if it sells with that markup, but it is not the net profit because selling expenses have not been deducted.

If the cost of advertising, utilities, wages, and other expenses translates to $20 for that item, the net profit is $12 ($32 markup – $20 expenses = $12 profit). If expenses are $32, no profit is made ($32 markup – $32 expenses = 0 profit). If expenses are more than $32, that item has created a loss for the company. Also, there is no guarantee that customers will buy that jacket at that marked-up price.

Markup is usually expressed as a percentage rather than a dollar amount. The *initial markup percentage* is the key element in guiding a retail company's price-setting decisions to try to achieve a specified profit.

There are two ways that retail markups are calculated. One is *markup percent of cost* or cost-plus pricing. The formula looks like this:

$$\text{Markup \% of cost} = \frac{\text{dollar markup (retail price minus cost)}}{\text{cost}}$$

The $32 markup on the jacket that originally cost $40 is a markup of 80% of cost, as shown below:

$$\text{Markup \% of cost} = \frac{\$32}{\$40} = 0.8 = 80\%$$

Another way that retail markups are calculated is as a *markup percent of selling price.* The formula looks like this:

$$\text{Markup \% of selling price} = \frac{\text{dollar markup}}{\text{selling price}}$$

Using the jacket example, the calculation would look like this:

$$\text{Markup \% of selling price} = \frac{\$32}{\$72} = 0.444 = 44.4\%$$

Store policy dictates which method is used to markup goods and the percentage amount to use. The easiest method is a percent of cost, since the cost is known from the invoice. If items are to be marked up 80% of cost, their purchase cost from the vendor is multiplied by .8 and added to the cost to get the selling price. In other words, it is calculated as 1.8 times cost.

However, most retailers use the selling price rather than the cost to compute their markups. This appears to be a smaller markup to consumers. It encourages retailers to think in terms of retail prices and their resulting profits. Also, it is easier to compare markups with other stores and published trade numbers since they are usually reported by percentage of net sales. When retail trade publications or business news articles discuss a certain percentage markup, it is assumed that they are talking about a markup percentage of the selling price.

The markup percent for the sum of all merchandise is figured in the same way. If total inventory cost (COGS) is $3,000,000 and total inventory at selling price is $5,400,000, the total dollar markup is $2,400,000 ($5,400,000 total selling price minus $3,000,000 total cost = $2,400,000 markup). This calculates to a 44.4% markup of the selling price as shown below:

$$\text{Markup \%} = \frac{\$2{,}400{,}000}{\$5{,}400{,}000} = 0.444 = 44.4\%$$

Computing the selling price is done from the known cost with the following formula:

$$\text{Selling price} = \frac{\text{cost}}{1 - \text{markup }\%}$$

If the cost is $40, and the markup is 44.4%, the calculation would be as follows:

$$\text{Selling price} = \frac{\$40}{1 - .444} = \frac{\$40}{.556} = \$71.94$$

The answer of $71.94 would round to $72 unless odd figure pricing is being used. This method is how most retail prices are established.

Since the markup plus the unit cost of an item is expected to cover the selling and administrative expenses as well as provide a profit, the markup percentage is usually similar (per unit) to the company's gross margin percentage. The gross margin percentage is generally used as the markup guideline for percentage of selling price.

A ***keystone markup*** is doubling the cost to arrive at the retail price. This is commonly done by small shops and is very easy to calculate (wholesale cost × 2 = retail price). The jacket with a purchase cost of $40 would have a retail price of $80 with a keystone markup. This would be a 100% markup of cost or 50% markup of the selling price.

Price Reductions

Reduction planning involves estimating a percentage of sales for markdowns, discounts, and stock that is damaged or stolen. These factors lower retail profits. Price reductions are discounts or markdowns on merchandise.

Discounts are reductions of the original retail price granted to store employees as special fringe benefits. They might also be offered to certain customers, such as senior citizens or store credit card holders, in recognition of their special status.

A *markdown* is the difference between the previously marked selling price of an item and the reduced selling price. It is a price reduction to stimulate the sale of merchandise. The objective of markdowns is usually to get rid of certain goods. However, sometimes popular items are marked down as a promotional device to increase store traffic.

Markdowns may be required if customers are unwilling to buy items at the originally marked-up price. This could be due to style changes, damaged items, lower prices at competing stores, or an original price that was too high to provide value. Items may be damaged due to fading, soiling, or careless handling.

Symbol Technologies, Inc.

19-6 Although you should know how to calculate price increases and decreases, much of this work is now done automatically with computerized equipment.

To get rid of these items, the retailer marks them down to a lower price.

Markdowns are usually considered to be caused by business errors, such as poor buying, overpricing, or other reasons. However, markdowns are a part of normal retailing and, just like other aspects of the business, need to be analyzed. These reductions in potential profit should be recognized and calculated. Today, this is often done automatically on individual items using electronic equipment, 19-6. Markdown calculations can also be done for an entire branch store or specific department.

Just as for markups, the two ways retailers compute markdowns are in dollar amounts or in percentages. A *markdown dollar amount* is the difference between the original selling price and the reduced selling price. An item originally ticketed for $100 that actually sells for $80 has a dollar markdown of $20.

Percentage markdowns are computed either as a percent of the original ticketed price or a percent of the marked-down selling price. *Markdown percent of the ticketed price* is often advertised to consumers, such as a sale in which everything in the store or on a rack is reduced by 20%. See 19-7. If the ticketed price is $100, the sale price would be $80. This is calculated by (1) deducting the percentage dollar amount or

19-7 It is unusual to mark goods down by more than 50%. However, to clear inventory, some retailers mark down certain items 60% or even 75% of the originally marked price.

(2) multiplying the ticket price by the complement of the percentage discount. Either method may be used as shown below:

(1) \$100 ticket price × .20 (% markdown) = \$20 markdown
 \$100 ticket price – \$20 markdown = \$80 selling price

(2) \$100 ticket price × (1 – .20) = dollar selling price
 \$100 ticket price × .80 = \$80 selling price

Conversely, if the dollar markdown and original ticketed prices are known, the markdown percentage of the original ticketed price can be calculated with the following formula:

$$\text{Markdown \% of original ticketed price} = \frac{\$\text{ markdown}}{\text{original ticketed price}}$$

For example:

$$\text{Markdown \% of original ticketed price} = \frac{\$20}{\$100} = 20\%$$

Markdown percent of the actual selling price for a merchandise item is calculated with the following formula:

$$\text{Markdown \% of actual selling price} = \frac{\$\text{ markdown}}{\$\text{ net sale}}$$

For example:

$$\text{Markdown \% of actual selling price} = \frac{\$20 \text{ (markdown)}}{\$80 \text{ (actual selling price)}} = 25\%$$

The example shows that an item with an original marked-up ticket price of \$100, which sells for \$80, has a dollar markdown of \$20. The markdown percent of the original ticketed price is 20% while the markdown percent of the selling price is 25%.

To relate markdown information to an entire department or store (profit center), or for a whole season or year, the same formula can be used. Retailers keep a record of the amount of markdowns and other reductions in each department for that period. Then they divide that total by the net sales in the department for the period. The following formula is used:

$$\text{Markdown \% on net sales} = \frac{\text{total \$ markdowns}}{\text{total net sales}}$$

For a store that had \$5,000,000 of total net sales and took \$500,000 of total markdowns, the markdown percent of sales for the period would be 10%, as shown below:

$$\text{Markdown \% on net sales} = \frac{\$\ 500{,}00}{\$5{,}000{,}000} = 0.1 = 10\%$$

The total markdown should be a smaller percent than the markdown percent on one item that has been reduced. This is because the total number also includes many items that were not marked down, but were sold at full price. This is the most common calculation, since it corresponds with the operating statement and other financial records that are based on net sales.

The markdown percent for a period of time, called the *markdown ratio*, is used as a tool by many retailers. It is calculated and compared over time to measure the performance of various departments and the entire business. Markdown ratios can also be used to compare the effectiveness of different buyers and salespeople in a store's departments. Over time, these ratios give management one measure of the performance of buyers, departments, or branch stores, rather than individual items.

Markdown Strategies

Markdowns are part of normal, everyday retailing. There are no hard and fast rules for determining the size of markdowns that retailers should take. However, markdowns should be large enough to attract customers' attention and induce them to buy. For planning purposes, past experience and trade averages are often used as the basis for determining price reductions. Some markdowns are taken to match competitors' prices. Rather than being viewed as a loss, many are used for promotional purposes of encouraging sales and increasing profits.

Among the considerations retailers should take into account when determining the size of price reductions are

- the type of merchandise,
- the time of the selling season or fashion cycle, and
- the size of the original markup.

Markdowns are generally greater for fashion merchandise than for staple goods. This is because of continual fashion movement, seasonal changes, and the difficulty of determining customer preferences for fashion items.

The optimal timing and amount of markdowns should be related to decreasing demand. Successful markdown strategy includes price reductions while there is still some customer demand to move the goods. Otherwise, the goods may not sell at all. First markdowns should be deep enough to immediately appeal to consumers so stock can be moved out quickly.

Also, markups and markdowns must be viewed together. For profits to be made, the higher the original markup percent, the less the impact of the markdown. Correspondingly, the lower the markup percent, with lower profit potential, the greater the impact of the markdown. With frequent retail price changes, many store branches, thousands of SKUs, and shifting strategic priorities these days, computerized pricing systems have gained widespread use. Input to the central computer by corporate pricing specialists results in immediate company-wide changes.

Sometimes markdown money is offered by suppliers. *Markdown money* is payment by a vendor to a retailer to compensate for losses from reduced selling prices of that vendor's goods. It is used as an incentive for retailers to buy the vendor's merchandise. Usually it is specified in advance on the purchase order or contract. With markdown money, the vendor and retailer share in the price reduction when items do not sell at full price. The potential loss of profit is shared by both parties.

Maintained Markup

A ***maintained markup*** is the difference between the total cost of the merchandise and its final selling price. A maintained markup equals the initial markup minus all retail markdowns or other reductions. It is what the retailer actually receives when products sell. When the maintained markup is expressed as a percent, it is the most important indicator of pricing success, since it is a combination of both markups and markdowns.

The calculation of the maintained markup percent attempts to establish the impact that markdowns for the period had on the original markup. In other words, it shows how much the total markdowns reduced the total markups. However, the problem is one of different entities. The markup percent is on goods *received* in the period, and the markdown percent is on goods *sold* in the period. They might not be the same goods. A solution is calculated with the following equation:

Maintained markup percent = Original markup % – ([100% – original markup %] × markdown %)

Thus, for a store that uses an original markup of 50% and has an overall markdown of 10% during the period, the maintained markup percent would be calculated as follows:

Maintained markup % = 50% – ([100% – 50%] × 10%) = 50% – (50% × 10%) = 50% – 5% = 45%

Summary

Careful planning and control of financial accounts is important to monitor and maintain firms' income, expense, and profit/loss conditions. A system of financial recordkeeping includes constant updating of ledger accounts, including cash receipts, cash disbursements, sales, purchases, payroll, equipment, inventory, accounts receivable, and accounts payable.

By comparing a series of monthly and yearly operating statements, firms can spot favorable or unfavorable trends, and take appropriate action to remedy problems. The net sales section shows returns and allowances from gross sales. Inventory cost calculations show the costs of beginning inventory, plus purchases, minus ending inventory. The final cost of goods sold is deducted from net sales to arrive at the company's gross margin. Finally, expenses are deducted to find the company's net profit or loss.

Comparative analysis is important to see how a company is doing versus results of previous periods, competitors, and the industry as a whole. Operating ratios can be shown with a column of percentage figures next to the dollar figures of the operating statement. Selling space performance is shown with sales per square foot and return on selling space. Other sales analysis includes stock turnover, stock-to-sales ratios, same-store sales growth, comparable-store sales, and sales productivity calculations. Expense management must also be considered.

Pricing takes into consideration overall profitability, sales volume, deterrence of competition, and image. Other pricing strategies might include odd-figure pricing, loss leaders, and the cost of overbuying.

Markups can be stated as dollar amounts, but are usually calculated as either a percent of merchandise cost or a percent of the selling price. Price reductions include discounts and markdowns on merchandise that are intended to stimulate sales. Markdown strategies take into account the type of merchandise, the price of the items, and the time of the selling season or fashion cycle. The maintained markup percent is the most important indicator of pricing success, since it is a combination of both markups and markdowns.

To Know

operating statement
cost of goods sold (COGS)
gross margin
net profit
comparative analysis
operating ratios
profit margin
sales per square foot
profitability range
same-store sales growth
comparable-store sales
expense management
fixed costs
variable costs
odd-figure pricing
loss leader
initial markup
keystone markup
maintained markup

To Review

1. What is the difference between cash receipts and cash disbursements?
2. Give the overall formula of factors that contribute to a fashion merchandising company's profit.
3. What is the main purpose of the operating statement?
4. How do you know that a number in the operating statement shows a loss or negative number?
5. What are returns and allowances?
6. What figures must be added and subtracted to determine the cost of goods sold during a year?
7. Name the three usual operating expense categories of businesses and give an example of each.
8. How are the basic operating ratios computed?
9. How can operating ratios be used most effectively?
10. What effect do high inventory turnover and low stock-to-sales ratios generally have on profits?
11. Name three measures of sales productivity.
12. Contrast controllable and uncontrollable expenses and give an example of each.
13. What are sales-below-cost laws?
14. List one advantage and one disadvantage of overbuying.
15. Why do most retailers use the selling price rather than the cost to compute percentage markups?
16. Why might customers *not* be willing to buy items at the originally marked-up price?
17. Why is total markdown percent for an entire month or year smaller than the markdown percent on one item that has been reduced?
18. What do retailers use as the basis for determining price reductions?
19. What is markdown money?
20. Why is the maintained markup the most important indicator of pricing success?

To Do

1. As best you can, write a summary of what you think the financial activity might be for a fictitious retailer's ledger accounts for one day. Make a chart of your work to show to the class. Be prepared to explain each of your entries.
2. Obtain a quarterly or annual report from a company, preferably a fashion merchandising firm. From the numbers shown in the company's income statement, calculate operating ratios for each major section.
3. Go through fashion advertisements in a newspaper to notice price reductions and the reasons given for specific sales (clearance, anniversary, holiday, etc.). Also notice the types of stores (discount, specialty, department stores, etc.) and the amounts of their price reductions. Write a paper summarizing your findings.
4. With a classmate, visit a nearby retail store. After identifying yourself to store or department personnel, look at specific merchandise that is reduced. Write down original ticketed prices, marked-down prices, odd-figure prices, items you feel are loss leaders, items that are not marked down, and any other information you find interesting. Prepare a report about your findings.
5. In a large mall or shopping area near you, analyze what you think the pricing strategies are for two different types of major stores. How are the price points for their merchandise coordinated with their overall profitability, sales volume, deterrence of competition, and image? Prepare a written report.

CHAPTER 20

Service, Safety, and Security

After studying this chapter, you will be able to

- summarize customer service, including service levels, quality, and features.
- explain aspects of consumer credit and payment processing.
- describe how safety relates to both customers and employees.
- tell about store security measures that deal with external and internal theft.

Though fashion retailers are in the business of selling apparel, many services must be provided to keep customers coming back to buy again. Many services involve the granting of credit and other payment services. In addition, safety measures protect both customers and employees. Security actions protect company property. A combination of excellent service, safety, and security are an important part of a company's strategy to maximize profits.

Customer Service

The end goal of retailers is to serve customers, 20-1. ***Customer service*** is the total of all enhancements offered to customers. Services are directly related to the sale of goods and include having the right items when customers want them. Customers reward businesses that keep them happy with the desired merchandise, efficient transactions by knowledgeable and courteous salespeople, in pleasant and comfortable surroundings. With so many smart and demanding consumers shopping among many competing stores, customer satisfaction directly affects each firm's profitability. Customer services can

20-1 Malls, as well as individual retailers, try to provide good customer service. At this mall customer service center, consumers can ask questions, receive assistance, and look at the directory.

20-2 Some service areas in stores are dedicated to payment of bills and credit card arrangements. Public rest rooms are often located here also.

create customer satisfaction that enables a store to stand out among the competition.

Retail customer services include such offerings as public rest rooms, credit, return privileges, and gift wrapping, 20-2. These services facilitate the consumer buying process and help the company establish a good relationship with customers. Customer services are more effective if done "proactively" by listening to, understanding, and acting upon customer desires. This is much better than treating customer service "reactively" with after-the-fact handling of complaints.

Offering only essential services gives a no-frills, low-price image. On the other hand, offering a full range of services usually gives an image of quality merchandise and prestige prices. Business strategies that include different retail price levels and products have traditionally been associated with certain levels of expected services, as shown in 20-3. The following are the three main levels of retail service:

- *Self-service retailing* uses a ***price positioning*** strategy in which customers locate products themselves, compare items, make unassisted decisions, and carry their selections to a checkstand or cash/wrap area, 20-4. Customers are willing to do this to save money. Discount stores operate with this strategy. It is used by sellers of convenience goods and fast-moving items of well-known brands for which shoppers consider low price more important than customer service.

  Self-service retailers offer only essential services that are basic and necessary to the process of transacting sales to customers. Essential services include maintaining safe and secure surroundings, regular store hours, convenient parking, and merchandise displayed on racks and shelves. They also include assisting with information and handling customer complaints.
- *Limited-service retailing* involves selling products for which customers need more information. These retailers offer additional services not often provided by self-service retailers. They also have slightly higher prices to cover their increased operating costs. Many national chain organizations, such as Sears and JCPenney, are limited-service retailers. They

Service Levels

	Self-service	Limited service	Full service
Characteristics	Very few (essential) services Low prices Staple goods Convenience items	Medium (expected) amount of services Goods with some selection and comparison features	Many (optional) services Upscale fashion goods and specialty items
Store Types	Discount stores Warehouse clubs Mail-order retailers Vending machines Supermarkets	Chain stores Department stores Door-to-door sales	Upscale department stores Specialty stores
	Least services offered		Most services offered
	Price positioning	Value positioning	Service positioning

20-3 These are the three main levels of customer service. However, retail experts sometimes rate stores into seven levels of service: unacceptable, poor, fair, good, excellent, superior, and exceptional.

20-4 Self-service retailing uses the discount philosophy of customers shopping without help from store personnel and taking their selections to a well-marked check-out area.

20-5 Limited-service retailers have some salespeople who offer assistance to customers as well as customer service desks where purchases are paid for and bagged.

follow a ***value positioning*** strategy, with middle price point merchandise and a medium amount of service.

Limited-service retailers offer expected services, as well as essential services. Services expected by customers include the acceptance of several credit cards, layaway privileges, shorter check-out lines, and more personalized answers to shopping questions, 20-5.

- *Full-service retailing* involves salespeople assisting customers one-to-one in every phase of the shopping process. Specialty stores and upscale department stores have more salespeople to wait on customers and provide many services. They pursue a ***service positioning*** strategy with higher prices to cover the personal services. The higher operating costs, resulting from so many services, are passed along to customers. A distinctive service mix can create competitive benefits that are long lasting and quite hard to imitate.

  Full-service retailers offer optional services, as well as essential and expected services. Optional services help retailers distinguish themselves from others with prompt, courteous service at all times and under all conditions. They might include some or many of the services listed in 20-6. Since shopping can be an emotional experience for consumers, these stores become memorable if some aspect is unexpectedly wonderful!

Assessing Service Quality

Service quality is how well services are performed. It is the degree to which a retailer approaches, meets, or exceeds customer expectations. Consumer expectation levels are rising, and competitive success is largely driven by what customers think of the quality of the services provided.

Retail services enhance customers' perceived value of each product purchase. Shoppers who are willing to pay a higher price for better goods also expect outstanding customer service. High service requires that salespeople and other employees be friendly, polite, approachable, trustworthy, and reliable. Employee training is very important so salespeople know how to listen well and provide customers with a pleasurable, hassle-free shopping experience. Consumers assess the quality of retail service by comparing it to their desires for fine facilities, merchandise, and all customer service offerings.

Service quality should be communicated to shoppers in such a way that they can fully perceive the uniqueness of the offerings. Then it is judged by customers according to the actions of the employees providing the services. Any service feature is only as

Optional Retail Services

- In-store events, product demonstrations, or guest appearances
- Art shows that feature works of local artists
- No-questions-asked return or exchange policies
- Almost unlimited customer freedom with merchandise
- Delivery to home, office, or anywhere else
- Free adjustments to all items purchased, such as clothing alterations or jewelry engraving
- Before- or after-hours shopping by appointment
- A formally-dressed musician playing a grand piano in the store
- Hospitality room and store give-aways (such as a tote bag) for conventioneers visiting the city
- A shopping service that will find a needed product at a competing store if it is not stocked by its store
- An employee book on regular customers that lists preferences, needs, buying history, and important dates
- Telephone and Web site orders
- Interest-free credit
- Bridal consultants and registries
- Personal shoppers to pick items out for customers
- Fashion shows, personal makeovers, or instructional seminars given in the community
- Call buttons in fitting rooms
- Cashing personal checks
- Interpreters for language assistance
- A newsletter to key customers telling about the newest fashions or best values
- An emphasis on environmentally friendly products
- A greeter at the entrance to offer help, give directions, and answer questions
- Information and complaint desks
- Complementary tea, cappuccino, cookies, etc.
- Thank-you notes for purchases
- Drinking fountains and elegant rest rooms
- Rooms/space provided for private, public, or club meetings or exhibits
- Children's play area and gifts
- A do-it-yourself gift wrap table for children and dads before Mother's Day
- Drawings and contests
- Free coat and package check
- Corporate gift service
- Customer phones and free 800 numbers for comments or questions

20-6 These optional services bring more customers to a store and encourage them to stay longer to make more purchases. However, more services increase costs, and once a particular service is offered, it can't be easily eliminated. Also, other stores copy it and customers soon come to expect it.

good as the actions of those who provide it. Most retail service complaints center around lack of respect for customers by store employees. Pleasant, customer-centered dealings should occur at all levels of the organization, 20-7.

To deliver consistently good customer service, retailers should evaluate whether customers are really satisfied. A clear, measurable assessment is needed of how their customers perceive their merchandise selection, service quality, billings, returns, delivery, and other areas.

An evaluation starts by determining the most important service requirements of the company's specific target market. Then information should be collected not only from customers, but also from salespeople and employees at all levels. Anonymous comment cards may provide a format for gathering such information. Finally,

20-7 All employees should be concerned with service to customers, including merchandise buyers, maintenance workers, salespeople, and specialized workers, such as this mall customer service representative.

the firm measures its performance against its requirements to see how effective it is in meeting customer needs. The company should be able to see how to take corrective action by improving service in those areas that are being performed at an unsatisfactory level.

Service improvement should be an ongoing commitment. It cannot be effective without employee teamwork and cooperation. A company-wide training and development program should emphasize attitude, caring, attentiveness, a sense of urgency, and courtesy. Training for employees should emphasize the importance of feedback about customer service, show how to positively improve customers' perceptions of services received, and offer rewards for new ideas about how to serve customers better. Customer satisfaction is fundamental to the success of any organization.

Customer relationship management (CRM) merges database information technology with customer service to analyze customers, respond individually to their needs, and build and maintain lasting relationships. Computer-collected customer information is used to provide customized services that give a competitive advantage. Companies understand their customers and please them with the correct goods, services, and ongoing communications. CRM brings customers back to retailers and encourages them to buy more while they're there. Also, retailers can determine which shoppers are the most loyal and profitable, and which require additional service. Loyalty reward programs can be provided for the best customers. Retail success increases because of providing consistent superior service.

Department of Consumer Studies; University of Delaware

20-8 Training about how to handle customer dissatisfaction is important to be able to resolve problems and create store loyalty.

Service Features

Service features are the actual service offerings. They include such features as accessible location and parking, convenient store hours, complaint resolution, knowledgeable salespeople, credit, and layaway. Other services include packaging, gift wrapping, fast checkout, delivery, alterations, and guarantees.

Accessible Locations and Parking

As mentioned in Chapter 13, consumers prefer to shop at convenient site locations. A location near a major highway or road that is easily entered and exited by car, or that has a bus stop near the entrance, is desired. Free parking or *validated parking* (the store marks the parking lot or garage stub as paid) is an expected customer service in many cases.

Also, customers appreciate a store that is easy to enter and has an interior layout that enables easy movement from area to area. These factors are not always thought of as customer service features, but they are very important to bring customers to the store and to satisfy their needs.

Store Hours

Store hours may be lengthened to satisfy changing consumer lifestyles or more competitive conditions. Evening, weekend, and holiday hours are now expected, but they increase retailers' costs of labor and utilities. They also increase personnel problems and security risks. Store hours may be limited due to various state or community legal restrictions, such as being closed on Sundays. Store hours should coincide with customers' social and religious attitudes that could affect the store's image.

Complaint Resolution

Complaint resolution is the settlement of customers' dissatisfactions with the store or its merchandise. Mutual agreement is reached between the two parties as to how to solve specific problems, including returns and adjustments, 20-8. It may involve resolving differences about price; damaged or imperfect goods; or mislabeled or mismatched sizes, styles, or colors. Some returns occur because customers make mistakes, change their minds, or are dishonest about their purchases. Customers may be given money off, money back, or an exchange. The spectrum of return policies among retailers runs from allowing no returns to a full cash refund with no questions asked.

Suggestions for Handling Complaints

- Be pleasant and businesslike with the customer.
- Encourage the customer to talk.
- Listen carefully, avoiding interruptions.
- Have a positive attitude, trying not to argue.
- Ask for suggestions.
- Apologize for the situation and inconvenience.
- Assure the customer of satisfaction.
- Show a sincere desire and effort to please.
- Act quickly to correct the situation.
- Sincerely thank the customer.

20-9 Retail employees should try to follow this list of actions for proper handling of complaints. How complaints are handled can leave lasting impressions with shoppers.

Lands' End Direct Merchants

20-10 High-service retailers offer gift wrapping free with purchases. Medium-priced retailers may offer gift wrapping for a fee, while discount stores usually do not offer any gift-wrapping service.

Complaint resolution can identify problems with the store's products or its services. It can show customer dissatisfaction with certain salespeople, such as incompetence, dishonesty, or selling methods used. How a company handles complaints is often more important to the customer than the actual adjustment. If problems are resolved quickly and well, it can be a source of customer satisfaction. They will likely tell others of how the store handled their complaint and recommend the store to others. If handled poorly, it is hard to regain dissatisfied customers, their families, and friends.

Good customer relations includes listening carefully to customer complaints, reassuring the customer, and apologizing for the situation. The employee helping the customer must be able to quickly analyze the problem and be prepared to help with an appropriate solution, 20-9.

Wrapping

The category of *wrapping* is comprised of bagging, store wrap, and gift wrap. *Bagging*, or putting merchandise into a sack, is almost always expected. It facilitates handling of purchases, especially with multiple products. It also protects the purchased merchandise from inclement weather and preserves the privacy of customer purchases. *Store wrap* puts customers' purchases in a distinctive store box, bag, or wrapping paper of a particular color and design. This helps to advertise the store and encourages gift buying from prestige stores. *Gift wrap* includes added features, such as colorfully designed paper plus a ribbon or bow, 20-10. Many retailers charge customers a fee for gift wrapping, which is usually done at one centralized location in the store.

Fast Merchandise Checkout

Time has increasingly become a premium commodity for consumers. Because consumers do not like delays, retailers try to make sure that items are always in stock, that merchandise is easy to find, and that customers can go through the check-out procedure quickly. Long checkout lines cause stores to lose customers who become frustrated when the wait is unacceptable to them. Sometimes they abandon their merchandise selections and leave the store. There are also problems with shoppers waiting to check out merchandise while salespeople speak to customers who phone in with questions or orders.

To counteract long waits, some stores have added more or newer checkout terminals for flexibility during busy times. New POS computers process transactions quickly and efficiently, as well as give information on inventory levels, the location of certain items, credit verifications, and the timing of new merchandise deliveries. Other stores have portable POS scanners that check out customers without the use of stationary registers. Salespeople can break into lines during peak times or go to the busiest departments to process transactions. The battery-powered bar-code scanners have a keypad with display, thermal printer for receipts, and magnetic stripe reader for credit cards. Since the terminals do not have cash drawers, only credit card transactions are processed away from the regular registers. The scanners are usually transported on a cart that contains bags for the purchased merchandise.

A few stores are now turning to total self-service selling with completely automated checkout systems. Some grocery and discount stores provide shoppers with hand-held electronic scanners to read codes on packages. It records the price of each item as shoppers place the items into take-home containers in their carts (or deducts the price if they change their minds). When the shopping is completed, the device

20-11 The United Parcel Service (UPS) is one of several independent delivery services hired by retailers to deliver merchandise to customers' homes or places of business.

prints out a bill and the shopper swipes a credit card to pay, then returns the scanner. The process is very fast, with no need to unpack goods at the checkout counter. However, spot checks are made to keep consumers honest!

Other stores use automated, do-it-yourself checkout machines that resemble regular checkout scanning stations. As the customer scans the code from each item, a small display screen shows the price while the machine's built-in voice verifies the price for the customer. When necessary, the voice also prompts the customer, such as if an item must be rescanned. Less stock shrinkage from theft occurs with this system since these stations are located in plain view and are overseen and assisted by cashiers who cash-out other customers.

Delivery Service

A store delivery service may be necessary for retailers that

- take telephone or mail orders;
- are located in large urban areas with customers who use public transportation;
- have a prestige image that they want to emphasize;
- sell large, bulky products, such as furniture or appliances;
- promote top service for items needed in an emergency, such as prescription drugs.

However, a delivery service is hard to plan, execute, and control. Problems include customers wanting the goods immediately, people who are not home to receive the items, and fluctuations in delivery demand that hamper planning. Other problems include damage in transit, inaccurate deliveries, and theft of goods from trucks or drop-off locations. Thus, most stores have discontinued their in-house delivery systems and now hire independent delivery services, such as UPS, 20-11. These businesses consolidate their deliveries for efficiency, offer cash-on-delivery (COD) services, make call-backs for undeliverable items, and assume liability for damaged or lost packages.

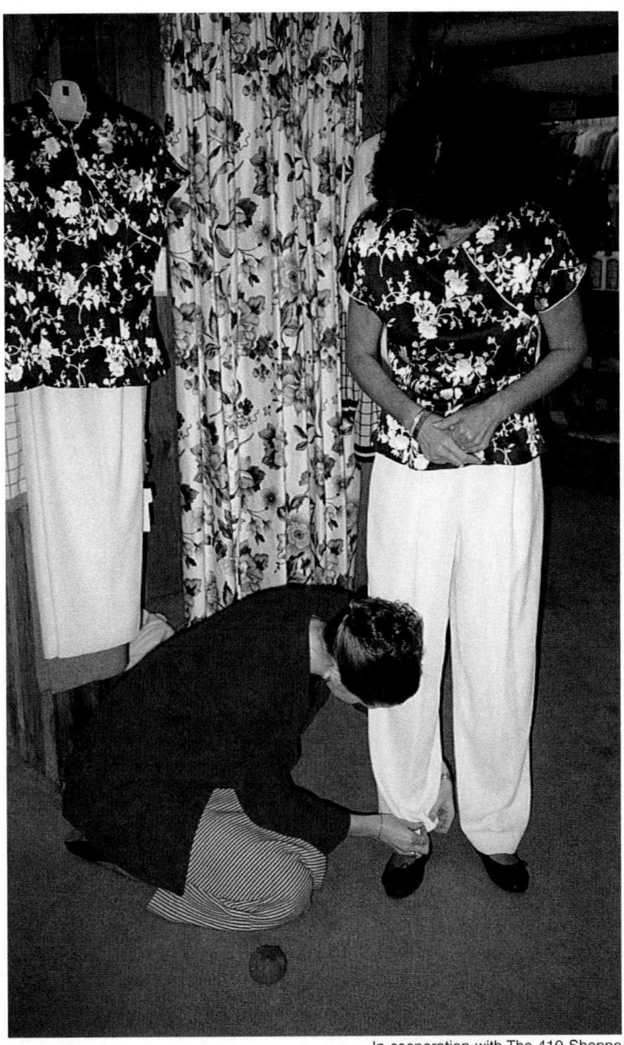

In cooperation with The 410 Shoppe

20-12 Better retailers offer alteration services to customers.

Alterations

Offering garment alterations can encourage the sale of goods and/or be an income-producing service, 20-12. Consumers expect free alteration services with expensive clothing purchases. For less expensive apparel, retailers charge for alterations.

Alterations can be done in the store or contracted out to private alteration services. In-store alterations permit direct control, but can create staffing and equipment problems. Contracting with private services eliminates these problems, but results in less control and longer waiting times for customers.

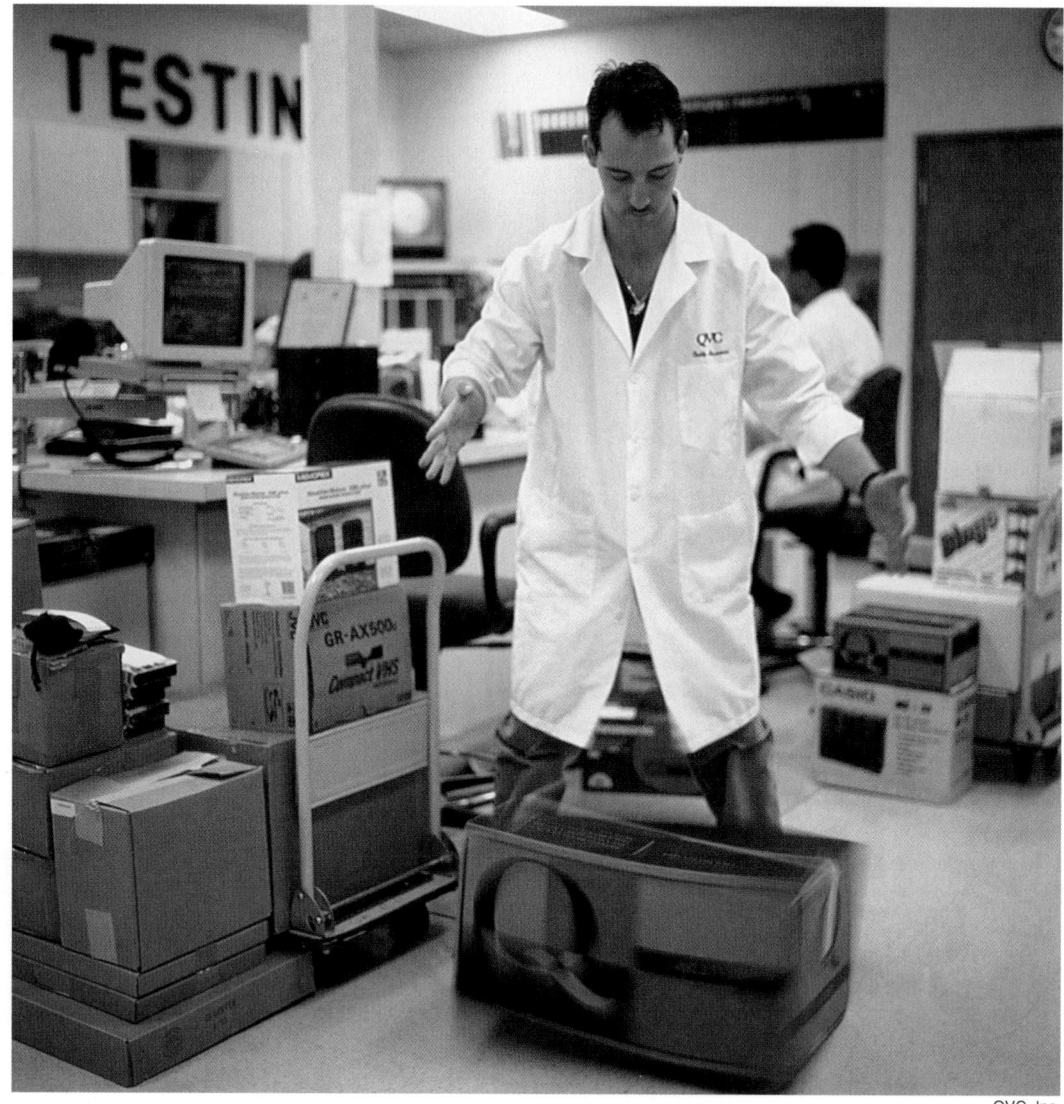

QVC, Inc.

20-13 To offer product guarantees, retailers may do their own testing of goods they sell to consumers.

Product Warranties

Warranties, also called guarantees, are assurances of product quality given to customers by manufacturers or retailers. Companies express their general responsibility for the quality and performance of the goods they make or sell. If customers are not satisfied with products, retailers offer return privileges and/or allowances. Jewelry stores may offer a certificate of registration for each gem setting, guaranteeing that the gems and mountings have no defects. If any are found, customers receive their money back.

Implied warranties are intended promises of product performance that are not expressed in written or oral form. These may relate to such factors as size, fit, construction, workmanship, colorfastness, or shrinkage. Some large retailers have testing laboratories so they can guarantee quality, 20-13. The success of such programs is hard to measure quantitatively, but sales do usually build because of repeat customers. Consumer complaints decrease, and satisfied customers increase.

Credit and Other Payment Services

Consumer credit allows customers to receive merchandise immediately and pay for it later. Offering credit has become essential for consumers and expected from retailers. It also stabilizes the timing of retail sales as credit purchases can be made throughout the month, rather than just near consumer paydays. Also, sales volumes increase because customers tend to buy more goods, and at higher prices, with credit. However, with money not coming in immediately, as it does for cash sales, offering credit may tie up funds in accounts receivable until bills are paid by customers.

The following are the three main types of credit plans offered by retailers:

- An *open account*, or thirty-day charge account. Also called a regular charge account, this plan is available to consumers with good credit ratings. All charges are to be paid in full within a specific time period, with no finance charge or interest added. The time within which it must be paid is usually thirty days from the billing date, but sometimes deferred billing allows a longer time to pay. A finance charge may be assessed for late payment beyond the due date.
- An *installment plan*, or installment credit. This plan requires a small down payment plus additional payments spread over several months or years. It is often used for expensive items. Equal ongoing installment payments are made until the total has been paid, plus interest. Installment agreements are legal contracts between retailers and consumers, with terms and conditions spelled out in writing and signed by both parties.
- A *revolving charge account*, or revolving credit, includes some features of both an open account and installment plan. Usually it is a regular thirty-day charge account, which may be paid in full by a certain date with no finance charge. It may also be paid in monthly installments, with interest charged on the unpaid balance. Sometimes a minimum fixed payment must be made each month. The customer may continue to add new purchases to the account until a predetermined credit limit is reached. Most major bank credit cards are of this type.

20-14 Most retailers have to accept credit cards in order to compete. Some offer their own cards, as well as accepting third-party credit cards.

Retail Credit Cards

A few retailers offer their own credit cards with the store's name and logo. Most stores also accept third-party credit cards, 20-14. A new offering is the secured credit card.

Proprietary credit cards are store-issued credit cards that are owned and managed by the retail firm. It is believed that proprietary credit cards, with instant store identity, increase customer loyalty and attract new customers with an image of product quality and service. Stores that offer these in-house cards try to establish goodwill and maintain a personal relationship with customers through special mailings and bill inserts. Stores get a great deal of market information about shoppers when customers fill out credit applications and use the credit to make specific purchases that are recorded. This creates a customer database for CRM programs. Also, retailers who form close relationships with their customers can adapt more quickly to changing customer expectations.

Although additional money can be made from proprietary credit card systems because of interest charged, there are also extra operating expenses. These occur from the need for more office space, personnel, equipment, and communications. To recover unpaid balances, fees and commissions must be paid to outside collection agencies. Some bad debts are never collected. Also, customer complaints sometimes necessitate adjustments to retail charge accounts. These might involve the correction of such errors as overcharging, improper recording, and incorrect dating.

Private label credit cards have the store's name and logo, but are issued and managed by a bank. Customer loyalty benefits and costs to retailers for these *co-branded cards* are similar to proprietary credit. Card issuers and retailers are working more closely as partners these days, for individualized database marketing programs. Retailers pay a fee to the bank which, in turn, bills customers. Many of the store's credit management problems are avoided by outsourcing the service to a financial institution. Small- to medium-sized retailers that offer credit cards often have private label systems rather than in-house systems.

Third-party credit cards are general use credit cards issued by outside institutions. Examples of these cards are Mastercard, Discover, American Express, and VISA. To accept this type of credit, stores do not need to establish or maintain a credit department, but must process the cards responsibly. They do not need to investigate credit applications, bill customers, or pursue collections. They can offer credit to a wider range of consumers, such as out-of-town visitors, rather than losing those sales. Also, they can maintain a steady cash flow from credit card institutions.

Stores that accept third-party credit must pay financial institutions a service charge, which is a percentage of the amount of money charged. Another disadvantage is that retailers cannot learn as much about their customers. In this information age, where emphasis is increasingly placed on knowing customers' desires, retailers are unable to track their customers' buying habits when they use third-party cards.

Some stores accept third-party cards, but also have in-house charge cards. They encourage customers to use their proprietary card, viewed as a marketing and promotional tool, and accept general cards only as a service to their customers.

Secured credit cards are now being offered to card applicants who might not qualify for most credit cards. Each secured credit card is linked to a savings account containing enough money to back up most or all of the credit line. With this service product, retailers are trying to create long-term loyalty with less credit-worthy shoppers.

Secured credit cards can be co-branded (store and bank) or proprietary (store managed). Since they are issued to consumers who are high credit risks, they tend to generate greater office work and higher costs. They are usually not moneymakers like regular credit cards. Instead, they are part of a marketing strategy, offered as an extra service and a defense against competitive stores.

A secured credit card program gives a retailer access to a new group of customers—consumers who cannot qualify for unsecured credit. These customers will probably be more loyal than average because of the confidence the merchant is showing by extending credit. A secured credit card program also serves as a "feeder system" into regular, unsecured credit cards.

Retail-Affiliated Credit Card Banks

The nation's largest retailers, all of whom have proprietary credit card programs, are now cashing in on the benefits of operating their own financial institutions. Retail credit card banks operate under federal charter and regulations that require all procedures to be well documented and stringently followed. However, they can "export" their late fees and interest rates. In other words, they can charge cardholders located anywhere the maximum interest rate permitted in the state where the credit card bank is located. Thus, they locate their banks in states with liberal interest rate laws that are also close to their retail operations.

Other Electronic Processing

Specialized financial companies offer credit card processing, check authorization, and other services to retailers. Replacing older, slow, paper-based procedures, these electronic database services can be tied to merchant locations nationwide and sometimes worldwide. Because of improved technology, they are very effective in fighting the serious problems of credit card and check fraud.

Credit Processing

Credit processing involves (1) initial credit approval when someone applies for a credit card and (2) ongoing authorization when credit transactions are made. Credit approval is done by checking with the consumer's bank and grantors of their other credit cards. A judgment is then made as to whether the individual is "credit worthy" or not.

For credit card authorization, the retailer enters a number into a special terminal. The terminal dials out to access the database, which then transmits back an "accept" or "decline" message. A decline message results if the consumer is using a card that has been discontinued, is over its credit limit, or has been reported stolen. Though transaction processing is becoming faster, it is slowest at peak shopping times such as during the holiday season. This is because thousands of retailers are electronically dialing into the system for authorizations at the same time.

After electronic authorization, the customer signs a credit slip to finalize the transaction. The customer is given a copy of the slip, the store keeps one for its records, and a third is sent to the bank or financial institution that issued the credit card. The store receives payment from the bank, minus a percentage of the amount charged as a fee for performing the service. The customer receives a bill from the bank that combines charges from all retailers and other credit transactions of that account for the month.

Check Verification

Most retailers also subscribe to service organizations with check verification (authorization) databases. ***Check verification*** minimizes the risk of accepting personal checks from customers and involves a similar procedure to credit card authorization. Recognizing that pooled information is the most efficient and cost-effective way to stop bad checks from being accepted, most retailers have joined the Shared Check Authorization Network (SCAN). Its value increases as the number of participants grows.

The central SCAN database is updated each night by members who transmit returned-check data to a central host computer. This provides a comprehensive and continually updated file that members can use in their check authorization processes. They search either by check number or driver's license number. If there is a match, the check is declined rather than being cashed or accepted as payment for merchandise. Retailers pay a flat fee each time they run a check authorization query.

In addition to retail bad-check data, SCAN is amended with data provided by financial institutions of stolen checks and checking accounts that have been closed. However, there is no guarantee that a check is good even if it has been approved through SCAN because it is matched only against what is already in the database. First-time bad checks, or those that pass outside of the network, are not flagged by the system.

With check verification, the merchant must accept the loss if the check bounces or pay a collection service to try to get the payment. Because bad checks have become so common, some stores are turning from check verification to the more certain alternative of check guarantees. With a ***check guarantee*** service, if any check is bad, the service firm reimburses the merchant and tries to collect the money on its own. The risk then falls on the bank or firm that authorized the transaction.

Check guarantee is more expensive than verification, costing a percentage of the face value of each check. However, many merchants feel the extra guarantee fees are worth it. By using it, the store does not have to turn down sales or have high staffing expenses and financial losses, especially from expensive items.

Debit Processing

Debit processing, also called *electronic funds transfer (EFT),* electronically takes the money for a purchase out of the consumer's bank account and puts it into the merchant's bank account. It is similar to a cash transaction, but a debit card is used and no money is actually handed from the shopper to the cashier. This is not a credit transaction because payment is made immediately, rather than at a later time. Some consumers also pay their bills this way, using their personal computer and a modem to transfer funds from their bank account into merchant bank accounts.

Another type of debit card is the *smart card*, or cash card. It looks like a credit card but contains a programmable microchip instead of a magnetic stripe. The microchip can store data or value, such as being loaded with a cash amount. The loading can be done from the consumer's bank account by phone or computer. The cards are also used for phone calls, highway toll collections, and medical information. They promote honesty since they are hard to duplicate. Special retail POS terminals are needed to read smart cards. Some stores are using the cards in place of paper gift certificates, as well as accepting them for check-out cash. Smart cards will also be used for secure online e-tailing payments in the future.

Retailers are also now using *electronic check conversion*, which converts paper checks into EFT at point-of-sale. The process reduces customer checkout time, shows if customers have sufficient funds or are presenting fraudulent checks, and gives merchants their money faster. Stores need special POS terminals that capture images of checks and convert them to electronic transactions, but fees are lower than for check verification or check guarantee services.

Safety

A safe environment helps to attract and keep customers coming back to a store. A safe workplace is also important for the well-being of the store's employees. Customer safety and employee safety are important concerns of fashion retailers in addition to product safety.

Customer Safety

Customer safety can be placed into two basic categories. Retailers want to protect their customers from criminal attack and they also want to protect them from accidental injury. The fear of crime has affected consumer shopping patterns. Customers patronize stores that enable them to shop safely. They spend more time and money where they have a secure feeling. Meanwhile, catalogs, television shopping channels, and Internet retailers tout the safety of shopping from home.

Retailers can do much to assure the safety of their customers. Examples of customer safety measures include providing rest room attendants and well-lighted stores and parking lots, 20-15. Also, guards in malls, high fences around parking lots, and surveillance camera systems help shoppers feel they are in a safe environment, 20-16.

Stores and shopping malls must provide safe shopping environments. They may be sued if accidents or personal crime occur as a result of their negligence. This is a liability that is worth each merchant's attention. Most retailers are very concerned about the personal safety of their shoppers. Employees must be taught to do everything reasonable and prudent to keep the store and its customers safe.

Store policies and rules are established for the safety and protection of customers and employees. Falls are the leading public liability claim. These can occur from wet floors when customers track in rain or snow. Floors can also be slippery after maintenance workers have waxed them. Cluttered aisles can occur when restocking shelves. Also, unmarked changes in floor levels cause shoppers to trip. "Caution—Wet Floor" or "Aisle Closed" signs should be posted to warn people of unsafe conditions. Companies are responsible when there is a dangerous condition of which they have knowledge and fail to try to rectify. Though unethical, some consumers try to get money for situations that are essentially beyond the control of retailers and mall operators.

Employee Safety

Companies should train their employees in accident prevention procedures. This will help to prevent injury from work-related causes. Almost all companies have safety programs to train and guide their employees. They include speakers, videos, handbooks, and specific rules to follow.

Lower accident rates can reduce the company's workmen's compensation insurance payments. They also reduce the extra pay for temporary replacement

Sensormatic

20-15 Retail stores or malls must be concerned with the safety of shoppers in the parking lots that they own.

Sensormatic

20-16 Surveillance camera systems have many cameras pointing at various places in retail stores, and they can be monitored from one location.

employees while injured employees are recuperating. These procedures also help to prevent lawsuits.

Policies relating to safety issues should be strictly enforced. This shows a company's commitment to the well-being of their employees. Companies that wait until they receive a complaint on workplace safety issues before taking action may find themselves in court.

Store Security

Store security involves loss prevention of merchandise, money, and other company possessions. Shortages from customer and employee theft are shockingly high, with estimates running at about 2 percent of all retail sales. Thus, for every million dollars in sales, $20,000 may be stolen. Store security also tries to prevent fires and other catastrophes, as well as being ready with emergency response plans.

Shrinkage, or stock shortage, is the difference between book inventory (according to records) and actual physical inventory. It is the reduction in total inventory value that is not recorded in the business accounts. Shrinkage can be the result of theft, clerical errors, or merchandise being damaged. Fashion merchandise can be damaged when customers try on garments, such as a zipper breaking or makeup getting on a garment. These items, then, cannot be sold.

External Theft

External theft is stealing by people who are not employed or otherwise associated with the firm. For retailers, external theft includes credit card fraud, check fraud, robbery, and shoplifting. Theft has also occurred by outsiders adjusting accounts via computer. However, secret codes and blocking methods are constantly being developed to counteract computer fraud. Fraudulent activities concerning credit cards and checks have already been discussed in this chapter.

Robbery is daytime burglary or after-hours theft. Retail stores have easy public access, available cash, employees disbursed or working alone, and after-dark hours that make them crime targets. *Closed circuit television (CCTV)* security systems are installed in stores and warehouses to ward off crimes and workplace violence. These systems can watch back entrances or detect and track unauthorized movement with intricate sensing devices. Alarm signals are automatically dialed and transmitted over telephone lines or cellular networks from the protected building to a central alarm monitoring station. The monitoring station immediately dispatches the police.

Shoplifting is the stealing of merchandise from a retail store by a person posing as a customer, 20-17. Apparel is traditionally one of the prime targets of shoplifters, as well as small, expensive items such as jewelry and electronic devices. Incidents of shoplifting have increased, mainly due to fewer salespeople on the selling floor. Professional shoplifting rings have also organized. These well-trained gangs move around the country hitting retailers swiftly and hard. They grab as many items as possible and flee in vans before officials can detain them. The stolen merchandise is then sold elsewhere, repackaged or with different tags.

Suspicious behavior and shoplifting should be reported to store security by anyone who observes it taking place. It is a serious crime, punishable by fine or imprisonment. Also, anyone who has a record of shoplifting will not be employed by retailers or other fashion merchandising companies.

Merchants can attempt to reduce shoplifting by

- training employees in shoplifting prevention;
- controlling exits;
- closing unmanned checkout areas;
- hiring security guards;
- using special detection equipment and anti-theft tags, 20-18; and
- placing monitors in secluded areas of the store.

Most stores do not want their shoplifting prevention efforts to be so obtrusive as to interfere with the store's pleasing atmosphere. On the other hand, the obvious presence of a security system helps to prevent theft. Shoplifters tend to go where it is easiest to steal.

Areas where shoplifters can conceal stolen merchandise include partially-open umbrellas, baby seats and strollers, unsealed packages from other purchases, and the bottom of shopping carts. Employees also need to be aware of customers with large coats and briefcases that can be used to hide stolen items. If cashiers notice concealed merchandise at the checkout terminal, they should ask the customer if he or she wishes to purchase the merchandise. This does not accuse the shopper of theft if it cannot be proven that the customer meant to conceal the merchandise. Also, the store then gets the money for the sale.

Electronic article surveillance (EAS) is a shoplifting prevention system that uses tags containing a small circuit that emits a radio signal. The tags are affixed to merchandise, sometimes inside UPC tickets, labels, or hangtags. The signal can be sensed by electronic pedestals or other devices placed at store exits, 20-19. Salespeople either pass the merchandise tag across a special deactivation unit or remove the entire tag with a mechanical device. Some POS scanners can deactivate tags at the same time as the item and price are entered into the system. If tagged merchandise leaves the store without the circuit being deactivated, an alarm alerts store personnel of theft.

Some vendors now apply the EAS tags to their merchandise before delivering it to the store, thus saving stores considerable time in attaching the tags. ***Source tagging*** is the process of integrating anti-shoplifting tags into product packaging at the manufacturing level. It combines security with floor-ready merchandise programs. Technology is continually improving source tagging.

Internal Theft

Internal theft is done by store employees. Theft can occur at the store level or elsewhere within the pipeline, such as at the supplier level. Recently, more losses are occurring from internal theft than from external theft, as shown in 20-20. New technology is being used in an attempt to reduce employee theft. Overhead cameras and other surveillance devices monitor employee behavior, backrooms, and cash registers. Hiring procedures include a more complete personal and job history and police checks of applicants. Multiple interviews and integrity screening programs also help in hiring honest employees. Additionally, employees can be trained to take an active role in preventing internal loss.

Pilferage is the stealing of a company's inventory or cash in small, petty amounts. Employees who take small items, such as pencils or pens, usually think it does not amount to much money. However, if many employees do this, the dollars lost add up quickly. Often this small theft builds to larger items and becomes a serious crime issue. Rolls of quarters, packets of dollar bills, skirts, sweaters, coats, VCRs, computers, and other items "walk out the door" undetected. Apparel manufacturers sometimes find themselves missing sewing machines!

Sensormatic

20-17 Shoplifting is often accomplished by hiding items under the garments the thieves are wearing.

There is a strong temptation for cashier theft. ***Sweethearting*** is providing discounts, uncharged items, or fraudulent returns to friends, relatives, or theft partners, 20-21. Cashier thefts are considered to be losses going out of the "front end" of the store. Retailers are fighting internal theft with "exception-reporting" software. This software uses artificial intelligence to analyze POS data. It recognizes unusual patterns of post-voids, returns, refunds, credit charges, or other fraudulent activity.

Closed-circuit television or video monitoring systems can read transaction tapes that prove illegal cashier activities. Suspected cashiers are tracked if their sales entries deviate from statistical norms, such as average item price, average items per minute, or high return rates. Publicizing such a surveillance system usually deters internal theft, reducing losses without further action.

"Back end" losses occur at such places as warehouses, loading docks, and stock rooms. Many retailers now require merchandise to contain electronic source tagging before leaving manufacturers' warehouses. Some electronic activation can be done in bulk as merchandise leaves a warehouse and the address is registered. Thus, manufacturers are source tagging items with dormant tags that can be activated when

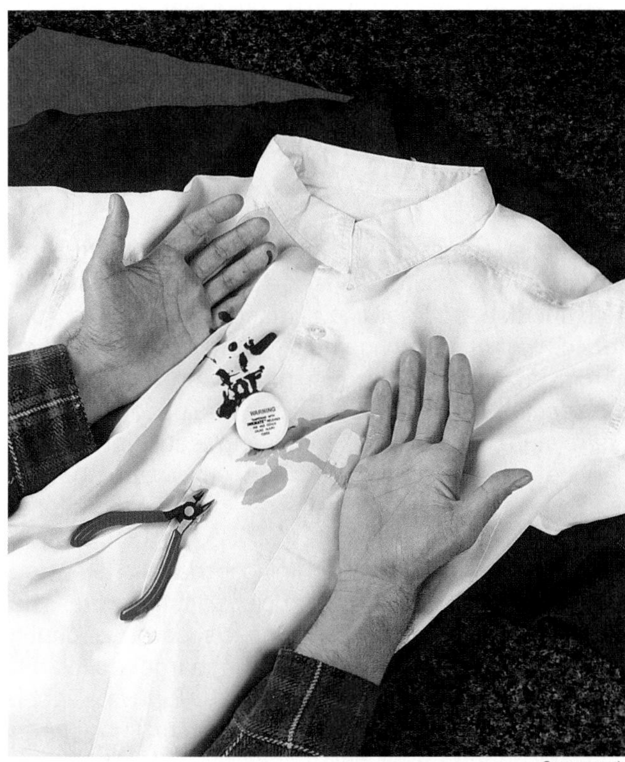

Sensormatic

20-18 Some anti-shoplifting tags release ink if not removed by a special tool at the retail cash register. This deters theft since the items cannot be used even if they are taken from the store.

Sensormatic

20-19 If this shopper was to take items from the store that did not have the EAS tags removed or deactivated at the cash register, the pedestals would cause an alarm to ring.

desired. For instance, some shoe products have electronic tags or magnetic strips placed inside shoe soles at the time of construction, replacing the need for tagging shoeboxes.

Causes of Retail Shrinkage	
Employee theft	42%
Shoplifting	34%
Administrative paperwork errors	18%
Vendor fraud	6%

National Retail Security Survey, University of Florida

20-20 These recent statistics show the percent of annual retail store losses that are attributable to various sources.

Stores are also sharing data on employee thefts through a national database of retail workers fired for stealing from their employers. Mutual protective associations have become an indispensable tool for reducing internal theft and keeping those guilty of such crimes out of the labor pool. It has been found that some people involved in employee theft are chronic criminals who, once caught and fired, merely apply for work at another store.

However, there are some drawbacks to the effectiveness of the system. The protective associations must abide by certain legal disclosure limitations. If employees are merely fired, without signing a statement of guilt or being prosecuted, they cannot be listed by the associations. They can move from one job to another, stealing cash and merchandise along the way. Prosecution is expensive, with legal fees and lost working hours for court visits. Also, criminal information is automatically purged after a certain number of years, in accordance with the Fair Credit Reporting Act.

Sensormatic

20-21 The woman posing as a shopper is really in a sweethearting crime. Her partner, the salesperson, has rung up her "purchases," voided the total so no money is owed, and will remove security tags and bag the items for her to take from the store.

Key Loss Prevention Methods
Screening of New Employees
Past employment verification Personal reference checks Criminal conviction checks Credit checks Pencil and paper honesty tests Driving history checks Education verification
Loss Prevention Awareness
Include in new employee orientation Periodic in-house security programs Bulletin board notices Training videotapes Anonymous telephone hotline Honesty incentives Employee newsletters
Loss Prevention Systems
Closed circuit television/video Observation mirrors Electronic anti-shoplifting tags Secured displays with cables and locks Plain-clothes security personnel Uniformed guards
Asset Control Policies
Refund controls Void controls Controlled access to cash Merchandise receiving controls Interstore transfer controls Price change controls Employee package checks Unobserved exit controls POS exception records POS bar coding/scanning Inventory bar coding/scanning Trash removal controls

National Retail Security Survey, University of Florida

20-22 These methods are used by many retailers to reduce losses and crime.

Loss Prevention Programs

Loss prevention (LP) strategies are being instituted by companies to prevent, recognize, and monitor security problems. Programs are aimed at reducing shrinkage from all causes. Suggested measures for minimizing losses are shown in 20-22. These programs often involve a combination of electronic article surveillance, closed circuit television surveillance, raised viewing platforms, mirrors, and point-of-sale monitoring. All of these provisions create extra costs. The markup on merchandise must be increased to cover shrinkage losses, as well as the overhead costs of hiring additional people and buying specialized equipment.

Summary

The end goal of retailers is to serve customers. Strategies that include different price levels and products include self-service, limited-service, and full-service retailing. Service quality enhances customers' perceived value of product purchases. Service features include accessible locations and parking, convenient store hours, and complaint resolution. Other services often provided include gift wrapping, fast merchandise checkout, delivery service, alterations, and products warranties.

Offering credit has become essential and expected from retailers, as a convenience for consumers. The three main types of credit plans are open accounts, installment plans, and revolving charge accounts. Retail credit cards include proprietary, private label, third-party, and secured credit cards. Some large retailers operate their own banks for their credit card sales. Besides credit approval and authorization, electronic processing is done for check verification and debit processing.

A safe environment helps stores attract and keep customers, who spend more time and money where they can shop safely. Employee safety programs reduce work-related injuries.

Losses from customer and employee theft are high. Retail external theft includes credit card and check fraud, as well as robbery and shoplifting. Internal theft has created front end and back end losses that recently have exceeded external theft. Loss prevention programs involve a combination of many methods to help reduce both internal and external losses.

To Know

customer service
price positioning
value positioning
service positioning
service quality
costumer relationship management (CRM)
consumer credit
proprietary credit cards
private label credit cards
third-party credit cards
secured credit cards
check verification
check guarantee
debit processing
shrinkage
external theft
shoplifting
source tagging
internal theft
pilferage
sweethearting

To Review

1. Explain proactive and reactive customer service.
2. Name the level of retail service associated with each of the following: essential services, expected services, and optional services.
3. At what service level do national chain organizations, which have middle price points for value-oriented consumers, usually operate?
4. How do full-service retailers cover the higher operating costs?
5. What is the first step in evaluating a store's customer satisfaction?
6. For a complaint about a purchase, what might be more important to the customer than the actual adjustment?
7. What three advantages does bagging of purchases provide for customers?
8. What do frustrated customers sometimes do when a store has unacceptably long checkout lines?
9. What advantages do independent delivery services offer?
10. Besides being a convenience for customers, what advantages result from offering consumer credit?
11. How do proprietary credit cards help stores get market information about shoppers?
12. For credit card authorization, why might a "decline" message be given?
13. Why do you think the SCAN database is considered to be a "negative" file?
14. Why do many stores feel that a check guarantee service is worth the extra fees that it costs?
15. What are the three categories of safety with which retailers are especially interested?
16. What type of accident is the leading public liability claim?
17. Name four ways merchants try to reduce shoplifting.
18. What is electronic article surveillance?
19. Where do losses that go out the "back end" usually occur?
20. List five methods of recognizing theft that may be included in loss prevention programs.

To Do

1. With two classmates, develop a list of customer service features for each of the following three retailers: a chain discount store, a medium-priced department store, a high-fashion boutique. If possible, visit an actual store of each type to investigate what services they offer. Make charts showing your lists and share your information with the class.
2. With a classmate, interview a local self-service retailer and a full-service retailer about their customer complaint resolution systems. Prepare a report indicating which system seems to be the most effective and why.
3. Develop a customer comment card to help retailers evaluate their customer services.
4. Do research and write a paper about how credit programs and electronic processing have evolved through the years. You might want to include the history of various types of credit plans, credit cards, and authorization procedures.
5. With one or two other classmates, develop a program to minimize external and internal losses at a specific store in your community. Contact store management to tell them of your project. Include ideas about technology, employee training, additional personnel, etc. Also note any safety concerns that might need to be corrected. Prepare a report that includes diagrams and descriptions of your plan.

PART 6

Fashion Promotion

CHAPTER 21

Fashion Promotion Through Advertising and the Press

After studying this chapter, you will be able to

- explain the purposes for, and levels of, fashion promotion.
- describe fashion promotion planning, follow-through, budgeting, and ethics.
- summarize the purposes for, and types of, fashion advertising.
- describe advertising agencies and freelancers.
- summarize advertising strategy and media.
- explain how to develop effective print advertisements.
- identify parts of print advertisements.
- define public relations and publicity.
- give examples of the fashion press.

Fashion promotion is one of the four major elements in the marketing mix of product, price, place, and promotion. (See Chapter 3.) Promotion is selling to the general public to increase buying response. It is considered nonpersonal because there is no person-to-person contact. Promotion is done locally, regionally, nationally, or internationally, depending on the scope of the company. It is aimed at communicating with the largest possible targeted audience.

The ***promotion mix*** is the combination of all types of persuasive communication used by an organization to market itself and influence sales. For fashion companies, the promotion mix usually includes advertising, public relations and publicity, visual merchandising, and special events. This chapter will explore advertising, public relations, and the fashion press. The rest of the fashion promotion mix will be described in the next two chapters.

Fashion Promotion

Different companies combine the various elements of the promotion mix in different proportions. This mix is based on the characteristics of their products and the market. Also, for each company, the proportions and emphasis of the mix might change over time. This might be in conjunction with changing economic conditions, seasons, and/or fashion cycles, 21-1.

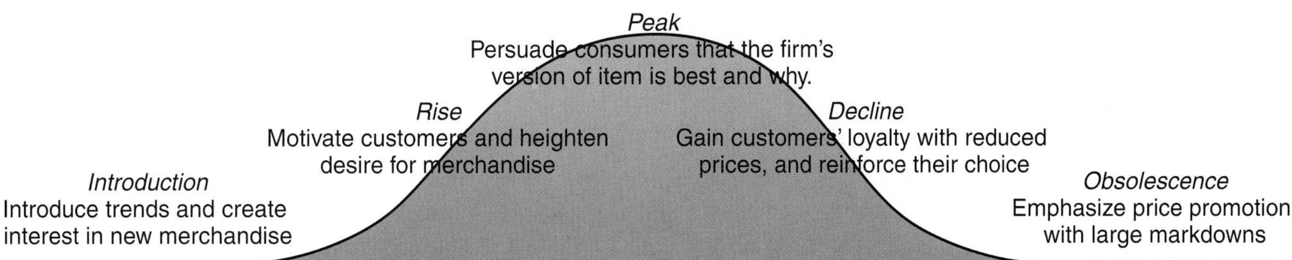

21-1 Different promotional approaches are used effectively during a fashion's various stages of the fashion cycle. Also, a merchant's target market, such as fashion followers, may naturally desire goods at only certain stages of the cycle, thus eliminating the need for promotion at other stages.

The Purposes of Fashion Promotion

Since merchandise does not sell itself, fashion merchandisers use promotion mainly to encourage customers to buy their goods. Promotion also helps to build a company reputation and develop good community relations.

Promotion should be designed to

- *inform*, by creating an awareness and understanding of companies or products. This is especially important when introducing new products, changing prices, or offering new services.
- *persuade*, to convince consumers about the benefits of using certain products or patronizing particular companies, especially in competitive situations.
- *remind*, which reinforces where products are available, encourages purchases, and stimulates additional purchases.

This informing, persuading, and/or reminding attempts to affect behavior by providing consumers with more information about companies and products. See 21-2. It serves to attract new customers, increase sales to existing customers, and boost brand name recognition. Consumers gain information about what they want, why they want it, and where and when to buy it. Continuing promotion confirms customer decisions and encourages additional purchases. Companies, in turn, achieve profitable sales and continued patronage from these customers.

Promotion Levels

Companies in every segment of the textile-apparel pipeline promote to consumers and to each other. The three main levels of promotion in the pipeline are shown in 21-3.

Consumer promotion is promotion directly to consumers, usually done on a national scale by companies that do not sell directly to consumers. The promotion is done even though retailers are the ones who actually sell the items to end users. Large textile and apparel manufacturers are mainly concerned with fashion marketing and preselling to consumers. They promote their lines to gain national or worldwide brand

21-2 This fashion ad by the Spiegel mail-order company informs people about the company's book, persuades them by mentioning its 600-page size and fashion contents, and reminds consumers that a toll-free telephone number and Internet address can get them a special offer.

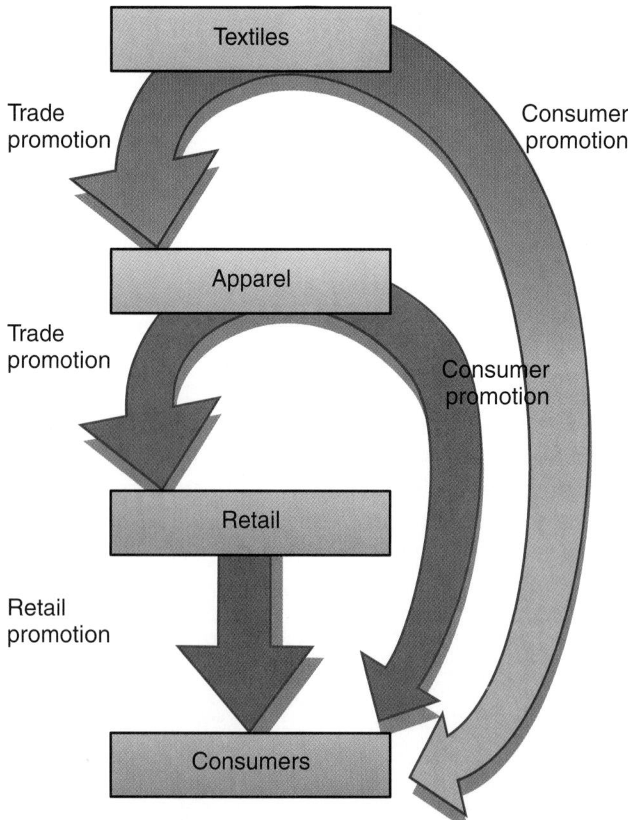

21-3 Some companies in every segment of the soft goods chain promote to end-use consumers with consumer promotion. They also promote to their direct customers in the next segment of the chain.

name recognition and eventual shopping preference from the public. Even if their promotion features specific styles, their main objective is to gain acceptance of their trade names and status labels.

Trade promotion is aimed within the industry, to the next segment of the distribution chain. For instance, fiber and fabric companies promote their textiles to apparel designers and manufacturers, 21-4. Apparel manufacturers promote their styles and lines to retailers. Promotion to a trade audience stresses how well the product performs, and projected profits if the product is purchased. Trade promotion may also involve conventions and trade shows, allowances (discounts), free goods, cooperative advertising, and markdown money.

Retail promotion is promotion by a store to its customers. It is essentially local or targeted consumer promotion. It has different objectives, sales appeals, and approaches than consumer and trade promotion. Stores promote the merchandise they have chosen for their particular target market, hoping to create demand for the items. They try to motivate their customers to buy the products from them by appealing to their desired lifestyles and standards of living. The promotion is often centered around seasonal peaks, traditional buying patterns, and special opportunities to increase sales volume during slow times.

HOT COLORS.
Xtreme Colors
Any wear. Any time.
Vivid new synthetic stretch fabrics from Warshow for today's flexible women's wear.
Call today for samples: 212-921-9200.
H. Warshow and Sons, Inc.

Reese, Tomases & Ellick, Inc., of Delaware

21-4 This eye-catching ad for "top-quality synthetic stretch fabrics" (in the latest colors and hands) is aimed at designers and manufacturers who are seeking new fabrics in which to manufacture their fashions.

Promotion Planning

Sales promotion must be well-planned to be effective. Promotion is more important lately because of increased competition and the similar merchandise offered by many manufacturers and retailers. Fashion merchandisers must differentiate their offerings from competitors to increase sales. Important advantages can be achieved by the way firms and their merchandise are promoted.

An important task of marketing and promotion management is to plan a promotion program. A ***promotion program*** is a written guide that details all of a company's promotion efforts for a certain period of time. It might include special sales, store displays, newspaper ads, television commercials, a community art show, and several fashion shows.

Retail promotion planning is usually done twice a year, for six-month periods that coordinate with retail buying plans (February through July, and August through January). Promotion planning calendars chart each promotion activity. They show month-by-month planning, budgeting, and preparation that builds up to the time of each promotional event and through to completion.

The promotion program is directed toward the company's target market and tailored to its fashion image. A typical fashion promotion program includes the following:

1. *Promotion goals and objectives.* These are usually based on past programs and should be well-defined. They form the basis for the rest of the planning and are used to evaluate the effectiveness of the program when it is finished. Goals and objectives might include selling certain merchandise, larger sales in general, or increased market share. They are influenced by such factors as how long the company has been established, how well it is known, its size and location, its merchandising philosophy, its fashion authority, and the nature of its competition.
2. *Message or theme.* This might stress elegance, patriotism, or spring/summer reawakening.
3. *Specific activities.* These should be chosen to effectively achieve the goals and objectives and promote the message or theme.
4. *Timing of the activities.* This includes how many messages to run, how often to run them, and over what length of time. For instance, activities might be geared toward Valentine's Day, Mother's Day, or Father's Day. Whatever the occasion,

advertising, displays, and other promotional activities should occur ahead of the maximum sales period. This stimulates early sales and generates a higher level of interest.

5. *The media mix to be used.* This deals with how much newspaper, radio, and other types of media space will be combined.
6. *Assignments of responsibility.* These specify people and departments for creating and carrying out the various aspects of the promotion program.
7. *Budget of expenditures.* Financial allocations are specified for each activity from the overall company budget.
8. *Evaluation methods.* These will be used to measure the effectiveness of the promotion after the program is finished. A thorough evaluation helps with the planning of future promotional efforts, so the successful parts can be repeated and the unsuccessful activities avoided.

Putting the Promotion Program into Action

The person responsible for promotion planning and follow-through varies depending upon the size of the firm. In small companies or stores, the owner or manager usually plans the promotional activities. Sometimes ads are used that are prepared by manufacturers. Some companies hire outside promotion consultants or advertising agencies to help. Small stores may only run ads at certain times, such as for holidays, end-of-season clearance sales, and back-to-school promotions. See 21-5. Additionally, an in-store trunk show or community fashion show may be held periodically.

Some specialty stores plan only a small amount of advertising, but promote themselves well with inviting entrance displays. Their stores are usually in highly visible locations or in popular malls where heavy consumer traffic can result in customers being attracted by the promotional displays, 21-6.

Large companies have promotion directors and departments that oversee their promotion programs.

21-5 During the busy back-to-school selling time, advertisements that small stores run in newspapers are supplemented with signs put up in the store.

21-6 Interesting displays of merchandise, placed near the walkways of malls, can sometimes beckon to shoppers more effectively than advertisements in various media.

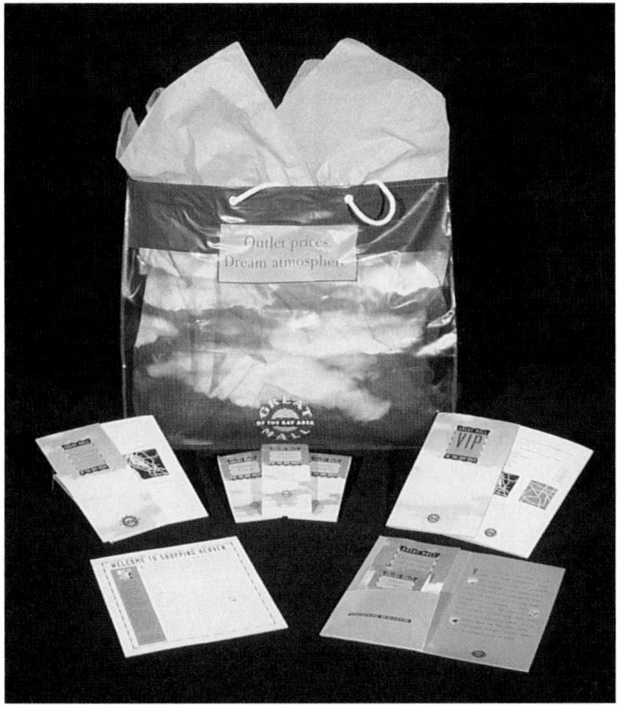

Great Mall of the Bay Area

21-7 This VIP Package includes a shopping bag, coupon book, store directory, and gift. The welcome program for shoppers who come with tour groups is supported by all tenants of the Great Mall of the Bay Area in California.

Mall of America

21-8 This Knott's Camp Snoopy is one of the attractions that appeals to families with children as they shop at the Mall of America in Minnesota.

They often work with an advertising agency on major campaigns or to develop television advertising involving special expertise. They combine this with in-house preparation of direct mail and other advertising not done by the agency. Merchandise buyers and managers with large retailers help with promotion planning and execution so the appropriate items and trends are promoted.

In shopping centers and malls, the stores, restaurants, and other tenants cooperate in promoting the center as a whole. See 21-7. Large malls employ a promotion director who coordinates the overall program. This might include combined newspaper advertising, or listings in the shopping center publication. At some times there are special events in the center of the mall, such as an antique or flower show, music, or celebrity visitations with picture-taking. Some malls attract customers by providing amusement rides, play areas for children, or unusual sights, 21-8. Through shopping center groups, small stores are able to participate in promotions that are planned by experts, with a percentage of the cost paid by each merchant.

Calculating Total Promotion Expenses

Although the promotion mix varies from company to company, promotion expenses are often substantial. A well-planned promotion program allows companies to achieve the best results with the most effective use of promotion money.

It is common to base the amount of money for promotion on a firm's anticipated annual sales dollars. Fashion manufacturers often allocate from five to eight percent of their anticipated sales for promotion. Their promotion activities often include trade show booths, giveaways, entertaining, and trade advertising. Fashion retailers may spend from one to four percent of anticipated sales. Their promotion is done with advertising, merchandise and seasonal displays, and special events.

One approach in determining a dollar amount for promotion is to use the previous year's expenditures as a base. Then a certain percentage is added or subtracted, depending on expected sales trends. For instance, if sales are expected to go up or down by eight percent, the budget would be increased or decreased by eight percent. This is an easy method, but assumes that the relationship between sales and promotional expenses was correct in the previous year and should be maintained. In reality, it may be smarter to increase promotional spending when business decreases, since the goal of promotion is to stimulate sales.

Sometimes companies calculate promotion expenses to relate to what competitors spend on promotion. However, it is often hard to obtain accurate information on the competitors' promotion budgets, so estimates are made. This thinking also assumes that the competitors' calculations are correct.

Allocating Promotion Budgets

Large firms involve many employees with promotion, and have large budgets that are dispersed according to promotion plans. These companies need very structured plans that assign funds in specific amounts to various activities and departments. Small firms make shorter-range plans with more flexibility, depending on their financial circumstances, as well as market pressures.

Three main methods are commonly used for allocating promotion budgets. They are

- *Top-down approach.* With this method, senior managers who are familiar with an organization's overall financial picture develop the promotion budget allocations. Decisions are based on the executives' past experiences and the need to control expenses. This is the most commonly used method in large fashion firms, but sometimes lacks personal commitment from lower-level employees who actually perform the promotional tasks.
- *Bottom-up approach.* This is a "goal and task" method of determining the promotion budget allocations. Based on objectives of specific product lines or departments, the types and amounts of promotion are decided upon by the employees involved with carrying them out and "living with" the results. Then calculations are made to estimate the budget for the departmental or divisional tasks. This encourages teamwork and accountability toward successful promotional efforts. However, it can result in overspending on promotion, assumes that merchandising employees understand media availability and costs, and requires upper management to give up some control.
- *Affordability approach.* The affordability approach is spending the amount that companies feel they can afford. This can maximize opportunities to stimulate sales and outdo the competition. It can bring short-term results, but lacks long-term continuity. Plus, some firms, especially small ones, miss market opportunities because they spend money for promotion only when they think they have ample funds. This seldom maximizes sales or profits.

Often a combination of the above approaches is used at different times. By using certain approaches when needed, companies can take advantage of the strong points of each, and minimize the weak points, as circumstances change.

Promotion Ethics

Ethics relate to acting or dealing in morally evaluated ways. Companies with good ethics have a system or code of conduct based on high integrity, values, and moral principles. They do business according to what is universally considered to be fair, proper, honest, and right. Company ethics are reflected through promotion, as well as through the actions of employees.

Promotional ethics can strongly affect how customers view a company and their beliefs about doing business with the company. Using poor or questionable ethics, or sending messages that cannot be believed or trusted, are good ways to damage the success of a business. Company messages and their practices must be consistent with each other, since customers easily recognize inconsistencies and will quickly take their business elsewhere.

Deceptive promotion occurs when information is presented in misleading ways. It is most commonly related to deceptive pricing practices, products, or sales practices:

- *Deceptive price promotion* occurs when retailers put higher original ticketed prices on items so they can mark them down to a "sale" price that is not really a bargain. Advertising claims of these merchants compare the lower price against what they say was the "original" or "regular" higher price. Sometimes they offer a certain amount of money off the regular price. Ethically, the retailer should use a former or regular price that has been well-established as the original selling price. Sometimes companies make false claims that their prices are lower than those of competitors. To do this, the company should determine that the compared price is the typical one that competitors regularly charge for identical products.
- *Deceptive product promotion* involves making false or misleading claims about actual products. For fashion products, this might include wrong information about fiber content, colorfastness, country of origin, care methods, size range, appropriate uses, or assured benefits. This also applies to information on packages and labels that is false or misleading about the exact quality and/or quantity of the package contents.
- *Deceptive sales practices* include ***bait and switch***, in which the consumer is baited by an advertised low price on a product that the retailer does not really plan to sell. The "switch" involves personal selling techniques that tempt the

customer to buy a higher priced product. Sometimes the store has not stocked the advertised product, but other times salespeople are encouraged to talk down that product, refuse to show the product, or deny credit if that product is purchased.

Government regulations have been enacted to limit promotion abuses. The Federal Trade Commission (FTC) oversees the legalities of promotion. Its rules say that all statements of fact must be supported by evidence, and sellers must not create an overall impression that is incorrect. The FTC accepts consumer complaints about promotion and can require companies to make good any implied offers they extend to consumers. The FTC also requires corrective advertising to be used by companies that are found to advertise deceptively. ***Corrective advertising*** uses promotional messages to correct previous false or unethical claims.

Self-regulation of corporate promotion departments, advertising agencies, the media, and many trade and professional associations causes higher standards to be set. This protects the public from unethical promotion. Also, some advertising-supported publications maintain commitment to the truth by not publishing slanted articles or editorials favoring only those companies that advertise in their publications. This could cause consumer distrust of the advertisers as well as the publications.

Advertising

Advertising is any paid form of nonpersonal sales message made by an identified sponsor through a mass communication medium. It is the best form of promotion to reach widely dispersed mass audiences quickly. For consumer items, such as fashion goods, it is more economical, with lower total cost, than direct person-to-person selling. It can presell goods and encourage customers to come to a store. Then direct selling can be done to bring about the final transaction.

Advertising is also the form of promotion over which the company has the most control. Ads of companies compete with each other to get consumer attention, arouse interest, activate desire, and stimulate a response. Much of the nation's and world's advertising is done by fashion merchandising firms.

Each year, billions of dollars are spent to advertise to specific target markets. Large companies are heavy advertisers, with the most promotion in highly competitive markets. Advertising can use a full range of creative approaches and media to convey the message.

The company paying for the ad is called the ***sponsor.*** In advertisements, sponsors can say whatever they want, as long as it conforms with the law and the moral and ethical standards of the advertising medium and trade associations. The firm sponsoring the message purchases the media space or time and controls the contents, appearance, and timing of the advertisement.

Purposes of Advertising

Advertising has many general purposes, such as to build a company's image, promote a product brand, announce a sale, or support a cause. Retail advertising has two specific purposes to get customers into the store and to contribute to the store's image. Advertising should be used continually to stimulate customer interest, provide useful information, and develop loyalty. It generates customer traffic and increased total sales and income. Fashion companies that do not make a serious effort to create productive and believable advertising lose more than just immediate sales.

Discount stores do the most advertising of all retailers, using newspaper ads, television, radio, and direct mail to get their message to consumers. Their advertisements are mainly product-oriented and emphasize low prices. Sometimes they suggest that consumers comparison shop to prove that they have the lowest prices. Discount operations also run frequent sales or special promotions, often tied to holidays, store anniversaries, or end-of-the-season clearance promotions.

Chain, department, and specialty stores often have large advertising budgets. National specialty chains advertise in general magazines, as well as major fashion magazines. Some mail special catalogs to their charge customers. Department stores advertise heavily in newspapers. Prestigious stores use direct mail, stuffing their monthly bills with advertising. They advertise some individual items and may feature a designer or new collection. They may also emphasize a new fashion trend rather than actual items.

Types of Advertising

The two main types of ads are product advertising and institutional advertising. Advertising may be done on a national, regional, or local level. Some are cooperative ads.

Product Advertising

Product advertising is designed to sell specific, identifiable merchandise items, lines, or certain services, 21-9. It aims at getting an immediate response. Product advertising identifies and describes products, and often mentions their price and availability. It may have a sense of urgency for a specific sale or limited time period. Most fashion advertisements are product ads, with the value and desirability of some items easier to communicate than others.

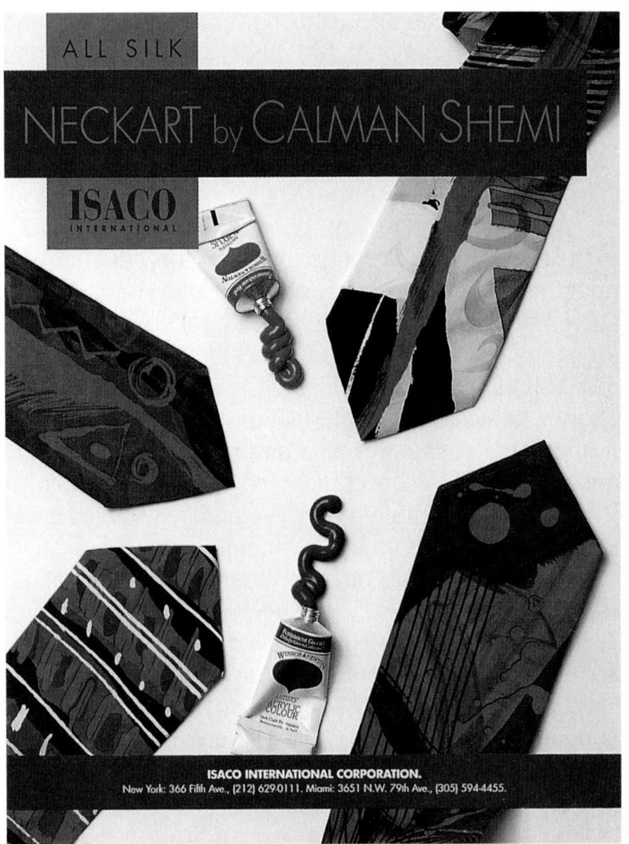

21-9 This trade advertisement, aimed at retailers, shows the types of neckties that are available in this manufacturer's line for the upcoming season.

21-10 This advocacy advertisement encourages others to support AIDS & Cancer Research. It only names the advertising sponsor (Roffe Accessories, Inc.) in small print across the bottom of the ad.

Fashion merchandisers who do product advertising must remember that ads cannot sell unwanted goods. Merchandise that has already been rejected by customers, or has passed its peak of acceptance, should not be featured. Instead, the spotlight should be on items that have the best selling potential. Otherwise, the advertising money and effort are wasted. Some companies have a policy of only advertising styles that are increasing in popularity. It is a mistake to rely on advertising to correct retail buying errors.

Institutional Advertising

Institutional advertising, also called image or corporate advertising, is designed to sell the reputation of an organization rather than a specific product. It projects the image of the firm as seen by others, possibly emphasizing fashion leadership, exceptional service, or community involvement. Such image advertising tries to build long-term patronage by customers, rather than seeking immediate merchandise sales. It is often used to promote the overall excellence of a retail store or an entire line of products. Some institutional ads use *advocacy advertising* to address public issues or influence public opinion, 21-10.

National, Regional, and Local Advertising

Ads can also be grouped as to their geographic scope. *National advertising* is sponsored by companies that sell products on a nationwide basis. Its objective is to create general demand for products. *Regional advertising* is done by retailers that have many stores only within several adjoining states or a confined section of the country. It tries to bring consumers into any of the stores. *Local advertising* is sponsored by local merchants. Its objective is to say that they have specific items, as well as to state the prices and quantities available.

Cooperative Advertising

Cooperative (co-op) advertising is the sharing of advertising and its costs by two or more organizations, 21-11. Producers of nationally sold brand-name goods may pay for some of the costs (often half) of local advertising with retailers that sell the items. This offers advantages to both parties. It enables both to afford

21-11 The cost of this cooperative ad is shared by the necktie manufacturer (Arden Cravats) and the supplier of the fabric protector (DuPont Teflon) that is being emphasized.

more advertising, promotes both the manufacturers and retailers of particular goods, and reinforces the images of the stores and producers.

Since cooperative advertising is mutually advantageous for companies, retail buyers should ask vendors if they offer cooperative advertising. However, retail buyers should not be tempted to order goods from suppliers just because co-op money is offered. This is especially true if the goods are not right for the stores' customers. Also, manufacturers sometimes place restrictions on retailers to qualify for co-op money which might interfere with the retailer's image or ethics. Advantages and disadvantages of cooperative advertising are summarized in 21-12.

Written cooperative advertising agreements avoid many arguments about the arrangements. Most large retailers have standard printed agreements for vendors that specify all details and provide legal protection to the store. Since all vendors receive the same treatment, no favoritism is shown.

Cooperative Advertising
Advantages
✱ Additional exposure for particular goods is gained by both parties.
✱ Lower advertising dollars are spent for coverage by each party.
✱ Producer prestige can be gained through public association with a well-known store.
✱ Retail prestige can be gained through public association with a well-known brand/label.
✱ Manufacturers get retailer feedback on the appeal of certain products.
✱ Local retail ads get better placement and lower costs for manufacturers than national ads.
Disadvantages
✱ It tempts retailers to buy goods from manufacturers that might not be bought otherwise, or which do not match the store's image.
✱ Lots of record keeping and accounting correspondence results between the companies involved.
✱ Sometimes retailers overcharge manufacturers, not disclosing/sharing their discounted space rate.
✱ Manufacturers and retailers lose control of how their ads look, deviating from their usual image of format because of the restrictions imposed by the other party.
✱ Stores with monthly/yearly contracts with newspapers may use manufacturer cooperative ads on poor selling days, so strong store promotions can be featured at better times.
✱ Competition among producers may cause them to overspend on cooperative advertising in order to sell their goods.
✱ Sometimes retailers end up promotionally launching lesser-known trade names.
✱ Extra retail coordination efforts are needed between buyers and their advertising departments.

21-12 Cooperative advertising can be a very smart way for manufacturers and retailers to advertise as long as the advantages and disadvantages are kept in mind.

Using Advertising Agencies and Freelancers

Advertising agencies are service firms that provide advertising expertise. They design, produce, and place advertisements in the media for their clients. They also research clients' markets, write press releases, and represent companies to the public. They plan advertising and marketing campaigns, develop artwork, write copy, create commercials, and design packaging. Client companies pay them for their creative abilities to carry out all aspects of campaigns to promote their products. However, less than half of ad agency revenues come from client payments.

Over half of the revenue of advertising agencies comes from commissions from the media into which they place ads. For instance, a newspaper might give a 15 percent discount on the cost of space to an agency that places ads in the paper. The agency then charges the client, for instance a retail store, the full amount (without the discount) for the newspaper ad space, as well as fees for their services. The retailer might have to pay that full amount for newspaper advertising space anyway. However, retailers that are regular, heavy advertisers often negotiate a lower rate on their own with print media on a yearly basis.

Advertising freelancers are also available on a part-time basis to help fashion merchandisers. They are artists, copywriters, photographers, or other creative professionals who are hired independently to produce advertisements.

Advertising Strategy

It is sometimes hard for companies to decide how much advertising to do, and how big the advertising budget should be. In general, the more that is spent, the higher the company's market share is likely to be. However, the resources of the firm, size and type of market, competitors' actions, and creativity of advertising also play important roles. Ads that are successful meet company goals in terms of sales targets, brand awareness, and/or brand recall.

An advertising platform is planned for each advertising campaign. An ***advertising platform*** is a plan that defines the target audience and summarizes the benefits and features of the product that will please that audience. It also indicates the general theme and tone of the message to be used to motivate buyers. It coordinates the advertising piece of the overall promotion program.

Fresh ideas, presented in clever ways, catch people's attention. However, they must also help to sell the company's products. Some of the most successful ads that sell consumer products (such as laundry or food products) are annoying. However, fashion and beauty ads are often based on sensuality, fantasy, and testimonials of famous people. Whether good or not, retailers have recently used "price-only" advertising that emphasizes special sales or the low prices they offer.

Forms of Advertising Media

Once the message has been developed, suitable media must be chosen to communicate it to the audience. The cost of media must be weighed against the effectiveness of each form. The right media is the one (or combination) that most effectively and efficiently reaches the largest portion of the company's target audience.

The advertiser plans a media mix that suits the size and type of the company, target market, media availability, and cost. The types of media chosen for the combination should support and strengthen each other for the overall advertising campaign. Decisions must also be made as to exactly when the advertising will appear in the media. This helps to make the most effective use of the company's advertising dollars.

Advertising is done through many ***media forms,*** or types of media. Print media include newspapers, magazines, outdoor, direct mail, and merchandise packaging. Broadcast media include radio, television, and video presentations. Web sites are also becoming an effective advertising tool. The strong and weak points of various media forms are summarized in 21-13.

The use of the particular ***media vehicle,*** or which particular newspaper, radio station, etc., depends on the availability and cost for the best total impact. Media vehicles with the largest circulation (readership) or audience, are more expensive than those with a smaller number of readers or listeners/viewers. Some have "media representatives" who are employees who sell advertising space and time, but also are specialists who can arrange to have company advertisements produced.

Often fashion merchandising companies use a mix of several advertising media such as newspapers, magazines, outdoor, direct mail, merchandise packaging, radio, television, video, and web sites.

Newspapers

Newspapers are the primary medium for local retail ads. The cost of reaching customers is lower, and the time needed for preparation and publication of newspaper ads is shorter, than with most other media. Advertisers can also measure the response to an advertisement when it runs, by checking their sales volume for that day or week.

Large stores dominate in newspaper advertising. Many of these companies contract with newspapers on a yearly basis and get lower space rates because of quantity buying. Thus, they pay lower rates than small users and communicate with customers more frequently and consistently. Sometimes preprinted "tabloid inserts" in full color, or advertising "circulars," are used, especially in Sunday editions of metropolitan newspapers.

Large company advertising causes smaller firms, who can only afford periodic ads, to have less desirable

Advertising Media Forms

Medium	Advantages	Disadvantages
Newspaper	Low cost for large coverage Geographic selectivity Products can be shown Different size/price ads available Frequent publication available Can be placed/changed on fairly short notice Fast response—used as shopping guide	Wasted circulation—not targeted Short life - hasty reading; papers thrown out Cluttered pages Hard for small stores to compete in dollars and placement Limited or poor color reproduction
Magazine	Longer life span of message Excellent quality of color and detail More targeted readership through specialty and regional coverage Tend to be believable	Limited demonstration value Space is expensive Some wasted circulation More professional preparation needed Long lead time limits fashion timeliness and ties up capital
Outdoor	Can select geographic location Repetitive viewing from audience Minimal cost per viewing if in high-traffic or high-exposure placement	Can only have short, general message Some wasted audience coverage Considered offensive by some people Cannot be clipped, kept, referred-to
Direct Mail	Control of what is sent Precise selectivity of receivers Can saturate market area Minimal wasted expense Results can be evaluated Flexibility of format and style Flexibility of timing for business conditions	High cost per receiver message Hard to get mailing lists Relies on strength of mailing list Consumer resistance—junk mail thrown out Prone to delivery delays
Merchandise Packaging	Small added expense Good customer relations Easily spread among target market	Limited audience—no mass distribution May be considered arrogant No product advertising—just image
Radio	Universally used medium Short preparation and lead time Fairly low cost Targeted through listening area, program content, station type Human voice is more convincing than print Effectively combined with newspaper ads	No opportunity for visual impact—can't show trends or demonstrate products Message is fleeting - short life Some wasted coverage Commercial clutter
Television	Very popular consumer medium Can reach large audiences Has sound, sight, and motion to show products and create image Some flexibility for content changes	High cost of time and production Message is fleeting Longer lead time needed Local TV not available everywhere
Video	Attracts attention near merchandise Has entertainment carryover Can be replayed many times Good educational value	Not effective advertising Need special expertise to produce
Web Sites	Interactive Current to reflect newest trends Instant worldwide market access E-mail allows feedback	Audience limited to computer users People can "click off" if not easy and understandable

21-13 Each advertising medium has specific strong and weak points. When these are known and kept in mind, an advertising campaign can use the best options and combine several media to be extremely effective.

locations in the paper and pay higher space rates for the ads. Since newspaper rates are higher in papers that have a large circulation, weekly suburban and community papers may be a better value for the ads of small retailers. Also the geographic area of circulation may more closely match the customer markets of the stores.

The affordability of newspaper advertising allows many merchants to advertise constantly. Many consumers check newspaper ads before going shopping. They clip ads about specific merchandise to remind them of what is being offered, where, and at what prices.

Magazines

Prestigious *magazine* advertising is done by large retailers and manufacturers who have widespread geographic distribution. Magazine ads usually run on a national basis, such as in fashion magazines, that are circulated to specific demographic or physographic groups. See 21-14. These magazine ads are very expensive. Regional and specialized magazines are available for more local or niche advertising to specific consumer groups.

Magazine ads offer opportunities to show more accurate color and detail. They can be very creative and beautiful. Magazine ads also have a longer circulation life than newspapers and gain added notice if there are accompanying articles about fashion trends.

Extensive preparation and long publication lead times are required for national magazines. This sometimes limits the timeliness of new trends and prices for fashion items and can tie up a firm's capital. Thus, institutional advertising is often done by nationally-known manufacturers and department stores.

Outdoor

Outdoor advertising includes billboards, public transit ads, posters, and free-standing signs. See 21-15. Most outdoor advertising is permanently placed for a certain length of time and has a short message that is

21-14 This nationally distributed fashion ad, which appeared in a Harper's Bazaar magazine, advertises the Christian Dior label in cooperation with three upscale retailers. It shows one merchandise item and presents the classy image of the label. It is a combination of cooperative, product, and institutional advertising.

21-15 Outdoor fashion advertisements are placed wherever prospective customers will see them. This ad for DKNY apparel is on the side of a phone booth near a busy metropolitan street corner.

21-16 This moving advertisement has high visibility. This colorful truck is likely to be noticed by consumers.

viewed quickly. This makes it most effective for institutional image advertising rather than emphasizing specific merchandise items. A monthly fee is usually paid according to an advertising lease, often for six months to a year.

Location is the most important factor for outdoor ads. Advertisers try to make a strong visual impact to the maximum number of consumers, 21-16. Billboards are expensive, but effective, where traffic is high. Manufacturers and retailers locate outdoor advertising space according to the consumers they want to attract.

Direct Mail

Direct mail is an advertising medium that includes catalogs, mailers, and bill enclosures mailed directly to customers' homes. The mailing list is often made up of charge customers or a specific list that has been developed of known and potential customers.

Direct mail does not have much "wasted circulation" since it only goes to the company's customers. With direct mail, companies can control what is sent, as well as how often and to whom. It can be a productive medium in terms of customer response, since only potential customers are contacted.

Direct mail is flexible and versatile. Its size and content is only limited by post office regulations and the cost of postage/delivery. The cost of direct mail varies according to how it is prepared and the method of delivery. Manufacturer-produced statement enclosures, often referred to as "bill stuffers," offer retailers low-cost selling opportunities. They are produced by manufacturers, inserted into a bill that is being mailed anyway, and may include a printed order form for additional sales. If possible, retailers should always enclose such a direct mail selling opportunity with bills to customers.

Direct mail advertising can be quite effective within certain volume limits. The design, message, audience, and cost can be closely regulated. It is often used by small, specialty retailers who cannot afford to compete with the mass media advertising of giant retailers. The results of a direct mail campaign with a specific objective, such as to invite customers to a special event, can be easily evaluated.

Merchandise Packaging

Merchandise packaging includes company names, logos, and slogans on shopping bags, gift boxes, and wrapping paper. It is institutional advertising. All purchases that customers carry from the store, or give as gifts, contain an advertisement of the retailer.

Radio

Radio is a broadcast medium that is popular with most consumers in their homes, cars (especially during morning and evening rush hours), and places of work and play. Sponsors can be selective about the types of audiences to which they advertise, since defined populations listen to various radio stations. Also, they can have the ad repeated at different times for a fairly low cost.

Radio ads have the flexibility of a short lead time for program scheduling. They also are quite easy to prepare because they do not contain visual material. Most are 10, 30, or 60 seconds long. Fees to the radio station depend on the length of commercials and times of the day or evening they are aired.

It is often hard to communicate fashion or style-trend messages with radio ads, since the merchandise items cannot be seen by the audience. Thus, radio advertising is usually used by retailers to advertise particular sales, special events, celebrity appearances, or store services and facilities. They are used effectively to back-up retailers' larger newspaper advertising campaigns with different ads that include voices, music, and sound effects.

Radio advertisements are also fleeting. In other words, they are gone from the customers' reach as soon as they have finished airing, as opposed to print ads that can be kept and referred to when convenient. Repetition is the key to having radio messages remembered.

Television

Television is another broadcast type of advertising. TV's increasing use is influenced by the fact that consumers are reading newspapers less and watching television more for their news and other information. Also, with customers dispersed among many outlying areas that are served by different newspapers and radio stations, regional stores with branches can reach the largest local audience with television ads.

National manufacturers, retail chains, and trade groups run costly ads on major network TV channels. These are mainly institutional ads that build brands or are lifestyle-oriented. Local retailers advertise on the many cable channels aimed at niche markets, and that have lower advertising rates. Some manufacturers and retailers do cooperative television advertising.

Fashion ads and home shopping sales are effective on television because mass audiences can be shown the actual products in color and motion. Merchandisers can create and reinforce their fashion authority in a fairly short time. TV commercials are 15, 30, or 60 seconds long, and are most expensive during prime-time evening hours.

The main drawback of television advertising is the high cost of time and production to prepare the ads. Writing and filming the ads require the creative talents of an advertising agency or film-making specialist. A longer lead time is needed for planning and executing the ads.

Video

Videos are sometimes set up in manufacturer's showrooms and in-store departments near the merchandise they are showing. They are designed to present fashion trends, promote merchandise, and build customer traffic. They attract the attention of passing customers, with sound and movement, to present the product's story. Videotaped fashion shows and interviews with designers encourage shoppers to stay in the department or store, 21-17. However, they have not had a strong sales effect.

21-17 Major fashion events, such as designer fashion shows, are usually videotaped so they can be used for promotional value at a later time.

Some fashion videos have been produced as music videos by manufacturers. They are shown on cable TV stations. They have strong entertainment value, without an obvious advertising sales pitch. They show the fashions, with the designer's name or trademark appearing often in the background, in hopes of being recognized when consumers are shopping. This is "soft sell."

Video walls have been used recently to get attention and stimulate fashion interest within malls and other large areas. *Video walls* are made up of many television screens (for instance eight rows of eight large screens for a total of sixty-four screens). The visual image on each screen is coordinated with the others to either form separate pictures, combined pictures on various sections of the wall, or one big picture with each monitor showing only one small part of the total image.

Even though advertising with videotapes has not been as successful as anticipated, merchandise videos are effective to teach sales personnel about the newest products and latest selling techniques. They are cost-effective, since they can be played over and over when desired. For instance, an employee fashion training seminar can be taped and shown at branch stores.

Web Sites

Advertising on Internet *web sites* is becoming increasingly popular. Companies try to attract people to their web pages with specialized art and copy that is entertaining and informative, just as for other media. The interactive process must be easy and understandable to those browsing the site or they will "click off." Also, the content of the site must be changed and refreshed constantly to reflect current trends and new merchandise. This requires company resources and maintenance. If used correctly, web pages are powerful for advertising. Up-to-the-minute messages can be communicated to the world immediately.

Since web site advertisers want action, they try to include ways to gauge their readers' interests, buying patterns, merchandise preferences, price points, etc. Usually, an e-mail link is included to gain important feedback. Companies also use Internet web sites to advertise employment opportunities when trying to fill specific job positions.

Developing Effective Print Advertisements

Print advertisements include those that are designed to appear in newspapers and magazines. The main components of these ads are created to try to motivate consumers into action. The components must be eye-catching and combined to communicate clearly and understandably to the target audience. The process must also be done to meet specific deadlines.

It should not be rushed, since changes are sometimes needed and unavoidable problems often arise.

The main parts of print advertisements are the headline, copy, illustration, logo/slogan, and white space. They are all put together according to a layout. As you read print advertisements, notice the following:

The *headline* of an advertisement is a condensed summary of the advertising message, usually in larger print. It implies what is to come. It should capture consumers' attention, suggest benefits, motivate readers to look at the rest of the ad, and arouse curiosity in the product being advertised. Sometimes there is also a *secondary headline* in a bit smaller print.

Copy is the reading material, or the words of an ad. Advertising copy should be written clearly to help consumers understand the message. It is best if the copy is short, simple, and concise. It is more readable if it has a conversational tone that is interesting, informative, and enthusiastic. It tries to convince its readers to act. It might describe products, give directions, or tell a story that accompanies the other parts of the ad.

The *illustration* is the visual part of the advertisement. Merchandise is often shown with photographs or artwork, for added consumer comprehension. It shows the fashion message or new trend being emphasized in the ad. It often shows product features, with the product actually being worn or used.

Merchandise items are often loaned to the company's advertising department, or outside advertising agency, to be drawn or photographed on models. Accessories should also be included by the fashion merchandiser, so the entire fashion story can be shown. Fashion trends that are expressed correctly, are more quickly accepted. Also, accessory sales can be increased if those items are shown.

Digital (electronic) photos are being used in most ads now. They provide better images, prevent time delays, and are more environmentally-friendly. Initial investment in the equipment is higher than older photography methods, but enhanced creativity and ease of retouching enable fashion companies to have better quality ads. No film is used and the images can be easily manipulated to reduce ongoing advertising costs.

The *logo* and/or *slogan* is the company's distinctive signature motif and/or marketing phrase that appears in all advertisements of that company. It identifies the firm and communicates its image and product offerings.

White space is the empty space that has no copy or illustration. It may not be white. It gives emphasis to the other parts of the ad by letting them stand out. Lots of white space, with a small amount of copy and one beautiful photo or sketch, often suggests quality and prestige. Cluttered ads, with very little white space, may suggest a low price, discount image.

The *layout* is how all the elements of the advertisement are put together. It is designed to first gain consumers' attention, then guide them through all of the ad's parts to absorb the message and meaning. Repetition of an ad layout format over a long period of time helps to create a strong identity with the sponsoring company.

Public Relations

Public relations (PR) activities are planned to build good relations with the various publics of an organization, such as customers, stockholders, government, community groups, and labor. PR activities are aimed at enhancing the long range "corporate image" through favorable news exposure, as well as handling or heading off unfavorable rumors, stories, and events. Public relations employees disseminate information through press relations, corporate communications, and lobbying.

Publicity is unpaid media coverage of news about an organization, or its products and activities, presented at the discretion of the media. Publicity accomplishes promotion by planting "public relations news" about the organization in media, not paid for by the sponsor. It differs from advertising in both payment and sponsorship, since it is free and unsponsored. It consists of news articles or programming that is carried by mass media, such as newspapers, television, radio, or magazines. The message must earn the media space or time by its newsworthiness of general public interest. In other words, it must be timely, have local interest, and appeal to the medium's audience.

Instead of buying advertising space or time, some companies seek favorable publicity to create interest in their company or merchandise. Fashion designers seek publicity about their collection showings. Retailers try to get publicity about new store openings, civic events held at their locations, or announcements about employee promotions. Factual stories about companies produce positive images and awareness.

To do this, designers, manufacturers, and retailers send out press releases and press kits about their activities or products. *Press releases* are written "news" stories sent as publicity to newspapers and magazines. They are formally typed, with facts and details in a standard format ready for the editor to accept.

Press kits are promotional portfolios that contain press releases and photographs and/or illustrations, 21-18. Apparel firms send out press kits with glossy photos of their best items, nicely accessorized and worn by models. Accompanying the photos are write-ups about the garments, as if written by a news reporter. Newspapers merely need to put the photos and copy in the paper for a fashion story. If used, the company that sent the press kit receives "free advertising." Some companies prepare videotapes for publicity on television news shows.

21-18 Press kits provide all the information needed for the company providing the kit to gain publicity about itself and its products in all types of print media.

Functions of the Fashion Press
* Communicate fashion information to consumers
* Publish advertisements for manufacturers and retailers
* Shop worldwide markets for newsworthy styles to feature
* Perform market research about consumer merchandise preferences
* Influence manufacturers to create projected successful items
* Serve as a general clearinghouse for industry information
* Encourage retailers to carry items they feature/endorse
* Give editorial credit to firm's whose items are featured
* Provide POS ads to retailers (hangtags, photo blow-ups, etc.)
* Provide information to firms, such as promotion/selling tips, merchandise sources, advance fashion trend projections
* Hold fashion shows and seminars for retail customers.

21-19. The print and broadcast fashion press serve many important functions to help the industry and consumers gather information and transact sales.

Large firms have their own public relations officer or an entire PR staff. They promote their firm during speeches before audiences, or hold press conferences. Smaller companies may hire the services of public relations firms. PR firms devise programs that project the company's public image through a planned program of activities. These might be aimed at employees, stockholders, the business community and/or the consuming public.

A public relations agency might create an entire multimedia campaign designed to shape or change the public's image of a client company. The original campaign blitz would be followed with ongoing activities to maintain the company's image or products.

Publicity is not only a bargain for the company, but it also seems more credible to consumers than advertising. On the other hand, the company has little control over how the content of the message is presented or the timing of its presentation. The medium's editors or producers decide if the message is of interest or entertainment for its audience, and how it will be presented. Thus, publicity can have a good or bad result.

The Fashion Press

The *fashion press* includes the print and broadcast media that present and interpret fashion and industry news. These publications and radio and television stations are also vehicles for paid advertisements. They provide fashion direction and information to all segments of the pipeline, from beginning fibers to end-use consumers. They satisfy a valuable communication niche, with enormous influence and authority in today's fast-paced global fashion environment. Functions of the fashion press are summarized in 21-19.

A wide range of publications report and interpret news, special events, and advertisements about fashion. *Fashion magazines* are aimed at consumers, and have an international fashion emphasis through articles, illustrations, and advertisements. A few examples are *Vogue, Harper's Bazaar, Elle, Town & Country,* and *InStyle,* as well as *GQ* and *Esquire* for men. See 21-20. These magazines help publicize the industry. *Trade publications* are magazines, newspapers, and books that deal specifically with a certain industry or segment of an industry. They were discussed in Chapter 4.

The editors of fashion magazines receive announcements of new collections and lines from designers and manufacturers. They also seek out and forecast fashion news and trends on their own. Editors from the leading fashion publications are seated in the front row at runway showings. They also attend key social events, such as parties, theater, and museum openings, to obtain a firsthand look at what the fashion leaders are wearing.

Fashion magazines receive the largest part of their revenue from the sale of advertising space, which is sold for tens of thousands of dollars per page. Thus, a large number of advertising pages, in relation to editorial content, means higher profits. Usually, advertising

21-20 Fashion magazines spread the latest fashion trends, news, and advertisements to consumers.

makes up at least half of the total number of pages in fashion magazines. However the ads also spread fashion ideas to consumers.

In addition to fashion magazines, many other publications report fashion news and trends along with other broader information. Women's magazines, such as *Redbook* cover fashion news regularly, as well as other women's interests. General interest and news magazines, such as *Time*, *Newsweek,* and *People* also have regular features that discuss, show, and advertise fashion designers, apparel trends, and fashion merchandising companies.

Major newspapers have a fashion editor and/or fashion department that researches and prepares articles. Sunday newspapers often have an entire fashion section with articles, photos and ads. Smaller papers pick up fashion-related stories from national news services.

Designers, manufacturers, and retailers try to gain editorial credit in magazines and newspapers. ***Editorial credit*** is mention in a publication of the manufacturer's tradename or specific retail sources for merchandise that is featured by the publication. Editorial credit is included as a service for readers, but is also free promotion, like an indirect endorsement, for companies and their products.

Television now disseminates a great deal of fashion news. Not only do actors and hosts wear the latest fashions, but short segments on fashion are often presented on news and talk shows. Also, fashion features are done on many cable channels on a regular basis. Shows combine behind-the-scenes footage of fashion shows, interviews with popular designers, and fashion commentary for the age groups and fashion tastes of their show's audience.

Summary

Promotion is used by fashion merchandisers to inform, persuade, and remind customers to buy goods. Promotion is done at consumer, trade, and retail levels. Retail promotion planning is usually done twice a year designed for the company's target market and tailored to its fashion image.

Different amounts and types of promotion are planned and done by different employees in various sizes and kinds of firms. Promotion budgets may be based on a percentage of anticipated sales, or based on what competitors spend on promotion. Budget allocations are made based on a top-down approach, bottom-up approach, or affordability.

Promotion ethics can strongly affect how customers view a company. Deceptive price or product promotion, or deceptive sales practices can harm a business. Self-regulation of those involved with promotion causes higher standards to be set.

Advertising is the best form of promotion to reach widely dispersed mass audiences quickly. It might build company image, promote a product brand, announce a sale, or support a cause. Most fashion ads are a combination of product and institutional advertising. Some are also cooperative ads. Advertising agencies or freelancers might assist fashion firms with their advertising strategy and campaigns. Advertising media forms and vehicles are chosen according to what best reaches the largest portion of a company's target audience.

The main parts of print advertisements are the headline, copy, illustration, logo/slogan, and white space. They are put together according to a layout.

Public relations activities try to enhance the long-range "corporate image" of companies and head off unfavorable exposure. PR tools include publicity, press releases, corporate communications, and lobbying.

The fashion press includes the print and broadcast media that present and interpret fashion and industry news. It provides fashion direction and information to consumers as well as to all segments of the pipeline.

To Know

promotion mix
consumer promotion
trade promotion
retail promotion
promotion program
ethics
bait and switch
corrective advertising
advertising
sponsor
product advertising
institutional advertising
advertising agencies
advertising platform
media forms
media vehicle
public relations (PR)
publicity
press kits
editorial credit

Review

1. List the three goals of promotion.
2. Why do large textile and apparel manufacturers do consumer promotion?
3. Why has promotion planning become more important lately?
4. When creating a promotion program, decisions should be made in what eight areas?
5. In large retail firms, why do merchandise buyers and managers help with promotion planning and execution?
6. What are two problems with promotion budgeting according to competitive equality?
7. List the three main methods commonly used for allocating promotion budgets.
8. Deceptive promotion is related most commonly to what three areas?
9. What government agency oversees the legalities of promotion?
10. What is corrective advertising?
11. What are the two basic purposes of retail advertising?
12. From what two sources do the revenues of advertising agencies come?
13. What company goals do successful ads meet?
14. What do media representatives do?
15. What is the most important factor for outdoor ads?
16. What constitutes merchandise packaging advertising?
17. What form of advertising media can be interactive?
18. What should a print advertisement layout be designed to do?
19. What is the major disadvantage of publicity?
20. Briefly describe three ways that television disseminates fashion news.

To Do

1. Identify a specific small fashion business, such as a retail shop or apparel manufacturer. Plan a six-month promotion program suited to its target market and fashion image. Prepare a promotion planning calendar that coordinates with the eight areas of promotion planning. Put your program together in booklet form.
2. Look through fashion magazines and general/news magazines. Photocopy or tear out a good example of each of the following: product advertising, institutional advertising, combination product/institutional advertising, national advertising, local advertising, and cooperative advertising. Make a bulletin board display with each type of ad labeled, or mount your ads on poster board. If you are able to find any advocacy advertising or corrective advertising, also include those.
3. With a classmate, visit three different types of retailers that sell apparel (department store, specialty store, discount store, etc.). After briefly explaining your fashion merchandising course to store management, request a sample of each type of the merchant's packaging. Show the examples to the class and lead a discussion about the pros and cons of this type of advertising in general, how well the examples represent each respective store's image, and the advertising effectiveness of each store's packaging.
4. After analyzing many newspaper fashion advertisements, create a newspaper ad that features fashion goods of a retailer's particular holiday sale or in-store promotion. Also listen to retail radio ads and write a 30- or 60-second radio ad that coordinates with the newspaper ad. Put these into a report and explain the music and any other audio that might give more emphasis or effect to the radio ad.
5. Cut out print advertisements of local fashion retailers. Mount them on poster board. Point out the headline, copy, illustration, logo/slogan, and white space of each. Then describe specifically how the layout gains consumer attention and guides readers through the ad to absorb the message and meaning. To what type of target market do you think each one is directed and what image is presented?

CHAPTER 22

Visual Merchandising

After studying this chapter, you will be able to

- explain the importance of visual merchandising.
- describe the two main areas of store layout.
- summarize the aspects of merchandise presentation.
- describe the components of in-store displays.
- list the advantages, disadvantages, and types of window displays.

Visual merchandising is the physical display of goods in the most attractive and appealing ways. The goal of visual merchandising is to please customer senses as shoppers enter and move around the store, 22-1. As opposed to advertising, visual merchandising reaches customers when they are at the store, resulting in immediate purchases.

In Cooperation with Saks Fifth Avenue

22-1 Visual merchandising attractively shows off items that are for sale in retail stores.

The Importance of Visual Merchandising

As with other types of promotion, the main purposes of visual merchandising are to sell goods and promote the store image. Additionally, visual merchandising can educate consumers about new item trends or show how new items can be worn or accessorized. Visual merchandising can also provide pertinent information, such as the price and special features of items. It gets attention for the store, introduces the store to prospective customers, and builds goodwill.

The world is now almost totally visually oriented, with a great deal of communicating being done through television and other created images rather than printed or spoken words. International travel and the coexistence of many different languages make visual merchandising important as a "common language." Also, visual merchandising is three-dimensional and real, which is more effective than flat drawings or photos.

To coordinate with fashion movement, visual merchandising must always try to be different, new, and creative. Ongoing planning is required. Although it must be done within a budget, extra money spent on store interior and display design is usually quickly returned in additional sales. Visual merchandising includes store layout and decor, merchandise presentation, and displays.

The Store Interior

Store layout refers to the interior arrangement of retail facilities. The two general interior areas of stores are the selling areas and sales support areas.

The ***selling areas*** are where merchandise is displayed and customers interact with sales personnel. The selling areas usually occupy 75 to 80 percent of

Jusco Co., Ltd./AEON Group

22-2 Most of the space in a store is devoted to selling, where customers can look at and choose the items they would like to purchase.

the total space, 22-2. Selling areas include space for departments, aisles, counters, fitting rooms, merchandise fixtures, displays, and other interior decor needs.

The ***sales support areas*** are devoted to customer services, merchandise receiving and distribution, management offices, and staff activities. Customer services include rest rooms, cashiers, gift wrapping, etc. Sales support areas should be located to facilitate customer convenience and employee productivity, 22-3.

When designing the store layout, a ***floor plan*** is drawn up to show the positioning of all selling and sales support areas. It presents an overall top view of the entire store, including the location of specific merchandise group areas, aisles, fixtures, and customer services. ***Fixtures*** are shelves, tables, rods, counters, stands, easels, forms, and platforms on which merchandise is stocked and displayed for sale, 22-4. Spaces or aisles between fixtures must be at least three feet wide. More expensive, upscale shops or departments should have four or more feet between fixtures.

22-3 Elevator and telephone areas do not contain merchandise for sale, but do provide for the convenience of customers.

Drawing floor plans allow retailers to meet their special requirements and minimize the limitations of their spaces before constructing the layout and stocking the store with merchandise. The amounts of materials needed can be estimated, such as flooring and lights. Also, all parts of the final layout can be planned in correct proportion to each other.

The layout may follow a grid or maze design. A ***grid layout*** has one or more primary (main) aisles running through the store, with secondary (smaller) aisles intersecting with them at right angles. All fixtures are positioned in line with the aisles. This provides an efficient use of selling space, plus good sight and security. It simplifies shopping for busy consumers, but also gives an uninteresting atmosphere for fashion retailing. Merchandise areas and aisles often have different flooring surfaces, such as carpet versus tile.

Jusco Co., Ltd./AEON Group

22-4 These special retail fixtures can clearly show the customers all the different styles of shoes offered.

A ***maze layout*** has a free-flowing arrangement. Fixtures are in informal, unbalanced placements. Paths of shoppers are determined by the positioning of the fixtures, often taking them past merchandise they would not have seen from the aisles of a grid layout. This presents a more interesting shopping environment, but some selling space is usually wasted.

Selling Area Layout

Selling area layouts are extremely important because they strongly influence in-store traffic patterns, shopping atmosphere, and operational efficiency. Store interiors are planned to use space effectively, with maximum flexibility for merchandise and display changes.

Large department stores and stores that carry better lines and career apparel seldom change the location of their departments. It is expensive and time-consuming to move departments, plus customers are accustomed to going directly to the location of their specific, desired brand. On the other hand, specialty stores often rotate the areas in which certain types of stock are located. Merchandise that is in greatest customer demand is placed in prime selling spaces.

Merchandise should be grouped logically and naturally in areas that help customers find, compare, and buy according to their needs. Each department should flow into an adjacent similar department. For instance, a woman who is unable to find a career dress may choose a suit in the adjoining department that she noticed from the dress department. Likewise, a men's active sportswear department would logically be located near departments that have running shoes and equipment bags. See 22-5. Customers should be able to understand and appreciate the organization.

Different selling locations within a store have different revenue-producing capabilities. The value, or sales expectations, of each space depends on its relationship with other departments and to traffic aisles. The same rules hold true for the placement of shops in malls in relation to other stores and to pedestrian traffic patterns.

The most valuable area of every store is near the entrance, which is the space most exposed to customers, 22-6. In small shops, the prime selling space is the first one-third of the store from the entrance. In multilevel stores, the main (entry level) floor is the most important. The value of other space decreases the farther it is from the entrance and main level, depending on how customers traverse the store.

On each floor, merchandise located along primary traffic aisles has more customer exposure than along

22-5 Merchandise items for camping and other outdoor activities are often located near each other to help customers fill all their specific needs.

22-6 The view that customers see first decides their impression of what a store has to offer, either from an open mall entrance or the street entrance of an independently located store.

secondary aisles. Thus, the best position is at the intersection of two primary traffic aisles. A good position is near one primary and one secondary aisle. The worst areas are only exposed to secondary aisles or are in the back of the store.

Store Decor

Decor is the style and appearance of interior furnishings. A decorating theme is carried throughout the store, to fit with the company's image. Examples might be a rustic look for a western apparel store, high-tech decor for a computer store, or French Provincial decor for an upscale women's apparel shop. See 22-7. The decor includes a distinctive style of lighting, colors, floor coverings, and display equipment.

Decor should coordinate with the store merchandise. In some areas of department stores, a different decor may be used in specific departments, to coordinate with the specific merchandise being sold. This might be in infant, sportswear, or other departments that have definite personalities. Whatever the theme, decor helps to attract attention and promote sales by serving as a backdrop for the merchandise.

Merchandise Presentation

Merchandise presentation includes the ways that goods are hung, placed on shelves, or otherwise made available for sale in retail stores. Merchandise might be

In Cooperation with The 410 Shoppe

22-7 A fashionable store in a country setting might compliment its garments and accessories with wooden accents and a flowered wallpaper border.

arranged on wall units or freestanding racks, counters, or shelves to expose the complete assortment of goods, 22-8. Arrangements vary with the amount of merchandise for sale.

Garments are often hung shoulder-out, but may also be shown face-forward. ***Shoulder-out presentation*** is

In Cooperation with Saks Fifth Avenue

22-8 Neatly organized assortments of specific garment classifications present merchandise nicely to customers.

the way most garments are hung in home closets with only one side showing from shoulder to bottom. Stores that have an abundance of merchandise usually use shoulder-out hangbars to hold as much stock as possible. This arrangement also creates an impression of fullness and implies price value through quantity. Tags should be placed on the outside of merchandise, on the customer side of hanging garments so they are accessible to be read.

Face-forward presentation, or face-out presentation, is the hanging of clothing with the front fully facing the viewer. This should always be done at entrances and aisles. Face-forward presentation is also used for focal points on walls, 22-9.

Presentation of merchandise assists customers in seeing items and making choices. Merchandise should be presented attractively in simple, logical groupings, such as by classification, color, or vendor. Sizing should be uniform, with the smallest size hanging on the left, graduating by size to the largest on the right. With a series of shelves or bin compartments, small sizes are placed at the top, down to large sizes on the bottom. Effective merchandise presentation is especially important in self-service retailing.

For variety, goods are placed at different levels using walls, pedestals, and platforms. Merchandise presentation heights might start at two feet from the floor and increase at six-inch intervals to a height of about five feet. This is reachable by most people, including those in wheelchairs. The height is determined by the items being sold. For instance, the bottoms of pants should never be higher than three or four inches from the floor to avoid an unnatural "high water" look. Items should also not drag on the floor. In stores where salespeople are available to use hooks or sliding ladders to retrieve items from walls, goods are sometimes placed up to 12 feet high.

Point-of-purchase (POP) displays near cash registers should be impulse-oriented, since every customer must pass that area. Small, high-margin items (such as pins, earrings, socks, or belts) can be sold as additional selections, made while customers wait to pay for their purchases.

Merchandise Fixtures

An appropriate fixture plan should coordinate with the store's merchandise style, inventory level, and budget. Merchandise fixtures should be arranged for maximum use of space as well as ease of customer shopping. Wall fixtures are attached to walls, 22-10. Floor fixtures stand on the floor, and usually have locking wheels so they can be moved around as desired. Common types of fixtures are listed in 22-11. Both wall and floor fixtures are available in capacity or feature types.

Capacity fixtures hold large amounts of merchandise. Most often they are positioned to the rear or interior of the store or department. However, during special promotional and clearance periods, sale merchandise is featured on capacity fixtures down the center of a small store or along the aisles of a larger store.

In Cooperation with Saks Fifth Avenue

22-9 When garments are hung face-forward along walls, customers can clearly view their features.

22-10 A variety of wall fixtures can be located anyplace in a store where there is a wall or sturdy partition.

Common Types of Retail Fixtures

A-frames. Pyramid-shaped fixtures in the shape of the letter A.

base cabinets. Cupboards below the merchandise presentation area that are closed and hold extra inventory or selling aids.

bins. A series of wooden, wire, or Plexiglas compartments (often 10" square and 16" deep) used to stock shirts, sweaters, or other clothing. They are usually on walls or in free-standing back-to-back units.

build-ups. A series of geometric shapes, often of Plexiglas or wood, used to display products at different heights.

card holders. Plexiglas or metal holders, available in many sizes, used to display informational signs within the store.

carousels. Circular racks that turn.

C-rack. Half of a round rack, sometimes called half-circle rack.

drapers. Mannequins or other forms that can be dressed with apparel items.

dump table or bin. A rimmed table or bin to hold sale or special merchandise on the sales floor, especially in discount operations; it has no formal arrangement.

four-way rack. A fixture with four extended arms, that permits accessibility to hanging merchandise all the way around; see "quad rack."

gondola. A counter with shelves at the top for merchandise presentation and storage space at the bottom for back-up stock; often freestanding and two-sided for use out on the floor.

grid units. Pinwheel, wall, gondola, or other units that can fit together into various arrangements to suit the changing needs of the store and its merchandise presentation.

hangbars. Rods that allow for the hanging of many garments.

pedestal units. Freestanding racks or other types of fixtures that have a stable base for support.

pegboard. A flat wallboard that contains holes into which hooks (pegs) are inserted at adjustable locations to hold items. Pegboard walls are used to hold most types of merchandise, and small pegboard units are used for such items as socks, hosiery, belts, and jewelry on cards.

quad rack. A 4-armed fixture with each arm extending out from a central, wide, cubed core.

rounders. Circular racks on which garments are hung around the entire circumference.

showcases. Glass display cabinets in which merchandise can be viewed but not handled. The tops of showcases are usually used as counters.

slatwall units. A wall section with permanent open horizontal lines (slats) into which merchandise presentation brackets and/or hangers can be inserted at any of the different levels.

spiral costumer. A circular descending waterfall extending out from, and around, a central upright post.

straight arm. A bracket or rod that comes straight out from a wall, on which garments are hung to face out to show their full front. One knob on the end prevents hangers from slipping off.

superquad. A floor fixture with four straight arms and/or waterfalls at different levels to each other, two aligned one direction and the other two aligned perpendicular to them.

tables. Flat surfaces held up from the floor with legs, upon which items are placed.

T-stand. Freestanding, two-way stand in the shape of a T, that holds clothes on hangers, sometimes with one straight arm and one waterfall.

tier tables or racks. Tables or racks with more than one level on which to place merchandise.

two-way racks. Same as T-stands.

wall standards and brackets. Method of attaching shelves or other fixtures to walls with a permanent long vertical piece of metal with openings (the standard) into which different types of brackets can be inserted at adjustable levels.

waterfall. A fixture with an arm that slants downward, that contains knobs to hold face-forward hangers with clothing at various levels.

22-11 Retail fixtures such as these are mixed and matched in retail stores to present merchandise in organized, attractive ways for shoppers.

22-12 Rounders with a larger diameter than 36 inches can hold even more garments, depending on their circumference.

22-13 Once again, estimating one garment per inch of the fixture means that four 22-inch arms can hold a total of 88 garments. The configuration of the fixture is shown by the base that has shorter arms than the upper garment hanging rods.

Examples of capacity wall fixtures are garment hanging rods and shelves. Straight, horizontal bars are designed to hang an average of one item per inch. Thus, a 12-inch long hangbar can ideally hold 12 garments. Examples of capacity floor fixtures are rounders, superquads, bins, and tables. A rounder (circular rack), as in 22-12, with a 36-inch diameter and a circumference of about 115 inches, can hold 115 garments (one garment per inch). A superquad with four 22-inch straight arms can hold an average of 88 garments. See 22-13. The capacity of bins varies, depending on the dimensions of the bin compartments and the thickness of the merchandise items.

Feature fixtures are designed to hold small amounts of merchandise that face outward toward shoppers. They are usually used for fashion forward items, featuring the newest and most exciting items in stock. They should be restocked with new items at least once a week, or more often, if possible. They should be positioned at the front of a small store, along aisles of a midsized store, or as a lead-in to each department of a large store.

Examples of feature fixtures are waterfalls, 22-14. ***Waterfalls*** are "slant arm" fixtures intended to hold one item per knob, 22-15. For design reasons and lack of confusion to customers, each waterfall or straight arm should feature just one style, color, and fabric at a time. Also, all feature fixtures used for two-piece separates should show both the tops and bottoms on that fixture.

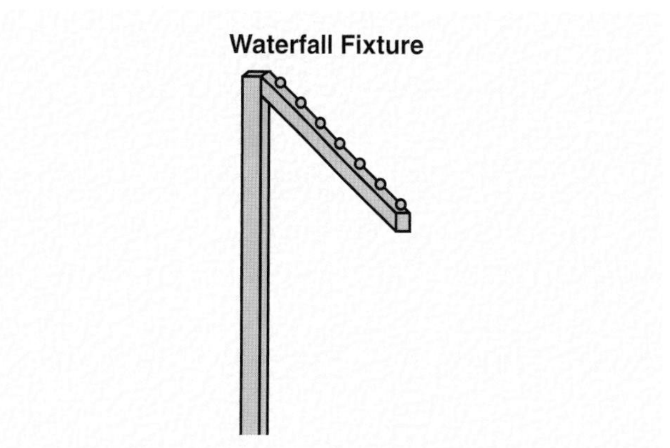

22-14 Waterfall fixtures, sometimes called "slant arms," are designed to hold one face-out hanger per knob, to present garments attractively.

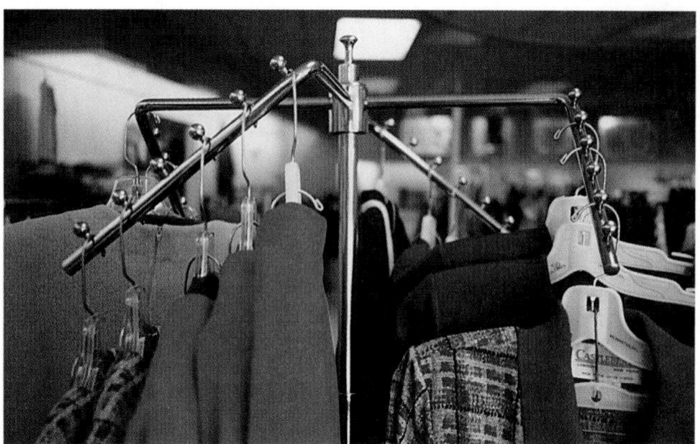

22-15 Waterfall arms can be of different thicknesses and the knobs can be square or round to coordinate with other fixtures in the store.

Usually tops are shown on a waterfall arm and bottoms on an adjoining straight arm.

Many conventional store hanging fixtures are made of chrome, which is a shiny silver metal. Hanging rod tubing is offered in square, rectangular, or round shapes. Waterfalls are available with varying amounts of round or square knobs. To provide uniformity in a store or department, just one shape of hanging rod tubing and one type of waterfall should be used.

A popular material for bins is Plexiglas. Shelves are usually of wood or glass, 22-16. Tables are of wood or metal. Often, tables do not have eye appeal or provide ease of selection. They have come to represent bargains to shoppers, and should not be overused by retailers.

In Cooperation with Saks Fifth Avenue

22-16 Glass shelves placed on adjustable supports are attractive for stacking many different types of folded items.

Sometimes furniture fixtures are used in upscale stores and departments. They include such pieces as hutches, desks, cupboards, and armoires (tall cabinets that serve as closets). Sometimes local craftspeople might be hired to build custom units.

Apparel manufacturers often supply free fixtures to stores for use with their lines. The fixtures usually have the producer's brand name on them. Some manufacturers will plan out entire shops for their merchandise, which gives them some control over how the merchandise is presented in the store. However, if a store uses too many fixtures and presentation suggestions from manufacturers, the store identity may be compromised.

Merchandise Arrangements on Walls

Wall areas are very important since customer attention focuses on them immediately after coming into the store. Wall areas should draw customers farther into the store. Walls are an excellent area for a store to present its merchandise and reinforce its image.

Wall presentations become more interesting by dividing large areas into smaller sections with architectural devices, such as columns or mirrors. Each section of the wall should then be individually merchandised as an independent unit, with one unified color group and fashion statement. For instance, if bright colors are featured, pastels would not be included. If swimwear is featured, golf shirts would not be included. This creates a natural sense of order and ease of selection for customers.

Wall standards are often secured to walls for merchandising flexibility. ***Wall standards*** are vertical strips with holes into which various types of brackets and fixtures can be inserted, 22-17. The most commonly used fixtures in wall sections are straight arms, waterfalls,

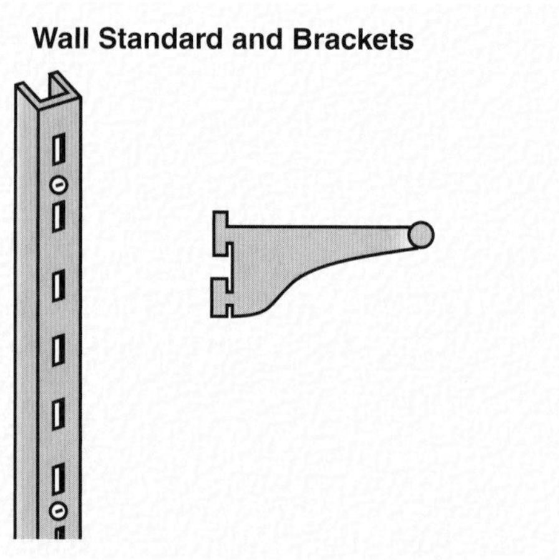

22-17 Many different types of brackets, inserted into wall standards, can be used for merchandise presentation. Shelves, hangbars, and other parts are used as needed.

In Cooperation with Saks Fifth Avenue

22-18 Hidden wall standards have been used here with a nice variety of brackets to provide an interesting mix of fixtures.

garment hangrods, and shelves. For interest, face-out units and shoulder-out garment rods should be intermixed along the walls of the store, 22-18.

Size-indicating rings are usually not placed in wall presentations because fewer garments are used and the presentation is so visible. If sizing is desired, the items should be placed from small to large, as described previously, depending on the type of fixture used. Also, sleeve lengths on shoulder-out wall garment rods should all be of similar length.

Wall fixtures should be positioned so there is only about five inches between garments hanging above and below each other. Otherwise there is an understocked look and items may become out of reach. Both tops and bottoms that coordinate should be shown together in a wall section to encourage complete outfits to be purchased. In almost all cases, merchandise bottoms are shown below tops. Only one style and one color of an item should be shown on each waterfall or straight arm in a wall section.

Interior Displays

Displays are individual and notable physical presentations of merchandise, 22-19. They are showings of products as attention-getting focal points. They use unique equipment or fixtures and feature distinctive merchandise. Good displays are color-coordinated, accessorized, and self-explanatory.

Displays are intended to

- stimulate product interest
- provide information
- suggest merchandise coordination

Almax USA Inc.

22-19 Displays show new items in fashionable ways.

- generate traffic flow
- remind customers of planned purchases
- create additional sales of impulse items
- enhance the store's visual image

Interior displays are important promotional tools. Print and broadcast advertising can get consumers to merchant locations, but then displays must take over for promotion.

Interior displays are placed in key locations throughout retail stores, 22-20. They are located near the merchandise lines being promoted or by cash registers, aisles, and entrances. A display at the store's entrance should establish a mood to get customers involved with the rest of the store merchandise and accessories. Department stores have displays in high traffic areas and often in each department to provide a clear impression of what is for sale in that area. See 22-21.

In Cooperation with Saks Fifth Avenue

22-20 This display is in a highly visible location along a major aisle of the store.

Successful floor displays make shoppers stop, look, and buy. Displays project current fashion trends and styles that represent what the store's target groups of customers want. They should be done with flair to make an impression on the viewers. This affects present and future sales.

Displays on the selling floor have gained in importance and influence. This is especially true since the indoor mall concept has removed walls, opening whole stores to the perusal of passing shoppers. Merchandise might be displayed in special ways on counters, ledges, columns, back walls, hangers from the ceiling, or specially designed racks, 22-22.

A mannequin with a perfect figure, wearing the latest look with a well-known label, reinforces the image of sexuality and attractiveness to customers. Display people reinforce images with the types of mannequins

Interior Retail Display Locations
Just inside the store entrance.
At the entrances to departments.
Near cash/wrap (point-of-purchase) counters.
Next to related items.
Across from elevators and the ends of escalators.
At the outer ends of aisles.
At open-to-mall or window areas.

22-21 Interior display locations should be chosen to maximize exposure of merchandise to increase sales.

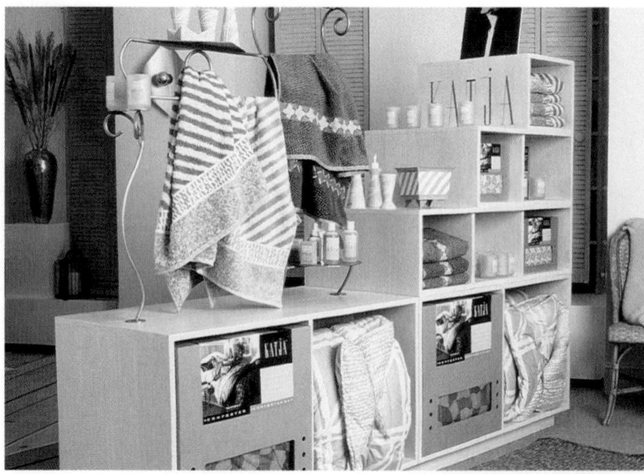

Revman Industries/AEON Group

22-22 Special display fixtures are available for particular product lines to maximize the appearance and exposure of goods to shoppers.

they show and by the manner in which the mannequins are dressed, positioned, and lit. To buy that product then makes customers imagine or feel particularly good or special. On the other hand, some newer mannequins have less than perfect features to appear more realistic.

Displays are carefully planned and scheduled in advance. Time is needed to acquire the components. Then display work is carried out in coordination with other promotional efforts of the store.

Components of Displays

All displays are made up of the same components, which are designed to give a pleasing visual impression. The main components of all fashion displays include merchandise, lighting, props, and signs.

Merchandise

The merchandise should be the central focus of any apparel and accessories display. Merchandise should be chosen carefully, according to store policies. It should be attractive, timely, and of interest to customers. In-store and window display space is best used for advertised, best-selling, high-margin, high-fashion merchandise. Considerations for what merchandise to choose for displays are listed in 22-23.

Display Merchandise Selection

Merchandise items chosen for displays should

- Be timely—as to current fashions, national and local events, the season, etc.
- Represent the stock carried by the store.
- Be stocked in enough depth and breadth to meet consumer demand created by the display.
- Represent the line of merchandise from which they were taken.
- Be in demand (of interest to shoppers, or best sellers that appeal to a large number of customers).
- Be new, to educate customers and let them know what is available.
- Encourage complementary or additional purchases of related items through coordination and accessorizing.
- Coordinate with the current promotional theme of the store.
- Look good on display so they have strong appeal to interest shoppers to be in the store.

22-23 Merchandise should be chosen carefully for displays, so the largest possible impact is achieved from the time, effort, and expense put into each display.

22-24 One distinctive or colorful gown, suit, or dress might be featured to gain the attention of shoppers.

Displays are more interesting if they feature an odd number of product items. This gives a more dramatic impression, which attracts attention better than an even number of items. Sometimes only one item is featured, 22-24. However, merchandise being displayed is most often grouped in one of the following ways:

- *One-category groupings*, or line-of-goods displays, highlight a specific kind of item, such as all skirts, children's dresses, holiday sweaters, or shoes. The items are very similar, but might be of different sizes or colors. A single manufacturer or brand name may be featured, referred to as a "vendor statement."
- *Related groupings* present ensembles of items that go together or reinforce each other. The items are meant to be used together, such as a tennis outfit plus a head visor, tennis racquet, balls, and carrying bag. This type of grouping suggests additional purchases to shoppers, showing that more than the featured item is needed, 22-25.

In Cooperation with Saks Fifth Avenue

22-25 This grouping shows related items that a fashionable man might need to complete an outfit.

In Cooperation with Saks Fifth Avenue

22-26 Notice the strong effect of the lighting in this display.

- *Theme groupings* display merchandise according to a particular setting, event, holiday, or other theme. They often show several different items of clothing, accessories, and props that support the theme. The number of possible display themes is unlimited, such as back to school, New Year's Eve, or football team spirit.
- *Variety or assortment groupings* display a collection of unrelated items that are all sold in the same store. This is often used for window displays of lower-priced retailers to show representative merchandise contained in the store.

Outfit coordination in displays might show unusual color, texture, and fabric combinations to achieve specific new looks. Trendy accessories might be added in a different way. Merchandise ideas can be obtained from fashion magazines, higher-end competitors, manufacturers, and by observing what fashion leaders are wearing.

Lighting

Lighting is used to direct customer attention to displays, 22-26. The colors of the items in the display and store placement of the display affect the amount of light needed. Because pastel colors reflect light, less lighting is needed for them. Dark colors absorb light, so more lighting is needed. Lighting fixtures should not be obvious or detract from the effect of displays. If possible, they are hidden behind props, merchandise, or sections of ceilings or walls.

Overlighting, from above the merchandise being displayed, can make items look washed out. *Underlighting,* from beneath, usually does not show merchandise as effectively as possible. Colored lights can be placed to create contrasts and special effects, but should be carefully used.

Effective accent lighting can be used to point out merchandise features, such as texture, color, and size, and give depth to displays. The ***beamspread*** is the diameter of the circle of light. The following beamspread techniques are often used to create desired effects:

- *Floodlighting* uses recessed ceiling lights to direct light over an entire, wide display area. *Wall washers* are floodlights that spread light across an area of wall.
- *Spotlighting* focuses attention on specific areas or targeted items of merchandise.
- *Pinpointing* focuses a narrow beam of light on a specific item. It is accomplished by placing a cover with a small hole in front of the light pointed at the item to be featured.

Different forms of bulbs can be used in adjustable fixtures and focused on the merchandise. Adjustable lights should be set at an angle, across the merchandise, rather than straight on. This reduces glare, maximizes the area that is covered, and gives more distance between the hot, fading light source and items being displayed.

Fluorescent lights are economical for general lighting in most stores. Special retail fluorescent bulbs do not distort the color of merchandise. Glare is reduced with *diffusers,* or light-softening shields over them. Metal halide lamps have become popular lately because they offer high intensity at very low operating cost. Low-voltage quartz lamps are used for high-impact window and in-store displays where beam control and color consistency is needed. However, both metal halide and quarts lamps are expensive to purchase. Regular incandescent recessed or track lighting is often used for display and accent lighting.

Props

Props are added objects that support the theme of the display. They must be appropriate for the display and should be kept clean and in good condition. The following types of props are used in displays:

* *Functional props* are used to physically support or hold merchandise. They include mannequins, stands, pedestals, panels, screens, or other apparel- or jewelry-holding forms. See 22-27. ***Mannequins*** are life-like human forms of men, women, and children. Forms of torsos, legs, hands, and heads may also be used, for instance, to only display shirts, hosiery, gloves, and hats. Steel tube forms or flat foam forms are sometimes used to show off clothing at a lower cost. Standard props can be obtained from display companies. Additionally, regular items, such as small chairs or tables, are used very effectively as functional props, 22-28.
* *Decorative props* are used to establish a mood or an attractive setting for the merchandise being featured. The sky is the limit for creativity with decorative props. They might include mirrors, plants, artificial flowers, bicycles, arches, pennants, seashells, surfboards, packing peanuts, mobiles, or antique books. See 22-29. Accent furniture pieces are often used. Any items that help attract interest, while adding to the display theme, can be used.
* *Structural props* are used to support functional and decorative props and change the physical makeup of displays. Boxes, support rods, stands, stairways, and cylinders are examples of structural props. These are usually covered or hidden from view as much as possible. Turntables or moving parts that operate from a small electric motor can add a special dimension to displays.

Options by Stafford/JCPenney

22-28 Retail display personnel are often very creative in their use of functional props.

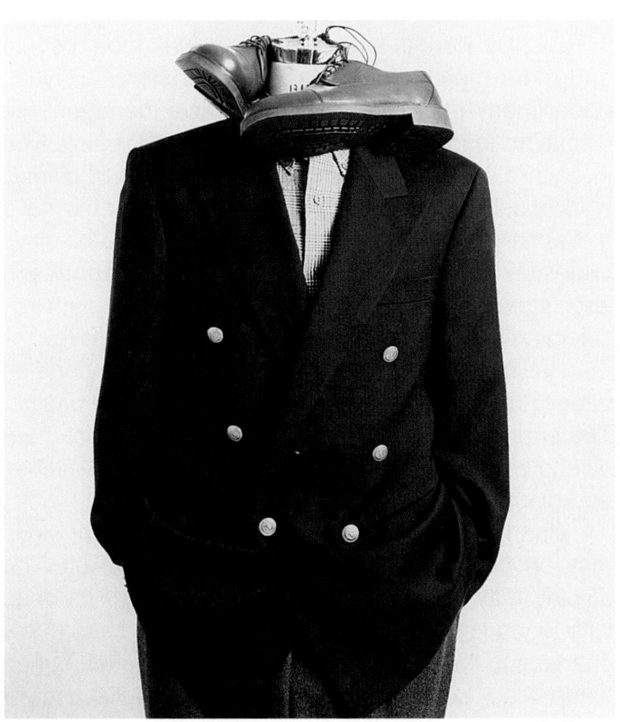

VanHeusen

22-27 This dressmaker's form is a functional prop used to display the shirt, jacket, slacks, and shoes assembled to show shoppers how men can put together a casual, yet fashionable, outfit.

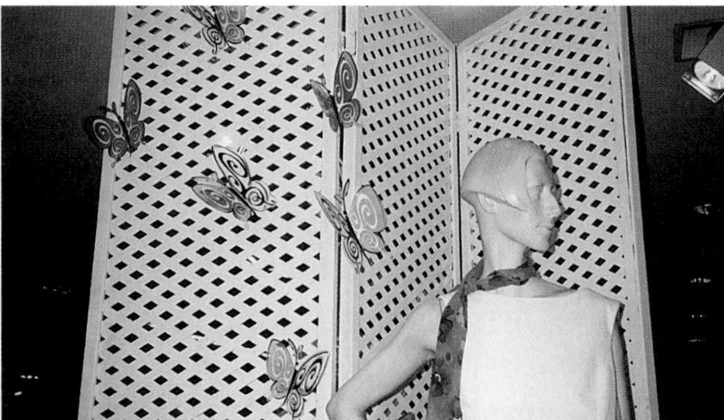

22-29 The lattice-work screen and stylized butterflies shown here are strictly decorative to set the tone for the summer outfit on the mannequin.

Signage

Signage includes individual letters and complete signs. Signs are often mounted in chrome or Plexiglas sign holders of standard sizes, 22-30. A variety of signs may be used, including counter signs, posters, hanging signs, banners and flags, elevator cards, and easels. However, if signs are overused, a confusing appearance will result, and none of them will stand out with a clear message.

In Cooperation with Saks Fifth Avenue

22-30 The small sign in the Plexiglas holder is a "showcard" that discreetly names the brand name of the items being displayed.

Signage can tell a story about goods, guide customers through the store, and do silent selling. It can generate customer interest and explain product benefits. Signage information should try to answer anticipated customer questions. It might include prices, sizes, styles, color names, features, construction, theme information, location of merchandise in the store, and the store logo. A store logo or slogan may be included in the same location on all signs to coordinate with advertising and other promotional vehicles. Use of a distinctive logo ties all merchandise to the image of the store and strengthens the store identity in the minds of customers.

The wording on signs should be informative and concise. Well-understood, common words should relate to the merchandise being featured. A theme can be briefly explained or accentuated with an appropriate phrase, such as "Happy Holidays" or "Celebrate Spring." Lettering should stand out with sharp contrast that attracts attention and should be large enough to be read from a distance.

Planning Interior Displays

In most small apparel and accessories stores, only a few items can be displayed. The selection is further reduced by several factors, including the season of the year, what has been displayed recently, and planned advertising. However, small stores also have the flexibility to change displays more often than large stores.

Display work in large stores involves more people and more merchandise than in small stores. Buyers, department heads, the merchandise manager, the display manager, and the display staff are all involved in each display. Communication and timing of display work must be carefully organized. Large stores have more merchandise to choose from and more displays to design. Also, displays are usually more elaborate in large stores and more time is needed between planning, selecting merchandise, and constructing displays.

Preliminary planning of displays should be done on paper, using the elements and principles of design. The arrangement is influenced by the type of merchandise to be displayed, display materials, props available, and display space.

Changes in merchandise, lighting, props, or signs may be needed as the display is being set up. The display may look too cluttered or too bare. However, with good preliminary planning, usually only a few changes to the display components are needed during setup. Also, experience in display work results in fewer mistakes. Ongoing maintenance is then needed, to keep the merchandise clean and everything in its place. See 22-31.

22-31 For this display to remain attractive, the tables, pottery vase, and mannequin tops must be dusted, and the dresses and flowers must be kept in order.

Displays can be expensive since they use store space, require props and materials, and take time to plan, set up, and maintain. However, good displays pay off. Records should be kept of each display, which include the date, description of the components, sketches or photos, and costs involved. Also, sales of the merchandise during the display period should be noted as well as any other pertinent comments.

Display Evaluation Questions

- How effective is the sales appeal of the merchandise?
- Was the display coordinated with store ads?
- Does the display help customers locate merchandise?
- Do the display materials and props enhance or detract from the merchandise?
- Is display signage both legible to read and easy to understand?
- Does display signage give the best selling points and answer the right customer questions?
- Are all displays working together to draw customers through the store?
- Have displays changed often enough to keep customers' interest?
- Are displays always kept clean and in good condition?

22-32 Display evaluation is an important step done to judge the effectiveness of current displays and to provide input for future displays.

Final evaluations of displays, and records kept about display details, help with ideas and improvements for future displays. The questions in 22-32, and others, might be asked to help with display evaluation.

Window Displays

Window displays are seen from outside the store, 22-33. They are the first contact that stores have with customers and often the main reason why customers enter stores. However, city window-shopping has decreased. People are too busy to window-shop for leisure or curiosity, and there are fewer street-facing windows used for displays.

22-33 Most flagship stores still maintain fashion displays in their windows.

Retail space is expensive in prime locations. Store area is more valuable if converted to interior selling space, storage, or dressing rooms, than if used to show only a few select pieces of merchandise to a few people who might look. Some stores have put fixtures and counters in place of window walls. Others have redesigned large, full-sized windows into small shadowboxes which require a lower budget and less decorating and upkeep time. However, most new higher-end strip shopping centers have expansive window display areas.

In some locations and for some stores, window displays are very important. The number, size, depth, and type of windows can substantially alter the exterior appearance of a store and general impression to consumers. Small stores may only have one display window or a pair of windows separated by the entrance.

Larger stores and specialty chains often have a series of several windows all in a row or one very long "run-on" window expanse of 30 or more feet. One long window allows for more flexibility and control. A large display using the entire expanse may be used at some times, and dividers added to separate the long stretch into individual display areas at other times. Wide storefronts that are open to shoppers in malls act as display windows without the glass.

Advantages and Disadvantages of Window Displays

Window displays can help distinctive retailers establish and maintain a unique image. They can stimulate and arouse the curiosity of shoppers to the point of having them enter the store, even if they are not motivated to buy the item on display. This allows the merchant many more opportunities to sell merchandise to those shoppers.

Although window displays can be eye-catchers, they are expensive to design, set up, and maintain. See 22-34. Special space, staff, props, and background

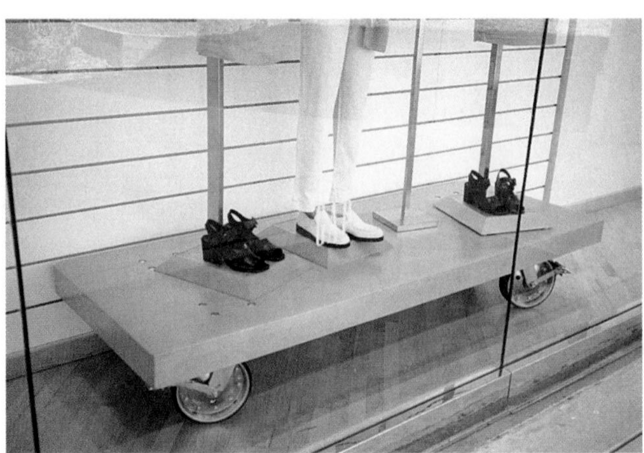

22-34 One way to ease the difficulty of window display setup is to use rolling platforms. This also gives a fun, casual feeling to the display.

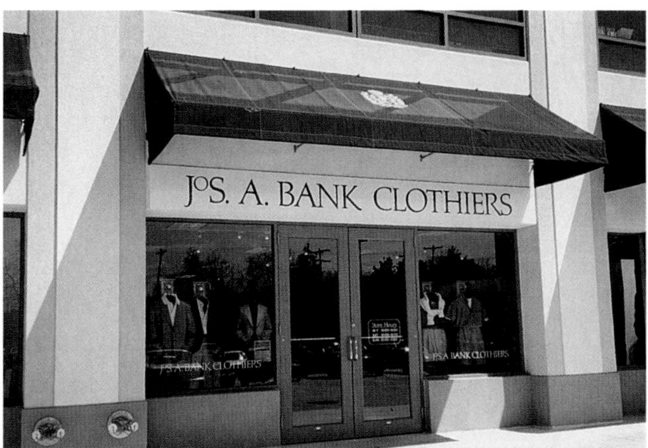

22-35 Although not all glare is eliminated with awnings, a great amount is removed and the merchandise on display is easier to see.

materials are needed. Sets, mannequins, and energy for lighting may be more elaborate than for interior displays. Additionally, window displays create wear and tear on merchandise and may have adverse effects from sunlight and heat.

An ongoing problem with display windows is the glare and reflection of the glass. This reduces the visibility of what is displayed in the window. Many retailers try to reduce glare and reflection with decorative awnings, 22-35. Awnings shelter shoppers on the outside from undesirable weather, giving them added comfort while entering the store. Awnings also protect merchandise in the windows from ultraviolet ray damage. Additionally, awnings enhance the store exterior. A store name/logo can be placed on both the front and sides of awnings, and they can be changed for special seasons or promotions.

Types of Display Windows

The two main types of display windows are enclosed windows and open windows. Variations of these include ramped windows, elevated windows, semi-enclosed windows, shadowbox windows, and island windows.

Enclosed Windows

Enclosed windows have a full background and sides that completely separate the interior of the store from the display window. It is the traditional type with a large glass window facing the sidewalk. It forms the ideal space in which to perfectly arrange a three-dimensionally created fashion picture.

Variations of enclosed windows include

- ramped windows, with the display floor higher in back than in front.
- elevated windows, usually located from one to three feet above sidewalk level.
- shadowbox windows that are small boxlike display windows, 22-36.

In Cooperation with Saks Fifth Avenue

22-36 Shadowbox windows are smaller than full-size windows and are usually at a height near eye-level. Notice that this is a double shadowbox, with a smaller shadowbox inside the regular shadowbox window.

Backgrounds of enclosed windows are usually painted or covered as needed, and changed often. They may be made of wallboard, fiberboard, paneling, corrugated board, draped or stretched fabric, or just painted a neutral color. When the window is "trimmed" or "dressed" (decorated), draperies, appliqués, or decorative panels, are used to set the stage for a merchandise theme. Contrasting colors and textured surfaces can emphasize the lines, shapes, sizes, textures, weights, and colors of merchandise. Photo murals or paper printed with scenes are also used. The back wall should never detract from the merchandise being displayed.

Lights are located at the ceiling, usually just above the window glass, and on grids and lighting tracks. This allows for flexible placement of lights, as well as space for the hanging of draperies, panels, streamers, and other decorative materials in the middle of the window.

The *side walls* of window displays should coordinate with the back wall and may have panels that are angled inward toward the back. This cuts down the width of the decorating space and concentrates the sight line of the viewer toward the center. It also hides any side lights that are used and gives a feeling of depth perception to the presentation.

The *floor covering* should blend with the background. Often neutral colors and basic textures are used, such as parquet wood tiles or broadloom carpeting. Fiberboard is often used over the permanent floor to change the look without damaging the permanent floor. It can be covered with paint, vinyl tiles, colored papers, cork chips, sand, rocks, fall leaves, artificial grass, straw mats, fabrics, or other creative surfaces. Padded surfaces allow for the use of pins and nails. Since the floor is seen by the viewers, it should be kept clean and neat at all times.

Semi-Enclosed Windows

Semi-enclosed windows have a partial background that shuts out some of the store interior from those viewing the window. A panel, screen, or curtain might be used to divide the window from the store interior. Often, the two finished sides have different surfaces, with a colored and textured background and a different treatment on the back that blends with the interior or merchandise of the store. This accentuates the merchandise featured in the window. Sometimes tall plants are used as dividers. Other choices might be semi-sheer curtains, beaded chains, or other see-through dividers that let daylight into the store for a feeling of greater openness. Also, some stores have removable back wall panels so enclosed windows can be converted to open windows or floor selling space.

Open Windows

Open windows have no background panel, and the entire store is visible to passersby through the window display. This increases the need for an inviting selling environment inside the store. New specialty store facilities in higher-end strip malls usually decorate their large, open glass expanses with dressed mannequins facing the sidewalk. The merchandise shown in the window is often enhanced and emphasized by having the same type and color merchandise in the selling space immediately behind it.

Open window displays are often done on a platform that raises the display area, or with raised props, 22-37. Some problems occur with lighting and background presentations, since the interior store merchandise and lighting are competing for the attention of the viewer. Also, window display lighting should not irritate the customers shopping inside the store.

Island Windows

Island windows are four-sided display windows that stand alone, often in lobbies. They can effectively highlight merchandise from all angles. Merchandise must be carefully selected and positioned to be interesting from all directions. Sometimes a turntable is used at the floor, allowing shoppers to see the entire display while standing in one place. However, internal lighting is difficult and external glare may be present on all four sides. Also, shoppers can see through the window to be distracted with action on the other side. Additionally, store liability exists with people walking into the glass.

22-37 If a platform is not present for open window displays, special props can be used on which to hang and set garments to increase visibility for window-shoppers.

Summary

The main purposes of visual merchandising are to sell goods and promote the store image.

The store interior includes selling and sales support areas. Selling floor layouts influence in-store traffic patterns, shopping atmosphere, and operational efficiency. Merchandise should be grouped logically to help customers find, compare, and buy according to their needs. Store decor reinforces the company image and is a backdrop for the merchandise.

Merchandise presentation varies with the amount of merchandise for sale. Appropriate fixtures should coordinate with the store's merchandise style, inventory level, and budget. Merchandise arrangements on walls should draw customers farther into the store. Point-of-purchase merchandise presentations near cash registers should be impulse-oriented.

Interior displays use unique equipment and feature distinctive merchandise. They should be located near the merchandise being promoted, or by cash registers, aisles, and entrances. Good displays are color-coordinated, accessorized, and self-explanatory. Small stores have fewer items to display and less space, but can change displays more often than large stores that have more people and merchandise.

Window displays are seen from outside the store and can convince shoppers to enter the store. However, they can be expensive to maintain and have glare from the outside. Types of display windows include enclosed, semi-enclosed, open, and island windows.

To Know

visual merchandising
store layout
selling areas
sales support areas
floor plan
fixtures
grid layout
maze layout
decor
merchandise presentation
shoulder-out presentation
face-forward presentation
capacity fixtures
feature fixtures
waterfalls
wall standards
displays
beamspread
props
mannequins

To Review

1. Why is visual merchandising more effective than flat drawings or photos?
2. What three advantages does the drawing of floor plans allow retailers to accomplish?
3. What two factors help to determine the value, or sales expectations, of selling spaces within a store?
4. Where is the most valuable area of every store located and why?
5. In what three general locations should face-out presentation of clothing be used?
6. In small, midsized, and large stores, where should feature fixtures be positioned, respectively?
7. Why should both tops and bottoms that coordinate with each other be shown together in a wall section?
8. What are the four main components of all fashion displays?
9. In a display category grouping, what is a vendor statement?
10. Where can merchandise ideas be obtained for display work?
11. Why should adjustable lights be set at an angle, across merchandise rather than pointing straight at the goods?
12. How are functional props used in displays?
13. What is the purpose of decorative props in displays?
14. What is the result of signs being overused?
15. What four factors affect the planning of display arrangements?
16. Name two reasons why city window-shopping has decreased.
17. Describe two advantages of window displays.
18. Name three advantages that retail exterior window awnings can provide.
19. What are the advantages of angling the side walls inward toward the back of window displays?
20. Briefly describe island windows.

To Do

1. With a classmate, visit two small stores to observe the layouts. Explain your project to the manager of each store and ask if you can tour the support areas that are not open to the public. Then draw the floor plan of a fictitious small store using graph paper, with 1/8 inch or 1/4 inch on the drawing representing one foot of the full-size store. Divide the total space into a small sales support area and a large selling area. Outline and label each general merchandise area. (You may want to lightly color in areas of the store to represent merchandise areas.) Draw a grid or maze traffic layout past or through the merchandise areas as well as showing the cash/wrap areas. Share your plan with the class, justifying the reasoning behind your work.

2. With a classmate, visit both a local expensive apparel store and a discount store. In a written report, describe and contrast the visual merchandising of the two stores. Include comments about the layout, decor, flooring, lighting, fixtures, width of aisles, number and types of displays, etc. What feeling is communicated to customers in each store? Is the visual merchandising appropriate for the target market of each store? Explain your thoughts about the comparison.

3. Visit a mall or department store and try to locate at least eight of the merchandise fixtures listed in 22-11. Include the name and a brief description (in your own words) of each one, and how the merchandise is placed onto it. Also state if each one is a capacity or feature fixture.

4. With a classmate, visit two stores that have similar target markets. Observe and sketch the merchandise presentation of two wall sections, one from each store. Show your drawings to the class. Have long wall areas been sectioned into smaller areas (and in what way)? Where are the wall areas located in each store and from what areas are they seen to draw attention? Do they make a specific color or fashion statement? Is there good spacing between the merchandise and a logical relationship between items? Is there any way that you would improve the wall presentations in the stores?
5. After obtaining permission from the store manager, take pictures of the several displays in a department store and its windows. Show the best photos to the class and describe each display. How are the elements and principles of design used? Is there a theme that coordinates displays storewide? Describe the type of merchandise groupings and props used. Is the displayed merchandise currently in fashion? What kind of lighting is used? Is signage appropriate for the displays? Also, ask the store manager what employees are involved in the planning, setting up, maintenance, and evaluation of the displays. Notice that same store's newspaper advertising and discuss how well the displays do or do not coordinate with the ads.

CHAPTER 23

Special Event Fashion Shows

After studying this chapter, you will be able to

- explain the many purposes of fashion shows.
- list the main types of fashion shows.
- identify the different aspects of planning for fashion shows.
- discuss the coordination of merchandise and models for the final lineup of fashion shows.
- summarize the coordination of the physical layout, music, choreography, and commentary of fashion shows.
- explain the aspects of promoting and presenting a smooth fashion show performance.
- describe the follow-up and evaluation procedures for fashion shows.

Special events are promotional activities held to build customer traffic, sell goods, and enhance the company image. They help distinguish a company from competitors. Special events are held in retail stores or elsewhere in the community. They may include visits by designers or celebrities, art exhibits, product demonstrations, contests, entertainment, charity sales days, and other such "happenings."

Fashion shows are some of the most exciting special events for those involved in the fashion industry. They are memorable occasions from the introduction of the newest fashions on Paris runways to the showing of ready-to-wear apparel in small stores or community programs across the country.

Fashion Shows Serve Many Purposes

Fashion shows are theatrical presentations of apparel and accessories on live models, 23-1. They are often presented at the beginning of fashion seasons to introduce new merchandise. Models wearing completely accessorized outfits promote fashion apparel better than flat photos or garments on hangers.

The American Printed Fabrics Council

23-1 Fashion shows are special events that parade outfits, such as this dress with coordinated shoes and hat, in front of audiences.

In Cooperation with The Fashion Association

23-2 Manufacturers' fashion shows can present all the style numbers in the company's line so retail buyers can pick their choices for their stores.

Fashion Institute of Technology/John Senzer, Photographer

23-3 This college fashion show is presented with creative flair by students who plan to become professionals in the fashion industry.

Fashion shows take place at several market levels. Couture designer collections are shown to elite customers and the press. Apparel manufacturers' lines are shown to retail buyers, 23-2. *Consumer fashion shows* are presented by retailers to consumers.

Using a fashion show for retail promotion makes a visual statement that helps sell merchandise in an exciting way. It educates customers about the latest trends in silhouettes, fabrics, and colors, while providing entertainment. It attracts new customers and keeps current ones by showing the retailer's fashion authority. It also indicates the depth and breadth of merchandise carried by the retailer, such as different brands, features of private label items, or special merchandise offerings.

Various designers or retailers may hold promotional fashion shows for business programs and social luncheons. Also, to provide goodwill within a community, stores may participate in fund-raising benefits for civic groups. Fashion show tickets are sold, with the proceeds going to a specified charity. Sometimes a local or national celebrity narrates the show.

Cooperative fashion shows are jointly sponsored, with expenses shared by two or more organizations. To promote both businesses, they may be cosponsored by

- a designer or manufacturer with a retailer that sells the designer's or manufacturer's merchandise.
- a fashion magazine with a retailer that carries the trends or lines featured in the magazine.
- a home sewing pattern company with a fabric store that sells the fabrics that have been made into garments from the patterns.

In other instances, retail salespeople learn from in-store-produced training shows, usually presented in the morning before the store opens. Such shows educate salespeople about specific trends and selling features of the apparel that will be for sale to customers during the upcoming season. Tips on merchandise presentation and coordination with the store's overall promotional plans are also given. The morale of employees improves, while their loyalty toward the fashion leadership of the store increases.

Fashion shows are also produced by fashion students, so they can show their creations and learn how to produce shows. See 23-3. The students learn how to model, and gain knowledge about planning, presenting, and evaluating fashion productions.

Types of Fashion Shows

Fashion shows can be large extravaganzas with months of preparation involving many people, or small, informal events with limited preparation and casual presentation. The most elaborate and expensive type of fashion show is the ***production fashion show***. It includes backdrops, lighting effects, and entertainment, 23-4. Modeling choreography is coordinated with live or specially produced music. ***Choreography*** is the planned arrangement of movement, such as with specific dance steps or gestured moves.

Production shows use many models and require a great deal of organization and advance planning. Sometimes they accompany a dinner and are part of

In Cooperation with The Fashion Association

23-4 This event featured the cast of the award-winning musical, *Bring in 'da Noise, Bring in 'da Funk.* Cast members modeled the latest designs of Marithe & Francois Girbaud as they did their tap dance routines to enthusiastic applause.

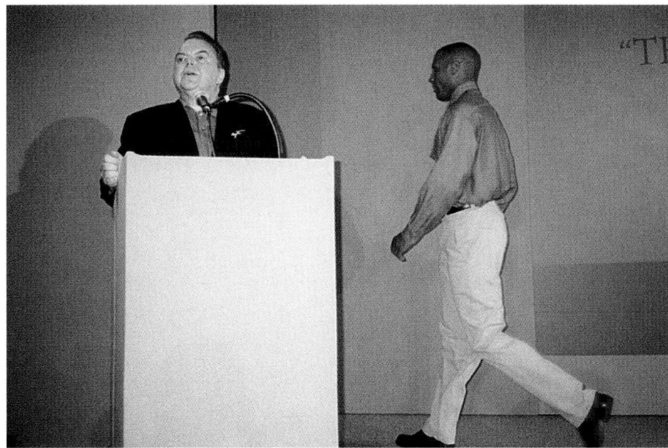

In Cooperation with The Fashion Association

23-5 As clothes are modeled in formal runway shows, a commentary explains the new trends. In menswear shows, examples of trouser features to be mentioned might be pleated or flat front, cuffed or straight hem, or spandex added to the fabric for comfort.

In Cooperation with The 410 Shoppe

23-6 Before restaurant patrons arrive, tearoom models are shown the restaurant layout and discuss the path they will take to show the clothes being featured.

a major charity fund-raiser for hundreds to thousands of people. Expensive fashion merchandise is featured.

The ***formal runway show*** is a typical presentation of fashion models parading on a runway in a certain order of appearance. It is held in an auditorium, hotel or restaurant, or salesroom. The merchandise and staging follows a theme, plus there is special lighting, music, and commentary. ***Commentary*** is a spoken explanation of what is going on, especially pointing out specific features of each outfit being modeled, 23-5.

Formal runway shows are aimed toward certain consumer groups or specialty retail buyers. They might be for career women, men's sportswear enthusiasts, or those interested in children's clothing. Runway shows present new lines and seasonal trends. Some type of refreshment is usually offered.

An ***informal fashion show*** is a more casual presentation of garments and accessories. Models walk through the manufacturer's showroom or the sales floor of a retail store. They may carry a sign, business card, or handout with information about the merchandise and how it can be purchased. This requires much less preparation since no music, lighting, or staging are used.

Another type of informal fashion show is ***tearoom modeling*** in which models walk individually from table to table in a restaurant to show and tell about what they are wearing. After going around in one outfit, the models change to a different accessorized garment to model the same way. They may give cards to interested consumers that entitle the holder to a certain discount on purchases at the store that is sponsoring the show. See 23-6.

Planning Fashion Shows

Advance planning of fashion shows is very important to enable the final presentation to run smoothly and professionally. Details include organizing the committees and jobs to be done. Both verbal and written communication are very important and should be encouraged. Written directions can help to eliminate misunderstandings among all those who are involved.

Responsibilities for a Large Fashion Show

Merchandise Committee	Promotion Committee	Commentary Committee
Merchandise selection/return Preshow fittings/alterations Dressing room supervisor Dressers Lineup and cue manager Starters	Publicity coordinator Advertising coordinator Photographer Invitations Ticket sales/distribution Program editor	Commentary writer Commentator General announcer
Model Committee	**Staging Committee**	**Hospitality Committee**
Model selection/training Model coordinator Choreographer Hair technician Makeup technician	Set and runway construction Props manager Music director Musicians or recordings Backstage manager Sound technician Lighting technician Safety and security	Site reservation Food/refreshments coordinator Servers, caterer, etc. Room and table decorations Seating host or ushers Gifts and door prizes Insurance

23-7 Although each show is different, committees such as these are organized according to the type and size of the fashion show. Each committee has a chairperson who reports to the fashion show director as well as people doing various sub-committee jobs.

The directions can be reviewed periodically so no details are forgotten or duplicated by more than one person.

Major advance planning decisions must be made about the audience, theme, time and location, and safety and security. Also, the budget must be carefully planned, with allocations for each type of expense.

The Fashion Show Coordinator

A ***fashion show coordinator*** is in charge of the entire presentation. In a retail company, this might be the fashion director. This person creates and coordinates the fashion image and buying program for one or many stores. For a small apparel shop, the fashion show coordinator is most likely the owner of the shop. For joint shows, an expert might be sent from a fashion magazine to coordinate the show. For school or civic fashion shows, a member of the group is chosen to be the coordinator.

The fashion show coordinator plans all arrangements, delegates responsibilities, and is accountable for all details. Jobs to be accomplished differ according to the complexity of the show. For a small runway show, a merchandise coordinator, model coordinator, stage manager, promotion coordinator, and commentator might be appointed. For a larger show, people might be assigned to specific jobs within several committees, 23-7.

The fashion show coordinator and committee chairpersons must continually review the progress of the plans for the show, making sure that deadlines are met by all those involved. They must try to foresee any problems and be flexible to solve or work around them. The fashion show coordinator should keep a diary that serves as a reminder list of details to be completed. Follow-up dates for various tasks and future needs for the show are written in it. After the show, it is a resource for planning future shows.

Pinpointing the Audience

Pinpointing the target market of the fashion show impacts all other decisions. The age, gender, income/spending habits, and lifestyle of the audience dictate the merchandise and theme for the event. Based upon the target audience, the theme might emphasize bridal, career, or casual wear. Appropriate garments and trends promoted in the show must match the needs of those who attend, 23-8.

Fashion shows can have a guaranteed or created audience. A ***guaranteed audience*** is established before the show is organized and will attend regardless of the show. For instance, a fashion show at a business luncheon or stockholders meeting is seen by those who would have attended even if no show was to be held.

A ***created audience*** is established after the show is planned, as a result of publicity and advertising. A created audience wants to see the new fashion trends and attend a social event. The audience might be created as a result of mailings to lists of store customers. General publicity and advertising may be done to the public, through local newspapers and radio stations. However, a specific audience profile is always targeted.

In Cooperation with The Fashion Association

23-8 Although not many fashion shows feature only formal wear, a show of bridal apparel or a benefit show for a ballet or opera guild might have a spectacular finish with tuxedos and gowns.

The size of the audience has an impact on the type of show and location, since all persons in the audience must be able to see the fashions from a comfortable location. The age of the audience influences the type of music and amount of extra entertainment to be included in the show. An older audience usually wants softer music and a more explicit, detailed commentary. A younger audience may prefer louder, faster music with more entertaining action and less commentary.

Deciding on the Theme

The theme of a fashion show is developed for the target audience, holiday or time of year, and merchandise to be featured. It is the basic idea of the show. Then a title is chosen for the show that indicates the content of the show. The theme and title are used in the coordinated publicity/advertising, merchandise, staging, and other planning of the show.

The theme might be "back-to-school" in late August, or evening wear just before New Years Eve. A current movie theme or travel destination might be enthusiastically received by certain audiences. If a designer/manufacturer, fashion magazine, or other organization is featured, that sponsor is usually included in the theme as a courtesy. This promotes the cooperative sponsor, can attract a larger audience if the name is well known, and can help the image of both the vendor and the store.

Timing and Location for the Show

The date and time for the show should not conflict with other events such as major community activities. Setting the exact time for the show must take into account travel time to and from the show for models, show workers, and the audience. An evening might be chosen if most of the audience is employed during the day. Retailers who want to attract customers who wear business apparel also sometimes stage breakfast or lunchtime shows. These feature a simple, quick meal and an entertaining, educational show during a time when these customers would be away from work.

Although a small show may last 30 minutes or less, consumer fashion shows often last about 45 minutes for the fashion segment. This fits the attention span of most audiences. An additional 15 minutes may be allowed for refreshments, announcements, and door prizes. This brings the entire event to one hour.

The location of the fashion show is coordinated with where the audience is and the purpose, type, and size of the show. People will travel farther to see larger productions. Small, informal shows must be located geographically close to the audience. During the holiday season and traditional wedding times, banquet rooms must be reserved more than a year in advance.

The date and place are booked after making sure there can be adequate seating arrangements, food service, and provisions for sound, lighting, staging, and dressing areas. Then details are finalized and put into a written contract. Details include what the site management will provide as far as room setup, food and beverages, public address system, cleanup, etc. Extra time may have to be rented to put up the staging and hold rehearsals. The contract is signed by representatives of both the site and the group using its services.

If informal modeling is done at a restaurant, a contract is probably not required. Some restaurants allow fashion shows to take place in their facilities during regular meal service. This can increase the restaurant's business while promoting fashion goods of a nearby store. However, adequate dressing room facilities must be available. Also, if the restaurant serves alcoholic beverages, models must be of legal drinking age.

If the fashion show is held for customers in a retail store, a large room can be set up for a formal show, with light refreshments being catered. A different format includes informal modeling that takes place on the floor of the store, during which the models talk to customers about what they are wearing and where it can be obtained. A runway may even be set up near where the merchandise is located.

With the date, time, and location of the show determined, a time schedule is planned for preparations. It outlines when certain activities will be done by all those who will participate in the show. Some preparations will start months ahead of the show, with more specific and frequent deadlines occurring as the date of the show draws near.

Safety and Security Considerations

The safety and security of merchandise, equipment, show participants, and the audience must not be overlooked in fashion show planning. Written policies about personal safety, and signed agreements about merchandise and equipment security, help prevent losses and legal problems later.

Merchandise used during rehearsals and the show must be protected from wearing damage, as well as from theft or vandalism. Access to the stage and dressing areas should be limited to only certain fashion show staff. The merchandise committee has the responsibility of organizing, labeling, transferring, and securing all goods from the retail location to the show area. All models and dressers should take responsibility for preventing harm to the show garments and accessories used in the show.

Security personnel may have to be hired to prevent theft or vandalism. Procedures should be followed that prevent accidents and injuries. Audience safety can be provided by preventing loose electrical cords from crossing the floor, meeting all fire code requirements, clearly marking emergency exits, and spacing aisles for easy access. Also, it is wise to buy insurance that covers all aspects of the show.

Budget Planning

Fashion show costs depend on the type and size of the show and location. Elaborate shows are more expensive, with high fees for professional models, large numbers of support staff, intricate staging, and room and equipment rentals. The least expensive shows are informal ones, presented at the point of sale, such as in the manufacturer's showroom or on the floor of a retail store.

The first step in planning a fashion show budget is to forecast expected *revenues* (incomes) for the show. All other aspects of financial planning are based on this estimate, since the amount of money going out must not exceed money available to use. Revenues come from ticket sales, money from cooperative sponsors, or allocations from the company's promotion budget. Retailers usually recover the costs of producing a fashion show from higher sales after the show.

Fashion show *expenditures* are divided among the different committees, according to the estimated needs they submit to the fashion show director. Written estimates are obtained from hotels, caterers, insurance brokers, and major equipment rental firms. Several bids from different organizations for each type of service may be solicited to obtain the lowest price and best contract.

There is no site rental cost if the fashion show is held in the manufacturer's showroom or at the retail store. When space is rented, the season, day of the week, and time of the day affect the price. Holidays, weekends, and evening times cost more than weekdays. Also, the cost of rehearsal time or additional space for rehearsals elsewhere must be considered. Refreshments may be part of the site rental fee or a caterer might be hired separately. Sometimes hotels will waive the rental charge for the room if a minimum amount of food and beverages are bought from them. An advance deposit is usually required when the site is booked and when a caterer is hired. Food might also be required for the models and show staff during rehearsal and setup times.

Fees for professional models are paid on either an hourly or daily basis, including time for fittings, rehearsals, and the show. Swimwear and lingerie models often receive higher rates than those who model conservative outfits. Well-known models in major market centers receive very high pay, such as $1,000/hour. Models in smaller markets often receive less. If amateur models are used for a retail or community fashion show, they are often given a gift, gift certificate, or discount on purchases.

Expenses for promotion include publicity and advertising preparation and media costs. Invitations, posters, tickets, and programs must be printed. Costs of press photographs, videotaping, and postage should not be overlooked. Someone hired to make a video or photo record of the show is paid. However, newspaper or television photographers sent by their employers are not paid by the fashion show organizers.

The budget must also include wages for people hired to build sets and do technical work, such as controlling the lighting or sound system, 23-9. If hair stylists, makeup artists, security personnel, and other support staff are hired, their pay must be anticipated. For charity shows, volunteers often make the decorations, provide transportation for merchandise and props, and serve as hosts, ushers, models and dressing helpers.

The budget must be realistic and flexible enough to be revised if circumstances change. It is updated on

In Cooperation with The Fashion Association

23-9 The pay for special craftspeople who are hired to oversee technical aspects of the show must be included in budget calculations.

a sheet such as the one shown in 23-10, as actual expenses are incurred. It is wise to include an emergency reserve in the budget, too. This is a "cushion" that covers unexpected costs or overruns of expenses. All participants should be aware that following the budget and controlling costs helps the show to be successful. Receipts should be saved by committee people and turned in for the final accounting.

Coordinating Merchandise and Models

Merchandise and models must be coordinated with each other, as well as with the fashion show theme and the type of audience. This involves merchandise selection, model selection, and the fittings and lineup.

Merchandise Selection

Merchandise selection involves choosing the best garments, shoes, and accessories for the show. The merchandise must represent the latest trends. This creates excitement and encourages purchases after the show. Retailers should have the items available in their stores at that time. For press and trade shows,

Fashion Show Budget

Show Title		
Date / Location / Time		
	Budget (planned)	**Actual**
Revenues:		
Ticket sales (quantity sold x price)	______	______
Cooperative sponsorship money	______	______
Company promotion allocation	______	______
Total revenues:		
Expenditures:		
Physical Facility:		
Site rental	______	______
Stage backdrop	______	______
Props	______	______
Runway design/construction	______	______
Lighting design/installation	______	______
Chairs	______	______
Tables	______	______
Decorations	______	______
Equipment and Technicians:		
Music	______	______
Public address system	______	______
Photographer/video crew	______	______
Hair stylist	______	______
Makeup artist	______	______
Publicity and Advertising:		
Press release preparation	______	______
Photography	______	______
Publicity distribution	______	______
Advertisement production	______	______
Media space/time	______	______
Tickets/invitations	______	______
Programs	______	______
Show Personnel:		
Models	______	______
Dressers	______	______
Starters	______	______
Commentator	______	______
Transportation	______	______
Hosts/ushers	______	______
Merchandise:		
Damages/repairs/losses	______	______
Security	______	______
Hospitality:		
Food/beverages	______	______
Entertainment	______	______
Gifts/prizes	______	______
Gratuities	______	______
Celebrity transportation/hotel	______	______
Insurance	______	______
Taxes	______	______
Emergency Reserve	______	______
Total expenditures:		

23-10 A budget is necessary for every fashion show. However, the categories used and the dollar amounts differ depending on the scope of the show.

workrooms of designers and manufacturers sometimes finish garments just before showtime to present their latest designs.

Fashion show merchandise should be chosen that matches the age, sex, lifestyle, and spending habits of the audience. Merchandise that seems too expensive intimidates customers, since they can't afford to purchase the items. On the other hand, merchandise that is less expensive than the taste of the audience is undesirable. Three-quarters of the merchandise in fashion shows should be items the audience will buy and wear. The other one quarter should be far-out and fun, as in 23-11, or exquisite items for the audience to dream about owning, as in 23-12!

Five to eight merchandise categories are usually included in a show. They may correspond to retail departments or lifestyle activities, such as casual/leisure clothing, exercise wear, or evening clothing. The strongest fashion statements should be made in the first and last categories of the show. The first category must capture the attention of the audience. The last items should leave a feeling of excitement and urgency for the audience to try on and buy some of the garments!

Merchandise categories usually build from the most casual to the most dramatic. A show of only careerwear may be divided according to different designers. A bridal show might have categories of traditional styles, bridesmaid dresses, mother of the bride outfits, sophisticated gowns, and others.

When retailers lend merchandise for a civic or school show, merchandise categories should be matched to the store offerings. If several retailers participate, more choices and ideas become available. Also, small stores with limited inventory can participate. Fashion show policies must be the same for all stores, to avoid favoritism.

The number of outfits to be shown is paced at one or two per minute. This gives the audience time to thoroughly absorb the trends, but not become bored. Thus, for a 45-minute show, 45 to 90 accessorized garments are shown.

Before merchandise is actually selected, an ***ideal chart*** is prepared that names all merchandise categories to be presented and the number of garments to be

In Cooperation with The Fashion Association

23-11 As a joke before showing men's fashion trends, this production paraded the first two models in "construction worker skirts" to get the attention of the audience!

Fashion Institute of Technology/John Senzer, Photographer

23-12 Fashion shows often end with some especially memorable items that audience members can be excited about seeing but probably would not buy.

In Cooperation with The Fashion Association

23-13 After doing a merchandise pull, all the apparel and accessories to be modeled in the show should be on racks in the storage area.

selected per category. This is higher than will actually be shown, since some will be eliminated during fittings and rehearsals. The ideal chart also lists important trends of each apparel category, including accessories.

Merchandise selection is coordinated with the fashion preferences of the audience and the ideal chart information. A ***merchandise pull*** is the removing of show items from the sales floor to a fashion show storage area, 23-13. This may be done about a week before the show date or when new merchandise is available. It should take place close enough to the show to include the latest items available, but far enough ahead to avoid a last-minute time crunch. Since merchandise pulled for the show is no longer on the selling floor of the store, the possibility of some lost sales must be considered.

When borrowing merchandise from stores, a professional working relationship should be maintained and precise details about the show should be provided. Show personnel are accountable for all items, including any that are lost or damaged. A *merchandise loan record* gives details of the borrowed merchandise, 23-14. A copy is held by both the store and the fashion show merchandise committee. Merchandise is expected to be returned to retailers ready for sale in the same clean, tagged condition as it was received.

Fashion show items are then grouped into the planned merchandise categories, emphasizing the trend details of the ideal chart and a pleasing flow of outfits. Within the categories, garments might be organized by color, styling details, or design sophistication.

Fashion Show Merchandise Loan Record

Show Title ______________________ Show Date ______________

Store Loaning Merchandise ______________________ Department ______________

Issued to ______________________ Loan Date ______________

Qty	Style #	Color	Size	Description	Price

Received back in stock by ______________________

Received from ______________________ Date ______________

23-14 A merchandise loan record is prepared for every store or department from which items are borrowed for the show.

Mix-and-match pieces modeled in different outfits should be on stage at the same time, or in succession, to show that they can be worn together.

Model Selection

Fashion models are the people who wear garments and accessories to promote them. They should be able to promote outfits to the audience by presenting them in a believable way. How models wear and accessorize clothing is aspired to by consumers who try to copy their looks. Models can be selected to represent different images and size ranges for fashion shows, such as junior, plus size, male, senior, or sophisticated high fashion. See 23-15.

Fashion show models must be attractive and well-groomed, with good hair and skin. They need not be beautiful, but should have a well-proportioned figure or physique that fits a standard clothing size. Many models have a fashion sense, with flair about how garments should be worn and accessorized. Even if they do not personally like some of the garments they must model, they should have a cooperative, professional attitude at all times.

Professional models have training and experience. They are hired through modeling agencies. The agencies show photos and tell about the models' experience for show planners to review. When the model list is narrowed to those being considered, a "go see" visit is scheduled at no charge. Models bring their portfolio of photos, try on garments, and answer questions. Those who are appropriate for the show are then "booked" through the agency. A written confirmation specifies the names of the models, date, time, and pay rate.

Amateur models are not trained or represented by agencies. If they are affiliated with the retail store, they are probably paid their regular wages during the fittings, rehearsals, and show. If they are from the sponsoring civic organization, they usually model for free. A few of them may have had some modeling experience, or may add interest and prestige to the show because they are community leaders.

Another way to get models is from modeling schools, located in most major cities. These models are receiving training and are seeking opportunities for experience. Students in fashion, acting, or dancing schools may also be willing to model just for the fun and experience of being involved, 23-16.

The fashion show budget usually determines whether professional or amateur models are used. For a smoother show, experienced models can handle last-minute changes and confusion. They are trained to remember directions and cues, be at appointments on

The American Printed Fabrics Council

23-15 For fashion shows that include children's apparel, children are needed as the models.

Fashion Institute of Technology/John Senzer, Photographer

23-16 Besides studying about fashion, these college students gain valuable experience by modeling in live shows.

time, respect the apparel, and present clothes in the best ways to the audience. A very small show might have five models, with only one on the stage at a time. A medium show might have 10 models, and a large show may have 20 or more models, depending on how many will share the stage at the same time.

Untrained models must be coached about walking, timing, posing, turning, and facial expressions. More models may be needed since untrained models take longer to change their outfits. They may not be of standard sizes, and may be vocal about what they do or do not want to wear. However, they can seem more believable in the clothes, and have great drawing power by attracting their friends and relatives.

After all models are selected for the show, a *model list* is prepared. It includes all model's names, telephone numbers, and apparel sizes. It should also list some substitute models in case a show model must cancel at the last minute.

A retail fashion office should create an ongoing file of models used in the store's shows. Index cards should include the name, address, telephone number, and sizes for each model. Additionally, comments about performance and reliability help with selecting models for future shows.

The Fittings and Lineup

The *model order* is the rotation of models in the show. It is kept in approximately the same order throughout the show, to give models the maximum time to change their outfits between appearances. It also helps them recognize who they follow in the lineup. The ***lineup*** is the order in which outfits will appear in the show. The model order is coordinated into a tentative lineup until it is finalized from the fittings and rehearsals.

Fittings are when the models try on the merchandise to see how each garment looks and fits. Advance preparation for the fittings saves time for all involved. Merchandise is pulled in the correct model sizes. Fitting supplies are organized, including pencils, pins, and measuring tapes. Underarm shields, and scarves or hoods that cover makeup, should also be included to protect garments. Fashion show tags are needed, to be attached to garments until the show. Each tag includes a brief garment description, category, model's name, and lineup number.

The lineup evolves as the model order is coordinated with *fitting sheets*. One fitting sheet is prepared per lineup number, 23-17. Then copies are made and put in order of appearance into notebooks. They are used for gathering accessories, organizing alterations

Fitting Sheet

Model (name) ______________________ Lineup number __________

Sizes: Dress ______________ Shoe ______________ Hosiery ______________

Garment description: (style, color, name of designer/manufacturer, etc.)	**Accessories:** (itemized description of shoes, jewelry, belts, scarves, etc.)
Alterations needed: (hem length, waist, etc.)	**Additional information:** (other remarks about the outfit, model, props, etc.)

23-17 A fitting sheet is prepared for each outfit to help with accessorizing, alterations, commentary writing, and finalizing the lineup.

In Cooperation with The Fashion Association

23-18 The accessories that Katrina will wear with the pants and white jacket are included. Brown boots are in the heavy plastic bag placed over the jacket hanger.

In Cooperation with The 410 Shoppe

23-19 Garments for fashion shows are carefully transported to show sites on hangers, protected from weather, soil, or any other damage.

that are done to make garments fit properly, and writing the commentary. Extra garments pulled from inventory should also be tried on by models and listed on fitting sheets, in case substitutions are made in the lineup before the show. Bags that contain the accessories for each outfit are looped over the tops of the garment hangers, 23-18.

Finally, the garments and accessories are covered with plastic bags, packed, and transferred to the show location, 23-19. Garments are pressed or steamed at the show site to eliminate wrinkles. See 23-20. Hang-tags are hidden or removed and reattached after the show. Shoes are kept in their original boxes, with masking tape applied to the bottoms of the heels and soles to keep them clean while being worn. Then they can be sold as new after removing the tape.

Individual model lineup sheets, 23-21, help models clarify their order of appearance, outfits, and other details. It has written descriptions, sketches, swatches, or whatever is needed. The instructions column might state whether the model is to appear alone or as part of a group, is to remove a coat, or should trade jackets with another model to show mix-and-match possibilities.

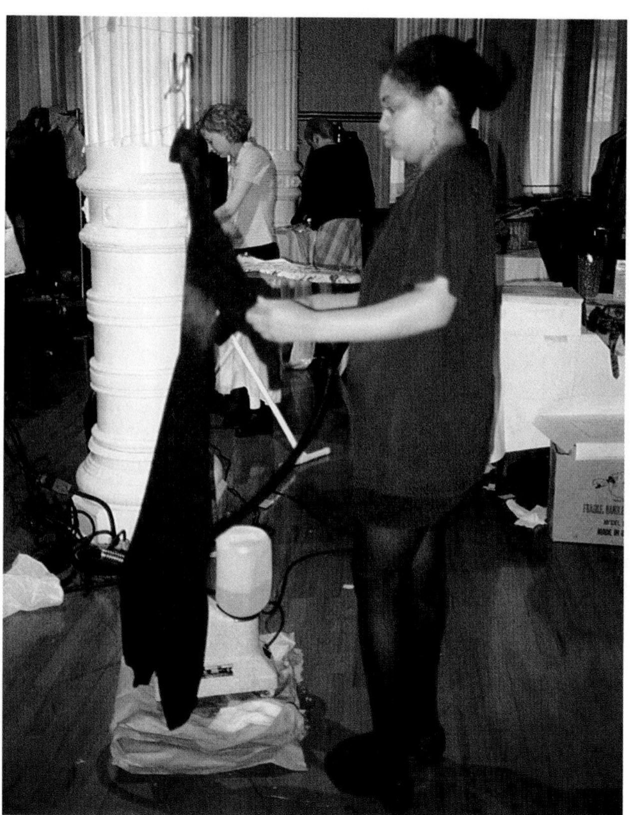

In Cooperation with The Fashion Association

23-20 A last-minute spruce-up is given to all garments so they will look their best when being worn in the fashion show.

Individual Model Lineup Sheet

Name of Model ____________ Title of Show ____________

Lineup #	Description of Apparel	Hosiery & Shoes	Jewelry	Accessories & Props	Instructions

23-21 An individual model lineup sheet is made for each of the models in the show. It quickly tells the model what is needed and in what order for his or her appearances.

Coordinating Physical Layout, Music, Choreography, and Commentary

The physical layout, music, choreography, and commentary must work together to enhance the theme and make the fashion show run smoothly. To the audience, the show should seem as if it is effortlessly produced, with the time passing pleasantly and quickly.

In Cooperation with The Fashion Association

23-22 By building the runway high off the regular floor level, audience members can see the fashions being modeled more clearly.

The Physical Layout

Work is done to the physical layout of the site, with stage decorations, backdrops, runways, lighting, and props that create a background and atmosphere for the fashion show. The *stage* is the background where models enter and exit the area within the view of the audience. ***Runways*** are elevated walkways for the models that project out from the stage, usually into the audience seating area, 23-22.

Informal fashion shows use no staging, just small props. Formal shows require staging. Large production shows require well-engineered backdrops and special effects.

The location and distance between the dressing area and runway are important. The best arrangement for fast outfit changes is a dressing area directly adjacent to the stage. More models are needed if it takes a long time to get to and from the dressing area. Also, to minimize confusion, the dressing area and stage should have specified entrances and exits for the models, 23-23.

The dressing area should be big enough for the amount of models, helpers, and merchandise being used. Space is needed for tables, chairs, and mirrors. Clothing racks need enough space to prevent the clothes from wrinkling. Each model should have an assigned space, according to the lineup, with his or her outfits placed together and marked with a label on each

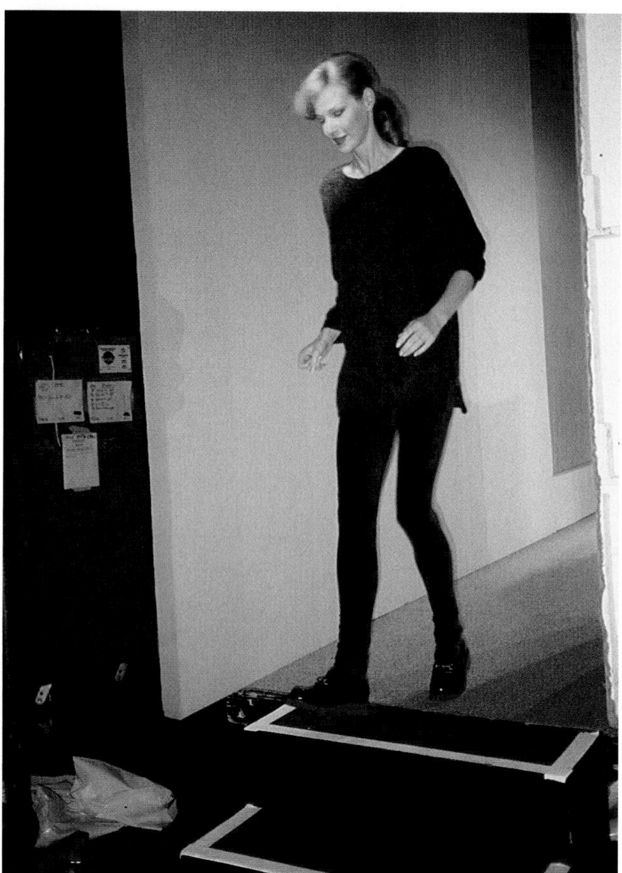

In Cooperation with The Fashion Association

23-23 For this fashion show, all models entered from the other side of the stage and exited at this side of the stage. By doing so, a clear pattern was established for the models and there was a minimum of confusion behind the scenes.

hanger. Models can most easily change when others with nearby spaces are out on the runway. A cloth sheet placed on the floor protects garments from dirt. A full-length mirror is located for a last-minute look where the models leave the dressing area, 23-24.

Most runways project straight out from the stage. They are long enough to allow enough time for the audience to react to each modeled outfit, but not be bored. The stage and runway should be drawn to scale ahead of time to plan the best dimensions, lighting, and building materials needed. This will also help in planning models' entrances, exits, choreography, and timing for the show.

Typical runways are from 32 to 40 feet long. A width of 4 feet enables two models to walk together or pass each other. Pieces of plywood that are 4 by 8 feet are the most popular construction material. Runways that are 6 or 8 feet wide enable three or four models to walk together. The height of the runway is ideally between 18 and 36 inches above floor level. Skirting or trim usually decorates the lower sides of runways.

Seating arrangements must let the audience see the show from every location without pillars or other obstacles in the way. Sometimes seats are reserved. *Theater seating* has rows of chairs lined up side by side, facing the runway. *Table seating* is used when a meal is served in conjunction with the show, often at round tables. During the show, all chairs are turned toward the runway. Programs and promotional gifts are sometimes placed on the chairs or tables in advance of the show.

In Cooperation with The Fashion Association

23-24 Somewhere along the pathway from the dressing area to the stage, a full-length mirror in a well-lit area must be available for adjustments and finishing touches.

The stage background should have an open and subdued feeling, enhancing the theme and clothing. A plain background may display only the logo of the designer or retailer. A simple doorway, archway, pillars, or screen can serve as an entrance for the models. Backdrops on movable flats may have scenes from

In Cooperation with The Fashion Association

23-25 Here, a cane is held by each of the models as a prop. The hat and gloves are part of the outfits rather than props.

nature or room interiors, and be changed for different show categories.

Props can be carried by the models or placed on the stage. Those that are carried might include a tennis racket, beach towel, briefcase, stuffed animal, or oriental fan, depending on the outfits being shown. See 23-25. Props that are strictly part of the stage background might include furniture, a beach umbrella, plants, or other theme items.

Lighting also sets the mood and shows off the clothing. Spotlights can follow the models, placed as high as possible to avoid shining in the eyes of the audience. Track lighting is effective if available. Round "globe" lights often line the edge of the runway. Lighting should change on cue as the show progresses, with different intensities and filters to add interest.

The Music

Music can be live or taped, instrumental or vocal. It must relate to the age and tastes of the audience. The right music sets the tempo and lends a great deal to the success of the show, especially if no commentary is used.

Live music is expensive, so a small musical group may be chosen. Sometimes only a piano player is used, who can adapt to the pace and actions of the show.

Large shows have a music director, who selects and makes arrangements to use the appropriate music. Permission may have to be obtained for copyrighted music. Smaller shows use a music technician who is in charge of the recorded music. Music directors or technicians attend all rehearsals that use music to coordinate cues of the commentator and models.

The *music mix* is the combination of different music selections to create specific moods. Music for the show should include a variety that matches merchandise categories and commentary. Soft music can play as the audience enters the room. For the show, it should start strong, flow easily during the middle, and end in a spectacular way!

Taped music is convenient, less expensive, and can provide a variety of sound. Ideally, each category presentation has music specifically mixed for it. Exercise wear requires a fast tempo, sportswear needs upbeat music; and eveningwear requires more sophisticated music. See 23-26. A music planning sheet is used to list the many appropriate selections that match the merchandise theme. Each song's title, recording artist, and length are included. This is edited to the final

Kellwood Company

23-26 If exercise apparel is modeled, the most appropriate music would have a fast beat—the type used for exercise routines.

In Cooperation with The Fashion Association

23-27 Sometimes the planned routine with more than one model on the runway will include handing a golf club to another model or exchanging jackets that coordinate with each other's outfits.

choices, combined to run smoothly together so the audience is not distracted by the changes.

Prerecorded selections can be copied onto two separate tapes to play through two systems. The tapes alternate for the merchandise categories, so one can fade out and the other fade in as the scenes change. Each recorded music segment should be a bit longer than the planned show category. This allows for flexibility since it can be played for a longer or shorter amount of time, and faded out according to the needs of the runway actions and/or backstage activities.

The Choreography

Choreography is used to plan the models' walking or dancing and the interaction of models on the stage and runway. Models move rhythmically to the music. The show choreographer plans entrances, cues, runway routines, and exits before the models arrive for the rehearsal. Choreography should reflect the theme of the show with a dramatic opening, good pace through the middle, and memorable finale.

The opening strives to get the audience involved with music, lights, and dancing. Then, the continuing pace should be fast enough to provide interest. The amount of time the models spend on stage can speed-up or slow-down the show. Amateur models sometimes walk too fast or too slow, which should be addressed during the rehearsal. Models should keep moving on the runway and stop to pose on the stage until the commentator has finished talking about the outfit being modeled.

Pivots and pauses are planned and rehearsed for specific times and places on the stage and runway. ***Pivots*** are turns that are most often done at the halfway point and end of the runway. Several different planned routes, as well as dancing routines, add variety and interest. Also, models may be on the runway alone, in pairs, or in groups, 23-27. Groups might enter together, pivot at the same or different times, separate, pass as in 23-28, and come together to exit. Before exiting, models are usually instructed to stop, turn, pause, and pose. This gives the audience one last look and time for the next model to enter.

The finale should leave an exciting last impression. All models return to the stage and runway wearing their last and most spectacular outfits. They may all be carrying a balloon, flowers, or other festive prop. For designer shows, the fashion designer is coaxed to join the models on stage during the finale to cheers and applause from the audience and the models!

The Commentary

The commentary describes the garments and accessories, especially those details that might be overlooked. It is meant to entertain the audience, put everyone at ease, and sell the merchandise. The commentary should use correct names for silhouettes, colors, fabrics, trims, garment parts, and other structural and decorative details. Going from general information to interesting details about each outfit, it builds with excitement toward the climax of the show. It should hold the audience's attention by creatively analyzing what is on stage. Mistakes that happen in the show should not be mentioned.

The *commentator*, or show narrator, should be a fashion expert who interprets trends for the audience, 23-29. A *public address system*, which includes a microphone, amplifiers, and speakers, should be used.

The commentary should tie the theme and fashion categories of the show together. *Commentary cards* may be prepared during the fittings and used for the narration of the show. Each large index card should include a description of the garment, accessories, and special selling features of an outfit. The cards include the model's name, show category, and lineup number. They are arranged in the order of the show. They can be rearranged if last-minute changes are made to the lineup.

Full commentaries have a script with every word written that will be said. This can sound stiff and may not

Fashion Institute of Technology/John Senzer, Photographer

23-28 When groups of models are on the runway, they usually pass between each other rather than to the sides to keep the focal point centered.

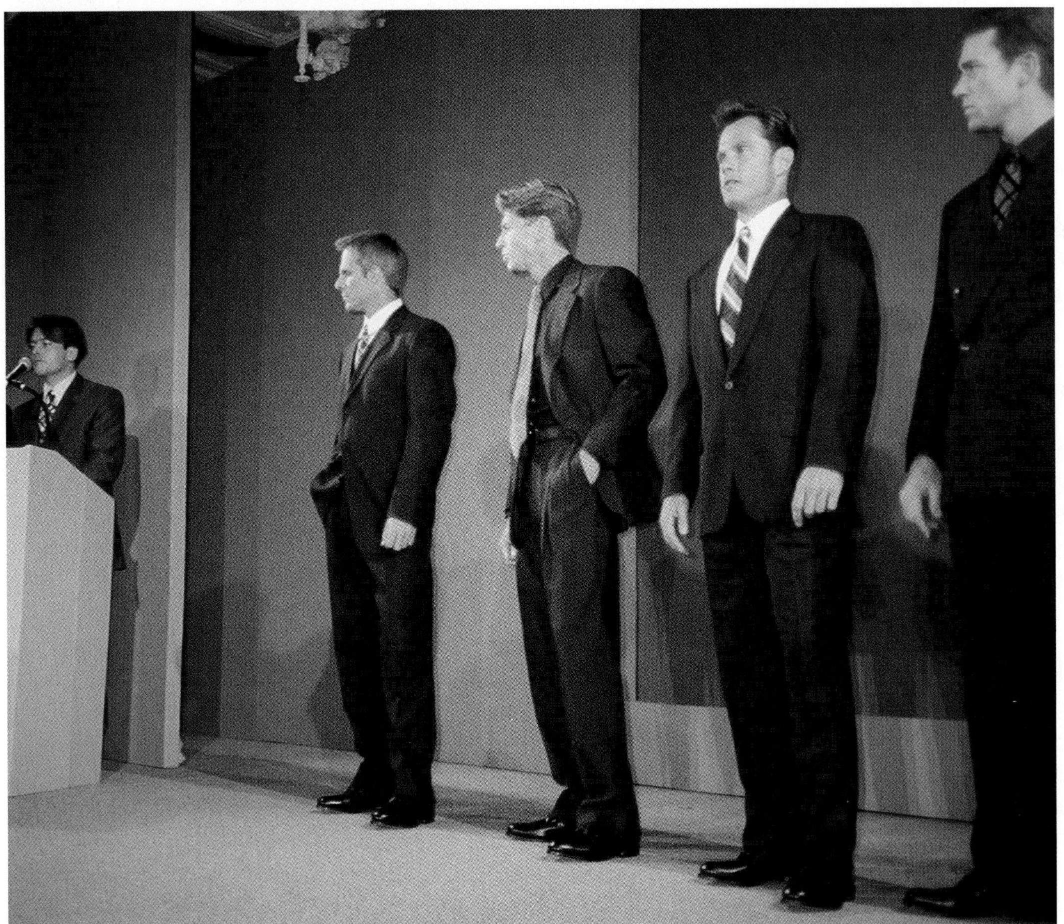

In Cooperation with The Fashion Association

23-29 The expert telling the audience about the necktie fabrics, patterns, and motifs on these models is Italian neckwear designer Gianfranco Zani, who designed the ties.

provide flexibility for last-minute changes. Full commentaries are used for production shows, in which all scenes, music, lighting, and model cues are noted on the script. However, the commentary may not describe garment details, which are printed in the program.

Partial commentaries list the major details of garments in outline form or short sections of script. This takes less time to prepare, but is more challenging to use during the show. The commentator gives descriptions as needed. Some filler commentary is also prepared to fill unexpected pauses during the show. Filler might be thank yous or credits to those who have contributed to the show or plugs for store services or departments.

Ad lib commentaries are created spontaneously during the show from brief cue cards. Many more fashion phrases than outfits in the show are accumulated on cards ahead of time for lead-ins and descriptions. A more natural delivery occurs in this way if the commentator has confidence and fashion knowledge. Highly experienced commentators may look at the outfits before the show and then speak about them without any prepared commentary. This can be conversational and spontaneous.

Manufacturers' fashion shows for prospective retail buyers do not have commentary. Music plays and style numbers are given. Buyers write their own observations onto printed buying guides that already contain information about each item, price, and minimum order required. Also, informal shows often do not have commentary, especially in restaurants where customers are conversing. The fashions are intended to speak for themselves. With tearoom modeling, models describe the outfits they are wearing only to people who are interested. See 23-30.

Consumer runway shows usually use informative commentary. Less fashion-aware audiences want more details and interpretation of trends. The commentary can slow a show that is going too fast, with additional remarks, or fashion information. On the other hand, it can also speed up the show by eliminating some details and by only noting key fashion looks.

In Cooperation with The 410 Shoppe

23-30 After dressing and before going out into the restaurant, a tearoom model studies a card with information that lists specific details about the outfit.

Promoting and Presenting the Show

The forms of promotion most used for fashion shows are publicity and advertising. Free publicity should be emphasized, supplemented with paid advertising if the budget permits it.

Press releases should be sent to all newspapers and magazines. If possible they should be sent directly to the fashion editor (or women's or community section editor) by name. It is best if different photos are sent to each publication, accompanied by captions. Publicity announcements are also sent to radio stations. Videos might be sent to television stations.

Press releases should arrive at the media two to four weeks before the event. This allows time for the editor to review the materials and, hopefully, deliver the message to the public just ahead of the event. Sometimes radio and television stations run free *public service announcements* if the fashion show is for a charitable event and of general interest to the community. Additionally, *press shows* are private fashion showings for the press before the public sees the fashions, 23-31. They are presented to gain publicity.

Media space can be purchased for advertisements. Newspaper ads are the most effective for fashion shows because they reach local audiences at a reasonable cost. Newspaper ads may be created by promotion committee members or by the newspaper advertising department as a helpful service. The fashion show advertising coordinator might submit rough sketches of a layout to the newspaper art department, which then produces a draft of a print advertisement, called a ***pasteup***. This is returned to fashion show personnel for review, changes, and/or approval. When the finalized ad has run in the paper, the newspaper sends a *tear sheet*, which is the advertisement torn directly from the paper. This shows proof of publication and can be saved for evaluation of the show.

Radio commercials can be effective if the station's audience is matched with the fashion show's target audience. Some local magazine and TV spot ads might be placed by a retailer if they are not too expensive. However, production of these ads costs more and must be done farther in advance. A professional advertising agency may be needed to produce effective, quality ads.

In Cooperation with The Fashion Association

23-31 Journalists attend press shows to gather information from written sheets that are distributed and to take pictures. The information is used for newspaper and magazine articles and for radio and television segments of fashion news.

Other fashion show promotion can be done with signs or posters in high traffic areas or by mailing out flyers and/or invitations. Membership and customer lists provide effective targeted promotion, but postage expenses add up fast. Additionally, retailers should inform all salespeople far in advance of the show so they can promote the event to their customers. A school or civic group should pass information to all members, encouraging them to tell others who may wish to attend the show.

Invitations, Tickets, and Programs

The promotion committee also handles the design and printing of invitations, tickets, and programs. Depending on the type of show, tickets are either sold or distributed free. If they are free, many extra tickets should be printed, since only a certain number of those who receive them will attend the show. The response rate is higher for specialized shows, such as for bridal attire. Better attendance also occurs if tickets must be picked up at a certain location, such as at a retailer's customer service desk.

The program serves as a guide to the merchandise for the audience. It's cover design and composition should follow the theme of the show. It lists the outfits in order of appearance, with a brief description, so attendees can keep track of items they may want to consider buying. Programs also acknowledge the designers, manufacturers, retailers, and staff members that have helped to make the show possible. This combines thank yous with publicity, and adds credibility to the group sponsoring the show. Sometimes advertising is sold and placed in programs, to raise additional money for a charitable cause.

Rehearsals and Show Time!

Most fashion shows cannot run smoothly without rehearsals. *Rehearsals* are practice sessions. Some are just run-throughs to work on choreography. The *full dress rehearsal* is a practice of the finished show, without an audience present. It includes all apparel changes, staging, lights, music, choreography, and other aspects.

Rehearsals prepare all people involved for a professional presentation, working through any problems and adding finishing touches. The finalized information and lineup are then distributed to all committees for coordination of the total show. The helpers and backstage manager depend on the final lineup that is posted in several backstage locations, 23-32.

When show time arrives, models should arrive half an hour to one hour before the scheduled start of the show. They should bring their own makeup and hair needs (unless makeup and hair technicians have been hired), classic shoes, and a selection of extra jewelry,

In Cooperation with The Fashion Association

23-32 The backstage manager has a copy of the lineup and commentary, can communicate with production staff members, and can inform models when they will be going onto the stage.

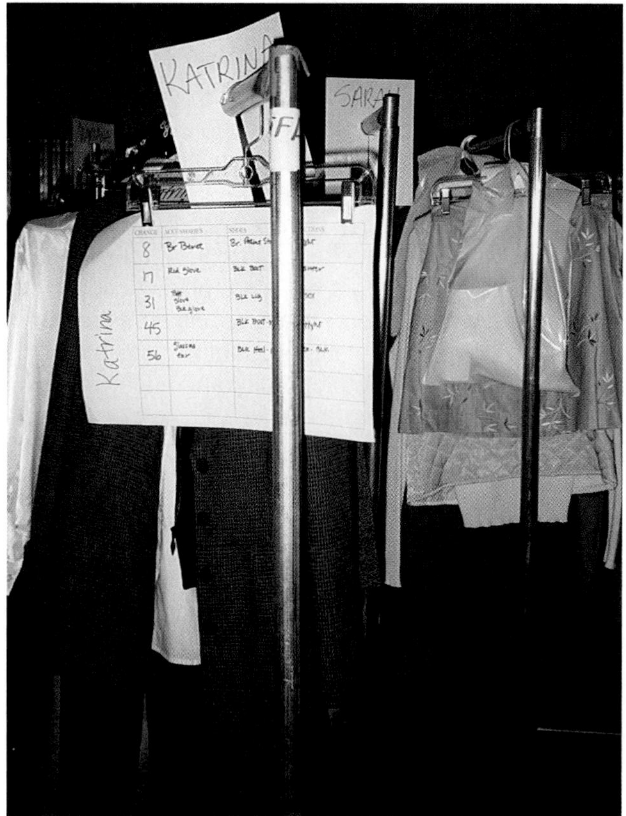

In Cooperation with The Fashion Association

23-33 When Katrina arrives for the show, she will check her garments, accessories, and lineup sheet to see that everything is in order for a smooth performance.

belts, scarves, hosiery, and undergarments. All models should check that the garments and accessories in their changing area are correct and arranged in order of appearance. See 23-33. If possible, garments should be unbuttoned and unzipped ready to go. Scarves might be pretied.

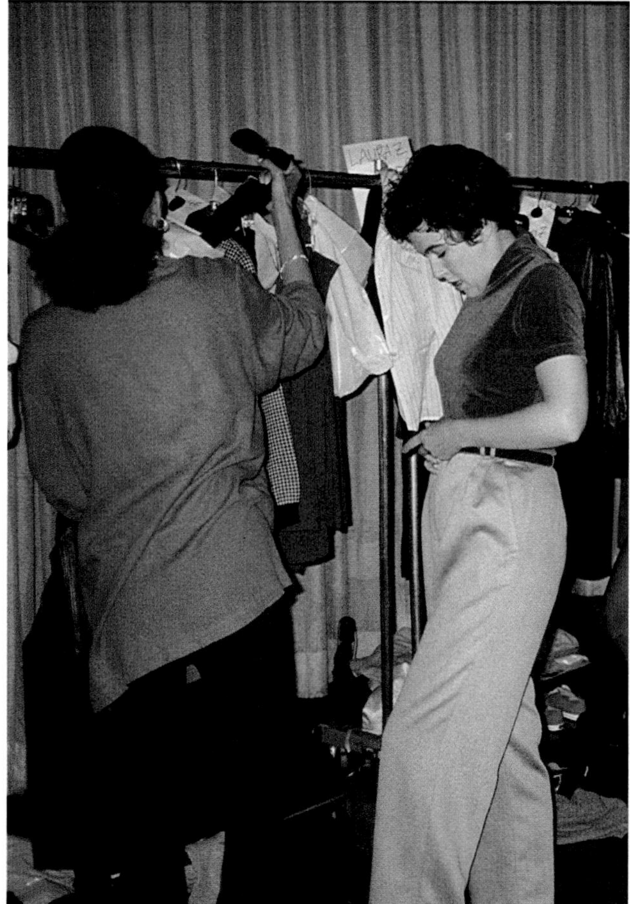

In Cooperation with The Fashion Association

23-34 When the model comes off the stage to the dressing area, the helper has the next outfit ready to put on and takes the previous outfit as the model removes it.

The backstage area can often be described as organized chaos! Only those with a job to do should be there. Talking should be eliminated or kept to whispers. ***Dressers*** help the models change and care for the clothes, 23-34. After quickly getting out of one outfit and into another, models must regain their composure before returning to the runway. After doing a last-minute check of the model's outfit and hair, ***starters*** cue the models onto the stage in the correct order, at the right time, guided by the lineup and commentary script. The audience can't see the starter, but the starter should be able to signal the commentator about changes or delays. Assistant starters or "runners" communicate with people in the dressing area if it is a distance from the stage.

The show should start on time. During the show, models must stay poised and cover up mistakes or unexpected events, such as tripping, forgetting a prop, or having a shoe strap slip off. A button might pull off as a model is dressing, causing that item to be eliminated from the show or modeled later, after the button is sewn back on. When mistakes occur, models should continue in a professional manner, without drawing attention to the situation.

If planning has been thorough, the fashion show will be a smashing success. Everyone in the audience should leave excited and inspired about the new fashions they have seen and heard about and know where to buy them.

Follow-Up and Evaluation

When the show is over, there is still work to be done. *Striking the stage* refers to physically disassembling the set and returning props and equipment. Most people involved with the show should help. Garments and accessories should be returned to retailers as soon as possible. They must be clean, pressed, and have their original hangtags attached. Merchandise loan records are completed as merchandise is returned.

Thank you notes should be sent as soon as possible after the show to businesses and individuals who provided merchandise, expertise, promotion, and/or time to the presentation. Fashion show bills should also be paid promptly.

The last important task is an evaluation of the show by all persons involved. This should take place within days of the show, while all details are fresh in people's minds. Retailers that present fashion shows often have evaluation forms on which to summarize all aspects of the show, with notes on what was especially good and what can be improved upon in the future. These are put into a binder with an accounting of the budget and expenses, model lineup sheets, merchandise loan records, and other information. The evaluation helps those involved to make the next show even better.

Summary

Special events provide promotion through celebrity visits, contests, and other ways. Fashion shows are popular special events, often used to introduce new merchandise at the beginning of fashion seasons. Accessorized outfits, worn on moving bodies, promote fashions better than flat photos or garments on hangers. Different types of fashion shows serve various purposes for certain target audiences.

Advance planning and communication of job assignments is important for professional presentations, headed by the fashion show coordinator. Pinpointing the age, gender, income/spending habits, and lifestyle of the audience dictates the merchandise and theme for the event. The time and location are coordinated with the needs of the audience. Safety and security must be considered for merchandise, equipment, show participants, and the audience. Budget planning must forecast expected revenues and expenditures.

Merchandise and model selection must be coordinated. Merchandise should be of the latest trends. The models should be able to present outfits to the audience in a believable way. The lineup is determined by the model order and fittings.

Stage decorations, backdrops, runways, lighting, and props create a background and atmosphere for the fashion show. The dressing area must be functional, and audience seating arrangements must provide visibility from every location. Music can be live or taped, instrumental or vocal. The models' entrances, cues, runway routines, and exits are choreographed ahead of time. The commentary is meant to entertain the audience, put everyone at ease, and sell the merchandise.

Fashion shows are promoted with publicity from distributed press releases. Advertising, signs, posters, and direct mailings are used, budget permitting. The promotion committee also handles the design/printing of invitations, tickets, and programs.

Rehearsals are held to practice all aspects of the show. A smooth performance starts on time and covers mistakes that happen. After the show, personnel strike the stage, return merchandise, write thank you notes, and pay bills promptly. An evaluation of the show helps to make future shows even better.

To Know

special events
fashion shows
production fashion show
choreography
formal runway show
commentary
informal fashion show
tearoom modeling
fashion show coordinator
guaranteed audience
created audience
ideal chart
merchandise pull
lineup
fittings
runways
pivots
pasteup
dressers
starters

To Review

1. Name five types of retail special events.
2. Briefly describe three market levels where fashion shows take place.
3. Name the three main types of fashion shows.
4. Describe the difference in music and commentary between older and younger fashion show audiences.
5. What is the usual length of time for the fashion segments of most consumer shows and why?
6. What are three formats for fashion shows in retail stores?
7. What are three possible sources for fashion show revenues?
8. Three-quarters of the merchandise in fashion shows should consist of what kind of items?

9. In what two categories of the show should the strongest fashion statements be made, and why?
10. Who keeps a copy of the merchandise loan record when merchandise is borrowed from stores?
11. Name three sources for amateur models.
12. Name four things about which untrained models must be coached.
13. Why is approximately the same model order kept through the show?
14. What are the purposes of fitting sheets?
15. Why should the fashion show stage and runway be drawn to scale ahead of time?
16. Name three advantages of taped music.
17. What are models usually instructed to do before exiting the stage?
18. Define commentator.
19. Why do fashion shows by manufacturers not need commentary?
20. What is striking the stage?

To Do

1. With the class divided into small groups, list all of the responsibilities for a small runway show that each group can think of for the following chairpersons: merchandise coordinator, model coordinator, stage manager, promotion coordinator, and commentator. Review the chapter so all duties are included. Compare the lists among the groups.
2. Develop a fashion show theme and title for each month of the year. Describe the merchandise categories that might be included and the target audience for each show. Assemble this into a report.
3. Select three merchandise categories for a fictitious upcoming fashion show. Research fashion magazines and retail stores for trend and accessory ideas to show and describe. Decide how you would organize your show and what trends you would emphasize. Report this information to the class, showing as many pictures and illustrations as possible.
4. Plan the physical layout for a fashion show at an actual ballroom, auditorium, or room in your school. Make a scale drawing of the dressing area, stage, runway, and seating arrangement. Also indicate model entrances, pivot spots, and exits. Make suggestions for lighting, stage backgrounds, and props. Put your finished drawing on a piece of posterboard to show the class or put on the bulletin board.
5. Clip six photos or sketches of fashion outfits (or separate garments and accessories for them) from fashion magazines or newspapers. Mount each outfit on a piece of paper. Write commentary cards about the items. Show your pictures to the class as you give the commentary about each outfit.

Hong Kong Trade Development Council

Fashion shows can be spectacular events designed to showcase designers' collections for the fashion press.

PART 7

Fashion Business in Today's World

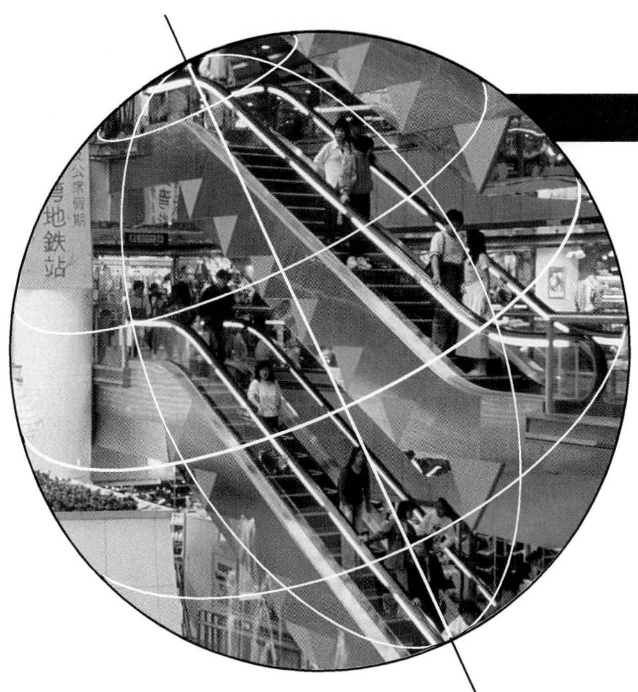

CHAPTER 24

A Global Perspective

After studying this chapter, you will be able to

- cite U.S. and world trade trends and policy.
- explain the relationship of textiles and apparel to developing nations.
- identify the world's major trading blocs.
- describe international sourcing for U.S. fashion importing.
- point out international market opportunities for U.S. fashion exporting.
- explain how to discover offshore sources and opportunities.

The international environment for fashion merchandising is constantly changing. This can be challenging, yet exciting. ***Globalization*** is the growth of international commerce and communications that makes national boundaries less important, especially in economic matters. Technological advances have brought about instant worldwide communication capabilities, through phone, fax, television, Internet, and other means. Airline connections exist to all parts of the globe. These factors have made the world seem smaller. With a "global economy" companies' customers, competitors, suppliers, facilities, and investors are throughout the world.

In recent years, due to changing trade trends and government policies, international trade has grown faster for fashion goods than for any other commodity. Challenges exist in trading with developing nations, and the world is dividing into major trading blocs. However, foreign countries are good sources of imported products for the U.S. fashion market, 24-1. Also, international market opportunities exist for the exporting of U.S. fashion goods and services.

24-1 Although these imported fashions from the Middle East are featured because of their cultural influence, most imports are produced to look American-made and are on the shelves and racks of almost all retail stores.

Trade Trends and Policy

Trade involves imports, exports, and exchanges of money. As stated in Chapter 10, imports are goods that come into a country from foreign sources, or what a country buys from other countries. The U.S. is the greatest consuming market of soft goods in the world, so other countries want to send their goods here. Imports to the U.S. have risen rapidly over the past few decades, with almost every country in the world competing for a large share of the U.S. consumer dollar.

Import penetration is the percentage of imports in a country's total market consumption. It measures foreign against domestic goods. Currently, imports account for about 60% of the total U.S. textile and apparel market. Mexico and China, provide the largest amount of imported textile and apparel items for U.S. consumers. Sweaters and jackets/coats are the apparel categories that have the highest import penetration.

Popular Import Categories

Category Number	Description
340	Men's and Boys' Woven Cotton Shirts
341	Women's and Girls' Woven Cotton Shirts and Blouses
347	Men's and Boys' Cotton Trousers, Slacks and Shorts
348	Women's and Girls' Cotton Trousers, Pants, and Shorts
359	Other Cotton Apparel
634	Men's and Boys' Coats of Manufactured Fibers
635	Women's and Girls' Coats of Manufactured Fibers
636	Dresses of Manufactured Fibers
639	Women's and Girls' Knit Shirts and Blouses of Manufactured Fibers
640	Men's and Boys' Woven Shirts of Manufactured Fibers
648	Women's and Girls' Trousers, Slacks and Shorts of Manufactured Fibers
659	Other Apparel of Manufactured Fibers
845	Vegetable Fiber Sweaters

24-2 Besides figuring square yard equivalents of imports, apparel items are categorized. Import comparisons are made between different categories as well as being compared to similar domestic goods.

Textile/apparel trade is important to most countries. The rules that regulate such trade affect governments, businesses, and consumers worldwide. A country's ***balance of trade*** is the relationship between the values of its imports and exports, described as being a deficit or a surplus. A ***trade deficit*** occurs when imports exceed exports. The U.S. has a large trade deficit with many more products coming into the market than being sent out to other countries. Textile/apparel products make up a large part of that deficit.

A ***trade surplus*** exists when exports exceed imports. Japan has a trade surplus because it sends more products out to world markets than it brings into the country. This also enables it to have a large amount of money that has been received in payment for its goods.

The amount of textile/apparel imports is determined by fabric quantity in *square meter equivalents (SMEs).* This helps to equate different items as fairly as possible, such as lightweight shirts, heavyweight pants, and bulky jackets. After determining the SME in items, they are organized by numbered fiber and garment categories to determine import amounts, 24-2.

A major consideration for businesses is the degree to which a foreign currency can be converted into the home country's money. The value of currencies (money) from the nations of the world fluctuates as conditions change. Currency is bought and sold based on the rates set in foreign exchange markets.

The exchange rate for the U.S. dollar becomes weaker or stronger against other currencies. When the value of the U.S. dollar falls, the weak dollar tends to improve the U.S. trade balance. This could decrease the trade deficit. A weaker U.S. dollar lowers the price of U.S. exports and makes imports more expensive. In other words, it takes more U.S. dollars to pay for foreign goods because the dollars are not worth as much compared to other countries' money. On the other hand, when the value of the U.S. dollar strengthens (or other currencies weaken), the opposite effects occur.

Free Trade Versus Protectionism

Free trade is a government's policy of allowing goods to flow freely in and out of its economy, without interference. ***Protectionism*** is the opposite of free trade and includes many government-imposed trade restraints, such as the barriers to free trade, 24-3. Most countries have policies between the two extremes of complete free trade or protectionism. Recently, trade referred to as "managed trade" has been more open throughout the world.

Government protection is aimed at reducing, limiting, or excluding foreign goods from entering a country's market. This is done to protect the country's industries and workers. Too many imports cause ***market disruption*** that seriously injures or threatens a particular industry that has products in direct competition with that industry. Increasing imports have caused shrinking sales of domestically-produced goods in the U.S. market and severe price competition that has weakened some industries.

Arguments for and against protectionism are listed in 24-4. There are sound issues on both sides. The U.S. must be careful about restricting trade. Curbing imports of fashion goods from other countries may bring retaliation from those countries. They might refuse to accept other types of goods that the U.S. exports to them. Governments must look at the total picture of trade, rather than just one segment of it. *International diplomacy*, or negotiating between nations while balancing political and economic issues, is important for trade.

Barriers to Free Trade

Tariffs (also called duties)—Charges (taxes) paid on goods coming into a country, which are often a percentage of the invoice cost. This raises the prices of imported goods coming into a market, making them less desirable. It also raises government revenue.

Quotas—Limitations established by the government on quantities of certain goods that can enter a country during a specified time span. This limits the number of each type of item (by square meter equivalent, fiber content, and style) that can be sold in a market.

Tariff-rate quotas—A certain number of imported items are allowed to enter free (or at a low rate), after which a higher tariff rate is assessed. This is a compromise that offers some lower import prices plus some industry protection.

Voluntary export restraints—A voluntary quota applied by exporting nations, usually because of pressure from the receiving nation against so many imports.

Standards—Certain levels of quality are specified (such as ISO 9000 standards) for imported goods to prevent inferior products from entering a country.

Subsidies—Direct payments by the producer's government to producers of certain goods so they can charge lower prices. This is done to compete with imports in a firms own country, or to export goods at lower prices. Subsidies can be in the form of cash, tax concessions, low cost loans, paid research and development costs, etc.

Other barriers—These include requirements concerning

- special licenses to bring goods into a country
- use of shipping vehicles only from the importing country
- intentionally slow customs processing
- government preferential treatment favoring domestic companies that bid on commercial projects
- embargoes (bans) or various pressures that are applied against foreign governments or categories of goods.

24-3 Trade barriers are imposed by governments to protect their domestic industries. They are meant to discourage or prevent foreign goods from coming into their countries.

Arguments For and Against U.S. Protectionism

For:

- Job protection for our workers, instead of helping the development of industries in other countries
- For strength and stability of weak and start-up industries, resulting in more investment into them, higher future productivity, and the ability to compete internationally
- Compensation for unequal international competition against low wages, lack of benefits paid, child labor, government subsidies, etc., of some other countries
- To maintain a strong manufacturing base for national security (to convert to a war effort if needed)
- To keep inferior and unsafe products from our market
- To reduce our trade deficit

Against:

- Protectionism encourages trade retaliation, which lowers exports of all industries
- Loopholes (unexpected interpretations) and corruption (fraud) enable merchandise to enter the market anyway
- Less damage to national interests
- Special treatment to certain industries is not as fair as encouraging all to compete equally
- It is hard to retract after it is in force
- It causes less competition, resulting in less innovation and weaker industries
- It penalizes consumers with fewer choices and higher prices

24-4 Depending on people's viewpoints, they argue either for or against protectionism. Years ago, manufacturing companies were in favor of protectionism, and retailers wanted free trade. Now more companies have a global perspective and want less trade protection.

Industry groups do a great deal of lobbying in Washington, DC, to try to influence trading laws. They represent textile and apparel manufacturers as well as retailers. The government's *Committee for the Implementation of Textile Agreements (CITA)* negotiates and administers individual agreements and quota programs. It has also tried to crack down on illegal transshipping and dumping of textile/apparel goods.

Transshipping is the rerouting of goods to evade quota limits. Quota items are sent through other countries

Some Reasons Why Companies Dump Products

- To carve out a market niche in an already competitive market
- To drive out competitors in a "price war"
- To get rid of inventories of slow-moving goods
- To retain market share and employees during slack periods by maintaining output
- To increase profits by increasing production volume (for economies of scale if fixed costs are already covered)

24-5 When foreign companies dump goods into another country's market, the domestic industry cannot compete with those goods. Thus, domestic companies go out of business or switch to other products.

that do not have or have not used their quotas. Papers are falsified with fraudulent registration information to imply that the goods were made in the country through which they have merely passed before entering the United States. For instance, some shipments from China, that would be kept out of the U.S. because of quotas, have come through Canada, with whom the U.S. has no quota restrictions. Shipping documents falsely say that the goods are from Canada, rather than China. Other fraudulent methods have also been used, such as misrepresenting quantities or classification of goods.

Dumping is the selling of goods at lower prices in foreign markets than in the home market. It might be done for the reasons listed in 24-5. Countries are not allowed to dump their goods into the American market because domestic companies cannot compete against these goods. Some Asian sources have had to pay duties to the U.S. several times because of dumping.

World Trade Organization

The ***World Trade Organization (WTO)*** is an international trade accord that reduces tariffs, quotas, and other trade barriers around the world. It is an agreement of more than 130 countries that negotiates and enforces global trade rules. It is meant to liberalize trade and serve as an international trade court for the settlement of differences.

The WTO agreement is phasing out, by 2005, the trade protections that U.S. textile and apparel producers had in the past, in exchange for access to send goods into the markets of the other member countries. Eventually, all countries are meant to compete with almost free trade. With new import access to fibers and fabrics produced elsewhere, domestic apparel manufacturers can be more competitive because they can import less expensive fabrics or have their lines produced overseas. We are moving toward a single world economy.

U.S. textile and apparel producers', as well as workers' unions, have finally accepted open global trading as a fact of life. Besides allowing more imports into the U.S., the WTO also should result in new overseas market opportunities for U.S. manufacturers and retailers. Sanctions can be imposed against countries that do not open their markets sufficiently. A problem, however, is that U.S. government income will decrease because of reduced tariffs.

The Relationship of Textiles/Apparel to Developing Nations

Before countries develop into world trading entities, they are generally agricultural societies. Most of what the people of undeveloped countries use in their lives is harvested from the land or animals, usually on a small scale by each family. There are few manufacturing or service industries. People make their own simple garments of natural fibers, and fashion movement is almost nonexistent. Examples of such areas of the world today are a few parts of Africa and Central Asia.

As countries begin to develop, companies form to make and sell specific products. Basic machines start to be used by the available labor. Eventually, these less-developed countries enter into international trade by exporting some of their manufactured goods. This, in turn, stimulates their economic growth. Examples of emerging countries in this stage of development are Pakistan, Malaysia, Vietnam, and Bangladesh.

Textile and apparel industries are usually the first internationally competitive industries to be formed in emerging economies. Because cut fabric garment parts are hard to handle by automation, apparel production remains labor-intensive. This offers manufacturing employment to low-skilled workers.

As countries develop further, the quality and quantity of textile/apparel production increases. World trading partners start to count on them for certain types of goods, and their workers' wages and company profits increase. As they move forward with technology, sophisticated processes are used for manufactured fiber production and garment design and construction. Hong Kong, Taiwan, and South Korea are at this industrialized stage today. Large trade surpluses build up, enabling these countries to buy commodities and invest in other countries.

Full maturity is eventually reached in the textile, apparel, and retail segments of countries. Japan and some European countries are at this point, with well developed fashion industries that are efficient and profitable. This advanced stage uses computerized design and production capabilities. See 24-6 and 24-7. Marketing pinpoints the needs of retail consumers. Employees must have higher skills.

Sulzer Ruti

24-6 Note the words in this computerized textile design system are not in English. This renowned weaving system, available throughout the world, is from a Swiss company.

Structural adjustment refers to the process of industries and economies adapting to long-term shifts in competitiveness. As nations develop, they respond to market supply and demand conditions with better education, training, and use of resources. The old, simpler production methods automatically transfer to lower-wage nations at the previous stage of development. This causes an ongoing global shift in apparel production.

Worldwide markets let nations focus on product categories in which they have a comparative advantage. A ***comparative advantage*** is the ability of one nation to produce certain goods or services better than other nations because of specific circumstances. Different amounts of resources, such as raw materials, labor, and capital are available for use in different amounts and skill levels as nations emerge through the development process.

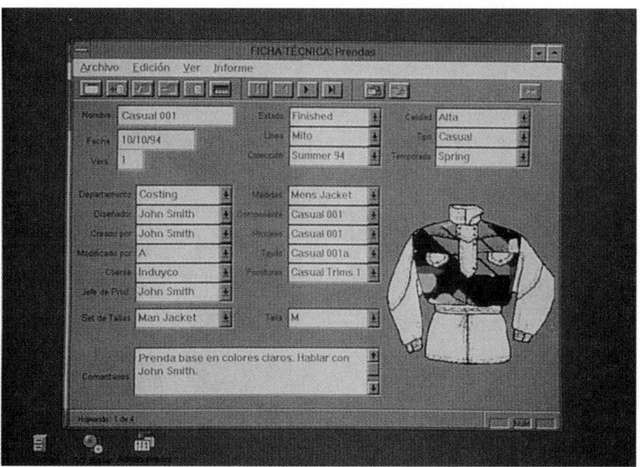

Investronica, Inc.

24-7 Although this advanced apparel design system is shown in the Spanish language, it also adapts to English, Portuguese, French, German, Turkish, Chinese, Japanese, Greek, Thai, and Hebrew. The home corporation for this technology is located in Madrid, Spain.

Countries' comparative advantages change over time. They exchange goods and services that they produce most efficiently for those that they produce less efficiently. In general, developed countries import more goods, and developing countries export more goods.

International trade today is broadening and accelerating. An oversupply of goods is resulting in the world. Production in developing countries has increased while consumption of the products in the markets of developed countries has decreased. This may result in ongoing problems for the soft goods chain if different products and alternate employment opportunities are not created.

Trade with Developing Nations

Before trading with developing nations, as much information as possible should be obtained. Companies should learn about the other countries' political stability, economic climate, infrastructure, and culture.

Political Stability

Political stability can influence the degree to which a country's laws and regulations are subject to change and are enforced. The laws of the U.S. and most other western and developed countries favor business. They remain quite constant over time, and are considered to be consistent and fair in most situations. In developing nations, this is not always the case.

Less developed countries, mainly with nonmarket economies (communist governments), may limit ownership of private industry. Instead, industries are operated and owned by the government. However, a few of these countries are now moving slowly toward privatization of industry. Also, some developing countries use what most people consider to be corrupt practices. For instance, U.S. regulations make it illegal for firms to pay any requested bribes or payoffs to do business in foreign countries. Additionally, terrorism, revolution, and chaos in countries must be evaluated before committing to business with those countries.

Economic Climate

The *economic climate* of countries affects businesses' abilities to earn profits in a reasonable amount of time. The economic climate of countries relates to:

- their purchasing power and standard of living. This indicates the amount of money people have to spend on themselves and their families.
- relative costs of doing business there, such as payments for rent, utilities, wages, etc.

In countries with low purchasing power and standards of living, low-wage manufacturing opportunities exist for U.S. firms if there are not barriers to doing business in that country. In countries with high purchasing power and standards of living, good retail opportunities exist if operating expenses are not too high. The

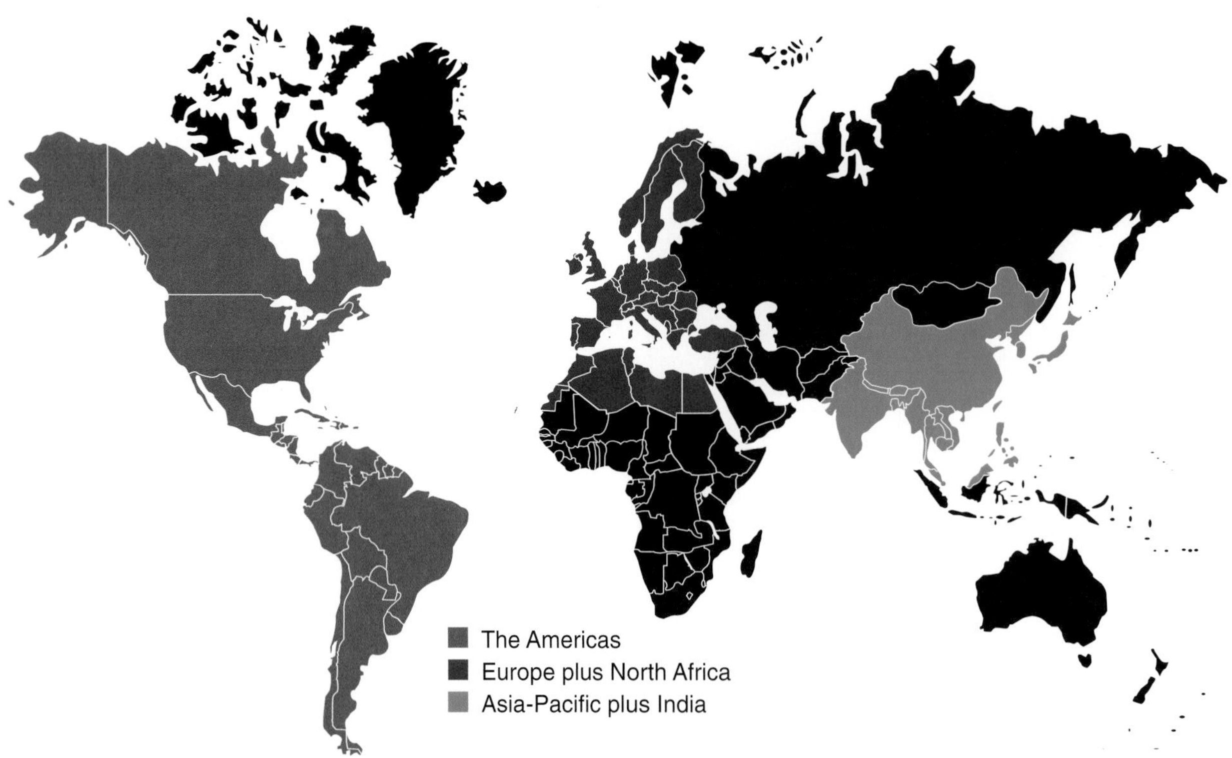

24-8 Countries within each main trade region are geographically close to each other and have relationships among their cultures.

number and size of established competitors should also be considered.

Infrastructure

A country's ***infrastructure*** involves the existence and condition of roads, transportation systems, electricity, telephones, mail delivery, etc. If U.S. companies do manufacturing in a foreign land, communication between the countries must be reliable. Also, finished goods must be able to be moved in a timely way by truck, train, airplane, or ship.

Culture

A nation's *culture* is its set of social norms or values. For instance, the ability to read and write may or may not be important to the people. Production workers might expect to have a siesta after lunch, and retail stores might close for several hours in midday. Also, work incentives that motivate employees in the United States may backfire elsewhere.

Companies that do business abroad cannot assume that other societies operate the same as theirs or feel the same way about certain issues. Nor should one country imply that their ways are best.

The World's Major Trade Regions

Neighboring countries are joining together into regional trade arrangements that are economically advantageous for the nations in each of those areas of the world. Within the regions, the countries with relatively high wage rates supply apparel designs and textiles to garment producers in nearby lower-wage countries, where items are sewn. Finished goods are returned to the original country, to be sold at retail. This synergy gives jobs and income to less-developed countries and maintains the high standards of living for the mature economies. It partners retailers with suppliers in close geographic proximity to reduce lead times. Trade alliances are negotiated and signed outside the auspices of the WTO.

The three main trade regions in the world today are Asia-Pacific plus India, Europe plus North Africa, and the Americas. See 24-8.

Asia-Pacific Plus India

Japan was the first to emerge in this part of the world. It is now an exporting leader because of its smart, aggressive marketing strategies listed in 24-9. Most of its apparel companies manufacture several different lines each, and sell them in company-owned stores.

Japan's development was followed by other "Pacific Rim" countries along the Pacific boundary of Asia, such as South Korea, Taiwan, Hong Kong, and Singapore. These industrialized nations each have a small land mass and limited natural resources. They must trade to survive. They import raw materials and food, use their labor and marketing skills effectively, and export quality manufactured goods. They have superb technology and efficiency.

Japan's Marketing Strategies

- ✸ Formulate long-range plans (as well as short-range) to build market share, including predatory pricing. *Predatory pricing* is charging very low prices at first to forego initial profits and lessen competition. This reduces other start-ups and causes existing uneconomical producers to go out of business so the price can later be raised for high profits.
- ✸ Use teamwork of government, finance, industry, and labor to achieve national goals of high industry performance. All entities support each other for the success of all.
- ✸ Invest heavily in technologies (robotics, computerization, etc.).
- ✸ Develop marketing information systems to obtain the latest worldwide information which is sent back to the country and its industries.
- ✸ Use government protection of the domestic market, by not allowing imports and encouraging exports.

24-9 Japan was aggressive in becoming a major exporting nation, with definite goals that other Asian nations have since followed to also become exporting nations.

As these Pacific Rim nations have advanced socioeconomically, their manufacturing of goods has been shifting to lower-wage parts of Asia and India. India has millions of individuals doing handicraft work and sewing in their homes. India exports millions of dollars of apparel each year but accepts no imports. They are a ripe potential market for the future. Meanwhile, many successful Pacific Rim family-owned businesses are shifting from manufacturing to becoming marketers, in hopes of sending finished goods to the biggest emerging market of them all–China.

China, which exports low-wage goods and has not allowed any imports into the country in the past, has been opening its borders to imports in order to become a member of the WTO. China is the largest exporter of manufactured textiles and apparel in the world. Countries that receive the goods, including the U.S., find opposition among consumers because of China's alleged human rights violations, transshipments, and other unfair trade practices.

Europe Plus North Africa

The *European Economic Community,* called the European Union (EU), includes 15 developed countries of Western Europe (Austria, Belgium, Britain, Denmark, Finland, France, Germany, Greece, Ireland, Italy, Luxembourg, the Netherlands, Portugal, Spain, and Sweden). This represents 20 percent of the world's gross domestic product (GDP) and more consumers than the U.S. market. Cyprus, as well as the former communist countries of the Czech Republic, Estonia, Hungary, Poland, and Slovenia are joining. The economies, political institutions, and societies of these Eastern "emerging" European nations are being intertwined with the advanced Western European states.

Eleven of the original EU countries have replaced their old national currencies with the *euro,* a common monetary unit. This will make it easier to do business—with common rules, standards, and practices. However, computer systems in Europe and internationally must overcome the technical challenges of the new currency.

There is now total free trade of goods, services, labor, and capital among European nations, with all customs border posts removed within the expanded internal economy. However, vast differences remain between the individual countries in respect to language, customs, product feature preferences, and retail store operations.

European businesses are efficient, competitive, and innovative. They are focusing on partnership linkages and technology to improve their operations. Advertising is upbeat, with effective marketing to the proper target consumers. Some low-wage production is done in North African nations. The U.S. also has agreements with North African (sub-Saharan) nations for manufacturing without trade barriers. Other European work is contracted in Turkey and Eastern European countries that are encouraging trade and capital investment. The growing industrialism and markets of emerging Europe are also providing business opportunities for some American apparel manufacturers and retailers.

The Americas

The Western Hemisphere is also becoming a unified trade region, 24-10. The ***North American Free Trade Agreement (NAFTA)*** set up an open trading zone among the United States, Canada and Mexico. All trade barriers on textiles, apparel, and other goods are being eliminated, creating a single North American market.

Canada has been a trading partner with the U.S. for a long time, exporting and importing many textile and apparel goods back and forth. It has a high wage rate. It sends upscale garments into the U.S. market.

Mexico has low wages for manufacturing and has caused some U.S. factories to close, taking away American factory jobs. However, Mexico also has a developing market as the country's standard of living increases. A huge potential exists for future retailing of apparel and other goods. Currently, Sears, JCPenney, Wal-Mart, Price/Costco, and others have stores in Mexican locations. Since NAFTA has been in effect, both imports and exports to and from Canada and Mexico have increased dramatically.

Many U.S. firms are entering into apparel production agreements in Mexico. U.S. companies that are investing in Mexico also consider the country as a launching pad for products into other Central and South American markets. Asian manufactures, which are

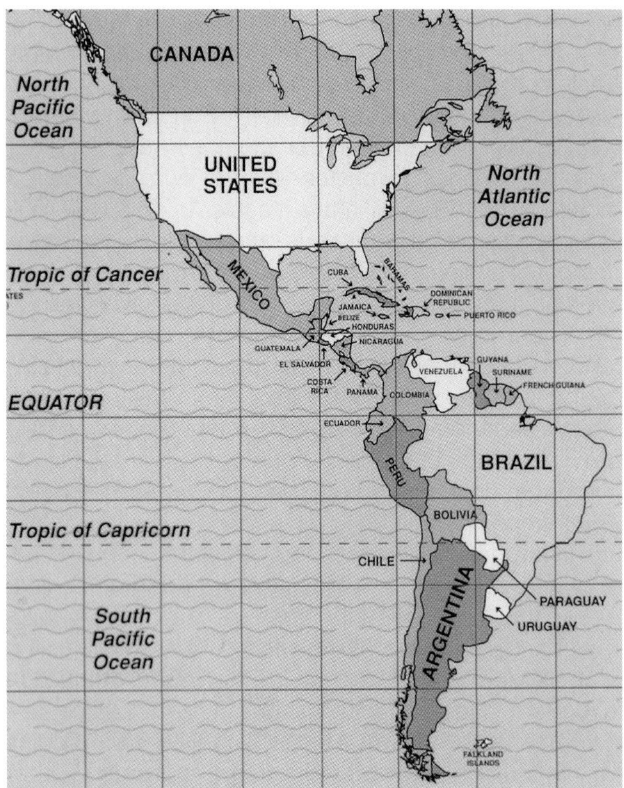

24-10 The Western Hemisphere, most of which is shown here, includes North America, Central America, and South America.

facing rising labor costs, are now shifting some of their production to Mexico. This also gives them access into the American market.

Mexican factories are eager to accept production jobs. Mexico has a large, young work force ready to be employed, but low education levels must be supplemented with training. Also, since many factories are equipped with old machinery and use outdated management methods, they are not as efficient as U.S. producers, which have been upgrading with new technology. Mexico has also had problems with smuggling of goods, illegal transactions, and electricity shortages to keep the plants running.

Most jobs have been with small Mexican companies in the past. New jobs are now evolving throughout the country. Some small factories are being bought and modernized by larger operations. Also, integrated networks are emerging, where several small companies are cooperating to combine their strength and minimize their weaknesses. Production is moving away from the border to areas where labor is more plentiful. Manufacturers are striving toward higher quality and more product diversity.

Item 807/9802

Item 807/9802 is a section of the U.S. Tariff Code that allows garment manufacturers to export cut components and trims of garments for assembly elsewhere. The garments are then reimported with duty being paid only on the value added. ***Value added*** is the increase in worth of products as a result of a particular work activity, such as the sewing. For instance, if the cut fabric parts of a jacket are worth $8 each when they are shipped offshore, and each sewn jacket is worth $10 when it comes back into the country, the value added while it was out of the U.S. is $2 per jacket.

Cooperative manufacturing has been done among countries of the Western Hemisphere for a long time, with U.S. manufacturers using nearby low-wage contract production. Developing areas of the Western Hemisphere have lower production costs than the U.S. and Asia, plus their proximity to the U.S. market gives shorter response times and lower freight rates. *Twin plant programs* use two manufacturing sites, with one in the U.S. and the other in a nearby low-wage country. Apparel design and cutting is done in the U.S., with the sewing and finishing done offshore. This combines U.S. materials, technology, and financing with offshore assembly. Finished products are of high quality, but have a lower cost. A later "809" arrangement allows yard goods to be shipped, so the cutting is also done offshore for full CMT (cut/make/trim) operations.

Caribbean Parity

U.S. Law now gives political, social, and economic stability to its neighbors in the Caribbean and Central America. By assisting the growth and development of these countries, it is believed that the U.S. is also helped economically and strategically. Caribbean and Central American countries have more employment and can earn money, plus U.S. companies can compete better against Asian imports.

24-11 The trade bureaus of countries that want to do business with other countries market their products by distributing informative materials.

Caribbean countries were not included in the original NAFTA. Thus, some of their work was transferred to Mexican factories. They then requested ***parity***, which is equal treatment. This was achieved with the *Caribbean Basin Trade Partnership Act (CBTPA),* passed in 2000. The CBTPA is helping to reform their economies with NAFTA-like provisions, for duty-free and quota-free trade. This significantly decreases U.S. company costs, because of low-wage manufacturing (lower than Mexico) and fewer record-keeping responsibilities to take merchandise through customs. It is also improving the standard of living of these nations because of income for workers and investments in facilities in the region.

Besides the Caribbean, it is expected that eventually the entire Western Hemisphere of North America, Central America, and South America will have a free trade agreement. This will result in more trade among all of the Americas.

Most countries want to send goods into the U.S., but may not be ready to open their markets to U.S. exports. Contract manufacturing is already being done in such places as Jamaica, Panama, Honduras, Brazil, Haiti, Argentina, Guatemala, Uruguay, Peru, and Ecuador. Colombia promotes its textile and apparel products, 24-11. Costa Rica, El Salvador, and the Dominican Republic are seeing a phaseout of U.S. quotas and tariffs because they are members of the World Trade Organization.

Additionally, Central and South American countries are trying to move their apparel industries toward ***full package production,*** focusing on supplying design and sample work, fabrics/findings/trims, all parts of construction, as well as packing and transportation arrangements. Full package design-through-distribution vendors supply everything up to shipping the orders. This vertically integrated service is especially important to the U.S. private label retail market.

International Sourcing for U.S. Fashion Importing

As previously discussed, sourcing products from low-wage countries is popular for labor-intensive apparel products. With many people needed to produce them, wage rates make a big difference in the final cost. Companies compete worldwide for price advantages, seeking the best possible goods for the least amount of money.

In the past, U.S. manufacturers favored protectionism. However, now U.S. textile and apparel manufacturing companies are using overseas plants and labor to produce their goods, instead of trying to compete against them. They are relying on foreign sources for fabrics, supplies, and assembly. The production for some lines may be spread among several different countries. Designing may be done in one country, fabric supplied by another, and cutting and sewing done in still another. The fashion industry has an unstoppable shift toward global production.

In general, retailers have always favored free trade. They want to stock what will sell for the highest profit. If the best values are not available domestically, U.S. retailers order them from overseas sources. If imports are cheaper for retailers to buy, and can be sold to consumers at about the same prices as domestic goods, retailers can benefit with higher margins. Most retailers feel that as long as the products can be obtained, sell well, and provide good profits, the problems involved with importing them are manageable.

Problems of sourcing goods from outside the home country include hidden sales, distribution, and management costs. There are added transportation and insurance costs and import fees. Long delays can occur in receiving merchandise because of shipping distances and customs procedures. It can be hard to monitor production, resulting in wide quality and fit variations. Employees often must travel to foreign lands, with high expenses plus time spent away from their other job duties. More employees might be needed and currency fluctuations can dramatically change profits. The pros and cons of importing apparel were listed in Chapter 15.

Large retail firms have groups of buyers who scour the world, looking for the best merchandise for their stores. Sometimes they can import new and different items that no other store has. Fashion innovation and garments that require lots of handwork may be absent from U.S.-made apparel. See 24-12. Also, foreign sources are more adventurous with design innovation and are willing to produce style numbers in smaller quantities. Often retailers have their own product development employees who contract with overseas plants to make specification goods and private label lines.

The Los Angeles area is the "gateway" for textile and apparel imports from Asia-Pacific. Japan has many trading companies that serve as middle-people in distributing Japanese products worldwide. The Far East is currently developing surpluses of production. The Western Hemisphere has supplied increasing amounts of apparel to the U.S. in recent years. Most Caribbean goods come into the U.S. through Miami.

Methods of Offshore Sourcing

To obtain import goods, U.S. companies can purchase items through domestic wholesale importers or buy directly from foreign sources. They can use foreign contractors to make their garments, or sign licensing or franchise agreements. Some American firms enter into joint venture agreements or have their own production facilities in developing countries.

Purchase Through Domestic Wholesale Importers

Purchases can be made in the U.S. from several different types of importers. *Import merchants* buy and import particular classifications of goods. A *resident sales agent* represents and is paid by a group of foreign

Kellwood Company

24-12 Fine quality leather goods are usually not produced in the United States. Therefore, they must be imported from Argentina, Italy, Israel, Indonesia, or other countries that make them.

manufacturers, usually from just one country or region of the world. The agent connects import buyers of those lines with the manufacturers and may or may not carry stocks of goods. An *import commission house* also serves as a brokerage between domestic buyers and foreign sources. A commission is collected from both the buyer and the vendor when deals are made.

Buying Directly from Foreign Sources

U.S. retail buyers often travel the world to find unusual or inexpensively-priced items to sell in their stores. Manufacturing orders are placed with agents in those countries. Orders can be written during market weeks in foreign locations or from export merchants or export sales representatives. Export merchants are foreign wholesalers who specialize in efficiently exporting goods from their countries. They serve as offshore sourcing commissionaires for the firms that hire them. *Export sales representatives* represent selected manufacturers, but do not maintain a wholesale inventory.

Global sourcing is now being done via the Internet. This has virtually eliminated national borders, time and costs, and offered flexibility. This also helps foreign companies bring goods to new markets quickly. E-mail permits conversations and digital cameras can show items immediately to buyers in other parts of the world.

Using Foreign Contractors

Manufacturing is often hired overseas by U.S. apparel producers, or retailers who want private label goods, produced for their stores. The U.S. firm becomes the importer of record. Foreign contract manufacturing dominates most high-volume, lower-priced apparel sourcing. Developing countries have many small low-wage producers. However, industrialized nations offer more advantages. They can often provide full package programs with extensive fabric choices, skilled operators, and experienced management. They also have reliable communication, transportation, and financial services.

Large U.S. manufacturers and retailers may have an American supervisor stationed in a foreign country, who keeps tabs on all of the contract production in that world region of the world.

Licensing Agreements

Licensing agreements allow U.S. companies to produce and/or market products of foreign firms in the U.S., in return for a royalty or fee. An American firm might obtain the rights to make and sell an Italian jacket line in the U.S., using the Italian pattern and label. The U.S. company would be responsible for maintaining the quality of the items and for advertising, promoting, and distributing them. In return, the U.S. company would pay the Italian firm a percentage of the income from sales of the goods. In this way, shipping costs and trade barriers are avoided.

Franchising

Retail franchises of foreign firms in the U.S. can be very successful. Benetton stores, which carry knitwear from an Italian franchiser, are examples of this. Chic, foreign boutiques are often found in American shopping malls.

Joint Ventures

Joint ventures are agreements that bring necessary skills or products of two companies together for added strength. Usually the expertise and technology are from the U.S., and the labor and plant sites are foreign. The two companies also share the investment costs and the profits of the business in percentages that are negotiated in advance. For best results, the U.S. firm should also be active in the training, quality, and delivery aspects of the business.

Company-Owned Foreign Facilities

The most comprehensive form of international business is to run a company operation in a foreign country. It might be a branch operation or a wholly owned subsidiary of the U.S. firm. A wholly owned subsidiary is a separate firm that is owned by the parent company. A company-owned facility might be established or bought from local owners. It can use available raw materials, send goods to the U.S., and have direct access to the foreign market. It can be highly profitable, but the U.S. firm may have problems with communications, labor relations, and foreign laws that are different from theirs. Thus, local nationals should be hired to work as managers as soon as possible.

Many foreign corporations have bought U.S. businesses or set up their own operations in the United States. A weaker U.S. dollar against other currencies and rising costs of foreign labor have made direct investment in the U.S. attractive to Asian and European firms. The branch factories or stores in the U.S. are controlled by the overseas company, which supplies them with the designs and materials needed for production or for their retail financing. For instance, Talbots now has Japanese ownership.

Foreign corporations with operations in the U.S. have automatic access to the American market. There has been an expansion of European retailers entering major U.S. cities, such as Gucci stores and Carrefour. However, some foreign retailers are having problems because they do not understand how to market to the diverse consumer base in the U.S. Foreign fashions are sometimes considered to be too expensive, awkwardly styled, and not sized to fit most Americans.

International Market Opportunities for U.S. Fashion Exporting

In the past, rapid U.S. economic growth brought domestic sales increases and expansion for retailers. Companies were busy keeping up with the demand for merchandise and new suburban stores in the United States. However, U.S. apparel market growth has slowed in the past two decades and competition is at an all-time high. Identifying and satisfying consumers in other parts of the globe is becoming more desirable and necessary.

Although American shoppers are more affluent than most overseas consumers, the number of people living in the U.S. represents less than five percent of the world's population. In buying power, our market is about one-quarter of that of the rest of the world. This leaves large market opportunities elsewhere.

Growth rates of certain international markets far outpace U.S. market growth. As freer world trade is opening new markets, smart U.S. fashion companies are competing for international sales, viewing the world as their customer. Textile products are among the first in demand when disposable income rises in developing economies. Rising living standards create a larger middle class with spending money.

It is easier for U.S. firms to start global expansion to developed countries with the same language and similar cultures, such as Canada and Great Britain. GAP and other specialty chains have expanded to these countries. See 24-13. Close proximity is also a consideration, such as exporting to Latin American countries.

Talbots, Inc./AEON Group

24-13 The origins of Talbots are American, so opening a store in England provided a location in another country with the same language and a similar culture.

Although established markets are easier to enter than developing markets, competition already exists there. Japan, Europe, and Canada account for most U.S. textile and apparel export sales. There is a demand for quality apparel, especially for sportswear with an American flavor, 24-14. The "Made in the USA" label is especially desired by the 16- to 35-year-old age group. See 24-15.

With higher U.S. productivity, American apparel producers are exporting some goods. However, export levels have not matched the rising numbers of imports. To improve U.S. export competitiveness, companies must be committed. In the past, the U.S. only sold unwanted goods abroad. These were not well accepted. Now it is known that to compete, the U.S. must identify markets and tailor goods to meet foreign tastes. Specific aspects to consider for export competitiveness are listed in 24-16. Benefits received from exporting products are listed in 24-17.

Although wage rates between American and foreign workers are narrowing as more countries become industrialized, competitiveness is not just based on wage costs. Some recent export growth of fashion goods

24-14 Disney products are examples of items that symbolize a U.S. lifestyle.

reflects specialization to satisfy certain market niches. Since the U.S. cannot compete on price with countries that inexpensively manufacture commodity goods, it can be more successful in creating differentiated premium products for which it can charge a higher price. However, automation is bringing U.S. costs down.

International business often involves logistical, financial, and political obstacles. Firms can learn to handle the extra calculations and "red tape," or turn these procedures over to specialists. Also, certification for ISO 9000 standards (explained in Chapter 7), concerning the ways businesses are run, is being requested by more international customers. However,

National Cotton Council

24-15 Blue jeans with a "Made in the USA" label are in demand among young adults throughout the world.

Ways to Improve U.S. Export Competitiveness

- Identify specific overseas markets.
- Make long-term commitments to develop those markets.
- Customize marketing practices for foreign preferences and cultural differences.
- Cater to specialized market niches.
- Use strategies to avoid trade barriers.
- Overcome warehousing and transportation problems.
- Strive to offer top service and reliability.
- Improve technology for reduced prices to compete.
- Invest abroad for effective production and market access.

24-16 For U.S. exports to compete in world markets, more of an effort must be made to satisfy market needs and to offer competitive value.

Benefits of Exporting Products

- More customers for increased sales.
- Market diversification with varied markets that react to different conditions (when one country's market is weak, conditions in another country might be strong).
- Increased profits from higher volume that gives lower average unit costs (economies of scale).
- Extended demand for seasonal products among the different world climates.
- Year-round production runs that increase productivity levels.
- Better domestic methods as a result of knowledge/technology learned overseas.
- Longer product life cycles because of transferring obsolete products to less sophisticated markets.

24-17 Many benefits result from taking advantage of export opportunities for fashion goods.

gaining export market access for some U.S. products can merely involve sales representatives directly calling on potential customers overseas.

International Retailing

International retailing, often called *cross-border retailing*, involves retail company operations that serve customers in multiple countries. Consumers all over the world need items that American companies have, and ambitious firms are taking advantage of these market opportunities. Mail order retailers send catalogs worldwide, and Internet retailers sell globally over Web sites. The opening of U.S. retail stores overseas also encourages the sale of American brands. See 24-18. Some U.S. real estate companies have developed malls in foreign countries, occupied by U.S. retailers.

U.S. companies are investing abroad to gain access to world markets. With joint ventures overseas, restrictions on local, direct investment are avoided. Since many countries will not allow foreign companies to own facilities, a local partner is needed to do business there.

Licensing deals also work, with a U.S. company licensing tradenamed goods in a foreign country. This puts U.S. products into foreign markets. It minimizes the risks of trying to enter a foreign market, while still obtaining a portion of the revenue from foreign sales.

U.S. retail store franchises overseas also minimize the costs and risks of foreign expansion and avoid trade restrictions. To develop and operate franchise stores abroad, stores sell their name and expertise to foreign organizations. The terms of the agreements specify the rights and responsibilities of each party in operating such stores.

Wholly owned foreign retail operations involve overseas stores that are completely owned and controlled by firms of another country, 24-19. Truly global retail enterprises have a worldwide presence to the point that their national affiliation becomes blurred. See 24-20.

There is more chance of failure and more financial investment involved with international operations than is usually encountered for a domestic business. However, high financial rewards are also possible. There have been many mergers and acquisitions among international businesses to strengthen those that exist.

Multinational corporations (MNCs) operate globally. They have direct investment in several different countries. From their research/development and plant sites, they can transfer technology and manufacturing know-how to their locations in various other countries. They can use their brand name identification, marketing skills, and management expertise throughout the world. See 24-21. By specializing in certain tasks in the best areas of the world, they take advantage of low wage and tax rates and other comparative advantages. They can also use profits from strong areas to subsidize efforts in developing markets.

Satisfying Market Differences

Effort is required to make profits from foreign business. Companies that sell goods in another country must understand the cultural attitudes and practices of the people of that country. There can be big differences in language, beliefs, religion, race, income distribution patterns, and customs from one country to another. See 24-22. Companies must adapt their marketing and ways of doing business to each country, while preserving the coherence and style of their goods and services.

U.S. manufactured goods have been more successful than retail stores in entering foreign markets. U.S.

Jusco Co., Ltd./AEON Group

24-18 Talbots of Japan uses the same store design and customer service techniques as are used in U.S. Talbot's stores. Merchandise is sent from the U.S. with an emphasis on petite sizes.

Jusco Co., Ltd./AEON Group

24-19 This JUSCO store has Japanese ownership and is located in Hong Kong, a previously British province of China.

Jusco Co., Ltd./AEON Group

24-20 Laura Ashley firms have a British origin and flavor, are located in major cities around the world, and some are jointly owned by a Japanese corporation.

Jusco Co., Ltd./AEON Group

24-21 The marketing skills and management expertise of the multinational corporation, AEON Group, helps promote the success of Talbots, Laura Ashley, JUSCO, and other retail chains that it owns.

Jusco Co., Ltd./AEON Group

24-22 Shoppers in Japan are accustomed to having store employees open the door for them and greet them as they enter. This is not done in the U.S.

retailers have had a hard time understanding different end-user tastes and preferences. Careful planning must be done to identify and evaluate the opportunities for foreign retail expansion.

To avoid problems, a product/market evaluation can discover different attitudes and preferences among consumers of various countries. It can indicate what consumers want, why they want it, and where and when people of certain countries shop. Each foreign market must be treated separately, with consumer differences taken into account for product adaptations. It is important to know size and fit expectations, influences on purchasing decisions, and how people use their money for goods and services. Local competition should also be evaluated. Then the market potential and demand for products can be estimated.

When starting the business, local input should be sought to prevent promotional errors or translation problems. Packaging must be adapted. The color of the package might need to be changed because of symbolism of certain colors in various countries. Other times the language must be changed on packaging and care labels. Trade names, when translated into other languages, sometimes have negative connotations. Computer searches can be done to create trade names that are easy to pronounce everywhere in the world and have no specific meaning anywhere.

Discovering Offshore Sources and Opportunities

The key to successful global business dealings is information. Picking the right countries and learning to think like the locals are key to international success. Customs, taxes, and employment laws are vastly different among different countries. This applies to both sourcing from foreign countries or selling to them.

Published reports prepared by foreign governments and private sources can provide preliminary information about foreign business environments. Computer searches and catalogs that list global information are available. There are also seminars and numerous sources of market research. Some companies hire consultants or do their own studies about countries where they are considering doing business. They seek out demographic data, factory and equipment cost estimates, retail sales dollars spent, and the number of stores in a certain locality.

The process of researching international markets is similar to the way market research is done domestically. The objectives of identifying customers' needs and supplying products that satisfy those needs apply wherever a company seeks business.

Awareness of differences, consultation with local people, and concern for host-country feelings reduce problems, save money, and increase profits. Questionnaires and marketing surveys can capture desired information when translated into the native language of the country. Paid services of an expert with knowledge of local dialects, or graduate business students from that country who are eager to gain experience are often used. After all, the language of international trade is not English—it is the language of the customer!

International trade shows have sections or pavilions by country. Sourcing fairs are hosted by various countries, either in a city in their region of the world, or in a U.S. city. China shows its merchandise and opportunities at its city of Canton twice a year. Bobbin Contexpo Apparel Show of the Americas, in Miami, Florida, has exhibits and seminars about how to do business in Latin America. Expotela is a North American textile show held in Mexico City for Mexican apparel manufacturers.

Summary

Technological advances have brought about instant worldwide communications and a global economy for international trade. U.S. textile/apparel imports have risen rapidly, with countries competing for a large share of the consumer dollar. Trade has been opening up throughout the world, with an elimination of barriers.

As countries develop, their textile/apparel industries go through a series of stages. They begin with simple, homemade garments of natural fibers. Eventually, specialization occurs with basic machines, leading to exporting. As the quality and quantity of products increase, processes become more sophisticated, finally leading to maturity. Before trading with emerging nations, companies should learn about other countries' political stability, economic climate, infrastructure, and culture.

The world's major trade regions are Asia-Pacific plus India, Europe plus North Africa, and the Americas. Japan was the first Asia-Pacific country to emerge, with neighboring countries following its lead. The developed countries of Western Europe are efficient and competitive. The Western Hemisphere is moving toward free trade among all of North America, Central America, and South America.

International sourcing for U.S. textile/apparel importing has traditionally been from low-wage countries. Manufacturers have favored protectionism while retailers have favored free trade. However, international trade is now a reality accepted by most businesses. To import goods, U.S. companies can purchase items through domestic wholesale importers, buy directly from foreign sources, or use foreign contractors. They can sign licensing or franchise agreements, enter into joint ventures, or have their own production facilities in developing countries.

There are vast international market opportunities for U.S. fashion exporting, including international retailing. To be successful in foreign markets, differences of each country must be satisfied. To discover import and export opportunities, information can be obtained from government reports, specific publications, computer sources, consultants, and trade organizations.

To Know

globalization
import penetration
balance of trade
trade deficit
trade surplus
free trade
protectionism
market disruption
transshipping
dumping
World Trade Organization (WTO)
structural adjustment
comparative advantage
infrastructure
North American Free Trade Agreement (NAFTA)
value added
full package production
parity
joint venture
multinational corporations (MNCs)

To Review

1. What country (economy) is the greatest consumer market of soft goods in the world?
2. At the current time, what is the import penetration of textile/apparel goods in the U.S.?
3. What apparel categories have the highest U.S. import penetration?
4. How are square meter equivalents used?
5. Why does a weak U.S. dollar tend to improve the U.S. trade balance?
6. What is international diplomacy?
7. What effect has the new World Trade Organization structure had on U.S. government income and why?
8. Why does apparel production remain labor-intensive, thus offering manufacturing employment to low-skilled workers?
9. Why is an oversupply of goods occurring in the world?
10. The economic climate of countries relates to what two categories of factors?
11. Within the world's major trade regions, how are high-wage and lower-wage countries using synergy to improve jobs, income, and standards of living?
12. Why must most Pacific Rim countries trade to survive?
13. What factors are causing Asian manufacturers to shift some of their production to Mexico?
14. Why are U.S. manufacturers no longer favoring protectionism?
15. What is a wholly owned subsidiary?
16. The number of people living in the U.S. represents about how much of the world's population and how much in buying power?
17. Since U.S. textile/apparel companies cannot compete on price with countries that inexpensively manufacture commodity goods, how can they be successful?
18. Name three types of business structures in which U.S. retailers are investing abroad.
19. What must companies that sell goods in another country understand and do?
20. What is the key to successful global business dealings?

To Do

1. Research textile and apparel trade at the library or through the Internet. Find out the total U.S. trade deficit (for all types of products), the amount of the trade deficit that relates to fashion goods, and the penetration of apparel imports in U.S. stores. Make a bulletin board display that illustrates your findings, with graphs that are labeled for clarity.
2. With two groups of students, debate the issue of free trade. One group of students should argue for totally free trade and the other should argue for complete protection for U.S. textile and apparel goods. One student can be the moderator and ask prepared questions. Do research to prepare the questions and your cases. Also answer questions from the class at the end of the debate. Then the moderator should sum up the main points to conclude the presentation.
3. From newspaper and trade journal references in the library, study the Uruguay Round of the GATT talks, the Multifiber Arrangement (MFA), and how the World Trade Organization came into existence. Discuss how the WTO has phased out MFA import protection and its effects on our soft goods pipeline. Write a report that also includes your feelings about the situation.
4. Using a large map of the world, explain to the class the advantages and disadvantages of doing textile and apparel trade with various parts of the world. Point out and describe the major trading blocs. Show why sourcing in the Western Hemisphere makes sense for U.S. retailers.
5. Visit a mid-priced apparel retail store. With permission of the store or department manager, read labels and record where 50 different garments were made. (Be very careful not to get pencil or pen marks on any merchandise.) After recording the information, figure out the percentage of garments that have come from each country. Analyze the significance of your results as far as cost level of production wages, intricacy of the garments produced in different countries, proximity to the U.S. market, etc. What is the total U.S. import penetration of the goods that you analyzed? Make a large chart of your results and explain your calculations, results, and thoughts to the class.

CHAPTER 25

The Latest Fashion Business Trends

After studying this chapter, you will be able to

- discuss the changing consumer market.
- explain niche specialization marketing.
- describe trends in retail formats.
- discuss the popularity and types of nonstore retailing.
- explain the current survival business strategies.
- summarize how technology is leading to customized goods.

Changes in the fashion industry are occurring at an increasing rate. Businesses that stand still become outdated and fail. Successful, innovative companies learn to use change as an opportunity, not a threat. They act positively toward the change, looking to the future rather than the past. They adjust to satisfy the demands of the changing marketplace.

The latest fashion business challenges involve satisfying a changing consumer market. Niche marketing is recommended to target specialized consumer groups. Trends in retail formats include discount retailing that dominates the market, with nonstore retailing gaining in strength. Survival business strategies include vertical and horizontal restructuring of the industry, employee training and service, and globalization. Additionally, technology is guiding the industry toward efficient customization of products.

Satisfying a Changing Consumer Market

Each year brings more sophisticated markets. Consumers are more diverse and harder to understand. Today's consumers are more discriminating and have less time to shop than ever before. They want more unique products that have better quality, lower cost, and are instantly available. Fashion businesses must gain a better understanding of emerging changes in consumer thinking. Then they must be flexible enough to develop product mixes and strategies that satisfy the desires of consumers. See 25-1.

Jusco Co., Ltd./AEON Group

25-1 Retailers must attune their strategies to consumers who now have less time to shop and want to find specific items quickly and conveniently.

Almost all consumers are price-conscious and "value-driven" demanding more and spending less. The earnings of families have not increased in relation to their wants and needs. This causes them to purchase less expensive items, avoid buying some things altogether, or delay various important purchases. Also, the term "sale" has lost its meaning because it has been overused and abused by retailers. See 25-2

Consumers have become wiser and cannot be fooled. They seek and recognize true value. Additionally there is no longer much customer loyalty to particular stores. Retailers have been addressing these situations with private label goods that provide consumer value and retailer profits, plus promoting their store names and merchandise as distinctive brands.

Almost all consumers are time-poor. With most people spending long hours at jobs, they have no time to browse or to waste time on unfruitful shopping. They require quick, convenient, one-stop shopping. Successful retailers must be open long hours, have merchandise in stock, have help available, and provide fast/easy checkout.

Cross-shopping is the consumer trend of combining purchases from both ends of the price scale. Consumers are buying from low-price mass discounters for most goods, and indulging themselves in a few expensive, distinctive items from upscale specialty shops. This is polarizing retailers on price, causing the demise of the middle-price market. A woman might wear an inexpensive skirt with a designer blouse. Consumers can no longer be stereotyped as bargain or premium shoppers. Studies have determined that quality is sometimes the same or better in less-expensive items, plus consumers feel they can discard them after a shorter period of time.

25-2 This sale, at the end of the summer season, probably offers good value for shoppers who need swimwear. However, some stores say their goods are "on sale" when they reduce falsely inflated prices.

Discount mass merchandisers are aggressively expanding their apparel departments. They are offering fashions that generate higher profits and more inventory turns than traditional types of stores. On the other hand, upscale apparel chains are opening new low-priced discount divisions that offer more casual attire than their regular stores.

Also, consumers now express their individual style instead of succumbing to fads. For instance, all skirt lengths are acceptable, 25-3. Thus, consumers do not need to update their wardrobes with the "right" skirt length. Men's apparel sales are growing faster than the

Sigrid Olsen

25-3 It is no longer expected that women wear their skirts at the same length, with fashion dictating where it should be.

Perry Ellis by Hartmarx

25-4 Men's apparel used to have fewer choices. Now there are many fashionable pieces that are mixed and matched for more interesting looks and self-expression.

women's fashion market. See 25-4. Sportswear sales are skyrocketing past all dressier types of clothing. Additionally, consumers are shopping "closer to need," rather than far in advance of each season.

The Importance of Demographics and Psychographics

A study of demographics and psychographics (described in Chapter 5) can supply a great deal of market information. For instance, age groups with strong spending power today include children and the mature market. Children influence their parents' spending, causing parents to spend more on their children's clothes. Also, many teenagers have jobs to earn their own spending money.

The mature market, over age 50, is getting larger as "baby boomers" move into it and people live longer. Much of the mature group is active and healthy and has large spending potential. They are self-confident and have a desire to buy what they want. They are less impulsive and are thinking and dressing younger than their ages might imply. Some of the group is made up of working women. Desires of the mature fashion market are described in 25-5. In short, mature shoppers want quality products, value pricing, outstanding service, and user-friendly stores.

Demographic shifts also include an explosion of ethnic populations in the U.S. To take advantage of this opportunity, some retailers are hiring Hispanic specialists to gain a better understanding of cultural desires. Also, they are advertising on Spanish-speaking radio and television networks. Latino malls exist in several locations. Special mail-order catalogs are targeted at African Americans, stressing the fashions, brand names, and cosmetics they prefer. Additionally, stores use ethnic mannequins and models in their displays and advertisements.

Consumer lifestyles, values, and attitudes have caused *cocooning,* or the preference of staying at home. This has brought an interest in home and family items,

The Fashion Association/Marithe & Francois Girbaud

25-6 People have become more casual and comfortable with their wardrobes.

Desires of the Mature Consumer Market
✷ Simple, lasting style rather than faddish fashion
✷ Functional fashion that is stylish, yet comfortable
✷ Easy-to-use garments that fit mature shapes
✷ High-quality, durable products
✷ Fair prices, good value
✷ Money-back guarantees with uncomplicated exchange and return policies
✷ Extra services, such as deliveries, alterations, phone ordering, etc.
✷ Good customer service with knowledgeable, helpful employees who listen and respond
✷ Safe, well-lit locations with convenient parking
✷ Clear signage and easy-to-read garment tags
✷ Pleasant shopping atmosphere with efficient store layout (merchandise easy to find)
✷ Items in stock and available immediately
✷ Real-life ads, rather than skinny supermodels in far-out costumes

25-5 A mature woman would find pleasure in quickly running into a nearby store to find high-quality, elegant-looking shoes that can be worn comfortably all day, available in her size, at a fair price.

such as furniture, linens, housewares, appliances, garden tools, and hobby items. There is less interest in dressy clothes as more casual, comfortable attire is preferred, 25-6. Also, consumers are increasingly concerned about health and fitness, and the environment. See 25-7. They enjoy traveling. These lifestyle interests override the purchases of some new, fashionable apparel.

At the same time, people are receiving intense visual stimulation from movies, TV shows, and news reports about crime and violence. This is desensitizing them to traditional forms of shopping entertainment. Sophisticated special events and shopping environments are needed to attract consumers to shop. Behavioral psychologists are being hired to steer retail promotion. Unusual types of recreation and store atmospheres are being created.

With consumers wanting "efficiency and fantasy," retailers are trying to provide fun, relaxed diversion to help them escape from their daily routines. They are updating stores and malls with renovations that create

Kellwood Company

25-7 Some demand for soft goods involves using and preserving a clean environment.

25-8 As shoppers walk in a sunny central court that has birds flying over a fountain surrounded by tropical plants, they feel good about where they are shopping.

inviting storefronts, elegant central courts, and activities for an image to remember and a desire to revisit, 25-8. Malls set up celebrity visits, musical bands, antique and car shows, and other enticing events. Retailers want more frequent and longer shopping trips from consumers.

Niche Marketing

The changing consumer market has led to the creation of many market segments that, in turn, contain specialized niches. This is illustrated in 25-9. Many of the niches are more profitable than general merchandise or market segment businesses. *Micro-segmentation* is the dividing of an industry's total market into extremely narrow target markets. Many of the markets are small, but can be developed for good profits.

To personalize customer relations, companies throughout the textile/apparel pipeline are choosing target niches carefully and positioning themselves to strongly identify with those niches. *Niche manufacturing* is the production of specific lines of goods for carefully defined customers. Sometimes manufacturers can fill a niche because they have special capabilities, certain machinery, or cheaper raw materials from by-products of other goods they make. Other firms might manufacture a mix of goods that customers previously had to buy from several different sources. Requirements for niche textile and apparel manufacturers are listed in 25-10.

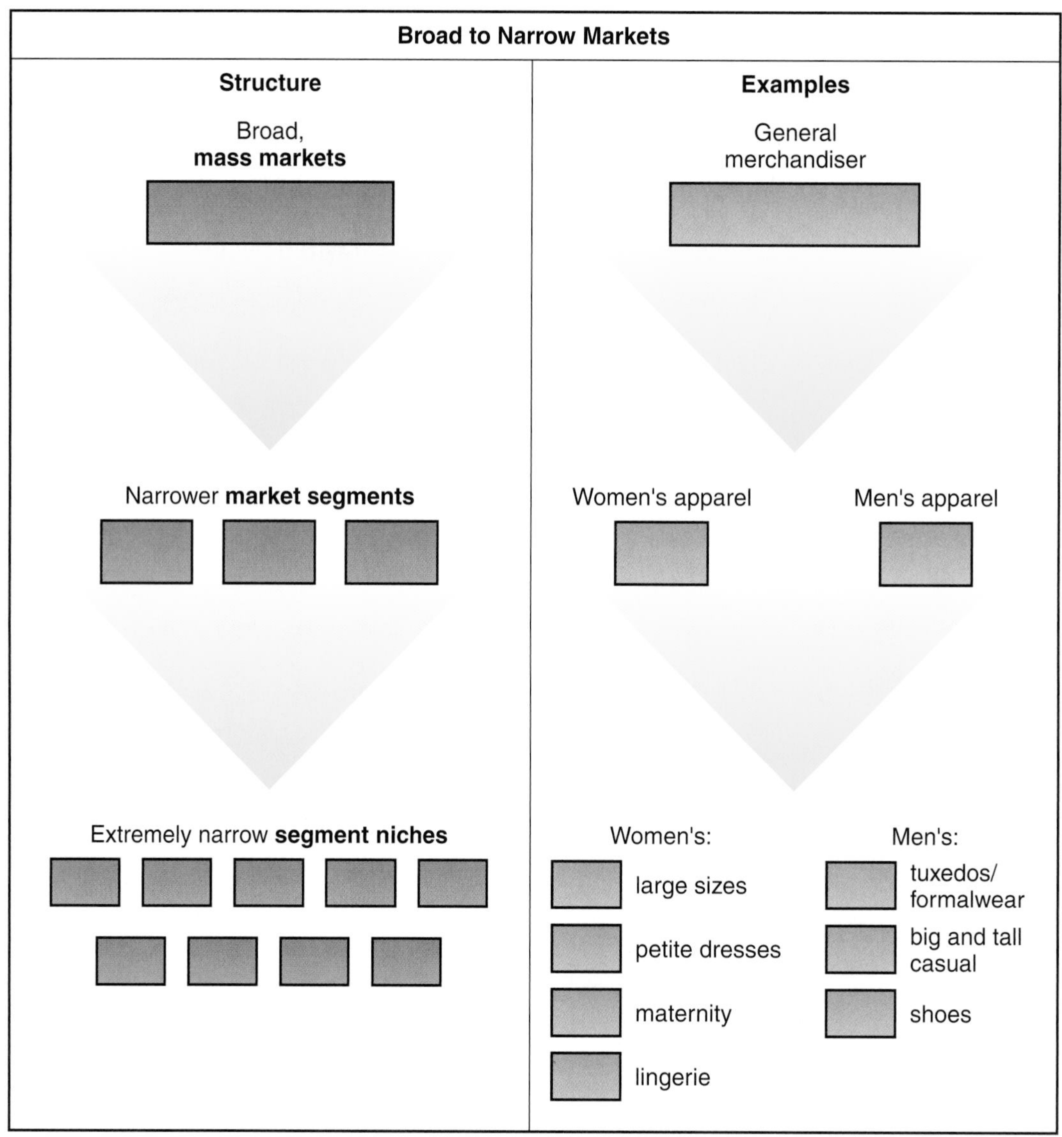

25-9 Certain specialized niches, within market segments, can be very profitable if the target need is recognized and exploited in the correct market area.

Requirements for Niche Manufacturing

- A clear vision of the planned direction to be pursued
- Knowledge of the company's special production and marketing capabilities
- Discovery of untapped company resources (materials, technology, human skills, etc.)
- A willingness to take the needed risks
- Creativity and innovation among all employees

25-10 By combining these requirements, a textile firm might discover that a by-product of one process is also a raw material that can be modified into a different unique product that is in demand. Possibly only the purchase of a small piece of equipment is needed to enter the new, profitable niche.

Specialized market positioning and merchandising is increasing in importance with today's tighter competition. Many companies, especially retailers, are all alike, but customers are all different. Today's consumers are more individualistic in their tastes and preferences. Consumers find an oversupply of general merchandise, but an undersupply of focused items for their diverse activities. See 25-11. With a clearer understanding of their target customers, fashion companies can operate with less stock and more inventory turnover.

Niche retailing is a specialty viewpoint in which departments or stores identify and closely target a specific set of fashion tastes. Companies are determining who their customers are, what those customers want, and how to provide it. When companies know what products they can offer at a profit, they can distinguish themselves from competitors and succeed against the competition.

Kellwood Company

25-11 Consumers who have specialized interests, such as jogging, may not find what they need in general merchandise stores. Niche retailers have opened stores catering to these specific market demands.

This is especially true for small retailers. They can't sell everything to everyone, or compete evenly against large, powerful stores. Small retailers need to complement big stores rather than compete against them. They should be highly focused, flexible, and creative to fill observed gaps between what consumers want and what mass retailing provides. Small fashion businesses can gain loyal customers. Midsized stores that deal with an entire market segment, rather than pinpointing a specific niche, are having trouble because of competition from discount and specialty stores.

Database Research for Niche Marketing

To thoroughly understand their customers, fashion businesses are doing sophisticated market research and database marketing. ***Database marketing*** is a general term for the use of electronically stored data that is gathered through market research, constantly updated, and used for company marketing activities. It has become easier to do with computer systems, direct mail, and point-of-sale information gathering. The data shows more than just the age, gender, and income level of customers. It also identifies the activities, thinking, and product style preferences of a company's niche market.

Market segmentation can pinpoint unsatisfied needs for more profitable opportunities. Then the market research results are combined with product design and development. Well-planned private label and confined merchandise can help provide a focused message about the company. Eventually, this will lead to the micro-merchandising of customized products that are carefully tailored to each buyer's expectations.

Fashion forecasting and market research are especially occurring at the retail level and moving backward through the chain to bring the right products to market. Also, companies must continually change as their research shows customers' needs changing. This includes offering "alternative shopping" that consumers want, such as nonstore retailing, as well as traditional store formats. See 25-12.

Database marketing enables fashion companies to provide better service and to use customer recognition devices that build loyalty. As mentioned in Chapter 20, customer relationship management (CRM) offers better service to customers, based on database information. That information is analyzed through ***data mining***, which uses software to discover patterns within a *data warehouse* (accumulated database) and derive actionable responses. Retail databases can identify individual retailers' most profitable shoppers. Purchases are tracked with proprietary (store) and private label (co-branded) credit cards. Companies can see where

QVC, Inc.

25-12 Market research, showing that certain consumers are dissatisfied with traditional shopping, has helped television retailing plan programming that pleases audiences.

customers use the cards and what they buy, providing a "transaction history." Data mining analysis attempts to determine why each customer purchased particular items and what products are now desired by that customer.

Data mining identifies the small percent of customers who generate the largest percentage of sales. Then individually tailored promotional messages and merchandise offers can be directed to these key customers. Special promotions or announcements are sent (often e-mailed) only to customers who purchase certain items, lines, or sizes. This is more effective than doing expensive promotions to large, general audiences. Some stores offer special amenities to particular customer groups, such as a percentage discount on purchases made by senior citizens on a certain day of every week.

Specialized services, such as personal shopping assistance by appointment and bonuses, may be offered to special customers. Also, frequent-shopper loyalty programs issue rewards for shoppers who are frequent credit card users or big spenders. These are aimed at keeping their customers shopping at the store and trying to reduce how much they shop the competition.

Innovative companies will continue to recognize voids in local markets and fill those voids through fast, efficient electronic data interchange (EDI) ordering. They will cater to individual consumers who are not having their needs met, and satisfy these consumers with the right merchandise and service. Instead of "batch-processing" entire clusters of customers, data mining is going toward customizing CRM for individuals.

Trends in Retail Formats

Retail saturation, or ***overstoring***, is the existence of too many stores and shopping centers in a retail trading area vying for limited consumer dollars. An overstored area has so many stores providing the same goods and services that they cannot achieve a fair return on their investment. The industry is saturated in most locations with much more merchandise supply than demand.

In spite of overstoring, retailers continue to expand with more and bigger stores. Retail expansion has grown much faster than growth in consumption. A good portion of annual soft goods shipments goes to fill newly added retail space, not to replenish consumer offtake. Goods remain as inventory–not sold.

The polarization of retailing into upscale shops and low-price discounters can be taken further. As was already discussed, successful small niche retailing combines unique merchandise, product expertise, and strong customer service. Now we will examine large discounters such as general mass merchandisers and niche specialist category killers, 25-13. Another condition is that retail saturation plagues the entire retail industry.

The Polarized Retail Market

Discount Stores: Centralized control, all alike, volume buying, and use the latest technology.

- General mass merchandisers (Wal-Mart)
- Category killers (Sports Authority)

Upscale Shops: Can be entrepreneurial and do local merchandising; some are small shops in malls with selective lines; others are independent boutiques.

25-13 With the polarization of retailing to large discount stores and small upscale shops, the department stores and medium-sized apparel chains in the middle are losing sales.

Also, nonstore formats, such as direct marketing, TV retailing, and online computer are taking market share from stores. Multi-channel retailing is evolving as the answer for retail success.

Discount Retailing

National discount mass merchandisers, off-price stores, factory outlets, and category killers are offering "value retailing." See 25-14. They stock brand-name merchandise, at low prices, in accessible locations. Their discounted shirts, sweaters, and other garments are almost identical to items in more expensive stores,

Great Mall of the Bay Area

25-14 Consumers like to shop in stores that have upscale names and value pricing.

so consumers are eager to buy them at lower prices. Sometimes, large discounters can even get trendy merchandise faster than smaller companies because of electronic transfer of market information. Large discount stores have expanded to carry more SKUs.

Discount retailing is very competitive, with low margins and companies often on the brink of failure. Although large retailers offer big assortments that give consumers greater variety and advantages, these assortments also involve retail management problems. It is hard to keep track of large product assortments and minimize out-of-stock situations.

National discount companies have more capital for innovation and risk-taking than regional stores. Regional discount merchandisers are often undercapitalized, with too much debt and no room for operational errors. Many are behind in computer technology and can't afford to advertise as much as national "power chains." Their stores are large, but unable to compete on volume, and they lack the expertise to find specialized niches. Thus, big national chains have consumed many smaller stores, resulting in an industry dominated by a few giants. For instance, about three-quarters of all discount retailing is controlled by only three companies–Wal-Mart, Kmart, and Target, 25-15.

The large national firms take advantage of buying clout, distribution power, and technology. ***Buying clout*** means that retailers use their power to get rebates, promotions, and additional discounts from their suppliers. Vendors are pushed to cut prices, give retailers exclusivity, and contribute advertising and promotional dollars. Vendors are expected to pay extra distribution costs, and are penalized when they don't conform exactly to rigid rules of retailers. Examples are the use of specific packing labels placed in an exact place on the carton, the use of particular trucking companies, or delivery at a certain date and time only. Too stringent logistical demands by retailers can ruin relationships with suppliers.

25-15 Wal-Mart is the largest retailer in the U.S., followed by Kmart and Target. These large discount chains know how to satisfy their millions of customers.

Charge-backs are penalties or claims against vendors for not following the many different rules set by each retailer. They are deducted by the retailer from the supplier's invoice, previously only for damaged merchandise, cooperative advertising costs, and the recovery of transportation charges for improperly routed merchandise. However, recently some rules and adjustments have become excessive, with suppliers being paid only a portion of what is owed them from retailers. With already low profit margins, many small suppliers have become more selective about their retail accounts. Some only ship on a *C.O.D.* (cash on delivery) basis, refusing to leave the goods unless they receive payment. Other suppliers have gone out of business.

To become more consumer-focused, many mass market discounters are using a category management strategy. ***Category management*** involves managing product groups as business units and customizing them on a store-by-store basis to better satisfy customer needs. It reassigns retail buyers as entrepreneurs, responsible for a small business within a larger enterprise.

For previous buyers to do these category manager tasks, training is required, especially on how to use new information systems for strategic decision making. Managers must gain the ability to turn data into information and actionable plans. The structure also necessitates stronger information-sharing alliances between retailers and suppliers. Ideally, a category manager chooses leading suppliers with whom to jointly develop category plans. The parties share information that was once considered confidential, assess the merchandise assortment, and develop new product programs.

Discounters have also upgraded their services, decor, and fashion images. Service is seen as the key to survival for retailers of every size and price point. Some of the best quick, efficient, and pleasant service is at the low price end today. Customer loyalty grows for stores that offer pleasant shopping.

Economical, but attractive, strip centers are being created for discount retailing because regular mall space is so expensive. Power centers have several large discount retailers on the same site, and usually in close proximity to a regional mall. Some of these mega malls now have up to several million square feet of retail space, with a dozen or so anchor stores. The sizes of some are overwhelming shoppers rather than improving the shopping experience. Regional malls are combating the power centers with more entertainment and leisure-time activities. See 25-16. However, the closing of mom and pop stores that could not compete has taken away the entrepreneurial flavor of some malls.

Outlet malls put manufacturers' stores all together as destination points for shoppers. Bus tours are encouraged. Affluent cross-shoppers are not ashamed to bargain hunt. It has become popular for shoppers to brag about their discount store "cheapskate chic" bargains that are fashionable.

As mentioned in Chapter 12, category killers are large stores that specialize in broad selections of one category of merchandise at a value price. These category-dominate "big boxes" have eliminated their competitors because of good selection and low prices. Category killers offer expertise and time-saving services for everything that consumers need for certain types of activities. They have seized market share from both department stores and specialty retailers. Most have become destination stores.

Nonstore Retailing

Since many consumers have lost interest in shopping, nonstore ***consumer-direct retailing*** formats offer convenience to those who want to shop from home. Nonstore retailing, described in Chapter 12, is gaining strength with consumers who like the variety of shopping choices. Nonstore retailing formats include direct mail catalogs, TV retail sales, and online commerce. Reasons for the popularity of nonstore shopping are listed in 25-17.

People are shopping in what they consider to be painless, more entertaining ways. Much more retail inventory is expected to be sold through consumer-direct retailing in the future. That will lower the inventory requirements of stores, since manufacturers and retail warehouses will ship orders directly to consumers. Consumers do, however, lose the experience of actually seeing, touching, and trying on the merchandise. This results in high rates of returns.

25-16 Besides offering some games and rides, many malls are providing a pleasurable experience where children can enjoy watching a waterfall and throwing pennies into the water.

To succeed with consumer-direct sales, retailers must develop the core competencies listed in 25-18. Since changes to retailing formats are accelerating, market share will go down for companies that do not improve their competencies. Non-store customers are time poor, and want customization of brands, immediate satisfaction, and savings. Consumer-direct retailers are revamping their selling methods, product development, logistics, and sourcing to offer consumers more time and money savings.

Reasons for the Growth of Home Shopping

- Convenience and safety: No hassles with traffic congestion, crime, inattentive or ill-informed store salespeople, limited assortment, long check-out lines, inadequate parking, inconvenient hours, etc.
- Comfort: No need to dress well, do hair, or put on makeup.
- Anonymity: No eye contact or identity recognition.
- Time saving: People work and are too busy to go out shopping when it can be done from home, 24 hours a day, whenever there is a spare moment.
- Improved sales presentation: Today catalogs are more colorful and well designed, TV shopping channels are better programmed, infomercials are more interestingly scripted, and computer web sites have become more user-friendly to disseminate more product information than is communicated at stores.
- Easy payment: Widespread use of credit cards (a necessity for nonstore retailing) gives consumers available credit, easy ordering, and payment convenience.
- Easy ordering: Toll-free phone numbers, or punching in account numbers via telephone or computer, allow for automatic transactions.
- Easy delivery: UPS, FedEx, U.S. mail and other delivery services bring packages quickly to people's homes or places of work.
- Declining fear of technology: People have become accustomed to using catalogs, telephones, and computers for purchases.
- Niche marketing: Specialized computer micro-segmented mailing lists enable sellers to target customers' wants and needs.
- Older, affluent consumer base: Mature population has a high level of discretionary purchasing power and low desire to go out in questionable conditions to shop.

25-17 Consumer-direct retailing is seen by shoppers to have many advantages over traditional shopping in stores. Because of this, it is increasing in popularity.

Core Competencies for Consumer-Direct Success

- Develop the technology to interact with the desired customers
- Strive for consumer intimacy and entertainment that substitute for the social experience of shopping
- Develop trust of descriptions for the look, feel, fit, and quality of items
- Provide consumer-friendly interaction with easy use of catalogs, programs, or systems
- Create access through experience, with an invitation to the next level at the proper time
- Make it affordable and efficient, such as offering discounts for shopping from home

25-18 It is becoming increasingly important to become competent in these areas in order to achieve success with non-store retailing formats.

Lands' End Direct Merchants

25-20 Consumers get to know which catalog companies offer quality goods at value prices and with helpful employees.

Direct-Mail Marketing

Direct-mail marketing is currently the largest, most established form of nonstore retailing. It uses catalogs, bill stuffers, and package inserts to initiate phone and mail sales. Direct marketers can cover a large market area and have low overhead and investment. However, the industry has experienced rapid paper, postage, and delivery cost increases. See 25-19. Also, the addition of more companies to the industry has tightened competition.

Niche catalogs focus on specific size ranges, lifestyles, and fashion levels, 25-20. Specialized catalogs are mailed to larger women, ethnic groups, and people with specific hobbies. Some mail-order companies have expanded globally, now mailing catalogs in Europe and Asia. Models used in the catalogs are sometimes older, black, Asian, Hispanic, or physically disabled, to represent real-life people.

Direct marketers have sophisticated forecasting systems. They understand their customers better than most other soft goods retailers and serve them around the clock with state-of-the-art logistics and fast service. See 25-21. They also have efficient sourcing of quality items from throughout the world.

Direct-mail merchants must be very customer-responsive. If customers are on hold for too long while trying to place an order, or the merchandise is on back-order, they quickly call another catalog company. Stock

Lands' End Direct Merchants

25-19 The business of direct-mail marketing depends on sending out catalogs and shipping merchandise. Increasing paper, postage, and delivery costs have a large impact on profits.

Lands' End Direct Merchants

25-21 Some catalog companies offer personalized monogramming services and are still able to send out the merchandise to consumers within just a few days.

outages have been a problem with some direct mail companies.

Some retailers, like JCPenney and Eddie Bauer, run both store and catalog businesses and use the synergies between them as a tool. New products and strategies are often tested in the catalog and the results monitored before store space is occupied with products. Stock of popular styles is then increased in both the stores and catalog. Lower-demand selections are eliminated.

TV Home Shopping Sales

Cable television shopping channels, such as QVC (Quality Value Convenience) and HSN (Home Shopping Network), sell household fashion items, 25-22. This retailing medium is being perfected as time goes on. Consumers watch these channels for live entertainment, information, and educational value.

TV home shopping channels have vast knowledge about their customers' buying habits. Their marketing lists are not sold or shared with vendors. The companies are diversifying their lines and moving higher in quality and price. Merchandise from well-known retail stores may be featured. Sometimes a free gift is offered with a purchase.

Television retailers try to sell at least $10,000 worth of merchandise per minute. The shopping channel's selling price is usually double the wholesale price. Jewelry accounts for almost half of the sales. Other successes are products that can be demonstrated, with their features and benefits emphasized. In retail stores those items would just hang on a rack or sit on a shelf, without being appreciated for what they can do.

TV retailing gives instant national feedback to fashion marketers in units and dollars about style, size, and color preferences. See 25-23. It can build brand names and increase a producer's customers. Also, since selling is done via live television, it can capitalize on demand, with high immediate sales of inventory. For instance, seconds after the end of a Super Bowl game, a large volume of football jerseys of the winning team can be sold quickly.

When goods are featured on a TV shopping channel, they must already be in the warehouse. Advanced inventory control systems are used. However, the inventory risk belongs to the vendor. If merchandise does not sell, the supplier gets it back within about two weeks instead of getting paid. Football jerseys of the team that lost in the Super Bowl may end up back with the supplier!

The TV home shopping industry is still in its marketing and technological infancy. Experts forecast growth of many more cable shopping channels in the years ahead. They will be segmented and specialized with particular fashion or product emphasis aimed at narrower markets. There will be advanced published listings of when certain shopping programs will air. Vendors are expected to have close ties with TV shopping channels, or sell their products directly to consumers through their own TV channels.

Home shopping television companies are becoming stronger, even though high numbers of purchased items are returned. The companies have a liberal return policy of 30 days with no questions asked. Also, since consumers usually buy on impulse, the companies try

QVC, Inc.

25-22 Stage sets and merchandise for TV home shopping sales are kept ready to provide entertaining sales presentations to consumers.

QVC, Inc.

25-23 Phone operators can see the program stages, and those on stage can see how the show looks on TV screens.

to ship out orders within 24 hours. "Fast-lane" sales have overnight delivery. In the future, TV shopping is expected to change from today's predominantly impulse-driven purchases to more planned purchases.

Infomercials are a more sophisticated format of TV home sales. They are heavy on information, to educate and build intimacy with customers. Home shopping companies are also entering the informercial format, even though it is more successful for selling gadgets than fashion items. Demonstrations are prepared and produced ahead of being broadcast, and the sponsors must pay to put them on the air. Some also rely on follow-up with purchasers, to sell extra items or for replenishment. This is especially true for cosmetics or other health and beauty aids.

Some TV home selling is done with two-way *interactive TV.* It consists of graphic and written presentations of merchandise shown on the screen. The merchandise can then be ordered by Touch-Tone telephone, computer modem, or a special set-top box. The set-top box has a keypad or credit card inserting device for ordering and printing a receipt. Eventually a satellite-based, wireless system will allow consumers to order simply by pointing a remote control device at the item on the screen.

Online Retailing

Online retailing is the selling of merchandise to consumers using personal computers with modems. This is also called electronic retailing. Instead of business-to-business (B2B) commerce it is *business-to-consumer (B2C) commerce.* It includes some CD-ROM, but mostly Internet sales. CD-ROMs are compact discs (read-only memory) that store large amounts of information. They can be distributed for use in computers. Most *Internet sales* are made through the World Wide Web (WWW) system with home computers.

Online retailing offers immediate choices through databases. This will be used more universally as consumers become more comfortable with the technology and Web sites are better planned for ease of use. With progress in computer technology and lower prices for equipment, more home computers are being used as time passes. This also enables retailing to be done globally. Challenges include getting customers to the Web site, getting them to buy, and getting them to come back again and again.

Companies have seen a need to develop security systems for Internet users to confidentially place orders and make transactions with encrypted credit card numbers. New programs are combating Internet payment fraud, providing online approval of credit cards, and offering digital receipts to print. The key is secure information collection and dissemination.

Internet retailers must also address the issue of consumer privacy by adopting clear policies on the use of personal data. Some consumers are reluctant to share information online, such as registering at Web sites. However, e-tailers would like to be able to individualize merchandise offers to specific customers. Some online retailers are posting their privacy policies or addressing users' privacy concerns other ways. The Better Business Bureau has set Internet privacy standards, and awards a certification logo for use on electronic retailing sites that meet them.

CD-ROM catalogs, which can be placed on the Internet, duplicate or exceed the inventory of some paper catalogs. CD-ROM discs do not need to be sent to customers if the catalog is placed on the Internet. This also allows for general access by all consumers (not just known customers) who have PC/modems and a service through which to log on, such as America Online, Netscape, or CompuServe. More and more screen-based catalogs, portals, and electronic shopping malls will evolve, with links to other retail sites that steer shoppers to similar merchandise.

Until now, online retailing has consisted mostly of promotion rather than selling. However, the number of computer shoppers today is expected to increase greatly in the future. Experts predict that the Internet will account for 10-12% of all clothing sales in the near future. Studies have found that an untapped source of consumers who enjoy shopping this way is affluent, well-educated men. Online customers usually spend more than traditional home shoppers.

Online retailing can reduce the high costs of paper and postage of mailed catalogs. Therefore, catalog companies are getting Web sites to sell their merchandise. Manufacturers and television retailers are also going online.

The appearance of merchandise differs between the mediums of mail-order and online catalogs. A paper catalog uses large photographs and a small amount of written description. On Web sites, it is hard to have a composed spread with many items. Big photos take a long time to download, so they must be kept small and light. However, there is more room for text to tell the story of each item. Improvements in computer graphics and speed will aid the process in the future.

The Internet Mall or portal concept enables shoppers to browse and make selections. Customers can summon product reviews, ask questions, and comparison shop. A shopper who selects the main category of "slacks" would be given a series of options to narrow the choices. The system might get down to specific brands of women's wool slacks in dark, solid colors and certain sizes. Plus, companies will track shoppers to see what they ask about and buy. This enables marketing databases to continue to be fine-tuned.

Technology is transforming how vendors and retailers do business. New start-up companies are based on innovative distribution ideas. Eventually, televisions, computers, and modems will combine into one piece of electronic retailing equipment. Customization of products will be done by shoppers asking questions of the system, for instance, to mix and match outfits. Other technologies may make different methods of electronic retailing available. At each stage of innovation, successful fashion companies will conquer the challenges by using it to their advantage when appropriate.

Multi-Channel Retailing

"Pure-play" Internet retailers, that sell only via Web sites, have not been very successful. It has been hard for them to establish their trade names and reliability with consumers, and costs have exceeded sales revenues. Thus, retailers are using a combination of several selling channels (stores, catalogs, Web sites, etc.). This is known as ***multi-channel retailing***. To be successful, e-commerce is being incorporated seamlessly into existing store or catalog businesses, with all the company's channels having the same product range, merchandise planning and stock systems, and customer relationship management (CRM). Companies need strong information technology (IT). Web sites strengthen existing customer relationships. Customers can shop any time, any place, anywhere. Those that do not perform well in all channels are at a disadvantage.

Many consumers are using the Internet for gathering information about purchases they plan to make in stores or by phone. Consumers do product research, check availability and pricing, and find special offers online. Thus, retail Web sites bring shoppers to store locations, as well as store locations showing products to shoppers that they can purchase online. With Web sites, retailers hope to attract new customers and reconnect with past customers. Similarly, manufacturers are using this "remote marketing" to explain their lines, take direct orders, and/or send shoppers to stores that carry their items.

Although large corporations often have their own IT departments, most fashion merchandising firms do not have expertise in Web site development and maintenance. Software is available to help retailers with this, but if not done correctly, poor Web sites anger "e-shoppers" and send them away. Thus, most retailers outsource this function to experts who know how to set up easy-to-use, secure sites and have done so for many companies entering the e-commerce arena.

Catalog and TV retailing companies were the first apparel retailers to add Internet sales, since it complements the ordering and shipping infrastructure of their businesses. Each company's mail-order catalog emphasizes their Web site address. Through the Internet, they have been able to reduce their costs of printing and mailing, as well as more effectively target consumers. On the Internet, they can also change their promotion and pricing on short notice. Additionally, via e-mail, customers can be sent automatic order updates, sale notices, and merchandise messages based on their shopping preferences. This enables companies to have ongoing dialogs of communication with customers.

Some traditional retailers have electronic storefronts. ***Electronic storefronts*** let consumers scroll through the departments of a store that has been simulated electronically, either by aisle, product category, or item. When the order is placed through the modem, it is immediately picked and delivered for a small charge. Wireless satellite ordering services will do this in the future.

There are now computer kiosks in stores and malls for consumers to use. Customers can "call up" information, view product demonstrations, and order merchandise. Some hotels and office buildings also have these "micromall" computer terminals. Shoppers can scroll through electronic catalogs and place orders to be delivered directly to their homes.

Survival Business Strategies

The fashion business today is increasingly complex, requiring strategic planning to gain market share and increase sales and profits. ***Strategy*** is large-scale, long-range planning for achieving an organization's objectives. It's slant can be very different from the short-term, bottom-line profit thinking that is often done to please stockholders.

The tougher fashion business climate is a result of an oversupply of goods and retailers, and the fact that consumers are not spending. To survive, there is both horizontal and vertical restructuring of the industry, as well as more emphasis being placed on employee training and service.

Restructuring involves examining a business to see what changes can make it better, reallocating resources and employees, and re-charting its course. Restructuring strategies might include making the company bigger, smaller, more efficient, more specialized, global rather than national, etc. The end results are aimed at higher revenues, lower expenses, and better profits.

Horizontal Restructuring of the Industry

One way retailers made money in the past was to continually open new stores. However, with decreasing domestic market growth, this no longer works. Fashion businesses are increasing profits, with better efficiency and increased market shares, through consolidation. ***Consolidation*** is the uniting of two or more parts into one. It is taking place at all levels of the industry. Jobs, departments, and divisions are being consolidated. Specialized work is being outsourced.

Horizontal consolidation of the industry is being accomplished with acquisitions, takeovers, and mergers. Downsizing and bankruptcies are other restructuring results of the high costs that have eaten into profits.

An ***acquisition*** is the purchase of another company, with the buying company gaining the controlling interest. For retailers to expand, buying another retail company is easier and less expensive than building new stores. Plus, it eliminates some of the competition. On the other hand, a company that is sold or sells part of its organization is said to transact a *divestiture.* See 25-24. Many previously well-established local stores with old family names no longer exist. They have been acquired to become divisions of large, corporate ownership groups.

A *takeover* is a change in the controlling interest of a corporation. It may be a friendly acquisition or a hostile takeover that tries to replace existing management. Hostile takeovers often destroy companies, resulting in high debt, the sale of some parts of the original firm, and loss of many employees' jobs. Companies that successfully resist takeover bids are also left in poorer financial condition because of the expensive legal efforts required to fight the takeover.

A ***merger*** is the joining of two companies to form a new one. Mergers can consolidate functions, such as combining the buying or advertising functions of both companies into one. They might also centralize data and credit systems for economies of scale. Distribution systems are streamlined, too. The chart in 25-25 gives many of the reasons why two companies might merge.

Downsizing is the reduction of the size of a business to reduce costs and become more efficient. Such reorganizing eliminates ineffective factories or stores and poorly performing divisions. The companies can then concentrate on making their profitable parts even better. Downsizing also gets rid of redundant levels of management and hourly employees who are not needed. This results in much flatter corporate structures, with leaner management hierarchies. Extra responsibilities are placed on the remaining personnel.

Retailers are downsizing by reducing the size of their stores, closing their least profitable branches, minimizing the size of their inventory holdings, and dropping unprofitable merchandise categories. In general, apparel categories have been kept, with hardlines dropped. This is because fashion items have higher margins per square foot and faster turnover than large, bulky items. Retailers try to downsize with no loss in volume by remodeling facilities and empowering employees. At the same time they are decreasing energy and interest costs and increasing theft prevention devices.

Bankruptcies, or the inability to pay debts, are also occurring among companies. The Bankruptcy Reform Act includes "Chapter 11," "Chapter 7," and other categories of bankruptcies.

The objective of "Chapter 11" bankruptcies is to get financial strength back and continue business operations. It is an orderly and fair settlement of obligations. The debtor keeps control of the business and its operation while it tries to work out of its difficulties. Implementation includes renegotiated payment schedules, restructured debt, reorganized management, and trimmed-down operations. Some divisions of the company may be sold. Companies that restructure under "Chapter 11" protection often emerge from bankruptcy in a few years as stronger firms.

25-24 This store has been sold to another retail company. After it closes, the new company plans to open it under new management and with a new name.

Reasons Companies Merge

- To increase market share with a larger customer base
- To open or enter new markets with a new customer base
- To consolidate capital (money, plants, equipment)
- To expand the line with a broader mix of products
- To eliminate one or more competitors
- To strengthen management or gain different expertise and viewpoints
- To obtain undervalued assets that are not competing well on their own
- To improve research/development by combining innovation activity
- To gain access to new technologies the other company has
- To gain access to foreign production or foreign markets
- To gain production capacity for synergies or economies of scale
- To consolidate buying, distribution, and service functions
- To get prestige and name recognition from the other company's name or brands
- To integrate vertically for more control of the distribution chain

25-25 Companies merge with each other for one or many of these reasons. With the company mergers that you know about, try to decide which of these reasons apply to their situations.

"Chapter 7" bankruptcy means going out of business, 25-26. It ends the company. The company ***liquidates,*** which involves selling off all assets and using the proceeds to pay outstanding debts on a percentage basis. The amount might be "25 cents on the dollar," in which case all parties that are owed money by the bankrupt business would receive one-quarter (25 percent) of the total owed to them.

Consolidation of retailers results in a concentration of fewer, more powerful companies that have huge buying power. Examples of power department store corporations are the Federated, May, and Dillard companies. Large buying volume is centralized, which makes it hard for smaller marginal retailers to compete.

The large companies have better merchandising, pricing, and store designs. They place more pressure on textile and apparel suppliers to provide low-priced, quality products. Also, large retailers have trimmed the number of vendors used. Some suppliers have been dropped and new ones have a hard time starting relationships with retail giants. However, producers have become more powerfully consolidated too, resulting in fewer, but larger, vendors. Retailers have closer ties to their suppliers.

Vertical Restructuring of the Industry

Vertical integration is also consolidation. Retailer and supplier lines have blurred. Manufacturers' factory outlets and retail private label goods provide companies with internal resources and supply chain efficiency. Their costs are lower since a middle layer has been eliminated. This allows them to compete against the stronger horizontally integrated companies.

More manufacturers are opening outlet stores to increase sales volume and control distribution. They stock the same as or different lines than they sell to traditional retailers. On the other hand, retailer's private label goods have become more accepted by consumers since national brands and designer merchandise are now in discount stores. Large retailers have their own design teams, quality labs, and manufacturing organizations. They promote entire lifestyle concepts with private label lines, 25-27.

Stores that offer types of fashion merchandise that are similar to competitors can achieve differentiation through private label programs. They must develop flexibility and speed of product development to satisfy market needs. It requires visionary leadership to respond to social, economic, and technological trends.

Since the entire globe is now integrated into a world economy, with foreign markets growing faster than the U.S. market, restructuring is being done by corporations on a worldwide basis. Companies are formulating strategies to aggressively go after retailing,

25-26 This store has not been sold. It has failed and is going out of business, selling all its assets.

Kmart

25-27 Kmart's private label Kathy Ireland ACTIVE line aims at combining comfort with fashion for active people.

as well as manufacturing, opportunities in the international marketplace.

Employee Training and Service

There are changing attitudes about workforce recruiting and performance, too. ***Organizational performance*** includes the individual quality of work done by each employee and the overall performance of the department or company as a whole. A team approach is emphasized now for higher productivity. Companies must find good workers and then train, utilize, and pay them better to accomplish this. See 25-28. Then employees will also feel better about their work.

Retailing has traditionally been plagued with high *employee turnover*, or rates of workers leaving and having to be replaced with new hirees. Money and time is needed to train new employees. Also, it takes awhile for the job performance or new workers to come up to the standards of experienced workers. Thus, worker retention is desired.

Better training of personnel takes time and effort, but is essential to provide the required service that increases profits. Employees must be taught to put customers first. They must be able to constructively deal with change, grasp the financial implications of their jobs and share in financial successes, plus understand how their work affects other employees and the company's goals. Employees can be empowered to use their training, experience, and judgment in dealing with issues as they arise. This encourages communication, creativity, adaptability, dedication, and leadership. Decision time is shorter when employees are more motivated to be responsive.

Companies are sending employees to more seminars, conferences, and development meetings. They are also hiring specialized personnel to perform specific tasks. In this way, companies can take advantage of emerging opportunities and develop key differential advantages. Their employees provide better customer service, which builds shoppers' loyalty.

Technology Leading to Customization

Companies must invest in technological developments to adapt to competition and trends. See 25-29. Success in today's faster, more flexible industry belongs to those who respond the quickest to market opportunities. In the U.S. this will be done through ***agile manufacturing,*** which is a "seamless" data capture system of production and delivery that makes information-based decisions quickly. It integrates information technology, mechanization, and team-based flexible manufacturing. It depends on communications being transmitted and received electronically. It allows consumers to be personally involved in selecting the exact clothes they want, also resulting in a perfect fit.

The agile manufacturing system combines

- quick response (QR) partnership alliances
- electronic data interchange (EDI) or Internet linkages
- radio frequency (RF) wireless transmission of point-of-sale information
- visualized data displays for manufacturers and retailers to track sales volume trends
- precise three-dimensional body scanning
- interactive design stations
- customized single ply cutting and digital printing
- flexible assembly with empowered team modules and robotics
- direct shipment of finished goods to consumers

Body scanning facilities to collect individual sizing information electronically are already in some retail

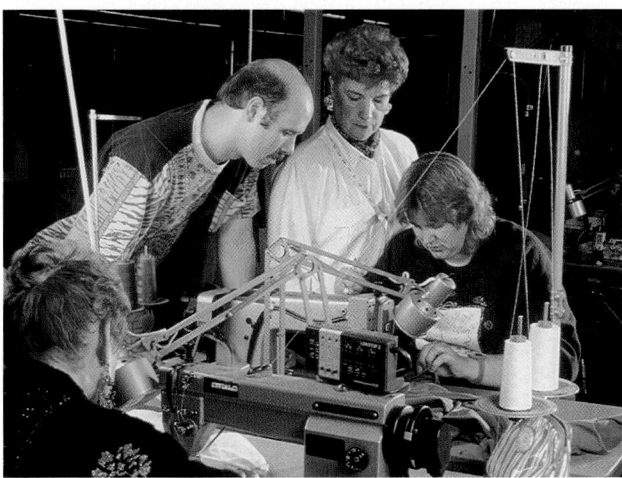

A and Z Industries, Inc.

25-28 Companies are striving for higher performance by training their employees well and encouraging team cooperation.

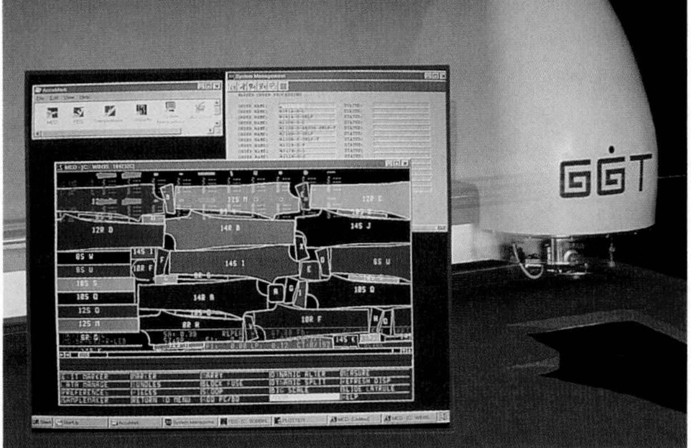

Gerber Garment Technology, Inc.

25-29 Apparel cutting equipment being used today sends pattern data instantly to an automated cutter for quick and economical cutting of garment parts. The marker is in the computer, not on the fabric.

Textile/Clothing Technology Corporation

25-30 Body scanning records the measurements and contours of a person's body so garments can be made specifically for that person.

centers and contained in some home equipment, 25-30. The information is stored on a smart card (updated as often as needed) that is inserted like a credit card to be read electronically. The smart card (introduced in Chapter 5) has a tiny integrated-circuit chip embedded in a credit card-sized piece of plastic. The chip allows the card to process and store the data.

Consumers can see new fashion trends in video catalogs, on screens at retail kiosks, through interactive TV, or on the Internet. Customers can then request specifications and suggest modifications. They can change colors, patterns, and accessories until they create the perfect selection. See 25-31. When they have garments the way they like them, they can see how those fashions look on them through virtual reality. ***Cyber-retailing*** shows consumers' own images on the screen to see how specific clothing will look on them. They can also see themselves in the outfits in appropriate settings.

A radio-frequency transmission of data exchange with a design workstation allows for the rapid design and pattern creation. Order information is sent electronically to manufacturing, where a computer generates a marker. The marker is sent to a single-ply laser cutter that cuts

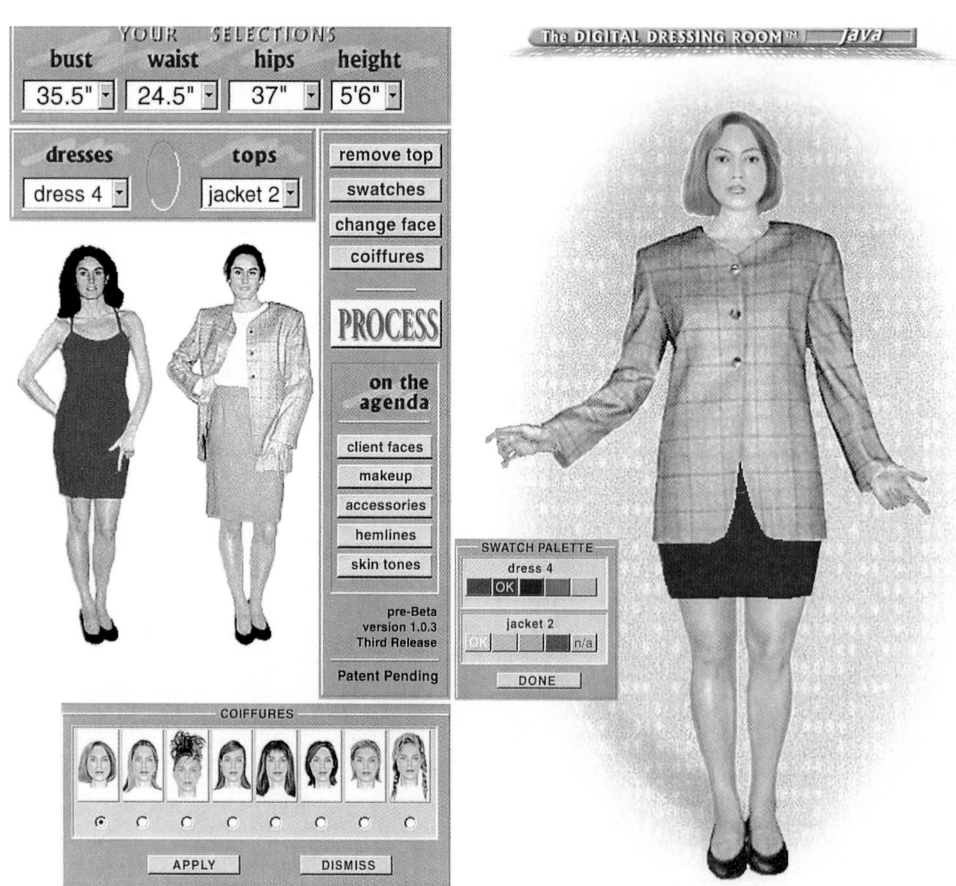

The Digital Dressing Room/Compucloz Corporation

25-31 Using this interactive program on the Internet, consumers can input their measurements, hair colors and styles, and other data to "try on" clothes they select. The concept was developed to license to retailers, department stores, and catalogs for electronic retail sales.

Textile/Clothing Technology Corporation

25-32 For customized computer apparel production, single-ply cutting of garment parts can take place extremely fast.

fabric at lightening speed, 25-32. White fabric is cut, which helps to avoid excess inventories of many different patterned materials. The cut parts are then surface-printed in the motif, style, and size specified by the order information received. Then the cut and printed parts are sent through flexible manufacturing, probably a module (team) approach with cross-trained operators for efficient manufacturing. Finally, the item is packed and shipped directly to the customer.

This ***mass customization,*** or offering individually-made items to everyone, will eventually change retail companies into order facilitators, since actual stock will not be needed in retail stores. All technology will be tied together to respond to the customer. Retail stores will be storefronts, with items not taken home from there.

Comparison of 20th and 21st Century Business Trends

20th Century	21st Century
A national economy	A global economy
An industrial society	An informational society
Paper systems	Electronic systems
Forced technology	User-friendly technology
Short-term considerations	Long-term strategy
Dominance of the northern U.S. states	Dominance moves south and west in U.S.
Society offers limited personal choices	A multiple-option society
Volume manufacturing—economies of scale	Flexible focus on customers' needs
Human-driven operations	System-driven operations
Mass marketing	Market creation and niche responsiveness
Push—move the product	Pull—respond to market demand
Service is only a routine function	Emphasis on service as value added
Unload unwanted goods offshore	Global markets have prime emphasis
R&D limited to improving products	Innovation for different product ideas
Tight control of employees	Empowerment of employees, teams
Layered management hierarchies	Leaner, flatter company structures
Telephone expediting	B2B purchasing
Closely guarded information	Information sharing for mutual benefit
Detached, analytical leadership (people told what to do)	Decentralized people development (people asked for participation value)
Obsession with internal company matters	Obsession with pleasing customers
Change considered a threat	Change viewed as opportunity
Companies/employees stagnate together	Companies/employees mix and match
Companies maintain same product mix	Changing product mix responds to market
Large inventories are ready to fill orders	No inventories—production fills orders
Constant throughput time is maintained	Faster throughput and deliveries
Employees methods are somewhat efficient	Technology raises efficiency
Quality is desired	Quality is expected and assured
Antagonism among pipeline segments	Partnership alliances among companies
Mid-sized companies with lack of direction	Horizontal and vertical consolidation
Effort to make old methods better	Revolutionary new methods used

25-33 This list, compiled from ideas presented in the speeches and writings of many business futurists, sums up what has occurred in recent history in the left-hand column. These are contrasted with ideas about the "new economy" of the future, in the right-hand column.

However, much of this technology is in the future. Stores will continue to provide merchandise for quite a while longer!

The agile manufacturing system is accomplished with trust-based partnerships that automatically and quickly execute information-driven decisions, through a flexible, empowered workforce. It takes the cost out of the process and puts in better quality through efficiency. There is no need for large warehouses of inventory. Long lead times are eliminated, with deliveries made in days (or hours) rather than months. Production risks of making the wrong styles in advance are eliminated. Consumers have limitless choices to get exactly what they want at affordable prices.

To understand how dynamic the latest fashion business trends are, compare the items on the left and right sides of 25-33. You can become an important part of the exciting new textile/apparel pipeline of the 21st Century!

Summary

Rapid changes are occurring in the fashion industry. Today's consumers desire goods of better quality, lower cost, and instant availability. Retailers are polarizing on prices, with the demise of the middle-price market. Demographics and psychographics are used to supply market information.

Microsegmentation of the market is providing opportunities for niche manufacturing and niche retailing. Sophisticated database research is pinpointing voids in the market, for which products are being developed.

The format of discount retailing is a strong trend. Discount general mass merchandisers, off-price stores, and factory outlets, as well as niche specialist discounters called category killers, offer value retailing. Large national firms take advantage of buying clout, distribution power, and technology. All types of retailers are plagued by retail saturation.

Nonstore retailing formats are gaining strength, offering convenience to consumers who want to shop from home, because they are time-poor, and want customization of brands, immediate satisfaction, and savings. Direct-mail marketing can cover a large market area with low overhead and investment. TV retailing provides entertainment, information, and educational value, besides selling goods. Online retailing is electronic business-to-consumer commerce. Multi-channel retailing is proving to be the most successful strategy.

Because of the tougher fashion business climate, consolidation is taking place in the industry. Horizontal restructuring is being done through acquisitions, mergers, and downsizing. Vertical restructuring is resulting in more manufacturers' factory outlets and retail private label goods. Additionally, better employee training and service are providing good service that raises profits.

Technology is enabling companies to be more flexible to respond quickly to market opportunities. Future customization will give consumers limitless choices to get exactly what they want at affordable prices. Exciting changes are occurring for fashion businesses in the 21st Century.

To Know

cross-shopping
database marketing
data mining
overstoring
buying clout
charge-backs
category management
power centers
consumer-direct retailing
online retailing
multi-channel retailing
electronic storefront
strategy
consolidation
acquisition
merger
downsizing
liquidate
organizational performance
agile manufacturing
cyber-retailing
mass customization

To Review

1. What do successful, innovative companies do about change?
2. How can retailers help consumers who are time-poor?
3. For what two reasons is the mature market (over age 50) getting larger?
4. Besides showing just the age, gender, and income level of customers, what does sophisticated database research identify?
5. What do frequent-shopper loyalty programs do?
6. In general, what three things do successful small niche retail companies combine?
7. What is a common financial situation for regional discount retailers?
8. With the overstored condition, a good portion of annual soft goods shipments go where?
9. What has the closing of mom and pop stores done to malls?
10. What is the main reason for the high rates of returns with nonstore retailing?
11. What inventory situation has been a problem with some direct-mail companies?
12. Who bears the inventory risk of goods that are featured on TV shopping channels? Explain.
13. How does two-way interactive TV work?

14. Give three reasons why online commerce will soon be used universally.
15. For what are consumers using the Internet before buying in stores or by phone?
16. In what four ways are retailers downsizing?
17. Why have many retail companies kept apparel categories and dropped hardline merchandise?
18. What does implementation of Chapter 11 bankruptcy include?
19. Why are costs lower as a result of vertical restructuring?
20. What is body scanning?

To Do

1. In a group of four students, try to be creative to develop retailing ideas for many years in the future. Two students should develop a market research form with many pertinent questions to be answered. Each of the two should interview at least six people (parents, friends, relatives, teachers, etc.). Try to discover how the market research subjects would most prefer to purchase their apparel including ways that possibly do not yet exist! Have them privately consider their time restraints, finances, quality expectations, fashion level preferences, etc. The other two students should do library research about where the latest national demographic and psychographic trends are headed. Relating that to knowledge of retailing, formulate some specific ideas for long-term strategy for a "different" industry in the future. Try to "dream" outside the current structure that exists. What "reengineering" of the industry might be done to provide quality products, quickly, with wonderful customer service? Then, altogether, use your imaginations and don't be embarrassed about ideas you think sound ridiculous! Then try to evaluate if you think a profit can be made at the same time as providing a pleasurable experience to consumers. Compile your combined results and give a report to the class about your market research and demographic/psychographic findings, and your futuristic ideas.
2. Visit two large discount merchandisers (regional or national) and two small niche retailers. Compare the merchandise fashion level, quality, and prices among them. Talk to the store managers, if possible, and ask if they do database research. Try to recognize how they operate (perform their merchandising, marketing, etc.). What target market are they trying to satisfy? Is it working? Why or why not? Compare their store locations. Are they in power centers, malls, strip centers, stand-alone, etc.? Prepare your findings, including an analysis, in a written report.
3. Collect at least six different mail-order catalogs (and more if possible). Analyze the marketing subtleties of each, such as personalized messages, entertaining copy, or other ways to get the attention of customers. What other ideas might help them sell to their market? How might they expand their business in the future? Describe your analysis to the class as you show them the catalogs. Ask for additional input and discussion from the class.
4. Reread the last section of the chapter ("Technology Leading to Customization"). Then, in a group of five students, with each student taking one of the other sections of the chapter (changing consumer market, niche marketing, retail format trends, nonstore retailing, and survival business strategies) prepare a presentation for the class that shows how technology is currently being used in these areas to progress toward the agile manufacturing system of the future
5. With another student, explain and "act out" the meaning of adjoining items in the two lists of 25-33. One student will represent 20th Century phrases and the other the new 21st Century phrases. Also field questions from classmates if they do not understand any of the concepts as you present them.

PART 8

Your Future in the Fashion Industry

CHAPTER 26

Is a Fashion Career in Your Future?

After studying this chapter, you will be able to

- assess popular views about fashion careers.
- describe how to select a career path.
- list educational requirements for fashion careers.
- describe how to gain preliminary work experience.
- explain what compensation can be expected in fashion careers.
- describe ethical and legal issues of employment.
- summarize the probable future for employment within the industry.

Since fashion is everywhere, fashion-related employment offers vast options and environments. Exciting, stimulating jobs in most areas of the textile/apparel pipeline are located throughout the United States and world. They offer different amounts of compensation and require different levels of education and training. Workplaces are becoming more diverse.

An Overview of the Field of Fashion

Fashion employment is often viewed as glamorous, involving beautiful merchandise and attractive people, 26-1. Fashion offers some of the world's most fascinating, challenging, and exciting careers. However, it also demands hard work and dedication. The advantages and disadvantages of fashion careers can depend upon a person's viewpoint. Few positions offer a typical nine-to-five workday. Long hours include evenings and weekends. Often retail stores must be staffed when other businesses are closed. However, sometimes there is a day off in the middle of the week to accomplish personal chores.

Lord West Formalwear

26-1 The view of fashion employment that is generally held by the public is exemplified by exquisite clothes being worn by slender, good-looking people. Although this is part of the industry, other less glamorous aspects also exist.

The Fashion Institute of Design and Merchandising, California

26-2 Companies in the fashion industry are employing well-prepared workers who can use new technology and efficient methods.

The seasonality of fashion work can result in hectic, heavy times followed by slow, dull times. Production schedules, stocks of holiday inventories, or other deadlines must be met at peak times. Often there are problems to solve, deadlines to meet, and pressures to make a profit.

Some people desire fashion careers that offer worldwide travel. Others want to remain close to home, commuting to an office, factory, or store. More people are telecommuting, or working at home with computer work stations, fax machines, and other home office resources. There are increasingly specialized fashion job opportunities in or near metropolitan areas that are large fashion centers. On the other hand, retail stores are located everywhere and need qualified, hard-working employees. Some companies require employees to relocate in order to advance.

Companies in the soft goods chain are improving their methods, technology, and image. They are trying to attract more competent and talented workers who have higher skills and knowledge than in the past. See 26-2. Computer literacy is a must. Good jobs in the dynamic, fast-moving world of fashion are not easy to get, but they are worth striving for as a goal.

Steps Along a Career Path

There is a difference between a job and a career. A ***job*** is a specific work assignment or position within an industry, with certain duties, roles, or functions. A *job description* is a written statement of what the employee holding a specific job is expected to do. It usually outlines specific tasks and responsibilities of a job, guidelines for the person holding the job to follow, authority of the employee, and expectations of accomplishments. See 26-3.

A ***career*** is a lifelong field of employment, or vocation, through which people progress. It includes various jobs that usually lead to higher levels of employment. The total of the jobs held make up a *career path*, or the order of jobs worked in a person's life. For instance, college graduates often begin with low-level jobs where they learn the industry "from the ground up." These jobs may eventually lead to executive-level positions.

Some fashion industry careers offer less occupational security than careers in other fields. Employees tend to change companies frequently because of the changeability and seasonal nature of much of the industry. However, that is also how some talented

Fashion Institute of Technology/John Senzer, Photographer

26-3 The job description for this fashion designer might be to oversee all the designs of a company, design one of the lines, or assist with certain designs, depending on her level of employment.

people move up the ladder of success. Others move up within the same company, by proving themselves at each job level.

Career planning is the process of outlining the steps involved in reaching a career goal. Based on your strengths and weaknesses, and commitment to the work, a certain level may be reached. You should plan to hold jobs that build on strengthening your skills and showing your talents, so you can progress toward your top goal. This may also involve working for several different companies.

Job Levels Along the Way

Fashion career paths can provide personal satisfaction. There are opportunities for unskilled, semiskilled, and skilled workers. Jobs at every level provide an opportunity to grow in knowledge and skills, and change career direction. Many require workers to move to or visit other geographic locations.

Entry-level jobs are beginning jobs in a career. They usually require little or no specific training or experience. They provide a "foot in the door" and a chance to learn about the business from the inside. They also provide a chance for employees to prove themselves, in order to move up in the industry in the future.

One of the most popular ways to start a career in the fashion field, if you have no higher education, is to gain experience with a job as a stock clerk or salesperson in retailing. See 26-4. You may eventually move up into management or buying positions.

26-4 The jobs of retail stock clerk and salesperson can be careers in themselves or jobs to gain experience for higher-level positions in the future.

The beginning level in retailing, if you are a college graduate, may be as a salesperson, assistant buyer, assistant manager, clerical assistant to a buyer, head of stock, or executive trainee. An aspiring fashion designer is likely to begin as a pattern maker, sample maker, fitting model, assistant designer, or helper who runs errands. The extra education and training enables you to have faster job advancement and higher pay.

Management positions are concerned with running the business. They deal with planning, organizing, controlling, implementing, and monitoring the program of the organization. They are involved with *administration,* or the tasks and employees concerned with the overall running of the company. Management employees must be able to think clearly, analyze information, and communicate their ideas. They supervise others and administer strategic decisions that try to result in the most efficient and profitable operations.

Lower management jobs are generally held by people newly hired after receiving college degrees. They move up to *middle management* positions after acquiring some experience and training. These jobs involve a higher degree of responsibility than a lower management level.

Talbots; AEON Group

26-5 Arnold B. Zetcher is President and CEO of the successful retail firm, Talbots, Inc. He is the top executive of the company.

Upper management is only achieved by devoted employees who prove themselves as strategic thinkers and hard workers. Men and women reach these positions after they have acquired maturity and a thorough knowledge of all aspects of the business. The *top management* level is only reached by a very few people. They might have the title of vice president, president, chief operating officer (COO), chief financial officer (CFO), or chief executive officer (CEO) of their company, 26-5. Each vice president is in charge of a large segment of the firm, such as domestic sales or overseas operations.

Selecting a Career Path

Those who want to enter the fashion industry should believe in themselves, yet try to avoid unrealistic perceptions when planning their futures. Good levels of success can be achieved with training, ambition, and energy. Those with a pleasing personality, genuine interest in people, and willingness to work hard and

General Fashion Career Categories	
Advertising	Personnel management
Apparel manufacturing	Product development
Display design	Promotion management
Distribution logistics	Public relations
Dressmaking/tailoring	Retail buying
Educator/trainer	Retail sales
Fabric sales	Showroom sales
Fashion buying	Special events coordination
Fashion design	Store management
Fashion illustration	Store planning/designing
Fashion journalism	Textile chemistry
Fashion photography	Textile design
Fashion show planning	Textile manufacturing
Fixture/prop design	Trend forecasting
International marketing	Wardrobe consulting
Market research	Wholesaling
Pattern making	Window dressing

26-6 These are some of the categories from which a person might select a fashion career. Other, more specific, directions might be discovered after entering the industry.

continue to learn almost always succeed in the fashion field. By nature, fashion means constant change, and many people enjoy the variety offered by fashion jobs.

Preparation for your career should include careful planning and study. Your career choice is very important and will influence all aspects of your adult life. It will affect your future lifestyle, self-esteem, and how others view you. It is wise to think about the effect the career might have on such things as where you will live, family life, income, degree of pressure and responsibility the job requires, number of hours devoted to the job, and social activities. The "right" fashion-related position exists for almost anyone who is interested. Several areas are listed in 26-6. A realistic evaluation of careers in relation to your goals will help to eliminate a mismatch between you and your career.

You will probably work for 40 years or more in your chosen career path. Thus, you owe it to yourself to choose a career carefully to ensure that your work years will be personally satisfying. Jobs do not need to be dull or routine. The most satisfying career for you has work activities that you enjoy and can give you the rewards you seek. By meshing personal needs with employers' needs, it can be a source of continued learning and pleasure.

To choose the right career path for you, first get to know yourself. Then learn as much as possible about various careers. With an understanding of yourself and careers, you can set goals and objectives to lead your efforts of obtaining rewarding life work. You can set your personal goals and aim for them. You can get the education and develop the skills needed for entry-level jobs in the area that seems most satisfying to you. Use the career planning chart in 26-7 as an outline for the process.

Outline of Career Planning Process

1. *Evaluate yourself* by assessing your aptitudes and interests, as well as your career and personal expectations.
2. *Investigate careers* to select what realistically suits you and sounds the best to you.
3. *Get the needed education and training* to increase necessary skills and have the proper credentials.
4. *Expand your competencies* through work experience during school years, or meaningful involvement in extracurricular activities, volunteer work, professional associations, and training seminars.
5. *Build a network of contacts* to spread the word about your availability and credentials.
6. *Package yourself* with a strong resume, professional-looking cover letters, sharp interviewing skills, and a terrific portfolio (if needed) to sell yourself to potential employers.
7. *Maintain ongoing awareness* of the direction of the industry and opportunities for you within it.

26-7 Use this outline as you go through your career planning process. Also, review it periodically as you progress through your long-term career path in later years.

Evaluate Yourself

A sincere self-assessment is needed to determine the kinds of work you would like to do and are able to do. Seriously consider your expectations concerning family issues, personal values, and general objectives. Begin to pay attention to your job-related interests and aptitudes. Then develop your skills.

Sample Fashion Activities	
Analyze lifestyle trends	Hire employees
Analyze public opinion	Illustrate fashion ideas
Arrange store merchandise	Improve production efficiency
Be responsible for a showroom	Make contact with new customers
Buy merchandise for stores	Manage a large sales staff
Calculate supply and demand	Manage a small retail shop
Choose fabrics and notions	Manage company expenses
Combine colors and textures	Model clothes
Compute production costs	Organize projects or work flow
Coordinate employee benefits	Oversee apparel manufacturing
Coordinate fashion outfits	Promote new fashions
Decorate store windows	Purchase production materials
Design clothes	Research new fiber innovations
Design fabric patterns	Research what/why people are buying
Design fashion show sets/props	Run a company
Design retail store interiors	Sell ideas
Design advertising, signage, etc.	Sell clothing lines to retail buyers
Design store displays	Set production schedules
Determine a budget	Supervise people
Draw floorplans	Survey public opinion
Explain sales techniques	Take fashion pictures
Figure sales increases	Test fabrics or apparel
Forecast fabric/fashion trends	Work in a creative team
Give fashion lectures/commentaries	Write fashion scripts
Help customers evaluate choices	

26-8 To help you decide in what direction to go with your career plans, consider which of these activities interest you. You will probably choose many of them. Some are similar and you may want to add others.

Interests

Interests are the things you like. You might determine your interests by deciding what job activities you would like to do. See 26-8. Evaluate your interests and match them with various career choices.

Aptitudes

Tests can determine your aptitudes. Your ***aptitudes*** are your talents—what you are naturally good at doing. They indicate the types of work in which you would probably excel. For instance, with an aptitude for

Bobbin, a Miller Freeman Inc. Company

26-9 People who are self confident, outgoing, and like to work with others have natural aptitudes to be in sales work.

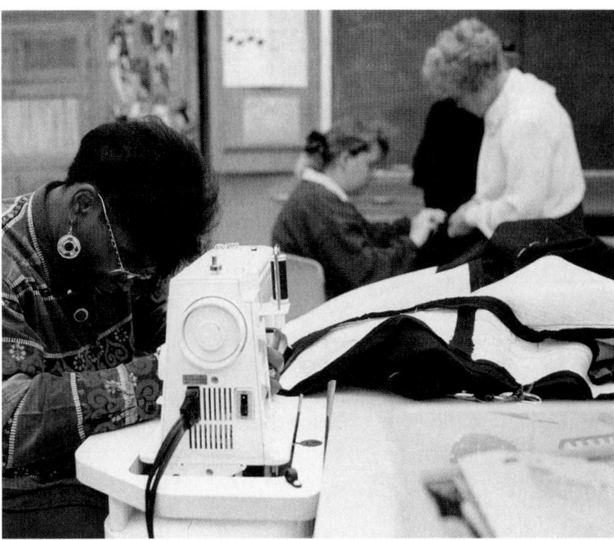

Ball State University, Indiana

26-10 For those who have aptitudes and interests in sewing, formal training in tailoring can greatly improve their skills.

writing, you could probably be successful in fashion journalism, advertising, and audio-visual work. With an aptitude for science, you might develop new textile fibers and finishes, or do product planning. Outgoing people usually excel in sales work and in public relations careers, 26-9. With a natural talent for working with others, you might want an education or personnel career. Visually creative people do well in design, display, advertising, photography, and illustration. Good health and stamina are needed for the demanding work of retail buyers, buying office representatives, magazine editors, and fashion coordinators. Those with mathematical reasoning and logical thinking tend to be good at managing factory production, market research, fashion assortment buying, or running entire retail units.

You have probably taken some aptitude tests in school, and know the results. If not, this can be arranged through your school vocational counselor. Also, think about your specific accomplishments at certain times, events, or jobs. You can make interesting self-discoveries as you "take stock" of these. Your accomplishments in school, at work, and during sports and leisure activities have provided you with good learning experiences. They also indicate some of your strengths, since you have used many abilities to achieve the accomplishments.

Skills

Skills, or abilities of doing specific tasks, in the areas of your aptitudes can then be developed with the right education and training. See 26-10. Good communication skills are required for almost every job these days. Most jobs are requiring workers to have more training, as newer technology is introduced into the workplace, 26-11.

Department of Consumer Studies; University of Delaware

26-11 Schools of higher education offer courses from the basic skills of the fashion industry to the most advanced technological innovations used in fashion companies.

Evaluate Careers

To make wise and realistic choices about your future vocation, you must also investigate specific careers and match them to your interests, aptitudes, and skills. Learn about the job possibilities that exist within different careers. Try to understand the personal qualifications and educational requirements needed for the careers that interest you. Many fashion careers demand a great deal of originality. Also, energy, courage, self-motivation, and patience may be needed. A good sense of humor always helps. You must plan ahead to find the most meaningful career for *you.*

Read library materials and sections of this book that describe individual jobs and various career paths

Aspects of Various Careers
✸ Duties and responsibilities
✸ Education and training needed
✸ Pay, fringe benefits, and other compensation
✸ Location
✸ Job security
✸ Advancement opportunities
✸ Working conditions and schedule
✸ Status and prestige
✸ Amount of challenge and pressure

26-12 When choosing your life's work, consider these aspects of jobs in the career path.

that especially interest you. Use your school's guidance or vocational counselor as a resource. Also, see what information is available online through the Internet. Check with your state employment office. Write for information from trade associations and professional organizations in the fields you are considering. Also talk with people in the careers that interest you. Ask about various jobs, the needed education and training, and what advancement you could expect.

Go through the list shown in 26-12 as you study the pros and cons of various jobs and careers. Then try some jobs to test them out. Work experience while you are still in school can help you decide what you might want to do. Perhaps you could find a job during evenings, weekends, or summers, 26-13. Also, remember that career paths may include some jobs you might not enjoy, but have to do to eventually reach challenging positions with interesting activities and high pay.

Achieving success is easier when your efforts are focused on a goal. Choose a field of employment that interests you and for which you are qualified or can become qualified. However, when setting career goals, beware of being too specific. An unanticipated career direction could open up anywhere along the apparel pipeline that might be just right for you if your eyes are open to the potential of it.

Strive Toward the Needed Training and Experience

To be able to aspire to a certain fashion career path, specific preparation is required. Various amounts and types of education are required for different

26-13 Summer jobs between your school years can teach you a great deal about the workings of each part of the textile/apparel pipeline.

careers. The prospects of advancement depend on your skills, personality, and attitude, as well as educational background. Also, certain experience must be obtained to gain the background needed to move forward toward your highest goal.

When hiring, employers often consider an applicant's *extracurricular activities*, such as clubs and sports outside of class, as well as academic records. Activities, especially those with leadership roles, can prepare students to deal with challenges in work situations. To succeed in the working world, employers know that people must have "life skills" as well as training in technical areas. Also, involvement in professional organizations outside of school allows students to meet people who are already in the working world. These can be excellent contacts for job opportunities.

Responsibilities of workers are increasing with leaner organizations and empowerment of employees.

Requirements for Fashion Industry Success
Future fashion industry employees will need to be
✱ flexible in their professional goals
✱ knowledgable about world economies
✱ oriented toward teamwork
✱ literate with the latest technology

26-14 The requirements for success in the fashion industry of the future are different from the easier, less technical requirements of the past.

Also, pay levels have increased for those who improve their skills. Read the latest requirements for fashion industry success in 26-14.

Educational Requirements

Some fashion-related jobs can be done while attending high school. Others require a high school diploma, vocational or technical certificate, or various college degrees. Education can be continued after high school at a trade school, college, or university. See 26-15.

The more creative, challenging career positions and those with potential for career advancement are all very competitive. They require higher education. Educated employees understand technology and the global economy. It has also been shown that employees with higher educations are eager to continue to learn throughout their careers. On the other hand, the earnings of those without advanced education are decreasing since technology is replacing some of them.

Fashion Institute of Technology/John Senzer, Photographer

26-15 Training in garment production can be gained from schools that offer comprehensive programs that prepare graduates for textiles, apparel, and/or retailing careers.

The Doneger Group/David Wolfe

26-16 An associate degree in fashion illustration would concentrate on how to professionally draw all types of fashion looks for the human form.

Most areas of the country have high school *vocational programs*, in which students learn the skills for entry-level employment. High school "vo-tech" (vocational/technical) programs sometimes offer retailing classes. *Certificate courses* are curriculums completed in trade schools. They might include photography or pattern making. An ***associate degree*** is earned with most community college programs, usually taking two years. Associate degrees might be offered in such areas as fashion merchandising, window and floor display, fashion illustration, and other trades. See 26-16.

A broader education is received in four-year college and university programs, usually offering more career choices and faster promotions through the later career path. A ***bachelor's degree*** is earned at the completion of most four-year programs. It can be a bachelor of arts or bachelor of science degree. A *major* is a specific field of study, such as textiles and clothing. It might even be more defined, such as fashion merchandising (retailing) or fashion design, 26-17. Fashion curriculums are offered by colleges of art, family and consumer sciences, or human resource sciences within universities.

The Fashion Institute of Design and Merchandising, California

26-17 A bachelor's degree in fashion design includes pattern making, draping, textiles, and design courses, as well as many in English, math, science, and other general knowledge courses.

More complicated careers may require advanced degrees. A *master's degree* in textile chemistry might be required to do research for a corporation that develops and manufactures fibers. A master's of business administration (MBA) degree, after receiving a bachelor's degree in another field of study, can offer extra opportunities in almost all career areas. A *doctorate degree* might be required to head a research lab or be a professor of fashion-related studies at a university.

Some universities that are far from fashion centers have *reciprocal agreements*, or exchange programs, with schools near the garment districts of such cities as New York, Los Angeles, Paris, and London. Students go there for a semester, year, or other recommended length of time. They see and learn about the actual workings of most aspects of fashion careers. They receive credits that transfer to their original institutions.

Finding Educational Opportunities

To find out about schools that offer training and education in fashion, consult your school guidance counselor, or check with computer Internet sources or a librarian. Several handbooks are available that index schools, and give the address of each one's admissions office, so you can request information. They also describe each school's curriculum, size, costs, student body, housing, and financial aid programs.

You might want to talk about schools with people who work in fashion careers. They can tell you which have the best reputations and the best results in placing their graduates into good jobs. After deciding which schools interest you, contact the admissions office for a catalog and any other information you need to know about the school and how to apply.

A variety of scholarships are available for those who make the effort to find out about them and apply. Most scholarships pay at least part of a student's college tuition and/or book costs. Other scholarships are for special learning experiences. For instance, The Fashion Group sometimes offers a scholarship for a paid four-week study trip to the Paris Fashion Institute. The winning student must be majoring in fashion merchandising at a two- or four-year U.S. college.

Distance learning courses, via television broadcasts or the Internet, are available to most people. Instead of attending classes in schools, students have the convenience of taping selected courses on TV and watching them at a good time for their personal schedule, or logging on to school Web sites. Distance learning courses are offered by trade schools, community colleges, and universities. Students must register for the courses and buy any required books or materials. Contact with instructors is done via e-mail, and attendance is required for exams.

Gaining Experience

Many schools offer ***work-study programs*** in which they team with employers to allow students to receive on-the-job training for their future careers. At high school and trade school levels of education, these are called *cooperative (co-op) programs*. At college levels, they are called *internships*.

In work-study programs, the students attend classes part-time, studying related career courses, and work at the job part-time. The work experience is supervised by a teacher, coordinator, or professor. Businesses have

Advantages of Participating in Work-Study Programs
✷ You acquire career skills and knowledge.
✷ You apply your school learning to a job.
✷ You can test interest and formulate more realistic career goals.
✷ You gain valuable work experience to show on your resume.
✷ You learn what employers and supervisors expect of employees.
✷ You learn how to communicate and work with customers, coworkers, suppliers, and others.
✷ You earn some pay as well as credits toward graduation.
✷ You partake in the transition from school to work.
✷ You meet valuable contacts for future career networking.

26-18 High school cooperative programs may offer jobs worked every afternoon or evening, with classes attended in the mornings. College internships may occur as full-time jobs during the summer break or during whole semesters between other semesters of taking courses.

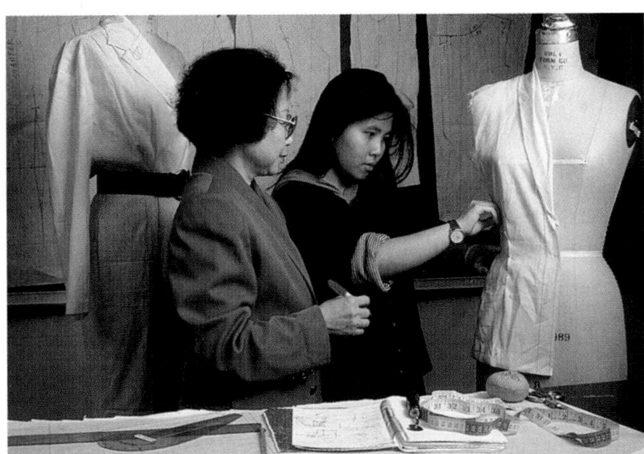

Fashion Institute of Technology/John Senzer, Photographer

26-19 After studying a trade in a school setting, an apprentice practices the skills with a seasoned professional who can give advice for each specific instance.

the advantage of gaining interested entry-level employees, possibly leading to trained full-time employees later. Students gain employment experiences and sometimes the offer of a full-time job after graduation. Students usually earn some pay, as well as school credits based on their work performance and class assignments. Other advantages are listed in 26-18.

In some work-study programs, students are placed in temporary jobs that alternate with their semesters of academic studies. In others, students work two days a week while taking a reduced course load, or spend a summer on a particular job. They gain valuable work experience, learn about different fashion-related jobs, and make important contacts in the industry. Also, the transition from a school environment to a full-time career is easier since the realities and responsibilities of a job are already recognized.

An *apprenticeship* is training for an occupation by working under the direction and guidance of a skilled worker. This often occurs after trade school or other formal training. While working with and learning from the expert, the trainee is paid entry-level wages. See 26-19. This might be done for jobs such as tailoring, photography, or jewelry-making. Work done by an apprentice to a fashion designer is shown in 26-20.

Most large companies offer their own on-the-job training programs to prepare employees for specialized jobs. Apparel manufacturers teach workers to operate the various sewing machines. Retail companies teach workers about store policies, how to operate checkout scanners, and what to do in cases of suspected shoplifting.

Executive trainee programs, also called *management training programs,* are general orientations offered by most large companies for new employees with college degrees. They first learn the store's selling systems and gain an understanding of the customers. The programs usually include both classroom and on-the-job training. They provide time on the selling floor and orientation to the entire store by rotating job assignments through all operational areas. Each company has its own policies and procedures that must be learned before employees are ready to take on their own responsibilities and advance to management positions.

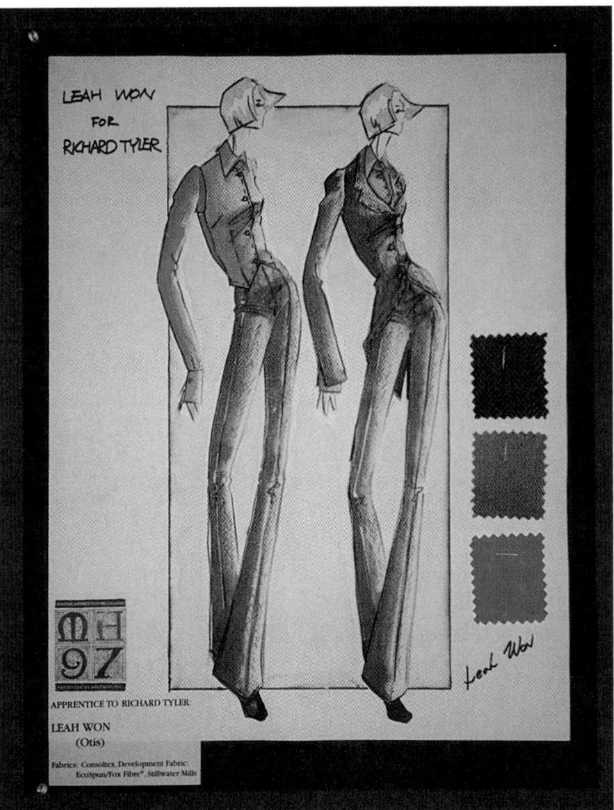

26-20 This swatched sketch by a design student, who was competitively selected to be an apprentice with a well-known fashion designer, shows the professional work that can be accomplished by combining education and training with talent.

College records for those chosen as executive trainees show that they have intelligence, leadership abilities, maturity, initiative, and alertness. In the program, they must be sensitive to conditions around them and able to take constructive criticism and stress. They should be goal-oriented, decisive, and self-confident, as well as enthusiastic, flexible, energetic, and not easily discouraged. They must look like professional fashion experts and be able to work with all the store's employees. They should also be available for evening, weekend, and holiday work.

Those who successfully complete executive trainee programs are usually the first to get jobs in the merchandising division when openings occur. They might become supervisors and eventually work into middle management positions or higher. This can lead to high status and incomes.

General Levels of Pay

	Amount Per Year	Per Month	Per Week	Per Hour
Low pay	less than $20,000	less than $1,670	less than $385	less than $9.50
Medium pay	$20,000 - 45,000	to $3,750	to $865	to $21.60
Good pay	$45,000 - 70,000	to $5,830	to $1,346	to $33.65
High pay	$70,000 - 100,000	to $8,325	to $1,920	to $48.00
Very high pay	$100,000 - 150,000	to $12,500	to $2,885	to $72.00
Extremely high pay	over $150,000	over $12,500	over $2,885	over $72.00

26-21 For ease of descriptions of job compensation, these categories of pay levels will be used through the rest of this unit. It is based on full time, year-round jobs done 40 hours per week.

What Compensation Can You Expect?

As you consider various career options, you may want to consider the pay you might receive. ***Compensation*** is payment for work done. A *compensation package* usually includes an hourly wage or salary, paid vacation time, and other benefits. Production workers may receive piecework pay. Sales employees sometimes earn a commission. General levels of pay are shown in 26-21. The categories of pay will be used in the following chapters to indicate pay levels of specific job categories. Also, sometimes the same job title pays different amounts in different parts of the U.S. and depending on an employee's skill and seniority. ***Seniority*** is the length of time an employee has been in a job compared to others who do the same job.

Lower level workers receive an ***hourly wage,*** or a certain predetermined pay rate per hour spent doing the job. These "nonexempt" employees usually punch in and out on a time clock. If they work *overtime*, or more than the usual 40-hour work week, they are paid an extra amount. This is usually calculated at one-and-a-half times the regular hourly wage. Work on Sundays or holidays may be paid at two times the regular rate. Most hourly wage jobs receive low to medium pay and do not require higher education.

Jobs that require the least amount of skill and responsibility might be paid the ***minimum wage,*** which is the lowest hourly rate established by law. For most jobs, an employer must pay at least the minimum wage to workers.

Retail sales jobs sometimes pay a commission on the amount of sales made by the employee. Rather than paying only a large percentage "straight commission," they usually combine a small commission on top of an hourly wage. Thus, an hourly wage is guaranteed for workers, but those who sell the most receive higher pay. The commission serves as an incentive to sell more merchandise.

A ***salary*** is a fixed amount of pay, usually received once or twice a month, for doing all that is required for a particular job. The salary amount is determined by the company's need for a person's services, education, and work experience. The annual (yearly) salary is divided into equal payments to be paid every week or two weeks, twice a month, or monthly. A salaried, or "exempt" employee does not receive overtime pay for extra hours worked or lose pay for hours missed. Most jobs that require college degrees or use highly skilled or experienced workers are salaried. Managers who have large responsibilities are usually salaried.

If you have had a job and received a paycheck, you know the amount of an employee's paycheck is less than the full amount of pay for the hours worked. Certain amounts, called *deductions,* are subtracted by employers and itemized on the stub attached to the check. Deductions are for federal and state taxes, as well as social security. Thus, "take-home pay" (net pay) is less than the total amount earned (gross pay).

Additional Compensation

Fringe benefits are employment rewards in addition to wages or salary. They include such extras as sick leave, medical programs, pension plans, group life insurance, and discount privileges for merchandise purchased. Some companies provide high school equivalency programs for their workers, tuition for higher education, or a child care center on-site.

Perquisites ("perks") are extras for those with high stature in the company. Examples might be flying first-class on business trips, limousine service to the airport, a country club membership, or eligibility to eat in the management dining room. Many special perks have been eliminated with corporate cost-cutting programs.

Some employers offer their workers a ***bonus,*** which is an extra payment in addition to regular pay. It might be an *incentive bonus* to reward high sales or productivity during a certain period of time. For instance, members of a production team might receive a bonus for exceeding their scheduled production. This encourages people to work hard. Another type is a *year-end bonus*, usually given at the end of the year. The amount of this payment depends on the company's profits and length of time a worker has been with the company. Employees with longer service and in higher positions of responsibility receive larger year-end bonuses than people with shorter service and lower positions. This encourages people to stay with the company.

Good hiring standards, training, and employee compensation and motivation programs can help companies maintain a good workforce. Some retail stores are now motivating their managers with monthly sales bonuses if their departments exceed the predetermined, reachable sales goals that have been set. This helps the managers feel more a part of the store's success and more intolerant of failure. Sometimes special parking spots or merchandise certificate dollars are given to the top salespeople of the previous month.

Companies say that good help is hard to find and keep. The best workers often take better jobs with other companies. Employees who are terminated usually qualify for unemployment compensation benefits from the government while they look for another job. They might have been fired because of unsatisfactory performance, laid off because of lack of work for them to do, or "downsized out" because of corporate restructuring.

Most beginning fashion jobs for college graduates have low pay compared to other fields. Pay goes up as employees gain experience and prove their dedication to the job. Those who work hard and are patient for advancement can often reap very high financial rewards. In fashion careers, people often gain responsibility and are given the chance to prove themselves in a fairly short period of time. People are rewarded if they achieve success with good sales figures and profits.

Ethical and Legal Issues of Employment

Employees and employers should be honest with each other. ***Business ethics*** involve using good moral values in business dealings. It concerns *how* a company does its business.

Most large companies have a *code of ethics*, which is a written statement that sets forth the legal principles that should guide the decisions of the organization. Some corporate ethical concerns are listed in 26-22. Topics covered in *value statements* deal with employee standards and "corporate culture-building." Examples of value statement items are listed in 26-23.

Topics Covered in Codes of Ethics
✷ Honesty and observance of the law
✷ Conflicts of interest
✷ Fairness in marketing and selling practices
✷ Use of inside information and securities trading
✷ Supplier relationships and purchasing practices
✷ Corrupt payments (bribes, kickbacks, etc.) to obtain business
✷ Acquiring and using information about others
✷ Questionable political activities
✷ Proper/improper use of company assets, resources, and property
✷ Protection of proprietary (confidential) information
✷ Pricing, contracting, and billing policies
✷ Representation to others (job applicants, stockholders, media)
✷ Industrial espionage (other company's trade secrets, employees)
✷ False/misleading advertising or promotion

26-22 Firms can combat many corporate legal problems with a strong code of ethics that is written, available to all, and supported from top management down.

Topics Covered in Value Statements
✷ Importance of customers and customer service
✷ Commitment to quality
✷ Commitment to innovation
✷ Respect for the individual employee (diversity differences)
✷ Corporate care for employee concerns (day care, furthering education, etc.)
✷ Importance of honesty, integrity, and ethical behavior
✷ Duty to stockholders
✷ Duty to suppliers
✷ Corporate citizenship in the community, country, and world (environmental matters, product safety, etc.)

26-23 Value statements set a corporate mood of concern for all stakeholders, or those who have a relationship with the business.

The most ethical companies have the best reputations and usually attract and hire the best people. If personnel activities are not handled properly, bad feelings can result and lawsuits can occur. Human resource employees and job applicants should know about employment laws. They should be clear about what they can and can't say in interviews and classified ads. Company representatives should have good recruiting, listening, and questioning skills. Short courses on these subjects are given by the *American Management Association (AMA),* a trade association for business executives.

Workplace Diversity

Workplace diversity is the blending of different races, cultures, genders, ages, socioeconomic backgrounds, personality types, and intelligence levels into a productive employment team. It involves encouraging and accepting people's differences, and using those differences to advantage.

As time passes, the U.S. work force continues to become more diverse. Employee relations departments are encouraging all workers to value others for their individual contributions. Previously untapped perspectives on issues are bringing new ways of solving work problems.

Employment discrimination is the treating of people differently, related to prejudice rather than work performance. It is illegal, but can occur company-wide through accepted policies and decision-making criteria. It also occurs with individuals, because of personal biases of those in authority who have decision-making power over others in employment matters.

Most large companies have worked hard to eliminate employment discrimination from their company practices. They try to provide equal pay for equal work, no matter who is doing the job. They encourage employees to cooperate with one another. To combat discrimination, companies try to treat all job applicants and employees uniformly, in a fair, equitable manner. To prevent possible legal actions later, they support all hiring and disciplinary actions by carefully documenting job interviews, and employee performance and behavior.

Passage by the federal government of the *Americans with Disabilities Act (ADA)* in the early 1990s made it illegal to discriminate against people with disabilities. Job applicants who are disabled should have the same chance of being hired as those without disabilities, if they are physically able to do a job. Also, the work environment must be made physically accessible for workers with disabilities. The soft goods chain offers numerous opportunities for people with disabilities.

Maintaining High Ethical Standards

Most companies that are especially concerned with business ethics will not do business with apparel contractors who violate basic human rights, often referred to as "sweat shops." Other matters involve environmental concerns, product safety, destructive hostile takeovers, or slanted government lobbying that hurts others. An example of poor ethics in fashion merchandising is the cooperation of vendors who inflate their "list prices" (not their actual prices) to help retailers secure above-average markups or hold false "sales."

Employees must also maintain high ethical standards or they will be fired. This includes avoiding pilferage and mishandling of personal expenses paid by company funds. It also relates to company loyalty, bribes and expensive gifts, conflicts of interest, substance abuse, and sexual harassment. Pilferage was described in Chapter 20. Personal expenses charged to the company would include private long distance phone calls on the company's lines or photocopying of personal papers. Employees must not reveal company secrets or file expense account reports for expenses that were not actually incurred. A *bribe* is money or a gift accepted by a trusted employee from an outsider trying to influence the employee's judgment or conduct.

Fashion Industry Future for Employment

A major problem facing the fashion industry in all developed countries, and especially the U.S., is one of attracting good employees. It stems from previous poor public relations of the industry, as well as the education system. High schools have not given importance to fashion careers, and colleges have not attracted high-caliber entrants. Many young adults seek the glamour of a fashion retail or promotion career, but are not excited about several years of education followed by hard work and possible low pay to enter the industry. Those who would otherwise consider manufacturing as a career may not be aware of the apparel industry's opportunities. However, more students are now becoming oriented toward international textile/apparel business, desiring studies abroad and international internships.

Public relations has begun to spread the good word! The industry's level of technology has become world class, and many challenges and rewards are available for those who obtain good preparation. For a healthy future, the industry must attract bright, new employees, 26-24. This is being done through more scholarship money from companies or trade associations, for educational endeavors in schools that offer curriculums in textiles, apparel, and retailing. The *American Apparel Education Foundation* is a nonprofit group that raises funds that go toward the ever-increasing costs of quality apparel education.

Firms that are successful in the global market need to continue to do a public relations job. They need to publicize the new successes, technology, and excitement taking place in the industry to attract the

Ball State University, Indiana

26-24 It is hoped that smart, enthusiastic, and well-educated young adults will choose to enter all the segments of the fashion industry.

people needed by the industry in the future. The media should be used to tell the story of the goods and services of the textile/apparel pipeline. Consumer and government confidence is needed in fashion products and manufacturing processes. You can become part of the revitalized industry.

Interested, well-trained employees are needed to expand the excellence of the industry–for improved products to be offered to consumers at reasonable prices. Change is occurring swiftly to bring about mass customization, body scanning, electronic retailing, and other ways of satisfying the individual desires of each consumer.

The industry must communicate its challenges and rewards to attract good employees. It can be done if companies combine the marketing and promotion of their fine products with news of their association with the entire industry.

Summary

Fashion-related employment offers vast options and environments. Some of the most fascinating, challenging, and exciting careers demand hard work and dedication. Employees can move through various jobs in different career paths.

Career paths should be selected thoughtfully. Evaluate your interests and aptitudes, and develop your skills. Research different careers to find a field that interests you and for which you can become qualified. Then strive toward the needed training and experience. Gain the right educational requirements. Do research to find the best educational opportunities for yourself. Also gain experience by coordinating work with your study schedule.

Compensation for work includes many different types of pay, depending on the work performed, job level, and seniority. Additional compensation includes fringe benefits, perquisites, and bonuses.

Ethical and legal issues of employment deal with how a company does its business. It includes codes of ethics, value statements, and workplace diversity. Both employers and employees should strive to maintain high ethical standards.

The fashion industry must strive to attract good employees. Good public relations efforts, updated school curriculums, and increased scholarship availability may encourage students to choose careers in the textile/apparel pipeline.

To Know

job
career
career planning
entry-level jobs
management positions
aptitudes
skills
associate degree
bachelor's degree
work-study programs
compensation
seniority
hourly wage
minimum wage
salary
fringe benefits
bonus
business ethics
workplace diversity
employment discrimination

To Review

1. Why does work in retail sometimes include evening and weekend hours?
2. What is a job description?
3. What are the two main ways in which talented people move up the ladder to success?
4. Name four beginning jobs that a college graduate might have in retailing.
5. What employees might reach upper management positions?
6. How long will you probably work in your chosen career path?
7. Name three fashion-related jobs/careers in which visually creative people can excel.
8. From what sources can you obtain information about specific fashion careers, besides from this book?

9. When setting career goals, why should you not be too specific?
10. Why do employers often consider a job applicant's extracurricular activities?
11. What are certificate courses?
12. What do scholarships offer?
13. What is an apprenticeship?
14. What does a compensation package usually include?
15. To be paid an extra overtime amount, how many hours must an employee work?
16. What is an incentive bonus?
17. What measures can help companies maintain a good workforce?
18. True or false. Most beginning fashion jobs for college graduates have low pay compared to other fields.
19. Name three ethical issues involved in fashion merchandising.
20. How can the fashion industry attract people needed by the industry in the future?

To Do

1. Cut three different types of pictures from magazines or newspapers that you think represent the glamorous public view of the fashion industry. In a report, explain the careers that are represented. Then tell what you think the preparation, work, and hours are for success in the careers.
2. Read a biography (or autobiography) of someone who has reached a high level in a fashion-related career (in retail, fashion design, etc.). A library computer database or a librarian can help you find an appropriate book. Prepare a book report that includes the person's career path, possible interests/aptitudes/skills, good and difficult times of the career, situations encountered, etc.
3. Look in the classified ads of your local newspaper to see if there are any entry-level retail jobs available as apparel stock clerks or salespeople. Also look for "help wanted" signs in store windows. Get the details about two of the jobs to compare the pay, work schedule, duties, and other details.
4. Make a list of your interests, trying to think of different types of things you like to do. Also use the chart in 26-8. Make a different list of your aptitudes, either from the results of aptitude tests or simply from what you know you are good at doing. Then list the skills that you have already developed or could develop in the future. Analyze the three lists to try to determine several types of work that might be right for your career.
5. Get admissions information (course catalog, entrance requirements, costs, etc.) from a nearby trade school or university that offers a fashion-related curriculum. Prepare a report about the degree(s) offered in various course concentrations, any reciprocal agreements, scholarships available, work-study programs, or other important facts about what the school offers.

CHAPTER 27

Textile and Apparel Careers

After studying this chapter, you will be able to
- describe careers in textile research and development, design, and production.
- summarize employment opportunities in apparel design and manufacturing.
- explain sales and distribution opportunities in textiles and apparel.

The textile and apparel segments of the soft goods chain are vital to the U.S. economy. They have a high number of firms, employees, and dollars invested. Fashion specialists are needed to design, manufacture, promote, sell, and distribute the products.

Producers of textile and apparel goods and industry trade associations offer a great number and variety of fashion careers. In small companies, several of the jobs discussed in this chapter may be combined and done by one employee. Large companies, with many more employees, have a larger number of more specialized positions, 27-1.

Textile and apparel manufacturing have always been labor-intensive, but are now becoming more capital-intensive because of industry restructuring, consolidation, and modernizing. They have also traditionally employed a high percentage of unskilled labor at below U.S. average wages. However, the skill level and wages are moving upward with automation, 27-2.

Burlington Industries

27-1 In large textile and apparel companies, employees do more specialized jobs, such as setting up yarn to flow smoothly and evenly onto weaving looms.

Sulzer Ruti

27-2 Computer automation, which is increasingly used in textile and apparel operations, is raising the skill level of needed employees.

Many textile jobs are located in New York City and other fashion centers. Other textile jobs are at the headquarters and plant sites of producers, such as in the Eastern and Southern states. Apparel jobs are also near fashion centers.

To get creative textile or apparel jobs that require design or artistic abilities, an excellent portfolio of original examples is needed. A ***portfolio*** is a case of loose, unfolded art or design papers showing a person's creative work. A professional-looking portfolio should contain a balanced representation of your best abilities. Each piece should be mounted neatly and have your name on it.

Both the textile and apparel segments require fashion-oriented people to guide their efforts. New product development, manufacturing, and distribution systems require employers trained in new technology. The best career opportunities arise for people with solid educational backgrounds and continually updated skills. High levels of success can be reached after employees have gained experience in several areas of the industry. The following sections describe the main career opportunities in the textile and apparel segments of the fashion industry.

Department of Consumer Studies; University of Delaware

27-3 Universities with textile curriculums have laboratories in which research is done. The research results can help industry introduce innovative products to the consumer market.

A Career in the Textile Industry

Many careers exist in the textile industry, from developing the initial fibers to selling the finished fabrics. The careers can be generalized into textile research and development, textile design, textile production, and textile sales. The latter will be discussed at the end of the chapter with apparel sales.

Textile Research and Development

Research and development (R&D) is a vital part of the textile industry. It leads to the development of new products and the improvement of old products. People in textile R&D careers work for fiber manufacturers, textile mills, and private testing laboratories. Government agencies hire chemists and lab technicians to see that textile products on the market meet government standards. Sometimes the researchers must develop the specifications for the standards. A great deal of research is also done at universities, often by graduate students who learn professional methods and gain experience while earning advanced degrees, 27-3.

Aptitudes to go into R&D include a creative imagination, curiosity, and attention to details, 27-4. A person in R&D should enjoy science and like to perform experiments alone, yet be able to clearly communicate precise, realistic, and practical results to others. Patience, persistence, and flexibility of working toward a solution are needed,

Fashion Institute of Technology

27-4 Researchers must take complete notes about all aspects of their experiments to be able to make a meaningful analysis of the results.

Fashion Institute of Technology/John Senzer, Photographer

27-5 Textile scientists develop synthetic fiber shapes and sizes and fabric construction patterns by computer. This allows for flexibility and speed in textile research work.

since it often takes months or years to invent a product or solve a technical problem.

Textile research scientists do R&D in several different textile areas to satisfy needs for specific end uses. They may develop new synthetic fibers that have certain characteristics, or blend fibers in new and better ways to create desired qualities. They work on different fabric constructions and find new finishes for better fabric performance, 27-5.

To be a textile research scientist, a college degree and usually an advanced degree is needed. Degrees might be in polymer chemistry, textile science, chemical engineering, or physics. Manufacturing experience in a textile plant, possibly through a work-study curriculum, is a great asset. Textile research scientists might be with a project from the initial idea to actual installation in a manufacturing plant.

Salaries are good for beginning textile research scientists and usually go up to high or very high pay with experience and proven abilities. Work hours are usually regular, with occasional overtime demands. Personal satisfaction can be great when complex problems are solved or something new is created. Also, there may be opportunities to broaden your career into other areas of the company, such as manufacturing supervision or marketing. See 27-6.

Textile laboratory technicians help conduct research, often working under research scientists. They have high school diplomas and usually technical trade school certificates. Many of the specific procedures they do, such as setting up equipment, writing down computations, and categorizing experiment results, are repetitive and are learned on the job. They may duplicate each step of a future manufacturing operation to evaluate its quality and efficiency. They may also test the serviceability of finished fibers, yarns, and fabrics. They receive medium pay.

Fashion Institute of Technology/John Senzer, Photographer

27-6 With good educational preparation as well as experience, textile researchers can move into other types of careers in the industry.

Sulzer Ruti

27-7 Testing that the quality of the product being developed matches the specifications required is an important part of textile research and production.

Pendleton Woolen Mills

27-8 Textile design employees must be able to coordinate artistic creativity with the fashion and performance needs of the market.

Technicians who are *textile testers* work for textile mills or independent testing labs. They test new products against required specifications of durability, colorfastness, and shrinkage. They check different fibers, yarns, fabrics, or finishes after they have been developed but before being introduced to the public. They also perform tests during the textile manufacturing process to assure good and uniform quality, 27-7.

Textile Design Employment

Textile design employees are responsible for the look of the final textiles. They should have a creative imagination and artistic ability, with a good sense of color. They need knowledge of the fashion field, as well as a love of beautiful fabrics. A wide knowledge of automated technology and the marketplace has also become important. Since apparel designers and manufacturers are guided by fabric offerings, textile design is important to companies later in the soft goods chain.

Fiber and fabric companies are at the beginning of the pipeline, so they work farther ahead of retail selling seasons than others in the chain. Textile fashion departments research and forecast upcoming trends. They interpret and guide company products toward meeting those trends, with the proper yarns, blends, textures, weights, and performance characteristics. See 27-8.

Fabric Designers

Fabric designers structurally and artistically develop the fabrics that apparel producers will want for their new lines. Fabric companies employ designers who have technical knowledge about fabric construction, as well as artistic ability. In small fabric mills that do not have a fashion director, the fabric designer makes the fashion decisions. In larger companies, decisions are shared that involve large capital investments for thousands of yards of new fabrics when a new season's line is prepared. Also, the resulting fabrics must be able to be sold within a specific price category.

Fabric structural designers interpret the findings and advice of their company's fashion department to create new woven or knitted patterns, or redesign existing ones, usually directed toward a specific market. Yarns of different textures or colors are combined in interesting ways. Rather than the old tedious method of doing calculated drawings on graph paper, a computer is now used to create the designs, 27-9. It shows the fabric structure and then controls the weaving loom or knitting machine. Small samples can be produced and approved for production before large quantities of fabric are made. Three specialized areas of fabric structural design are woven, knit, and lace/embroidery designing.

For fabric structural design, an understanding of technical processes and manufacturing equipment capabilities is needed. Fabric designers and equipment technical people may cooperate to achieve the necessary production automation. The designer must know about new fibers, dyes, and finishes. Textile colleges offer four-year degrees that are technical, but have an art emphasis. Some two-year schools of design or technology also offer preparation for this type of work.

Fabric surface designers translate the company's color choices and applied print looks onto fabrics. They

Burlington Industries

27-9 Designs that fabric structural designers develop on computers can control the looms or knitting machines that manufacture the fabrics.

may specialize as print/repeat artists, colorists, or strike-off artists. These may be entry-level positions requiring an associate degree.

A ***print/repeat artist*** does original textile surface designs, which may include color combinations and repeats. After sketching out one ***motif*** (design idea or theme), the motif is combined with repeats of itself to form a continuous pattern. See 27-10 and 27-11. This is often done in response to customer requests.

Colorists work out different color combinations for the designs. A colorist might give new colors to previous designs for a new seasonal line, or adapt designs for specific customers or markets. The same motif may be produced in several different color combinations, shown with computer printouts before the final versions are tried on fabrics.

Fashion Institute of Technology/John Senzer, Photographer

27-10 When the idea is finished, this textile design motif might be printed continuously to fill the entire surface of yard goods.

Philadelphia University

27-11 When a fabric is printed, the motif in the design is combined into a continuously running pattern that repeats itself over and over again.

A ***strike-off artist*** arranges prints on fabrics after the motifs and colors have been established. He or she interprets the intentions of the surface design department to the plant. Sometimes the strike-off artist must modify a design or color combination because of quality or production restraints.

Fabric surface design jobs are available with fabric mills, textile converters, and garment producers that make their own fabrics. They are also available at fabric design studios, forecasting services, retail private label product development offices, interior decorating fabric companies, and computer graphics design firms. Almost all jobs require CAD skills.

For fabric surface design jobs, the portfolio should show versatile skills, especially with computer work. It should indicate your ability to meet professional standards. Successful job applicants must also be able to follow directions and meet deadlines.

Fabric Stylist

A ***fabric stylist*** serves as a bridge between the creative and business aspects of the company, coordinating fabric design, production, and sales. This high level job requires knowledge of textiles, long-range planning, fabric design, the entire fashion industry, and the consumer market. Company sales depend on the stylist's ability to gauge demand and stimulate interest in new fabrics. He or she also guides the production staff at the plant to produce the correct amounts of fabrics in the right qualities. Many years of textile industry experience and a wide range of industry contacts and resources is helpful for this job. The pay level is high or very high.

Fabric stylists organize fabrics into lines each season, grouping them to be shown and sold to customers. Swatches and color cards are put together for sales presentations in the company's showroom, as well as being sent to prospective customers. Also, large enough samples can be requested by apparel designers/manufacturers to make samples of their new designs. When the stylist receives feedback about garments to be produced with the company's fabrics, the information is used for promotion to the press, retailers, and consumers.

An entry-level job with fabric companies is an *assistant to the stylist.* This person sets up appointments for the stylist and does clerical work. He or she also acts as a go-between with the company's plants or mills, and works with clients and salespeople in the stylist's absence. This should not be confused with the job of *assistant stylist,* which is a middle management position in large fabric firms or textile design studios. This person works with the stylist in compiling lines, preparing storyboards, and doing forecasting. He or she gives assignments to the fabric designers and some directions to the plants.

Fashion Director

The ***fashion director***, sometimes called the *merchandiser,* heads the fashion department. The fashion director determines the fashion direction the business will take, and communicates that information throughout his or her organization. This person attends worldwide fashion events and keeps in close touch with sources of fashion information. Sometimes sample fabrics are bought abroad. When the fashion director of a fiber producer learns that the upcoming season will feature a certain color or silhouette, he or she works with the fabric mills that use the company's fibers, to develop the correct types of yard goods for the market.

Fashion directors send fabric presentations to apparel designers, manufacturers, buying offices, fashion magazines, and retail companies. They help these companies with fashion-related problems, and set up fashion exhibits for the trade. They must be able to coordinate apparel and accessories, stage fashion shows, and work well with the press. They have proven themselves in the industry before being appointed to this position. They have high esteem and receive very high pay.

Depending on the size of the firm, the fashion director may have one or many assistants. An *assistant to the fashion director* is often involved in glamorous activities such as running a fashion show of a designer's collection made from the company's fibers or fabrics, or helping to entertain influential people. However, usually the assistant takes care of routine chores, such as follow-up phone calls, scheduling meetings, and sending out correspondence. This job is sought after by lower level employees who aspire to be fashion directors someday. See 27-12.

A fashion-related college degree is becoming more necessary to be an assistant to the fashion director. The pay can be low, medium, or good, depending on the company and the number and levels of assistants that are employed.

Western Kentucky University

27-12 At Fruit of the Loom, Inc., the fashion director and assistant fashion director discuss the latest yarns and colors for the knit products being coordinated for a new fashion season.

Other Design-Related Textile Positions

An organization chart that illustrates fabric line development is shown in 27-13. Fabric designers might become assistant stylists and eventually work up to stylist. The ***department manager*** at the top of the chart is responsible for the entire fabric type (such as polyester knits or cotton broadcloth), or market category (such as women's career wear or men's sportswear). In a smaller company that markets only one fiber type or to one market category, the *vice president of merchandising* would likely be at the top, with no department managers.

A ***fabric librarian*** is in charge of the fabric library that most manufactured fiber companies, natural fiber trade associations, and home sewing pattern companies maintain, 27-14. These visual collections that change each season show everything that is new and important in fabrics made from the organization's fibers. Fabric swatches are clipped to cards on which detailed descriptions and sources of supply are recorded. The librarian must be able to discuss the latest fashion trends, fibers, and fabrics with interested fabric and apparel designers and manufacturers.

Also assisting this process are ***market analysts*** who conduct market research to try to discover future textile needs. They are alert to supply and demand shifts. They keep track of what their competitors are

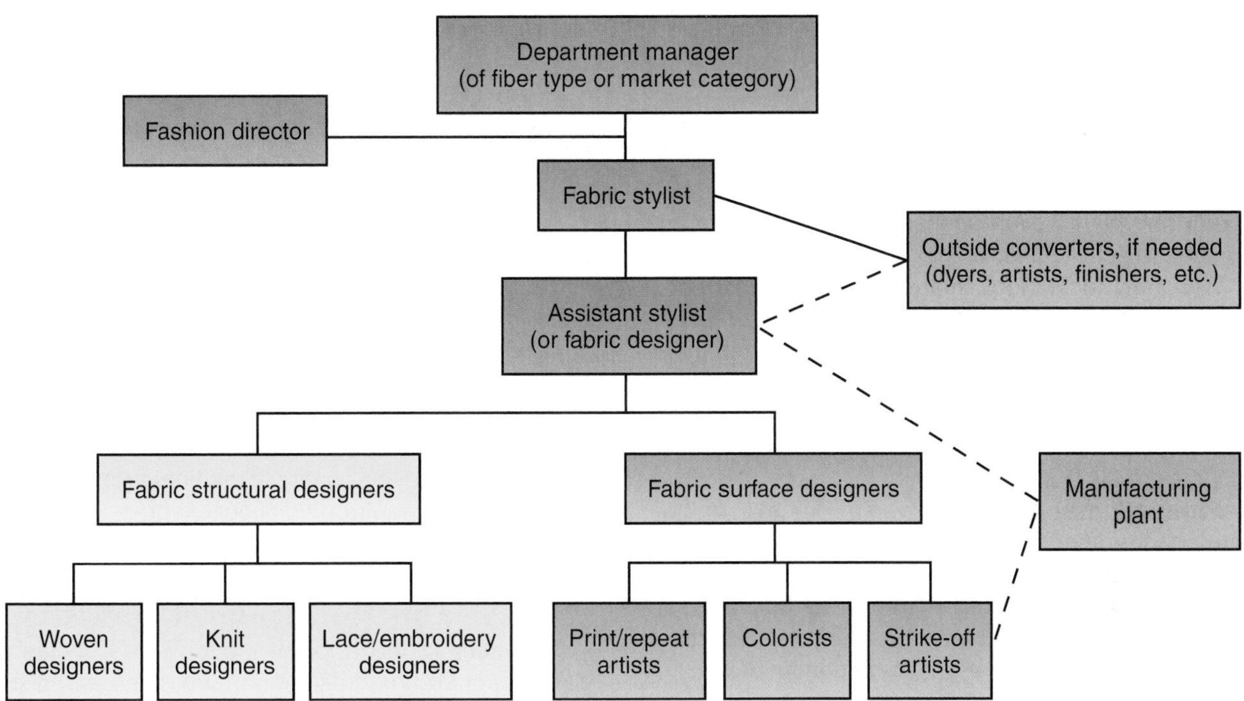

27-13 Many textile experts contribute to the development of a company's fabric lines. They have different amounts of expertise and responsibility, for which they receive different compensation. Also companies of different sizes have more layers of employees and various titles for jobs. Dotted lines mean they interact but do not have direct authority over these functions.

doing in long-range pricing and supply, and work closely with their firm's stylists so the right products are offered at the right time. They know every aspect of the industry and have training in textiles, business, marketing, economics, psychology, and statistics.

McCall Pattern Company

27-14 Fabric librarians organize and oversee the collection of fabric samples that are updated to show the textiles for a particular season.

Textile Production

Textile production involves the largest single portion of textile industry employees. *Textile production workers* operate the machines that perform the manufacturing procedures, 27-15. They have high school diplomas and are usually trained on the job. They may have taken courses in trade or vocational schools. They should have good mechanical aptitude, physical

Pendleton Woolen Mills

27-15 Textile production workers run looms, knitting machines, and other equipment used in the manufacture of fibers and finished fabrics.

coordination, vision, and manual dexterity. Most textile production workers are people who enjoy routine tasks. Some belong to unions.

Work is done during day, evening, and night shifts, with extra pay for those who work the evening and night shifts. The average textile worker's earnings have moved from the low pay into the medium pay category. Fringe benefits and working conditions are generally good. Many plants even sponsor recreational, social, and athletic activities for employees and their families.

With new technology, many production jobs now require computer skills. Electronic equipment is used for such tasks as forecasting amounts of raw materials needed and computing how much of each type of fiber or fabric to produce. Computers do statistical analysis for quality control, as well as automatic weaving and knitting from CAD instructions.

Production supervisors oversee various manufacturing operations to maintain the highest worker productivity and product quality. College graduates with degrees in engineering, textile technology, business, or chemistry might begin their careers as production supervisors. The companies that hire them usually offer management training programs. Also, most firms send their production supervisors to periodic seminars, workshops, and classes to help them keep up with developments in the industry.

Textile *quality control inspectors* work in all phases of production to analyze the quality of fibers, yarns, or fabrics. They check to see that precise standards and specifications are met, 27-16. They identify quality problems, try to find solutions, and report on their findings. They should have good analytical skills and enjoy detail and follow-up work. Most quality control inspectors have completed a textile technology or production college program.

Burlington Industries

27-16 Quality control inspections are done regularly during the production of fibers and fabrics to guarantee top quality results after manufacturing is completed.

Plant engineers make sure all environmental systems are operating properly. If the heat, air conditioning, electrical, materials handling, noise reduction, or other systems are not functioning well, the plant engineer modifies or repairs them. A college degree in engineering is desirable. The pay is good or high.

Industrial engineers are cost and efficiency experts who save companies time and money. They study each operation to determine the most efficient, least expensive, and safest method to get it done. They decide what machines are needed and are constantly looking for better ways of performing production tasks without reducing the quality of the final product. Preparation for this requires a college degree in industrial engineering or textile manufacturing.

A Career in the Apparel Industry

Careers in the apparel industry exist in fashion design, apparel manufacturing, and sales and distribution. The latter will be discussed at the end of this chapter with textile sales.

Fashion Design

The job of *fashion designer* is to create new ideas that combine function and beauty. The goal is to have the firm's garments at the leading edge of fashion. Designers might specialize in womenswear, childrenswear, menswear, or they might design in more specific areas such as swimwear, bridal attire, or shoes, 27-17. The success of the manufacturer's business depends on the salability of its designs.

Fashion Institute of Technology/John Senzer, Photographer

27-17 Lately, the menswear design field has expanded, with male consumers becoming more interested in fashion as well as the acceptance of different types of menswear for casual and business occasions.

Most fashion design jobs are full-time. However, a few work on a freelance basis for several small firms that do not have their own designers. Fashion designers often work long, hectic days especially when a line is being finished for a showing. Designers find that expressing their creativity and being responsible for successful collections is very rewarding. A degree in fashion design is needed from a college or vocational school. See 27-18.

The greatest number of design employees work for manufacturers who mass-produce low priced items. Instead of originating ideas, these *design stylists*, also called *copyists*, adapt higher priced fashion designs to the price ranges of their customers. They may select the fabrics, coordinate the lines, and oversee other details. They receive lower salaries and less prestige than designers of more exclusive lines. However, entry-level jobs may be available to gain experience in the industry.

Moderately priced apparel is usually produced by medium-sized manufacturers that have several designers. Each designer has an assistant or design room staff. These designers are not well-known because their names are not publicized or sewn into the clothes they design. They are strictly important employees working for their firms. They usually design on CAD systems and receive good to high pay.

Very high-priced apparel firms employ only the most talented designers. A designer must be recognized as being gifted in the field to fill one of these scarce positions. The salary is extremely high. Aspiring designers often work as assistants for top designers, to learn the trade. They receive good pay and invaluable experience.

An *assistant designer* might follow-up on a designer's sketches through draping, pattern making, sample cutting, or sample making. He or she might contribute some design ideas, or help the designer select fabrics and trimmings. Clerical duties involve keeping records of fabric, notions, and trim purchases. The assistant might also make appointments, answer telephones, and run errands. It is important to be able to follow directions accurately and work well under pressure.

Most opportunities for assistant designers exist in ready-to-wear manufacturing firms. A few are available in companies that create home sewing patterns. Assistant designer jobs might also be available as summer

Philadelphia University

27-18 After learning all aspects of fashion design at a school of higher education, graduates can enter fashion design jobs with the confidence of doing a good job.

employment during college years or as work-study programs. When applying, you must present a portfolio of your own fashion design ideas.

The Qualifications and Work of Fashion Designers

Fashion designers need imagination and creativity for a constant flow of ideas. They must be aware of changing social and economic trends so their designs satisfy market demands. A natural fashion flair, supplemented with education and experience, should provide a strong sense of color, line, texture, balance, and proportion. Also, enthusiasm, determination, and drive to succeed are necessary for this demanding career.

Fashion designers must have technical knowledge of fabrics, trimmings, and fit. Expertise in pattern making, draping, and sewing are especially important, 27-19. Designers must understand manufacturing processes and costing, so they can stay within the production capabilities and marketing plans of their firms. They must be able to visualize a finished, three-dimensional garment before it is made. Patience is necessary, since design specifications may have several revisions. Also, flexibility and cooperation are needed as well as the self-assurance to sell design ideas to others.

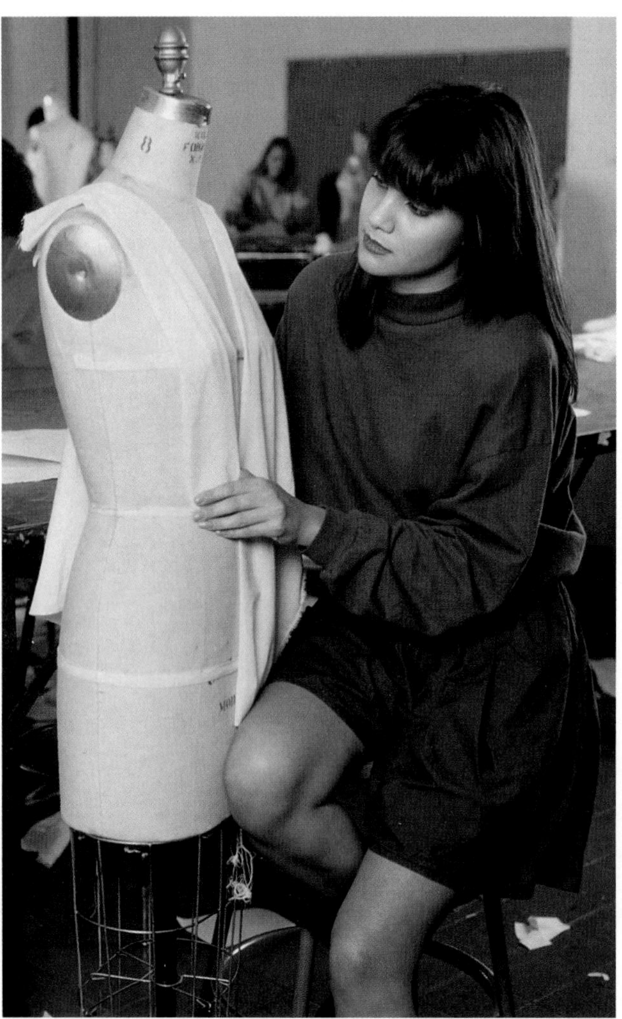

The Fashion Institute of Design and Merchandising, California

27-19 Draping enables fashion designers to understand how fabrics fit the human form. Even if the final designing is done by computer, having draping skills is part of the combined expertise for success.

Sources of design inspiration were discussed in Chapter 9. Some designers visualize their ideas by sketching on paper or by draping fabric onto a dressmaker's form (mannequin). However, most now use CAD equipment, often with three-dimensional programs that allow the garment to be turned and viewed from all sides. The designer can add more or less fullness where desired, work with different color combinations, and see how various trims might look. When the design is just right, it is saved and printed in realistic color. Some equipment makes photographic slides that can be enlarged into fashion pictures.

Finished designs are submitted to top management for approval. Management discussions sometimes result in changes, which are entered into the CAD system, and patterns are created. Then a prototype of each design is cut and sewn, often in muslin, to work out all details and to edit the line. Finally, samples are made in the chosen fashionable fabrics to be used by salespeople and shown to retail buyers.

Designers must plan and supervise the work of their staff, such as assistant designers, sample cutters, and sample hands. They deal with fabric salespeople and retail buyers. They also work with management, production, and promotion/publicity employees.

Sketching Employees

Fashion firms sometimes employ ***sketchers***, who do freehand drawings of the ideas that designers have draped onto mannequins in fabric. This work is good for those who can draw precise, accurate accounts of other people's ideas at a fast pace. It requires outstanding sketching skills and a fashion sense, but not much original design creativity. The work is quite confining, except when asked to meet customers, do promotional work, and assist with presentations of new collections.

Sketching assistants are employed by large manufacturing firms and pattern companies, 27-20. They mainly record designs in precise, technical detail. They point out all construction and design features of a seasonal line of samples to be kept with the company records. They "swatch" the sketches by attaching fabric and trim samples. They also do some clerical work, filling out a specification sheet of construction details for each item.

Sketching employees receive low to medium pay. They need training in art or fashion illustration after high school. When applying for a sketching position, a

McCall Pattern Company

27-20 Sketching employees make detailed drawings of fashion ideas. They work for design firms, large manufacturers, or pattern companies.

portfolio of artwork must be presented. Candidates should be fashionably well-groomed, poised, and articulate.

Sample Workers

A *sample cutter* cuts out sample parts, and a *sample maker* (also called a sample hand) sews sample garment designs together, following the designer's pattern, sketch, and specifications. He or she does all the required sewing and finishing. This tests the pattern in fashion fabrics, after which final changes or refinements are made to the design.

This is exacting work. Sample makers must be skilled in all construction techniques, and able to interpret someone else's ideas into garments. This can be an entry-level design job, but usually a factory sewing machine operator moves up to this position because of skill, hard work, and a good attitude. Sometimes he or she has taken vocational school courses. The low to medium pay is higher than that of most sewing machine operators in the factory.

Apparel Manufacturing

Ready-to-wear apparel is mass-produced in large quantities. Apparel factories are located in many areas of the U.S. and the world. The labor-intensity of apparel manufacturing requires many workers. However, the number of U.S. apparel industry production workers has been decreasing. This is mainly because of imports and the use of higher technology. Most companies specialize in only certain types of apparel.

Preproduction Employees

Pattern makers translate apparel designs into the right number, size, and shape of pattern pieces needed for mass production. A precise master pattern is made in the company's basic size, while trying to keep fabric yardage at a minimum. Most of this work is done by computer, rather than by hand cutting heavy paper patterns. See 27-21. However, for intricate or expensive designs, some fashion experts feel the flair and judgment of a skilled traditional pattern maker cannot be duplicated by a machine.

Based on the master pattern, *pattern graders* cut patterns in all of the different sizes produced by the manufacturer, by enlarging or reducing the pattern pieces exactly the right amounts. This technical and precise work must often be done under the pressure of production schedules. Pattern grading may be done by the pattern makers who originally created the designs. Or, the computer program grades the design patterns, on command, into the needed sizes.

Markers are employees who figure out how the pattern pieces can be placed most efficiently for cutting. They place the pattern pieces in the tightest possible layout, on a paper marker, so the least amount of fabric is wasted during cutting. Computerized plants are doing this electronically now.

Pattern makers, graders, and markers are employed wherever there are apparel firms. Even if factory sewing is done off-shore, the design, pattern making, and grading may take place domestically. Pattern employees need a good background in flat pattern making, draping, design, fabrics, and clothing construction. They must understand body proportions and garment fit.

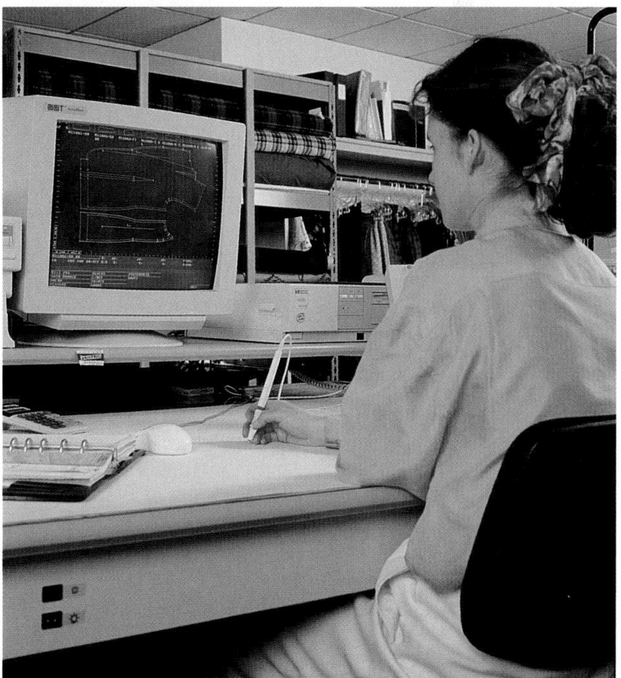

Pendleton Woolen Mills

27-21 Computer pattern making is done by knowledgable employees who understand patterns and are proficient with the computerized process.

Lands' End Direct Merchants

27-22 Spreaders lay out the many layers of fabric that will be cut into garment parts to begin the manufacturing process.

They should have at least two years of vocational education, studying pattern making technology.

Experienced traditional pattern makers, graders, and markers can receive good salaries. Those with computer skills receive high pay. The jobs in this industry are changing as competition encourages high-tech production. Old methods are being replaced by faster, more accurate procedures requiring fewer but more educated workers.

Cutting, Sewing, and Finishing Jobs

To begin the factory production process, *spreaders* lay out the chosen fabric for cutting. These employees guide bolts of fabric back and forth to form smooth, straight layers, 27-22. In the past, this job required no higher education, with the skills learned at the plant. However, with computerized equipment, vocational training is needed to operate the new systems. Often this job is done by cutters.

In older factories, *cutters* use power saws, knives, or shears to carefully cut out stacks of garment parts. In more modern factories, they control the computer cutting equipment. In that case, no paper marker is used—the layout arrangement and pattern piece outlines are in the memory of the computer, 27-23. Sometimes only one layer is cut at a time, extremely fast, by a computer-controlled laser.

Cutters who use hand-held equipment need physical strength, good manual dexterity, and excellent

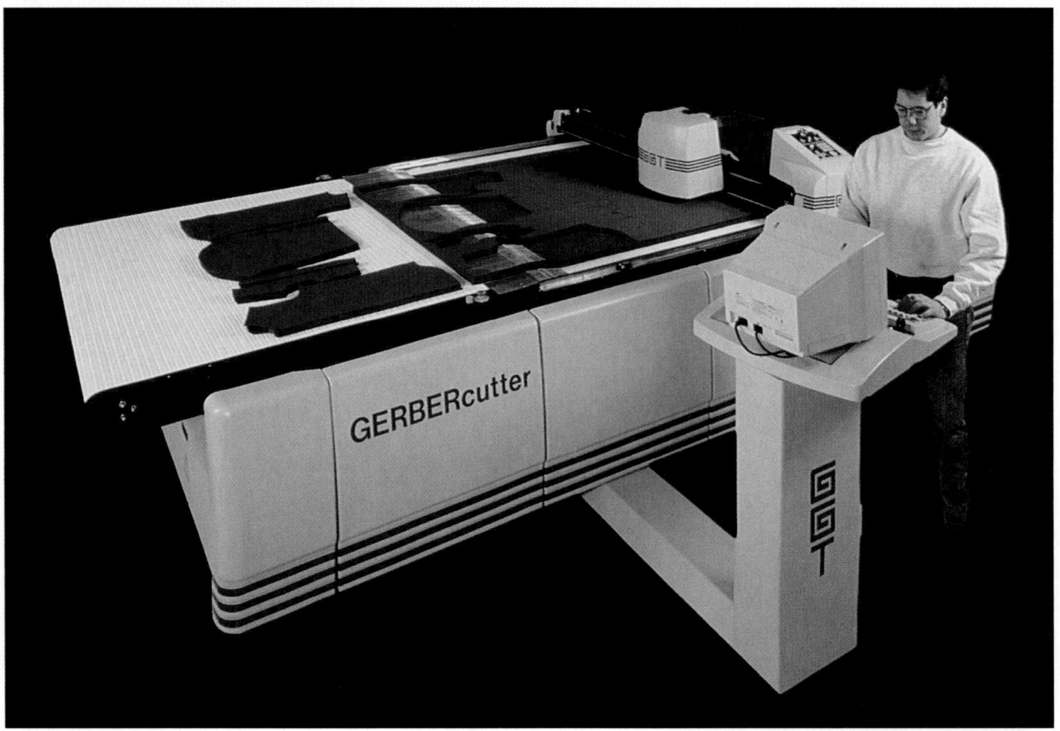

Gerber Garment Technology, Inc.

27-23 With this automated production cutting system, consistent and accurate cutting is controlled through the computer by this trained employee.

eyesight. They must take pride in accuracy. They often have some vocational training, but learn the actual job at the plant site from experienced cutters. However, computerized plants need people with education in computer operations and programming, combined with apparel production technology.

Assorters (also called assemblers) prepare the cut garment parts for production sewing. For progressive bundle manufacturing, they sort and tie the parts into bundles of 12, mark any construction details, and put them into rolling bins. Later in the production process, they bring parts together, such as slacks with their corresponding zippers and waistbands. Factories that use computer-aided manufacturing (CAM) need fewer assorters. Here the parts may be loaded together for each garment on an overhead carrier that will automatically take it through the operation, 27-24. Some assorters may also fold and package finished items.

Sewing machine operators, sometimes called *sewing technicians*, construct apparel on fast industrial power machines. In some factories, they sit and do just one specific task over and over again. When the operators develop more skill and versatility, they can advance to more complicated jobs. If a factory uses stand-up, hand-off modules, the team sewing machine operators have higher skills. They are trained to operate many machines for many different assembly procedures.

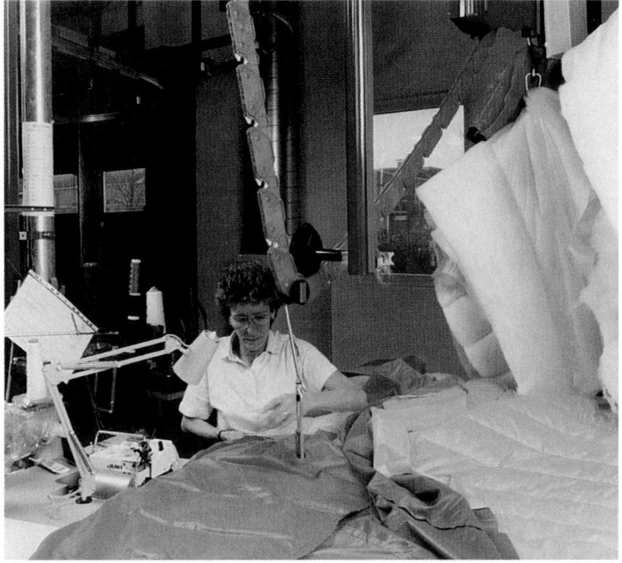

Eton Systems, Inc.

27-24 An assorter has loaded this overhead carrier with sleeping bag parts to go through the sewing production operations.

Sewing machine operators need a basic knowledge of sewing construction and should enjoy doing routine tasks. They must have good manual dexterity, coordination, and eyesight to handle materials and use equipment, 27-25. They must be able to do neat,

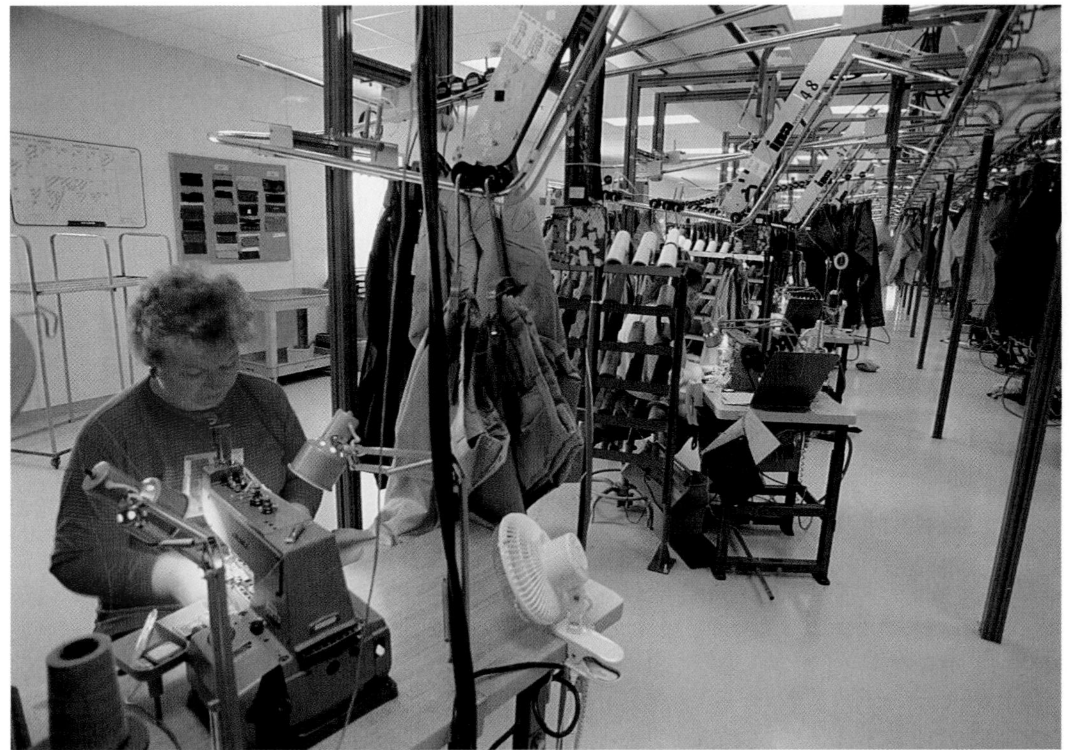

Lands' End Direct Merchants

27-25 Sewing machine operators might do one or several steps in the manufacturing process at specialized machines that must be controlled in various ways.

steady, and accurate work at a fast pace in a compact work area. The work can be tiring because of the rapid pace and pressure for high performance. Also, sewing machine operators should not be bothered by the loud noise of many machines buzzing at top speed.

Sewing machine operators usually work regular hours. Many belong to workers unions. Earnings are low to medium, but increase with higher skills needed for the new technology of the industry. A high school diploma is recommended. Trade and vocational schools offer some training, and manufacturing companies give on-the-job training in the specific construction techniques for their garments.

Finishers are employed mainly by better quality, higher priced lines. They finish garments, such as hand-attaching fasteners, trimmings, hems, or linings. They must have good eyesight and finger dexterity to do rapid, accurate hand sewing. There are few opportunities, but the pay may be higher than that of a machine operator. No higher education is required.

Inspectors/trimmers cut off loose threads, pull out basting stitches, and remove lint and spots from garments. They examine garment parts during production, as well as finished garments after production, to check for flaws or poor quality. They pull out unsatisfactory items and arrange for minor repairs. Bad sewing is sent back to the operator responsible or to *alteration hands* in the factory who correct the production defects. Alteration hands need experience in clothing construction to skillfully perform all techniques.

Pressers flatten seams, iron garment surfaces, and shape garments with steam-pressing machines. Pressing is done during construction of better garments, as well as to garments in all price ranges at the end of construction. Pressers should have a high school diploma and possible vocational school training. They must be willing to learn on the job from a supervisor and have a tolerance for steam and heat.

Production Management

Production management employees oversee the work of others. They study and prepare reports, attend business meetings, and guide the operations so the company can reach its goals. They have college degrees in apparel management, apparel production, or engineering. They may start as *management trainees.*

Production managers with large companies may be transferred to different locations during their careers, moving to plant sites in small U.S. towns and/or to international locations. Good communication, math, computer, and problem-solving skills are needed. A combination of production, technical, administrative, and marketing knowledge is required. People with maturity, the ability to work with varied personalities, and a good sense of organization can advance fairly quickly.

Product managers are in charge of every aspect of one of the company's lines or a specific category of garments within a line. They oversee the design, manufacture, and sales/distribution of that line or category of goods, 27-26. They may work with suppliers, set prices, coordinate promotional activities, and work with their salespeople. They look for new market opportunities and respond to trends, competitor's products, and the image and goals of their company. For instance:

- Do the colors mix and match with other clothes being sold?
- Will the prices be competitive?
- Is the plant's production machinery able to produce them?
- Can existing sales methods and retail outlets be utilized?
- Can manufacturing and delivery dates be met?

If the answers to these questions are "No," design ideas must be changed or rejected.

Product managers are practical with a good business sense. They have college degrees, such as in fashion merchandising, and lots of industry experience. They receive good or high pay. They report to a *marketing manager* who plans and directs all marketing endeavors of the company.

A ***plant manager*** is in charge of all operations and employees at a manufacturing plant. This person is responsible for estimating production costs, scheduling the flow of work in the factory, and hiring and training new workers. He or she oversees the purchasing, cutting, sewing, pressing, quality control, shipping, and all other aspects of production. It is a complex task that is rewarded with very high pay. This job is achieved after years of working up to it through lower plant management jobs.

Lands' End Direct Merchants

27-26 A product manager might be in charge of all items the company sells within a specific category of goods.

Production assistants do detail work and record-keeping for plant managers. They keep track of materials, assist with production schedules, and keep tabs on factory work flow. They control inventory, incoming deliveries, and outgoing shipments. They also keep customers informed about their orders, and expedite certain deliveries. To do this, production assistants need good math, organizational abilities, and spoken and written communication skills. They should be accurate, assertive, thorough, and have a high tolerance for stress. They probably have a college degree in apparel production management or engineering.

As in textile manufacturing, *production supervisors* oversee the workers in the factory. They make sure there is a smooth flow of work, solve problems, and try to motivate the operators to achieve the highest quality and speed of production. They receive medium or good pay.

Piece goods buyers are purchasing agents who research and buy the fabrics, trims, and notions that are chosen by designers and approved by management. See 27-27. Piece goods buyers try to get the highest quality materials at the lowest possible prices. They also keep tabs on any production problems that occur with the fabrics or trims. They should have an interest in and knowledge of fabrics and production methods. They need good math, communication, and organizational skills. Specialized training in textiles, fashion merchandising, or apparel production management is recommended. They receive good or high pay.

Costing engineers determine the overall price of producing each item, including the cost of fabrics and notions, wages for the operators who produce it, and all other manufacturing expenses. To price each separate design in an upcoming collection, they may have to travel to various plants to view production operations and consult with plant managers. They sometimes have *costing clerks*, who assist them by noting and analyzing the figures on specification sheets. Also, CAD systems now include automatic costing calculations when products are being developed.

Just as in the textile industry, quality control engineers develop specifications and maintain standards for the products, plant engineers oversee the physical sites, and industrial engineers are efficiency and safety experts. Industrial engineers also plan the layout of production lines, work station progression, and storage areas. Their time and motion studies establish piece rates for pay of sewing machine operators.

McCall Pattern Company

27-27 Piece goods buyers are specialists who purchase the materials needed to manufacture the company's products.

Textile and Apparel Sales and Distribution

Textile producers and apparel manufacturing companies have similar important career opportunities in sales and distribution. For most of these, experience within the industry and some specialized skills are as important as a knowledge of fashion. The jobs offer a variety of interesting tasks at a fast pace.

Sales employees should represent their companies in a professional manner, while providing their clients with good service. They communicate and sell the textile or apparel company's products to customers. Fiber salespeople sell to yarn producers or fabric manufacturers. Greige goods producers sell to converters. Firms with finished fabrics and notions sell to apparel designers and manufacturers, 27-28. Apparel manufacturers sell to buying offices and retailers, 27-29.

Bobbin, Miller Freeman Inc. Company

27-28 The piece goods buyers described in the previous section do their purchasing of fabrics and notions from sales employees in the segment preceding theirs. The salesperson (standing) is explaining apparel appliqués to the buyers (seated).

Atlanta Apparel Mart

27-29 Apparel salespeople sell their lines to retailers and corporate buying offices.

Sales employees must be friendly, likeable, and ambitious. They must have thorough knowledge of their products to communicate reputable advice and service to each customer. They also need to follow through on details. They should understand the entire soft goods chain, and be able to think quickly to present merchandise with flair and enthusiasm.

As the link between the firm and its customers, salespeople must have integrity to gain and keep the trust and respect of customers. Honesty about quality, dates of delivery, price, and other matters set the groundwork for future sales. Creativity and sensitivity are needed to make the best of each situation and respond to the views of others.

Sales representatives must have poise, self-confidence, maturity, and personalities that can stimulate desires for their products. They should be outgoing, yet sincere, and able to get along with all kinds of people. They must be hardworking and organized to make their own appointments and set their own hours. They must give attention to both the needs of the customers and the interests of the company, using feedback to advise their managers, market analysts, and stylists on fashion directions in the marketplace. Salespeople are the communication link between their company and the market. Line editing and manufacturing are adjusted accordingly.

Sales is a very competitive area of the textile and apparel segments and is not for everyone. It requires stamina, and the ability to withstand pressure and maintain enthusiasm for the company's line. See 27-30. Salespeople are given responsibilities and earnings in proportion to their job performance. For those with the right aptitude and interest, the opportunities and financial rewards can be great. Pay is often a base salary plus a commission on the amount sold. Also, there are opportunities to advance into a marketing or sales manager's job.

It is desirable for sales employees to have completed a program in textiles, apparel, fashion merchandising, business administration, marketing, the sciences, or

EAT, Inc.; The DesignScope Company

27-30 With the activities of talking to others face-to-face and on the telephone and writing out calculations and sale contracts on the computer, the challenging and hectic work of being a salesperson is exciting to those who enjoy it.

liberal arts. Necessary skills include techniques for showing a line, making a presentation, handling objections, and closing a sale. Sales employees should have excellent grooming, be fashionably dressed, and show poise and confidence.

Sales Positions

Showroom salespeople are "in house" sales employees at the firm's sales offices who present the goods to visiting buyers. They show buyers the newest features and colors of the line. Many fashion industry showroom salespeople work in New York City, Los Angeles, Dallas, or other market cities or marts. Hours for showroom salespeople are usually regular, but are long during market weeks. The pay is medium or good. *Sales trainees* learn how to be effective in sales by working under experienced salespeople. They learn about the firms' products, production processes, merchandising techniques, and customer needs.

Showroom salespeople get to know the buyers of the company's important accounts and try to service their needs. For instance, a fabric salesperson might show sample garments made of the fabrics to apparel manufacturers. An apparel salesperson might suggest ways retailers can present and display the merchandise in their stores. Some apparel companies have *merchandise coordinators* who make sure their merchandise is presented as effectively as possible within retail stores. This job, with medium pay, is less stressful and demanding than sales, but is very interesting.

The *showroom manager* supervises all of the personnel and activity in the showroom. He or she makes sure all items are attractively displayed and that all samples are in stock for the buyers. He or she handles any buyers' problems that occur, and trains new showroom employees. This position receives good pay.

Traveling sales representatives make up the "outside" sales force that sells away from the firm's sales offices/showrooms. They travel around for constant contact with customers and the marketplace. Usually they cover a certain geographic selling "territory" for the company by car. They are given sample textile swatches or garment samples at home office sales meetings just before each new line is launched.

Traveling sales reps make appointments with their accounts to inform them about developments such as price changes or new styles added to the line. They may offer displays to customers to promote their products, prepare demonstrations, or present fashion or trunk shows at stores. They try to get new accounts and plan exhibits and do selling during market weeks at marts or convention centers. They take orders and follow through on them to make sure delivery commitments are kept by the plant. They must also deal courteously with customer complaints. Some are called *account executives*, since they work with specific customers in determining their needs and providing products to suit those needs.

Most traveling sales reps are away from home much of the time. They may work long and unusual hours, especially during peak times. Sometimes they are transferred to a different territory. The job can be exhausting, exciting, and very satisfying for those who enjoy both people and fashion. With commissions, the financial rewards for successful reps can be high.

Sales managers supervise several sales representatives in an established "district" of the country or a division of the company. They set sales quotas and guide their salespeople to achieve or surpass the quotas. To direct a smooth flow of products from the plant to the customer, they must understand every step of the industry, through research, design, production, sales, and distribution. Successful sales managers have a good sense of fashion and sound judgment about what customers want.

Sales managers must relate well to people and have strong administrative abilities to achieve top sales. The job is demanding and stressful, with high or very high pay. A college degree is required, and some sales managers also have an MBA degree. Success in the job can lead to top management. Most sales managers were successful salespeople before being promoted to this position.

Distribution Jobs

The physical distribution of goods is a large and dynamic field with many career opportunities. It is recommended that professional distribution employees have knowledge of quantitative methods, finance, accounting, and marketing. ***Traffic managers*** manage distribution centers (DCs) and try to get products quickly from manufacturing to the customer, 27-31. Computers are used to keep records of shipments.

27-31 Traffic managers are in charge of the many details involved in the distribution of goods.

27-32 Distribution jobs involve moving individual orders of merchandise to the proper locations.

Workers are needed to pack and ship the merchandise. Bins of fabric bolts or racks of garments must be moved from place to place, to storage areas, or to the shipping department. Orders must be received, processed, and sent from the manufacturer to each separate account in the right quantities, colors, and other specifications. See 27-32. Quick Response partnership agreements must be honored.

It is important to meet delivery dates to satisfy customers and to check incoming goods accurately. Some of these jobs do not require education beyond high school. However, these workers must be accurate with details and conscientious about doing a good job. Some of the job titles for distribution center workers include clerk, order picker, checker, packer, and transportation specialist.

Summary

Many careers exist in the textile and apparel segments. Industry restructuring, consolidation, and modernizing is increasing the skill levels and pay for employees. The best career opportunities arise for people with solid educations and continually updated skills.

Textile research and development careers are available with fiber manufacturers, textile mills, private testing laboratories, and government agencies. Research work is done by university students, textile research scientists, laboratory technicians, and testers.

Textile design departments try to predict trends far ahead of retail selling seasons, to develop the correct types of yard goods for the market. Fabric designers determine the structural and surface looks of their company's textiles. Fabric lines are developed for each fashion season.

Textile production involves the largest single portion of textile industry employees. Production jobs have such titles as production workers and supervisors, quality control inspectors, and plant and industrial engineers.

Fashion designers create new ideas that combine function and beauty. These employees need imagination and flair, as well as technical knowledge of fabrics, trimmings, fit, pattern making, draping, and sewing. Sketching employees sometimes record designer's ideas with drawings, swatches, and written details. Sample workers make sample garments of the designs.

Apparel manufacturing requires many workers. Preproduction employees make and grade patterns, and make markers. Spreaders, cutters, and assorters prepare garment pieces for sewing machine operators. Finally, the garments are finished, inspected, and pressed. Production managers oversee the manufacturing work.

Textile and apparel sales employees communicate and sell their company's products to customers. They are also the link between their company's design staff and market feedback. There are showroom and traveling sales jobs, as well as administrative positions. Distribution employees try to get the merchandise to the right places at the right times.

To Know

portfolio
research and development (R&D)
print/repeat artist
motif
colorist
strike-off artist
fabric stylist
fashion director
department manager
fabric librarian
market analyst
production supervisor
plant engineer
industrial engineer
sketcher
product manager
plant manager
piece goods buyer
costing engineer
traffic manager

To Review

1. What should a professional looking portfolio contain?
2. Why do researchers need patience, persistence, and flexibility to work toward a solution?
3. College degrees for textile research scientists might be in what subject areas?
4. Name two different places where textile testers might work.
5. When the fashion director of a fiber producer learns that the upcoming season will feature a certain color or silhouette, what does he or she do?
6. Name three types of organizations that maintain fabric libraries.
7. What training should market analysts have?
8. What do fabric surface designers do?

9. What involves the largest single portion of textile industry employees?
10. Name three tasks that electronic (computer) equipment does in textile production.
11. What do design stylists or copyists do?
12. Why must fashion designers understand manufacturing processes and costing?
13. What are three ways that designers might visualize their ideas?
14. What are the three reasons why the number of U.S. apparel industry production workers has been decreasing?
15. Why might the work of a sewing machine operator be tiring?
16. In general, what do production assistants do?
17. How are piece rates established for pay of sewing machine operators?
18. How do sales representatives of apparel production firms affect line editing and manufacturing adjustments?
19. What is a traveling sales representative's "territory"?
20. Professional distribution employees should have a knowledge of what areas?

To Do

1. Try your hand at fabric surface design. Draw a motif that could be continuously printed onto yard goods. Also notice what colors are especially fashionable this season. Combine those colors artistically and add them to your motif. Create two final versions of your motif on paper to be displayed on the classroom bulletin board. Each should have completely different color combinations, possibly on colored backgrounds, as if the fabric was dyed before the print was added.
2. Obtain a course catalog for a nearby trade school, vocational college, or university that offers a curriculum relating to the textile industry or apparel design and manufacturing. Possible references to find schools are *The College Handbook* or the *Index of Majors* in the library or guidance counselor's office, *Career Opportunities in the Apparel Industry and College Directory* from the American Apparel and Footwear Association, or through Web site links on the Internet. Give a report to the class about the requirements to enter the program, contents of specific courses to be taken, length of study to receive particular degrees, anticipated entry-level jobs after graduation, and lifetime career path that could be expected. Answer questions from classmates and encourage discussion about this and other programs.
3. Make arrangements to talk with an employee of a textile or apparel manufacturing plant. Ask about the specialized machines and the skill levels required to operate them. Ask about the use of new technology, especially computer systems. What are the educational requirements for jobs at the plant? What company training is provided? Do people work regular hours or alternating shifts? What are the average pay levels for various jobs? What fringe benefits are offered, as well as social or recreational activities? Compile your findings into a written or oral report.
4. Pretend you are an apparel design stylist. Cut out three fashion drawings or photos from magazines, catalogs, advertisements, or newspapers. Redraw each of the designs, keeping the same general look, but including fewer seams and details, simpler trim, etc. Mount your examples, including an explanation of the types of materials that would be used.
5. Pick one of the jobs in this chapter that sounds especially interesting to you. Do extensive research about it from books, trade journals, computer on-line references, and by talking to people in that profession. Write a report about the job. Analyze your own interests, aptitudes, and skills in relation to possibly pursuing that as your career.

CHAPTER 28

Retail Careers

After studying this chapter, you will be able to

- explain retail career generalities.
- describe retail sales positions.
- summarize the merchandise management career track.
- explain the store management career track.
- describe the jobs of other retail employees.

Almost everyone buys apparel either for themselves or others. Thus, fashion merchandising will always be necessary. You can be on the "cutting edge" in retailing as the industry moves forward with new ideas and technology! Fashion merchandising is exciting for those who want to combine fashion with business.

As this book has discussed, the field of fashion merchandising/retailing involves all of the functions of planning, buying, and selling. The selling activity is split between direct selling done by retailers, and indirect selling or promotion. Careers in promotion will be discussed in the next chapter.

Is a Retail Career in Your Future?

Many career opportunities exist in retailing for people who are interested in textiles and fashion. A steady flow of merchandise must be planned, bought, and sold as efficiently and profitably as possible. Hours might be long, but the excitement of working with new merchandise, as well as receiving a discount on purchases, are fringe benefits. As retailing has become more competitive, employees with higher levels of education and skills have been hired. Individuals who enjoy working with people and understand the needs and wants of consumers are the most likely to succeed.

Retail jobs are available in all geographic locations, with large and small stores, mail-order operations, and electronic retailing. See 28-1. However, because of industry consolidation and the use of new technology that has automated some retail tasks, the number of

Lands' End Direct Merchants

28-1 Retail jobs are available with many different job descriptions. They are located in all sizes and types of communities and in all parts of the world.

In Cooperation with Kmart

28-2 Retail stores offer wonderful opportunities for young adults to fit work into their schedules, while they also learn about retailing.

In Cooperation with The 410 Shoppe

28-3 The owner or manager of a small retail shop must do most of the planning, buying, and selling—including arranging the displays and keeping the store in order.

retail jobs has stopped growing. But many opportunities still exist, especially with mass merchandisers and chains. A good way to start is with part-time or summer retail jobs during your school years or a work-study program, 28-2. People without experience must be willing to start at the bottom. Those with education and training can move up more quickly and to higher levels. The chances for advancement are good for talented, hard-working people.

Retailing has many levels of employment and degrees of responsibility. The division of job duties varies among different stores. Generally, the smaller the store the greater the variety of job responsibilities and tasks performed by an employee. See 28-3. This is because many of the duties are combined. One or two people might do all of the planning, buying, receiving, pricing, advertising, displaying, selling, bookkeeping, and janitorial chores.

As retail stores become larger, managers may be hired to assist the owner/operator. A ***two-functional organization*** has one manager employed to oversee all merchandising duties and another manager in charge of store operations. More salespeople are hired as growth occurs. Eventually, a financial manager is added for a ***three-functional organization.*** These structures are shown in 28-4. With continued growth, a promotion manager would probably be hired.

In large stores or chains, specialized tasks are assigned to different employees, with each concentrating his or her efforts on only those certain tasks.

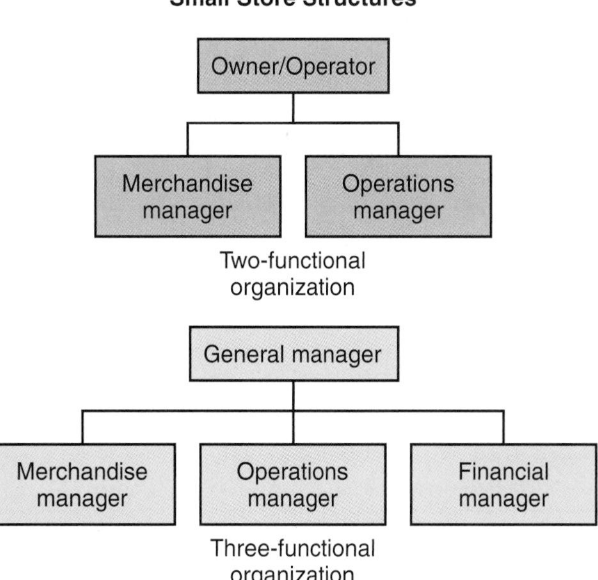

28-4 As an owner/operator or mom and pop store becomes larger, it begins to specialize slightly into merchandise and operations divisions. With more growth, a manager is added to oversee financial matters, resulting in a three-functional form.

Additionally, there are supervisory and executive levels. A typical organizational chart for a large retail store is shown in 28-5. These positions will be described in this chapter. Besides fashion personnel, large retail companies need a legal staff, real estate experts, store planners and designers, auditors, maintenance workers, and other types of employees.

People who want to pursue a career in fashion retailing should be outgoing, well organized, and able to handle figures and details well. They need energy and stamina, and the ability to move and think quickly. They must be able to get along well with others, and work under stress. Also, excellent grooming and a sense of fashion are important. Good leadership abilities and self-confidence enable advancement.

For a professional career, a program in fashion merchandising is recommended. Courses include product planning and development, marketing, sales promotion, fashion buying, merchandise math, and consumer motivation, 28-6. Other subjects studied are retail operations, business law, computer science, and small store management. A knowledge of textiles, garment construction, advertising, economics, accounting, and psychology is also recommended. Retail selling experience is very valuable.

Most large retailers offer management training programs for those with college degrees. In large retail organizations, there are two main career paths for professional employees. One is the merchandise management track, concerned with merchandise planning and buying. The other is the operations management track, concerned with salesforce management and store operations. These two career progressions are shown in 28-7. Employees start both of these as executive trainees, after finishing their formal educations.

Executive (management) trainee candidates are interviewed for management track careers shortly before they graduate from college. They are selected carefully by retail managers for the limited openings. They must be serious about having retailing as a career and willing to learn the business from the ground up. Executive trainee programs exist with large, specialty chains, department stores, and mass merchandisers. The organized programs last between six months and two years.

Executive trainees learn about the store's branches, selling departments, nonselling jobs, cost control, and promotional techniques. They are trained in the areas of supervising and motivating salespeople, sales techniques, customer service, and merchandise classification and presentation. They also learn about pricing,

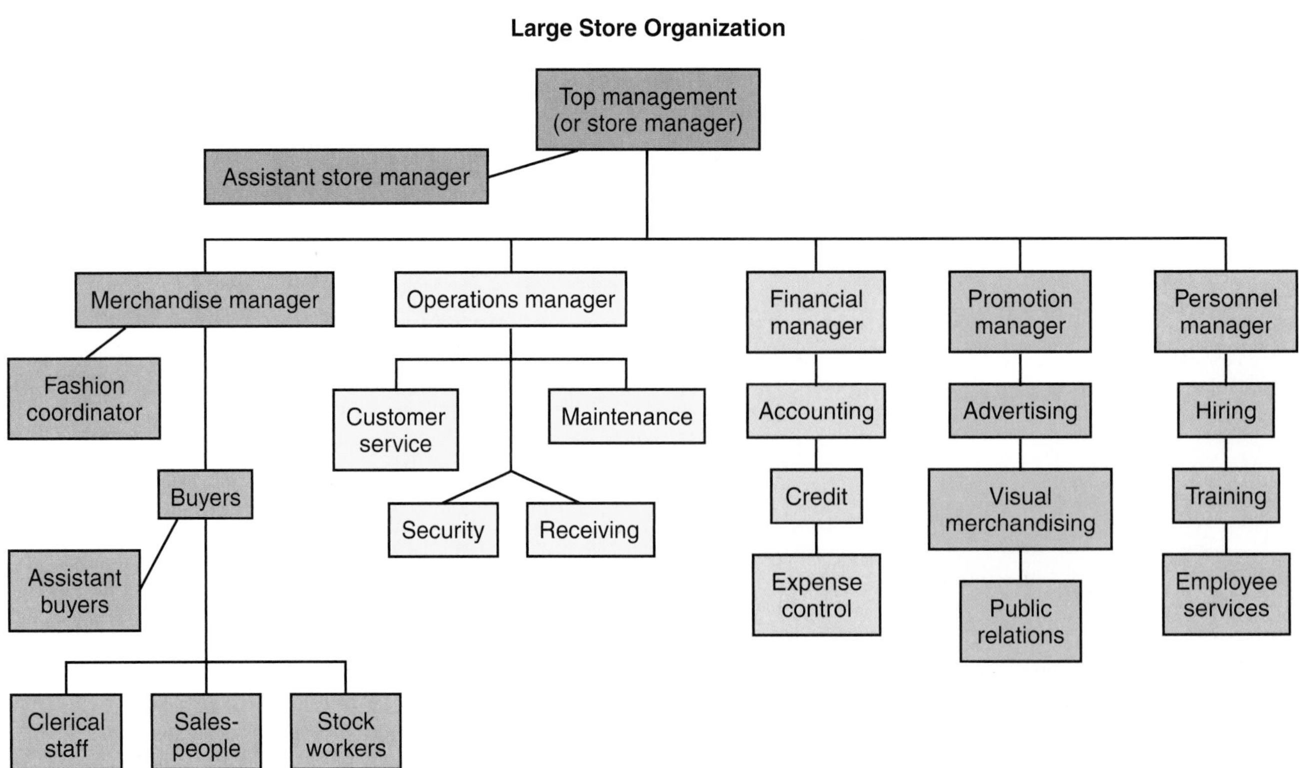

28-5 A large retail store has many layers of jobs with each employee performing only specific duties. Also, the typical organization chart varies from firm to firm.

Fashion Institute of Technology/John Senzer, Photographer

28-6 Courses within a fashion buying and merchandising curriculum prepare students for a professional career in fashion retailing.

Merchandise Management	Operations Management
Vice pres.—merchandising	Vice pres.—operations
General merchandise manager	Regional manager
Divisional merchandise manager	District manager
Buyer	Store manager
Assistant buyer	Assistant store manager
	Department manager
	Assistant dept. manager

Executive trainee

28-7 With a centralized organization, managers either move up the merchandise career path or the store operations track, depending on their interests, aptitudes, and skills.

time management, and reports and statistical analysis. They receive a low salary during the training period, but may emerge as head of stock, an assistant department manager, or an assistant buyer with medium pay. In several more years, depending on job performance, a candidate might advance to a buyer or other merchandising job, or become a department or store manager in the operations track.

Retail Sales Positions

The largest number of employees in most retail companies are involved with direct selling. *Retail salespeople* sell goods directly to customers. There are opportunities in every geographic location, with job openings resulting from turnover of employees. Retail sales tasks may be done on the selling floor of a store or over the telephone. Some people spend their entire careers in direct sales, while others move up to higher level merchandising or store management jobs. The salesperson job is often used as an entry-level position for retailers to evaluate employees for future advancement.

Salespeople are valuable retail employees. They meet the public and represent the company and its image to the outside world. They should be neatly-groomed, get along with many types of people, and always be courteous and pleasant. They must know every aspect of the company's merchandise and be

Symbol Technologies, Inc.

28-8 Most duties of retail jobs, including in-store receiving, involve continuous standing or walking.

quick to understand what customers do or do not want. They must have good communication skills and the ability to show, explain, answer questions, and recommend merchandise in an enticing and enthusiastic way.

Salespeople in ready-to-wear departments may be expected to assemble various fashion looks for customers. They must find appropriate styles and sizes, show customers into the fitting rooms, and check with them periodically to see if another size or style is needed. They must also make sure the merchandise stays in good condition. Displays must be replenished as merchandise is sold.

Salespeople may assist in stock counts and suggest reorders of fast-selling items. They must be able to use the scanning and cash register equipment, compute sales tax, and handle cash, checks, or credit card transactions. They must have basic math skills and be able to give the right change and package the purchases neatly. They may also have to accept returns and refund money. Honesty and reliability are required.

Retail sales work can be tiring, with most of the time spent walking or standing, 28-8. Good health and physical endurance are needed. The job is sometimes available part-time or during holidays, summers, and school breaks. See 28-9. For a permanent job, a high school diploma may be needed.

New salespeople receive in-store training about procedures with sales slips, cash registers, exchanges, and refunds. They are told about stock arrangements and how to deal with specific situations that might occur. They get advice about what should and should not be said to customers. Then they work with an experienced salesperson until they are proficient with all tasks.

The pay for apparel sales work is generally low to medium. It may be based on an hourly wage, commission, or a combination of the two. Most salespeople must work some weekends, evenings, and holidays. Longer hours may be necessary during busy times, such as holiday seasons, special sales, and inventory time. A big advantage is the employee discount, offered

28-9 Many opportunities exist for seasonal retail jobs, providing good work experience for future careers in the retailing field.

28-10 Checkout cashiers must be pleasant and proficient at scanning bar codes, operating the cash register, processing credit cards, gaining approval for checks, making change, and bagging merchandise.

by most employers, on merchandise bought at the store. Other benefits for full-time employees are paid vacation time, sick days, and insurance. The pleasant working surroundings are usually well-lit, air-conditioned, and clean.

Sales work provides an excellent background for almost any higher level job dealing with fashion. The training value of selling experience should not be underestimated. With good performance, a salesperson may advance to assistant buyer or head of stock. For higher positions, a college degree is usually needed.

A *checkout cashier* does not sell, but rings up customer purchases, collects and records payments, makes change, and bags the items. See 28-10. This may be a high school graduate who has been trained by the store to use the checkout equipment—electronic cash register, credit card imprint machine, security tags removal tool, etc. This entry-level job is readily available in self-service retail stores throughout the country, and is a good way to gain experience. Pay is low and a great deal of standing is done. Checkout cashiers must be honest and trustworthy. They must be thorough in performing their duties, plus be friendly and have a pleasant appearance.

The Merchandise Management Career Track

The merchandise management career track moves executive trainees to assistant buyer, buyer, and up through merchandise management positions. These jobs deal directly with decisions about the fashion lines that are selected and sold in the stores where these employees spend their careers.

Retail Buyers

The job of *retail buyer* was introduced in Chapter 15. The job varies with different sizes and types of retail organizations. It is considered to be true merchandising.

In the traditional department store format, a ***departmental buyer*** plans and purchases goods for only his or her own department. He or she is also responsible for the sales and profits of the department. The buyer is the boss of the department's salespeople, and in smaller stores is the department manager, 28-11. The buyer often has an office where calculations are made concerning the budget, merchandise coordination, inventory levels, and other matters. See 28-12.

Departmental buyers instruct salespeople about new merchandise at meetings. They train employees to sell the goods using the best possible techniques. They decide when and how much to reduce the price of goods that are not selling well. They supervise the handling of complaints about merchandise and sometimes do direct selling on the floor to keep in touch with the views of customers. There are hardly any departmental buyers anymore, because single-store, independent department stores have closed or have been purchased by large retail corporations.

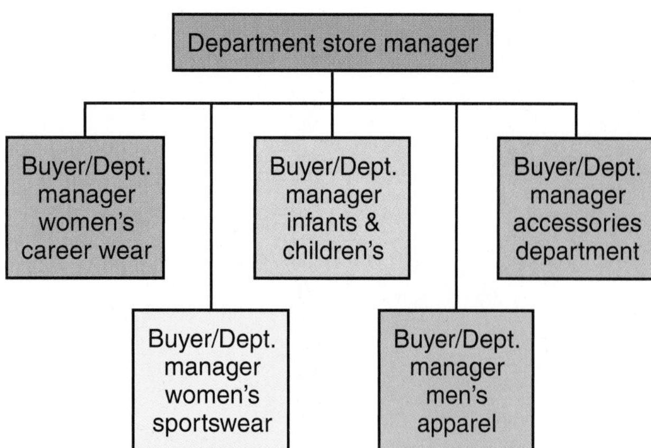

28-11 With the traditional department store structure, each buyer may be in charge of the merchandise, salespeople, finances, and all other activities of his or her department.

Today's huge retail organizations have centralized the procedures of both buying merchandise and distributing goods to stores. They use many ***classification buyers,*** also called *central buyers,* who specialize in only one category of goods. They plan, choose, purchase, price, and promote one classification for all the stores in a chain or large store organization. The classification might be women's sweaters, men's suits, or infant goods. The buyer becomes an expert in that category.

In Cooperation with The Fashion Shop

28-12 Since most space in the store is allocated for merchandise selling, the buyer's office is usually small. The office must contain many resources and records pertaining to merchandise orders, sales transactions, and other business matters.

Most classification buyers work at a central headquarters buying office of the retail company. They may visit all major markets in the U.S., as well as Europe and Asia. Just like other types of buyers, they locate new and exciting sources of merchandise, make selections, and place orders. They reorder the goods that sell well. However, they are not responsible for publicizing or selling the merchandise. Thus, in large stores, the buying and selling functions are separated. However, the classification buyer does disseminate trend and other information to individual stores. Department managers (discussed later) oversee the selling and other tasks in these stores.

The central buying system aims at being very efficient, but has been accused of not being responsive to various store customers or different geographic locations. Thus, some stores are moving toward category management, as described in Chapter 25. *Category managers* oversee business units that customize merchandise and service for individual stores, to better satisfy local needs. It is sometimes hard for traditional buyers to change to the ways of category management, since the job involves more strategic planning and analytical analysis of electronic data.

The Buying Job

The principles of buying are the same regardless of the type of merchandise being purchased or the organizational structure. A buyer who understands the job should be able to adapt quickly to buying different price lines or types of merchandise. To do purchasing, all types of buyers must locate reliable vendors of goods. They go to market several times a year to visit manufacturers' showrooms in major cities or apparel marts. They might travel internationally to source unusual items from foreign manufacturers at good prices. Sometimes they are assisted by resident buyers in market cities they visit. Other times, sales representatives from manufacturers call on buyers at their stores. They do a great deal of research, planning, and recordkeeping. With experience, responsibilities increase as buyers progress to larger departments or more important classifications.

The retail buying procedure is changing. For one thing, long-term Quick Response partnership linkages have streamlined some of the buying duties. Midseason decisions to reorder or not to reorder are based on electronic data collected about sales. Computer-based replenishment systems automatically record, analyze, and act on sales trends, short-term profit opportunities, and inventory levels. Buyers are spending less time interacting with retail customers, and doing more market planning and merchandise specifying.

Additionally, more private label merchandise is being featured, which involves product development or

Lands' End Direct Merchants

28-13 Product managers oversee all aspects of a private label line, coordinating the styles, fabrics, and quality with the company's standards and image.

specification buying. Buyers sometimes become ***product managers,*** responsible for developing, coordinating, executing, and delivering private label corporate programs. See 28-13. They might become ***product sourcers,*** who identify, research, open, and develop production sourcing markets and vendors that meet their company's long-term product supply needs. Apparel sourcing might be done from Europe, Asia, the Middle East, the Caribbean, Central or South America, or the U.S.

College graduates in apparel design or apparel production might start their retail-related careers as *product development trainees* at the central buying office of a large retail company. Beginning duties might include gathering fashion trend information, doing some overseas communications, and handling order follow-up details. More complex duties include working with product development managers and buyers to coordinate styles, prepare specs, locate resources, approve samples, deal with clients, and negotiate deliveries. The final lines must meet buyers' expectations of quality, price point, and timing.

All buyers must make sure the orders from vendors are delivered on time and ready to sell, often arriving in floor-ready condition. Buyers authorize payment for goods, or issue instructions for returns, if defective. They make pricing decisions, see that items are properly marked, and deal with paperwork, computer data, and merchandising finances. They also help promote, display, and advertise the merchandise. Top-level buyers develop an enormous range of contacts with fashion writers, manufacturers, fabric companies, designers, and buying offices.

Buyers put in long, irregular hours, and work some weekends and holidays. They may get only short amounts of time off. The work is competitive, stimulating, exacting, and done under pressure. However, there is opportunity for travel to the fashion centers of the U.S. and world. There is satisfaction, too, when record sales are made with items the buyer chose or helped to develop. Buyers try to outdo the success of competitors as well as their own records from previous years. With success, a buyer can move to a larger department or a more important classification of goods. Eventually, he or she can move up the merchandise management ladder. Retail companies usually pick their top executives from the best buyers.

Buyers' Qualifications

Buyers should love fashion and have good taste to anticipate what styles and prices will be accepted by their customers. They must keep up with fashion trends to know when something is increasing in popularity or has peaked. They must have originality and good ideas of how to promote and sell merchandise. They also must have good grooming and flair with their personal appearance, always being attractively and appropriately dressed.

Buyers must have technical knowledge about the merchandise, as well as a keen business sense. They must be creative and able to organize their work and that of others. They must be outgoing, self-confident, and able to unite their workers into a cooperative team. They must also have patience and tact to deal with manufacturer's representatives, coworkers, and customers.

Retail insiders say that buyers need strong feet and a sense of humor! Actually, they do need enthusiasm and dedication to their work, with good emotional and physical health. They need lots of energy and the ability to remain unruffled when working closely, under pressure, with many people. They need mature judgment and openness to other people's opinions. They also must be able to communicate well with many people, taking and giving directions clearly.

Buyers must be good with figures and details to evaluate sales, margins, markdowns, and inventories. They must know what style numbers have been ordered and what items have been sold. Computer skills are essential, to interpret and react to trends indicated by the data.

Buyers are paid medium to good salaries, that relate to their abilities and responsibilities. Fringe benefits include a discount on store merchandise, paid vacation time, group health insurance, and a retirement plan.

To become a buyer, it is best to have a college degree in merchandising, fashion, or business. Experience, hard work, and proven talent are required. Most buyers are promoted from assistant buyer. Some have worked for fashion magazines before going into retail work. Others have had responsible jobs with fabric or apparel manufacturers.

Assistant Buyers

An *assistant buyer* is an entry-level job for a college graduate, usually after completing the management training program. Assistant retail buyers learn the buying job by helping to present merchandise to retail staffs at sales meetings and assisting with displays and advertising. They keep track of sales and inventories at branch stores, coordinating transfers of merchandise when needed. Sometimes they go to market with the buyer to help select merchandise.

Assistant buyers help trace items during shipment, return unsatisfactory goods, and place reorders. They do clerical work for buyers, calculate markdowns, fill out reports, and step in during the buyer's absence. In these ways, they learn the buying techniques and sources of goods.

Extremely large firms also have the job of ***buyer's clerical,*** which involves keeping accurate records, scheduling appointments, answering phones, and doing follow-up work. Assistant buyers and buyer's clericals must be organized and have the ability to carry out jobs accurately and quickly. They must be able to communicate well, get along with all kinds of people, and remain calm under pressure. They receive low to medium pay.

Resident Buying Office Buyers

RBO buyers help their member retail firms do a better buying job, but have no responsibilities over retail sales or profits. They research wholesale markets and report on trends through written fashion news bulletins. Sometimes they present merchandise clinics or previews of items of one or more leading resources. They recommend suppliers, arrange appointments, and get samples for buyers to see before purchasing decisions are made. Sometimes they visit vendors in the market with member buyers. If requested, they make some buying decisions for their members, as well as placing reorders. They follow up on deliveries, adjustments, and complaints about merchandise.

Resident buying office buyers should have excellent communication skills. They must be able to handle work under pressure and manage several tasks at the same time. They must have a highly developed sense of fashion, both personally and professionally. They work regular weekday hours during most of the year, but have a hectic schedule during market weeks. Their offices are located in major fashion cities.

Merchandise Managers

A ***merchandise manager*** coordinates the merchandise of several retail departments. This manager oversees a group of classification buyers or store departments. Merchandise managers compete with each other for larger sales and profits, and try to beat their own previous records so their parts of the business grow and prosper. They search out new and different sources of items and try to be creative in developing new merchandise ideas or special store departments.

Merchandise managers have usually been promoted after proving their hard work and abilities in lower jobs for a long time. Retail buyers are often promoted to these positions. The managers act as consultants and teachers by sharing knowledge and ideas with employees under them. They must gain and keep the respect of employees at all levels in the company, with patience, diplomacy, and enthusiasm. The responsibility, prestige, and pay are high.

In large companies, the merchandise manager works directly under the divisional merchandise manager. In smaller retail organizations, this job is the same as the divisional merchandise manager. A ***divisional merchandise manager (DMM)*** supervises a group of buyers and/or coordinates the merchandise of several related departments, divisions, or stores—to maximize profits. A division is a segment of the business, divided according to customer or merchandise types. Examples are women's ready-to-wear or men's casual wear.

Divisional merchandise managers serve as liaisons between upper management and buyers in presenting and interpreting company merchandising policies. They have probably been successful buyers for many years. They advise buyers about budget control, and work out problems with vendors and confer with them about market conditions. They oversee merchandise distribution to their group, plan new departments for stores, and implement plans requested by higher management.

In most retail organizations, all divisional merchandise managers report to a ***general merchandise manager (GMM).*** This executive is responsible for the total retail merchandising operation. The GMM is management's link to the divisional merchandise managers and buyers. In smaller organizations, the GMM is the *vice president of merchandising.* In large firms, the GMM reports to the vice president of merchandising. The GMM represents the merchandising organization with top management in determining, interpreting, and executing merchandising policies. General merchandise managers guide those below them to achieve the best profits for the company.

Fashion Director

A retail company's *fashion director* makes sure that all buyers, fashion departments, and stores of a large retail business are kept updated on the latest trends. Just as in the textile industry, fashion directors combine what fashion forecasters say with their own tastes, ideas, and instincts to advise about buying or product development. They inform buyers and merchandise managers about new fashions, and tie the merchandise of store departments together to create a fashion whole. They make sure the company's fashion image is projected to the public. When a color or style of apparel is featured, accessories must be available, too, for complete wardrobe selections. Sometimes fashion directors also run training seminars to update sales personnel. They do not work with budgeting or inventory control.

Fashion directors also assist with promotions of the goods, assembling and harmonizing what goes on display. A theme for each season is suggested to the display manager, with garment and accessories chosen accordingly. Direction is given for publicity and advertisements, to emphasize the right goods in the best ways. When fashion shows are presented, the retailer's fashion director usually supervises the preparations and serves as commentator, pointing out fashion news to the audience. This person tries to make store employees and customers excited about the new fashions.

Retail fashion directors cover worldwide fashion centers to get advanced information. They attend trade shows to see new ideas and investigate product research and development. Then they develop buying and selling strategies for all parts of the complete "fashion story," and transmit that to the employees who buy, promote, and sell the goods. This is time-consuming, demanding, glamorous, and challenging. It requires long hours with considerable pressure. Yet, the excitement of this executive position has stiff competition and is sought by many aspiring retail people.

To be a fashion director, you must be familiar with fashion cycles and understand what affects consumer acceptance or rejection. A highly developed fashion sense is required, as well as an awareness of style lines that leading designers will be using. You must know the contents of all American and foreign fashion magazines. You must be aware of changing social patterns, and be resourceful and flexible.

Fashion directors must have poise, good grooming, enthusiasm, and creativity. They must be able to schedule their time well and make sound decisions, while adapting to many situations. They must be able to work tactfully with others and be comfortable and confident about speaking to large audiences. Most have had lots of successful retail experience, and they are still selling at the executive level. They may have moved up from assistant fashion director or buyer.

An *assistant fashion director* helps the fashion director with details. He or she sets up appointments, makes telephone calls, books models, and runs errands. The assistant helps put on fashion shows, write fashion bulletins, and observe market trends. This scarce, competitive job is only available in large retail firms. Excellent grooming and a keen sense of fashion are required. Poise, self-confidence, and a good speaking voice are also important.

The Operations Management Career Track

For the store operations management track, an executive trainee would first become an assistant department manager. An *assistant department manager* helps the department manager run the area smoothly. He or she might arrange merchandise on the selling floor, manage markdowns, and transfer merchandise. This person may also try to spend a great deal of time on the selling floor to determine customer preferences before moving up to a department manager.

A ***department manager*** runs a department or group of departments *(group department manager)* according to the framework of the company's overall plan. This person is the liaison between the buyer and the sales staff, providing feedback about sales and inventory. The department manager sees that goods are arranged well on the selling floor, merchandise counts are accurate, and reorders are made when needed for the assigned area. He or she trains and supervises the salespeople, opens and closes the registers, does employee scheduling, and handles customer complaints.

Department managers try to maximize volume and profit, while maintaining their company's reputation for quality and customer service. This competitive position usually reports to the store manager or assistant store manager. Previous experience in sales and lower management jobs is desirable. The salary is most often in the medium range.

Assistant store managers help in all phases of store operations, including sales, display, buying, inventory control, and accounting. These positions are often available with specialty chains.

A ***store manager*** is the top person in charge of every aspect of one store's operations. Through subordinate managers, he or she organizes and directs the stocking and selling of goods, and the hiring, training, and scheduling of workers. Store managers are in charge of overall customer service, promotional activities, financial accounts, and community relations. They negotiate contracts for services, such as security and maintenance. They must solve any large or storewide problems, but also receive the credit when things go well. They give instructions and guidance to those who report to them about expected results and procedures.

Store managers must have initiative, lots of energy, and leadership abilities to deal with many people in a friendly, yet firm, manner. They should have a good memory, communication skills, and business sense. They need an outgoing personality and fashionable appearance. Store managers may have to relocate if transferred to different geographic locations. They sometimes work evenings, weekends, and holidays. However, with dependable and well-trained personnel, the store should run smoothly without their constant presence. The salary is medium or good, especially with bonuses for profitable results. The manager has probably been named to this position after being a successful assistant store manager.

For department store organizations that are growing ever larger, the job of ***branch coordinator*** is becoming more important. This person keeps tabs on all the branches to see that their stock, selling techniques, and general operations coordinate with the main store's or headquarters' policies. This executive position is gained after much retail and management experience.

At a higher level, specialty store chains would promote a successful store manager to ***district manager,*** responsible for growth and volume of possibly up to a dozen stores. Above the district manager is a ***regional manager,*** who oversees several districts. The regional manager might have responsibility for up to 75 or 80 stores. He or she reports to the *vice president of stores.*

Average annual salaries for retail merchandise and operations management personnel are shown in 28-14. Merchandising jobs generally pay higher salaries than operations management, but also require more fashion aptitude, flair, and decision-making pressure.

Other Retail Employees

There are many other important tasks that must be accomplished to help retail stores operate smoothly and efficiently. One area of responsibility is stockkeeping.

Stockkeeping Employees

In general, stockkeeping involves receiving goods, protecting them, and controlling their movements. Tasks concerned with *receiving* include checking incoming goods against the numbers of each item ordered, assessing quality, making any necessary adjustments, checking or attaching tags, and authorizing payment of invoices. *Protecting* involves securing and properly storing the merchandise to prevent shoplifting, internal theft, and damage. *Controlling* the goods includes sales analysis to evaluate which items are selling rapidly or slowly, transferring merchandise between stores, and handling returned items.

A *stock clerk* is an entry-level position for someone without college training. People in this job receive merchandise from delivery trucks that bring the apparel to the store. They open containers, unpack items, and compare delivery records with the actual goods that are received. They check the condition of items and file a report if any damage or soiling is found. Then new stock items are entered into computerized stock control lists, often by scanning bar codes on the cartons and/or the items.

Retail Management Average Annual Pay	
Chief Executive Officer (CEO)	$500,000
Vice President—Merchandising	215,000
Vice President—Operations	160,000
Fashion Director	145,000
General Merchandise Manager (GMM)	138,000
Director of Product Development	125,000
Director of Distribution Planning	115,000
Divisional Merchandise Manager (DMM)	105,000
Distribution Center Manager	96,000
Regional Manager—Stores	87,000
Sales Promotion Manager	75,000
Merchandise Buyer	56,000
District Manager—Stores	50,000
Store Manager	32,000

28-14 From industry surveys, these were the average annual incomes for retail executives in the early 2000s. The numbers represent a base salary, plus a bonus. Employees with these titles may receive substantially more or less than these figures.

Stock clerks prepare the merchandise for selling, with price tags or hangers if needed. Then the merchandise is taken to the proper departments and stockroom records are updated accordingly. Stock clerks may also place the items on shelves or racks in the sales area to keep all displays neatly filled. They help count items during inventory time and send back returned merchandise to the manufacturer. They must always know what is on hand and be able to find it. They also fill special orders and keep the stockroom in the proper order.

The job of stock clerk is methodical, with merchandise being handled carefully, quickly, and accurately. It can be physically tiring because it involves lots of lifting, bending, and pushing. It requires good health, stamina, and fine eyesight, as well as dependability, a helpful attitude, and legible handwriting. A knowledge of math, typing, filing, and computers is helpful. However, no higher education is needed after high school. The store provides training in their procedures, records, and forms. Hours are regular, and wages are low. However, regular benefits are often provided and there is usually an employee discount on purchases.

The ***head of stock*** is the employee in charge of the merchandise for a given department or area. He or she keeps stock on the selling floor in good order, maintains merchandise in reserve, and monitors inventory levels. This job is sometimes equated to assistant departmental buyer. It is an entry-level position for a college graduate, or the person may have been promoted from stock clerk or salesperson. The head of stock reports to the department manager or buyer.

Large retailers have ***distribution planners*** at their central or regional distribution centers who keep track of the thousands of units of merchandise through computerized records. Breakdowns of each style are done by sizes and colors for distribution among their branch or chain stores. They communicate with buyers and merchandise coordinators to allocate various needed items of stock, and immediately update records of all movements of goods. This is an entry-level job for a college graduate of business or merchandising. Strong knowledge of fashion, math, and data analysis is required. Higher jobs are *distribution center manager* and *corporate director of distribution planning.*

Additional Retail Jobs

There are many other important jobs in retail stores. For instance, ***training supervisors*** give orientation classes in large retail companies, to new salespeople. Training supervisors might also teach current salespeople about new equipment or procedures. Sometimes new fashion colors, styles, and promotional plans are stressed. Training supervisors also help plan and run the company's executive training programs. In smaller companies these duties are combined with another supervisory job.

Training supervisors receive medium or good salaries. A college degree may be required, and retail experience is a must. Training supervisors must be self-confident, organized, and businesslike. They must be able to meet people easily and communicate ideas clearly. The job combines office work, teaching, and promotional activities.

As in other industries, the following employees are needed by retail companies:

- *Personnel director:* This manager oversees the hiring and benefits of employees. Sometimes this person must also dismiss an employee who has done an unsatisfactory job, is unreliable, or has been dishonest. The personnel director has probably not advanced through direct selling jobs, but must know what tasks are done and what qualifications are needed for each job.
- *Customer service managers:* These people serve as intermediaries between their store and its customers. They handle complaints, special orders, and home delivery. They also oversee courtesy needs, such as credit purchases, gift wrapping, returns, and exchanges. They investigate and try to solve problems that consumers have with the store or its merchandise to keep customers happy. They make sure each salesperson treats shoppers fairly. They also keep records of all matters, and guard customers against illegal business practices. The manager must have experience with the store, talent for dealing effectively with all kinds of people, and the ability to solve problems. The salary is medium or good.
- *Alterations experts:* Alterations experts are employed by stores that do not send out their alteration work. This person takes in, lets out, and reshapes garments that do not fit the purchasing customer properly. This employee must be proficient at all garment fit/adjustment techniques and sewing procedures, 28-15. Such skills are learned from high school or trade school courses, plus lots of sewing experience. The pay is low to medium.
- *Garment fitters:* If an outside alteration service is used, a garment fitter may be available to mark or pin changes wherever they are required. See 28-16. The alterations are then recorded and specific instructions are attached to the garment.
- *Comparison shoppers:* These employees compare the prices, services, and displays and advertisements of competitors with that of their own company. They note the amount of merchandise and its fashion level. They make purchases in their store (without the sales clerk knowing they are an employee) and in other stores to evaluate sales and service techniques. They keep company managers informed so problems can be anticipated and eliminated, and good programs can be expanded. Sometimes, this is part-time employment or a temporary job. There are limited positions available, and pay is quite low. No higher education is needed, but some retail experience is desirable to evaluate selling techniques and merchandise quality and price value. Comparison shoppers should be able to communicate clearly and be organized enough to evaluate their findings into meaningful conclusions.
- *Personal shoppers:* Also called ***fashion consultants,*** these employees select merchandise in response to customers' mail or telephone requests. At other times, they accompany customers in the store to offer fashion advice and help them choose the best items for their needs. Thus, personal shoppers must be familiar with current fashion trends and the standards of dress for various professions and lifestyles. They must have a pleasant, tactful personality, as well as the ability to listen and respond to requests. Education beyond high school may not be required, but extensive retail experience and a flair for fashion are needed.

In Cooperation with The Fashion Shop

28-15 The alterations expert of an upscale fashion store would be available to fit garments on customers as they try them on and to do the alterations in a backroom of the store.

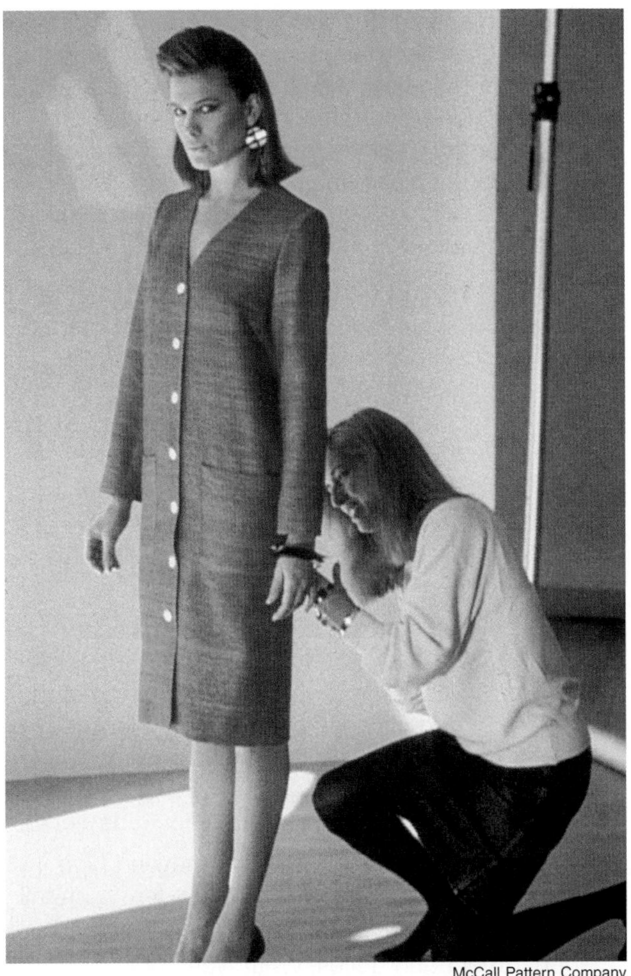
McCall Pattern Company

28-16 Salespeople are often trained to mark garments for alterations. If this is not the case, a garment fitter is needed so the proper changes can be made by the outside alteration service used by the store.

- *Quality assurance testers:* These employees evaluate merchandise to determine if quality standards have been met as established by the retail firm. Only a few large companies maintain their own product testing laboratories.

Summary

Many career opportunities exist in retailing–to plan, buy, and sell merchandise as efficiently and profitably as possible. Various levels of retail jobs are available in all geographic locations. More specialized tasks are done by employees of large stores or chains.

The largest number of employees in most retail companies do direct selling. Sales employees represent the company to the public. They must know the merchandise and make sure it stays in good condition. They need good communication skills and physical endurance. Sales work provides an excellent background for most higher level jobs dealing with fashion.

The merchandise management career path includes buying jobs. Retail buyers might be departmental, classification, or resident buying office buyers. They locate reliable vendors, and do planning, recordkeeping, and purchasing. Quick Response partnerships and private label product development have changed the buyer's job. Buyers should love fashion, and have knowledge about merchandise and business. With success, they might become a merchandise manager, divisional merchandise manager, general merchandise manager, or vice president of merchandising. Fashion directors update merchandisers about the latest fashion trends, as well as assisting with displays and fashion shows.

The operations management career path goes from department to store to district to regional managers. It is headed by the vice president of operations at the corporate level.

Stockkeeping employees receive, protect, and control the movement of goods. Jobs include stock clerk, head of stock, distribution planner, distribution center manager, and director of distribution planning.

Other retail employees include training supervisors, personnel directors, customer service managers, alterations experts and garment fitters. Comparison shoppers, personal shoppers, and quality assurance testers are among the many other important jobs with fashion retail firms.

To Know

two-functional organization
three-functional organization
executive (management) trainee
departmental buyer
classification buyer
product manager
product sourcer
buyer's clerical
merchandise manager
divisional merchandise manager (DMM)
general merchandise manager (GMM)
department manager
store manager
branch coordinator
district manager
regional manager
head of stock
distribution planner
training supervisor
fashion consultant

To Review

1. What career field combines fashion with business?
2. Why has the number of retail jobs stopped growing?
3. With continued growth of a three-functional organization, what is the next manager who would probably be hired?
4. What characteristics should people who want to pursue a career in fashion retailing possess?

5. In large retail organizations, what are the two main career paths for professional employees and the thrust of each?
6. With what kinds of retail companies do executive trainee programs exist?
7. What entry-level job is often used by retailers to evaluate employees for future advancement?
8. Why are salespeople such valuable retail employees?
9. On what is the pay for apparel sales work based?
10. Where do most classification buyers work?
11. Buyers must have patience and tact to deal with what three types of people?
12. Why are computer skills essential for buyers?
13. When retail organizations present fashion shows, what role does the fashion director usually have?
14. In the operations management track, what is the first job after completing an executive trainee program?
15. Who is the liaison between the buyer and the sales staff, providing feedback about sales inventory?
16. In general, what three functions does stockkeeping involve?
17. Why is the job of stock clerk physically tiring?
18. From what three backgrounds might the head of stock come?
19. What three types of work activities are combined for training supervisors?
20. What do quality assurance testers do?

To Do

1. Make an appointment to interview someone in a fashion retail position that interests you. Be prepared with a list of questions. Ask about particular qualifications or educational requirements for the position, job responsibilities, particular skills used, company training offered, hours worked, job duties, type of pay (salary, commission—not amount), fringe benefits, advantages, disadvantages, etc. Give an oral report to the class about your findings. Also, write a thank you note that mentions how you shared the information with the rest of the class.
2. Select a fashion retailing position of interest to you. Investigate it further from library or Internet references, supplemented by looking at help-wanted classified ads in your local paper. List some of the businesses in your area that employ people in the job and the types and number of positions currently open. Summarize hours, wages, and specific working conditions. Also evaluate the pros and cons of the job for you, personally.
3. With another student, create a bulletin board display that shows the two major career tracks in retailing. With each of you taking one side of the display, put job titles in bold letters, followed by a list of job responsibilities for each position, personal requirements, skills, pay level, and any other pertinent information that should be noted.
4. Assume the fictitious identity of a retail buyer for a particular department of a local department store. Write a report that describes your department and duties. What types of merchandise would you buy for the department to sell? Clip pictures from catalogs or advertisements of specific items that you would stock, and explain why you selected the items. Tell how you would increase your department's profits and encourage the sale of items that were not selling well.
5. Interview the owner/manager of a small apparel store. Ask how his or her position differs from that of a retail buyer or a merchandise manager in a large chain or department store. Ask the pros and cons of working in a small store versus a large store. Prepare a report about your findings.

CHAPTER 29

Promotion Careers

After studying this chapter, you will be able to

- explain how fashion is communicated by models, photographers, writers, illustrators, and audiovisual workers.
- describe visual merchandising careers.
- give examples of fashion advertising employment.
- explain public relations job opportunities.

Just imagine—if you had a career in fashion promotion, you would be able to show the excitement of new trends to the public! Fashion promotion is the indirect selling function of merchandising. It includes modeling, photography, fashion writing, illustration, and audiovisual work. It creates market demand among the general buying public for the latest garments and accessories. For retailers, it builds the company's fashion image, increases store traffic, fosters goodwill with the community, and sells merchandise.

Fashion promotion is done by a network of supporting auxiliary businesses to the fashion industries. Promotion activities are used to some degree by all fashion firms. Internal sales promotion of large retail companies is often divided into visual merchandising, advertising, and public relations departments, 29-1.

Communicating Fashion

The latest in fashion merchandise is communicated to business people and consumers through fashion promotion work. Many exciting, challenging, and rewarding jobs are available in these career areas.

Modeling

As described in Chapter 23, fashion models wear garments and accessories to show how they look when

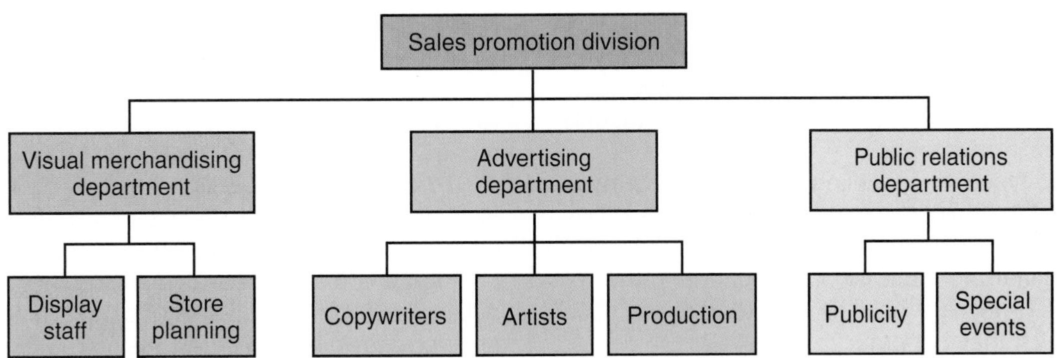

29-1 Many specialized jobs are required for retail promotional activities. They all work together in a coordinated team effort.

Kellwood Company

29-2 Accessorized outfits shown on live models are more clearly portrayed than if they are promoted on hangers or with just written descriptions.

Fashion Institute of Technology/John Senzer, Photographer

29-3 Runway models can show apparel in very animated ways since they parade in front of audiences who are assembled to watch the fashion show.

Department of Consumer Studies; University of Delaware

29-4 Fit models put on design samples to show the look and fit of the garments to designers and other company decision makers. They also model the manufacturer's garments for retail buyers who want to see the line.

being worn, 29-2. Modeling is a combination of advertising and performing. The model must stand, turn, and walk to demonstrate the features of the clothing. Models also pose for photographs.

Several types of modeling jobs exist. ***Runway models*** work in front of live audiences. See 29-3. This might be done at restaurants, retail stores, community events, seminars, on television, or at trade shows or conventions. They are paid by the hour or for each show in which they perform.

Some models work in design areas and showrooms of designers or manufacturers. This "mannequin work" is done by fit models. ***Fit models*** try on and model samples for the company's management and help to sell the line to retail buyers. These models are hired to fit the proportions of the company's clothing. See 29-4. They work full-time, regular hours, and receive salaries and company benefits. Extra part-time models are hired during the buying seasons.

Photographic models pose in front of cameras for pictures used in press releases or advertisements of manufacturers and other firms. See 29-5. Their photographs may appear in fashion magazines, trade publications, newspapers, and pattern catalogs. They are also shown in mail-order catalogs, direct-mail fliers, garment packaging, billboards, and computer online services. They are paid by the hour, day, or assignment.

Monsanto Fibers

29-5 Many pictures are taken of photographic models in various poses wearing several outfits during photo shoots.

Cesarani

29-6 Although the finished photos may look glamorous and spontaneous, a photographic model may work under the hot lights for many hours, wearing warm sweaters, suits, or coats.

JCPenney

29-7 Youthful models are needed to show consumers the children's fashions available at retail locations, especially during the back-to-school season.

Photographic models must be photogenic and responsive to direction. They must be able to convey pleasure, surprise, or other feelings. They may work long hours in hard-to-hold poses under bright lights, 29-6. Slimness may be important since photos make the model's body look heavier than it really is.

The typical model is young, tall, and thin because our society considers those attributes to be "ideal." Most models are in their early 20s, but there is a growing demand for older or heavier models, or models with disabilities. These images represent the way people really are. Some very young models are needed to model children's clothes, 29-7.

Because of the desire for youth, a modeling career may only last a short time. For female models, the average working time is about 10 years. For male models, it is about 20 years. Models should realize they may have to go into another line of work in the future. Modeling can be a stepping-stone to other apparel careers.

Because of pressure to maintain a certain image for modeling, eating disorders and drug use sometime develop. These are extremely damaging to the body, energy level, and ability to work, and harm the chances to be a model. To maintain their health and fitness, models should get plenty of sleep, eat balanced meals, and exercise regularly. They must be ready for a job at any time, and able to adapt to unusual schedules. Models need perfect grooming, a fashion sense, good posture, and above average appearance. They must have physical stamina, as well as determination and patience. They should have poise, style, and flair to move effectively in the clothes they wear. They also need self-confidence and pleasant, outgoing personalities.

Professional modeling is very competitive, demanding work. It can be glamorous, however, employment is often unpredictable and earnings can be irregular. Fees increase as a model becomes more experienced and better known.

To go into modeling, you might want to consider enrolling in an accredited modeling school. There you would learn techniques of how to stand, pose, and move properly. You would study posture, speech, hairstyles, and makeup. Additional training or experience in dance, drama, art, fashion design, and retail sales would also be helpful. However, none of this guarantees you a modeling career. Make sure the school has a job placement service before you decide to attend. Thoroughly read any contracts you are asked to sign.

A modeling employment agency arranges job opportunities and interviews for models. Often, modeling agencies also train models. To register with a modeling agency, several enlarged, unretouched photos are needed that show you in various poses. One should be full-length, one close up, and at least one smiling. You will fill out an application form listing your name, address, age, height without shoes, weight, and body measurements.

Although New York City has the greatest number, modeling jobs are available in most other major cities. Large businesses almost always hire models through agencies. However, you may apply directly to advertising agencies, newspapers, retail stores, or apparel manufacturers. In each case, include photographs and a resume, listing training, experience, and personal specifications.

Kellwood Company

29-8 A fashion photographer has decided the interesting texture, neutral background, and outdoor feeling is a perfect setting in which to photograph this outfit.

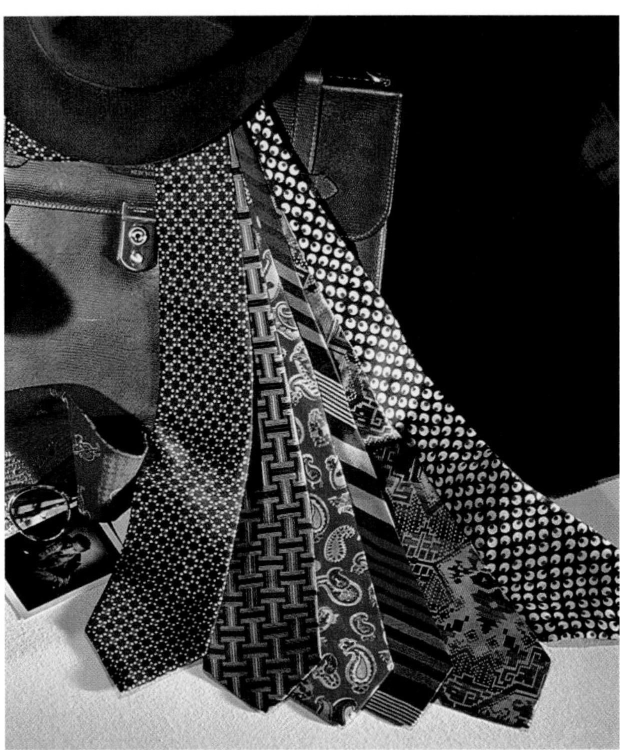

Cesarani

29-9 Interesting arrangements of merchandise are photographed as still shots for some types of promotion.

Fashion Photography

Fashion photographers take still pictures that show fashionable clothes and accessories looking their best. They also try to express moods through the settings and compositions of their photos. They use creative props and interesting backgrounds, 29-8. Photographers may take pictures of fashion apparel on live models or still shots of fashion merchandise, 29-9.

When using a model, a fashion photographer often tries to make the picture look like the model is in motion. The model moves and poses for many pictures. After printing, the best ones are chosen.

Photography is considered to be one of the most flexible forms of artistic expression in fashion communication. Photographers are hired by photo studios, advertising agencies, publications, and large retailers. Their work may require some travel. They may work as salaried employees or as freelancers. Only top talent receives top pay.

A fashion photographer should have an interest in all art forms, fashion trends, and people. Besides talent and imagination, photographers must have sound technical training. They must understand lighting techniques, effects with black-and-white and color film, and how to use professional cameras and other equipment. See 29-10. A knowledge of darkroom procedures is also necessary.

Fashion photographers need to take photography classes after high school to learn the technical aspects

29-10 This photographer is recording the window displays of a department store along Fifth Avenue in New York City. He must know all the technical aspects of using his equipment, using available lighting, and avoiding glare from the glass of the windows.

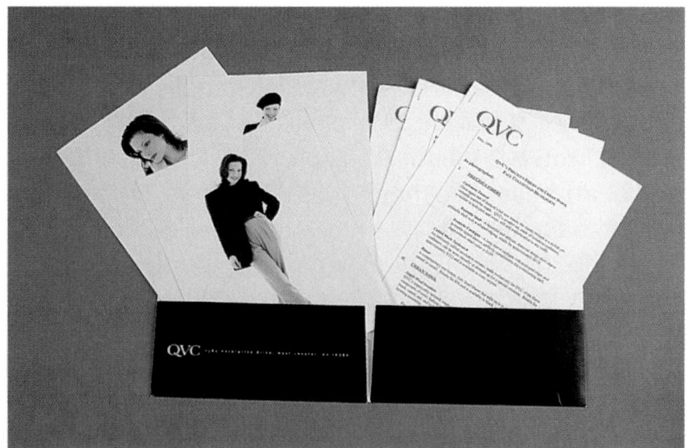

In Cooperation with QVC

29-11 Press kits make the job of fashion reporting easier because photos and accompanying text are included. The reporter can choose to use a large or small amount of what the kit contains, or to do completely independent research.

of photography. They should also study fashion display and advertising design. A portfolio must be prepared to show prospective employers the types and quality of work the photographer is capable of doing.

Assistant photographers are apprentices getting on-the-job experience under professional photographers. They test the lighting, take sample photos, and help prepare sets and props for backgrounds. When they have proven their technical abilities, they also work with the darkroom equipment to develop the pictures.

Photo stylists book models, accessorize apparel, obtain props, pin up hems, iron garments, and pick up and return merchandise. They work in photography studios, advertising agencies, or as freelancers. They must understand both fashion and photography, and may work long hours during demanding times. They need enthusiasm, stamina, flexibility, resourcefulness, a high tolerance for stress, and a strong sense of style and color.

Fashion Writing

Fashion journalists write, edit, and pass along fashion information through the mass media. They work mainly for newspapers and fashion magazines, and sometimes for trade journals. Fashion authors might also write books on topics such as wardrobe planning, colors for individuals, fictionalized fashion novels, or fashion-related textbooks.

A ***fashion reporter*** or *fashion editor* for a newspaper may write a daily or weekly column, or periodic feature stories. He or she may write about fashions seen at important social and cultural events. Some fashion writers do freelance work part-time from home. For monthly magazines, full-time writers usually do more than one article. These often are accompanied by several fashion photos or illustrations.

Press kits from manufacturers, advertisers, or trade organizations are sometimes used as sources of information for fashion journalists. Press kits contain photos, along with descriptions or short articles about a company's latest designs, 29-11. Generally, fashion writers write their articles based on their own research. They gather material from personal interviews, phone calls, and fashion events. Some fashion news items come over the wire service.

A writer often covers a specific subject area, such as fabrics, accessories, knitwear, or couture designers. Sometimes the writer serves as a technical consultant to other staff members, photographers, and advertising people. Writers may travel to market centers to see the latest fashions during fashion press weeks. They must keep in touch with key people in textile production, fashion design, and apparel manufacturing.

Fashion writers must be creative and write precisely, while being under the pressure of deadlines. The latest interesting and useful information must be researched and explained to the proper audience. The information must always be presented clearly and thoroughly.

Members of the "fashion press" must have a flair for writing and a keen sense of fashion. They must keep up with changes in the industry and have the ability to spot newsworthy trends or feature material. They must be able to organize their time and work well alone. They must also be outgoing to arrange and conduct interviews. Writers must be able to think and act quickly, to obtain as much information as possible from each interview.

To become a fashion writer, you should have a college degree in journalism, combined with merchandising, apparel, and advertising courses. Computer skills are essential. You should also read fashion publications to analyze the styles of various writers. When you apply to publications that allot space to fashion, become familiar with the newspaper or magazine beforehand and take appropriate samples of your writing with you. Then you can point out your specific qualifications that blend well with that publication.

Beginning salaries in fashion journalism are low or medium, with increases for education, experience, and ability. Fringe benefits vary among employers. Working hours may be irregular, depending on events to be covered and deadlines to be met. The work is exciting and offers challenges and variety. However, lots of competition exists for a limited number of jobs, most of which are located in large cities.

Copywriters

Copywriters compose the word messages that describe items that are being promoted in advertisements, brochures, magazines, and catalogs. See 29-12. They write the information as editorial text, or as blurbs

DuPont Company/Supplex®

29-12 A copywriter has written the upbeat descriptive text that accompanies the photographs on this page from a trade advertisement.

that accompany photographs or illustrations. Often fashion items must be accurately described with as few words as possible. Copywriters work from essential information that is given to them, such as description, price, fabric credits, or stores where available.

Copywriters should be creative, mature, and able to translate ideas into words quickly and under pressure. They must be thorough, flexible, and able to spot trends and identify resources. They also need good computer skills. A degree in English, advertising, or journalism, with a fashion emphasis, helps to develop these attributes. Trade schools also offer training in advertising and communications. When applying for a job, a copywriter should have a portfolio with examples of his or her written copy.

Editors

Editors usually supervise fashion writers and copywriters. They might be in charge of one or more departments of a publication, such as fabrics or accessories. They should have extensive experience in their fields of expertise. They are administrators, as well as journalists, who set policies and give assignments. They sometimes supervise photography sessions. They are responsible for all information being accurately and creatively presented to the correct readership audience. Eventually an editor might advance to become editor-in-chief of a fashion magazine.

The activities of fashion editors vary according to the importance that each publication and its readers attach to fashion information. For large general publications, the fashion editor is assisted by a fashion staff that might include photographers, illustrators, and writers. The editor is the publication's authority on all aspects of fashion and apparel. He or she interprets fashion news, influences the acceptance of fashions, and advises manufacturers about the fashion interests of the publication's readers.

Editors must have imagination, integrity, vision, and administrative skills. They should be confident and alert at important social events. Besides flair and proven ability, they must have a business mind, know the apparel industries, and be well-organized. Editing is hard work. However, most editors have high prestige and high to extremely high pay, depending on the job level and publication.

Fashion Illustration

Fashion illustrators draw garments that have been designed and produced by others, showing complete accessorized outfits. Illustrators try to show the good points of apparel to promote and sell the fashions. They are employed mainly by retail stores, pattern companies, and advertising agencies. Some are hired by fashion publications, design or display studios, and forecasting or buying offices. Textile and apparel manufacturers also employ fashion illustrators or sketchers, previously described in Chapter 27.

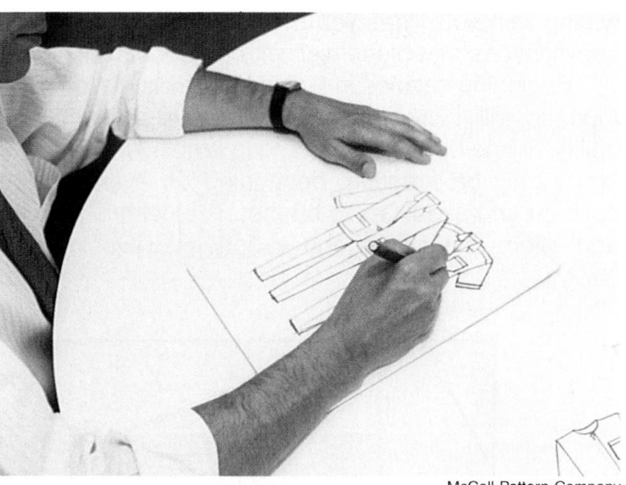

McCall Pattern Company

29-13 An illustrator for a pattern company must do detailed drawings that accurately show seams, darts, gathers, and other structural details.

Fashion illustrators who work for a pattern company give emphasis to seams and trimming details of the apparel. This gives the sewer an idea of the construction required, 29-13. For fashion magazines or trade publications, the illustrator might point out trends or garment features being described by the fashion writers. For retailing and advertising uses, exotic background touches might be added to catch the attention of viewers and tempt them to buy what is shown. Illustrations done for forecasters show trend predictions. Buying office illustrators draw the latest fashions to show their member retailers. Those employed by textile firms illustrate fashionable uses for their company's line of fabrics. In manufacturing firms, the drawings often record a season's line.

To be a fashion illustrator, you must be artistic and have a knowledge of fabrics and fashions. You need flair, initiative, and determination. You must be able to work quickly under the pressure of deadlines. You should keep up with current art and fashion news through trade publications, magazines, art and costume exhibits, fashion shows, and displays.

Competition for illustration jobs is keen, with most opportunities being in big cities. When seeking a fashion illustration job, a portfolio is needed with examples of your best work. Your illustrations should be of interest to the type of employer you contact. The salary for these jobs is generally medium, but depends on the person's talent, as well as the size or type of firm. Illustrators usually work regular hours.

To succeed in this field, your natural artistic talent should be further developed at a trade school or

Fashion Institute of Technology/John Senzer, Photographer

29-14 Educational curriculums in fashion illustration can provide strong skills and practice in developing a personal style of drawing garments on the human figure.

college. In these programs, art courses concentrate on drawing the human figure. See 29-14. There is also training in advertising design, all art media, and the use of art studio equipment. Many people develop their own distinctive styles of illustrating. Some become freelance illustrators after gaining on-the-job experience and making many good contacts. Freelance work can be more challenging, satisfying, and profitable than staff work, but is usually less steady.

Audiovisual Work

Fashion-related ***audiovisual work*** involves radio, television, and multimedia presentations. Job activities for those behind the camera include planning programs, writing scripts, getting props, and producing the presentations. These workers must have a knowledge of fashion as well as all areas of communications. They must be able to write descriptive, informational dialogue quickly and accurately, and present ideas clearly and simply.

Other jobs are available for those who are in front of the camera or who appear in the presentations. They must be confident and outgoing, while sounding natural and sincere. They should have a pleasing voice and appearance.

The audio tape, video, or film productions may be local or national commercials, promotional fashion tapes, interviews with designers at their collection showings, telecommunications shopping programs, or entertainment talk shows with fashion themes. The productions might be used to sell products, educate consumers or students, train or update industry people, or strictly for entertainment. See 29-15.

The Fashion Association and JCPenney

29-15 Elsa Klensch, of the CNN television network, plans and appears in regularly scheduled fashion programs. Here she gives an acceptance speech after designer Donna Karan has presented her with the ALDO (excellence in fashion journalism) Award for Lifetime Achievement.

29-16 Audiovisual workers must stay up with the latest techniques and equipment in order to make effective audiovisual presentations.

For this work, you must have good organizational skills and be detail-oriented. You must deal with tight schedules, frequent deadlines, long rehearsals, and irregular schedules. To be successful, you should be able to meet and get along with people under all circumstances and work with poise and self-confidence. It helps to stay up-to-date on new fashion trends.

A degree in audiovisual communications is recommended for this work. Courses in writing, speech, drama, and the use of equipment are especially needed, 29-16. You may also enter this field through experience in fashion, advertising, or journalism. Employment might be with a broadcast station, an advertising agency, a marketing firm, or a video production company.

Visual Merchandising

As discussed in Chapter 22, visual merchandising is intended to show customers what merchandise is available and how items can be combined and accessorized. Each retail wall, counter, rack, or display should be eye-catching to encourage consumers to select and buy merchandise, 29-17. If retailers do not have their own visual merchandising department, they can contract with a freelance service to do their displays at scheduled times. Large chain organizations draw up visual merchandising plans at their central headquarters and send them with instructions to local store managers for implementation.

Display managers are head employees of retail display staffs who oversee all display work. They often work for retail stores. When planning displays, they consult with the company's buyers and merchandise

Western Kentucky University

29-17 This visual merchandiser was hired by JCPenney after receiving the needed credentials to do his job.

managers, and advertising and public relations people. Like other merchandisers, they must know what to feature, to whom, and why and when it should be presented. They might emphasize holiday seasons, a new color, a fashion trend, or a community event. They prepare rough sketches, outline ideas, and make blueprints or models for the display staff to follow, staying within a certain budget. They sometimes arrange for television monitors to show videotapes for customers to view in particular locations.

Display designers and *window dressers* (also called window trimmers) do the interior and window displays. These designers must understand techniques with lighting and props. They must have a good imagination and know how to use design elements and principles. A knowledge of carpentry and sewing is helpful, as well as merchandising, accessorizing, lettering, and painting, 29-18. These skills can be learned in display design programs in vocational schools and colleges. See 29-19. Education is usually followed by an apprenticeship with a display designer, window dresser, or manager.

Fashion Institute of Design and Merchandising, California

29-19 Visual merchandising students learn specific ways of presenting merchandise in the most appealing ways.

Fashion Institute of Design and Merchandising, California

29-18 Schools with curriculums in visual merchandising supplement their design theory courses with the practice of actually creating interior and window displays.

Fashion Advertising

People in fashion advertising try to attract and inform audiences to encourage them to buy products. They may work for retail stores, manufacturers, advertising agencies, or publications. To succeed, people in advertising must know the merchandise, as well as effective approaches to reach the right customers. They must formulate and follow complete advertising programs for products. A variety of jobs are available in fashion advertising. Most jobs require hustle, enthusiasm, creativity, and aggressiveness.

Advertising Director

Advertising directors work for retail stores, supervising their companies' ad departments and publications. Similar jobs with manufacturing firms are called *marketing specialists.* Other advertising directors work with publications and advertising agencies. All of them direct the planning and budgets of advertising and promotional campaigns. This includes the preparation of print and broadcast advertisements, as well as the creation of selling aids, labels, signs, and other advertising materials. See 29-20.

A retail advertising director coordinates the design and distribution of all the store's newspaper ads, catalogs, and other direct-mail pieces. He or she helps plan promotions, keeps track of each buyer's advertising budget, and supervises the art department.

STS Systems

29-20 An advertising director or marketing specialist would oversee the promotional campaign that includes this presentation of the features that STS Systems can offer retailers.

The advertising director of a publication is in charge of selling and arranging ad space in the publication. He or she interacts with the account executives at advertising agencies. This person also works with the advertising directors of individual firms to coordinate their advertising in the publication.

Advertising directors must have good organizational skills and administrative abilities to see that deadlines are met. They need self-confidence, persuasiveness, and the ability to communicate well. They must be imaginative, alert, ambitious, and able to deal with creative people. Besides enthusiasm and physical stamina, they must have the ability to originate and develop ideas that are sound and practical, yet new and unusual. They must be capable of doing market research, media analysis, and mass communications planning.

Advertising directors usually have college degrees in liberal arts. They have taken courses in advertising, psychology, fashion, business, writing, English, printing, photography, and art. This position requires both education and experience, either with an advertising agency or fashion promotion department. Advertising directors earn very high salaries, but work hard for their pay and status.

Account Executive

An advertising agency employee in charge of selling to and handling specific advertising accounts is an ***account executive.*** This person is the liaison between the ad agency and clients. Clients may be medium to large textile or apparel manufacturers, and small to medium retailers. Most large retailers have their own in-house advertising departments.

Account executives work closely with merchandising and marketing people from the businesses they represent. Some advertising agencies are devoted entirely to apparel, while other agencies have a fashion advisor on their staff.

Often ad agency account executives continue to represent the same businesses year after year. They relate the client's message to the creative staff, explaining client ideas and objectives, and spelling out exactly what should be communicated through print or broadcast. They supervise and coordinate the development of total corporate advertising campaigns consisting of a series of ads and/or other promotional products. Usually, a campaign has a theme, with all advertising corresponding to it. The ads are aimed at reaching as many customers of the business as possible.

To maintain good working relationships with clients, account executives need to be personable, diplomatic, and sincere. They must be innovative, and up-to-date on the fashion news of the businesses they represent. They must be aware of consumer desires, able to identify target audiences, and know where to place ads to create the greatest impact.

Media Buyers

Media buyers select and buy the best media for clients' ads. They handle arrangements for broadcasting commercials on radio and TV, publishing ads in newspapers or magazines, or mailing promotional materials directly to the public. Media buyers are visited by media salespeople who try to convince them that their station or publication is the most effective. Media buyers bargain for the lowest rates and make deals for good advertising broadcast times and the best positions in publications.

Art Director

Art directors are sometimes called advertising designers. Most are employed by ad agencies and retail stores. Only a few art directors are employed by buying offices, textile producers, apparel manufacturers, and trade organizations.

Art directors conceptualize the ads for newspapers, magazines, direct-mail flyers, radio, television, signs, and outdoor media. They try to design the best advertising for the budgeted price. Besides advertisements, they also design ***collateral materials,*** which include brochures, annual reports, packaging, hangtags, and other corporate image projects. The collateral materials often accompany products for sale, giving important information, sometimes required by law, while they catch the customer's eye to help sell the product.

There is stiff competition in advertising design. Job titles and responsibilities differ, depending on the size of the agency or firm, and on the types of projects to be done. Salaries, fees, or commissions also vary widely. Creative work must often be done under the pressure of deadlines, with long hours and limited time off.

To become an art director, education is needed after high school in a college or vocational school. Courses include basic design, drawing, painting, lettering, photography, typography, advertising, and promotion. Most schools have typesetting and printing facilities, as well as well-equipped radio and television labs to learn audiovisual skills. Computer graphics and computerized typesetting skills are universally required in the advertising field, too.

Other Advertising Design Jobs

Graphic designers come up with the visual representation for advertisements and collateral materials, based on the ideas of the art director and copywriter. When they have clearly illustrated the ideas and gained approval from the art director, agreement must be obtained from the clients. Finally, the finished work is prepared by the graphic designer or junior members of the staff. Most work is done with computer graphics programs.

Entry-level jobs that can lead to graphic design positions include layout artist and pasteup/mechanical artist. ***Layout artists*** design the layouts for ads. They specify the typefaces and do sample renderings that show what the finished ads will look like when they are printed. ***Pasteup/mechanical artists*** put together the actual elements of the layout, such as the type, line drawings, and photographs, for final printing. In some agencies, these jobs are combined and done by one person. However, they are becoming less important because all of this is now being done by graphic designers, directly on computers, for automatic printing executed with the software.

People seeking art positions in fashion advertising should be able to work quickly, under pressure, to meet deadlines. They must be good at details and have the ability to follow instructions and take criticism. They must have excellent computer design skills. Most employers require applicants to have a degree in advertising design, art, or illustration. See 29-21. A portfolio is needed, showing creativity and precision in doing advertising layouts. Since it is hard to get an entry-level job in large advertising agencies, college graduates have a better chance of starting in a small agency. There is less pay and "glitz," but the opportunities to work and learn

Fashion Institute of Technology

29-21 Many colleges offer advertising curriculums with courses that prepare students to become advertising designers for fashion and other types of companies.

are good and provide the experience needed to qualify later for a better job with a major agency or retail company.

Public Relations

Public relations (PR) includes publicity and special events. *Public relations agents,* or ***publicists,*** are company employees or independent publicity consultants hired to help companies project their public image. They tell the story of a firm or its products through various media. They also try to anticipate problems a company may have with the buying public. Complaints against the corporation are often handled by PR people. Public relations agents try to gain public information media space with newsworthiness and present their company and products better than the competition.

Publicists strive to get editorial mention and photographs in publications, "plugs" on broadcasts, and favorable remarks in public speeches. They tell about products at meetings, conferences, and conventions, or arrange speaking engagements for company officials. They also try to get endorsements from, or tie-ins with schools and universities, sport teams, celebrities, or special events. They prepare and send out press releases, or stage special events worthy of media attention, such as fashion shows. They produce and present filmstrips, posters, movies, transparencies, booklets, and promotional/educational kits. They publish and distribute newsletters, reports, and bulletins to teachers, researchers, store buyers, students, and consumers.

Creative people are hired by PR firms or public relations departments of manufacturers, retail stores, and trade associations. Large retail companies have their own public relations departments. In chain organizations, these activities are planned by headquarters PR departments and coordinated with local stores. Small stores may hire independent public relations agencies to oversee important news or events.

Public relations agents must have lots of imagination and be able to speak and write clearly and persuasively. They need a thorough understanding of their products and skill to find or create news value to promote them. They must be able to anticipate and predict trends. They must be familiar with all kinds of advertising media and selling techniques and know how to schedule their time wisely. They must be convincing, yet tactful, and have confidence and drive. They should not be shy about speaking in front of groups and should know how to use visual aids. They should enjoy some traveling, have social poise, and a pleasing voice and appearance.

Most PR employees work in large cities and have college degrees. Publicity assignments often evolve from copywriting jobs. A background in English, journalism, communications, or liberal arts is helpful. A portfolio of publicity campaigns is needed when applying for a public relations job. Pay is high after experience and success are achieved.

Summary

Promotion is done by a network of supporting auxiliary businesses to the fashion industries. Fashion models wear garments and accessories to show how they look when being worn. Fashion photographers take pictures of fashion apparel on live models or shots of arrangements of fashion merchandise. Fashion writing is done by fashion journalists who might be reporters, copywriters, or editors. Fashion illustrators draw garments that have been designed and produced by others, showing complete accessorized outfits. Audiovisual work involves producing and/or being in radio, television, and multimedia presentations.

Visual merchandising shows what retail merchandise is available, and how items can be combined and accessorized. A display manager might oversee the work of the display designers and window dressers of a retail company.

Fashion advertising attracts and informs audiences to encourage them to buy products. Advertising directors, account executives, media buyers, art directors, and other employees must know the merchandise and the outlet selling it. They must also use effective approaches to reach the right consumers.

Public relations employees use various methods and media to tell the story of a firm or its products. They also anticipate public problems and handle complaints about the corporation.

To Know

runway models
fit models
photographic models
photo stylists
fashion journalists
fashion reporters
copywriters
editors
fashion illustrators
audiovisual work
display managers
display designers
advertising directors
account executives
media buyers
art directors
collateral materials
graphic designers
layout artists
pasteup/mechanical artists
publicists

To Review

1. What four general purposes does fashion promotion serve for retailers?
2. Sales promotion of large retail companies is often divided into what three departments?
3. On what basis are fit models hired?
4. Why is slimness especially important for photographic models?

5. What six pieces of information will you need to supply on a modeling employment agency application form?
6. What types of businesses might hire fashion photographers?
7. Name three activities that assistant photographers might perform.
8. What do press kits that are sent to fashion journalists contain?
9. When you apply to publications that allot space to fashion, why should you become familiar with the newspaper or magazine beforehand?
10. What prestige and pay levels do most fashion editors have?
11. What is emphasized when fashion illustration work is done for a pattern company and why?
12. Why do fashion illustrators sometimes add exotic background touches to their work?
13. Name at least three job activities behind the camera in audiovisual work.
14. For what types of companies might an audiovisual professional work?
15. How is visual merchandising planned for local chain stores?
16. When display managers plan displays, with whom do they consult?
17. What is the title of the employee who supervises a manufacturing firm's ad department and publications?
18. Why do advertising agency account executives usually not interact with large retailers?
19. Advertising art directors conceptualize the ads for what types of media?
20. What are the two branches of fashion public relations?

To Do

1. Read a book and do other research about techniques of modeling (how to pivot, pose, etc.). If possible, also watch some TV presentations of collection showings or other fashion shows to observe actual models doing their jobs (or tape them to show the class). Practice modeling in front of a mirror at home until you are confident enough to give a report and demonstration about modeling for the class. Also review for the class the various types of professional modeling.
2. Cut out the five best fashion photographs you can find. Mount them as a part of a bulletin board display. Next to each one, place a description of the mood, setting, apparent motion, composition, creative props, interesting backgrounds, use of lighting, or other points about how the fashion is accentuated by the fashion photographer.
3. After reading fashion articles in magazines or newspapers, decide on a fashion-related article that you could write. Do research on the subject, organize the points of your information, and write an article of your own on a word processor. Edit your article carefully for good organization, spelling, and grammar before printing a final copy.
4. With a classmate, visit a shopping area to look at a major interior display and a window display. Write down the techniques used for lighting, props, and other display elements used to accentuate the items being featured. What knowledge and skills were needed to put the displays together? Do you think the displays were extremely effective or would you have done the job differently? Draw up each display as best you can to show the class and explain your observations and conclusions.
5. Try your hand at composing a fashion advertisement that will attract and inform those who view it, encouraging them to buy the product(s) being featured. Use drawings or photos cut out of catalogs and do your own copywriting, lettering, and composition. Show your ad to the class, describing the merchandise, the retailer(s) selling it, and the target customers you are trying to reach. Also tell where you would probably place the ad (media and time/location) to reach the desired audience. Encourage discussion from class members.

CHAPTER 30

Entrepreneurship and Other Fashion-Related Careers

After studying this chapter, you will be able to

- describe the personal traits needed and opportunities available for entrepreneurs.
- explain fashion careers in the home sewing industry.
- tell about the field of theatrical costuming.
- summarize clothing care and preservation careers.
- describe careers for those who want to teach.

Besides the fields already studied, there are additional interesting career paths that relate to fashion. You may want to have your own business. If so, there are many types of activities that can be developed into a business. You may want to be associated with the home sewing industry, theatrical costuming, or clothing care and preservation. Maybe a career in education suits your fancy. This chapter will describe these opportunities in detail.

Entrepreneurship

Do you think you might want to go into business for yourself someday? An ***entrepreneur*** is a person who organizes, launches, and directs a new business venture and assumes the financial risks and uncertainties of the enterprise. The business might be run from a person's home, an office, or a store. It might focus on retail sales, provide a service, or produce a line of goods, 30-1. Successful entrepreneurs are able to turn innovation, flexibility, and creativity into a functioning business operation.

Independent small businesses make up a rapidly growing area for U.S. employment. More than half of all working Americans are employed by small businesses.

30-1 An entrepreneur might start with a small line of items in a certain niche, such as lingerie, and expand with a larger line as the sales volume increases.

Small companies can often meet the particular needs of a market better than large companies. Some small businesses operate as franchises of established corporations. Entrepreneurs also buy existing small businesses in hopes of making them better and stronger. Many entrepreneurs start new, independent businesses.

For new businesses to become profitable, it usually takes at least two years. Owners must be able to sustain themselves through this start-up time. Great satisfaction is received from a venture that becomes a success. Most of the well-known businesses of today started as small companies. On the other hand, many new businesses fail each year. Most business failures are due to lack of experience, poor planning, and inadequate capital.

Personal Traits to Succeed as an Entrepreneur

Entrepreneurship is not for everyone. The responsibility of self-employment requires self-confidence, ambition, and drive. The owner must be good at time management and have discipline to schedule work and meet deadlines. Entrepreneurs must make the best possible use of their human, material, and financial resources. Long work hours are often required, and thoughts about the business usually linger after hours. There may be no opportunity to take time off for a vacation. Sometimes employees must be hired and trained, and work delegated. A site may have to be rented, and equipment, supplies, and inventory purchased before any income can be generated, 30-2. Advertising or other types of marketing must be carried out to inform potential customers about the business.

Haggar Clothing Company

30-2 An entrepreneur may begin with only essential equipment in an otherwise bare office to start building a successful business for the future.

Successful entrepreneurs have certain qualities in common. Most entrepreneurs are optimistic. They believe in themselves and their business. They are self-starters with the energy and initiative to see what needs to be done and then doing it. Creativity is typical of entrepreneurs as they create new products, services, or sales techniques. Small business owners are also willing to take risks, or they would not hazard losing their investment, self-esteem, and community standing with a new business venture.

Entrepreneurs should be able to set goals and execute plans that will enable them to reach their goals. Small business owners should be flexible, since circumstances sometimes steer the business in a different direction than originally planned. They also must be decisive—able to make decisions and to act on them. Their time, interest, and dedication are what make the business successful.

Factors to Consider When Starting Your Own Business

Potential entrepreneurs should consider many factors when deciding to start a new business. It is advisable that they have work experience with the type of product or service they hope to offer in their own company. More preparation can be obtained by taking business courses and specialized continuing education classes. Community college classes are offered in the evenings to help entrepreneurs get started.

To start your own business, seek information from your local chamber of commerce. In addition, the ***Small Business Administration (SBA)*** is a government agency that offers helpful counseling, workshops, videotapes, and free publications. It has regional business development centers around the country. Experienced people in the Service Corps of Retired Executives (SCORE) can also give advice.

Potential entrepreneurs should ask themselves the questions listed in 30-3 before starting a business. They may also want to conduct a market survey to identify potential customers and assess the market need for the business.

Entrepreneurs should then develop a ***business plan*** that defines the idea (purpose), operations, and financial forecast of their proposed company. It should specify the products, market opportunities, competition, and strategy for the venture. Business plans help entrepreneurs crystallize their thinking about their ventures. Also, a business plan is needed in order to borrow money from lending institutions. The entrepreneur should also contact a lawyer to help set up the business structure. An accountant can give advice to establish a financial record-keeping system. An insurance agent is needed for advice about business insurance.

Some Questions to Ask Before Starting a Business

* What is the specific definition of my business?
* What is my target market?
* What image do I want to project?
* Will the business satisfy a real need in the market?
* Is the demand growing for my products or services?
* How will I promote my business?
* How will I price my products or services?
* Do I have the education, experience, and drive necessary to succeed in this field?
* What resources are available for any special help I may need (courses, workshops, consultants, etc.)?
* What organizations should I join that can offer professional advice and assistance?
* Do I have a network of helpful industry contacts?
* Who are my competitors? What are their strengths and weaknesses?
* What are the opportunities I should build on and the threats I must counteract?
* Where is the best location for my business and why?
* How and where will I get the capital I need to finance the venture?
* Am I willing to put in lots of long hours and hard work, possibly at the expense of my personal time?

30-3 Ask yourself questions such as these before deciding to start a business of your own.

Entrepreneurs must understand all aspects of their business. They should have the knowledge and skills to buy the right supplies, keep complete financial records, and manage people in a way that they can be highly productive. They should know where to seek specific types of help when needed, such as from a consultant, agency, or trade organization. Entrepreneurs need to project a professional image with well-designed business cards and letterhead stationery. They must set up business bank accounts and provide their own pension funds, health insurance, and other benefits. They must also understand taxes and government regulations, some of which are described in 30-4.

Legalities to Check Before Starting a Business

License Requirements
State or local general business registration fees and special licenses are often needed to make, sell, or provide certain goods or services. Contact your local town hall, Economic Development Office, or Small Business Administration for information.
Zoning Ordinances
To control land use, most communities designate certain areas for residential homes and other areas for commercial or industrial use. Businesses usually cannot be located in a residential zone. Also, commercial zones may be further restricted to certain types of businesses, such as offices, light industry, or heavy manufacturing. This assures orderly growth plus adequate roads and government services. For zoning information, check with your local Planning Commission.
Operating Requirements
Special regulations, such as being open on Sundays, trash pickup, number and width of entrances and exits, sign placement, etc., may exist. These will need to be checked at your local town hall.
Sales Tax
Many states have a sales tax on certain categories of items that are sold directly to consumers. If your goods or services are within one of these categories, you must collect the tax from your customers and pay it to the state. Check with your County Clerk's Office about sales tax procedures.
Labeling
If you plan to manufacture apparel items, even on a small scale, certain information must be included on permanent, sewn-in labels. A business lawyer, library reference materials, or the Federal Trade Commission can provide you with specific details about labels.
Registering a Business Name
The name of your business can be registered if no one has already registered it for their use. This protects the name for your use only. Consult a business lawyer or contact your County Clerk's Office.

30-4 These are some of the many details that must be taken care of before going into business for yourself.

Entrepreneurial Opportunities

Many entrepreneurial opportunities exist that can be operated from a home, store, factory, or warehouse. Small boutiques or specialized stores can be found anywhere there are consumers. You might want to open a dressmaking or tailoring shop, or an apparel production business. A trading company is a possibility or a mail-order business. Freelancing and consulting are other options. Technology enables small business owners to keep in touch with both suppliers and customers.

A Home-Based Business

More and more people are working from their homes. For instance, you might use a knitting machine to produce individualized sweaters or a monogramming machine to personalize shirts and jackets. You could sew specialized items to sell at craft shows, on consignment in retail shops, or through a traveling sales representative who visits retail shops. You could also sell a line of apparel or accessories from your home or through a home party system. Writing fashion articles for publications is another opportunity for a home-based business.

There are some advantages to operating a home-based business. By working out of your home, you are not committed to a commercial lease for any period of time. You have no commuting time or parking expenses. You may not need a business wardrobe. A home-based business might allow you to combine family and income-producing responsibilities. You can run a load of family laundry or put dinner into the oven and continue working. Your children might even gain training in business methods.

A home-based business also has tax advantages, since a portion of your home expenses can be allocated to the business. This can be explained by an accountant, tax expert, or by reading publications for small businesses. Careful records must be kept of legal and professional fees, supplies, business publications, and business-related travel. Educational expenses might even be deductible.

There are also disadvantages with a home-based business. Family matters can be distracting and disrupt your job. It may be too easy to work evenings and weekends without taking time off to relax. Clients may intrude on your personal time or not take your business seriously because it is at your home. Also, neighbors may object to having a business near them.

Independent Sales Representative

For this job, you could have an office at home, but make calls out of the home. Independent sales representatives (reps) often handle several different product lines for many small manufacturers that are not large enough to have their own sales staffs. For instance, they might sell several small manufacturers' lines that are not in competition with each other. However, the retail accounts to which they sell the items should be the same. For instance, a self-employed rep in menswear might sell a line of shirts from one producer, slacks from another, neckties from another, and sweaters from another—all to

Retail Store Start-Up Costs
✷ Physical space must be rented or purchased.
✷ Renovations must be done to suit the space to the business (walls, doors, dressing rooms, receiving area, etc.).
✷ Furnishings must be acquired (counters, racks, display props, cash register system, etc.).
✷ The original inventory must be bought so there is something to sell.
✷ Wages must be paid to hired employees.
✷ Advertising and other promotion is needed to announce the opening of the store to consumers.
✷ Operating overhead bills for heating, air conditioning, and electricity must be paid.
✷ Funds for unexpected emergencies and delays must be available.

30-5 To open a new retail business, all these expenses must be covered before there are any sales revenues available.

men's apparel retailers. By "repping" many lines, if one does not sell well, commission income can still be made from the other lines. Also, a bad line can be dropped and replaced with other merchandise as needed.

Owning a Retail Shop

Though there are many giant retail firms, the vast majority of stores are small and privately owned. There are various ways to become the owner of a retail shop. You can buy a business that is already in operation or buy a partnership in it. Another way to become a store owner is to start a new retail business on your own. Some people choose to buy a franchise. A franchise may cost more initially, but there is less risk involved since the parent firm provides some guidance, protection, and promotional assistance. In addition, the franchise name may be well established.

In all cases, a loan will probably have to be acquired from a bank or other source to cover start-up costs. ***Start-up costs*** are the initial expenses involved in starting a new business venture. Typical start-up costs for a retail business are shown in 30-5.

Small shop owners often employ one or two other people to help operate the store. As the owner of the new business, you must be willing and able to do whatever needs to be done. This might include locating sources for merchandise, buying the merchandise, receiving the goods, determining pricing, and marking the merchandise. You would have to offer credit and personal services to customers, arrange displays, and do all the paperwork. You might also do selling, promotion, store operations, and janitorial duties! You may not have any personal income until the store becomes well-established with satisfied customers.

Owners of retail shops must cater to their target market with the proper merchandise and image. They must know their competition and carry goods that meet a need or are in demand. They must know how to control costs and build sales to achieve a profit. In addition, they should have good relations with people in the community. Expertise in the areas outlined in 30-6 is also recommended.

Expertise Needed to Own a Small Retail Shop
✷ How to organize and analyze financial data to improve business performance.
✷ How to establish and maintain good vendor relationships.
✷ How to develop seasonal merchandise plans and time inventory for the "fashion calendar."
✷ How to maximize buying dollars while getting appropriate merchandise for target customers.
✷ How to assure proper inventory levels with good sales/stock ratios.
✷ How to overcome slow or nondeliveries of merchandise.
✷ How to obtain and use the latest technology, such as inventory control and checkout systems.
✷ How to build good credit ratings with financial institutions.

30-6 Knowledge in these areas can be gained through reading, attending courses and seminars, and having work experience in similar businesses.

A Dressmaking or Tailoring Shop

Dressmakers/tailors are expert sewers who make custom garments or do apparel alterations and repairs. Sometimes they specialize in wedding gowns or tailored suits. They may do alterations for specialty clothing shops, dry cleaners, or department stores.

A dressmaking/tailoring shop can be started with a relatively small investment. However, it may become harder to make a good living doing this in the future with body scanners enabling manufacturers to make customized garments. Rather than working from a rented storefront, tailoring may be better as a home-based business, especially for someone with young children at home.

Dressmakers/tailors should have a fashion sense to help clients choose flattering styles and appropriate fabrics. They must understand form, proportion, fit, and color. They should also enjoy sewing and be able to work with speed and accuracy. Good eye-hand coordination is needed, as well as finger dexterity.

Paula B. Sampson/Ball State University, Indiana

30-7 This display depicts the skills and supplies that a dressmaker or tailor would need to do a professional job for customers.

Dressmakers/tailors take customers' measurements, construct garments, check fit, and do all required finishing. They might follow a commercial pattern, modify a pattern, or create a garment from a sketch or picture. The skills of pattern making, draping, and professional techniques of clothing construction are required, 30-7. They must be neat, accurate, patient, and tactful with people.

Vocational or trade school courses in fashion design, pattern making, clothing construction, and textiles are helpful for people preparing to be dressmakers or tailors. Sometimes adult education courses offer "sewing for profit" workshops. Some people master this trade through apprenticeships. A helpful trade group is the Custom Tailors and Designers Association of America. The best preparation is to study textiles and clothing in college, with business courses taken as electives.

An Apparel Producer

Another entrepreneurial opportunity is to start an apparel production firm. Someone with design ideas or product development skills may want to produce his or her own apparel designs. The designer begins by creating samples with which to sell the designs, 30-8. Manufacturing may be accomplished with a cottage industry arrangement. A ***cottage industry*** uses the labor of individuals working in their homes with their own equipment to manufacture goods. This arrangement offers low overhead costs and lots of flexibility, but must adhere to government labor laws. Another option is to hire contract factories to produce the designs.

From the production side of business, you could start your own contract factory to make other people's designs. Capital is required for cutting and sewing equipment, building rent, utilities, and wages and training for workers. Sometimes there is demand for

Fashion Institute of Technology/John Senzer, Photographer

30-8 A fashion entrepreneur might develop a line of samples to show to prospective accounts. Then garments can be made in quantity according to the orders received.

Brother International Corporation

30-9 A contract factory might specialize in sewing embroidery designs onto garments that are produced elsewhere.

Haggar Clothing Company

30-10 The costs of traveling to foreign lands to transact business would be deductible expenses for an entrepreneur who owns a trading company.

specialized production, such as sewing appliqués or embroidery onto garments, 30-9. In such a case, a niche can be filled very successfully by a manufacturing entrepreneur.

Small apparel manufacturers often have the advantage of being able to act quickly to take advantage of sudden fashion shifts. They often set the fashion pace for the industry because they create more fashion-forward designs. With the right marketing, profits can go up quickly. However, a single season with a bad line can wipe out a small, undercapitalized firm.

Apparel production entrepreneurs are often people with design talent, as well as experience with large firms, who want to go out on their own. They should be acquainted with retail buyers, fashion editors, suppliers, and contractors. Personal appearances in stores that carry their goods can help promote their lines and gain customer feedback for improvements. Editorial mention in fashion articles can give their labels a big boost.

Once again, a bachelor's degree in textiles and clothing or an associate degree in fashion design is recommended. Small business centers and trade schools offer courses in how to start new businesses. Students learn how to develop a sales force, manage personnel, and work with contractors. They also learn various finance methods relating to sales and production. Workshops are taught by industry leaders and consultants, with guest speakers in specific fields of expertise.

A Trading Company

You may want to start a company that imports or exports fashion goods. Most trading companies specialize in a certain product category, such as silk apparel from China or leather handbags from Israel.

A trading company may be run by one or two people who have some warehouse space and a small office. To start this type of a business, product line expertise is required. Contacts are needed with international suppliers and domestic retailers. A great deal of traveling is done, with the costs being business expenses, 30-10.

A Mail-Order Business

Many entrepreneurs have started mail-order businesses selling fashion goods. They may manufacture their own fashion products or source from elsewhere. Mail-order businesses place ads where they will be seen by people who might use their products, or they send out promotional materials to a select group of people from a mailing list.

Inventory planning for a mail-order business can be tricky. There is no sure way of knowing how many orders will be received. You could be swamped with orders you cannot fill fast enough. On the other hand, if you build up an inventory anticipating large orders that do not materialize, you could be stuck with unsold products. The printing and postage costs for catalogs can also add up quickly.

A mail-order company must have warehouse space for inventory, but the location is not of prime importance.

Lands' End Direct Merchants

30-11 A mail-order entrepreneur would have to employ helpful and cheerful order-taking employees who represent the company to customers.

Oregon State University

30-12 A freelance fashion promotion specialist has expertise in advertising design techniques, fashion illustration, and marketing.

Mail-order businesses often rent post office boxes instead of using their street addresses. A toll-free telephone number, and possibly a Web site, encourage customers to place orders, so order-taking employees are required, 30-11.

Running a mail-order business requires organizational abilities and a talent for selecting products that people will want enough to make the effort of ordering. The market for the products must be identifiable and easy to reach. The prices must attract customers, while providing a realistic profit. Ideally, mail-order items should be fairly lightweight and easy to package and ship.

Owners of mail-order businesses must obey Federal Trade Commission and post office regulations. Products and prices cannot be misrepresented in advertisements. Wearing apparel must have proper labeling. All products must be safe for consumers to use. Also, if orders cannot be filled within 30 days of receipt, the customers must be contacted and given the opportunity to cancel with a refund or accept later shipment.

Freelancing and Consulting

Freelancing is the selling of expert skills to accomplish particular tasks. There are many freelance opportunities related to fashion. For instance, freelance fashion designers sell their designs to manufacturers. Illustrators make drawings of manufacturers' lines for market week order pads. Freelance photographers take pictures of modeled garments for promotional materials. Promotion specialists prepare advertising campaigns for producers and retailers, 30-12. Some freelancers do window displays, store planning, and fashion show presentations. Others do personal shopping for clients.

Consulting is selling a person's expert ideas and advice as a service business. Consulting opportunities related to fashion can involve selling advice about financial improvements, production efficiency, or improved ways of marketing a company's products. Expertise can be offered for sales training programs, public relations campaigns, and other ways to improve business effectiveness. Some consultants work with consumers, advising them on personal images, wardrobe coordination, accessorizing, or color analysis, 30-13. Wedding consultants are also in demand.

Freelancers and consultants may work independently on individual, short-term jobs or on a contractual basis for several clients. Their jobs end when each assignment is completed. They generally have few inventory requirements. Advertising materials are usually distributed to announce and promote the service. Successful experience is needed, however, to establish credentials as an expert.

Colour Concepts

30-13 Color analysis consultants advise customers about which colors are the most flattering for them to wear.

Freelancers and consultants often charge $100, $500, or $1,000 an hour, depending on their expertise. This compensates for their preparation time for which they are not paid. Also, they may not work forty hours a week, fifty-two weeks per year. Some charge a daily fee rather than an hourly fee.

Evening courses offer instruction in establishing freelance or consulting businesses. They teach people how to promote themselves and their talents, develop client lists, and minimize financial risks. Methods of building financially rewarding businesses are discussed.

Other Fashion-Related Careers

You may be interested in other fashion-related careers that require some different aptitudes and skills than the careers already described. For instance, there are many opportunities in the home sewing industry, or how about the creative excitement of theatrical costuming? Does work in the fields of clothing care or preservation sound interesting to you? Rewarding careers in education also provide good income, self-esteem, and personal satisfaction.

The Home Sewing Industry

Businesses in the *home sewing industry* deal with nonindustrial sewing machines, notions, fabrics, and patterns. There are fabric stores, books, magazines, radio and TV shows, advertisements, videotapes, and mail-order catalogs aimed at home sewers and professional dressmakers. All of these firms need fashion-oriented personnel.

Fabric store salespeople have similar duties to other retail salespeople. In addition, they must have a thorough understanding of fibers, fabric construction and finishes, care of textiles, and sewing procedures. Salespeople must be able to interpret information from pattern envelopes in order to advise customers. They measure and cut fabrics for customers.

Employment with Commercial Pattern Companies

Employees of commercial pattern companies design, produce, package, and sell the patterns that are purchased by home sewers, 30-14. These people combine their artistic talents and technical expertise as a team. Most of the design and manufacturing work is now done using computers.

Many of the jobs with pattern companies are similar to related positions in apparel manufacturing and fashion promotion. Pattern company *marketing employees* collect consumer statistics that are used to guide design and production decisions. *Fashion directors* seek out and interpret the latest trends about silhouettes, colors, fabrics, and accessories. *Merchandising directors* figure out what the company's customers will want in patterns and try to anticipate sales. Then *designers* create garments within the many pattern categories offered. Designers might specialize in such areas as dresses, sportswear, or children's patterns.

Pattern makers make patterns for the new designs, and *seamstresses* construct samples. *Fit models* try on the samples to check fit, drape, and movability. After approval from the design staff and management, *pattern graders* make larger and smaller versions of the pattern pieces for each design. *Checkers* look over patterns to see if notches line up, facings match their corresponding garment parts, and that other cutting and sewing markings are properly included. *Markers* calculate pattern layouts and fabric yardage requirements.

Simultaneously, *fabric editors* obtain samples of the latest fabrics for the company's fabric library and for specific designs. *Accessories editors* research and obtain the latest styles of buttons, jewelry, shoes,

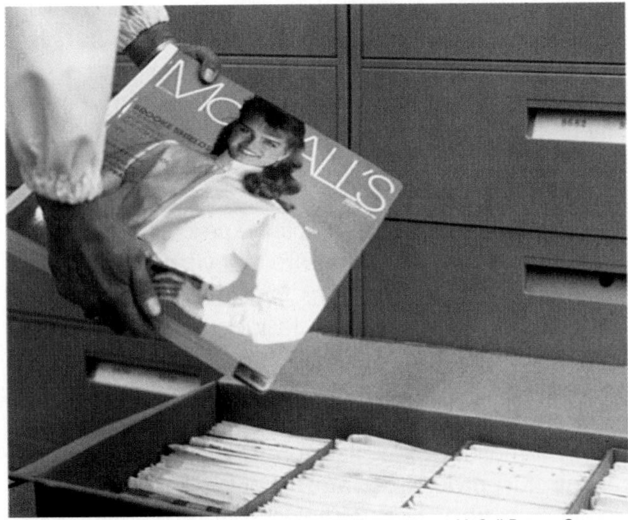

McCall Pattern Company

30-14 Many employees are involved in the design and printing of commercial pattern company catalogs and patterns.

scarves, and belts for the accessories room. These are used to create finished ensembles for illustrations and photographs.

Pattern guide sheets and envelopes must also be produced. *Technical writers* create clear sewing directions that are easy to read and follow. These writers combine journalism skills with a knowledge of sewing construction, fabrics, notions, and patterns. *Diagram artists* create the technical drawings to accompany the written directions on the guide sheet. *Illustrators* make a finished fashion drawing of each design for the pattern envelope and the company's catalog that is used in fabric stores. *Layout designers* assemble the guide sheet copy and diagrams, as well as the pattern envelope layout, for printing. Then the finished pattern pieces, guide sheets, envelopes, and catalogs are ready for production and distribution.

Sales and promotion employees include home office staff members and field staff people who call on accounts in geographic territories. *Retail coordinators* are fashion and promotional liaisons between pattern companies and retail fabric stores. *Copywriters* provide press releases and publicity for the media. *Educational representatives* prepare teaching materials such as booklets, posters, and videotapes. They must have top construction skills to answer questions about sewing problems that customers ask them.

Theatrical Costuming

Theatrical costuming is creating wardrobes for performers in operas, ballets, stage plays, circuses, movies, advertisements, television shows, and parades. A costumer might work for a theater company, movie or television studio, or costume shop. Some costumers are freelance designers hired to work with the wardrobing staff for certain shows.

Theatrical costumers work from scripts to appropriately clothe the characters in the production. Costumers need to know how to portray moods and desired effects with apparel. Appropriate dress for certain income levels, cultures, and time periods must be created, 30-15. Theatrical costumers design outfits that look right under various lighting conditions and with different props. They also must work within certain limitations, such as the size of the stage or budgetary restrictions.

An entry-level job is that of a costume technician, also called a *wardrobe helper.* ***Costume technicians*** organize the costumes and accessories for a production by character and scene. They help with research to make sure the designs are authentic, and do shopping and other footwork to collect everything that is needed. They help the actors dress for the production, and they care for the wardrobes between performances. They also do repair work on the costumes before, during, and after performances.

Department of Consumer Studies; University of Delaware

30-15 Theatrical costumers must be able to accurately clothe characters that portray a certain national origin, time period, income level, or place in society.

With experience and proven flair, a wardrobe helper might work up to ***wardrobe designer.*** This head of the costume department is rewarded with high pay and industry recognition. Wardrobe designers are named in the credit lines of movies or programs of stage productions. As with other types of fashion designing, only a few people make it to the top of the field. However, there are important contributions and enjoyable careers for those at all levels of theatrical costuming.

To do theatrical costuming, you need creativity and a thorough knowledge of lighting, staging, and special effects. You also need a solid background in art, design, and history, 30-16. The ability to work with emotional and artistic performers is also an asset. Fashion school

McCall Pattern Company

30-16 A wardrobe designer may create costumes that "swish" when a character turns to add to the drama of a theatrical plot.

training and an apprenticeship usually provide a good range of skills, including sketching, pattern making, draping, and sewing.

Clothing Care

Clothing care is a leading service industry with many small and privately owned commercial laundries and dry cleaning establishments, 30-17. Jobs in them require a high school education and training under skilled workers.

In a dry cleaning or laundry business, employees are needed to receive items to be cleaned from customers, attach identity tags, and inspect for pocket contents and stains. Other employees operate the dry cleaning or laundering equipment and do pressing and other finishing, 30-18. A sewing employee may be hired to do repairs and alterations. Some of these jobs require a well-groomed appearance and courteousness. Others require technical skills and mechanical ability. The work requires accuracy and concentration in order to maintain high standards. All employees must have a knowledge of textiles, clothing construction, dyes, and cleaning agents.

International Fabricare Institute

30-17 Commercial laundries and dry cleaning establishments deal with fashion products from a different perspective.

International Fabricare Institute

30-18 Well-trained dry cleaning and laundry employees know how to clean and press textile products so they look their best.

Clothing Preservation

Textile/apparel preservation gives special attention to the long-term care of fabrics and clothing. Such apparel items include wedding gowns that are to be saved for future generations or antique clothing for museum collections, 30-19. Soil that could prematurely age and damage the fabrics is first removed from garments. Then they are wrapped in "archival" acid-free paper and placed in boxes that protect them from strain, discoloration or fading, and insects such as moths.

Costume curators (or *conservators*) locate, identify, and determine the age of textiles, apparel, and accessories from the past. Electronic scanning microscopes are used to determine the age and condition of fibers and threads used in constructing the items. Broken and frayed areas are repaired. Then the items are stored flat in rooms with controlled temperature and humidity. Curators also make sure the items are kept in darkness or under low lights without ultraviolet rays.

Costume curators care for the historic costume collections of museums, libraries, and universities, 30-20. They must have a thorough knowledge of the apparel of past eras and other cultures. Curators prepare exhibits that display the historic garments. Inaugural gowns and

The Fashion Institute of Design and Merchandising, California

30-19 Collections of antique clothing are preserved so they can be displayed, studied, and enjoyed by ongoing generations.

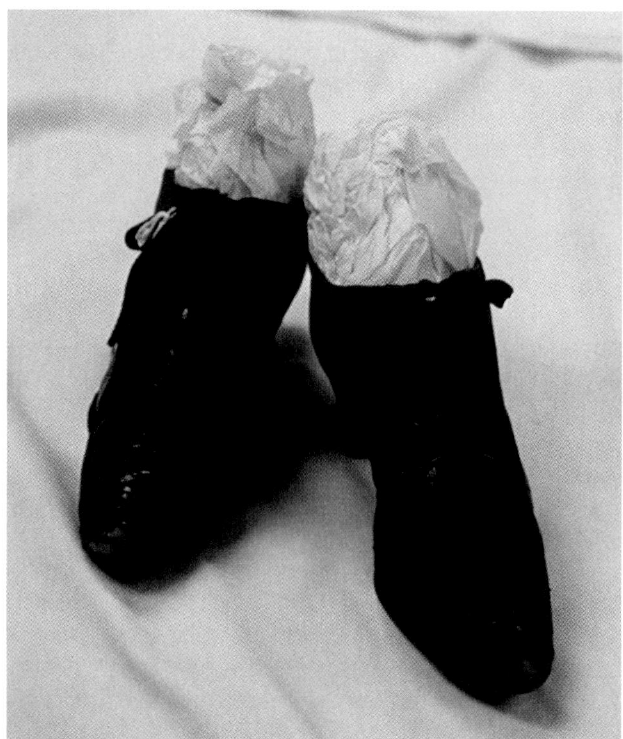

Department of Consumer Studies; University of Delaware

30-20 Articles of antique wearing apparel are a part of collections that are often owned by the textile and apparel departments of universities.

other ceremonial apparel are often included in historic collections. Everyday clothes of long ago are quite rare, but often tell a lot more about what life was like in former times than special garments do.

Costume scholars collect and catalog old and new fashion drawings, clippings, slides, photos, films, and books. They have access to detailed information that can date, describe, authenticate, and classify old apparel. These costume scholars help people find specific information by researching what has been written about various aspects of clothing. Sometimes they assist the wardrobe designer for an historic film. They might also give lectures showing slides of historic costumes and describing their influence on modern fashions and textiles.

Costume curators generally have college degrees in science, textiles and clothing, or art history. Many have advanced degrees. Apprenticeship training or graduation from an art conservation training program is recommended. The work can be stimulating and personally and professionally rewarding, but patience is required in doing the tedious research.

Education

Fashion educators give instruction in school clothing and fashion merchandising classes and adult education courses. Apparel educators demonstrate products and procedures, and share knowledge and enthusiasm with their students. When fashion concepts are taught, the educator might assume the role of designer, stylist, or fashion director. Educators may be required to make purchasing decisions about textbooks, sewing machines, mannequins, and other equipment and supplies.

Classroom Teacher

Clothing classes are taught in family and consumer sciences or home economics departments in junior and senior high schools. Subjects may include textiles, fashion, design, grooming, clothing selection and care, sewing construction, and apparel-related careers. Many high schools have fashion merchandising classes.

Classroom teachers in vocational schools provide training that can lead the students directly to gainful employment. They teach courses in commercial clothing construction, alterations and repair, pattern making, modeling, art, and retailing. Trade school instructors teach fashion design, illustration, retailing, apparel production, photography, and other fashion subjects. College and university professors teach such courses as textile science, tailoring, merchandising, display, education, fashion journalism, and promotion, 30-21.

Teaching provides a routine with variety. Instructional plans follow a master curriculum, but the specific

Department of Consumer Studies; University of Delaware

30-21 Teaching fashion subjects in a college setting requires a higher level of education, as well as exposure to what is happening in the industry.

Western Kentucky University and Auburn University

30-22 This assistant professor, who has a Ph.D., is qualified to teach upper-level textiles and apparel courses, as well as advise students and do research and writing about innovative ideas.

content of courses can vary. Teachers continually learn more about their subject matter as they read and study to stay up-to-date. They have some flexibility and freedom in their work to teach their courses to best meet the needs of their students.

Teachers must like to work with and help people. They need good communication skills to explain facts, give directions, demonstrate procedures, answer questions, and discuss ideas. They must be flexible, fair, patient, and able to tactfully give constructive criticism. Energy is needed to do a good job.

Public school teachers need at least a college bachelor's degree, but many have a master's degree. Teachers in vocational schools have work experience and job expertise in the areas in which they teach. To teach in college, a master's degree is required and a doctorate is preferred.

Most teaching jobs have good fringe benefits and retirement programs. The pay for teachers is good, but usually not as high as similar work in private industry. However, the great amount of vacation time is a bonus. Teachers can use that time to conduct personal business, enjoy hobbies, travel, or pursue further studies. Those teachers who have children have more time to spend with them when schools are closed in the summer. Though the official workday for teachers ends in mid-afternoon, they often must correct papers or prepare lessons after school hours. College instructors have shorter teaching hours. However, they have other duties in professional areas, advising students, and doing research and writing, 30-22.

Extension Agent

Extension agents are staff members of land-grant universities who work as family and consumer scientists in all counties in the United States, including both urban and rural areas. They teach apparel, nutrition, consumer economics and other homemaking skills to groups such as 4-H clubs, community organizations, and senior citizen groups. Programs and workshops are developed based on the needs of the people in their respective counties. Sometimes extension agents work with individuals on a one-to-one basis. States often have an extension agent who is a *clothing specialist* and is also on a university staff.

Extension agents speak to groups, attend meetings, and plan and put on demonstrations. They write newspaper columns and educational materials. Radio and television stations often ask extension agents to appear on programs where their knowledge can be shared with listeners and viewers. Because of their many responsibilities, lots of time is spent traveling within their territories.

Extension agents' salaries are similar to those of teachers. They usually have longer work hours and shorter vacations than teachers, but they have more freedom to plan their own work. Usually deep satisfaction is felt from working closely with the people in their communities. Personal qualities and skills needed by extension agents include being:

- well-organized
- resourceful
- imaginative
- good at solving problems
- able to get along with all types of people
- able to communicate well through all media
- desirous to improve people's knowledge, skills, and lives

Adult and Consumer Education

Adult education courses are special-interest classes for adults that are taught at local schools or community centers. These classes are usually offered at night since most of the adult students work during the day. Classes related to clothing that might be offered include pattern alterations, basic clothing construction, tailoring, sewing with new fabrics, or making certain craft items. The teachers usually have developed the skills they teach through work experience, and this is often a part-time or extra job for them. Some are high school or vocational school teachers during the regular workday.

Consumer education combines teaching with business promotion. This is frequently a full-time professional position with manufactured goods companies. These professionals are often called *educational representatives* because they promote their firms' products by teaching about them. Educational representatives

- instruct dealers and consumers about sewing machines, patterns, notions, textiles, laundry equipment, or other products;
- hold in-store classes;
- give demonstrations at trade shows;
- prepare and distribute educational and promotional materials about the use and care of their products;
- provide an important link between their companies and consumers.

A consumer educator employed by a fabric store might teach specialized sewing classes to the store's clientele. Sewing of vests, quilts, or Christmas gifts might be taught. In a yarn store, one might teach knitting, crocheting, or macramé to promote the store's goods. The educators often have to prepare instructional leaflets and make samples to show. Pay is either a flat fee per session or a percentage of the total fees collected. Sometimes the educator is given all the fees since the class brings customers into the store. These are often part-time positions with retail stores.

Consumer educators should be well-groomed, poised, and have a pleasing personality. They should be creative and well-skilled in the area they teach. They need good communication skills, self-confidence in front of groups, and loyalty to their firms. Pay varies according to job responsibilities and personal qualifications.

Gaining Success in the Fashion Industry

After studying the many fashion-related careers described in this book, perhaps you have a career in mind for yourself. With careful planning and the needed preparation, you should be able to get into the type of work that suits and interests you.

The people who become the most successful in their careers are those who treat change as opportunity. They look for and accept new challenges to make things happen. To learn and grow in your profession, it is recommended that you participate in professional organizations, take advanced courses and seminars, and read trade journals and other publications. Often someone with less talent can work harder and achieve more than others who do not use their talents to capacity. Sincere enthusiasm for your work is one of the first requirements for success.

Whatever career you choose, you should give it your best effort. Fashion-related jobs require a neat appearance, good grooming, and good health and energy. You need pride, a cooperative manner, and a sense of taste. The responsibility of confidentiality must also be taken seriously, so new fashion designs, company policies, or research discoveries are not revealed inappropriately. To get ahead, you must follow instructions, take suggestions and criticism well, and finish all tasks. You must be honest and willing to do more than you are asked. Perseverance is an important trait for success. With dedication and hard work, you, too, can achieve success in the fashion industry.

Summary

Being an entrepreneur is demanding, but it can be very rewarding. The responsibility of self-employment requires self-confidence, discipline, ambition, drive, and other personal traits. To be an entrepreneur, you should have gained preliminary work experience, as well as educational preparation.

Fashion-related entrepreneurial opportunities include having a home-based business or being an independent sales representative. You might own a retail shop or dressmaking/tailoring shop. You could become an apparel producer, or start a trading company or mail-order business. Freelancing or consulting in some fashion specialty might be for you.

Careers in the home sewing industry include fabric store sales or mail-order sales. Commercial pattern companies employ people with many different kinds of expertise. Theatrical costuming combines the performing world with the fashion world. Clothing care involves work in commercial laundries and dry cleaning establishments. Clothing preservation specializes in the conservation of historic textile products. Fashion education provides many opportunities at various school levels and in many subject areas. For instance, some extension agents are clothing specialists, and some people teach adult and consumer education based on their work experience.

To gain success in the fashion industry, careful planning and preparation are needed. You should have enthusiasm for each job, giving your best effort. With dedication and hard work, you can succeed in the fashion industry.

To Know

entrepreneur
Small Business Administration
business plan
start-up costs
dressmakers/tailors
cottage industry
freelancing
consulting
theatrical costuming
costume technicians
wardrobe designer
textile/apparel preservation
costume curators
extension agents
adult education
consumer education

To Review

1. What proportion of working Americans are employed by independent small businesses?
2. What are the three main factors that cause entrepreneurial business failures?
3. What should a business plan define and specify?
4. Why is it recommended that an independent sales representative handle many lines?
5. Why might it be harder to make a good living as a dressmaker or tailor in the future?
6. When starting a contract sewing factory, what is capital specifically required for?
7. What two things are needed to start a trading company?
8. Why is inventory planning tricky for mail-order businesses?
9. Name three types of consulting work with consumers.
10. What is the overall goal of employees of commercial pattern companies?
11. What do pattern company checkers do?
12. Why are technical writers hired by pattern companies?
13. What types of organizations hire theatrical costumers?
14. What are the advantages of becoming a wardrobe designer?
15. What education and training is usually required to work in the clothing care industry?
16. What kind of equipment do costume curators use to determine the age and condition of fibers and stitching threads?
17. What is meant by the phrase "teaching provides a routine with variety"?
18. Name one advantage and one disadvantage of being a teacher.
19. What do educational representatives of manufactured goods companies do?
20. What is recommended in order to learn and grow in your profession?

To Do

1. Choose a fashion-related entrepreneurial business that might interest you in the future. Find out as much as you can about the business, then answer the questions listed in Figure 30-3. Prepare this as an oral or written report.
2. Read the biography of an entrepreneur who is not in the fashion field. Then write a two-part report. The first part should be a summary of the entrepreneur's life or experiences. The second part should relate some of the basic entrepreneurial lessons learned from reading the biography to the field of fashion or a specific fashion career.
3. Watch a television movie or special program to study the costumes. Then prepare a report about the theatrical costuming that was done for the characters in the production. What moods and effects were portrayed through apparel? How were income levels, time periods, and cultures represented? Did it seem that costumes were coordinated among the characters that appeared together and with the settings or props? Could the costumes be purchased at retail stores or do you think they had to be custom made? Tell about any other observations.
4. Obtain a commercial pattern and mount the pattern pieces, guide sheet, and envelope on poster board for an oral report. Describe the jobs of at least ten of the employees who contributed to the design, production, packaging, and selling of the pattern.
5. Try being a teacher or educational representative. Pick a specific fashion-related topic to teach or an apparel-related product to demonstrate. Give a 5- or 10-minute educational lesson or talk that includes appropriate charts, handouts, or samples that would be needed. Be prepared to answer questions from your classmates.

Glossary

A

absorbent. Having the ability to take in moisture. (6)

accented neutral color scheme. Plan that combines white, black, or gray with a bright color accent. (8)

accessories. The articles added to complete or enhance outfits. (1, 14)

accessories editor. Commercial pattern company employee who researches and obtains the latest available styles of accessories to create finished ensembles. (29)

account executives. Sales representatives who work with specific customers in determining their needs and providing products to suit those needs. (27, 29)

accounts. Records of debits (subtractions of money) and credits (additions of money) as a result of transactions. (19)

accounts payable. The balances the company owes to others. (19)

accounts receivable. Credit due to a company; money owed by customers who have bought goods. (19)

acquisition. The purchase of another company, with the buying company gaining the controlling interest. (25)

active listening. The process of asking open-ended questions, paying careful attention to the replies, and then asking further questions to probe more deeply and clarify confusing points. (17)

active sportswear. Garments for sports participation which are also worn during leisure time. (14)

adaptation. A design that reflects the outstanding features of another design but is not an exact copy. (9, 21)

added visual texture. Finishes and designs applied to the surface of fabrics; applied texture. (8)

add-ons. Additional merchandise items, such as related items to create complete outfits. (18)

ad lib commentary. A fashion show commentary created spontaneously during the show from brief cue cards. (23)

administration. Tasks and employees concerned with the overall running of a company. (26)

administrative expenses. Management salaries, office supplies, postage, and other miscellaneous administrative costs. (19)

adornment. Attractive decoration. (1)

adult education. Instructional courses held for adults at night. (30)

advance buying. Retail ordering of merchandise well ahead of the desired shipment date, usually at a lower price. (15)

advance orders. Merchandise orders with a longer lead time before the delivery date. (16)

advance ship notices. Electronic notification interchanges that detail the contents of shipments, and tell how and when shipping will take place. (11)

advertising. Any paid form of nonpersonal sales message made by an identified sponsor through a mass communication medium. (21)

advertising agencies. Service firms that provide advertising expertise and design, produce, and place ads in the media. (21)

advertising and promotion agents. Employees who plan, develop, and execute campaigns to tell customers about the firm's products, create demand, and encourage sales. (29)

advertising director. Retail employee who supervises the advertising department and publications. (29)

advertising freelancers. Artists, copywriters, photographers, or other creative professionals who are hired independently to produce advertisements. (21)

advertising platform. A plan that defines the target audience and summarizes the benefits and features of the product that will please that audience. (21)

advocacy advertising. Institutional ads that try to address public issues or influence public opinion. (21)

agile manufacturing. A seamless data capture system of production, and delivery that makes information-based decisions quickly. (25)

allowances. Price reductions on items that are not quite right, but that customers decide to keep at the lower price. (19)

alta moda. The high fashion design industry of Italy. (9)

alteration hands. Apparel production employees who correct production defects. (27)

alterations. Changes to existing items. (20)

alterations expert. Employee who takes in, lets out, and reshapes garments that do not fit the purchasing customer properly. (28)

ambiance. Atmosphere. (13)

American Apparel Education Foundation. A nonprofit group that raises funds that go toward the costs of apparel education. (26)

American Apparel and Footwear Association (AAFA). National trade association representing all types of U.S. apparel producers. (11)

American Association of Textile Chemists and Colorists (AATCC). Trade association concerned with the "wet processing" aspects of textile finishing. (7)

American Fiber Manufacturers Association, Inc. Trade organization for producers of manufactured fibers in the U.S. (6)

American Management Association (AMA). A trade association for business executives. (26)

American Printed Fabrics Council, Inc. A trade organization that recognizes creative achievements in printed fabrics. (7)

Americans with Disabilities Act (ADA). A U.S. law making it illegal to discriminate against people with disabilities. (26)

American Textile Manufacturers Association, Inc. (ATMI). Large and influential trade organization for the textile industry. (7)

analogous color scheme. Plan using adjacent colors on the color wheel. (8)

anchor stores. Major chain and department stores that provide the attraction needed to draw customers to shopping centers or malls; "destination stores." (12)

apparel jobbers. Outside shops that never produce any of their own goods. (10)

apparel marts. Buildings or complexes that house permanent showrooms of apparel manufacturers. (11)

applied design. Surface design added onto a fabric. (7)

apprenticeship. Training for an occupation by working under the direction and guidance of a skilled worker. (26)

approval buying. An arrangement in which merchandise is shipped to the retailer's store for inspection before the final purchase decision is made. (16)

aptitudes. Natural talents. (26)

art director. An advertising designer who conceptualizes ads for newspapers, magazines, direct-mail flyers, radio, television, signs, and outdoor media. (29)

artificial intelligence (AI). Computer systems that display behavior that would be regarded as intelligent if it were observed in humans. (17)

artificial suede. Nonwoven polyurethane/polyester fabric that looks and acts similar to real suede. (7)

as ready. Term denoting that a manufacturer promises to ship orders when they are completed, rather than by an exact date. (16)

assistant. One who helps or aids another in doing a job. (28)

associate degree. An educational degree earned with most community college programs, usually of two years in length. (26)

assorters. Apparel manufacturing employees who prepare cut garment parts for production sewing; also called assemblers. (27)

assortment. Diversification of goods, range of stock, or total selection offered. (13)

assortment breadth (width). The number of different categories or classifications of merchandise offered. (13)

assortment depth. The quantity of each item offered in the assortment categories or classifications carried. (13)

assortment plan. A buying plan that projects the variety and quantity of specific stockkeeping units to be carried by a store or department to meet customer demand. (15)

attitudes. An individual's feelings or reactions to people, things, or ideas. (1)

audio-visual work. Employment doing radio, television, and multimedia presentations. (29)

automated conferencing. Simultaneous communication between geographically dispersed people, including audio conferencing, video conferencing, and computer conferencing. (17)

automation. The use of machinery to perform physical tasks that are normally performed by humans. (10)

auxiliary group. Organizations that support or help businesses associated with the soft goods chain. (4)

avant-garde. The most daring and wild designs. (1)

B

B2B EC. Business-to-business electronic commerce using the Internet. (5, 25)

B2C commerce. Business-to-consumer commerce; electronic retailing to the general public. (25)

bachelor's degree. An educational degree earned at the completion of most four-year college programs. (26)

back orders. Merchandise orders that have not been filled within the time specified and have not been canceled by the buyer. (16)

backward integration. Combining a business at one step of the distribution channel with another toward the beginning of the chain closer to the raw materials. (4)

bagging. Putting merchandise into a sack for better handling, protection, and privacy of customer purchases. (20)

bait and switch. A deceptive sales practice in which consumers are "baited" by an advertised low price on a product that the retailer does not plan to sell, and then "switched" with selling techniques that tempt the customers to buy a higher-priced product. (21)

balance. Principle of design that implies equilibrium or steadiness among the parts of a design. (8)

balanced assortment. Stock situation with sufficient items to meet demand, with breadth and depth to satisfy the varied spectrum of customers, while maintaining a reasonably low investment in inventory. (15)

balanced (even) plaid. Design of crossing lines and spaces that are the same going out in both the lengthwise and crosswise directions. (7)

balance of trade. The relationship between the values of a country's imports and exports, described as being a deficit or a surplus. (24)

bankruptcy. The inability to pay debts. (25)

bar code printer. A mechanical device used to mark merchandise tags or labels with bar codes. (5)

bar codes. Standardized symbologies used on merchandise tags for electronic identification and collection of product data. (5)

basic stock plan. A proposed purchase list composed mostly of basic staple goods. (15)

basket weave. Variation of the plain weave with two or more filling yarns passing over and under the same number of warp yarns. (7)

beamspread. The diameter of the circle of light created by a light source. (22)

beauty. A quality that gives pleasure to the senses. (1)

belts. Accessories that go around the waist and usually buckle. (14)

benchmarking. The continuous process of measuring a company's products, services, and practices against world class companies that are renowned as leaders. (11)

benefits. Favorable outcomes received. (18)

bias grain. Diagonal grain of fabric. (7)

blanket orders. Promises to buy from favored vendors over a period of time, with no detail of colors, sizes, or shipment until later. (16)

bleaching. Chemical process that removes color, impurities, or spots from fibers or fabrics during fabric finishing or garment laundering. (7)

blend. Yarn made by spinning together two or more different fibers, usually in staple form. (6)

Bobbin. Magazine of the apparel production industry, as well as a yearly trade convention with the AAMA. (11)

body build. Total human structural form established by relationships or proportions of body parts. (8)

body language. Communication through body movements. (17)

body scanning. A procedure to collect individual sizing information electronically. (25)

bonding. Process of laminating two or more materials together with adhesives, plastics, or other methods. Also, the process of salespeople doing everything possible to strengthen relationships with customers. (7, 18)

bonus. Extra payment in addition to regular pay. (26)

border print. Design pattern that forms a distinct border, usually along one or both selvage edges of a fabric. (7)

boutiques. Small stand-alone shops or distinctive areas within a larger store that sell unusual, few-of-a-kind apparel, accessories, or decorative items. (12)

boys sizes. Clothing sized 8 to 22 for boys in grade school through adolescence. (14)

braiding (plaiting). Intertwining three or more strands to form a regular diagonal pattern down the length of the resulting cord. (7)

branch coordinator. Employee of a large retail organization who keeps tabs on all the branches to see that their stock, selling techniques, and general operations coordinate with the main store or headquarter's policies. (28)

branch stores. Smaller additional retail units owned and operated by a parent store that are usually located in the suburbs or in metropolitan shopping areas. (12)

brand-line representative. In cosmetics retailing, a trained salesperson who advises customers on the proper use of the cosmetics line being sold. (14)

brand name. *See* trade name. (6)

bribe. Money or a gift accepted by a trusted employee from an outsider trying to influence the employee's judgment or conduct. (26)

bridge jewelry. Good quality jewelry made to look like fine jewelry but less expensive. (14)

bridge lines. Secondary or "diffusion" lines of well-known designers priced between the designer and better categories. (9)

budget. An estimate of income and expenditures for a specified period of time. (15, 23)

business cycle. Fluctuations in the level of economic activity that occur with some regularity over a period of time. (3)

business ethics. The use of good moral values in business dealings. (21, 26)

business plan. A written definition of the idea (purpose), operations, and financial forecast of an entrepreneur's proposed company. (30)

buyer's clerical. Retail employee who keeps records, schedules appointments, answers phones, and does follow-up work for a buyer. (28)

buying clout. Power in the marketplace that enables companies who have it to get promotions, rebates, and additional discounts from suppliers. (25)

buying motives. The reasons people buy what they buy. (13)

buying plan. A plan that describes the types and quantities of merchandise to purchase for a department or store for a specific time period and for a set amount of money. (15)

C

CAD. *See* computer-aided design. (7)

CAM. *See* computer-aided manufacturing. (7)

capacity fixtures. Merchandise presentation fixtures that stock large amounts of merchandise. (22)

capital. Money and equipment that support a business. (10)

capital intensive. Using mainly machines and advanced technology to make products, rather than relying heavily on labor. (10)

card-control. An inventory management system with a separate card for each item stocked. (15)

career. A lifelong field of employment or vocation through which people progress. (26)

career path. The order of jobs worked in a person's life. (26)

career planning. The process by which managers and employees lay out employees' futures with a firm, based on the firm's needs and each employee's strengths and weaknesses. (26)

cart. *See* kiosk. (12)

cashiers. Salesclerks who make transactions. (18)

cash register. A piece of equipment that records transactions, performs mathematical operations, calculates tax, holds money, and generates a sales slip. (18)

casual lookers. Classification of customers who are simply browsing or killing time. (18)

catalog showrooms. Stores that display sample items of merchandise mainly sold through catalogs. (12)

category killers. Large, discount specialty chains than carry huge selections of merchandise in a single product category at such low prices that they destroy the competition in their specialty area. (12)

category management. A retail strategy of managing product groups as business units and customizing them on a store-by-store basis to better satisfy customer needs. (25, 28)

caution. Admission or entrance fee required by haute couture houses from commercial customers to attend showings. It is intended to deter copying and is applied toward purchases. (9)

CD-ROM. Computer compact disks with read-only memory that can store and provide users with large amounts of information. (25)

cellulosic fibers. Fibers composed of or derived from cellulose from plants, such as cotton, linen, rayon, acetate, and triacetate. (6)

central business district. A downtown retailing cluster. (13)

central buyer. *See* classification buyer. (15, 28)

certificate courses. Curriculums completed in trade schools. (26)

chain. A group of stores (usually twelve or more) that is owned, managed, merchandised, and controlled by a central office. (12)

Chambre Syndicale. Trade association for top designers of the Paris couture. (9)

channel of distribution. The route that products take from the original source through all middle people to the end user. (4)

charge-backs. Penalties or claims against vendors for not following the many different rules set by each retailer. (25)

checker. Commercial pattern company employee who sees that cutting and sewing markings are properly included and lined up. (30)

check guarantee. Personal check acceptance program in which the risk falls on the bank/firm that authorizes the transaction. (20)

checkout cashier. A retail employee who does not sell, but rings up customers' purchases, collects and records payments, makes change, and bags the items. (18, 28)

checkout counter. *See* checkstand. (18)

checkout terminal. *See* cash register. (18)

checkstand. The table or station where customers bring merchandise to pay and to have it bagged or wrapped. (18)

check verification. Electronic authorization of the probable risk of accepting individual personal checks from customers. (20)

chemical finishes. Finishes that become part of the fabrics through chemical reactions with the fibers. (7)

cherry picking. Buyers' practice of selecting only a few items from each vendor that represent the best of their lines. (16)

children's apparel. Clothing for girls ages 3 through 13 and boys ages 3 through 16. (14)

children's sizes. Apparel sizes for preschoolers who are taller and more slender than toddlers. (14)

choreography. The planned arrangement of movement, such as specific dance steps or gestured moves in a fashion show. (23)

Civil Rights Act. Government legislation outlawing job discrimination. (26)

classic. A style or design that continues to be popular over an extended period of time, even though fashions change. (1)

classification buyers. Retail employees who plan, choose, purchase, price, and promote one classification of goods for all the stores in a chain or large store organization. (28)

classification buying. Activity of purchasing only one category classification of merchandise, often done by chain store buyers. Also called central buying. (15, 28)

classification resources. Suppliers that are specialists in given classifications. (15)

classroom teacher. Educator in charge of school classes. (30)

clearance merchandise. Low-priced promotional goods, usually featured in off-price discount stores or as sale items. (15)

client book. A salesperson's book of customer's names, addresses, phone numbers, sizes, and important dates. (18)

closeout goods. Selected, discontinued goods, usually of various sizes and colors, sold at a low price. (15)

closing the sale. Getting a commitment from the customer to buy the merchandise. (18)

clothing specialist. State extension agent who is often a university staff member. (30)

cocooning. The preference of people to stay at home. (25)

code of ethics. A written statement that sets forth the legal principles that should guide that organization's decisions. (26)

C.O.D. send. A cash-on-delivery sale that is sent to the customer, with payment made through the delivery company. (18)

collateral materials. Extra advertising or corporate image materials, such as brochures, annual reports, packaging, hangtags, logos, and trademarks. (29)

collection. The total number of garments in a designer's or apparel manufacturer's seasonal presentation, especially for high-priced garments. (9)

color. Element of design; hue. (8)

color analysis. A study to analyze a person's skin tone to determine what colors are most flattering for that person to wear. (30)

colorfast. Term designating that the color in a fabric will not fade or change with laundering, dry cleaning, or time and use. (7)

colorists. Employees who work out different color combinations for fabric surface designs. (27)

color scheme. Plan for harmonious combination of colors. (8)

color wheel. A circular diagram used to show hues, how they are related to each other, and how to choose and combine them. (8)

combination yarn. A ply yarn composed of two or more yarns, each of different fibers. (6)

commentary. A spoken explanation of what is going on in a fashion show, especially pointing out specific features of each outfit being modeled. (23)

commentary cards. Cards prepared during fashion show fittings, used for the narration of the show. (23)

commentator. Fashion show narrator who interprets trends for the audience. (23)

commercial pattern company. A firm that designs, produces, packages, and sells patterns for home sewers. (30)

commission. Payment based on a percentage of the dollar amount of sales made by a hired person. (7, 18)

commissionaires. Independent foreign buying agents who help retailers buy goods from their countries. (16)

Committee for the Implementation of Textile Agreements (CITA). Government group that negotiates and administers individual agreements and quota programs. (24)

commodity fibers. Generic fibers not identified with any specific manufacturer. (6)

commodity products. Staple goods that hardly ever change in design and are in constant demand. (4)

communication. The exchange of information for results. (17)

communication process. The transmission of meaningful messages that are not only heard, but also understood. (17)

community shopping center. A medium-sized cluster of 15 to 50 stores that serves a community market within a five to six mile radius. (13)

comparable-store sales. An analysis of a retailer's sales in relation to close competitors that have similar corporate or store sizes, expense structures, merchandise lines, departmental structures, and ways of operating. (19)

comparative advantage. The ability of one nation to produce certain goods or services better than other nations because of specific circumstances. (24)

comparative analysis. The periodic examination and comparison of financial data to try to measure the effectiveness of the company's overall strategy. (19)

comparison shoppers. Retail employees who check the merchandise assortments, prices, ambiance, and services offered in competing and noncompeting stores, as well as the advertising, displays, and knowledge and demeanor of salespeople. (15, 28)

compensation. Payment and benefits for work accomplished. (18, 26)

compensation package. Wage, salary, and other compensation such as paid vacation time. (26)

competition. Rivalry between two or more independent businesses to gain as much of the total market sales, or customer acceptance, as possible. (3)

complaint resolution. The settlement of customers' dissatisfactions with a store through mutual agreement on how to solve specific problems. (20)

complementary color scheme. Plan using hues across from each other on the color wheel. (8)

complementary products. Items that supplement or accessorize other basic products. (15)

completion date. The date designated by the retailer on the purchase order specifying when the goods are needed and should be delivered. (16)

compliance. Using the uniform standards for bar codes that are accepted throughout the soft goods chain. (5)

complimentary close. The sign-off of a business letter before the signature. (17)

composites. Textiles combined with other materials, such as for use in commercial hose, belting, car fenders, and boat hulls. (4)

computer-aided design (CAD). A computer system used for designing textiles, apparel, and other products. (7)

computer-aided manufacturing (CAM). Electronically controlled production. (7, 10, 11)

computer database. Market information formulated from consumer actions and purchases recorded into comprehensive computer records. (5)

computer graphics. The use of computers to draw or chart. (17)

computer hardware. Electronic equipment consisting of keyboards, monitors, and printers. (5)

computer-integrated manufacturing (CIM). A combination of many electronic steps of a production system, toward "hands-off" manufacturing. (11)

computerized knife cutter. Electronically controlled machine that cuts multiple layers of fabrics into garment parts. (10)

computer network. An inter-connection of computing equipment using data communications circuitry. Also, an inter-connected group of people. (17)

computer retailing. Selling goods via computer and telephone technologies. (12)

computer software. Electronic operating systems that tell the computer to do the required procedures. (5)

confined. Selling only to one retailer within a certain geographic trading area on an exclusive basis, or only to a particular chain of retail stores nationally. (11)

conformity. Obeying or agreeing with some given standard or authority. (1)

conservator. *See* costume curator. (30)

consignment. Placing merchandise for sale in a store and being paid a percentage of the retail price if and when the merchandise is sold; the supplier retains ownership of the goods rather than the retailer taking title. (6, 15)

consolidated shipping. Merchandise from two or more companies are put together into a truckload to lower transportation costs. (11)

consolidation. The uniting of two or more parts into one. (25)

consulting. The selling of a person's expert ideas and advice as a service business. (30)

consumer confidence. Consumer feeling of certainty to spend money. (3)

consumer credit. The use of credit cards or other purchase charges that allow consumers to have merchandise immediately and pay for it later. (20)

consumer-direct retailing. Nonstore selling to consumers who shop from home. (25)

consumer education. A combination of teaching and business promotion. (30)

consumer fashion shows. Fashion shows presented by retailers to consumers. (23)

consumer panel. A market research method that has participants keep diaries. (5)

consumer promotion. Promotion directly to consumers, usually done on a national scale by companies that do not sell directly to consumers. (21)

consumers. People who buy and use finished products. (3)

continuum. A sliding scale from one extreme to another with infinite possible responses falling at different points along it. (3, 9)

contract. A written agreement between a buyer and seller, detailing all conditions of the sale. (11)

contractors. Independently owned sewing factories that produce goods for apparel firms. (10)

controllable expenses. Costs over which companies have direct control. (19)

controlling retail goods. Doing sales analysis to evaluate how items are selling, transferring merchandise between stores, and handling returned items. (28)

convenience goods. Necessities that consumers purchase regularly, with a minimum of shopping, from the most accessible retail outlets. (15)

converters. Businesses that convert greige goods to finished fabrics and distribute those fabrics. (7)

cool colors. Hues from green to violet on the color wheel that represent water and the sky. (8)

cooperative advertising. Advertising done jointly and with costs shared by more than one organization, such as a manufacturer and retailer. (6, 21)

cooperative buying office. A resident buying office that is jointly owned and operated by a group of similar independent stores, with expenses divided among the member stores. (16)

cooperative fashion shows. Jointly sponsored fashion shows, with expenses shared by two or more organizations. (23)

cooperative (co-op) programs. Work-study programs at the high school and trade school levels of education. (26)

copy. The reading material of words, lettering, or numbers that appear in type in an advertisement. (21)

copyist. *See* design stylist. (27)

copywriter. A fashion writer who composes the word messages describing items promoted in advertisements, catalogs, and brochures. (29)

corporate buying office. A resident buying office owned and financed by a store ownership group or syndicate. (16)

corporation. A chartered enterprise organized as a separate legal entity with most of the legal rights of people. (3)

corrective advertising. Promotional messages used to correct previous false or unethical claims. (21)

cosmetics. Products to be applied to the face, skin, or hair to improve appearance. (14)

cost-effective. The benefits outweigh the expense. (7)

costing. Procedure of calculating the estimated expenses of producing something. (10)

costing clerks. Employees who assist costing engineers by noting and analyzing the figures on specification sheets. (27)

costing engineers. Manufacturing employees who determine the overall price of producing each item. (27)

cost of goods sold (COGS). An accounting of what has been spent on goods that have been sold to customers during the period. (19)

costume curator. Person who locates, identifies, and determines the age of textiles, apparel, and accessories from the past. (30)

costume jewelry. "Fashion jewelry" that is inexpensive, often made of plated metals and artificial stones. (14)

costume technician. Theatrical wardrobe helper who organizes the costumes and accessories by character and scene. (30)

cottage industry. Manufacturing that uses the labor of family units working in their homes with their own equipment. (30)

cotton. A natural cellulosic fiber obtained from the boll of the cotton plant. (6)

Cotton Incorporated. Marketing and research trade organization for cotton growers. (6)

Council of Fashion Designers of America (CFDA). Trade association of top U.S. designers. (9)

counterfeit fashions. Fashion goods with false producer labels or designer logos. (11)

couture. Custom-made designer segment of the fashion industry for the highest priced "class" market. (9)

couturier. High fashion designer. (9)

Crafted With Pride in U.S.A. Council (CWP). An industry-wide organization to strengthen the competitive position of the U.S. soft goods chain by conducting an ongoing "Buy American" campaign. (5)

craze. Passing love for a new fashion that is accompanied by a display of emotion or crowd excitement. (1)

created audience. A fashion show audience that is established as a result of publicity and advertising after the show is planned. (23)

creative director. Advertising agency executive who oversees all the agency's advertising output. (29)

credit processing. Electronic credit approval and ongoing authorization of credit transactions. (20)

crimped. Process that curls or waves manufactured fibers to give them elasticity and resiliency, similar to natural fibers. (6)

cross border retailing. *See* international retailing. (25)

cross dyeing. Method of dyeing blend or combination fabrics to two or more shades by using dyes with different affinities for the various fibers. (7)

cross-shopping. The consumer trend of combining purchases from both ends of the price scale. (25)

crosswise grain. Direction of the filling yarns across the fabric from selvage edge to selvage edge. (7)

culmination stage. The top popularity of the fashion cycle when a fashion is in great demand by almost everyone. (2)

culture. A set of social norms or values. (1, 24)

curved lines. Elongated marks that are rounded or somewhat circular. (8)

customer relationship management (CRM). The merging of database information technology with customer service to analyze customers, respond individually to their needs, and build and maintain lasting relationships. (20)

customer service. The total of all enhancements offered to customers, not directly related to the sale of specific products. (20)

customer service manager. Retail employee who serves as an intermediary between the store and its customers. (28)

custom-made. Made-to-order apparel with individual fit for the client and one-of-a-kind exclusiveness. (9)

Customs Service. U.S. agency responsible for keeping track of and enforcing trade barriers at points of entry into the country. (24)

cutters. Apparel producers; "cutting-up" or needle trades. Also, employees who cut out garment parts. (10, 27)

cyber-retailing. The showing of consumer's own images on the screen to see how specific clothing will look on them. (25)

D

Daily News Record. Newspaper that reports the textile and menswear industries. (4)

data. Numbers, statistics, facts, and figures. (17)

database marketing. A system of electronically stored data that is gathered through market research, constantly updated, and used for company marketing activities. (25)

data integration. The combining of several steps into one continuous computerized process. (10)

data mining. Analysis of computer database information from retail sales, using software to discover patterns and derive actionable responses. (25)

data processing. The input of information into computers, relating to sales, shipping, billing, inventories, and payroll. (11)

debit processing. The money for each purchase is taken directly out of the consumer's bank account and electronically put into the merchant's bank account; electronic draft capture. (20)

debt level. The amount of money that is borrowed. (19)

decided customers. Customers who know exactly what they want and why, preferring to make their purchase quickly. (18)

decoding. Message receiver's process of translating the meaning of a message. (17)

decor. The style and appearance of interior furnishings. (22)

decorative lines. Applied lines created by adding details to the surface of clothing rather than with structural joining. (8)

decorative props. Display objects used to establish a mood or an attractive setting for merchandise being featured. (22)

deductions. Certain amounts of money subtracted from paychecks, such as for taxes and social security. (26)

demand. The amounts of a good or service that consumers are willing and able to buy at a certain time and price. (3)

demand flow manufacturing (DFM). Computerized custom production that responds to single orders of desired goods. (11)

demographics. Vital statistics of human populations, broken down by such factors as age, gender, race, education, religion, income, occupation, and geographic locations. (5)

denier. Term to describe fiber (usually filament) thickness or diameter. Higher numbers indicate thicker threads. (6)

departmental buyer. A traditional department store employee who plans and purchases goods for only one department and is responsible for the sales and profits of the department. (28)

departmental buying. Activity of department store buyers who purchase merchandise for only their own departments. (15)

department manager. Executive responsible for an entire type of merchandise or market category or running a retail department. (27, 28)

department stores. Large scale general merchandisers with a fashion orientation that offer many varieties of merchandise grouped into separate departments. (12)

design. A particular or unique version of a style because of an original or individual arrangement of parts, form, color, fabric, line, and texture. Also, the plan used to put an idea together. (1, 8)

designer patterns. Patterns for replicas of actual designer fashions offered to home sewers by commercial pattern companies. (9)

designing. The process of creating new versions for garments, accessories, or other items. (4)

design stylist. Person who redesigns existing garments rather than creating new fashion designs. Also, one who advises about styles in apparel or other categories of goods. (9, 27)

desktop publishing. Computer creation, editing, and production of documents that are of a similar quality to that produced by typesetters. (17)

diagonal lines. Elongated marks that slant rather than being vertical or horizontal. (8)

diagram artist. Commercial pattern company employee who does technical drawings to accompany the written directions of the guide sheet. (30)

digital printing. Computer-driven textile printing that rolls fabric through an extra-wide ink-jet printer. (7)

diffusers. Light-softening shields. (22)

direct competition. Rivalry between two or more companies using the same type of business format. (13)

directional print. Fabric design with an up and down direction. (7)

direct-mail marketing. Mail-order retailing. (12)

director of distribution planning. Corporate executive who oversees all distribution centers and activities for a company. (28)

direct selling. The exchange of merchandise to individual consumers in return for money or credit; personal selling. (16, 18)

discounts. Reductions of the original retail price granted to store employees or special customers. (19)

discount stores. Retail establishments that sell merchandise at lower than recognized market level prices. (12)

display designer. An employee who does interior merchandise displays. (29)

display manager. Head of the retail display staff and all display work. (29)

displays. Individual, special visual presentations of merchandise. (22)

disposable. Thrown away after use, rather than being reused. (7)

distance learning. Educational courses available via television broadcasts or the Internet. (26)

distribution. Activities involved in physically transferring goods from where they are produced to the proper locations for consumption. (3)

distribution center manager. Person in charge of a particular distribution center. (28)

distribution planner. Retail stockkeeping employee who keeps track of all units of merchandise through computerized records. (28)

district manager. Chain store employee who is responsible for growth and volume of up to a dozen stores. (28)

divestiture. A transaction of a company selling part or all of its organization. (25)

divisional merchandise manager (DMM). Retail executive who supervises a group of buyers and/or coordinates the merchandise of several related departments, divisions, or stores. (28)

division of labor. Breaking up the total manufacturing process into small, individualized jobs that are each repeatedly done by one worker. (10)

dobby attachment. Loom attachment that permits the weaving of geometric figures. (7)

doctorate degree. A high educational degree after many years of university study and possibly research. (26)

dollar/closeout chains. Discount stores that sell limited items at low prices. (12)

dollar merchandise plan. A financial buying budget for planned stock, sales, and profit of a department or store for a six-month period. (15)

domestic market centers. Buying areas in one's own country. (16)

domestic production. The manufacturing of goods in one's own country. (10)

domestics. Bed, bath, and kitchen textiles. (4)

double knit. Fabric made on a weft knitting machine with two sets of needles and yarns knitting two fabrics as one. (7)

double-ticket. Marked with two combined but similar-size numbers in different categories. (14)

down. A fluffy feather undercoating of geese and ducks used as a lightweight insulator in apparel. (6)

downsize. The use of smaller size numbers for equal body measurements in expensive fashions. (14)

downsizing. The reduction of the size of a business to reduce costs and become more efficient. (25)

dress code. A set of written or unwritten rules of appropriate attire. (1)

dressers. People who help fashion show models change and care for the clothes. (23)

dressmakers/tailors. Expert sewers who make custom garments or do apparel alterations and repairs. (30)

dual distribution. The selling of products in two steps of the channel of distribution, such as a manufacturer selling goods to regular retailers as well as operating company-owned retail outlets. (11)

dual sizing. A combination of two size dimensions, such as neck plus sleeve length combinations (men's shirts), waist plus inseam combinations (men's slacks), or chest measurement plus short or long (men's sportcoats). (14)

dumping. The selling of goods at lower prices in foreign markets than in the home market. (24)

durable finish. Fabric finish that lasts through several launderings or dry cleanings, but loses its effectiveness over a period of time. (7)

dyeing. Method of giving color to a fiber, yarn, fabric, or garment with either natural or synthetic dyes. (7)

dyes. Coloring agents. (7)

E

economic climate. A country's purchasing power, standard of living, and relative costs of doing business. (24)

economies of scale. Cost reductions per item resulting from large-scale mass production. (3)

edit. When a manufacturer changes and revises the designs in an apparel line, or a retail buyer prioritizes the available goods for a buying plan. (16)

editor. Supervisor of fashion writers and copywriters. (29)

editorial credit. Mention in a publication of a manufacturer's trade name, or specific retail sources for merchandise featured by the publication. (21)

educational representatives. Commercial pattern or manufacturing company employees who promote their firm's products by teaching about them. *See* consumer education. (30)

electronic article surveillance (EAS). A shoplifting prevention system that uses specially designed tags containing a small circuit that emits a signal that, if not deactivated, is sensed by devices at exits. (20)

electronic check conversion. A computerized system that converts paper checks into electronic funds transfers at point-of-sale. (18)

electronic data interchange (EDI). Communication of information or transactions through computer linkages between companies. (5)

electronic feedback tests. A market research method that uses computers to receive both quantitative and qualitative information. (5)

electronic funds transfer (ETF). See debit processing. (20)

electronic graphics interchange. In software, computer design options that can be combined according to the final goal of the designer. (9)

electronic mail. The sending, storing, and receiving of messages via networked computers. Also called e-mail. (17)

electronic mailbox. A computer holding-file that can only be accessed by someone with the proper code. (17)

electronic point-of-sale (EPOS). Computerized stock control equipment. (15)

electronic retailing. A combination of computer and telephone technologies with marketing and merchandising so shoppers can view merchandise on their computer monitors at home and order by telephone modem. (12, 25)

electronic storefront. A computer-simulated store that consumers can scroll through by aisle, product category, or item. (25)

elements of design. Building blocks of design that include color, shape, line, and texture. (8)

elevated windows. Display windows with the floor above sidewalk level. (22)

emotional behavior. A response based on feelings. (13)

emphasis. Principle of design that uses a concentration of interest in a particular part or area of a design. (8)

employee turnover. Workers leaving a company and the hiring of new, replacement workers. (25)

employment discrimination. The different treatment of people according to prejudice rather than work performance. (26)

empower. To give official authority, responsibility, and autonomy to employees to make their own work-related decisions. (25)

enclosed windows. Display windows with a full background and sides that completely separate the store's interior from the display window. (22)

encoding. Message sender's process of putting thought into symbolic form to be meaningful for the receiver. (17)

enterprise resource planning (ERP). Use of computer databases to manage companies' entire global production supply chains. (11)

entrepreneur. A person who organizes, launches, and directs a new business venture, and assumes the financial risks and uncertainties of the enterprise. (30)

entry-level jobs. Beginning jobs in a career. (26)

ergonomics. Human engineering that matches worker performance to the tasks performed, the equipment used, and the environment. (10)

essential services. Services that are basic and necessary to the exchange process, offered by self-service discount stores. (20)

ethics. Acting or dealing in morally upstanding ways. (5, 21)

European Economic Community (EEC). A trading bloc that includes the developed boundaries of Western Europe. Also called the EC (European Community) or the EU (European Union). (24)

even plaid. *See* balanced plaid. (7)

everyday low pricing (EDLP). Retail strategy of consistently offering fair prices and good values at all times. (13)

exchange rate. The price at which one country's money can be converted into another country's money. (15)

exclusive market coverage. Using one retail location to serve either an entire market area or some major segment of that market. (13)

executive trainee. College graduates who are hired to train with a company for future management positions. Also called management trainee. (28)

executive trainee programs. General orientation offered by most large companies for new employees with college degrees. Also called management training programs. (26)

expansion. An economic growth in national income, employment, and production. (3)

expected services. Services offered by value-oriented retailers that include the acceptance of several credit cards, layaway privileges, shorter checkout lines, and more personalized answers to shopping questions. (20)

expenditures. Money spent. (23)

expense management. The process of planning and controlling operating costs. (19)

export cooperative. An export trading company formed and operated by several firms. (24)

export merchants. Foreign wholesalers who specialize in efficiently exporting goods from their countries. (24)

exports. Commercial products sent out of a country to other countries. (10)

export sales representatives. Foreign natives who represent selected manufacturers but do not maintain a wholesale inventory. (24)

export trading companies (ETCs). Intermediaries between U.S. exporters and foreign buyers. (24)

extenders. "Multipliers" that can be mixed and matched within a wardrobe for more outfits. (14)

extension agents. Educators hired and paid by state land grant universities to work as family and consumer scientists in various counties or an entire state. (30)

external theft. Stealing by those who are not employed or otherwise associated with a firm. (20)

extracurricular activities. Clubs and sports outside of school classes. (26)

F

fabricated products. Sewn garments, accessories, and other manufactured items. (4)

fabrications. Fabrics, leathers, furs, or other materials used in making fashion products. (10)

fabric designers. See fabric structural designers and fabric surface designers. (27)

fabric librarian. Employee of a manufactured fiber company, natural fiber trade association, or home sewing pattern company who is in charge of the fabric library. (27, 30)

fabric library. A collection of sample fabrics for the upcoming fashion season. (6)

fabrics. Long pieces of cloth. (4)

fabric store salespeople. Retail sales help in fabric stores. (30)

fabric structural designers. Textile company employees who interpret fashion into new woven or knitted patterns. (27)

fabric stylist. Textile company employee who serves as a bridge between the creative and business aspects of the company, coordinating fabric design, production, and sales. (27)

fabric surface designers. Textile company employees who translate the company's color choices and applied print looks onto fabrics. (27)

face-forward. Face-out presentation of apparel merchandise by hanging with the front fully facing the viewer. (22)

facsimile transmission. The use of special equipment to electronically transmit visual images; "fax." (17)

factors of production. Resources of land, labor, capital, and entrepreneurship needed to manufacture products. (10)

factory outlets. Manufacturer-owned and operated discount stores that sell only the merchandise the manufacturer makes, at reduced prices. (12)

fad. A temporary, passing fashion that has great appeal to many people for a short period of time. (1)

fashion. The display of the currently popular style of objects or activities. (1, 7)

Fashion Association, The (TFA). A nonprofit public relations arm of the apparel industry. (11)

fashion consultant. *See* personal shopper. (28)

fashion cycle. The ongoing rise, peak, and fall in popularity of specific styles or shapes. (2)

fashion designers. Employees who create ideas that combine function and beauty into new garments. (27)

fashion director. Executive who determines the fashion direction the business will take and communicates that information throughout his or her organization. Also called merchandiser. (27, 28)

fashion editor. Head fashion reporter for a newspaper or magazine. (29)

fashion educator. Person who gives instruction in school clothing and merchandising classes, extension work, and adult and consumer education courses. (30)

fashion followers. Individuals who wear a fashion look only when it is firmly accepted. (2)

Fashion Group, The. A global professional association of women executives who represent every segment of the fashion industry. (4)

fashion illustrator. An artist who draws garments that have been designed and produced by others. (29)

fashion journalist. A writer who passes along fashion information through the mass media. (29)

fashion laggers. Individuals who are the last to adopt accepted styles. (2)

fashion leaders. The few "fashion forward," trendsetting individuals with enough confidence and credibility to start new fashions. (2)

fashion look. A total accessorized outfit. (1)

fashion magazines. Magazines for consumers that have international fashion emphasis through articles, illustrations, and advertisements. (21)

fashion marketing. The making and selling of apparel and accessories that are desirable to customers. (3)

fashion merchandising. The planning, buying, and selling of apparel and accessories. (12)

fashion models. People who wear garments and accessories to promote them. (23, 29)

fashion movement. Ongoing change in what is considered to be fashionable. (2)

fashion photographer. Job of taking pictures that show fashionable clothes and accessories looking their best. (29)

fashion piracy. The stealing of design ideas. (9)

fashion press. The print and broadcast media that present and interpret fashion and industry news. (21)

fashion products. Goods that are always changing, having style and timing risk. (4)

fashion reporter. A fashion writer for the media. (29)

fashion seasons. Retail selling periods. (10)

fashion show coordinator. The person in charge of an entire fashion show presentation. (23)

fashion shows. Theatrical presentations of apparel, accessories, and other fashion products on live models to audiences. (23)

fashion trend. The direction in which fashion is moving. (2)

fashion weeks. *See* market weeks. (9, 11)

feature fixtures. Merchandise presentation fixtures that stock small amounts of merchandise that face outward toward shoppers. (22)

feedback. Response communicated to the sender or source. (17)

felt. Nonwoven fabric made by applying heat, moisture, and pressure to matt fibers together; often of wool. (7)

fiber dyeing. The dyeing of fibers before they are spun into yarns. (7)

fiberfill. Staple fibers used without spinning to fill pillows, mattresses, sleeping bags, and comforters. (6)

fibers. Very thin, hair-like strands that can be quite short or very long; the basic units in making textile products. (4, 6)

figure. Shape of a girl's or woman's body. (8)

filaments. Long, fine, continuous threads found naturally as silk and extruded as manufactured fibers. (6)

filling knits. *See* weft knits. (7)

filling yarns. Crosswise yarns running from selvage to selvage at right angles to warp yarns in a woven fabric; weft yarns. (7)

film. Thin sheet, usually of vinyl or urethane, sometimes used as a coating over fabrics. (7)

financial control. The retail function that deals with supervising the budget and overseeing the spending activities of the store or retail firm. (12)

findings. Materials for the functional parts of garments, such as linings, zippers, hooks, snaps, thread, and labels. (10)

fine jewelry. Expensive jewelry, usually of very high quality, of genuine metals and gemstones, and retailed by jewelry stores. (14)

finished goods. Completed, post-production manufactured items. (11)

finishers. Apparel production employees who do hand work to finish better-quality, higher-priced garments. (27)

finishes. Coatings applied to fabrics to improve the appearance, feel, and performance for the product's end use. (7)

first cost. The wholesale price for goods in a foreign country of origin, exclusive of shipping costs and duties. (16)

fiscal period. A financial accounting. (11)

fiscal year. An accounting period of one year, which might or might not coincide with the calendar year. (19)

fit model. A design room or showroom model who tries on and models samples for the company's management and retail buyers. (29)

fittings. Before a fashion show, the trying on of merchandise by models to see how each garment looks and fits. (23)

fitting sheet. A written form for each lineup number in a fashion show. (23)

fixed costs. Overhead expenses that remain the same regardless of sales volume. (19)

fixtures. Shelves, tables, rods, counters, stands, easels, forms, and platforms on which merchandise is stocked and displayed for sale. (22)

flagship store. The parent or original main store of a retail company, which usually houses the executive, merchandising, and promotional offices for the entire operation. (12)

flax. Plant from which the natural fiber linen is obtained. (6)

flexible manufacturing. *See* modular manufacturing. (10)

flocking. Method of cloth ornamentation using a glue substance on material in a pattern, with finely chopped fibers sprinkled on top to produce a design with texture. (7)

floodlighting. Light directed over an entire wide display area with recessed ceiling lights. (22)

floor fixtures. Merchandise presentation fixtures that stand on the floor. (22)

floor plan. A drawing showing arrangement of physical space, such as showing the positioning of merchandise groups and customer services for a retail store. (22)

floor-ready merchandise (FRM). Vendor-shipped items in a condition to be put directly on the retail shelf or fixture without any additional preparation. (15)

focus group. A dozen or so people in a room with a facilitator who leads a discussion about a particular subject or product line while company representatives watch to gain feedback. (5)

footwear. Accessories that include dress shoes, casual shoes, boots, slippers, and athletic shoes. (14)

ford. A style or design that is produced at the same time by many different manufacturers at many different prices. *See* runner. (1)

forecasting services. Consultants that foresee the colors, textures, and silhouettes to predict coming fashion trends. (7)

foreign market centers. Buying areas outside of one's own country. (16)

formal balance. Equilibrium created in a design with symmetrical parts, such as design details being the same on each side of a center line. (8)

formal business reports. Business writings with covers, title pages, tables of contents, executive summaries, and complete subject matter that analyze complex issues. (17)

formal runway show. A typical fashion show presentation with models parading on a runway in a certain order of appearance. (23)

forward integration. Combining a business at one step of the distribution channel with another farther toward the end of the chain (closer to the end user.) (4)

four-groups approach. A way of showing the flow of goods from fiber to retail that includes the primary, secondary, retail, and auxiliary groups. (4)

fragrances. Products that add a pleasant scent. (14)

franchisee. The person (or group) that owns a franchise business. (9)

franchising. Business arrangement in which a firm grants a retailer the right to use a famous or established name and trademarked merchandise in return for a certain amount of money. (9, 24)

franchisor. The person or firm with the famous or established name used by franchisees. (9)

freelancing. The selling of expert skills to accomplish particular tasks. (30)

free-market system. A market-directed economy in which the way people spend their money determines which products will be produced and what the products will cost without government intervention. (3)

free trade. A government's policy of allowing goods to flow freely in and out of its economy without interference. (25)

freight-forwarding agent. A commercial service business that assists with handling shipping details in offshore production from foreign countries. (24)

fringe benefits. Employment rewards in addition to wages or salary. (26)

full commentary. A fashion show commentary with a script that has every word written that will be said. (23)

full dress rehearsal. A practice of a finished show without an audience present. (23)

full-fashioned. Knits produced on a flat knitting machine that have been shaped by adding or reducing stitches. (7)

full package production. Design-through-distribution contracting, which focuses on supplying design and sample work, fabrics/findings/trims, all parts of construction, as well as packing and transportation arrangements. (24)

full-service retailing. Stores with salespeople who assist customers one-to-one in every phase of the shopping process. (20)

functional props. Objects used to physically support or hold merchandise in a display. (22)

fur. Soft, hairy coat of an animal. (6)

furrier. Manufacturer of fur items. (6)

fusible web. A sheet of binder fibers that can act as an adhesive because its softening point is relatively low. (7)

G

gainsharing. All members of a group share in extra incentive rewards when the group exceeds work expectations. (10)

gallery programs. The traditional sales method for large furniture items displayed in showrooms. (4)

garment. An article of wearing apparel, such as a dress, suit, coat, evening gown, or sweater. (1)

garment district. Area within a fashion city where most of the apparel companies are located. (10)

garment dyeing. The dyeing of constructed garments by apparel manufacturers to fill retail orders for requested colors. (7)

garment fitter. Employee who pins altering folds or marks changes with chalk wherever alterations to garments are required. (28)

garment parts. Components of garments, such as the sleeves, cuffs, collar, and waistband. (1)

gauge. The number of stitches or loops per inch in a knitted fabric. (7)

general expenses. Costs of rent, utilities, and other operating overhead.(19)

general merchandise manager (GMM). High retail executive who is responsible for the total retail merchandising operation. (28)

general merchandisers. Retailers that market all types of goods in multiple price ranges and try to satisfy many needs of a broad range of customers. (12)

generic groups. Identification of families of manufactured fibers, categorized according to similar chemical composition. (6)

geotextiles. Industrial textiles that relate to the earth's surface. (4)

gift wrap. Fancy wrapping such as colorfully designed paper and a ribbon or bow. (20)

girls sizes. Apparel sizes from 7 to 16, for girls of those corresponding ages. (14)

globalization. The rapid growth of international commerce and communications that makes national boundaries less important, especially in economic matters. (24)

gloves. Handwear for warmth, grip, or fashion. (14)

goods. Physical products that are made by manufacturers. (3)

good taste. Sensitivity not only to what is artistically pleasing, but also to what is appropriate for a certain situation and a specific individual. (1)

gradation. A gradual increase or decrease of similar design elements used to create rhythm in a design. *Also* called progression. (8)

grading. Scientific process of making garment patterns into larger or smaller sizes. (10)

grain. The direction of the lengthwise and crosswise yarns or threads in a woven fabric. (7)

graphic designer. Advertising employee who comes up with the visual representation for advertisements and collateral materials. (29)

greige goods. Yard goods in an unfinished state. (4)

grid layout. A retail floor plan that has one or more primary (main) aisles running through the store, with secondary (smaller) aisles intersecting with them at right angles. (22)

gross margin. The sum of money available to cover expenses and generate a profit; gross profit. (19)

gross profit. *See* gross margin. (19)

gross sales. The total dollar amount received from sales; gross revenues. (19)

group department manager. Retail employee who runs a group of departments. (28)

growth features. Attributes of garments that allow them to be expanded as children grow. (14)

guaranteed audience. A fashion show audience that is established before the show is organized and will attend regardless of the show. (23)

H

half-sizes. Apparel sizes for heavier, short-waisted women. (14)

hand. The way fabrics feel to the touch. (7)

handbags. Purses. (14)

handkerchiefs. Pieces of fabric used to blow the nose or for a fashion statement. (14)

hangtags. Detachable heavy paper signs that are affixed to the outside of garments as a form of promotion to help sell products. (18)

hardlines. Also called hard goods, these are nontextile items such as major appliances. (14)

harmony. Pleasing visual unity of a design created by a tasteful relationship among all parts within the whole. (8)

haute couture. The high fashion designer industry of France (or elsewhere) that creates original, individually designed fashions. (9)

headline. The condensed summary of an advertising message or other written communication. (21)

head of stock. Retail employee in charge of the merchandise for a given department or area. (28)

headwear. Hats and caps, sometimes called millinery. (14)

heat transfer printing. Method of printing fabric by transferring the design from preprinted paper by contact heat. (7)

high fashion. Items of the very latest or newest fashions; high style. (1)

home furnishings textiles. Fabrics used for furniture coverings, window treatments, and miscellaneous decorative home accessories. (4)

home sewing industry. Businesses that deal with the production and selling of nonindustrial sewing machines, notions, retail fabrics, patterns, and publications. (4, 30)

horizontal integration. The combining under common ownership of several chains or companies that are at the same location on the channel of distribution. (12)

horizontal lines. Elongated marks that go from side to side like the horizon. (8)

hosiery. Stockings, including panty hose, tights, knee highs, leg warmers, and all other socks. (14)

hourly wage. A certain predetermined pay rate per hour spent doing a job. (26)

house boutique. Small retail shop owned by a couturier that sells items with the couturier's label. (9)

hue. The name given to a color. (8)

hypermarkets. Huge, warehouse-type "supercenters" that sell almost every type of merchandise and target time-stressed consumers who want to do all their shopping in one trip. (12)

I

ideal chart. A fashion show planning device that names all merchandise categories to be presented and the number of garments to be selected per category. (23)

identification. The process of establishing or describing who someone is or what they do. (1)

illustration. The visual part of an advertisement, such as photographs or artwork. Also, the drawing of a fashion design. (21, 29)

image. How something or someone is perceived by others, or nonverbal communication of a store in customers' minds. (13)

import commission house. A brokerage between domestic buyers and foreign sources. (24)

importers. Merchants that bring in products from overseas. (15)

import merchants. Individuals or companies that buy and import particular classifications or categories of goods. (24)

import penetration. The percentage of imports in a country's total market consumption, which measures foreign against domestic goods. (24)

imports. Goods that come into the country from foreign sources. (10, 24)

impulse purchases. Sudden buying without much planning. (14)

incentive bonus. A bonus that rewards high sales or productivity during a certain period of time. (26)

incentives. Prizes or rewards meant to stimulate people to do better work toward achieving results. (18)

income statement. *See* operating statement. (19)

indirect competition. Rivalry between two or more companies using different types of business formats to sell the same type of merchandise. (13)

indirect selling. Nonpersonal promotion aimed at the public or a large general audience. (15, 18)

individuality. Self-expression that distinguishes one person from another or makes each person unique. (1)

individual model lineup sheets. Written descriptions, sketches, and swatches to help models clarify their order of appearance, outfits, and other details when they are in a fashion show. (23)

industrial engineers. Cost and efficiency experts who save companies time and money. (27)

industrial textiles. Technical fabrics sold to commercial business customers according to specifications and performance quality rather than a fashion look. (4)

infant's apparel. Clothing for babies and toddlers younger than 3 years old. (14)

infomercial. A television home sales technique that is heavy on information to educate and build intimacy with customers. (25)

informal balance. Equilibrium in a design created with an asymmetrical arrangement in which design details are divided unequally from the center. (8)

informal business reports. Shorter, less rigid business papers, such as those prepared about sales, work progress, market research, or business calls. (17)

informal fashion show. A casual presentation of garments and accessories without a runway or commentary. (23)

informal organization. The network of interactions that is not part of a company's formal structure, but influences how the organization accomplishes its goals. (17)

information. Processed, meaningful, useful data that is relevant, accurate, timely, and complete. (17)

information management. The activities that generate an orderly and timely flow of relevant information to support business activities. (17)

information systems. Computer components that work together by combining collection, classification, storage, retrieval, and dissemination of data toward a certain outcome. (5)

information technology (IT). See information management. (17)

infrastructure. A country's existence and condition of roads, transportation systems, electricity, telephones, and mail delivery. (24)

initial markup. The difference between merchandise cost and the selling price originally placed on merchandise. (19)

ink-jet printing. Computer-driven printing on a machine with many micronozzles that spit droplets of colors onto materials moving through them. (7)

innovation. The creative, forward-thinking introduction of new ideas. (6)

inside address. The complete name, business title, and address of the person to whom a business letter is written. (17)

inside shop. Apparel firm that does all stages of garment production itself, from design concept and fabric purchasing, through all sewing procedures, to the shipment of finished garments. (10)

inspectors/trimmers. Apparel manufacturing employees who cut off loose threads, pull out basting stitches, and remove lint and spots from garments. (27)

installment plan. Credit agreement with a small down payment and additional payments spread over several months or years. (20)

instant gratification. The unwillingness of consumers to defer fulfillment of their wants to some future time. (15)

institutional advertising. Image or corporate advertising designed to sell public awareness and the reputation of an organization as a whole, rather than selling specific products. (21)

intensity. The brightness or dullness of a color. (8)

intensive market coverage. Blanket coverage to serve all customers of a market. (13)

interactive. Allowing for two-way communication that reacts to people's responses. (5)

interactive TV. Two-way television selling that consists of graphic and written presentations of merchandise that is shown and can be ordered through the technology. (25)

interests. The things a person likes. (26)

intermediate hues. Colors made by combining equal amounts of adjoining primary and secondary hues. (8)

internal theft. Stealing by employees. (20)

international diplomacy. Negotiating between nations while balancing political and economic issues. (24)

International Linen Promotion Commission. Trade association that promotes linen fibers. (6)

International Organization for Standardization (ISO). An organization of over 90 nations that has developed "ISO 9000" standards to certify the quality of goods and services internationally. (7)

international retailing. Retail operations of a company that serve customers in multiple countries. (24)

Internet. A global network connecting millions of computers that all work together to share information. (17)

Internet sales. Retail transactions made through the World Wide Web system with home computers. (25)

internships. Work-study programs at the college level. (26)

intimate apparel. The general women's category that includes foundation garments, lingerie, and loungewear. (14)

intrepreneurship. Risk-taking, innovative thinking within companies. (25)

inventory. Goods held on hand for the production process or to be sold to customers. (11, 19)

inventory control. The process of maintaining inventories at a level that prevents stockouts and minimizes holding costs. (11)

inventory management. Activities that ensure a flow of merchandise from vendors to stores to consumers; stock control. (15)

inventory-to-sales ratio: *See* stock-to-sales ratio. (15)

inventory turns. See stock turnover. (15)

invoicing. Billing for materials sent. (5)

irregulars. Items with imperfections, such as slight mistakes in manufacturing. (15)

island windows. Four-sided, lobby display windows that stand alone and can be viewed from all sides. (22)

Item 807/9802. A section of the U.S. Tariff Code that allows garment manufacturers to export cut components and trims for sewing elsewhere, and reimport them, paying duty only on the value added. (24)

J

Jacquard loom. Machine that weaves large and intricate designs with a series of programmed punch cards. (7)

jagged lines. Lines that change direction abruptly and with sharp points like zigzags. (8)

jewelry. Accessory items, such as pins, necklaces, earrings, bracelets, and cuff links. (14)

job. A specific work assignment or position within an industry, with certain duties, roles, or functions. (26)

jobber. *See* apparel jobbers *and* textile jobber. (7, 10)

job description. A written statement of what the employee holding a specific job is expected to do. (26)

job lot. A broken or unbalanced assortment, priced low by a vendor for quick sale to a retailer; odd lot. (15)

joint venture. An agreement that brings necessary skills or products of two companies together for added strength. (24)

junior. Apparel size category for fully developed, small-boned, and short-waisted females. (14)

junior department stores. Smaller department stores that do not carry as wide a range of goods. (12)

just-in-time. An inventory system with a continuous process of inventory control that, through pipeline teamwork, seeks to deliver a small quantity of materials where and when needed. (5,11)

K

key resources. Vendors preferred because of excellent past dealings, consistent orders, good profitability, image, and best satisfaction to store customers. (15)

keystone markup. Doubling the cost price to arrive at the retail price. (19)

kiosk. A cart or open sales pavilion, usually centrally located in a shopping mall such as in a main walkway. (12)

knitting. Fabric construction method done by looping yarns together. (7)

knock-off. Copy of another, usually higher-priced, garment. (9)

L

labels. Small pieces of ribbon or cloth attached to garments on the inside that contain printed information. (18)

labor intensive. Requiring many workers to make the products, rather than relying heavily on machines and technology. (4, 10)

lace. Fancy openwork fabric made by crossing, twisting, or looping yarns into designs. (7)

laser-beam cutter. Machine that vaporizes a single layer of fabric almost instantaneously with an intense, powerful beam of light. (10)

layaway. A deferred purchase arrangement in which the store sets aside a customer's merchandise until the customer has fully paid for it. (18)

layout. How all the elements of an advertisement or other visual arrangement are put together. (21)

layout artist. Advertising employee who designs layouts for ads. (29)

lead time. Amount of time between placing an order for merchandise and the desired delivery date. (10)

leased department. Area within a retail store that is stocked and operated by someone else. (6, 12)

leather. A tough, flexible material made from animal hides. (6)

leave paper. Retail buying term for writing completed orders with vendors, usually during market week. (16)

ledger. A book or computer program containing ongoing accounts of the company. (19)

lengthwise grain. The direction the warp yarns run in a fabric, parallel to the selvages. (7)

leno weave. Fabric construction that produces an open effect using crossing pairs of warp yarns. (7)

liability. Legal responsibility for debts and obligations. (3)

licensed merchandise stores. Concept shops built around licensed merchandise. (12)

licensees. Manufacturers of products with a well-known name owned by others. (9)

licensing. Arrangement whereby a manufacturer is given the exclusive right to produce and market goods that bear the famous name of someone who, in return, receives a percentage of wholesale sales. (9, 24)

licensors. Designers or owners of well-known labels. (9)

lifestyle competition. Rivalry between businesses for consumers' pastimes and spending money. (13)

limited-service retailing. Value-oriented stores that offer expected services and sell products for which customers need some information. (20)

line. Element of design that is a distinct, elongated mark as if drawn by a pen. Also, a group of styles and designs that will be produced and sold as a set of new selections for a given season. (8, 9)

linen. Natural cellulosic fiber obtained from the stalk of the flax plant. (6)

linens. Table and bath textiles. (4)

lines of authority. Levels of responsibility within a company's structure, usually shown on an organization chart. (17)

lineup. The order in which outfits will appear in a fashion show. (23)

liquidate. Selling off all assets and using the proceeds to pay outstanding debts on a percentage basis. (25)

local advertising. Ads sponsored by local merchants that provide details about where to find products and their prices and quantities available. (21)

logistics. The handling details of storing and physically moving merchandise to the proper locations. (11)

logo. Symbol that represents a person, firm, or organization; often combined with a slogan in company advertising. (9, 21)

long-run fashions. Styles that take a long time to complete the fashion cycle. (2)

loss leaders. Low-priced articles on which stores make little or no profit because of lowering the price for promotional reasons. (19)

loss prevention programs. Action strategies to prevent, recognize, and monitor security problems. (20)

M

machine technicians. Manufacturing company employees who keep the complex factory equipment in good working order, or who operate the machines. (27)

machine vision. The identification of bar codes or goods with video cameras that read signatures, such as size, shape, or package color. (5)

magnetic stripe. An information-containing band on a credit, financial, or security card that is read by swiping through a special reading machine. (5)

mail-order retailers. Companies that sell through catalogs they distribute to consumers. Also called direct-mail marketers. (12)

maintained markup. The difference between gross merchandise cost and the net selling price of merchandise; the initial markup minus all retail markdowns or other reductions. (19)

major. A specific field of study in college. (26)

management information systems (MIS). Departments in corporations and independent consultants that specialize in computer communications. (17)

management positions. Jobs concerned with running a business. (26)

management trainees. Entry-level employees who have college degrees; executive trainee. (27)

management training programs. *See* executive trainee programs. (26)

mannequins. Lifelike human forms. (22)

mannequin work. Employment as a model for a designer or manufacturer to check fit and show samples. (29)

manufactured fibers. Fibers created through technology and produced artificially from substances such as cellulose, petroleum, and chemicals. (6)

manufacturers. Companies that make goods. (3, 10)

manufacturing resource planning (MRP II). A computerized method of planning production materials and levels of inventory. (11)

margin. The difference between the price received by a company for its products and the cost of providing them; profit per item. (9)

markdown. The difference between the previous selling price of an item and the reduced selling price. (19)

markdown money. Payment by a vendor to a retailer to compensate for losses from reduced selling prices of that vendor's goods. (19)

marker. Long piece of paper that has a drawing of the layout of all the pattern pieces for fabric cutting in garment manufacturing. (10)

markers. Apparel manufacturing employees who figure out how the pattern pieces can be placed most efficiently for cutting. (27)

market. Group of potential customers; a geographic area where buyers and sellers meet to exchange money for products and services, usually with many sellers in close proximity to each other. (11)

market analysts. Employees who conduct market research to try to discover future market needs. (27)

market centers. Concentrated areas where goods are produced, sold, and bought at wholesale prices; a geographic area where buyers and sellers meet to exchange money for products and services. (16)

market coverage. The amount of concentration a retailer has in a customer area, such as intensive, selective, or exclusive. (13)

market directory. A mart showroom guidebook listing locations, phone numbers, merchandise lines, and sizes offered. (16)

market disruption. A situation, usually caused by too many imports, that threatens a particular industry with products that are in direct competition with that industry. (24)

market growth. An increase in the size of the entire market, with more products sold and higher total dollars of sales. (5)

marketing. The process of finding or creating a profitable market for specific goods or services. (3, 7)

marketing manager. Executive who plans and directs all marketing endeavors of a company. (27)

marketing mix. A blend of features that satisfies a chosen market, including product, price, place, and promotion. (3)

marketing specialist. Advertising director with a manufacturing firm. (29)

marketing triangle. A way of relating price to volume, showing that lower-priced products will sell in larger quantities than higher-priced products. (3)

market research. The process of systematically gathering and analyzing information, such as consumer tastes and changing trends, relating to a particular market. (5)

market segmentation. Dividing the total market into smaller groups that contain similar characteristics. (5)

market segments. Smaller groups of a total market that contain similar characteristics. (5)

market share. The part of the total market controlled by a firm, usually computed by sales and indicated as a percentage of the total industry. (5)

market weeks. Scheduled periods of time during which producers officially introduce their new lines of merchandise and retail buyers shop the various lines. (11, 16)

markup (markon). The amount added to the cost of merchandise to determine the selling price. (19)

mass customization. Offering individually made items to everyone. (25)

mass fashion. Styles that are produced in volume and widely sold at lower prices. (1)

mass market cosmetics. Inexpensive lines sold by discount and other lower-priced retailers. (14)

mass merchandisers. Retailers of large amounts of staple goods and mass-produced garments. (12)

masters degree. An advanced college degree that is higher than a bachelor's degree but not as high as a doctorate degree. (26)

materials handling. All activities of goods not involved in actual production processes, such as moving, storing, packing, and transporting of the raw materials, semi-finished parts, or final garments. (11)

maze layout. A free-flowing retail floor plan arrangement. (22)

mechanical finishes. Finishes that are applied mechanically rather than chemically. (7)

mechanical spinning. Method of pulling (drawing) and twisting staple fibers together to obtain continuous lengths of yarns. (6)

media buyers. Advertising employees who select and buy the best media for clients' ads. (29)

media forms. Types of media available for advertising. (21)

media vehicles. Specific media forms from which to choose or combine for an advertising campaign. (21)

memorandum. An informal written message from one person or department to another person, group, or department in the same company; memo. (17)

memorandum buying. An arrangement in which the retailer takes title to goods when they are received, but unsold goods may be returned to the vendor after a specified time. (15)

mercerization. A treatment under tension with caustic soda that gives luster, strength, and dyeability to cellulosic textiles. (7)

merchandise acceptance curve. A bell-shaped curve that shows the stages of the fashion cycle. (2)

merchandise blend. The right products being at the right place at the right time in the right quantity at the right price with the right appeal. (3)

merchandise broker. Middleperson who connects producers and retailers for the selling and buying of goods. (16)

merchandise buying. Obtaining planned merchandise through vendors or other suppliers. (15)

merchandise coordinators. Manufacturing company employees who make sure their merchandise is presented as effectively as possible within retail stores. (27)

merchandise fashion level. The emphasis of presenting goods in the early or late stages of the fashion cycle. (2)

merchandise items. Articles that are distinguishable by specific, unique characteristics. (14)

merchandise loan record. A sheet on which is written details of the borrowed merchandise for a fashion show. (23)

merchandise manager. Employee who coordinates the merchandise of several retail departments. (28)

merchandise planning. Activities of estimating consumer demand and how it can best be satisfied. (16)

merchandise presentation. The ways that goods are hung, placed on shelves, or otherwise made available for sale in retail stores. (22)

merchandise pull. The removing of fashion show items from the sales floor to a show storage area. (23)

merchandiser. *See* fashion director. (27, 28)

merchandise selection. Process of choosing the best garments, shoes, and accessories for a fashion show. (23)

merchandise selling. Promotion and/or exchange for money of merchandise. (15)

merchandising. The process through which products are obtained (designed, developed, or bought for resale) and promoted to the point of sale, trying to match those products to established market requirements to make a profit. (3, 12)

merchandising cycle. A circle of ongoing planning, buying, and selling activity. (15)

merchandising director. Executive who figures out what the company's customers will want. (27)

merchandising policies. Specific guidelines established by management for the company to follow to keep inventory choices on track. (13)

merger. The joining of two companies to form a new one. (25)

message media channel. In communication, various approaches to how a message might be transmitted. (17)

microdenier fibers. Extremely thin filament manufactured fibers that are soft, luxurious, and drapable. (6)

micro-segmentation. The dividing of an industry's total market into extremely narrowly defined target markets. (25)

middle management. Jobs that involve a higher degree of responsibility than lower management jobs. (26)

minimum wage. The lowest hourly rate established by law. (26)

misses. Apparel size category for fully developed women of average height, weight, and proportions. (14)

missionary selling. Convincing customers that they need a product before trying to sell it to them. (6)

model. *See* fashion model. (23, 29)

model lineup sheets. Individual forms for each model in a fashion show, giving the order of appearance, outfits, and other details. (23)

model list. A list of all the models that will be in a fashion show, including names, telephone numbers, and apparel sizes. (23)

model order. The rotation of models in a fashion show. (23)

model stock plan. A proposed purchase list composed mostly of fashion merchandise with ever-changing appeal. (15)

modem. An electronic device that transmits computer data over telephone lines. (5)

modesty. The covering of a person's body according to the code of decency of that person's society. (1)

modular manufacturing. Flexible apparel production method where employees are divided into independent module work groups that sort out problems and agree on their own work assignments and schedules. (10)

Mohair Council of America. The promotional organization for U.S. mohair producers. (6)

mom and pop stores. Independent owner-operated stores run by a husband and wife, or a proprietor and a few employees. (12)

monochromatic color scheme. Plan that uses different tints, shades, and intensities of one color. (8)

monofilament yarns. Single filaments used as yarns, usually of a high denier. (6)

monopoly. A market structure in which there are no direct competitors in an industry; one company controls the industry and market. (3)

more than one. Suggestion selling of more than one of the same or similar item. (18)

motif. A design idea or theme. (27)

multifilament yarns. Yarns consisting of many continuous filaments or strands twisted together. (6)

multi-channel retailing. Retailers' use of a combination of several channels, such as stores, catalogs, Web sites, etc. (25)

multinational corporations (MNCs). Companies that operate globally with direct investment in several different countries. (24)

music mix. The combination of different music selections to create specific moods, such as for a fashion show. (23)

music planning sheet. For fashion shows, a list of the many appropriate selections that match the merchandise theme. (23)

N

nap. A layer of fiber ends raised from a fabric surface. It appears different when viewed from different directions. (7)

national advertising. Ads sponsored by companies that sell products on a nationwide basis to create general demand for products. (21)

National Cotton Council. The central organization of the cotton industry, which disseminates information and lobbies for trade legislation. (6)

National Retail Federation (NRF). The world's largest retail trade association. (12)

natural fibers. Textile strands from plants and animals. (6)

neckties. Narrow lengths of material of various fabrics and surface designs worn at the shirt collar. (14)

need. Something that a person must have for existence or survival. (1)

needle punched. Mechanically interlocked fibers with a needle loom to make a nonwoven fabric characterized by regularly placed punched holes. (7)

needle trades. Term referring to the garment manufacturing, or apparel, industry. (10)

neighborhood shopping center. A small cluster of 5 to 15 stores that services local consumers in surrounding neighborhoods. (13)

net. Openwork fabric made by crossing, twisting, or looping yarns together in a regular pattern. (7)

net loss. A resulting negative number after expenses have been deducted from the gross margin figure, which is shown in parentheses. (19)

net profit. A resulting positive number after expenses have been deducted from the gross margin figure. (19)

net sales. The actual dollars earned and kept from sales during an accounting period (gross sales minus returns and allowances). (19)

network. An interconnection of computing equipment using data communications circuitry. (17)

networking. The exchange of ideas, information, or services among an interconnected group of people. (4)

neural computing. Electronic programs that can learn internally from their previous activities. (17)

neutrals. Black, white, and gray rather than true hues. (8)

never-out list. A list kept by retailers of key items or best selling goods that should always be on hand and on display. (15)

never-outs. Best-selling merchandise items that account for a significant sales volume and must always be available. (15)

niche manufacturing. The production of specific lines of goods for carefully defined customers. (25)

niche retailing. A specialty viewpoint in which departments or stores identify and closely target a specific set of fashion tastes. (25)

noise. Static, distortion, or interference during the communication of a message. (17)

noncellulosic manufactured fibers. Synthetic fibers made of various petrochemical mixtures. (6)

nonprofit corporation. A corporation that exists to provide a social service rather than to make a profit. (3)

nonstore retailing. Selling without a conventional store facility, such as through mail-order catalogs, telecommunications, personal selling, and vending machines. (12)

nonverbal communication. The sending and receiving of messages without using words. (17)

nonwoven fabric. A compact web of fibers, not yarns, held together with a combination of moisture, heat, chemicals, friction, and/or pressure. (7)

North American Free Trade Agreement (NAFTA). A trading bloc that includes the United States with Canada and Mexico. (24)

novelty fabrics. Fashion fabrics that change with style trends. (7)

O

objections. Feelings of concern or disapproval. (18)

obsolescence factor. The rejection of recently used items in favor of newer ones, even though the old items retain their utility value. (2)

odd-figure pricing. The retail pricing of merchandise a few cents less than a dollar denomination. (19)

odd lot. *See* job lot. (15)

off-price discounters. Retailers that sell brand name or designer merchandise at lower than normal prices. (12)

offshore production. Manufacturing that is done overseas. (10)

offshore sourcing. Buying goods from overseas producers, or contracting with foreign manufacturing plants. (15)

oligopoly. A market structure with only a few large rival firms that produce the products, dominate the market, and react to each other's actions. (3)

online retailing. The selling of merchandise to consumers through personal computers with modems. (25)

open account. A charge account, to be paid in full within a specific time period (usually thirty days), with no finance charge or interest. (20)

open distribution policy. The selling and shipping of goods to anyone who can pay for the merchandise. (11)

open-ended questions. Questions that require multiple-word answers rather than merely a yes or no. (17)

open order. An order placed with a resident buyer or vendor with no restrictions as to style, color, price, or delivery. (16)

open systems. Computer components from different suppliers that are compatible with each other to be mixed and matched. (5)

open-to-buy (OTB). The dollar or merchandise unit amount that buyers are permitted to order for their stores, departments, or apparel category or classification for a specified time period. (15)

open windows. Display windows that have no background panel at all, with outside visibility into the store. (22)

operating ratios. Mathematical relationships of income and expense figures that measure firms' effectiveness in generating sales and managing expenses. (19)

operating statement. A summary of the financial results of a firm's operations over a specified period of time; income statement. (19)

operational policies. Specific guidelines, established by management, to make the store appealing for the target market through physical appearance and customer services. (13)

optical scanners. Electronic light beam readers that feed bar code information to computers. (5)

optional services. Top services offered by full-service retailers that distinguish those retailers from others. (20)

organizational climate. The feeling that employees have about their opportunities, value, and rewards for good performance. (18)

organizational performance. The individual quality of work done by each employee and the overall performance of the department or company as a whole. (25)

organization chart. Diagram or visual representation of a company's official structure, indicating lines of authority. (17)

outside shop. Apparel firm that handles everything but the sewing and sometimes the cutting, using contractors to do those production steps. (10)

outsourcing. The hiring of independent specialists to do particular work, rather than using company employees. (5)

overall print. A printed design that is the same across all of a piece of fabric. (7)

overlighting. Lighting from above the merchandise in a display. (22)

overrun. When more product has been made than was ordered by customers. (7)

overstoring. The existence of too many stores and shopping centers in a retail trading area, all vying for limited consumer dollars. (25)

overtime. Time worked beyond the usual 40-hour workweek. (26)

P

packaging. The covering, wrapper, or container in which some merchandise is placed. (18)

parity. Equal monetary value or treatment by the law. (24)

partial commentary. A fashion commentary that lists the major details of garments in outline form or short sections of script. (23)

partnership. An unincorporated business that is co-owned and operated by two or more persons. (3)

paste up. A draft of a print advertisement. (23)

paste-up/mechanical artist. Advertising agency employee who puts together the actual elements of an ad layout. (29)

patronage motives. Reasons customers choose to shop at one store rather than another, based on reputation and image, merchandise assortments, convenience of location, customer services, price, or other factors. (13)

pattern graders. Manufacturing employees who cut patterns in all the different sizes produced by the manufacturer. (27)

pattern makers. Manufacturing employees who translate apparel designs into the right number, size, and shape of pattern pieces needed for mass production. (27)

perceived difference. The idea in customers' minds that items stand out from others, usually because of image and quality. (9)

performance standards. Product ratings according to suitability for specific end uses. (7)

permanent finish. Fabric finish that lasts the life of the garment. (7)

permanent press. A resin finish applied to certain fabrics to help them retain their original shape and resist wrinkling. (7)

perquisites. Extra niceties for employees with high stature in the company. (26)

personality. The total characteristics that distinguish an individual, especially his or her behavioral and emotional tendencies. (1)

personal selling. Moving merchandise directly to customers through door-to-door sales, selling parties, or showings in homes or work environments. *See* direct selling. (12, 18)

personal shopper. Fashion consultant who chooses merchandise in response to customers' requests or accompanies customers to offer fashion advice and selection help. (28)

personnel. The retail function that deals with hiring, training, rewarding with pay and benefits, and other human relations efforts of the company. (12)

personnel administrator (or director). The person who oversees the matters of company employees. (28)

petite. Apparel size category for short females. (14)

photographic model. A model who poses in front of cameras for pictures used in press releases or advertisements of manufacturers and other firms. (29)

photo stylist. Employee who books models, accessorizes apparel, obtains props, pins up hems, irons garments, and picks up and returns merchandise for fashion photo shoots. (29)

physical inventory. An inventory audit done by counting and recording actual stock at a certain time. (18)

physique. Shape of a boy's or man's body. (8)

piece dyeing. The dyeing of yard goods in fabric form after weaving or knitting rather than as fibers, yarns, or garments. (7)

piece goods buyers. Purchasing agents who research and buy the fabrics, trims, and notions that are chosen by designers and approved by management. (27)

piecework. Manufacturing in which one specific task is assigned to each person along an assembly line. (10)

pile fabrics. Material with a surface effect of tufts, loops, or other projecting yarns. (7)

pilferage. The stealing of a company's inventory or cash in small, petty amounts. (20)

pill. To accumulate little balls of fibers on the surface of a spun yarn fabric usually caused by rubbing and wearing. (6)

pilot plant. A small-scale trial production facility that uses commercial factory methods. (6)

pinpointing. Lighting that focuses a narrow beam on a specific item on display. (22)

pinsonic thermal joining. The use of ultrasonic vibrations to quilt fabrics together with a series of "welds" in a chosen design. (7)

pivots. Turns made by models in fashion shows, most often at the halfway point and end of the runway. (23)

plain weave. Simplest and most common fabric weave in which each filling yarn passes successively over and under each warp yarn, alternating each row. (7)

plaiting. *See* braiding. (7)

plant engineers. Manufacturing employees who make sure all environmental systems are operating properly. (27)

plant manager. Executive in charge of all operations and employees at a manufacturing plant. (27)

ply. Each strand of yarn in a ply yarn. (6)

ply yarns. Yarns of two or more single yarns twisted together for extra strength, added bulk, or unusual effects. (6)

point-of-sale (POS). Merchandise data collected electronically when consumer purchase transactions are recorded. (5)

political stability. The degree to which a country's laws and regulations are subject to change and are enforced. (24)

polymers. Chainlike chemical structures of molecules from which many manufactured fibers are made. (6)

portal. A starting Web site with links to many specific sites for a certain subject, such as shopping. (12)

portfolio. A case of loose, unfolded art or design papers showing a person's creative work. (27)

power centers. Shopping areas with several large discount retailers on the same site, and usually in close proximity to a regional mall. (25)

preselling. Maintaining contacts with previous customers to start the selling steps all over again. (18)

pressers. Apparel industry employees who flatten seams, iron garment surfaces, and shape garments with steam-pressing machines. (27)

press kit. A promotional collection of materials presented as a portfolio with press releases and photographs and/or illustrations. (21)

press releases. Written news stories sent as publicity to newspapers and magazines. (21)

press show. Private fashion showing for the press before the public sees the fashions. (23)

prestige cosmetic lines. Cosmetic products sold by department and specialty stores, with high-quality, exclusive images. (14)

prestige pricing. A policy of setting high prices on items to attract customers who want quality goods or the status of owning expensive and exclusive merchandise. (13)

prêt à porter. The French designer ready-to-wear (pret) industry. (9)

preteen sizes. Girls sizes that offer more sophisticated styling. (14)

preticketing. *See* vendor preticketing. (15)

price. The amount of money charged for a product or service. (19)

price look-up (PLU). Feature of computerized POS systems that automatically adjusts prices to the correct amount when bar codes are scanned at checkout. (18)

price point. The dollar amount at which an item is offered for sale. (13, 19)

price-positioning strategy. Self-service, discount retailing with only essential services offered. (20)

price promoting. Advertising special price reductions of goods to bring in shoppers who will then buy other items as well. (13)

price war. When competition drastically lowers their prices to try to attract customers by underselling each other. (13)

primary group. Suppliers of raw materials (textiles, leathers, and furs) in the soft goods chain. (4)

primary hues. The three basic colors of red, yellow, and blue. (8)

principles of design. Rules of balance, proportion, emphasis, and rhythm concerning how the design elements should be used. (8)

printing. Process for adding color, pattern, or design to the surface of fabrics. (7)

print/repeat artist. Fabric designer who does original textile surface designs of motifs, color combinations, and repeats. (27)

private (central) buying office. A resident buying office that is owned and operated by a single retail organization. (16)

private corporations. Companies with stock that is not available to the general public. (3)

private label. Goods that are produced only for a particular retailer and have the retailer's special trademark or brand name. (4)

private label credit cards. Charge cards with the store's name and logo, but issued and managed by a bank. (20)

proactive approach. An attempt to make processes and situations better before problems occur, doing everything right the first time. (11)

procurement. Buying at the wholesale level for resale at the retail level. (16)

product advertising. Advertising designed to sell specific, identifiable merchandise items or lines, or certain services, and aimed at getting an immediate response. (21)

product development. The process of carrying a product idea through stages from initial conceptualization to actual appearance in the market. (5)

product development directors. Retail employees who are production experts. (15)

product features. Physical characteristics of items. (18)

product guarantees. Policy statements by companies expressing their general responsibility for the products they sell. (20)

production. The transformation of resources into a form that people need or want. (10)

production assistants. Employees who do detail work and recordkeeping for plant managers. (27)

production show. The most elaborate and expensive type of fashion show, with entertainment, backdrops, and lighting effects. (23)

production supervisors. Manufacturing company employees who coordinate and direct various manufacturing operations. (27)

production workers. Employees who operate the machines that do the manufacturing procedures. (27)

productivity. A measure of how efficiently or effectively resources (labor supply, machines, materials) are used, calculated by dividing output by employee hours expended to achieve that output. (10)

product managers. Manufacturing executives who are in charge of every aspect of one of the company's lines or a specific category of garments within a line. Retail employees who develop, coordinate, execute, and deliver private label corporate programs. (27, 28)

product mix. A company's entire selection of goods and services. (13)

product motives. Qualities or images of certain products that affect consumer purchases, such as materials, construction, style, fit, or guarantees. (13)

products. Economic goods or services that fulfill a market need and are exchanged for payment. (3)

product sourcers. Employees who identify, research, open, and develop production sourcing markets and vendors that meet their company's long-term product supply needs. (28)

product warranties. Specific statements by sellers of the quality or performance capabilities of their products. (6)

profit. Money left over after expenses and taxes have been deducted from what was received from the company's sales. (3)

profitability range. The difference between the most profitable and the least profitable lines of merchandise, based on profit per square foot of selling space. (19)

profit margin. Ratio that measures profit as a percentage of net sales; return on sales (ROS). (19)

progression. *See* gradiation. (8)

progressive bundle system. Piecework apparel manufacturing in which cut garment parts are packaged into bundles of dozens to go through the sewing operations. (10)

promotion. Selling to a large audience to increase buying response. (3)

promotion buying. The purchase of items at special low prices, often late in the ordering calendar, to be retailed at reduced prices. (15)

promotion mix. The combination of all types of persuasive communication used by an organization to market itself and influence the purchase of merchandise. (22)

promotion program. A written guide that details the company's promotion efforts for a certain period of time, as well as for single important events. (21)

proof. Word ending for fabric finishes that give complete protection; for instance, waterproof. (7)

prophetic fashions. Styles that are identified early as future best sellers in many price ranges. (9)

proportion. Principle of design concerning the spatial, or size, relationship of all the parts in a design to each other and to the whole. Also called scale. (8)

proprietary. Exclusive to the source of the information or product, and secret or unavailable to others. (5)

proprietary credit card. Store-issued charge card that is owned, operated, and managed by the company; in-house credit card. (20)

props. Added objects that support the theme of a display. (22)

prospect. To search for customers who have the willingness to buy and the ability to pay for the company's products. (18)

protection. Physical safeguards. (1, 28)

protectionism. The opposite of free trade, which includes many government-imposed trade restraints. (24)

protein fibers. Natural fibers of animal origin, such as wool, silk, and specialty hair fibers. (6)

psychographics. Statistics that try to explain consumer behavior through such variables as lifestyle, values, attitudes, and self-concept. (5)

public address system. A sound system consisting of a microphone, amplifiers, and speakers, such as for a fashion show. (23)

public corporations. Companies that offer their stock to the general public, usually on national exchanges. (3)

publicists. Public relations agents who help companies project their public image. (29)

publicity. Unpaid media coverage of news about an organization, or its products and activities, presented at the discretion of the media. (21)

public relations (PR). Activities that try to build good relations with the various publics of an organization or product line. (21)

public relations agents. Employees who tell the firm's story to stockholders and the press. (29)

public service announcements. Announcements run free of charge by radio and television stations for events, such as fashion shows, that are for charity and of general interest to the community. (23)

purchase order (PO). A written document authorizing the delivery of certain goods at specific prices and times. (16)

purchasing agents. Employees who buy materials, equipment, and services needed for the company to function. (27)

purchasing behavior. The way consumers act in the market. (13)

pure competition. A market structure in which no company in an industry is extremely large or powerful enough to influence or control prices. (3)

pure wool. New wool fibers or yarns that have never been used. (6)

purl knit. Reversible knitted fabric with prominent crosswise ridges with superior stretch and recovery in both directions. (7)

Q

qualitative. What people feel or want. (5)

quality. The degree of excellence of a product. (7, 11)

quality assurance tester. Retail employee who evaluates merchandise to determine if quality standards have been met. (28)

quality control inspectors. Employees who work in all phases of production to analyze the quality of items being manufactured. (27)

quality standards. Product ratings according to levels of defects. (7)

quantitative. How strongly people feel about or want things. (5)

Quick Response (QR). An industry-wide program that ties together the entire textile/apparel pipeline using bar code data, EDI technology, and long-term customer-supplier partnerships. (5)

quilted fabrics. Three-layer fabrics with batting in the middle, usually held together by machine stitching. (7)

R

rack jobbers. Wholesalers that sell specialized goods, especially through self-service retailers, where they provide setup, mark prices, and maintain the fixtures for their product lines. (18)

radiation. Rhythm in a design created by lines emerging from a central point like rays. (8)

radio frequency (RF) data communication. Wireless data collection done through airwaves. (5)

rag trade. Old insiders' term for the garment manufacturing industry. (10)

rain check. A certificate that entitles the customer to buy an out-of-stock advertised special at a later time at the same advertised price. (18)

ramie. A cellulosic fiber from the stalks of a woody-leafed plant called China grass. (6)

ramped windows. Enclosed "raked" windows with the display floor higher in back than in front. (22)

raschel knit. Patterned or intricate knit fabric made on a raschel knitting machine. (7)

rational behavior. A response of conscious reasoning. (13)

raw materials. Preproduction resources, such as fabrics, trimmings, and notions for apparel production. (4, 11)

reactive approach. Fixing problems after they occur. (11)

ready-to-wear (RTW). Garments, especially women's apparel, produced in factories according to standard sizes. (9)

receiver. Destination of a message or shipped goods. (17)

receiving. The physical exchange of goods between the vendor's transporting agent to the retailer. Also, the checking-in of goods. (18, 28)

recession. An economic decrease in national income, employment, and production. (3)

reciprocal agreements. Exchange programs with schools in other parts of the country or world. (26)

recycled wool. Wool fibers recovered from previously used wool. (6)

reduction planning. Estimating a percentage of sales for stock shrinkage, markdowns, and discounts. (19)

refabricate. Apparel designs with high sales volumes in the previous season that are retained for the next season with only minor changes. (10)

regional advertising. Ads within an area of adjoining states or a confined section of the country. (21)

regional manager. Chain retailer executive who oversees several districts. (28)

regional shopping center. A group of many stores, often in an enclosed mall with several shopping levels and one or more full-line anchors. (13)

regular orders. Stock order for line merchandise. (16)

regular price-line buying. Buyers' systematic writing of purchase orders and normal reorders with vendors. (15)

rehearsals. Practice sessions, such as for fashion shows. (23)

renewable finish. Fabric finish that is temporary but can be replaced or reapplied. (7)

reorders. Additional orders of the same merchandise as ordered previously. (16)

repellent. *See* resistant. (7)

repetition. Method of creating rhythm in a design by repeating lines, shapes, colors, or textures. (8)

reporting/consulting services. Organizations that collect, tabulate, and report information on certain product lines and/or merchandising activities. (16)

repricing. Price increases and decreases on goods that are in stock. (19)

research and development (R&D). Innovation to discover new knowledge, develop new products, and improve old products. (27)

resellers. Wholesalers who serve to distribute goods between producers and retailers or users. (4)

resident buying office (RBO). A service organization located in a major market center that reports market information, acts as a market representative, and performs other related services to a group of noncompeting stores. (16)

resident buying office buyer. Employee who helps member retail firms do a better buying job but has no responsibilities over retail sales or profits. (28)

resident sales agent. A representative in a country who connects buyers of other countries with local manufacturers of particular types of goods. (24)

resilient. Having the ability to spring back when crushed, stretched, or wrinkled. (6)

resistant. Second word of a phrase for fabric finishes that indicates partial protection, such as water-resistant. (7)

resources. Industrial materials and manufacturing capabilities. *See* suppliers and vendors. (3)

response. The reactions of the receiver of a communication after being exposed to the message. (17)

response time. The amount of time it takes to produce and deliver merchandise after it has been ordered. (10)

responsive selling. Responding to the customer's presence rather than going out to find customers. (18)

restructuring. Examining a business to see what changes can make it better, reallocating resources and employees, and re-charting its course. (25)

retail buyers. Merchandising executives who are responsible for selecting and purchasing goods for their companies and for selling the goods at a profit. (15, 28)

retail coordinators. Fashion and promotional liaisons between pattern companies and retail fabric stores. (30)

retail corporate ownership groups. *See* store ownership groups. (12)

retailers. Companies that sell merchandise in small quantities to end-use consumers. (3)

retail group. Stores, catalogs, TV home shopping channels, and other retail enterprises that sell finished goods to those who want to buy and use them. (4)

retailing. The business of selling merchandise or services directly to final consumers, for their use, through a store or other method. (3, 4)

retail positioning. Where a store situates itself in the consumer market, which guides how it satisfies its market while differentiating itself from competitors. (13)

retail promotion. Promotion by a store to its customers. (21)

retail salespeople. Store employees who sell goods directly to customers. (28)

retail saturation. An overabundance of stores for the size of the market; overstoring. (25)

return on sales (ROS). *See* profit margin. (19)

returns. When customers are given a full refund or credit for goods brought back to the store. (19)

returns to vendors (RTV). Goods that are shipped back to a supplier by a store. (18)

revenue. Income. (23)

revolving charge account. An open account that has no finance charge if paid in full within thirty days, and interest on the unpaid balance if not paid in full. (20)

rhythm. Principle of design concerned with the pleasing arrangement of the design elements to produce a feeling of continuity or easy movement of the observer's eye. (8)

rib knit. Double knit fabric with pronounced lengthwise ridges and great crosswise stretch. (7)

rib weave. A plain weave with a corded effect created by using coarser yarns in one direction and regular yarns in the other direction. (7)

robbery. Violent or after-hours theft; burglary. (20)

robotics. Mechanically accomplished tasks done by automated equipment. (11)

roller printing. Inexpensive, simple, high-speed method of applying color directly to fabric with a series of metal rollers engraved with the design. (7)

rotary screen printing. A combination of roller and screen printing in which dye is pushed through a perforated cylindrical screen to apply each color. (7)

runner. A best-selling style that sells in large quantities at all price levels. *See* ford. (1)

runway model. A model who works in front of live audiences. (29)

runways. Elevated fashion show walkways for models that project out from the stage, usually into the audience seating area. (23)

S

S corporation. A small corporation with no more than thirty-five shareholders and taxed like a sole proprietorship or partnership. (3)

salary. A fixed amount of pay, usually received once or twice a month, for doing all that is required for a particular job. (26)

sales associates. Retail employees who use more formal or creative selling skills than just ringing up sales; "order getters." (18)

sales-below-cost laws. State laws that attempt to preserve competition by restricting lower than usual pricing. (19)

sales catalogs. Source to purchase basic goods, containing photos or drawings of items, and sometimes fabric swatches. (15)

salesclerks. Retail employees who facilitate routine sales transactions; "order takers." (18)

sales forecasting. Predicting the quantity of each item that will be sold during a particular future fiscal time period. (11)

sales managers. Supervisors of several sales representatives in an established district of the country or a division of the company. (27)

sales per square foot. A retail comparison figure to determine success versus previous years or against others, calculated by dividing total sales by total square feet. (19)

sales presentations. Formal, well-prepared showings of a company's goods to potential customers. (11)

sales productivity. Retail effectiveness and efficiency shown through such results as average sales per hour, average items sold per transaction, and average dollars per transaction. (19)

sales promotion. The retail function that involves advertising, display, public relations, publicity, and special events to encourage public acceptance of goods or services to try to result in their sale. (12, 13)

sales quotas. Projected volumes of sales (units or dollars) assigned to a selling department or person for a certain time period. (18)

sales slip. A cash register receipt that shows money amounts for items, tax, and the sales total of transactions. (18)

sales support areas. Store spaces devoted to customer services, merchandise receiving and distribution, management offices, and staff activities. (22)

sales tax. An extra percentage of a purchase collected by retailers in most states to be paid to the state government. (18)

sales trainees. Employees who are learning how to be effective in sales by working under experienced salespeople. (27)

salutation. The beginning greeting of a business letter. (17)

same-store sales growth. A barometer for success that compares the results of each succeeding year against previous years, usually shown in a percentage increase or decrease. (19)

sample cutter. Apparel company employee who cuts out sample parts to be sewn together. (27)

sample maker. Apparel company employee who sews sample garment designs together. Also called sample hand. (27)

samples. Trial garments or prototypes made up exactly as they will look when sold. (10)

sampling. A sales promotion technique that encourages consumers to try products by giving them free samples. (10)

samplings. Small quantities of garments placed in retail stores to get indications of consumer reactions to them. (10)

satin weave. Basic fabric weave that has long yarn floats on the surface giving a smooth, lustrous appearance. (7)

saturation. Market state of having been supplied with the most it will absorb of a fashion. (2)

scale. *See* proportion. (8)

scarves. Decorative wraps of various sizes, colors, fabrics, and designs. (14)

screen printing. Printing method similar to stenciling in which the dye is forced through untreated areas of a fabric screen onto the material being printed. (7)

seamstress. Person who constructs garments by sewing. (27)

seasonal products. Products that change in popularity or demand with the seasons of the year. (4)

secondary group. The manufacturing segment of the soft goods chain that makes fabricated products. (4)

secondary hues. The colors of orange, green, and violet made by mixing equal amounts of two primary hues together. (8)

secondary lines. Ready-to-wear collections of renowned designers. (9)

seconds. Merchandise factory rejects with defects that may affect wearability. (15)

secured credit cards. Charge cards linked to a savings account containing enough money to back up most or all the credit line. (20)

security guard. Employee who protects against theft and usually also handles health and safety in emergencies. (20)

selected distribution policy. Selling only to a limited number of stores per area to maintain exclusivity. (11)

selective market coverage. Having enough locations to adequately cover selected target markets. (13)

self-help features. Attributes of garments that enable children, as well as people with disabilities or older people, to dress themselves. (14)

self-service retailing. Stores in which customers locate products themselves, compare items, make an unassisted decision, and carry their selections to a checkstand. (20)

selling areas. Store layout areas where merchandise is displayed and customers interact with sales personnel. (22)

selling expenses. Costs of payroll (wages) for the sales staff, advertising, delivery costs, and other costs for the selling function. (19)

selvage. Strong lengthwise edges of fabric that do not ravel, formed when the filling yarns turn to go back the other direction. (7)

semi-enclosed windows. Display windows that have a partial background that shuts out some of the store interior from those viewing the window. (22)

sender. The source of a message or shipped goods. (17)

seniority. The length of time an employee has been in a job compared to others who do the same job. (26)

service. An intangible activity or benefit that is performed and that has value. (3)

service features. The actual service mix offerings. (20)

service-positioning strategy. Retailing with a distinctive service mix, often used by specialty stores and upscale department stores. (20)

service quality. How well services are performed to approach, meet, or exceed customer expectations. (20)

Seventh Avenue (SA). New York City's "Fashion Avenue," along which designers' showrooms and apparel industry company offices are located. (10)

sewing machine operators. Manufacturing employees who construct apparel on fast industrial power machines. (27)

shade. A darkened color made by adding black to a hue. (8)

shadowbox windows. Small, enclosed, boxlike display windows at eye level. (22)

shipping container marking (SCM). Standardized bar coding and scanning among vendors, distributors, and retailers, for merchandise containers. (11)

shoplifting. The stealing of merchandise from a retail store by a person posing as a customer. (20)

short-run fashions. Styles that are popular for a brief period of time, usually for only one selling season. (2)

shoulder-out. A way of hanging garments with only one side showing from shoulder to bottom. (22)

showroom manager. Supervisor of all personnel and activity in a company's showroom. (27)

showrooms. Company-owned sales areas where merchandise is displayed and selling staffs answer questions and take orders. (11)

showroom salespeople. In-house sales employees at a firm's sales offices, who present goods to visiting buyers. (27)

shrinkage. The difference between book inventory (according to records) and actual physical inventory; stock shortage. (20)

signage. The total of all the signs of a store or location. (13, 22)

silhouette. The overall form or outline shape of an outfit or clothing style. (8)

silk. A natural protein fiber obtained from cocoons spun by silkworms. (6)

single knit. Stretchy knit fabric constructed on a single needle, weft knitting machine. (7)

sketchers. Apparel company employees who do freehand drawings of ideas that designers have draped onto mannequins in fabric. (27)

skills. A person's abilities of doing specific tasks. (26)

sloper. A basic pattern in a certain size, or to particular body measurements, from which fashion patterns are created. (10)

Small Business Administration (SBA). A government agency that offers helpful counseling, workshops, videotapes, and free publications to entrepreneurs. (30)

smart card. Plastic card for consumers that contains a small microprocessor that stores information or electronic cash. (5)

soft goods chain. The channel of distribution for apparel and home decorating textiles. (4)

soft lines. Products made from textiles, sometimes called dry goods. (14)

sole proprietorship. A business owned by just one person. (3)

solution dyeing. Process of adding color to a fiber solution before it is extruded, giving a clear, rich color with high colorfastness, since the pigment is part of the fiber. (7)

solutions. Answers to problems. (18)

solution spinning. The making of multifilament yarns simultaneously with extrusion from the spinneret. (6)

source tagging. The integration of anti-shoplifting tags into product packaging at the manufacturing level. (20)

sourcing. The seeking of vendors or producers of desired goods. (10)

sourcing consultants. Experts hired to guide companies to identify countries and factories that give the best opportunities for their apparel production. (10)

special events. Promotional activities held to build customer traffic, sell goods, and enhance the company's image. (23)

specialized merchandisers. Retailers that offer limited lines of related products targeted to more defined customers. (12)

special offer. When an additional item can be obtained as a result of purchasing an item. (18)

special orders. Orders for merchandise to satisfy individual customers rather than for regular stock. (16)

specialty chains. Specialty retailers that are part of a regional or national chain. (12)

specialty goods. Merchandise items that are well-known to consumers by brand identification, high quality, or other specific characteristics.

specialty stores. Retailers that carry large selections of limited classifications of merchandise. (12)

specification buying. When a retailer submits definite specifications to a manufacturer about the quality of materials, workmanship, style, and fit of items, rather than looking for goods already produced. (15)

spinneret. Nozzle with many tiny holes through which liquid fiber-forming solutions are forced to form manufactured filaments. (6)

spinning. Process of drawing, twisting, and winding individual staple fibers into long, cohesive strands or yarns. Also, the extrusion of manufactured filaments. (6)

spin-off stores. New retail stores as divisions of established retailers, with distinct images and names. (12)

split complementary color scheme. The use of one color with the two colors on each side of its complement on the color wheel. (8)

sponsor. The company that pays for an advertisement. (21)

spotlighting. Lighting that focuses attention on specific areas or targeted items of merchandise. (22)

spreaders. Machines that hold bolts of fabric and roll back and forth to spread yard goods onto long tables in high stacks for garment cutting. Also, employees who lay out the fabric for cutting. (10, 27)

spreadsheets. Computer programs that calculate numbers that are placed in rows (across) and columns (up and down). (17)

spun yarns. Yarns made by spinning (mechanically pulling and twisting) staple fibers together into a continuous length. (6)

square meter equivalents. Fabric quantity measure used to value the penetration of textile/apparel imports. (24)

standard of living. The level of necessities and luxuries enjoyed by a population for various levels of comfort and status. (3)

staple fabrics. Commodity textile products made continuously each year, with little or no change in construction or finish. (7)

staple fibers. Short lengths of natural fibers under eight inches, or of filament fibers that have been cut. (6)

starters. People who cue fashion show models onto the stage in the correct order and at the right time, guided by the lineup and commentary script. (23)

start-up costs. The expenses to turn a new business venture into reality. (30)

status. A person's position or rank in comparison to others. (1)

stock clerk. Retail stockkeeping job that receives merchandise from delivery trucks, open containers, unpack items, and compare delivery records with the actual goods received. (28)

stock control. *See* inventory management. (15)

stock dyeing. The dyeing of natural fibers in staple form. (7)

stockkeeping. Merchandising function that includes receiving, preparing, protecting against damage or theft, and controlling the merchandise before it is sold. (18)

stock keeping unit (SKU). The smallest unit for which sales and stock records are kept. (15)

stock-out. Situation of being out of a particular item, especially because too few were ordered or produced to meet customer demand. (15)

stock shortage. *See* shrinkage. (20)

stock-to-sales ratio (inventory-to-sales ratio). A calculated number that shows dollar sales volume in relation to the dollar value of average inventory. (15)

stock turnover. The number of times the average inventory on hand is sold and replaced in a given period. (15)

store layout. The interior arrangement of retail facilities. (22)

store manager. The top employee in charge of every aspect of a store's operations. (28)

store operations. The retail function concerned with physically managing and maintaining the store. (12)

store ownership groups. Corporations formed by individual stores joining together into central ownership. Also called retail corporate ownership groups. (12)

STORES magazine. Trade publication of the National Retail Federation. (4, 12)

store security. Function of loss prevention of merchandise, money, and other company possessions. (20)

store wrap. Putting customer purchases in a distinctive store box, bag, or wrapping paper of a particular color and design. (20)

straight lines. Elongated marks that are not curved or jagged. (8)

strategy. Large-scale, long-range planning for achieving an organization's objectives. (25)

strike-off artist. Employee who arranges prints on fabrics after the motifs and colors have been established. (27)

striking the stage. Physically disassembling the set, for instance of a fashion show, and returning props and equipment. (23)

strip mall. An unenclosed shopping area with a line of stores along an outside walkway. (13)

structural adjustment. The process of industries and economies adapting to long-term shifts in competitiveness. (24)

structural design. Texture or interest built into fabrics when they are manufactured. (7)

structural lines. Constructed lines in clothing (seams, darts, pleats, tucks, and edges) that are formed when a garment is made. (8)

structural props. Objects, usually hidden from view, used to support functional and decorative props. (22)

structural texture. A fabric's hand that is determined by its fibers, yarns, and method of construction. (8)

stub-ticket control. An inventory management system of removing and saving a specific portion of the price ticket when the item is sold. (15)

style. A design, shape, or type of apparel item distinguished by the particular characteristics that make it unique. Also, possessing a characteristic or distinctively "smart" way of doing things. (1)

style number. Number assigned to a particular apparel design that identifies it for manufacturing, retail ordering, and distribution. (10)

sub-specialty stores. Retailers that specialize in extremely narrow lines of merchandise. (12)

substitutable goods. Items that can be used in place of each other. (14)

suggestion selling. Increasing sales by adding to the customers' original purchases. (18)

suit separates. Jackets and trousers (or skirts) that mix and match into many different outfits. (14)

super-regional centers. The largest malls and shopping areas, also called "power centers" or "mega malls." (13)

suppliers. Resources for goods; vendors or resources. (3, 15)

supply. Quantities of a good or service that producers are willing and able to provide at a particular time at various prices. (3)

survey. A market research method of asking questions to consumers via mail, telephone, or mall intercepts. (5)

sweater knit. A loosely knitted stretchy fabric made with large yarns. (7)

sweeteners. New items added to a manufacturer's line between design seasons. (10)

sweethearting. Cashier activity of providing discounts, uncharged items, or fraudulent returns to friends, relatives, or theft partners. (20)

synergy. Cooperative interaction of parts resulting in a total effect that is greater than the sum of the parts added together separately. (5)

T

table seating. Fashion show seating, often at round tables, when a meal is served in conjunction with the show. (23)

tailors. *See* dressmakers. (30)

tailor system. Manufacturing system in which all sewing tasks to make a garment are done by a single operator. (10)

takeover. A change in the controlling interest of a corporation. (25)

tanning. Process of preserving animal hides to make leather. (6)

target market. The specific segment of a total market that a company wants as customers, and toward whom it directs its marketing efforts. (3)

target marketing. Defining of the specialized niche of the market to whom the company wishes to make its greatest appeal. (5)

taste. The prevailing opinion of what is and is not attractive and appropriate for a given person and occasion. (1)

tea-room modeling. Presenting fashions informally by walking from table to table in a restaurant to show and tell about what is being worn. (23)

tear sheet. An advertisement torn directly from the print medium in which it appeared. (23)

technical writer. Commercial pattern company employee who creates clear sewing directions that are easy to read and follow. (30)

technology. Scientific discovery or modification of products and methods, usually advanced through research and development. (7, 9)

technology transfer. Spread of technological knowledge. (11)

telecommunication. The transfer of information using telephone lines, or other communicating signals, and computers. (17)

telecommunication retailing. Selling with communication devices, including television retailing and electronic (computer) retailing. (12)

telecommuting. Working out of one's home, using a computer. (17)

teleconferencing. *See* automated conferencing. (17)

telephone tag. The activity of people alternately returning calls to others who are out or unavailable. (17)

television retailing. Selling to consumers by showing and describing merchandise on certain television channels. (12)

temporary finish. Fabric finish that lasts until washing or dry cleaning. (7)

tenant mix. The particular assortment of different types of stores grouped together in a cluster, shopping center, or mall. (13)

terms of sale. The conditions governing a sale, as set forth by the seller. (16)

textile/apparel pipeline. *See* soft goods chain. (4)

textile/apparel preservation. The giving of special attention to long-term care of fabrics and clothing. (30)

textile broker. Individual or company that matches the needs of sellers and buyers to each other for a commission. (7)

Textile/Clothing Technology Corporation ([TC]^2). A not-for-profit, industry-wide organization that researches high-tech innovations in apparel production equipment and processes, and helps the industry implement them. (5)

textile jobber. Wholesale distributor (reseller) that buys textiles at low prices from companies that can't use them and sells them in various size pieces to companies that can use them. (7)

textile laboratory technicians. Textile industry employees who help conduct research, often working under research scientists. (27)

textile performance. How a fabric performs, measured by durability, colorfastness, stain resistance, and other attributes. (4)

textile research scientists. Employees who do R&D in several different textile areas to satisfy needs for specific end uses. (27)

textile testers. Textile industry employees who test new products against required specifications or standards of quality. (27)

texture. Element of design concerned with the tactile quality of goods, or how the surface feels and looks. (8)

textured. Fibers or yarns processed with chemicals, heat, or special machinery for added visual surface characteristics. (6)

textured knit. Knitted fabric made of filament yarns that have been permanently crimped, coiled, curled, or looped. (7)

theater seating. Rows of chairs lined up side by side, facing a stage or fashion show runway. (23)

theatrical costuming. Wardrobing for operas, ballets, stage plays, circuses, movies, advertisements, television shows, and parades. (30)

third-party credit cards. General purpose credit cards issued by outside institutions. (20)

three-functional organization. A retail company structure that has merchandise, operations, and financial managers all reporting to a general manager. (28)

tint. A lightened color made by adding white to a hue. (8)

toddlers. Children who are actively moving around and walking. (14)

toiletries. Personal care products used in grooming. (14)

top grain leather. High-quality "genuine leather" used in most consumer products. (6)

top management. The highest level of company executives. (26)

total costs. The sum of a company's fixed and variable expenses. (19)

total quality management (TQM). An ongoing process focusing on internal requirements to deliver the right products in the best way for continuous improvement of service and satisfaction beyond customers' expectations. (11)

trade. International commerce that involves imports, exports, and exchanges of money. (24)

trade associations. Nonprofit, voluntary organizations made up of businesses that have common interests. (4)

trade deficit. The amount by which the value of imports exceeds exports. (24)

trade name. A brand name that identifies the product and/or its manufacturer. (6, 15)

trademark. A trade name or logo that associates a product with a particular manufacturer or seller. (11)

trade promotion. Promotion aimed within the industry to the next segment of the distribution chain, stressing how well the product performs and the projected profits if purchased. (21)

trade publications. Magazines, newspapers, and books that deal specifically with a certain industry or segment of an industry. (4, 21)

trade regions. Areas of the world that have free trade within them, with neighboring countries joining together for advantageous production and sales of goods. (24)

trade shows. Periodic temporary exhibits scheduled throughout the year in various trading centers. (16)

trade surplus. The amount by which the value of exports exceeds imports. (24)

trading up. Obtaining larger sales by selling higher-priced, better-quality merchandise to customers. (18)

traffic managers. Employees who manage distribution centers and try to get products quickly from manufacturing to the customer. (27)

trainees. Employees who are learning how to do a job. (26, 27)

training supervisors. Manufacturing employees who train new workers to do specific tasks or to use specialized machines. Also retail employees who give orientation classes to new salespeople. (27, 28)

transshipping. The rerouting of goods to evade quota limits. (24)

traveling sales representatives. Manufacturers' "reps" who sell producers' lines around the country by making individual sales calls. (27)

triad color scheme. Plan that uses three colors equidistant on the color wheel. (8)

trial confirmation. A salesperson's questions to a customer to get an indication of what needs to be done to close the sale. (18)

trickle-across theory. The assumption that fashion moves horizontally through groups at similar social levels from fashion leaders to followers. (2)

trickle-down theory. The assumption that fashion trends start at the top of a "social ladder" and gradually progress downward through lower social levels. (2)

trickle-up theory. The assumption that fashion trends start among the young or lower income groups and move upward to older or higher income groups. (2)

tricot. Drapable, warp knit fabric that does not run. (7)

trimmings. The decorative materials of fashion items, such as buttons, laces, belts, and braids that are added to enhance the design. (10)

true bias. Grainline that runs at a 45 degree angle, or halfway between the lengthwise and crosswise grains of a fabric. (7)

trunk show. Bringing a collection of a designer's or producer's samples into a store for a limited amount of time, during which orders are taken directly from customers for later delivery. (11)

turnaround time. How soon a vendor can deliver finished items after goods are ordered. (15)

twill weave. A basic fabric weave characterized by diagonal wales produced by a series of staggered floats. (7)

twin plant program. The use of two manufacturing sites, with one in the U.S. and the other in a nearby low-wage country. (24)

two-functional organization. A retail company structure that has one manager employed to oversee all merchandising duties and another manager in charge of store operations. (28)

U

uncontrollable expenses. Costs over which companies have no control and that, in the short run, cannot be adjusted to current operating needs. (19)

undecided customers. Classification of customers that need an item, but seek pertinent information about products. (18)

underlighting. Lighting from beneath the merchandise in a display. (22)

uneven plaid. A design of crossing lines and spaces that are different in one or both directions. (7)

uniforms. Articles of clothing that are alike and specific to everyone in a certain group of people. (1)

unit production system (UPS). CAM piecework system in which the cut pieces of a garment are hung (loaded) together on an overhead product carrier that moves them through the production line. (10)

Universal Product Code (UPC). The most familiar bar code of dark bars and white spaces of varying widths. (5)

upper management. High-level jobs held by strategic thinkers who are devoted employees. (26)

up-selling. See trading up. (18)

V

validated parking. A customer service in which the store marks the parking lot/garage stub as paid. (20)

value. The lightness or darkness of a color between almost white to almost black. Also, the degree of worth or measure of benefit of something, such as highest quality for lowest price. (8, 25)

value added. The increase in worth of products as a result of a particular work activity. (11, 24)

value-positioning strategy. Limited service, mid-price retailing with expected services offered. (20)

value pricing. The selling of items below the price suggested by vendors of the goods. (13)

values. Ideas, beliefs, and material items that are important to an individual. (1)

value statement. A written document that deals with employee standards and corporate culture building. (26)

variable costs. Expenses that increase or decrease with the volume of sales or production. (19)

variant. A manufactured fiber modified slightly (within its generic group) during production resulting in a change in the properties of the fiber. (6)

variety stores. Small town dime stores that offer a few items in many classifications of lower-priced merchandise. (12)

vendor-managed inventory (VMI). Situation in which suppliers control stock level replenishment from retail POS data. (15)

vendor preticketing. Manufacturer-attached labels and price tags as specified by the retailer. (15)

vendors. Suppliers of goods; resources. (15)

verbal communication. Sending messages with the use of words. (17)

vertical competition. Rivalry between businesses at different levels of the supply chain, such as competing with a company's own customers. (13)

vertical integration. The combining of two or more steps of the pipeline within one company and under one management. (4)

vertical lines. Elongated marks that go up and down. (8)

very small aperture terminal (VSAT). Technology based on satellite network communications that allows users to broadcast information to other locations. (5)

vice president. A corporate executive who usually oversees a particular function of company business. (28)

videotex. Using a computer to access material that is within the database of a larger system. (17)

video wall. Promotional wall made up of many television screens to present visual images. (21)

virgin wool. Wool fibers that have never been used before. Also called pure wool or 100 percent wool. (6)

virtual reality. Computer generated "cyberspace" that stimulates the user's senses to create a perception of being in another environment. (5)

visual aids. Communication instructional display items that appeal mainly to peoples' vision. (17)

visual merchandising. The physical presentation of goods in the most attractive and understandable ways to increase sales. (22)

vocational programs. Educational programs in which students learn the skills for entry-level employment. (26)

voice mail. The use of recording devices to accept messages from callers when the recipient is not available. (17)

voice recognition. Computer response to human voices for data input and/or operating commands. (5)

volume fashion. *See* mass fashion. (1)

W

wall fixtures. Merchandise presentation fixtures that are attached to walls. (22)

wall standards. Vertical strips used on walls, with holes into which all types of brackets and fixtures can be inserted. (22)

wall washers. Floodlights that spread light across an area of wall. (22)

want. A person's desire for something that gives that person satisfaction. (1)

want books/slips. Retail forms on which salespeople record customer inquiries or requests about products not carried or out of stock. (15)

wardrobe designer. Head of a theatrical costume department. (30)

wardrobe helper. Costume technician for theatrical costuming. (30)

warehouse. A holding facility for storing backup stocks of supplies or finished goods. (10)

warehouse clubs. *See* wholesale warehouse clubs. (12)

warm colors. Hues from red to yellow on the color wheel that represent fire, sun, or brilliance. (8)

warp knits. Fabrics made on flat knitting machines using many yarns and needles, with loops interlocking in the lengthwise direction. (7)

warp yarns. Yarns that run lengthwise (parallel to the selvage) in woven fabrics. (7)

waterfall fixtures. Slant arm merchandise fixtures intended to hold one item per knob. (22)

water-jet cutters. Machines that cut small stacks of fabric layers with a thin stream of very high-pressure water. (10)

weaving. Procedure of interlacing two sets of yarns at right angles to each other, usually done on a loom. (7)

Web site. An individual location on the Internet, sponsored by a company or organization. (17, 21)

weft knits. Fabrics knit with one continuous strand of yarn going crosswise. Also called filling knits. (7)

weft yarns. Name for the crosswise yarns in a woven fabric. (7)

wheel of retailing theory. An evolutionary process in which stores that feature low prices gradually upgrade themselves. (12)

whitespace. The empty space of an advertisement or other written or printed page that has no copy or illustration. (21)

wholesalers. Middlepeople, also called resellers or distributors, who purchase large quantities of goods from manufacturers and sell small quantities to retailers. (15)

wholesale warehouse clubs. Retailers that combine wholesaling and retailing on a no frills, cash-and-carry basis. (12)

wholly owned subsidiary. A separate firm that is owned by the parent company. (24)

wicking. The dispersing or spreading of moisture or liquid through a given area, such as pulling body moisture to the surface of a fabric where it can evaporate. (6)

window dresser. Employee who does window displays. Also called window trimmer. (29)

winners. Best-selling items in a manufacturer's line that are recut for production the next season. (9)

women's. Apparel size category for females with larger proportions. (14)

Women's Wear Daily. Trade newspaper covering all aspects of the women's fashion industries. (4)

wool. A natural protein fiber obtained from the fleece of sheep. (6)

Wool Bureau, Inc. Trade association of U.S. wool growers. (6)

woolen. Less expensive wool fabric, made of short fibers, that is relatively dense and has a soft, fuzzy surface. (6)

word processing. The activity of entering, editing, storing, and printing words with a computer. (17)

work design. The ergonomic matching of jobs and equipment to employees, the company's output requirements, compensation plans, and worker behaviors that are reinforced. (10)

work-in-process (WIP). Partially completed goods going through production. (11)

work-study programs. A team approach between employees and educational institutions that gives students on-the-job training for future careers. (26)

workplace diversity. The blending of different races, cultures, genders, ages, socio-economic backgrounds, personality types, and intelligence levels into a productive employment team. (26)

World Trade Organization (WTO). An international trade accord that reduces tariffs, quotas, and other trade barriers around the world. (24)

World Wide Web. Total of all the Web sites on the Internet. (17)

worsted. Fine quality wool fabric, made from long combed fibers, that has a tight smooth surface. (6)

wrapping. Activity comprised of bagging, store wrapping, and gift wrapping. (20)

Y

yarn dyeing. The dyeing of yarns before they are woven or knitted into fabrics. (7)

yarns. Continuous strands of textile fibers spun into a form suitable for processing into fabrics. (4)

year-end bonus. A bonus, usually given at the end of the year, based on the company's profits and length of time a worker has been with the company. (26)

Index

D

G

H

I